The Complete Book of Life's Questions

THE COMPLETE BOOK OF

LIFE'S QUESTIONS

WITH ANSWERS FROM THE BIBLE

RONALD A. BEERS
V. GILBERT BEERS

Tyndale House Publishers, Inc.
CAROL STREAM, ILLINOIS

Visit Tyndale's exciting Web site at www.tyndale.com

TYNDALE and Tyndale's quill logo are registered trademarks of Tyndale House Publishers, Inc.

The Complete Book of Life's Questions: With Answers from the Bible

Copyright © 2007 by Ronald A. Beers. All rights reserved.

Cover photo of teacher copyright © by Bonnie Jacobs. All rights reserved.

Cover photo of newspaper copyright © by Johnny Lye. All rights reserved.

Cover photo of battleship copyright © by Nillo Tippler. All rights reserved.

Cover photo of gas pump copyright © by Craig Veltri. All rights reserved.

Cover photo of baby copyright © by Digital Images/Getty Images. All rights reserved.

Cover photo of coins, wedding couple, and map copyright © by iStockphoto. All rights reserved.

Designed by Ron Kaufmann

Scripture compilation by Amy E. Mason

Scripture quotations are taken from the Holy Bible, New Living Translation, copyright © 1996, 2004. Used by permission of Tyndale House Publishers, Inc., Carol Stream, Illinois 60188. All rights reserved.

Library of Congress Cataloging-in-Publication Data

Beers, V. Gilbert (Victor Gilbert), date.
  The complete book of life's questions : with answers from the Bible / V. Gilbert Beers, Ronald A. Beers.
      p. cm.
  Includes index.
   ISBN-13: 978-1-4143-0730-5 (sc)
   ISBN-10: 1-4143-0730-6 (sc)
   1. Bible—Miscellanea. I. Beers, Ronald A. II. Title.
BS612.B44 2007
220.3—dc22   2006100942

Printed in the United States of America

13   12   11   10   09   08   07
7   6   5   4   3   2   1

TABLE OF CONTENTS

V

W

INTRODUCTION

This book was more than ten years in the making. It was born out of the frustration of being asked lots of questions about God, life, and the Bible and not having good answers and not knowing where to find the answers.

If the Bible is a blueprint for living, then it should have something to say about all of life. It should address any question you might have about why certain things happen to you, how life works, and God's role in it all. So, for the past ten years, we've been collecting questions—thousands of them—from Christians and non-Christians alike. And we've been searching the Bible for answers. In every case, we found that God, the creator of life, has already addressed every question one might ask about life. The answers aren't always what you might expect, and they aren't always neat and tidy. In some cases, they require more than an easy formula—they require a journey, because the Christian faith is often complex and mysterious. But it is amazing how clearly and thoughtfully God's Word answers any question one can devise.

After a decade of collecting questions and searching for answers in the Bible, we felt confident enough to offer this book to you, in hopes that you might better know the God who cares about *all* of your life and not just some of it.

In this book, you will find more than three hundred topics for daily living and more than 1300 questions—most of them questions you've probably asked at one time or another. Following each question you will find one or more Bible verses that directly address the question, followed by a short application note to stimulate further thinking. You can read through this book front to back devotionally, or use it again and again as a reference guide.

Perhaps nothing reveals the heart of human emotion more than questions. Questions reveal who you are, what you're thinking about, what you long to know, and what drives you. Questions come out of curiosity, a thirst for knowledge, a desire for relationship, frustration, anger. Not a day goes by that people don't ask questions, either of themselves, of another person, or of God. The human heart longs for answers to the "whys" of life.

Some people need answers to get them started on their faith journey. Some need answers to help confirm their faith. Some need answers to deepen their faith or help them through tough times. Some need answers to reconnect to a God they have begun to doubt or long to know more intimately. And some are just curious, thoughtful people who wonder if there is a God and just how involved he gets with humankind. All these kinds of questions are addressed in this book. There are questions for everyone—the seeker, the student, the pastor, the Bible-study leader, the layperson.

God has anticipated your questions and has responded to them. You just have to know where to find the answers. In this book, we've tried to make that process of discovery easier.

Though we could not cover every possible question someone might ask, there is probably no other book that answers as many questions as you'll find in these pages. Our prayer is that this book will encourage you to begin a journey of deliberately searching God's Word. May you find God's answers and allow him to be your daily guide in all matters of life.

~

All Scripture is inspired by God and is useful to teach us what is true and to make us realize what is wrong in our lives. It corrects us when we are wrong and teaches us to do what is right. God uses it to prepare and equip his people to do every good work.

2 TIMOTHY 3:16-17

~

Your laws are my treasure; they are my heart's delight. . . . I rejoice in your word like one who discovers a great treasure.

PSALM 119:111, 162

~

Your word is a lamp to guide my feet and a light for my path.

PSALM 119:105

ABANDONMENT *See also* Loneliness, Neglect, Rejection

One of our greatest fears is the termination of a cherished relationship. Whether it is a result of abandonment, being forsaken, giving up, death, or divorce, our fear is of being left alone, of losing someone for whom we really care. Sometimes the hardest consequence of being abandoned is that it threatens our feelings of self-worth. How comforting it is to know that God will never abandon us! But the question is, have we abandoned him?

Has God abandoned me during my difficult times?

Even if my father and mother abandon me, the LORD will hold me close.
PSALM 27:10

God is always at hand. There will be times when even those closest to you will neglect or even desert you, but God never will. In fact, your difficulties can become the means to experience God's presence even more intimately.

Is there ever a circumstance where God will abandon me?

The Spirit of the LORD had left Saul. 1 SAMUEL 16:14

God doesn't abandon you; but he does move on to do his work through others when you make it clear that you do not want or need him in your life. If you walk away from him, he will make repeated attempts to bring you back. But there comes a time when he moves on because you have willfully and completely closed your heart to him. There is nothing more frightening than God leaving your life, because you lose the connection with the only one who can truly help and comfort you and secure your eternal future.

Does my suffering mean that God has abandoned me?

The LORD will not abandon his people. 1 SAMUEL 12:22

Suffering does not mean that God has left you. In fact, it is through suffering that you can experience God's comfort more than ever. To abandon you, God would have to stop loving you—and he cannot do that because he cannot act against his loving nature. Rather than abandoning you when you suffer, our compassionate God moves in closer to help, strengthen, and comfort you with his presence.

ABILITIES *See also* Gifts, Strength

Deep within the human spirit is a desire and a capability to do wonderful things. Because we are made in the image of God, we inherited from him the desire to create, to accomplish, to make things happen. But God wouldn't give us the desire without the means to carry it out, called abilities, or talents. They are the gifts God has given us to help us accomplish great things for him and to live fulfilling lives. How we use or misuse these abilities determines our quality of life—*quality* being defined not as comfort or the accumulation of things, but as character, joy, and lasting satisfaction. Our goal is to first discover our abilities, then develop them, and finally channel them toward what is good, helpful, productive, and God honoring.

How should I use my abilities?

Well done, my good and faithful servant. You have been faithful in handling this small amount, so now I will give you many more responsibilities. MATTHEW 25:21

For reasons we cannot explain, God seems to give more ability to some people than to others. To those with more ability, he provides more resources. But he also requires more responsibility from them. He expects you to maximize the effectiveness of your abilities in proportion to his gifting. While the most talented people may seem the most blessed, they must also be the most responsible.

How can my abilities become a danger?

Beware that in your plenty you do not forget the LORD your God and disobey his commands, regulations, and decrees that I am giving you today. For when you have become full and prosperous . . . be careful! Do not become proud at that time and forget the LORD your God. DEUTERONOMY 8:11-14

When your abilities bring you success and blessing, you are in danger of becoming complacent and forgetting that God gave you those abilities to serve him and others. Another danger of having great abilities is becoming proud and thinking you no longer need God's help or advice from others.

Do my limited abilities limit my ability to serve God?

He takes no pleasure in the strength of a horse or in human might. PSALM 147:10

It is not by force nor by strength, but by my Spirit, says the LORD of Heaven's Armies. ZECHARIAH 4:6

God is more impressed by your faith than your ability. He uses your abilities only in proportion to your faith in him. If you want to delight God, say yes to him, step out in faith, and watch him accomplish great things through you. Abilities give you the potential to do good; faith gives you the power to do good. Neither potential nor power alone is sufficient. They must work in harmony. If God is asking you to do something, he will give you the ability and the extra resources to get the job done.

ABORTION *See also* Euthanasia

A great controversy rages today concerning abortion. For some, abortion is about personal convenience and rights. But the real issue is the sacredness of human life and the identity of the unborn child. Is this merely a fetus, or is this a person? Is there a specific time when the fetus becomes a viable human being, or is it a human being from conception? Another part of the controversy is whether there are justifiable reasons for abortion. Most Christians argue against abortion as a means of birth control. But some argue that abortion is acceptable if it will save the life of the mother, if the pregnancy is a result of rape or incest, or if the unborn child is known to be brain damaged or deformed. Ultimately the core questions are these: In the process of conception and birth, when does human life begin, and what value do we place on the developing unborn child? God's Word is surprisingly clear on this issue.

When does life begin?

I was born a sinner—yes, from the moment my mother conceived me. PSALM 51:5

The Bible makes it clear that human life begins at conception.

What is the value of an unborn child?

You made all the delicate, inner parts of my body and knit me together in my mother's womb. Thank you for making me so wonderfully complex! Your workmanship is marvelous—how well I know it. You watched me as I was being formed in utter seclusion. . . . You saw me before I was born. Every day of my life was recorded in your book.
PSALM 139:13-16

God is present continuously during the nine months of pregnancy—forming, watching, creating, and even scheduling each day of the unborn baby's life. Before you were born, God knew you personally and intimately, and he had already established a purpose for you. The value of an unborn child is priceless because he or she is already a friend of God.

Don't I have the final say over what happens to my body?

Don't you realize that all of you together are the temple of God and that the Spirit of God lives in you? God will destroy anyone who destroys this temple. For God's temple is holy, and you are that temple. 1 CORINTHIANS 3:16-17

You say, "I am allowed to do anything"—but not everything is good for you. And even though "I am allowed to do anything," I must not become a slave to anything. You say, "Food was made for the stomach, and the stomach for food." (This is true, though someday God will do away with both of them.) But you can't say that our bodies were made for sexual immorality. They were made for the Lord, and the Lord cares about our bodies.
1 CORINTHIANS 6:12-13

Your body was created by God and designed by him as a place where his Spirit can live. Even though you can choose what to do with your body, what you choose is not necessarily right in God's eyes or good for you. Abortion fails on both these counts. It is not right in God's eyes because it terminates a human life. And there is no medical evidence to suggest that abortion is good for you. In fact, medical evidence clearly indicates it is harmful—for your body, your mind, and your emotional state. The long-term consequences of terminating a pregnancy are far worse than carrying that child to birth.

Does the Bible say anything specifically about abortion?

Do not permit any of your children to be offered as a sacrifice to Molech, for you must not bring shame on the name of your God. LEVITICUS 18:21

The Bible doesn't specifically refer to the practice of abortion, but it does address child sacrifice, a big issue in Old Testament days. Ironically, child sacrifice actually continues today in a different form, in the flourishing industry called abortion. Things haven't changed much over the centuries: Parents still sacrifice their children to the gods of convenience and economy. Many believe that their own rights take precedence over the rights of their unborn child. When personal preference becomes more highly valued than another human life, spiritual priorities are completely compromised.

Is abortion absolutely wrong?

Anyone who murders a fellow human must die. If anyone takes a human life, that person's life will also be taken by human hands. For God made human beings in his own image. GENESIS 9:5-6

You must not murder. EXODUS 20:13

The Bible makes it clear that life begins at conception, not birth. Therefore aborting an unborn child is terminating the life of that child and is absolutely wrong. If you are considering an abortion, you must clearly understand the Bible's position on this issue. If you have had an abortion or encouraged someone to have one, you must also clearly understand the wonder of God's grace and mercy and accept his forgiveness (see 1 John 1:9).

Can God forgive me for having an abortion?

I recognize my rebellion; it haunts me day and night. . . . Create in me a clean heart, O God. . . . Restore to me the joy of your salvation. PSALM 51:3, 10, 12

[The LORD says,] "Though your sins are like scarlet, I will make them as white as snow. Though they are red like crimson, I will make them as white as wool." ISAIAH 1:18

Just as King David experienced the joy of total forgiveness after committing adultery and murder, so you can know God's forgiveness—for any sin—if you confess your sin to him.

No matter how great your sin, God's forgiveness is greater. God can cleanse and heal you from any and all sin, no matter how big or terrible it might be. No matter what you may have done in the past, let God restore you to wholeness through his amazing, boundless love.

The abortion issue has nothing to do with me. Why worry about it?

Rescue those who are unjustly sentenced to die; save them as they stagger to their death. Don't excuse yourself by saying, "Look, we didn't know." For God understands all hearts, and he sees you. He who guards your soul knows you knew. He will repay all people as their actions deserve. PROVERBS 24:11-12

Every child needs a champion, especially the unborn child. Perhaps God is calling you to be a voice for the unborn or to help support a cause that helps the unborn. Maybe he wants you to adopt a baby or help a new mother cope with her new child. Pray and ask God how he might want you to help the unborn.

ABSENCE *See also* Loss

We all experience absence in some way. Sometimes our friends or family members leave us for a period of time, or maybe they were always absent from our lives. Sometimes our own absence causes us to miss important opportunities. And in difficult situations, we can feel as though God is absent or has moved away from us. Whatever the cause of an absence in your life, it is important to know that God is never absent. He sent his Holy Spirit to be present with us always.

Why do I sometimes feel that God is absent?

[Jesus said,] "Be sure of this: I am with you always, even to the end of the age."
MATTHEW 28:20

The greater your troubles, the farther away God sometimes seems. In your darkest hour, you may feel that God has left you. When it seems like God is absent, don't trust your feelings; trust God's promise that he will never leave you. Rely on what the Bible tells you is true, not on what your feelings tell you.

Listen! The LORD's arm is not too weak to save you, nor is his ear too deaf to hear you call. It's your sins that have cut you off from God. ISAIAH 59:1-2

When God seems far away, it may be because you have moved away from him, not because he has moved away from you. Sometimes it is your own persistent, willful sin that causes you to feel cut off from God and miss the joy of fellowship with him. If you want to feel God's presence again, you need to acknowledge your sin to God. Then through prayer and time with him, you will begin to sense his presence again, and you will see evidence of his work in your life.

Is God absent in my times of intense pain and loneliness?

Even when I walk through the darkest valley, I will not be afraid, for you are close beside me. Your rod and your staff protect and comfort me. PSALM 23:4

God never promised that following him would free your life from trouble, but he does promise to be with you at all times and to help you move through your problems with more wisdom and less fear. It is in your darkest moments, when you need him most, that he is ready and able to help when you ask him. Sometimes God takes away your problem immediately. But more often God allows you to struggle so you can learn and grow stronger because of it. Either way, he knows your trouble and walks beside you through it.

Why is it important for us not to be absent in our relationships (from our families, from our jobs, from the church, etc.)?

Two people are better off than one, for they can help each other succeed. If one person falls, the other can reach out and help. But someone who falls alone is in real trouble.
ECCLESIASTES 4:9-10

Your presence provides physical and emotional support to others. Two or more can form a team and accomplish much more together than separately. When someone needs a "lift" emotionally, an inanimate object doesn't do much; that person needs a smile, a kind word, a hug, or a touch from someone who cares.

Come, let us tell of the LORD's greatness; let us exalt his name together. PSALM 34:3

They all met together and were constantly united in prayer. ACTS 1:14

Your presence provides spiritual support to others. God's people should meet together in God's presence for worship, prayer, and to encourage each other.

When Joseph's brothers saw him coming, they recognized him in the distance. . . . Some time later, Reuben returned to get Joseph out of the cistern. When he discovered that Joseph was missing, he tore his clothes in grief. GENESIS 37:18, 29

When you are absent, you miss crucial opportunities to help others. Much good can be done by just being there.

Are there times when it is best for me to be absent?

Esau hated Jacob because their father had given Jacob the blessing. And Esau began to scheme: "I will soon be mourning my father's death. Then I will kill my brother, Jacob." But Rebekah . . . sent for Jacob and told him, "Listen, Esau is consoling himself by plotting to kill you. . . . Flee to my brother, Laban, in Haran." GENESIS 27:41-43

Sometimes it's better to leave a violent or inflammatory situation (see also 1 Samuel 19:11-12).

[David] told Uriah, "Go on home and relax.". . . But Uriah didn't go home. He . . . replied, "The Ark and the armies of Israel and Judah are living in tents, and Joab and my master's men are camping in the open fields. How could I go home to wine and dine and sleep with my wife? I swear that I would never do such a thing." 2 SAMUEL 11:8-11

There may be times when a higher duty calls for your absence from your family, but these times shouldn't become a way of life. The pattern for family success is personal presence.

ABSOLUTES See also Truth

In recent years, tolerance has become a virtue—you believe what you want and I'll believe what I want and everyone will be happy. But if everyone did what they wanted, it wouldn't take long for chaos and anarchy to reign. Thus, there must be some absolute truths, set in place from the beginning of time, that apply to all people in all times and places. When people live by these truths, the world functions well. Ironically, tolerance embraces every kind of religion, idea, and belief but denies the existence of absolutes: "The only absolute is that there are no absolutes!"

The Bible makes it clear that absolutes do exist and that absolute truth begins with God. God's Word reveals the truths that make the world work, that make relationships work, and that determine our future. By studying these truths and living by them, we discover the way life really works. God's truth sets us free from a meaningless and chaotic life to a certain and eternal future where life will always make sense and will always be fair, just, and full of joy.

What is absolute truth?

The very essence of your words is truth; all your just regulations will stand forever.
PSALM 119:160

Truthful words stand the test of time, but lies are soon exposed. PROVERBS 12:19

Anyone who accepts his testimony can affirm that God is true. JOHN 3:33

All Scripture is inspired by God and is useful to teach us what is true and to make us realize what is wrong in our lives. It corrects us when we are wrong and teaches us to do what is right. 2 TIMOTHY 3:16

Absolute truth has been defined as "that which is true for all people, for all times, for all places; absolute truth is objective, universal, and constant." Absolute truth originates from God, who didn't just create truth but who *is* truth.

Why do we need absolutes? Can't we just do our own thing?

Your job is to obey the law, not to judge whether it applies to you. JAMES 4:11

We can see examples from the beginning of time of individuals who did what was right in their own eyes, which resulted in catastrophic consequences for themselves and others. Scripture teaches that you are born with the desire to sin; thus, doing your own thing will always lead you away from God, the source of absolute truth. Your job is not to pass judgment on God's ways by devising your own way, but to follow God and all he says. If you buy something that needs assembling and you build it contrary to the instruction manual, what you assemble will not work properly. It's the same with life. Follow God's instruction manual, the Bible, and life will work much better.

There seem to be so many gray areas when it comes to right and wrong. How can I tell what is absolutely right?

If you love me, obey my commandments. JOHN 14:15

God has given us his Word, the Bible, which clearly tells us all things that are absolutely right or absolutely wrong.

What are some of the absolutes of the Christian faith?

God gave the people all these instructions: . . . "You must not have any other god but me."
EXODUS 20:1, 3

God gave us the Ten Commandments (see Exodus 20:1-17). They are absolute truths that apply to all people in all cultures for all time. Obeying these commandments will point your life in the right direction, make your life more fulfilling and satisfying, save you from much harm, and keep your focus on the only one who can grant you eternal life.

Jesus Christ is the same yesterday, today, and forever. HEBREWS 13:8

God's character is unchanging. He is consistently all-powerful, absolutely good, the originator of truth, all-wise, and consistently faithful, and he loves us unconditionally.

Jesus told him, "I am the way, the truth, and the life. No one can come to the Father except through me." JOHN 14:6

The wages of sin is death, but the free gift of God is eternal life through Christ Jesus our Lord. ROMANS 6:23

There is absolutely only one way for a person to enjoy eternal life in heaven. Salvation is a gift from God, available to us through faith in Jesus Christ.

Through this man Jesus there is forgiveness for your sins. Everyone who believes in him is declared right with God. ACTS 13:38-39

God's forgiveness is absolute. When he forgives you, it is forever. He never takes it back.

He was buried, and he was raised from the dead on the third day, just as the Scriptures said. He was seen by Peter and then by the Twelve. After that, he was seen by more than 500 of his followers at one time. . . . He is the first of a great harvest of all who have died. 1 CORINTHIANS 15:4-6, 20

The resurrection of Jesus Christ is an absolute truth of the Christian faith. Because he was raised from the dead, he has conquered death; therefore, his promise of eternal life to all who have faith in him is certain.

You Gentiles have also heard the truth, the Good News that God saves you. And when you believed in Christ, he identified you as his own by giving you the Holy Spirit, whom he promised long ago. The Spirit is God's guarantee that he will give us the inheritance he promised and that he has purchased us to be his own people. EPHESIANS 1:13-14

The presence of the Holy Spirit is an absolute guarantee to those who believe in Jesus Christ as their Lord and Savior.

ABSTINENCE *See also* Fasting, Sacrifice

Abstinence in a general sense means refraining from doing something you want to do because it's not good for you. For a Christian, abstinence usually involves obeying God and refraining from doing things he has told us are harmful to us. But sometimes abstinence can also mean giving up something—even something good—for a period of time in order to more completely focus on God. These days, abstinence is a rare discipline. We hear people say that abstinence cramps their freedom. But that is a distortion of the truth. Avoiding harmful behaviors really results in freedom—freedom from fear, disease, addiction, and other painful consequences. Abstinence, therefore, is substituting short-term pleasure (and its long-term consequences) for long-term joy (with the consequence of giving up some short-term pleasure). Abstinence is the discipline of refraining from one thing in order to more fully and continuously experience something better.

Why should I abstain? What are the benefits?

Do not let sin control the way you live; do not give in to sinful desires. Do not let any part of your body become an instrument of evil to serve sin. Instead, give yourselves completely to God, for you were dead, but now you have new life. So use your whole body as an instrument to do what is right for the glory of God. ROMANS 6:12-13

Abstaining from sin brings God's blessings.

Soldiers don't get tied up in the affairs of civilian life, for then they cannot please the officer who enlisted them. 2 TIMOTHY 2:4

Abstinence can be a way to show the Lord your thankfulness, devotion, and obedience to him.

It is better not to eat meat or drink wine or do anything else if it might cause another believer to stumble. ROMANS 14:21

Abstinence may be necessary to keep others from stumbling in their relationship with God. It is necessary at times to stay away from things that might cause those who look to you for guidance to go against their conscience.

Give honor to marriage, and remain faithful to one another in marriage. God will surely judge people who are immoral and those who commit adultery. HEBREWS 13:4

Abstaining from sexual sin before marriage provides great blessings of trust and intimacy to you and your spouse after marriage.

From what should I abstain?

Keep away from anything that might take God's place in your hearts. 1 JOHN 5:21

Abstain from anyone or anything that takes God's place of first priority in your life. God desires a heart totally devoted to him.

Put to death the sinful, earthly things lurking within you. Have nothing to do with sexual immorality, impurity, lust, and evil desires. Don't be greedy, for a greedy person is an idolater, worshiping the things of this world. . . . But now is the time to get rid of anger, rage, malicious behavior, slander, and dirty language. COLOSSIANS 3:5, 8

Abstain from sin as much as humanly possible—from sinful thoughts as well as sinful actions. A heart that allows thoughts of evil, lust, anger, rage, or impurity to linger is a heart that will draw you into greater sin.

Don't you realize that your body is the temple of the Holy Spirit, who lives in you and was given to you by God? You do not belong to yourself. 1 CORINTHIANS 6:19

Since your body is the temple of the Spirit of God, be careful what you allow to enter it. You don't want to profane your temple with the misuse of food, alcohol, drugs, or foul thoughts.

How do we practice abstinence?

Clothe yourself with the presence of the Lord Jesus Christ. And don't let yourself think about ways to indulge your evil desires. ROMANS 13:14

Don't be drunk with wine, because that will ruin your life. Instead, be filled with the Holy Spirit. EPHESIANS 5:18

Abstinence is possible through the power of the Holy Spirit, God's gift to every Christian. The more you make a place in your heart for the Holy Spirit, the less space you have for sinful, harmful influences.

Don't even think about it; don't go that way. Turn away and keep moving. PROVERBS 4:15

There are times when the best way to practice abstinence is to physically remove yourself from a tempting situation.

What happens when we don't abstain?

Don't you realize that those who do wrong will not inherit the Kingdom of God? Don't fool yourselves. Those who indulge in sexual sin, or who worship idols, or commit adultery, or are male prostitutes, or practice homosexuality, or are thieves, or greedy people, or drunkards, or are abusive, or cheat people—none of these will inherit the Kingdom of God. Some of you were once like that. But you were cleansed; you were made holy; you were made right with God by calling on the name of the Lord Jesus Christ and by the Spirit of our God. 1 CORINTHIANS 6:9-11

A lifestyle of indulging in sin has eternal consequences. When you willfully go against what the Bible says is wrong, you are rebelling against God. It's that simple. When you try to abstain from sin, you are showing your desire to please God by showing your respect for his Word and his ways. God and sin cannot live side by side in the inner places of your heart. You must always try to abstain from sin so you can be devoted to God.

ABUSE See also Oppression, Violence

In our lifetime, we are given many gifts: people, talents, possessions, and opportunities. What we do with what we receive is a reflection of who we are and how worthy we are to be entrusted with more. We can maximize these gifts, we can ignore them, or we can abuse them. Abuse comes in many different forms. It can be violent, or it can be as subtle as neglect or abandonment of a trust. Abuse is harmful to both the abused and the abuser and, thus, creates two victims. Not only can God heal the abused, he can also change the heart of the abuser through forgiveness, and he can give both a new way to live.

How do I heal the wounds of abuse?

Get rid of all bitterness, rage, anger, harsh words, and slander, as well as all types of evil behavior. Instead, be kind to each other, tenderhearted, forgiving one another, just as God through Christ has forgiven you. EPHESIANS 4:31-32

Recognize how bitterness and desire for revenge only poison your own soul. For those who have been a victim of abuse, the hurt is real and there are scars—physical and emotional. When justice doesn't happen as it should—when life doesn't seem fair—that's when bitterness can consume you. It's essential to recognize and deal with the bitterness before the bitterness overwhelms you. Otherwise you will not be able to find healing and move on.

Love your enemies! Pray for those who persecute you! MATTHEW 5:44

If you forgive those who sin against you, your heavenly Father will forgive you.
MATTHEW 6:14

This may be the hardest act in your Christian life: forgiving those who have wronged you terribly, without any expectation that they will change. Forgiveness is the only way to purge your soul of the toxins of bitterness and a vengeful spirit. The only way to forgive fully is to understand and accept that Jesus has forgiven your sins, even though you did not deserve it. Only when you seek forgiveness for your sins can you be filled with God's Spirit. And when you are filled with his Spirit, you are filled with his power. It is through his power that you can find the strength and the grace to forgive others. And when you forgive others, your heart is changed so you can move on. Forgiving does *not* mean that the hurt isn't real or that the event didn't matter or that you will put yourself in a position where you might be harmed again. Forgiving means that you refuse to let the abuser have any more control in your life. The act of forgiveness occurs between you and God. Leave your hurt with God, and allow his power to heal you from the inside so you can have a fresh start.

Fix your thoughts on what is true, and honorable, and right, and pure, and lovely, and admirable. Think about things that are excellent and worthy of praise.
PHILIPPIANS 4:8

As you fill your mind with good and pleasant thoughts, you have less room and less time to dwell on the past. Focus on the future and on God's promises to you.

Will God forgive a person who is guilty of abusing others?

Manasseh also sacrificed his own sons in the fire in the valley of Ben-Hinnom. . . .
When he prayed, the LORD listened to him and was moved by his request.
2 CHRONICLES 33:6, 13

Manasseh was one of the most wicked kings in Judah's history, abusive to the point of burning his own sons as human sacrifices. Later in life, however, he sought God's forgiveness. God did forgive him, and Manasseh became a man who did great things for his nation. No sinner is too wicked for God to save; no sin is too vile for God to forgive. His mercy is available to all who call on him, regardless of their past. If you are an abuser, you must still accept the consequences of your sins, but you are not out of reach of God's forgiveness if your heart is truly sincere in desiring change.

What is the best way to prevent abusing others?

Love does no wrong to others. ROMANS 13:10

Love restrains us from abusing others—physically or in any other way. This is not a roller-coaster love based on feelings but a rock-solid commitment to protect and nurture regardless of our feelings at a particular moment. Violence or abuse against a loved one is a sign that anger is stronger than love.

ACCEPTANCE *See also* Equality, Prejudice, Tolerance

The welcome mat is out, and the door is open. A guest walks across the threshold into your home or into your life. That person is accepted into your presence because you have invited him or her. A loved one is accepted because she is family. A stranger may be accepted because of the recommendation of a mutual friend. Acceptance is the essence of relationships. Without acceptance, we are condemned to rejection and loneliness. With acceptance, we can live joyfully together in a kaleidoscope of friendship, love, bonding, and family ties. We accept into our lives not only persons but their gifts, acts of kindness, and expressions of love. The Bible also calls us to accept those the world deems unacceptable—the poor, homeless, handicapped, elderly, prisoners, and addicts.

I feel so unworthy—does God really accept me? What makes me acceptable?

God showed his great love for us by sending Christ to die for us while we were still sinners. ROMANS 5:8

Nothing in all creation will ever be able to separate us from the love of God that is revealed in Christ Jesus our Lord. ROMANS 8:39

You are accepted by God because he made you and created you in his image. Nothing you do could cause God to love you more, because he already loves you completely. And nothing you do will cause God to love you less. In fact, God accepts and loves you so much that he sent his own Son to die for you, to accept the punishment that you deserve for sin. He died in your place so that you can be accepted into eternity with him.

Will God accept me into heaven?

God loved the world so much that he gave his one and only Son, so that everyone who believes in him will not perish but have eternal life. JOHN 3:16

If you confess with your mouth that Jesus is Lord and believe in your heart that God raised him from the dead, you will be saved. For it is by believing in your heart that you are made right with God, and it is by confessing with your mouth that you are saved. ROMANS 10:9-10

There is a big difference between being loved and accepted by God for who you are and being accepted into heaven. If you are convicted of a crime, you must pay the consequences, no matter how much someone loves you. In the same way, all people are guilty of the crime of sin against God. Jesus actually paid the consequences for your crimes, but you must believe and accept what he did. Then you will be accepted into heaven to live with him forever. Your sin separates you from a holy and perfect God. But faith in Jesus removes your sin and makes you holy and acceptable in God's sight.

How can I accept others, especially people I dislike?

Love your enemies! Pray for those who persecute you! MATTHEW 5:44

Pray for those you dislike. Through prayer, God can help you see them through his eyes. Then don't be so quick to make up your mind about who they really are and what they can or can't do. Judging others is better left to God because it is so easy for us to misjudge them. God sets the standard for accepting others.

What should I do when other people don't accept me?

Even if my father and mother abandon me, the LORD will hold me close. PSALM 27:10

Take comfort that God's love endures even when people are fickle and cruel. Demonstrate Christlike love to all people, even those who don't accept you. You will be surprised how many people accept you when you accept them first.

What if a person has committed a terrible sin? Should I still accept that person?

Accept each other just as Christ has accepted you. ROMANS 15:7

God has loved and accepted you, even though sin separated you from him. In the same way, you must love and accept others, no matter how great their sin. This does not mean you accept or condone their sinful actions or ignore the appropriate discipline, but you view and accept them as a unique and special creation of God. It is only through love that you bring a sinful person into fellowship with God and others.

What should I never accept?

[Josiah] destroyed the pagan altars and the Asherah poles, and he crushed the idols into dust. He cut down all the incense altars throughout the land of Israel. 2 CHRONICLES 34:7

Never accept or tolerate sin in your life. Never feel satisfied that you sin less than someone else. All people have a sinful nature, and they have certain sins to which they are particularly vulnerable. Left unchecked in their life, those sins, no matter how small, will begin to grow and spread like a malignant tumor, affecting all they think and do.

ACCOMPLISHMENTS *See also* Productivity, Work

To accomplish something is to complete a task, whether it is finishing the dishes or winning the Super Bowl. The Bible mentions many physical accomplishments, but it also highlights spiritual accomplishments, which we so often overlook—an active prayer life, Christian maturity, telling a neighbor about your faith, a moral victory over temptation, a tender word of encouragement to a child. These kinds of accomplishments need to take priority in our life.

What kind of attitude should I have toward my accomplishments? Is it wrong to be proud of them?

[Jesus said,] "I tell you the truth, anyone who believes in me will do the same works I have done, and even greater works, because I am going to be with the Father. You can ask for anything in my name, and I will do it, so that the Son can bring glory to the Father. Yes, ask me for anything in my name, and I will do it!" JOHN 14:12-14

You have been created, called, and equipped to serve God in significant ways. Your achievements, however, are always to be understood as the result of God's grace in you, not your own efforts. Your greatest accomplishment is allowing God to carry out his plans through you.

Can my accomplishments ever be dangerous? How?

As the people migrated to the east, they found a plain in the land of Babylonia and settled there. They began saying to each other, "Let's make bricks and harden them with fire." (In this region bricks were used instead of stone, and tar was used for mortar.) Then they said, "Come, let's build a great city for ourselves with a tower that reaches into the sky. This will make us famous." GENESIS 11:2-4

Although it is good to be committed to significant achievements, the construction of the tower of Babel serves as a warning not to pursue accomplishments solely for your own glory. Achievements are to glorify God, not yourself.

How can I achieve my God-given potential?

Jesus told them, "I tell you the truth, if you have faith and don't doubt, you can do things like this and much more. You can even say to this mountain, 'May you be lifted up and thrown into the sea,' and it will happen." MATTHEW 21:21

[Jesus said,] "I am the vine; you are the branches. Those who remain in me, and I in them, will produce much fruit. For apart from me you can do nothing." JOHN 15:5

Stay in a healthy love relationship with God. The product of such a relationship is a deepened faith in who he is and what he can do. Achieving God-given potential is accepting what God has given you to do and using his power to accomplish it.

What is the greatest thing that can be accomplished?

This Good News tells us how God makes us right in his sight. This is accomplished from start to finish by faith. As the Scriptures say, "It is through faith that a righteous person has life." ROMANS 1:17

Salvation, the greatest of accomplishments, is not accomplished through your own work but through the work of God in your heart. It is simply by faith—believing that Jesus Christ died for your sins—that you can live forever with God.

ACCOUNTABILITY *See also* Boundaries, Self-Control, Stewardship

Accountability means answering to someone. It is literally giving an account of yourself—

where you've been, what you've been doing, what your motives were. Accountability also suggests that the one who is holding you accountable has the freedom to ask for an account. Most of us don't like to be accountable because it puts too many restrictions on us. It also forces us to open up dark corners of our lives we'd prefer to keep hidden. But real accountability keeps us honest, moral, and on the right path. It's not always comfortable, but it's necessary. On a deeper level, God holds us accountable. He sees all and knows all; nothing is hidden from him. On the day of final judgment, we will have to give an account to him of how we lived our life.

How do I become more accountable?

"Can anyone hide from me in a secret place? Am I not everywhere in all the heavens and earth?" says the LORD. JEREMIAH 23:24

If you're going to take accountability seriously, you have to begin with God. You will better understand what you are doing and why you are doing it when you understand for whom you are doing it. God knows all the secrets of your heart anyway, so why try to hide anything from him? Be honest with God, and tell him the struggles you have in following him.

How can a young person stay pure? By obeying your word. . . . Now teach me good judgment and knowledge. PSALM 119:9, 66

To become more accountable, follow God's commands as outlined in his Word, the Bible.

Oh, why didn't I listen to my teachers? Why didn't I pay attention to my instructors? PROVERBS 5:13

Part of being accountable is being a good listener and observer. You can learn much about your own behavior by observing others and listening to wise friends you respect.

You must commit yourselves wholeheartedly to these commands that I am giving you today. Repeat them again and again to your children. Talk about them when you are at home and when you are on the road, when you are going to bed and when you are getting up. Tie them to your hands and wear them on your forehead as reminders. Write them on the doorposts of your house and on your gates. DEUTERONOMY 6:6-9

Knowing God's Word and talking about it with others help keep you accountable. Writing down your spiritual journey and insights will also help keep you accountable and help you remember the fervor of your early faith.

Why is accountability so important?

Two people are better off than one, for they can help each other succeed. If one person falls, the other can reach out and help. But someone who falls alone is in real trouble. . . . A person standing alone can be attacked and defeated, but two can stand back-to-back and conquer. Three are even better, for a triple-braided cord is not easily broken. ECCLESIASTES 4:9-12

A person standing alone against the world is vulnerable. You need support and companionship. Enlisting a Christian friend as an accountability partner will more than double your spiritual strength. Include the Lord in that relationship and you will become "triple-braided."

What happens when there is no accountability?

All the people did whatever seemed right in their own eyes. JUDGES 17:6

Left unaccountable, people will always lean toward sin. The consequences of sin eventually hurt you and others, and pull you away from God.

A Jew named Apollos, an eloquent speaker who knew the Scriptures well, had arrived in Ephesus from Alexandria in Egypt. He had been taught the way of the Lord, and he taught others about Jesus with an enthusiastic spirit and with accuracy. However, he knew only about John's baptism. When Priscilla and Aquila heard him preaching boldly in the synagogue, they took him aside and explained the way of God even more accurately. ACTS 18:24-26

Even those trying to do good need accountability. Sometimes your own good intentions can be sabotaged by wrong information or even your enthusiasm.

How can I effectively hold someone else accountable?

He must not be arrogant or quick-tempered. . . . He must live wisely and be just. He must live a devout and disciplined life. TITUS 1:7-8

Before you can help others be accountable, you must not only know God's commands but also consistently obey them and always work to develop good judgment. If you are going to minister to others by holding them accountable, you must be wise, honest, godly, trustworthy, and kind yourself.

The people of Israel followed all of the LORD's instructions to Moses. Then Moses inspected all their work. When he found it had been done just as the LORD had commanded him, he blessed them. EXODUS 39:42-43

When you are in leadership, you are accountable for the work of others. Inspection and evaluation are necessary accountability tools.

Think about it: Just as a parent disciplines a child, the LORD your God disciplines you for your own good. DEUTERONOMY 8:5

God uses loving discipline to hold you accountable, and you can follow his example when you are responsible for others.

Does God really hold me accountable for all my actions?

We don't live for ourselves or die for ourselves. If we live, it's to honor the Lord. And if we die, it's to honor the Lord. So whether we live or die, we belong to the Lord. Christ died and rose again for this very purpose—to be Lord both of the living and of the dead. . . . Yes, each of us will give a personal account to God. ROMANS 14:7-9, 12

Live today as though you will be with God in eternity tomorrow. One day you will have to give an account to God for how you lived here on earth. So lead a life of obedience, pleasing to God.

What kinds of things am I accountable for?

Anyone who believes in God's Son has eternal life. Anyone who doesn't obey the Son will never experience eternal life but remains under God's angry judgment.
JOHN 3:36

You are accountable for your own disobedience to God.

No accounting of this money was required from the construction supervisors, because they were honest and trustworthy men. 2 KINGS 12:15

You are accountable for your own character.

Oh, why didn't I listen to my teachers? Why didn't I pay attention to my instructors?
PROVERBS 5:13

You are accountable for your own spiritual growth.

You must give an account on judgment day for every idle word you speak.
MATTHEW 12:36

You are accountable for the words you speak.

When someone has been given much, much will be required in return; and when someone has been entrusted with much, even more will be required. LUKE 12:48

You are accountable for the work you are given to do.

If you are untrustworthy about worldly wealth, who will trust you with the true riches of heaven? LUKE 16:11

You are accountable for your resources: how you spend your money, time, energy, and talents.

ACCUSATIONS *See also* Blame, Criticism

We live in a world where our sinful nature urges us to look out for ourselves first. Rather than take responsibility for our own actions and faults, our instinct is to accuse someone or something else—anything to take the focus off ourselves and avoid the consequences of our mistakes. But accusations are often justified—when a crime is committed, a costly mistake is made, or a sin is committed that threatens a relationship. In these cases, it is important to accuse the one who did wrong so that justice can be served and restitution made. Before we accuse, we must be very careful to have all the facts and to make the accusation in a way that focuses on righting the wrong, not on destroying the accused. Accusations have the power to destroy another person, so we must be extremely careful before we assign blame. Remember that God knows all motives, and he will bring justice to the guilty in his time.

Why do Christians seem to face more accusations and criticism than others?

We are not fighting against flesh-and-blood enemies, but against evil rulers and authorities of the unseen world, against mighty powers in this dark world, and against evil spirits in the heavenly places. EPHESIANS 6:12

Spiritual forces of darkness battle against all who believe in Jesus as Lord, and they are often behind the criticism and antagonism we face.

Is there a proper way to accuse someone?

Why worry about a speck in your friend's eye when you have a log in your own? How can you think of saying to your friend, "Let me help you get rid of that speck in your eye," when you can't see past the log in your own eye? Hypocrite! First get rid of the log in your own eye; then you will see well enough to deal with the speck in your friend's eye. MATTHEW 7:3-5

Self-examination should precede accusation: When you recognize your own wrongs, you may be less hasty to accuse.

If another believer sins against you, go privately and point out the offense. If the other person listens and confesses it, you have won that person back. But if you are unsuccessful, take one or two others with you and go back again, so that everything you say may be confirmed by two or three witnesses. If the person still refuses to listen, take your case to the church. MATTHEW 18:15-17

If you feel you have been wronged by another believer, Jesus instructs you to go to that person and work it out privately. This helps you gain an understanding of his or her motives and keeps the problem from becoming public. Don't talk about it to anyone else first, which may cause undue damage to the other person's reputation. Only after that person has refused to listen should you involve another believer or two.

You must not convict anyone of a crime on the testimony of only one witness. The facts of the case must be established by the testimony of two or three witnesses. DEUTERONOMY 19:15

Multiple witnesses are necessary to determine the facts equitably. More than one witness reinforces the credibility of the other witnesses.

Don't pick a fight without reason, when no one has done you harm. PROVERBS 3:30

Double-check your motives. Make sure you are not accusing someone simply out of anger or to cover any mistakes you've made. Falsely accusing another may cast suspicion on a person's reputation, cheating that person of his or her innocence.

What are the consequences of falsely accusing others?

If a malicious witness comes forward and accuses someone of a crime, then both the accuser and accused must appear before the LORD by coming to the priests and judges in office at that time. The judges must investigate the case thoroughly. If the accuser has brought false charges against his fellow Israelite, you must impose on the accuser the sentence he intended for the other person. DEUTERONOMY 19:16-19

False accusations are as bad as the crime itself. To falsely accuse another is to destroy that person's reputation, so it demands justice and appropriate punishment. Ironically, false accusations often work like a boomerang, returning to accuse the person who let them fly. If you falsely accuse someone, you may be punished instead.

How should I respond to accusations against me?

They shout, "Aha! Aha! With our own eyes we saw him do it!" O LORD, you know all about this. . . . Rise to my defense! Take up my case, my God and my LORD. Declare me not guilty, O LORD my God, for you give justice. Don't let my enemies laugh about me in my troubles. PSALM 35:21-24

If God is for us, who can ever be against us? ROMANS 8:31

Your first line of defense is to draw strength from the assurance that God is for you, not against you. Realize that God has full knowledge of the accusation and the truth and that he has the authority and ability to handle the situation. If you are innocent, defend yourself. But don't forget to ask God to defend you and see that justice is done.

"Who told you that you were naked?" the LORD God asked. "Have you eaten from the tree whose fruit I commanded you not to eat?" The man replied, "It was the woman you gave me who gave me the fruit, and I ate it." Then the LORD God asked the woman, "What have you done?" "The serpent deceived me," she replied. "That's why I ate it." GENESIS 3:11-13

When you're accused, your first reaction is probably to blame others. However, you need to accept any blame that is rightfully yours. If an accusation against you is true, you need to own up to it, ask forgiveness from those you hurt, and make restitution.

When you are brought to trial in the synagogues and before rulers and authorities, don't worry about how to defend yourself or what to say, for the Holy Spirit will teach you at that time what needs to be said. LUKE 12:11-12

Be sensitive to the Holy Spirit's guidance as you respond to accusations. He may give you help you never thought possible.

Love your enemies! Pray for those who persecute you! MATTHEW 5:44

Don't underestimate the power of prayer. As hard as it is to love someone who falsely accuses you, pray for them, and you will begin to see them as Jesus does.

When the leading priests and the elders made their accusations against him, Jesus remained silent. "Don't you hear all these charges they are bringing against you?" Pilate demanded. But Jesus made no response to any of the charges, much to the governor's surprise. MATTHEW 27:12-14

In some instances it is best to remain silent. There are times when your silence shouts that you are innocent.

ADDICTION *See also* Drinking/Drunkenness, Drugs, Gambling

Who in his right mind would volunteer to become a slave, chained forever to a life of bondage? Yet that's just what addiction is: self-imposed slavery, selling oneself into a lifetime of bondage to a habit or substance. While we typically think of addiction as a problem related to drugs or alcohol, there are other addictions that are just as destructive. People can become addicted to work, laziness, television, computer games, unhealthy food—the list goes on and on. You can even be addicted to good things. For example, you can actually exercise too much or eat too much good food.

We all have our addictions, whether they are "minor" bad habits or serious dependencies. One thing we are all dangerously addicted to is sin. We consistently and daily disobey God's Word (through bad thoughts, bad words, wrong motives). And we can't help it. The only cure is to submit to the control of God and his Holy Spirit. We are still controlled, but his control is always for our benefit and health, not our destruction. God's transforming power is the only thing that can ultimately heal us of all addictions.

How do addictions begin?

[These false teachers] promise freedom, but they themselves are slaves of sin and corruption. For you are a slave to whatever controls you. 2 PETER 2:19

Addiction is about control—what controls you. Whenever you have a master, you are a slave. Addiction begins when you relinquish yourself to the control of something or someone else. Sin, your greatest addiction, is often alluring and attractive, offering short-term pleasure. It is easy to justify giving in "just this once" because you think you have things under control. But soon you realize that what you are giving in to has become a habit that you can't stop. It is now controlling you. Sin's control often comes from the loss of self-control.

Can addiction include more than substance abuse?

Jesus told him, "If you want to be perfect, go and sell all your possessions and give the money to the poor, and you will have treasure in heaven. Then come, follow me." But when the young man heard this, he went away sad, for he had many possessions.
MATTHEW 19:21-22

Possessions can be addictive.

That is why God abandoned them to their shameful desires. Even the women turned against the natural way to have sex and instead indulged in sex with each other. And the men, instead of having normal sexual relations with women, burned with lust for each other. Men did shameful things with other men, and as a result of this sin, they suffered within themselves the penalty they deserved. ROMANS 1:26-27

Sexual perversions can be addictive.

Those who love pleasure become poor; those who love wine and luxury will never be rich.
PROVERBS 21:17

Pleasure, a luxurious lifestyle, and wealth can be addictive.

All our busy rushing ends in nothing. PSALM 39:6

Jesus said, "Let's go off by ourselves to a quiet place and rest awhile." MARK 6:31

Work can be addictive. Make sure you find time to rest and refresh your body and spirit.

How can God break the power of addiction in my life?

The Holy Spirit produces this kind of fruit in our lives: love, joy, peace, patience, kindness, goodness, faithfulness, gentleness, and self-control. GALATIANS 5:22-23

God can break the power of addiction when you give him control of your life. He will come into your life and change your heart and your desires. Surrender to the Holy Spirit, and God will replace addictive drives with life-affirming desires.

Don't you realize that you become the slave of whatever you choose to obey? You can be a slave to sin, which leads to death, or you can choose to obey God, which leads to righteous living. ROMANS 6:16

Submission is the choice to obey something or someone. Every day you stand at the crossroads, choosing sinful ways or God's ways. The choice is yours. Admit your need to God in prayer, release all your anxieties to him, and rely fully on the promise of God's help.

Two people are better off than one, for they can help each other succeed. If one person falls, the other can reach out and help. But someone who falls alone is in real trouble. . . . A person standing alone can be attacked and defeated, but two can stand back-to-back and conquer. Three are even better, for a triple-braided cord is not easily broken.
ECCLESIASTES 4:9-12

It is almost impossible to overcome addiction by yourself. You need the consistent support of other people who love you, tell you the truth, and hold you accountable. Participating in an addiction recovery support group is often valuable, perhaps even essential in order to overcome an addiction. God often works through other people to help you.

If we shouldn't let anything control us, why should we submit to the Holy Spirit's control?

Letting your sinful nature control your mind leads to death. But letting the Spirit control your mind leads to life and peace. ROMANS 8:6

God's control is the only kind of control that produces completely positive results.

The Lord is the Spirit, and wherever the Spirit of the Lord is, there is freedom.
2 CORINTHIANS 3:17

The Holy Spirit works in you to bring freedom from the drives and desires that distract you from living for God.

ADOPTION *See also* Infertility

Adoption is a beautiful expression of God's love for humankind. Adoption gives children a new life that they could not achieve on their own. In the same way, Jesus came for us at just the right time to give us eternal life in heaven—a new life we could never achieve on our own. Just as parents lovingly nurture and teach an adopted child as their own, God nurtures and teaches us as his children through the Holy Spirit. We can all be adopted into God's family, and his blessings are given to us in both this life and eternity. This hope in our spiritual adoption sustains us as we or those we know experience the frustrations and joys of earthly adoption.

Is adopting a child right for me and my family? How can I know for sure?

[Jesus said,] "Anyone who welcomes a little child like this on my behalf is welcoming me."
MATTHEW 18:5

There are some things in life you can't know for sure, but the Bible is clear on this: God puts a high priority on loving children. If you adopt a child and welcome him or her into your heart and life, you are demonstrating the kind of love Christ showed for you.

How should I tell others about my decision to adopt?

Children are a gift from the LORD; they are a reward from him. PSALM 127:3

The best thing you can do is lovingly explain the journey you took to get to this point. Tell them that God loves all children equally and that you feel God brought this child to your family for a particular purpose.

How has God adopted me?

To all who believed him and accepted him, he gave the right to become children of God.
JOHN 1:12

When the right time came, God sent his Son, born of a woman, subject to the law. God sent him to buy freedom for us who were slaves to the law, so that he could adopt us as his very own children. GALATIANS 4:4-5

When you accepted Jesus Christ as your Savior, God adopted you into his family.

Why would God want to adopt me?

God decided in advance to adopt us into his own family by bringing us to himself through Jesus Christ. This is what he wanted to do, and it gave him great pleasure.
EPHESIANS 1:5

God chose you to be his adopted child because he loves you. Adopting you as his child has been part of God's plan since the beginning of time.

How do I know I've been adopted by God?

All who are led by the Spirit of God are children of God. . . . You received God's Spirit when he adopted you as his own children. . . . For his Spirit joins with our spirit to affirm that we are God's children. ROMANS 8:14-16

The Bible assures you that if the Holy Spirit lives in you, then you have been adopted by God. The Holy Spirit also speaks to your heart, assuring you that you are part of God's family.

Those who have been born into God's family do not make a practice of sinning, because God's life is in them. So they can't keep on sinning, because they are children of God. So now we can tell who are children of God and who are children of the devil. Anyone who does not live righteously and does not love other believers does not belong to God. 1 JOHN 3:9-10

A new lifestyle of obedience and love is evidence that you have been adopted as a child of God.

What are my responsibilities as God's adopted child?

You must live as God's obedient children. Don't slip back into your old ways of living to satisfy your own desires. You didn't know any better then. But now you must be holy in everything you do, just as God who chose you is holy. For the Scriptures say, "You must be holy because I am holy." 1 PETER 1:14-16

As God's child, try to develop the character of your heavenly Father, modeling obedience, holiness, purity, mercy, kindness, humility, gentleness, patience, and love.

My child, don't reject the LORD's discipline, and don't be upset when he corrects you. For the LORD corrects those he loves, just as a father corrects a child in whom he delights. PROVERBS 3:11-12

God disciplines his children. When he disciplines you, he reminds you that you are his child. Part of your responsibility as his child is to pay attention and learn from his correction.

What are some of my privileges as God's adopted child?

Now all of us can come to the Father through the same Holy Spirit because of what Christ has done for us. EPHESIANS 2:18

You have the privilege of a relationship with God the Father.

We praise God for the glorious grace he has poured out on us who belong to his dear Son. He is so rich in kindness and grace that he purchased our freedom with the blood of his Son and forgave our sins. He has showered his kindness on us, along with all wisdom and understanding. EPHESIANS 1:6-8

You are the beneficiary of God's kindness and a recipient of his blessings and good gifts.

We have a priceless inheritance—an inheritance that is kept in heaven for you, pure and undefiled, beyond the reach of change and decay. 1 PETER 1:4

The privilege of being a child of God does not stop on earth but continues through eternity. You will always have a relationship with God. Even your inheritance is eternal, for you will live with God in his heavenly home forever!

ADULTERY *See also* Betrayal, Marriage, Sex/Sexuality

What the Bible says about adultery stands in stark contrast to today's casual view of sexual encounters. The issues of adultery relate to sex, but much more profoundly, they relate to vows and faithfulness. Marriage vows promise faithful commitment to one person, just as our vows to God promise our faithfulness to him. God insists on being the one divine love in our lives; we must not elevate any other person, object, or deity to his level. The marriage union is symbolic of that commitment. As we remain faithful to our mate, we understand more of what it means to be faithful to God. This faithfulness allows us to share an intimacy and a common purpose that is not possible in casual relationships and is destroyed by adulterous relationships. The vow starts with God's commitment to us. He will never leave us or forsake us. He also expects that same degree of commitment from us. The sexual dimensions of human love are God's provision for marital commitment to find expression in a unique, rich, and rewarding way that reflects our love relationship with God. That is why God guards the marriage relationship as something special and pure.

What is the definition of adultery?

Give honor to marriage, and remain faithful to one another in marriage. God will surely judge people who are immoral and those who commit adultery. HEBREWS 13:4

Adultery is being unfaithful to one's mate. In general, this involves forming a sexual relationship with someone other than your spouse. But an intimate emotional relationship with another person or even unfaithful thoughts can become adulterous if they take you away from your first love. Similarly, in the spiritual realm, you commit adultery against God when you are unfaithful to him by worshiping anything or anyone except him.

Why is adultery dangerous?

The man who commits adultery is an utter fool, for he destroys himself. PROVERBS 6:32

Like most sin, adultery is a momentary act of pleasure that has dire consequences—a lifetime of regret and pain. The consequences of adultery are severe and lasting.

How do I protect myself from getting into an adulterous relationship?

From the heart come evil thoughts, murder, adultery, all sexual immorality, theft, lying, and slander. MATTHEW 15:19

The seeds of adultery are planted in the garden of the heart. Guard what is planted in your heart—through what you read, watch, or think about—to avoid growing the fruit of adultery.

Wisdom will save you from the immoral woman, from the seductive words of the promiscuous woman. PROVERBS 2:16

God promises wisdom to those who ask him for it (see James 1:5). When you have wisdom, you will have the discernment to know how to avoid adultery. You still must make the choice to avoid it, but wisdom helps you recognize the early warning signs that you are moving in the wrong direction.

The lips of an immoral woman are as sweet as honey, and her mouth is smoother than oil. But in the end she is as bitter as poison, as dangerous as a double-edged sword.... So now, my sons, listen to me. Never stray from what I am about to say: Stay away from her! Don't go near the door of her house! If you do, you will lose your honor and will lose to merciless people all you have achieved. PROVERBS 5:3-4, 7-9

When faced with situations that could lead to adultery, you might be tempted to think that you can handle it, but the best course is to run away and not look back (see Genesis 39:1-21).

Drink water from your own well—share your love only with your wife.... Let your wife be a fountain of blessing for you. Rejoice in the wife of your youth. PROVERBS 5:15, 18

Adultery is more likely if you allow discontentment to creep into your heart. But you won't be tempted to "shop around" when you are content with your mate and rejoice over the blessing he or she is to you.

Can God forgive my adultery?
I have swept away your sins like a cloud. I have scattered your offenses like the morning mist. Oh, return to me, for I have paid the price to set you free. ISAIAH 44:22

If your heart is broken over your actions and you are truly sorry for what you've done, go to God and seek his forgiveness. He promises to forgive you and to bring healing to your heart. You will suffer the natural consequences of your sin, but you will be able to move forward and pick up the pieces.

How can I recover from adultery?
If we confess our sins to him, he is faithful and just to forgive us our sins and to cleanse us from all wickedness. 1 JOHN 1:9

Confess your sin to God with a humble heart, and he will forgive you. Confess your sin to your spouse and ask for forgiveness. Your spouse may not forgive you, but you should still seek it.

Let the Spirit renew your thoughts and attitudes. EPHESIANS 4:23

True repentance should lead to a change in behavior.

ADVICE *See also* Discernment, Listening, Will of God

What should I do? This is a commonly asked question. In an age of conflicting claims and confusing directions, many search for wise counsel. Maybe that's why counselors are in such great demand and advice columnists are in every newspaper. But there is often a critical difference between wise counsel and well-meaning advice. God's wisdom is the best because he is all-knowing. Why not begin by seeking advice from the one who knows everything that will happen tomorrow and every tomorrow to come? Then advice from others can be better measured and interpreted.

Where do I look for good advice?

The godly offer good counsel; they teach right from wrong. PSALM 37:30

Let the message about Christ, in all its richness, fill your lives. Teach and counsel each other with all the wisdom he gives. COLOSSIANS 3:16

Seek advice from God through prayer and reading his Word, the Bible. Next, seek advice from godly people who have a gift for giving wise counsel. These are people who have proven themselves to be faithful, godly, honest, and trustworthy. They can be counted on to give you counsel that comes from God's Word.

I will ask the Father, and he will give you another Advocate, who will never leave you. JOHN 14:16

God gave us his Son as our Counselor; both Jesus' life and words counsel us. God also gave us the Holy Spirit, who is called the Counselor, or Advocate. He will stay with you at all times to give you wisdom and guide you in any circumstance.

Without wise leadership, a nation falls; there is safety in having many advisers. PROVERBS 11:14

It is often wise to seek more than one opinion, especially on major issues, and to compare that advice with God's Word and his ways.

How do I evaluate the advice of others?

You can identify [false prophets] by their fruit, that is, by the way they act. MATTHEW 7:16

One way to evaluate advice is to evaluate the advisers. Do their actions match their words? Most important, when evaluating advice, check it against the truth of God's Word. If it contradicts the Bible, then it is bad advice.

Caleb tried to quiet the people as they stood before Moses. "Let's go at once to take the land," he said. "We can certainly conquer it!" NUMBERS 13:30

What is the basis of the advice—fact or opinion? Caleb's advice was fact because God had promised a victory. (See Numbers 10:9.)

[Ahaziah] did what was evil in the LORD's sight, just as Ahab's family had done. They even became his advisers after the death of his father, and they led him to ruin. 2 CHRONICLES 22:4

Think through what the results of following the advice could be. Where will it lead you in the long run?

Do I need advice from others? Why can't I just rely on my own wisdom?

The instruction of the wise is like a life-giving fountain; those who accept it avoid the snares of death. PROVERBS 13:14

Plans go wrong for lack of advice; many advisers bring success. PROVERBS 15:22

Good advisers bring perspective, new information, expertise, and experience to whatever challenges and problems you face. No one is wise enough to anticipate all the possibilities of a situation or to grasp all the issues related to a problem. But the right counsel can make the difference between success and failure, joy and sorrow, prosperity and poverty, victory and defeat.

How do I give good advice to others?

Fix your thoughts on what is true, and honorable, and right, and pure, and lovely, and admirable. Think about things that are excellent and worthy of praise. PHILIPPIANS 4:8

When you give advice, make sure your motives are right—to offer the best possible advice for the situation, not to offer advice that might improve your own situation. Point to God's Word, and don't use advice as an excuse to lecture. Pray about what you need to say, and have the other's best interests in mind. Words are like medicine; they should be measured with care. An overdose may do more harm than good.

As Samuel grew up, the LORD was with him, and everything Samuel said proved to be reliable. 1 SAMUEL 3:19

It is not because I am wiser than anyone else that I know the secret of your dream, but because God wants you to understand what was in your heart. DANIEL 2:30

Some people always seem to have good advice because they have a good adviser. People listened to Samuel and Daniel because their words came from the wisdom of the Lord God himself.

Let the message about Christ, in all its richness, fill your lives. Teach and counsel each other with all the wisdom he gives. COLOSSIANS 3:16

Know God's Word so that you can refer to it as you provide advice. Then your words will be wise and helpful.

Spouting off before listening to the facts is both shameful and foolish. PROVERBS 18:13

Make sure you have all the facts. Thoroughly understand a person's situation before giving advice.

What happens when I follow good advice?

Oh, the joys of those who do not follow the advice of the wicked, or stand around with sinners, or join in with mockers. PSALM 1:1

Following godly advice results in joy because it leads to blessing; following bad advice robs you of joy because it leads to sorrow and disaster.

People who despise advice are asking for trouble; those who respect a command will succeed. PROVERBS 13:13

Following good advice helps prevent failure and promotes success.

If you reject discipline, you only harm yourself; but if you listen to correction, you grow in understanding. PROVERBS 15:32

Get all the advice and instruction you can, so you will be wise the rest of your life. PROVERBS 19:20

Your understanding and wisdom increase as you follow good advice. You learn something from each situation to help you in the future.

How do I know when to give advice and when not to?

Instruct the wise, and they will be even wiser. Teach the righteous, and they will learn even more. PROVERBS 9:9

Give advice to those who ask for it. Wise people seek further wisdom; fools never do.

Dear brothers and sisters, if another believer is overcome by some sin, you who are godly should gently and humbly help that person back onto the right path. And be careful not to fall into the same temptation yourself. GALATIANS 6:1

It is your duty to give counsel and gently correct a fellow Christian who has fallen into sin.

Timely advice is lovely, like golden apples in a silver basket. PROVERBS 25:11

There is a right time to give advice. Be sensitive to the Holy Spirit, the circumstances, and the people involved.

Everyone enjoys a fitting reply; it is wonderful to say the right thing at the right time! PROVERBS 15:23

Make sure your advice applies to the situation at hand. Sometimes we give good advice, but it doesn't apply to that particular person or circumstance.

Are there certain areas of life where I don't need advice?

The LORD directs the steps of the godly. He delights in every detail of their lives. Though they stumble, they will never fall, for the LORD holds them by the hand. PSALM 37:23-24

No area of life is too small or unimportant to seek advice from the Lord. The only kind of advice you should not seek is from ungodly people who try to tell you not to seek advice from God!

AFFECTION *See also* Friendship, Intimacy, Romance

Many times we think of affection as romantic gestures between two people: a kiss, a hug, or holding hands. More generally, our affections are simply responses to those things we care most about. This is why it is important to be sensitive to the Holy Spirit and to love God so that our affections do not become misguided. When we begin showing affection toward the wrong things or for the wrong reasons, we are in danger of being drawn away from God, our first love. Misguided motives lead to misguided affections that lead to misguided actions. Our affections are indicative of what we care about the most.

Where should I focus my affections?

Whom have I in heaven but you? I desire you more than anything on earth.
PSALM 73:25

If your greatest affection is for God, your priorities are in the right place. As you develop a relationship with God by reading the Scriptures, you will love him more and more. Develop a love for the church as well, for it is God's house where you can worship him in a special way.

The second [commandment] is equally important: "Love your neighbor as yourself." No other commandment is greater than these. MARK 12:31

Your second priority is to show affection toward others.

How does God express his affection for me?

God showed how much he loved us by sending his one and only Son into the world so that we might have eternal life through him. This is real love—not that we loved God, but that he loved us and sent his Son as a sacrifice to take away our sins. 1 JOHN 4:9-10

God gave up his own Son, Jesus, as an expression of his love for us. Jesus died so that we can live forever. This is real love.

How can I express my affection for God?

If you love me, obey my commandments. JOHN 14:15

Obedience to God and his Word is evidence of your affection for him. Obeying God is the highest expression of love, for it demonstrates the desire to honor him.

With my whole being, body and soul, I will shout joyfully to the living God. PSALM 84:2

Your words are evidence of your affection for God, both in what you say and what you don't say. Show your affection for God by telling him how great and awesome he is, and avoid saying anything that would displease him.

What should I do if I feel my affection for God waning, or if I feel some of my affections are misplaced?

Put me on trial, LORD, and cross-examine me. Test my motives and my heart.
PSALM 26:2

Be willing to let the Lord test your affections, and be open to what he reveals to you. Ask him to show you what might have become more important than he is. But if you ask, be ready for him to expose any misplaced affections, and then be willing to change.

Guard your heart above all else, for it determines the course of your life. PROVERBS 4:23

Be careful to guard your affections, realizing how improper desires often have a disastrous effect on your life and your family. Whatever you regard with high affection will determine the direction of your life. Be sure your highest affections will direct you to life's greatest goal—a vital relationship with Jesus.

AFFIRMATION *See also* Encouragement, Praise, Criticism

We all have a need to feel affirmed—to know that our life has value and is valued by others. Sadly, people don't always offer the affirmation we need, and as a result, we might feel rejected, alone, or worthless. When no one else offers words of affirmation, we can feel affirmed that an almighty God chose to create us in his image and to have a relationship with us. God draws us to himself, even to the point of sacrificing his own Son to die for our sins so that we could have the opportunity to live with him forever. God's words and actions affirm that he desires us more than anything else and that we matter to him.

How does God affirm me?

You bless the godly, O LORD; you surround them with your shield of love. PSALM 5:12

May God be merciful and bless us. May his face smile with favor on us. PSALM 67:1

In his kindness God called you to share in his eternal glory by means of Christ Jesus. So after you have suffered a little while, he will restore, support, and strengthen you, and he will place you on a firm foundation. 1 PETER 5:10

God affirms you through his love, his blessings, his mercy, his forgiveness, and his gift of salvation. What greater affirmation can you receive than approval from the Creator of the universe?

How do I affirm God?

Enter his gates with thanksgiving; go into his courts with praise. Give thanks to him and praise his name. PSALM 100:4

To give or receive a blessing is a great affirmation. You affirm God through your praise, worship, and thanksgiving. As God affirms you, so you should affirm him.

How do I affirm others? Why is it so important?

Encourage each other and build each other up, just as you are already doing. . . . Show them great respect and wholehearted love because of their work. And live peacefully with each other. 1 THESSALONIANS 5:11-13

You affirm others through encouragement, praise, and building them up. This gives you and others a great sense of worth.

AGING/OLD AGE *See also* Death, Retirement, Wisdom

If God continues to give us life, old age is inevitable. Though old age will bring changes and limitations, we serve a changeless and unlimited God. The Lord loves us throughout our lives and has a unique purpose for us in each stage of life's journey. We can have confidence that God gives new mercies and fresh possibilities for whatever stage we are in.

Does the age of a person matter to God?

[Caleb said,] "I am as strong now as I was when Moses sent me on that journey, and I can still travel and fight as well as I could then." JOSHUA 14:11

"O Sovereign LORD," [Jeremiah] said, "I can't speak for you! I'm too young!" The LORD replied, "Don't say, 'I'm too young,' for you must go wherever I send you and say whatever I tell you. And don't be afraid of the people, for I will be with you and will protect you. I, the LORD, have spoken!" JEREMIAH 1:6-8

God uses people of every age to do his work. No one is too old or too young to have an impact for God. People look at outward appearance and age, but God looks at the heart. Godly hearts come in people of all ages, from little children to those in the golden years.

Will I still be useful in my old age?

The godly will flourish like palm trees. . . . Even in old age they will still produce fruit; they will remain vital and green. They will declare, "The LORD is just! He is my rock! There is no evil in him!" PSALM 92:12-15

Zechariah said to the angel, "How can I be sure this will happen? I'm an old man now, and my wife is also well along in years." LUKE 1:18

The Bible is filled with stories of older people whom God used. Even if your physical abilities are limited, you can serve God in valuable ways, such as ministering in prayer and encouraging and telling others of God's goodness. No matter how old you are, you never outlive your usefulness to God.

What are some of the benefits of old age?

The glory of the young is their strength; the gray hair of experience is the splendor of the old. PROVERBS 20:29

One benefit of growing older is the wisdom that can come from a lifetime of experience. Living a long time gives you the opportunity to pass on to the next generations the lessons of a lifetime of faithfulness to God, the blessings he showers on you through the years, or even warnings as a result of your mistakes.

What are some responsibilities older people have?

Teach the older men to exercise self-control, to be worthy of respect, and to live wisely. They must have sound faith and be filled with love and patience. Similarly, teach the older women to live in a way that honors God. They must not slander others or be heavy drinkers. Instead, they should teach others what is good. These older women must train the younger women to love their husbands and their children, to live wisely and be pure, to work in their homes, to do good, and to be submissive to their husbands. Then they will not bring shame on the word of God. TITUS 2:2-5

Older people should mentor the young in God's ways of living. Those who are older have a wealth of experience and insight to share, and it should be shared in a gracious and godly manner.

Now that I am old and gray, do not abandon me, O God. Let me proclaim your power to this new generation, your mighty miracles to all who come after me. PSALM 71:18

Share how you have seen God's hand in your daily life as well as in your lifelong experiences. God's work in your life can be an encouragement to others who follow behind you. Candid recognition of your failures can also be an encouragement, for you will help new Christians avoid some of the pitfalls you experienced.

What are some responsibilities the young have toward older people?

Honor your father and mother. Then you will live a long, full life in the land the LORD your God is giving you. EXODUS 20:12

Honor your parents. This is the only one of the Ten Commandments that comes with a promise, showing how important this is to God.

Now, in my old age, don't set me aside. Don't abandon me when my strength is failing. PSALM 71:9

Don't ignore or abandon the elderly. Instead, thank them for their contributions to your life, your family, your church, your community, and your nation. Even in old age people still have much to offer, and you can learn from them until their dying day.

AIDS *See also* Compassion, Healing, Sickness

AIDS is a fatal virus that affects men, women, and children alike. AIDS can be contracted in several ways, but often we think of AIDS as being indicative of an immoral lifestyle. With many people, this is the case, but there are millions of innocent people who contract this disease as well. When someone has AIDS, it's easy to assume the worst and judge their lifestyle. But Jesus' first response would be compassion, a desire to help the sick. All of us have a dreadful disease that has reached epidemic proportions: It is called sin. God will judge us for that because it truly is based on lifestyle. Our job is to leave the judging to God and to minister to the physical and spiritual needs of those who are hurting, showing them the love of Jesus in the process.

Why is there AIDS?

By the sweat of your brow will you have food to eat until you return to the ground from which you were made. For you were made from dust, and to dust you will return. GENESIS 3:19

When Adam and Eve disobeyed God, sin entered the world, and all of life changed. As a result, there is sickness, pain, and death. AIDS, like any disease, is one of the results of living in a fallen world.

What should be my response to people with AIDS?

Don't just pretend to love others. Really love them. ROMANS 12:9

Most of you opposed [the man who caused all the trouble], and that was punishment enough. Now, however, it is time to forgive and comfort him. Otherwise he may be overcome by discouragement. So I urge you now to reaffirm your love for him.
2 CORINTHIANS 2:6-8

Regardless of how someone acquired AIDS, Scripture commands us to treat that person with the same love that Christ would show. This does not mean we condone immoral lifestyle choices, but the love of Christ must be shown equally to all people. Only then can God's message of grace and forgiveness and healing break through.

A man with leprosy came and knelt in front of Jesus, begging to be healed. "If you are willing, you can heal me and make me clean," he said. Moved with compassion, Jesus reached out and touched him. "I am willing," he said. "Be healed!" MARK 1:40-41

He comforts us in all our troubles so that we can comfort others. When they are troubled, we will be able to give them the same comfort God has given us. 2 CORINTHIANS 1:4

Leprosy was the AIDS of Jesus' day. Lepers were shunned and led lonely lives. Just as Jesus touched and healed a leper out of great compassion, so we should respond to those with AIDS. Bring "healing" in any way you can—take a meal to them, spend time with them, offer words of encouragement and hope, be a friend. God calls you to love, serve, and have compassion for all people.

AMBITION *See also* Desires, Goals, Greed, Success, Work

Ambition can be compared to fire—both have the potential to be wonderfully productive or terribly destructive. When fire is kept in a fireplace, it creates the benefits of heat and light. But when used improperly, fire threatens to consume the home and all those inside. So it is with ambition. The Bible encourages us to learn to distinguish between godly ambition, which produces great benefits, and selfish ambition, which can become like a fire burning out of control.

When is ambition good?

Joyful are people of integrity, who follow the instructions of the LORD. Joyful are those who . . . search for him with all their hearts. PSALM 119:1-2

The purest ambition of all is to know God and to do what he asks.

Make it your goal to live a quiet life, minding your own business and working with your hands, just as we instructed you before. 1 THESSALONIANS 4:11

Ambition is good when it is directed at the quality of our character, not at self-promoting accomplishments.

A tree is identified by its fruit. . . . A good person produces good things from the treasury of a good heart. LUKE 6:44-45

A good ambition is to be productive serving God. Just as a vibrant fruit tree produces good fruit, so we should produce "fruit" as we do the work God has given us. God's people are to live lives that bear the fruit of righteousness, justice, and obedience.

When does ambition become destructive or sinful? What is the danger of ambition?

Let's build a great city for ourselves with a tower that reaches into the sky. This will make us famous. GENESIS 11:4

Ambition becomes wrong when its goal is to bring glory to yourself instead of God, who gave you your talents and abilities.

"I will give it all to you," [the devil] said, "if you will kneel down and worship me." MATTHEW 4:9

Ambition can become destructive if Satan uses it to lure you away from God. You can test your ambitions by asking if what you want to do will lead you closer to or further away from God. If you're not sure, then it is leading you away from him.

What kind of ambition does God want me to have?

God blesses those who hunger and thirst for justice, for they will be satisfied. . . . God blesses those who work for peace, for they will be called the children of God. MATTHEW 5:6, 9

Go and make disciples of all the nations. . . . Teach these new disciples to obey all the commands I have given you. MATTHEW 28:19-20

Let love be your highest goal! 1 CORINTHIANS 14:1

Working toward justice, peace, and love in the world and bringing people into fellowship with God are ambitions worthy of your time and energy.

My ambition has always been to preach the Good News where the name of Christ has never been heard. ROMANS 15:20

Paul demonstrated a "holy ambition" to do great things for God. A holy ambition is a large vision rooted in the will and service of God—a cause so large only God can pull it off. But this cause can degenerate into a selfish pursuit unless it is continually realigned with God's plan and energized by the Holy Spirit.

How do I guard against selfish ambition?

Don't be selfish; don't try to impress others. Be humble, thinking of others as better than yourselves. PHILIPPIANS 2:3

Priorities change when you concentrate on others instead of focusing on what they think of you. Rather than trying to impress others with yourself, impress upon them their worth and value as individuals made in God's image.

If others have reason for confidence in their own efforts, I have even more! . . . I once thought these things were valuable, but now I consider them worthless because of what Christ has done. Yes, everything else is worthless when compared with the infinite value of knowing Christ Jesus my Lord. . . . I focus on this one thing: Forgetting the past and looking forward to what lies ahead, I press on to reach the end of the race and receive the heavenly prize for which God, through Christ Jesus, is calling us. PHILIPPIANS 3:4, 7-8, 13-14

Selfish ambition fades as truth dawns. In reality, earthly achievements cannot compare with knowing Jesus Christ. In fact, they can get in the way, distracting you from depending fully on God. At the end of your life, only what's done for him will matter.

ANGELS *See also* Spiritual Warfare

A man walks away from a deadly car crash without a scratch. A stranger pulls a child from the path of an oncoming vehicle and then disappears. Were both the man and the child saved by angels? We may never know for sure. But we do know that angels exist because the Bible provides eyewitness accounts from real people who have seen them. We also know that angels are God's special messengers who sometimes intercede on earth to bring God's justice, to carry out God's will, or to take care of us. Angels play a special role for God both on earth and in heaven, a role we will never fully understand until the day God reveals his mysteries.

Are angels real?

Then the LORD opened Balaam's eyes, and he saw the angel of the LORD standing in the roadway with a drawn sword in his hand. Balaam bowed his head and fell face down on the ground before him. NUMBERS 22:31

My God sent his angel to shut the lions' mouths so that they would not hurt me, for I have been found innocent in his sight. DANIEL 6:22

Gabriel appeared to her and said, "Greetings, favored woman! The Lord is with you!" . . . "Don't be afraid, Mary," the angel told her, "for you have found favor with God!" LUKE 1:28-30

Suddenly, there was a bright light in the cell, and an angel of the Lord stood before Peter. The angel struck him on the side to awaken him and said, "Quick! Get up!" And the chains fell off his wrists. ACTS 12:7

Angels are supernatural, celestial beings. Like humans, they are created by God. The reality of angels is documented by many people in the Old and New Testaments.

How do angels compare with humans?

I, John, am the one who heard and saw all these things. And when I heard and saw them, I fell down to worship at the feet of the angel who showed them to me. But he said,

"No, don't worship me. I am a servant of God, just like you and your brothers the prophets, as well as all who obey what is written in this book. Worship only God!" REVELATION 22:8-9

Both humans and angels are created to serve God.

I heard the voices of thousands and millions of angels around the throne and of the living beings and the elders. And they sang in a mighty chorus: "Worthy is the Lamb who was slaughtered—to receive power and riches and wisdom and strength and honor and glory and blessing." REVELATION 5:11-12

A primary function of both humans and angels is to worship God.

You are like an angel of God in discerning good from evil. . . . You are as wise as an angel of God, and you understand everything that happens among us! 2 SAMUEL 14:17, 20

Both humans and angels are intelligent beings.

There is joy in the presence of God's angels when even one sinner repents. LUKE 15:10

Both humans and angels have emotions.

God did not spare even the angels who sinned. He threw them into hell, in gloomy pits of darkness, where they are being held until the day of judgment. 2 PETER 2:4

Humans and angels were created with free will; therefore, both are imperfect. Humans and angels are accountable to God, so both are subject to judgment.

As I, Daniel, was trying to understand the meaning of this vision, someone who looked like a man stood in front of me. And I heard a human voice calling out from the Ulai River, "Gabriel, tell this man the meaning of his vision." DANIEL 8:15-16

Angels have some human characteristics and can even appear fully human.

They will never die again. In this respect they will be like angels. They are children of God and children of the resurrection. LUKE 20:36

Humans are mortal; angels are immortal.

"Don't be afraid!" Elisha told him. "For there are more on our side than on theirs!" Then Elisha prayed, "O LORD, open his eyes and let him see!" The LORD opened the young man's eyes, and when he looked up, he saw that the hillside around Elisha was filled with horses and chariots of fire. 2 KINGS 6:16-17

Angels can be visible or invisible.

Those who . . . despise authority . . . are proud and arrogant, daring even to scoff at supernatural beings without so much as trembling. But the angels . . . are far greater in power and strength. 2 PETER 2:10-11

Angels are stronger and more powerful than humans.

When the dead rise, they will neither marry nor be given in marriage. In this respect they will be like the angels in heaven. MATTHEW 22:30

Relationships between angels differ from earthly relationships between humans.

What do angels do?

All heaven will praise your great wonders, LORD; myriads of angels will praise you for your faithfulness. For who in all of heaven can compare with the LORD? What mightiest angel is anything like the LORD? The highest angelic powers stand in awe of God. He is far more awesome than all who surround his throne. PSALM 89:5-7

Heavenly angels worship and praise God.

The Spirit then compelled Jesus to go into the wilderness, where he was tempted by Satan for forty days. He was out among the wild animals, and angels took care of him. MARK 1:12-13

Angels ministered to Jesus while he was on earth.

The rider standing among the myrtle trees then explained, "They are the ones the LORD has sent out to patrol the earth." Then the other riders reported to the angel of the LORD, who was standing among the myrtle trees, "We have been patrolling the earth, and the whole earth is at peace." ZECHARIAH 1:10-11

The angel said to [John], "Everything you have heard and seen is trustworthy and true. The Lord God, who inspires his prophets, has sent his angel to tell his servants what will happen soon."... "I, Jesus, have sent my angel to give you this message." REVELATION 22:6, 16

Angels are God's special messengers. God uses angels to give people guidance and direction and to complete special missions on earth.

The LORD sent an angel who destroyed the Assyrian army with all its commanders and officers. So Sennacherib was forced to return home in disgrace to his own land. And when he entered the temple of his god, some of his own sons killed him there with a sword. 2 CHRONICLES 32:21

Then there was war in heaven. Michael and his angels fought against the dragon and his angels. And the dragon lost the battle, and he and his angels were forced out of heaven. This great dragon—the ancient serpent called the devil, or Satan, the one deceiving the whole world—was thrown down to the earth with all his angels. REVELATION 12:7-9

Heavenly angels are God's warriors. God's angels are in constant battle against Satan's angels. God's angels are stronger than Satan's angels and will one day defeat them when God says it is time.

The two angels reached out, pulled Lot into the house, and bolted the door. Then they blinded all the men, young and old, who were at the door of the house, so they gave up trying to get inside. GENESIS 19:10-11

Angels are sometimes called upon to protect God's people.

"Don't be afraid," he said, "for you are very precious to God. Peace! Be encouraged! Be strong!" As he spoke these words to me, I suddenly felt stronger and said to him, "Please speak to me, my lord, for you have strengthened me." DANIEL 10:19

Angels offer encouragement.

You deliberately disobeyed God's law, even though you received it from the hands of angels. ACTS 7:53

Angels can convey God's laws to people.

That night the angel of the LORD went out to the Assyrian camp and killed 185,000 Assyrian soldiers. 2 KINGS 19:35

Instantly, an angel of the Lord struck Herod with a sickness, because he accepted the people's worship instead of giving the glory to God. So he was consumed with worms and died. ACTS 12:23

Angels execute God's judgment.

Praise the LORD, you angels, you mighty ones who carry out his plans, listening for each of his commands. Yes, praise the LORD, you armies of angels who serve him and do his will! PSALM 103:20-21

Angels carry out God's will.

Do I have a guardian angel?

[The Lord] will order his angels to protect you wherever you go. They will hold you up with their hands so you won't even hurt your foot on a stone. PSALM 91:11-12

Angels are only servants—spirits sent to care for people who will inherit salvation. HEBREWS 1:14

The Bible does not say whether there is one specific angel assigned to each believer. It does say that God uses his angels to counsel, guide, protect, minister to, rescue, fight for, and care for his people. Whether he uses one angel specifically assigned to a particular individual or a host of angels to minister to a host of human needs, it is God's choice and your blessing. Chances are that angels have played a greater role in your life than you realize.

Are there really evil angels? Can they harm us?

We are not fighting against flesh-and-blood enemies, but against evil rulers and authorities of the unseen world, against mighty powers in this dark world, and against evil spirits in the heavenly places. EPHESIANS 6:12

You say you have faith, for you believe that there is one God. Good for you! Even the demons believe this, and they tremble in terror. JAMES 2:19

Evil angels do exist, and they know there is a God.

God did not spare even the angels who sinned. He threw them into hell, in gloomy pits of darkness, where they are being held until the day of judgment. 2 PETER 2:4

Angels were created by God and given a will. Amazingly, after tasting heaven, some chose to rebel against God and follow Satan.

Then the devil, who had deceived them, was thrown into the fiery lake of burning sulfur, joining the beast and the false prophet. There they will be tormented day and night forever and ever. REVELATION 20:10

God has judged and condemned the devil, his angels (called demons), and all their followers to eternity in hell. Christians have authority and victory over Satan and his angels because of the victorious death and resurrection of Jesus Christ.

ANGER *See also* Hatred, Jealousy, Temper, Violence

Of all the emotions, anger may well be the most passionate, for it has the power to fuel hatred and smother love. Anger itself is not wrong. God himself gets angry. But there is a difference between righteous anger and sinful anger, and that difference is determined by the object of our anger, our motive, and the outcome. Anger that is self-righteous, self-centered, prideful, or self-willed is dangerous. If allowed to continue unchecked, it consumes us, leads to bitterness and hatred and violent behavior, and obliterates compassion and forgiveness. God's anger, however, is directed against sin and unrighteousness. His anger is a consuming fire, but his focus is to eradicate sin, not destroy the sinner. Our anger usually has the opposite effect—it spreads sin, and it consumes others and even ourselves. God's anger burns against evil. It is a cleansing fire that burns away impurities and allows the gold to emerge, making us fit for the Master's use.

Why do I get angry?

The LORD accepted Abel and his gift, but he did not accept Cain and his gift. This made Cain very angry, and he looked dejected. GENESIS 4:4-5

When Haman saw that Mordecai would not bow down or show him respect, he was filled with rage. ESTHER 3:5

Anger is often a reaction to hurt pride. When you are confronted, rejected, ignored, or don't get your own way, anger is a defense mechanism used to protect your ego. It is common to feel angry when someone confronts you about your own sinful actions, because you don't want others to know you have done something wrong.

This made Saul very angry. "What's this?" he said. "They credit David with ten thousands and me with only thousands. Next they'll be making him their king!" 1 SAMUEL 18:8

Anger often shows itself as jealousy of what others have or what they have accomplished.

What are the effects of anger?

A gentle answer deflects anger, but harsh words make tempers flare. PROVERBS 15:1

Anger leads to conflict and arguments.

Esau hated Jacob because their father had given Jacob the blessing. And Esau began to scheme: . . . "I will kill my brother, Jacob." But Rebekah heard about Esau's plans. So she sent for Jacob and told him, ". . . Get ready and flee to my brother, Laban, in Haran." GENESIS 27:41-43

Anger isolates you from others.

Saul boiled with rage at Jonathan. . . . "As long as that son of Jesse is alive, you'll never be king. Now go and get him so I can kill him!" 1 SAMUEL 20:30-31

Anger spawns evil motives and leads to ungodly actions. Left unchecked, anger can produce thoughts of violence and even lead to murder because it blinds you to what is right and good. Saul's jealous anger blinded him to the fact that God had already chosen David to be the next king because of his godly character. As a result, Saul plotted to kill David.

What makes God angry?

God is my shield, saving those whose hearts are true and right. God is an honest judge. He is angry with the wicked every day. PSALM 7:10-11

God cannot tolerate sin and rebellion against himself; therefore, any kind of sin or evil angers him. But he is ready to forgive because he is kind and merciful. Those who humbly confess their sin and turn to God in faith receive his abundant love and mercy instead of anger.

"At that time I will put you on trial. . . . I will speak against those who cheat employees of their wages, who oppress widows and orphans, or who deprive the foreigners living among you of justice, for these people do not fear me," says the LORD *of Heaven's Armies.* MALACHI 3:5

God gets angry when people neglect or abuse the unfortunate and those in need.

How can I control my anger?

A gentle answer deflects anger, but harsh words make tempers flare. PROVERBS 15:1

Christ suffered for you. He is your example, and you must follow in his steps. . . . He did not retaliate when he was insulted, nor threaten revenge when he suffered. He left his case in the hands of God, who always judges fairly. 1 PETER 2:21, 23

Jesus teaches that giving in to anger is sin. In addition, giving in to anger gives power to the cause of your anger. Striking back invites the other person to strike back harder.

When anger wells up inside you, quickly ask God to help you respond appropriately, without retaliating or escalating the conflict.

Don't sin by letting anger control you. Think about it overnight and remain silent.
PSALM 4:4

Thinking through an issue ahead of time and planning a gentle response will help you restrain yourself instead of reacting impulsively. Then you will not only keep from sinning, but you will also earn respect for having good sense and self-control.

[Love] is not irritable, and it keeps no record of being wronged. 1 CORINTHIANS 13:5

Love is the mightiest weapon in overcoming anger. It is hard to stay angry at people when you concentrate on their lovable qualities and how much you love them or how much God loves them.

What are the benefits of restraining anger?
Sensible people control their temper; they earn respect by overlooking wrongs.
PROVERBS 19:11

Rarely will you regret having controlled your temper. Whereas venting anger breeds more anger, restraining anger often cools the fires of conflict. It indicates your mature character.

When I am angry, what should I avoid?
As David played his harp, Saul hurled his spear at David. 1 SAMUEL 19:9-10

Avoid acting on impulse in the heat of anger. You may do something that will haunt you for the rest of your life.

When is anger appropriate?
The LORD said to Moses, "Phinehas . . . has turned my anger away from the Israelites by being as zealous among them as I was. So I stopped destroying all Israel as I had intended to do in my zealous anger." NUMBERS 25:10-11

[Jesus] drove out the sheep and cattle, scattered the money changers' coins over the floor, and turned over their tables. Then . . . he told them, "Get these things out of here. Stop turning my Father's house into a marketplace!" Then his disciples remembered this prophecy from the Scriptures: "Passion for God's house will consume me."
JOHN 2:15-17

Anger at sin is not only appropriate but necessary.

APATHY *See also* Complacency, Laziness, Procrastination
In the book of Revelation, apathy is compared to lukewarm water (see 3:16). Cold water quenches thirst and refreshes a parched mouth. Hot water is used for cooking and sanitizing. But lukewarm water has little appeal. Apathy is much the same. When apathy settles in, it means that passion and purpose have gone away. Those who are apathetic don't care about

much. Apathy is like a disease that feeds on your cares and motivations and wastes your talents and gifts. Fortunately, there are antidotes: Hard work, a thankful heart, and acts of service toward others can help fight off feelings of apathy and renew your focus on God's purpose for your life and the blessings he has given you.

What causes apathy?

They have no sense of shame. They live for lustful pleasure and eagerly practice every kind of impurity. EPHESIANS 4:19

Sinful living causes apathy. Sin turns the spotlight onto yourself and selfishness, so concern for others fades away.

As soon as they were at peace, [the] people again committed evil in [God's] sight. NEHEMIAH 9:28

Success, prosperity, or easy living can lead to apathy.

What are some warning signs of apathy?

Who will listen when I speak? Their ears are closed, and they cannot hear. They scorn the word of the LORD. They don't want to listen at all. JEREMIAH 6:10

Ignoring or neglecting God's Word is a warning sign. When you cut yourself off from God, you cut off your lifeline to the one who gives you purpose and joy.

Lot rushed out to tell his daughters' fiancés, "Quick, get out of the city! The LORD is about to destroy it." But the young men thought he was only joking. GENESIS 19:14

Not taking sin seriously is a warning sign. When you can't find anything bad enough to outrage your soul, you have become apathetic to what God says and what he values. You may be falling in step with Satan rather than walking with God.

Listen, you women who lie around in ease. Listen to me, you who are so smug. ISAIAH 32:9

Becoming more and more lazy is a warning sign. It's hard to win a race and enjoy its rewards from a rocking chair.

Our ancestors in Egypt were not impressed by the LORD's miraculous deeds. They soon forgot his many acts of kindness to them. Instead, they rebelled against him at the Red Sea. . . . Yet how quickly they forgot what he had done! They wouldn't wait for his counsel! PSALM 106:7, 13

Forgetting God's past acts of mercy and love is a warning sign. When your memories of God's blessings fade, so will your contentment with life.

What can I do when I am feeling apathetic?

Watch out! Don't let your hearts be dulled by carousing and drunkenness, and by the worries of this life. Don't let that day catch you unaware. LUKE 21:34

Jesus warns his followers to be alert to spiritual apathy. You don't want to be caught at the end of your life having neglected your relationship with God because you've been so focused on "living the good life."

I am shriveled like a wineskin in the smoke, but I have not forgotten to obey your decrees.
PSALM 119:83

Obey God's commands even when you don't feel like it. This takes tremendous effort, but it's hard to be apathetic when you're so focused on something. Whatever takes great effort is also stimulating and engaging. This will help keep you close to God.

Don't look out only for your own interests, but take an interest in others, too.
PHILIPPIANS 2:4

The more interested you are in something, the less apathy you will have. So, the more interested you become in the lives of those around you, the more you'll care about them. Getting involved in the lives of others will not only keep you from becoming indifferent but will challenge you to find ways to reflect the love of Christ to them.

Lazy people want much but get little, but those who work hard will prosper.
PROVERBS 13:4

One of the best cures for apathy is hard work! When you work hard, you become productive. The more productive you are, the more you are satisfied and fulfilled. And when you see your hard work as an act of service to God, you gain even more energy because you see God working through you to bless others.

The LORD gave [Jeremiah] this message: "I knew you before I formed you in your mother's womb. Before you were born I set you apart and appointed you as my prophet to the nations." JEREMIAH 1:4-5

You can stimulate your passion for life by realizing that God has a purpose for you. God created you to make a difference for his kingdom! Purpose stirs passion, and passion drives apathy away.

What happens if apathy is allowed to grow in my life?

How long must this land mourn? Even the grass in the fields has withered. The wild animals and birds have disappeared because of the evil in the land. JEREMIAH 12:4

Without God, life ultimately becomes empty and withered because you wonder if anything you've done really matters or will really last. Without God, your sinful nature is allowed to eat away at you unchecked, eventually turning your soul into a wasteland. When you invite God into your life, he begins to clean out the sin so your soul can thrive and flourish.

Tremble, you women of ease; throw off your complacency. Strip off your pretty clothes, and put on burlap to show your grief. Beat your breasts in sorrow for your bountiful farms and your fruitful grapevines. For your land will be overgrown with thorns and briers. Your joyful homes and happy towns will be gone. ISAIAH 32:11-13

Ironically, apathy causes you to lose what you want the most. If a man is apathetic toward his wife, he is in danger of losing her. If you are apathetic about investing your money, you will not have much of it for retirement. If you are apathetic toward God, you are in danger of losing the priceless rewards that await his followers in heaven. Not only is apathy a passive force that lulls us to sleep, but it can also be an aggressive force that prevents us from keeping what is most meaningful and important.

Son of man, you live among rebels who have eyes but refuse to see. They have ears but refuse to hear. EZEKIEL 12:2

Apathy can lead to rejection of God. If you don't care about what's really true or what God wants you to do, then you are in fact rebelling against him. Having an "I don't care" attitude about God is the same as saying to him, "Stay away from me."

APOLOGY *See also* Confession, Forgiveness, Reconciliation

Saying "I'm sorry" for something you have done wrong is one of the most difficult things to do. You have to recognize your fault, face it head-on, and then humble yourself enough to admit it to someone else. A true apology is the first step in changing your behavior and committing to do the right thing from now on. Refusing to apologize when you know you're wrong is a clear sign of pride, which has devastating effects on your life and relationships. But a simple apology demonstrates humility and will open the door to healing and blessing.

Why should I apologize? What are the benefits?

People who conceal their sins will not prosper, but if they confess and turn from them, they will receive mercy. Blessed are those who fear to do wrong, but the stubborn are headed for serious trouble. PROVERBS 28:13-14

It was also written that this message would be proclaimed in the authority of his name to all the nations, beginning in Jerusalem: "There is forgiveness of sins for all who repent." LUKE 24:47

Confess your sins to each other and pray for each other so that you may be healed. JAMES 5:16

When you apologize, you receive forgiveness, mercy, healing, refreshment, and courage. In confessing your sins to God, you receive eternal life! Refusing to apologize will prevent you from receiving all these blessings. Often you will still experience the consequences of your wrong actions because the harm has already been done. But God's forgiveness restores your relationship with him.

To whom should I apologize?

Against you, and you alone, have I sinned; I have done what is evil in your sight. PSALM 51:4

First, apologize to God. Any wrong you do saddens your Creator, who desires your obedience. Sometimes you sin only against God, as is the case with your thought life. Make sure you confess these sins to him. He will always forgive.

So if you are presenting a sacrifice at the altar in the Temple and you suddenly remember that someone has something against you, leave your sacrifice there at the altar. Go and be reconciled to that person. Then come and offer your sacrifice to God.
MATTHEW 5:23-24

When you have done something wrong that has hurt someone else, it is essential to apologize to that person. An apology may not remove the consequences of your actions, but it will make room for forgiveness, remove some of the pain, and bring about restoration of the relationship. This will give you a clear conscience and a fresh start.

When should I apologize?

You know that afterward, when he wanted his father's blessing, he was rejected. It was too late for repentance, even though he begged with bitter tears. HEBREWS 12:17

Apologize as soon as you realize you have done something wrong. Timing is critical for an apology: It is never too early to seek forgiveness, but later it may be too late. If you need to apologize to someone, don't wait!

How do I apologize?

[Moses said,] "Please pardon the sins of this people, just as you have forgiven them ever since they left Egypt." Then the LORD said, "I will pardon them as you have requested."
NUMBERS 14:19-20

"I'm sorry, brothers. I didn't realize he was the high priest," Paul replied, "for the Scriptures say, 'You must not speak evil of any of your rulers.'" ACTS 23:5

"I'm sorry" is a good start. Admitting you are wrong and sincerely feeling bad about it shows humility and a desire to change. It opens the door to forgiveness and restoration.

His son said to him, "Father, I have sinned against both heaven and you, and I am no longer worthy of being called your son." LUKE 15:21

Apologize with honesty and humility. Don't try to justify what you did or blame others. Take ownership of your wrongs, and seek forgiveness.

If someone steals an ox or sheep and then kills or sells it, the thief must pay back five oxen for each ox stolen, and four sheep for each sheep stolen. EXODUS 22:1

Zacchaeus stood before the Lord and said, "I will give half my wealth to the poor, Lord, and if I have cheated people on their taxes, I will give them back four times as much!"
LUKE 19:8

An apology may need to include restitution. Sometimes you must overcompensate for your wrong to show that your apology is truly sincere.

How do I accept an apology?

David confessed to Nathan, "I have sinned against the LORD." Nathan replied, "Yes, but the LORD has forgiven you, and you won't die for this sin." 2 SAMUEL 12:13

The Lord welcomes a broken and repentant heart. He is quick to forgive and offer mercy. That's the example you must show when someone apologizes to you.

He returned home to his father. And while he was still a long way off, his father saw him coming. Filled with love and compassion, he ran to his son, embraced him, and kissed him. His son said to him, "Father, I have sinned against both heaven and you, and I am no longer worthy of being called your son." But his father said to the servants, "Quick! Bring the finest robe in the house and put it on him. Get a ring for his finger and sandals for his feet. And kill the calf we have been fattening. We must celebrate with a feast, for this son of mine was dead and has now returned to life. He was lost, but now he is found." So the party began. LUKE 15:20-24

When someone apologizes to us, we're often tempted to punish them further, to lash out in anger, to make them suffer a little more. But in this parable, Jesus tells us the father not only forgave his son at once, he threw a party to celebrate this great event in his son's life—being restored to his family. True forgiveness is not grudging or sparing but joyful, generous, and healing.

APPEARANCE *See also* Modesty, Status

In so many cultures, looks are everything. Those who are physically attractive get better breaks and get to enjoy more of the good life. If you make your boss look good, even if it means sacrificing your integrity, you improve your position in the company. And the person who has mastered the art of what to say and what not to say in a social setting is the most popular. In almost everything we do, appearances matter. But should they? God also says that appearances matter, but he has some very different ideas about what we should be looking at. How you look on the inside is more important than how you look on the outside. How you look in the Lord's eyes is far more important than how you look in your boss's eyes. And how you accurately reflect the characteristics of Jesus is more important than anything you might do to win popularity with your peers.

How much does appearance matter?

People judge by outward appearance, but the LORD looks at the heart.
1 SAMUEL 16:7

Don't be concerned about the outward beauty of fancy hairstyles, expensive jewelry, or beautiful clothes. You should clothe yourselves instead with the beauty that comes from within, the unfading beauty of a gentle and quiet spirit, which is so precious to God.
1 PETER 3:3-4

Appearance does matter; just make sure you're looking at the right things. Your outward appearance, including your body, face, and clothes, reflects your earthly shell, which is in a constant process of aging and decay. Your soul and character reflect your inner being, which is ageless and eternal and reflects who you really are. Walking with God causes you to reflect his beauty. There's nothing wrong with paying attention to your physical appearance, but you should not neglect your spiritual appearance.

How can appearances be deceiving?

When [Jesse's sons] arrived, Samuel took one look at Eliab and thought, "Surely this is the LORD's anointed!" But the LORD said to Samuel, "Don't judge by his appearance or height, for I have rejected him. The LORD doesn't see things the way you see them. People judge by outward appearance, but the LORD looks at the heart." 1 SAMUEL 16:6-7

The condition of your body does not reveal the condition of your heart.

He was despised and rejected—a man of sorrows, acquainted with deepest grief. We turned our backs on him and looked the other way. He was despised, and we did not care. ISAIAH 53:3

What you see is not always what you get because appearances can be misleading. Jesus came to earth as a plain-looking man and was not recognized as God's Son despite the perfect condition of his heart. Be careful not to judge people based on how they look.

What is the danger in evaluating others based on appearance?

These people are false apostles. They are deceitful workers who disguise themselves as apostles of Christ. But I am not surprised! Even Satan disguises himself as an angel of light. So it is no wonder that his servants also disguise themselves as servants of righteousness. 2 CORINTHIANS 11:13-15

A beautiful cover on a book does not make it good literature. In the same way, nice appearances can cover up a lot of faults. A smooth talker can cover up a lack of substance—for a while. A lot of religious activity may appear good, but it can sometimes be a cover for self-centered interests. Make sure to focus on substance, not on image.

How do I see beyond appearances?

You can identify them by their fruit, that is, by the way they act. . . . A good tree produces good fruit, and a bad tree produces bad fruit. A good tree can't produce bad fruit, and a bad tree can't produce good fruit. . . . Yes, just as you can identify a tree by its fruit, so you can identify people by their actions. Not everyone who calls out to me, "Lord! Lord!" will enter the Kingdom of Heaven. MATTHEW 7:16-21

All God's people must be "fruit inspectors," looking beyond appearances and words to the actual fruit of a person's behavior and character. Obedience to the Bible is an essential mark of authentic faith in Jesus Christ. Good works alone are not sufficient. There must be consistency between words and works, character and conduct.

Is there any value to maintaining a good appearance?

Don't you realize that your body is the temple of the Holy Spirit, who lives in you and was given to you by God? You do not belong to yourself, for God bought you with a high price. So you must honor God with your body. 1 CORINTHIANS 6:19-20

You should not be obsessed with your physical appearance, but neither should you ignore it. How you present yourself is in part a reflection of who you are and plays a role in your ability to interact with others. Your body is the house in which the Holy Spirit dwells, so you should take care of it. The more you take care of your body, the more energy you have to serve God. Keeping yourself clean and pleasant looking allows more opportunities to become involved in other people's lives and to influence them with the Good News of Jesus. How you present yourself can help you in the way you represent Jesus Christ.

APPROVAL *See also* Peer Pressure, Respect, Judging Others

What causes us to approve of some people and not others? Too often it comes down to appearance or performance. We don't like the way someone looks, or we don't like something someone has done. Or perhaps the shoe is on the other foot, and we've found it hard to win the approval of someone we care about or work for. We may never get that approval, no matter how good we look or how well we perform. The most important thing to understand about approval is the ground rules. It's appropriate for your boss to disapprove of your work if you are not meeting his standards of performance. It's appropriate for God to disapprove of your behavior if you are living a lifestyle that is contrary to his commandments.

But there's another kind of approval that everyone needs and that must never be based on performance—the unconditional love we all long for. In a good family, you find love and acceptance no matter how you look or what you do. This is a picture of what it's like to be in God's family. As a child of God, created in his image, you are loved and accepted for who you are. The fact that God has created you gives you great worth. He loves you and approves of you because you are his, no matter what you think about him or what others think about you. This knowledge should motivate you to do all you can to please God more.

Can I earn God's approval?

Nothing in all creation will ever be able to separate us from the love of God that is revealed in Christ Jesus our Lord. ROMANS 8:39

When I tried to keep the law, it condemned me. GALATIANS 2:19

You cannot earn God's approval because he already approves of you! His approval is based not on your performance but on the fact that you are his creation. Your performance is an expression of your gratitude to God, not the basis for his approval.

Everyone has sinned; we all fall short of God's glorious standard. . . . If you confess with your mouth that Jesus is Lord and believe in your heart that God raised him from the dead, you will be saved. ROMANS 3:23; 10:9

Nothing can ever separate us from God's love. ROMANS 8:38

While God loves you unconditionally, he does not approve of your sinful behavior. When you understand that it is your sin that separates you from God and that Jesus died and rose again to take away your sin and restore you to God, you realize how much he values you. When you confess your sins to him, seek his forgiveness, and commit to following Jesus, you have been approved to enter heaven for eternity. There's a difference between God's unconditional love (he doesn't love some people, even Christians, more than others) and his conditional salvation (he saves only those who admit they have sinned and need his forgiveness). Understanding that difference is a matter of life and death.

What are the things I should not approve of?

We must live decent lives for all to see. Don't participate in the darkness of wild parties and drunkenness, or in sexual promiscuity and immoral living, or in quarreling and jealousy. ROMANS 13:13

You should not approve of anything that contradicts God's Word.

Do not let sin control the way you live. ROMANS 6:12

You should not approve of sinful behavior or allow sin to control the way you live.

How should I give my approval to others?

Don't just pretend to love others. Really love them. Hate what is wrong. Hold tightly to what is good. Love each other with genuine affection, and take delight in honoring each other. ROMANS 12:9-10

Loving and serving others affirms their value and worth as God's creations and shows them you approve of them.

How do I respond when others disapprove of my faith?

The LORD is my light and my salvation—so why should I be afraid? The LORD is my fortress, protecting me from danger, so why should I tremble? PSALM 27:1

Your ultimate purpose is to please God, who made you and redeemed you, no matter what others may think of you. Focus on God and feel his approval.

[Jesus said,] "Your approval means nothing to me." JOHN 5:41

Jesus' strong words came out of his unwavering confidence in God's approval and his own freedom from being a slave to human opinion. You too can live free from the bondage of human opinion and criticism when you truly grasp God's love and approval.

ASSUMPTIONS See also Judging Others

We make dozens of assumptions every day. In fact, it would be difficult to function if we couldn't make assumptions about weather, traffic, food, work, and relationships. Many of our assumptions are harmless, and many are necessary (like assuming that gravity will continue to keep our feet on the ground as we walk). On the other hand, assumptions can also be wrong and harmful, causing us to react in ways that have negative effects. For example, when we see a kid with pink hair and dressed in black, we might assume he's into drugs, only to find out later he's involved on a Christian ministry team. These wrong assumptions happen all the time, which is why it is important to recognize that some assumptions can be harmful and get us into trouble. We need to get the facts instead of jumping to conclusions. In this way, we can act wisely and avoid hurting ourselves and others.

What is the danger in making assumptions?

"My thoughts are nothing like your thoughts," says the LORD. "And my ways are far beyond anything you could imagine." ISAIAH 55:8

Our natural assumptions rarely align themselves with the way God thinks. If you want to understand how God acts, you must work to understand how he thinks.

The Ammonite commanders said to Hanun, their master, "Do you really think these men are coming here to honor your father? No! David has sent them to spy out the city so they can come in and conquer it!" 2 SAMUEL 10:3

Fear can cause you to assume the worst about people and their intentions. If you consistently assume the worst about others, you will become suspicious and paranoid. You may also hurt others as you try to keep them away from you.

Don't be in a hurry to go to court. For what will you do in the end if your neighbor deals you a shameful defeat? PROVERBS 25:8

Assumptions are often made too quickly. As the old saying goes, "Haste makes waste." When you are too quick to judge before having all the information, you make poor decisions, which you may later regret.

[Sarah] laughed silently to herself and said, "How could a worn-out woman like me enjoy such pleasure, especially when my master—my husband—is also so old?" GENESIS 18:12

Assumptions made from a human viewpoint lead to actions from a human viewpoint, often closing the door to God's miracles in your life. When you are open to the possibilities of God working in your life, you begin to see his work around you more clearly.

As she was praying to the LORD, Eli watched her. Seeing her lips moving but hearing no sound, he thought she had been drinking. "Must you come here drunk?" he demanded. "Throw away your wine!" "Oh no, sir!" she replied. "I haven't been drinking wine or anything stronger. But I am very discouraged, and I was pouring out my heart to the LORD. Don't think I am a wicked woman! For I have been praying out of great anguish and sorrow." 1 SAMUEL 1:12-16

Assumptions are often unfair because they judge another person before the facts are known.

When God saw what they had done and how they had put a stop to their evil ways, he changed his mind and did not carry out the destruction he had threatened. . . . So [Jonah] complained to the LORD about it. JONAH 3:10; 4:2

Sometimes an assumption causes you to give up on people instead of seeing them through God's eyes. Jonah assumed that the Ninevites could never be saved. When you judge the spiritual condition of others, you doubt that almighty God has the power to change lives.

Moses assumed his fellow Israelites would realize that God had sent him to rescue them, but they didn't. ACTS 7:25

Sometimes an assumption can cause misunderstandings that damage relationships. If an assumption begins with a flawed premise, it will surely lead to a flawed conclusion.

What are some assumptions I should avoid?

Don't just say to each other, "We're safe, for we are descendants of Abraham." That means nothing, for I tell you, God can create children of Abraham from these very stones. Even now the ax of God's judgment is poised, ready to sever the roots of the trees. Yes, every tree that does not produce good fruit will be chopped down and thrown into the fire. MATTHEW 3:9-10

Jesus told him, "I am the way, the truth, and the life. No one can come to the Father except through me." JOHN 14:6

Don't just assume you will go to heaven. The Bible says the only way to heaven is by accepting Jesus Christ as Savior and Lord.

"I have always loved you," says the LORD. But you retort, "Really? How have you loved us?" MALACHI 1:2

Don't assume God doesn't care, for the evidence clearly shows he does.

"Sir," Gideon replied, "if the LORD is with us, why has all this happened to us? And where are all the miracles our ancestors told us about? Didn't they say, 'The LORD brought us up out of Egypt'? But now the LORD has abandoned us and handed us over to the Midianites." JUDGES 6:13

Don't assume God won't help you or doesn't want to help you, for he has already done so in more ways than you know and he will continue to do so. Don't assume you know better than God the best way through your problems.

"But Lord," exclaimed Ananias, "I've heard many people talk about the terrible things this man has done to the believers in Jerusalem!" . . . But the Lord said, "Go, for Saul is my chosen instrument to take my message to the Gentiles and to kings, as well as to the people of Israel." ACTS 9:13-15

Don't assume people can't change; you may miss out when they want to give their best. Like Saul, renamed Paul, the worst of sinners can become the mightiest of Jesus' followers.

When Moses' father-in-law saw all that Moses was doing for the people, he asked, "What are you really accomplishing here? Why are you trying to do all this alone while everyone stands around you from morning till evening? . . . Select from all the people some capable, honest men who fear God and hate bribes. Appoint them as leaders. . . . They will help you carry the load, making the task easier for you." EXODUS 18:14, 21-22

Don't assume that you are the only person who can do a certain job; others might do it better or at least help you. We all can benefit from the help and advice of others.

Then the LORD answered Job from the whirlwind: "Who is this that questions my wisdom with such ignorant words? Brace yourself like a man, because I have some questions for you, and you must answer them." JOB 38:1-3

Don't assume that you have all the answers, for you do not even understand all the questions. Only God knows everything.

ASTROLOGY *See also* Dreams/Visions, Idolatry

For centuries, many people have consulted astrologers for help in making important decisions, especially decisions about the future. Horoscopes, sun signs, and psychics all operate on the assumption that celestial events determine what happens in people's lives. Those who believe in astrology worship the creation over the Creator—the sun, moon, and stars have the greatest authority, not God, who made them. Looking to anything other than God for guidance is idolatry because only God has the answers to your biggest questions. He is the ultimate authority on the future.

Is astrology wrong?

You must not have any other god but me. EXODUS 20:3

Manasseh also sacrificed his own son in the fire. He practiced sorcery and divination, and he consulted with mediums and psychics. He did much that was evil in the LORD's sight, arousing his anger. 2 KINGS 21:6

Astrology is wrong because it involves worshiping the heavens instead of God, who created the heavens. Worshiping anything or anyone other than God is idolatry.

Can astrology give me direction?

God made two great lights—the larger one to govern the day, and the smaller one to govern the night. He also made the stars. God set these lights in the sky to light the earth. GENESIS 1:16-17

God controls all celestial events, so don't seek advice from the stars. Seek it from God, the Creator of the stars. He created you too, so only he can give you direction for your life. You should never worship the creation over the Creator.

Can God use celestial events to influence human events?

The sun stood still and the moon stayed in place until the nation of Israel had defeated its enemies. . . . The sun stayed in the middle of the sky, and it did not set as on a normal day. There has never been a day like this one before or since, when the LORD answered such a prayer. JOSHUA 10:13-14

After this interview the wise men went their way. And the star they had seen in the east guided them to Bethlehem. It went ahead of them and stopped over the place where the child was. When they saw the star, they were filled with joy! MATTHEW 2:9-10

Because God created all things, he can use celestial events to influence human events. It is absurd to think that the sun, moon, and stars have a mind of their own. Science has proven that this is impossible.

ATHEISM *See also* Idolatry, Salvation, Truth

Atheism is the belief system that says there is no God. Atheists spend much time and energy trying to prove God doesn't exist. What we decide about the existence of God is literally a choice between life and death. It is not enough to decide that he exists; we must then decide how we will respond to his clear message in the Bible.

What are the characteristics of atheism?

You did not know the covenant promises God had made. . . . You lived in this world without God and without hope. EPHESIANS 2:12

Living in ignorance of God. An atheist either has no knowledge of God or chooses to live like one who does not know God.

Who is a liar? Anyone who says that Jesus is not the Christ. Anyone who denies the Father and the Son is an antichrist. 1 JOHN 2:22

Denying Jesus Christ. Those who deny Jesus here on earth will be denied access to heaven at the time of judgment.

"Is that so?" retorted Pharaoh. "And who is the LORD? Why should I listen to him and let Israel go? I don't know the LORD." EXODUS 5:2

Defying God and his message. Picking a fight with the Creator of the universe is not a wise thing to do.

They even mock God and say, "Hurry up and do something! We want to see what you can do. Let the Holy One of Israel carry out his plan, for we want to know what it is." ISAIAH 5:19

Denying God's ability to intervene in human events. To deny that God takes an active interest in this world is the same as saying that God doesn't care about you or that God is not powerful enough to help you.

Do not bring shame on the name of your God by using it to swear falsely. I am the LORD. LEVITICUS 19:12

Showing contempt for God's name. Those who profane the name of God are cutting off their only lifeline to eternity.

What is God's desire for the atheist?

His purpose was for the nations to seek after God and perhaps feel their way toward him and find him—though he is not far from any one of us. ACTS 17:27

The Lord isn't really being slow about his promise, as some people think. No, he is being patient for your sake. He does not want anyone to be destroyed, but wants everyone to repent. 2 PETER 3:9

God's desire for the atheist is repentance, salvation, and a personal relationship with him. God loves even those who do not love him. There is no greater love than that.

What does the future look like for the atheist?

They know the truth about God because he has made it obvious to them. For ever since the world was created, people have seen the earth and sky. Through everything God made, they can clearly see his invisible qualities—his eternal power and divine nature. So they have no excuse for not knowing God. ROMANS 1:19-20

God has given plenty of evidence for his existence. He even created humans with a certain knowledge of himself. There is no excuse for not knowing him and recognizing his presence in creation.

What hope do the godless have when God cuts them off and takes away their life? JOB 27:8

The future for an atheist is hopeless. Those who deny the existence of God have cut themselves off from a relationship with him. The Bible is clear that only those who acknowledge God as Lord have the hope of living forever in heaven with him.

How can I know there is a God?

All who see this miracle will understand what it means—that it is the LORD who has done this, the Holy One of Israel who created it. "Present the case for your idols," says the LORD. "Let them show what they can do," says the King of Israel. "Let them try to tell us what happened long ago so that we may consider the evidence. Or let them tell us what the future holds, so we can know what's going to happen. Yes, tell us what will occur in the days ahead. Then we will know you are gods. In fact, do anything—good or bad!" ISAIAH 41:20-23

Remember the things I have done in the past. For I alone am God! I am God. . . . Only I can tell you the future before it even happens. Everything I plan will come to pass, for I do whatever I wish. ISAIAH 46:9-10

Fulfillment of prophecy. The record of the prophets, who spoke long before the prophesied events, confirms that what they spoke was truth—God's truth.

God has made everything beautiful for its own time. He has planted eternity in the human heart. ECCLESIASTES 3:11

Even Gentiles, who do not have God's written law, show that they know his law when they instinctively obey it, even without having heard it. They demonstrate that God's law is written in their hearts, for their own conscience and thoughts either accuse them or tell them they are doing right. ROMANS 2:14-15

Your inner conscience. In your heart you know there is someone out there much bigger than you. This awareness is the work of your conscience, which God has built into your heart and the heart of every human being. If you listen to your conscience, it will convict you of your need for God.

The LORD answered Job from the whirlwind: "Who is this that questions my wisdom with such ignorant words? Brace yourself like a man, because I have some questions for you, and you must answer them. Where were you when I laid the foundations of the earth? Tell me, if you know so much." JOB 38:1-4

The heavens proclaim the glory of God. The skies display his craftsmanship. Day after day they continue to speak; night after night they make him known. PSALM 19:1-2

O LORD my God, how great you are! . . . You stretch out the starry curtain of the heavens; you lay out the rafters of your home in the rain clouds. You make the clouds your chariot; you ride upon the wings of the wind. The winds are your messengers; flames of fire are your servants. PSALM 104:1-4

He never left them without evidence of himself and his goodness. For instance, he sends you rain and good crops and gives you food and joyful hearts. ACTS 14:17

The design of nature. All creation testifies to the Creator. Nothing can be made without a maker.

[Paul] used to blaspheme the name of Christ. In my insolence, I persecuted his people. But God had mercy on me because I did it in ignorance and unbelief. . . . "Christ Jesus came into the world to save sinners"—and I am the worst of them all. But God had mercy on me so that Christ Jesus could use me as a prime example of his great patience with even the worst sinners. Then others will realize that they, too, can believe in him and receive eternal life. 1 TIMOTHY 1:13-16

The testimony of others. When God changes lives, like he changed Paul's, it is clear to others that a divine miracle has occurred.

ATTITUDE *See also* Character, Emotions, Thoughts

Your attitude plays a huge role in how you live your life. What you think about something determines whether you will do anything about it. If something is important to you, you'll care enough to make time for it. If you don't care about something, you'll ignore it. Your attitude affects your actions. But the opposite is also true—your actions can affect your attitude. If you consistently practice a certain behavior, your attitude about that behavior will likely change the behavior. For example, if you always take care of yourself first, your attitude will be self-centered. On the other hand, if you begin helping at a homeless shelter on a regular basis, whether you want to or not, you will probably develop the attitude that helping those in need is important.

The same principle applies to your relationship with God. When your actions focus on serving him, you will begin to develop an eternal perspective about life that changes the way you look at the world. The bottom line is this: How you react to your circumstances is more important than what actually happens to you. Your attitude makes the difference between being content and happy or discontented and miserable. It's your choice.

What kind of attitude does God want me to have?

Love is patient and kind. Love is not jealous or boastful or proud or rude. It does not demand its own way. It is not irritable, and it keeps no record of being wronged. It does not rejoice about injustice but rejoices whenever the truth wins out. Love never gives up, never loses faith, is always hopeful, and endures through every circumstance.
1 CORINTHIANS 13:4-7

An attitude of love.

You must have the same attitude that Christ Jesus had. . . . He gave up his divine privileges; he took the humble position of a slave and was born as a human being. When he appeared in human form, he humbled himself in obedience to God and died a criminal's death on a cross. PHILIPPIANS 2:5-8

An attitude of humility.

Always be full of joy in the Lord. I say it again—rejoice! Let everyone see that you are considerate in all you do. Remember, the Lord is coming soon. Don't worry about anything; instead, pray about everything. Tell God what you need, and thank him for all he has done. PHILIPPIANS 4:4-6

An attitude of joy for all God has done for me and an attitude of dependence on him for all my needs.

What kind of attitude is displeasing to God?

"Why are you so angry?" the LORD asked Cain. "Why do you look so dejected? You will be accepted if you do what is right. But if you refuse to do what is right, then watch out! Sin is crouching at the door, eager to control you. But you must subdue it." GENESIS 4:6-7

Responding with resentment to God's discipline separates you from his help and makes you vulnerable to sin.

"Why have you brought us out of Egypt to die here in the wilderness?" they complained. "There is nothing to eat here and nothing to drink. And we hate this horrible manna!"
NUMBERS 21:5

Complaining shows a lack of appreciation for what God has given you.

Haughtiness goes before destruction. PROVERBS 18:12

An attitude of pride causes you to think you don't need God's help.

What are the practical benefits of a faith-filled attitude?

I have learned the secret of living in every situation, whether it is with a full stomach or empty, with plenty or little. For I can do everything through Christ, who gives me strength. PHILIPPIANS 4:12-13

Your attitude changes everything. Faith is an attitude of trust that the events in your life happen according to God's direction rather than chance. This allows you to view your life, and live it out, from a whole new perspective.

What is the key to having a good attitude?

Letting your sinful nature control your mind leads to death. But letting the Spirit control your mind leads to life and peace. ROMANS 8:6

Let God's Holy Spirit be in control instead of your sinful nature.

Don't copy the behavior and customs of this world, but let God transform you into a new person by changing the way you think. ROMANS 12:2

As you give God control of your life, his attitudes begin to become yours.

AUTHORITY *See also* Discipline, Employers/Employees, Leadership, Obedience, Submission

We're all used to answering to some higher authority, whether a parent, a boss, or the government. Sometimes people abuse their authority. It's hard to submit to someone who takes advantage of you or misuses power. Another problem occurs when a society elevates individuals above the community, and everyone becomes his or her own authority. When people think they can do whatever they want, rules go out the window and chaos reigns. People follow their own laws and seek first to satisfy their own personal desires. Perhaps God instituted positions of authority because he knew that if human nature is left unchecked, individuals assume personal authority, with disastrous results. People in authority must be careful how they view and use their authority. There is a delicate balance between using authority to serve others and using it to gain personal power.

Why is human authority necessary?

In those days Israel had no king; all the people did whatever seemed right in their own eyes. JUDGES 21:25

God has appointed human authorities, such as governments, to bring order and security to society. We also have authority figures in other areas, such as in the church and in the family. Authority properly exercised is essential for teaching others, taking care of others, and holding each other accountable.

Should I submit to the authority of the government?

Everyone must submit to governing authorities. For all authority comes from God, and those in positions of authority have been placed there by God. So anyone who rebels against authority is rebelling against what God has instituted, and they will be punished. ROMANS 13:1-2

The Bible says it is important to obey those in authority over you.

*Peter and John replied, "Do you think God wants us to obey you rather than him? . . .
We must obey God rather than any human authority."* ACTS 4:19; 5:29

If those in authority order you to denounce God or deliberately disobey him, you
must not follow their orders. God is the highest authority, and you must obey him first,
above all others.

How should authority be used?

*The officer said, "Lord, I am not worthy to have you come into my home. Just say the
word from where you are, and my servant will be healed. I know this because I am
under the authority of my superior officers, and I have authority over my soldiers. I
only need to say, 'Go,' and they go, or 'Come,' and they come. And if I say to my slaves,
'Do this,' they do it." When Jesus heard this, he was amazed. Turning to those who were
following him, he said, "I tell you the truth, I haven't seen faith like this in all Israel!"*
MATTHEW 8:8-10

The centurion displayed humility and faith in his understanding of authority. He
knew both the power and the limitations of his own authority. He did not presume that
because he held a position of authority in the military he could order Jesus around. He
humbled himself for the sake of helping his own servant. This understanding of authority invites voluntary submission rather than demanding or forcing compliance. Authority should be used to serve others.

What can be dangerous about authority?

*O Egypt, to which of the trees of Eden will you compare your strength and glory? You, too,
will be brought down to the depths with all these other nations. You will lie there among
the outcasts who have died by the sword. This will be the fate of Pharaoh and all his
hordes. I, the Sovereign LORD, have spoken!* EZEKIEL 31:18

*It is not that we think we are qualified to do anything on our own. Our qualification
comes from God.* 2 CORINTHIANS 3:5

Authority and its corresponding power are intoxicating because with them come recognition, control, and often wealth. Each of these things feeds pride, and pride leads away
from God and into sin. This is why the power that comes from authority so often corrupts.
If you are in a position of power or authority over someone, two things will help you use it
wisely: accountability and service. When you have to explain your motives to others, you
will be more careful what you do and say. And when you serve others with your authority,
rather than yourself, you will gain support and loyalty from those you serve.

What if I have a bad attitude toward authority?

*The Holy Spirit says, "Today when you hear his voice, don't harden your hearts as Israel
did when they rebelled, when they tested me in the wilderness. There your ancestors*

tested and tried my patience, even though they saw my miracles for forty years. So I was angry with them, and I said, 'Their hearts always turn away from me. They refuse to do what I tell them.'" HEBREWS 3:7-10

Sometimes it gets tiring being told what to do; you want to chart your own course and become your own person. Being your own person is one thing, but being rebellious is quite another. Authority is not always a bad thing—it's the abuse of authority that is bad. God's authority and his rules not only save your life but show you how to be successful and blessed. Don't rebel against that authority lest you jeopardize your very soul. Being your own person doesn't mean doing whatever you want to; it means using your God-given personality and talents to serve him by serving others.

What should I do when I have authority over others?

Whoever wants to be a leader among you must be your servant. MATTHEW 20:26

He must become greater and greater, and I must become less and less. JOHN 3:30

If you want others to look up to you, you should have a servant's heart, be willing to take responsibility for your actions, refuse to stay silent when things are wrong, and avoid seeking glory for yourself. The world has taught you the opposite. But in the end, the people who have consistently shown kindness, integrity, and a deep love for God will be respected and honored.

What is the ultimate source of authority?

Jesus said, "You would have no power over me at all unless it were given to you from above." JOHN 19:11

God is the ultimate source of authority. Not only does he have authority over each person's life, he has authority over governments as well.

All Scripture is inspired by God and is useful to teach us what is true and to make us realize what is wrong in our lives. It corrects us when we are wrong and teaches us to do what is right. 2 TIMOTHY 3:16

Because Scripture is the Word of God, it is the guiding authority over your life.

AVOIDANCE/AVOIDING *See also* Excuses, Procrastination

Avoiding a particular thing can either harm you or help you—the key is understanding the difference. Staying away from metal during an electrical storm can save your life. But the strong metal frame of a car can save your life in an auto accident.

In matters of faith, sin is something you should try to avoid at all costs—it is deadly. But avoiding God's divine guidance can be just as deadly. The opposite of *avoiding* is *approaching*. God alone knows what is around the corner in your life, and he wants you to approach him to find out. As you approach him, you develop a relationship with him and learn what you should and should not avoid.

What should I avoid?

Stay away from every kind of evil. 1 THESSALONIANS 5:22

Avoid sin as much as you possibly can.

Dear children, keep away from anything that might take God's place in your hearts. 1 JOHN 5:21

Avoid worshiping anything or anyone except God.

Avoid all perverse talk; stay away from corrupt speech. PROVERBS 4:24

Avoiding a fight is a mark of honor; only fools insist on quarreling. PROVERBS 20:3

Do everything without complaining and arguing. PHILIPPIANS 2:14

Don't get involved in foolish, ignorant arguments that only start fights. 2 TIMOTHY 2:23

Avoid gossiping, complaining, quarreling, or saying things that are inappropriate or hurtful to others.

Are there things I shouldn't avoid?

Jonah got up and went in the opposite direction to get away from the LORD. He went down to the port of Joppa, where he found a ship leaving for Tarshish. He bought a ticket and went on board, hoping to escape from the LORD. JONAH 1:3

You should not avoid doing what God has called you to do. You will miss out on the joy and satisfaction of accomplishing something important for him, and like Jonah, you will be miserable for it.

Do not withhold good from those who deserve it when it's in your power to help them. PROVERBS 3:27

You should not avoid doing good for those in need. Helping others reflects the love of Jesus.

How do I avoid the things I am supposed to avoid?

The LORD asked Satan, "Have you noticed my servant Job? He is the finest man in all the earth. He is blameless—a man of complete integrity. He fears God and stays away from evil." JOB 1:8

Keeping a close relationship with God helps you avoid sin. The closer you are to God, the further you are from evil and the less likely you are to sin.

Do not waste time arguing over godless ideas and old wives' tales. Instead, train yourself to be godly. 1 TIMOTHY 4:7

Instead of getting involved in worthless talk, spend your energy on spiritual training.

Why do I often want to avoid the things I should do?

Don't harden your hearts as Israel did when they rebelled, when they tested me in the wilderness. HEBREWS 3:8

Perhaps you think that your plan is better than God's or that his plan is too inconvenient for you. Realize that God's call to you deserves and requires an immediate response. He will not ask you to do anything without giving you the resources you need to accomplish it. If you avoid the opportunities God gives you, you will miss his blessings as well.

B

BACKSLIDING *See also* Compromise, Temptation

Because of our sinful nature, it's easy to drift away from God. Often the drift is subtle; we don't even notice when we take a small step away from him. But several small steps can cover a long distance. Then we suddenly realize just how far from God we have strayed. We commit ourselves to getting back to God, and for a while we make great progress. But before long, we find ourselves sliding back into our old sinful ways.

We can prepare ourselves ahead of time to guard against backsliding. Every day we have a choice to make: We can take a step toward God, or we can take a step away from him. It takes conscious effort to step toward him; it takes no effort to step away, for our sinful nature is always pulling us in that direction.

What do I do when I've fallen away from God?

Finally, I confessed all my sins to you and stopped trying to hide my guilt. I said to myself, "I will confess my rebellion to the LORD." And you forgave me! All my guilt is gone.
PSALM 32:5

If we confess our sins to him, he is faithful and just to forgive us our sins and to cleanse us from all wickedness. 1 JOHN 1:9

It happens to you, as it does to almost everyone: You suddenly realize you are far away from God. It worries you, maybe even scares you. Don't ignore that internal warning. Look at how you got where you are—was it simple neglect, or was it a sinful habit that you didn't want to give up? Recognize what you've done, and confess it to God. Only then can you be forgiven and begin the process of restoring your relationship with him. Confession is the act of acknowledging that your sin has separated you from God. It is an expression of your desire to move back toward him. God's forgiveness will bring you back together.

How can I avoid backsliding?

Keep watch and pray, so that you will not give in to temptation. For the spirit is willing, but the body is weak! MATTHEW 26:41

You must live as God's obedient children. Don't slip back into your old ways of living to satisfy your own desires. You didn't know any better then. 1 PETER 1:14

Obedience to God's Word, persistence in prayer, and resistance to temptation will help you avoid backsliding.

How does it affect others when I backslide?

What sorrow awaits the world, because it tempts people to sin. Temptations are inevitable, but what sorrow awaits the person who does the tempting. MATTHEW 18:7

When you sin, it almost always affects someone else as well. Your sinful actions might tempt someone else to sin. Then your sin has doubled its effect. God warns that the consequences for causing someone else to sin will be terrible. Like a pebble tossed into a quiet pool, one small sin may spread out in ever-widening circles.

BALANCE *See also* Burnout, Overwhelmed, Priorities

We get out of balance when we overemphasize one aspect of our responsibilities at the cost of others. Balance means using our gifts, time, and resources to live a life that honors God and cares for others and ourselves. God assures us there is time for everything he calls us to do. During his time on earth, Jesus completed all God had planned for him to do—no more and no less.

How do I live a balanced life?

Letting your sinful nature control your mind leads to death. But letting the Spirit control your mind leads to life and peace. ROMANS 8:6

When you let the Holy Spirit have control of the way you think, he will help you bring everything into balance, giving you life and peace.

Be satisfied with what you have. HEBREWS 13:5

Often life gets out of balance when you become dissatisfied with what you have. Contentment frees you from the constant pursuit of things.

I run with purpose in every step. I am not just shadowboxing. I discipline my body like an athlete, training it to do what it should. 1 CORINTHIANS 9:26-27

When you fully understand the work God has given you to do, you can focus on that and remove the distractions that throw your life out of balance.

How did Jesus live a balanced life?

Jesus explained, "I tell you the truth, the Son can do nothing by himself. He does only what he sees the Father doing. Whatever the Father does, the Son also does." JOHN 5:19

Jesus carefully followed God's example. Since God created life, he knows best how life should be lived. The Bible, God's Word, tells you exactly how to live a life of perfect balance.

Jesus grew in wisdom and in stature and in favor with God and all the people. LUKE 2:52

Jesus grew in all areas: physically, mentally, spiritually, and emotionally. Focusing on only one or two of these areas can throw the others out of balance.

Jesus said, "Let's go off by ourselves to a quiet place and rest awhile." He said this because there were so many people coming and going that Jesus and his apostles didn't even have time to eat. So they left by boat for a quiet place. MARK 6:31-32

The next day there was a wedding celebration in the village of Cana in Galilee. Jesus' mother was there, and Jesus and his disciples were also invited to the celebration. JOHN 2:1-2

Jesus saw the importance of spending time with people as well as the importance of rest and reflection. Life should have a balance between work and rest, between investing in people and quiet time for restoration.

How do I find the proper balance in life?

Accept the way God does things, for who can straighten what he has made crooked?
ECCLESIASTES 7:13

A godly life is a balanced life because God's way is always balanced. By consistently studying God's instructions for life, found in the Bible, you will find balance.

Think clearly and exercise self-control. Look forward to the gracious salvation that will come to you when Jesus Christ is revealed to the world. 1 PETER 1:13

A life of self-control is a balanced life. As your thinking is transformed to be like Christ's, your new perspective helps you exercise self-control.

Fan into flames the spiritual gift God gave you when I laid my hands on you.
2 TIMOTHY 1:6

A balanced life makes full use of God's gifts.

You see me when I travel and when I rest at home. You know everything I do.
PSALM 139:3

A balanced life includes proper rest, sleep, quiet, and reflection. If you go without these things, it won't be long before you feel unbalanced.

What causes our lives to become unbalanced?

People who long to be rich fall into temptation and are trapped by many foolish and harmful desires that plunge them into ruin and destruction. 1 TIMOTHY 6:9

Don't love money; be satisfied with what you have. For God has said, "I will never fail you. I will never abandon you." HEBREWS 13:5

Feelings of dissatisfaction often result in an unbalanced life because we focus too much on what we cannot have, should not have, and may never have. It's important to meet your needs for food, shelter, and clothing, but focusing too much on yourself will cause you to neglect one of God's greatest mandates: Help others who are in need. The more you focus on yourself, the more dissatisfied you become because you can never get everything you want. When you balance your needs with meeting the needs of others, you find contentment.

[False teachers] promise freedom, but they themselves are slaves of sin and corruption. For you are a slave to whatever controls you. 2 PETER 2:19

Anything that controls you—drugs, alcohol, work, or even a hobby—will knock your life out of balance.

It's not good to eat too much honey, and it's not good to seek honors for yourself.
PROVERBS 25:27

They furnish wine and lovely music at their grand parties—lyre and harp, tambourine and flute—but they never think about the LORD or notice what he is doing. ISAIAH 5:12

Sometimes too much of even a good thing can cause you to neglect other important areas of your life.

What are the benefits of living a balanced life?

This is what the LORD says: "Stop at the crossroads and look around. Ask for the old, godly way, and walk in it. Travel its path, and you will find rest for your souls." JEREMIAH 6:16

If you look carefully into the perfect law that sets you free, and if you do what it says and don't forget what you heard, then God will bless you for doing it. JAMES 1:25

God's blessings flow from a balanced life—today and for eternity. But if we willingly mess up our lives, it's hard to ask God to bless the mess. When you know and do what God's Word says, you live in balance—that is, you live with the proper perspective on life.

Letting your sinful nature control your mind leads to death. But letting the Spirit control your mind leads to life and peace. ROMANS 8:6

When you let the Holy Spirit control your life, the balance he brings gives you peace of heart and mind. When you try to accomplish everything you want to get done, you usually feel overwhelmed. If you let him, God will show you what he wants you to get done each day, and that will be enough.

BETRAYAL *See also* Adultery, Deceit/Deception, Trust

Betrayal is one of the saddest realities of human relationships. It can be bold and direct (committing treason against your country or committing adultery) or it can be quiet and subtle (flattering friends to get something from them or telling a little white lie to make yourself look better than someone else). Whether great or small, betrayal involves the breaking of trust and confidence in a relationship.

On a deeper level, we often betray God. Every day, we break the trust of the one who created us and gives us life and purpose. Fortunately, by God's grace through Jesus' death on the cross, we can confidently trust that God will never betray us when we enter into a relationship with him.

How do we betray God?

Their hearts were not loyal to him. They did not keep his covenant. PSALM 78:37

Anyone who has become a Christian has pledged loyalty to God. Betrayal is the opposite of loyalty. You are disloyal to God when you allow something else to become more important than him or when you look to something or someone else to help you rather than acknowledging God or asking for his help first.

I have discovered this principle of life—that when I want to do what is right, I inevitably do what is wrong. I love God's law with all my heart. But there is another power within me that is at war with my mind. This power makes me a slave to the sin that is still within me. ROMANS 7:21-23

Your sinful human nature causes you to betray God even when you don't want to. Your heart betrays you, and then it betrays God. You deceive yourself into believing that it is okay to deceive God.

Despite all this, they were disobedient and rebelled against [the Lord]. NEHEMIAH 9:26

You betray God through your disobedience. You disobey when you do something God's Word tells you not to do, or when you don't do something God's Word tells you to do.

Give the following instructions to the people of Israel: If any of the people—men or women—betray the LORD by doing wrong to another person, they are guilty. NUMBERS 5:6

When you do wrong to another person, you also betray God because you are breaking your pledge of loyalty and obedience to him, which includes doing what is right and loving toward his people.

How can we avoid betraying God?

Everyone has sinned; we all fall short of God's glorious standard. Yet God, with undeserved kindness, declares that we are righteous. He did this through Christ Jesus when he freed us from the penalty for our sins. ROMANS 3:23-24

If we confess our sins to him, he is faithful and just to forgive us our sins and to cleanse us from all wickedness. 1 JOHN 1:9

You can't avoid betraying God. Every person has sinned and will continue to sin against God. But if you realize you have a sinful heart and if you confess your sins to God, he will forgive you. He will look at you and treat you as though you have never betrayed him.

How can we avoid betraying others?

Never let loyalty and kindness leave you! Tie them around your neck as a reminder. Write them deep within your heart. PROVERBS 3:3

Love, loyalty, and kindness require practice, just like anything else. They don't come naturally. The more you practice, the better you will become and the more you will enjoy watching others benefit from your loving actions.

Do to others whatever you would like them to do to you. MATTHEW 7:12

Practice the Golden Rule. You don't want to be betrayed, so don't betray others.

A gossip goes around telling secrets, but those who are trustworthy can keep a confidence. PROVERBS 11:13

Telling lies about others is as harmful as hitting them with an ax, wounding them with a sword, or shooting them with a sharp arrow. PROVERBS 25:18

Never lie or gossip about others because you always betray someone else when you do so.

A friend is always loyal, and a brother is born to help in time of need. PROVERBS 17:17

Loyalty says, "No matter what happens around us or between us, there is no fear, doubt, or hurt that can make me turn my back on you." When loyalty is present, a relationship is secure and solid, and the chances of betrayal are slim.

What should I do when I am betrayed?
This High Priest of ours understands our weaknesses. HEBREWS 4:15

There is comfort in knowing that, because Jesus was betrayed, he personally understands your pain. He who has the power to help you has experienced your hurt himself. When others are unfaithful to you, take great comfort in God's unwavering faithfulness.

Esau ran to meet him and embraced him, threw his arms around his neck, and kissed him. And they both wept. . . . "My brother, I have plenty," Esau answered. "Keep what you have for yourself." But Jacob insisted, "No, if I have found favor with you, please accept this gift from me. And what a relief to see your friendly smile. It is like seeing the face of God!" GENESIS 33:4, 9-10

Jacob betrayed his brother, Esau, but Esau forgave him after years of separation. Continue to love those who betray you, as Jesus did (see John 13:38; 21:15-19). While you don't excuse the betrayal, you are to love and forgive the betrayer. Forgiveness is the only way to stop the downward spiral of retaliation and revenge.

Even your brothers, members of your own family, have turned against you. They plot and raise complaints against you. Do not trust them, no matter how pleasantly they speak. JEREMIAH 12:6

Be as shrewd as snakes and harmless as doves. MATTHEW 10:16

When you realize you cannot trust a particular person, act wisely and take steps to keep from getting hurt again. If you think someone is going to betray you, prepare yourself. Think through how you will respond. You can do this with kind words and a forgiving heart instead of retaliation. You can avoid revenge and grant forgiveness while still exercising prudent self-protection.

If you forgive those who sin against you, your heavenly Father will forgive you. MATTHEW 6:14

Forgiveness is the only way to move past betrayal. Nothing anyone has done against you compares with what you have done against God. Refusing to forgive another means you don't realize how much God has forgiven you. A forgiven person forgives.

BIBLE *See also* Absolutes, Authority, Truth

How remarkable that the God of the universe would actually want to communicate with us! We are creatures of a physical world to which we relate through our five senses. God is a spiritual being. In our physical state, we cannot see him, hear him, or touch him, so how can he communicate with us? Through the Bible. Over several centuries, God inspired a select number of people to write down what he wants us to know about him and what we need to do in order to live with him forever in heaven. These writings have been collected into a book called the Holy Bible—*holy* because it contains the sacred words of almighty God. In a miraculous way, the Bible speaks generally to all people and specifically to each individual. Its truths apply across generations, across cultures, across all life experience, because it is written by the one who created life itself.

Can we truly trust the Bible as God's Word?

All Scripture is inspired by God and is useful to teach us what is true and to make us realize what is wrong in our lives. It corrects us when we are wrong and teaches us to do what is right. 2 TIMOTHY 3:16

The Bible has stood the test of time more than any other document in human history. It has been faithfully preserved because it is God's very words to us, and he will not let his words disappear from the face of the earth or his truths be altered by human hands.

How can a book written so long ago be relevant for me today?

The grass withers and the flowers fade, but the word of our God stands forever. ISAIAH 40:8

The word of God is alive and powerful. It is sharper than the sharpest two-edged sword, cutting between soul and spirit, between joint and marrow. It exposes our innermost thoughts and desires. HEBREWS 4:12

Because the Bible is the Word of God, it is the only document that is "living"—in other words, it is relevant for all people, in all places, in all time periods. It is as contemporary as the heart of God and as relevant as your most urgent need.

Why is it so important to read God's Word every day?

You will know the truth, and the truth will set you free. JOHN 8:32

Reading the Bible tells you how to be set free from sin.

The people of Berea were more open-minded than those in Thessalonica, and they listened eagerly to Paul's message. They searched the Scriptures day after day to see if Paul and Silas were teaching the truth. ACTS 17:11

Reading the Bible helps you recognize true and false teaching.

This regular reading will prevent him from becoming proud and acting as if he is above his fellow citizens. DEUTERONOMY 17:20

Reading the Bible helps you keep a right attitude toward God and others.

They are a warning to your servant, a great reward for those who obey them. PSALM 19:11

Your laws please me; they give me wise advice. PSALM 119:24

Reading the Bible warns you about things that will harm you and provides good counsel about your problems.

How can a young person stay pure? By obeying your word. PSALM 119:9

Your word is a lamp to guide my feet and a light for my path. PSALM 119:105

Reading the Bible guides you in daily living and helps you stay close to God.

Your promise revives me; it comforts me in all my troubles. PSALM 119:50

Reading the Bible gives you comfort and hope for the future.

Why is it important to read the Bible to others?

Preserve the teaching of God; entrust his instructions to those who follow me.
ISAIAH 8:16

God wants you to pass his Word on to others, teaching them as you have been taught. As the Word has changed your life, when you pass it on to others, it can change theirs also.

Why is it important to memorize Bible verses?

They have made God's law their own, so they will never slip from his path. PSALM 37:31

I have hidden your word in my heart, that I might not sin against you. PSALM 119:11

When you fill your heart and mind with God's Word, you keep yourself close to God and far from sin. Memorizing Scripture allows you to meditate on God's life-changing words at any time.

What special promises does the Bible contain?

All praise to God, the Father of our Lord Jesus Christ. It is by his great mercy that we have been born again, because God raised Jesus Christ from the dead. Now we live with great expectation, and we have a priceless inheritance—an inheritance that is kept in heaven for you, pure and undefiled, beyond the reach of change and decay. 1 PETER 1:3-4

The greatest promise in the Bible is God's vow to forgive your sins if you confess them to him. This promise is true because Jesus not only died on the cross to take the punishment for your sins, but he also rose from the dead. God promises that those who believe this will live forever with him in heaven, where there will be no pain, suffering, or evil. When you take God at his word, you enter into a life with a future that is far beyond what you can imagine.

BITTERNESS *See also* Anger, Blame, Jealousy, Resentment

Bitterness is anger that has settled in for the long term. It is anger that has birthed resentment, the feeling that you have been treated harshly, unfairly, or carelessly. Left unchecked, bitterness can eat its way deep into your mind, heart, and even your soul, turning you into a hostile, hardened person. The poison of bitterness can destroy you. And the most dangerous thing about bitterness is that it makes forgiveness impossible, which puts your relationship with God and others on hold.

What are the signs of bitterness?

This made Saul very angry. "What's this?" he said. "They credit David with ten thousands and me with only thousands. Next they'll be making him their king!"
1 SAMUEL 18:8

Anger that is allowed to fester and grow turns into bitterness. If you want to deal with your bitterness, deal first with your anger.

As all the people heard of the king's deep grief for his son, the joy of that day's victory was turned into deep sadness.... [Joab said to David,] "You seem to love those who hate you and hate those who love you. You have made it clear today that your commanders and troops mean nothing to you. It seems that if Absalom had lived and all of us had died, you would be pleased." 2 SAMUEL 19:2, 6

Prolonged grief that has turned into despair creates bitterness. It looks as if life is meaningless and is always against you.

Jacob soon learned that Laban's sons were grumbling about him. "Jacob has robbed our father of everything!" they said. "He has gained all his wealth at our father's expense."
GENESIS 31:1

Resentment causes you to look at other people's success with suspicion. Perhaps you begin to think they became successful by taking some opportunity away from you. This creates a bitter spirit.

As the believers rapidly multiplied, there were rumblings of discontent. The Greek-speaking believers complained about the Hebrew-speaking believers, saying that their widows were being discriminated against in the daily distribution of food. ACTS 6:1

Discontent and jealousy cause you to think you aren't getting what you deserve. When you focus on yourself and what you aren't getting, bitterness quickly sets in.

Miriam and Aaron criticized Moses because he had married a Cushite woman. They said, "Has the LORD spoken only through Moses? Hasn't he spoken through us, too?"
NUMBERS 12:1-2

When you focus on what others do wrong, you are in danger of bitterness controlling your life.

Leah angrily replied, "Wasn't it enough that you stole my husband? Now will you steal my son's mandrakes, too?" GENESIS 30:15

Jealousy leads to anger. Unresolved anger leads to bitterness. If the anger is allowed to grow, bitterness can lead to harmful and even violent behavior toward those you envy.

Why am I feeling bitter? How did I get this way?

Esau hated Jacob because their father had given Jacob the blessing. GENESIS 27:41

Bitterness comes when you resent not receiving the blessings you wanted.

Haman was a happy man as he left the banquet! But when he saw Mordecai sitting at the palace gate, not standing up or trembling nervously before him, Haman became furious.
ESTHER 5:9

Bitterness comes when you want more honor than you deserve or receive.

Abner shouted down to Joab, "Must we always be killing each other? Don't you realize that bitterness is the only result?" 2 SAMUEL 2:26

Bitterness comes when you retaliate for wrongs done against you.

It is time to forgive and comfort him. Otherwise he may be overcome by discouragement.
2 CORINTHIANS 2:7

Make allowance for each other's faults, and forgive anyone who offends you. Remember, the Lord forgave you, so you must forgive others. COLOSSIANS 3:13

Bitterness comes when others hurt you and you refuse to forgive.

Watch out that no poisonous root of bitterness grows up to trouble you, corrupting many.
HEBREWS 12:15

Bitterness comes when you forget God's grace. It is like a toxin that affects not only you but everyone around you.

How do I cause others to feel bitter?

You twist justice, making it a bitter pill for the oppressed. You treat the righteous like dirt.
AMOS 5:7

You cause bitterness in others when you are unjust or unfair in your dealings with them, particularly toward those who are poor and oppressed. Treat others with the same respect and fairness with which you expect to be treated.

How do I deal with my bitterness toward others?

Get rid of all bitterness, rage, anger, harsh words, and slander, as well as all types of evil behavior. Instead, be kind to each other, tenderhearted, forgiving one another, just as God through Christ has forgiven you. EPHESIANS 4:31-32

Forgiveness is the antidote to bitterness. It lifts burdens, cancels debts, and frees you from the chains of unresolved anger.

I want you to know, my dear brothers and sisters, that everything that has happened to me here has helped to spread the Good News. PHILIPPIANS 1:12

Instead of becoming bitter, remember that God can use your difficult situation for good. Paul was traveling the world, preaching the Good News about Jesus. Then he was thrown into prison for sharing his faith! That could have made him bitter. Instead, he was happy because he saw it as an opportunity. He knew that God takes even the worst situations and brings good out of them, if we allow him to. Paul couldn't wait to see the good that God would bring out of his prison time. While in prison, Paul wrote many of the New

Testament letters, which have brought countless millions to faith in Jesus. That's a lot of good out of a bad situation! God is waiting for you to let him do the same in your difficult situations.

BLAME *See also* Accusations, Excuses, Responsibility

"He made me do it!" "She started it!" How many times have parents heard these words come from their children's mouths? We all learn at a young age how to blame others for our own actions. We blame others for many reasons, but it often boils down to fear—from the fear of getting into trouble to the fear of looking foolish in front of others. Blame shifts the spotlight to someone else, temporarily getting us off the hook. It's human nature to pass the blame to someone else. Accepting responsibility for our mistakes can be difficult and embarrassing. Cleaning up our own problems is messy business.

Pride is another cause of blaming others. We're often too proud to admit we're part of the problem. The opposite of blaming others is taking responsibility, which forces us to accept the consequences of our actions and work to fix the problem.

Why do we blame others?

"Who told you that you were naked?" the Lord God asked. "Have you eaten from the tree whose fruit I commanded you not to eat?" The man replied, "It was the woman you gave me who gave me the fruit, and I ate it." Then the Lord God asked the woman, "What have you done?" "The serpent deceived me," she replied. "That's why I ate it." GENESIS 3:11-13

Aaron took the gold, melted it down, and molded it into the shape of a calf.... When... Moses saw the calf ... he turned to Aaron and demanded, "What did these people do to you to make you bring such terrible sin upon them?"... Aaron [said,] "You yourself know how evil these people are." EXODUS 32:4, 19-22

We blame others to deny our own guilt. But it is pointless to say, "It wasn't my fault," when the Lord sees everything.

[The people] said to Moses, "Why did you bring us out here to die in the wilderness? Weren't there enough graves for us in Egypt? What have you done to us? Why did you make us leave Egypt? Didn't we tell you this would happen while we were still in Egypt? We said, 'Leave us alone! Let us be slaves to the Egyptians. It's better to be a slave in Egypt than a corpse in the wilderness!'" EXODUS 14:11-12

We blame others when things don't turn out the way we want. We rationalize our criticism by dwelling on what might have been. We say, "If only this" or "If only that." We try to take the responsibility off ourselves and pin it on someone else.

Sarai said to Abram, "This is all your fault! I put my servant into your arms, but now that she's pregnant she treats me with contempt. The Lord will show who's wrong— you or me!" GENESIS 16:5

We blame others because of pride. We are too proud to admit that the problem is our own fault. We don't want others to see how weak and vulnerable we are.

What should I do when others blame me?

The sailors were terrified when they heard this, for he had already told them he was running away from the LORD. "Oh, why did you do it?" they groaned. And since the storm was getting worse all the time, they asked him, "What should we do to you to stop this storm?" "Throw me into the sea," Jonah said, "and it will become calm again. I know that this terrible storm is all my fault." JONAH 1:10-12

Take responsibility for any wrong thoughts and actions, and accept whatever blame you deserve without passing it to someone else. When you earn blame, you should keep it.

When [the delegation] arrived in the land of Gilead, they said to the tribes of Reuben, Gad, and the half-tribe of Manasseh, "The whole community of the LORD demands to know why you are betraying the God of Israel. How could you turn away from the LORD and build an altar for yourselves in rebellion against him?" . . . Then the people of Reuben, Gad, and the half-tribe of Manasseh answered the heads of the clans of Israel: "The LORD, the Mighty One, is God! The LORD, the Mighty One, is God! He knows the truth, and may Israel know it, too! We have not built the altar in treacherous rebellion against the LORD." JOSHUA 22:15-16, 21-22

Sometimes others blame you unjustly. Do your best to correct these misunderstandings in a calm and loving way. Expect that people will jump to the wrong conclusions from time to time. When it happens, don't react defensively or start a fight. Usually when you explain your side of the story, people will realize they were wrong and back down.

What should I do when I feel like blaming someone else?

You cry out, "Why doesn't the LORD accept my worship?" I'll tell you why! Because the LORD witnessed the vows you and your wife made when you were young. But you have been unfaithful to her, though she remained your faithful partner, the wife of your marriage vows. MALACHI 2:14

Before you blame someone else, especially God, consider how you might be the cause of your problem. The people Malachi spoke to wanted to blame God for abandoning them, but God had made it absolutely clear that only if they sinned (in this case by divorcing their wives and leaving them destitute) would he abandon them. It wasn't God who abandoned them, but they who abandoned God.

David confessed to Nathan, "I have sinned against the LORD." 2 SAMUEL 12:13

O people, the LORD has told you what is good, and this is what he requires of you: to do what is right, to love mercy, and to walk humbly with your God. MICAH 6:8

We are each responsible for our own conduct. GALATIANS 6:5

Be honest in assessing your motives and actions before you automatically blame someone else.

Satan left the LORD's presence, and he struck Job with terrible boils from head to foot. . . . His wife said to him, ". . . Curse God and die." But Job replied, ". . . Should we accept only good things from the hand of God and never anything bad?" So in all this, Job said nothing wrong. JOB 2:7-10

Sometimes you are not to blame for your problems. We live in a fallen world where pain and suffering come to everyone and where the devil persecutes God's people. You should accept responsibility for your actions when you do something wrong, but you should not blame yourself for trouble that isn't your fault.

What can I do to live a blameless life?

[God] has reconciled you to himself through the death of Christ in his physical body. As a result, he has brought you into his own presence, and you are holy and blameless as you stand before him without a single fault. COLOSSIANS 1:22

There is no way that you, by your own efforts, can ever live a blameless life. It is only through Christ's death on the cross that you become blameless in God's eyes. When you confess your sins to God and accept Jesus as Lord of your life, his forgiveness cleanses you. He took on the blame that you deserve. This doesn't mean you no longer sin, but God looks at you as though you have not sinned.

BLASPHEMY *See also* Idolatry, Rejection

Blasphemy is claiming to be God or damaging the reputation of God. When Jesus claimed to be God, he was accused of blasphemy by the religious leaders of his day. In their minds, Jesus was just a human being; to say he was God was to claim that an all-powerful, divine God had stooped to take on mortal human characteristics. Ironically, that's exactly what Jesus did!

Christians sometimes wonder if blasphemy is the "unforgivable sin" (see Matthew 12:31). If it were, all Christians would be forever barred from heaven, because we all treat God with less respect than we should. We all blaspheme God when our words and actions do not give him the honor he deserves. The Bible does say, however, that *blasphemy against the Holy Spirit* is a sin that cannot be forgiven. Why? Because when you reject the Holy Spirit, you reject the only one who can bring you to God so that your sins can be forgiven. And without forgiveness of sins, there is no salvation and eternal life. It's not that God won't forgive you; it's that you won't put yourself in a position to be forgiven. God offers forgiveness for *all* sins if we simply ask. Blasphemy against the Holy Spirit is refusing to ask.

What is blasphemy? Why is it sinful?

In your great pride you claim, "I am a god! I sit on a divine throne in the heart of the sea." But you are only a man and not a god, though you boast that you are a god. EZEKIEL 28:2

Jesus said to the paralyzed man, "Be encouraged, my child! Your sins are forgiven." But some of the teachers of religious law said to themselves, "That's blasphemy! Does he think he's God?" [Jesus said,] "I will prove to you that the Son of Man has the authority on earth to forgive sins." MATTHEW 9:2-3, 6

Jesus replied, ". . . In the future you will see the Son of Man seated in the place of power at God's right hand and coming on the clouds of heaven." Then the high priest tore his clothing to show his horror and said, "Blasphemy! Why do we need other witnesses? You have all heard his blasphemy." MATTHEW 26:64-65

The Jewish leaders tried all the harder to find a way to kill [Jesus]. For he not only broke the Sabbath, he called God his Father, thereby making himself equal with God. JOHN 5:18

Blasphemy is claiming to be God or claiming to be equal to God. It is applying his characteristics to yourself. Ironically, the teachers of religious law accused Jesus of claiming to be God—and he is!

During the fight, this son of an Israelite woman blasphemed the Name of the LORD with a curse. So the man was brought to Moses for judgment. LEVITICUS 24:11

Job scraped his skin with a piece of broken pottery as he sat among the ashes. His wife said to him, "Are you still trying to maintain your integrity? Curse God and die." JOB 2:8-9

Blasphemy is cursing God.

How long, O God, will you allow our enemies to insult you? Will you let them dishonor your name forever? . . . See how these enemies insult you, LORD. PSALM 74:10, 18

Jerusalem will stumble, and Judah will fall, because they speak out against the LORD and refuse to obey him. ISAIAH 3:8

Blasphemy is damaging the reputation of God.

"Is that so?" retorted Pharaoh. "And who is the LORD? Why should I listen to him and let Israel go? I don't know the LORD." EXODUS 5:2

Come back to your God. . . . But no. . . . Israel boasts, "I am rich! I've made a fortune all by myself! . . . My record is spotless!" HOSEA 12:6-8

You say, "I am rich. I have everything I want. I don't need a thing!" And you don't realize that you are wretched and miserable and poor and blind and naked. REVELATION 3:17

Blasphemy is thinking you are on a level with God. In essence, it is making yourself a god by believing you don't need the one true God, that you can do everything on your own.

If you do not listen to me or obey all these commands, and if you break my covenant . . . treating my regulations with contempt . . . I will punish you. LEVITICUS 26:14-16

*Those who brazenly violate the L*ORD*'s will . . . have blasphemed the L*ORD*, and they must be cut off from the community. Since they have treated the L*ORD*'s word with contempt and deliberately disobeyed his command, they must be completely cut off and suffer the punishment for their guilt.* NUMBERS 15:30-31

*Sennacherib's officers further mocked the L*ORD *God . . . heaping insult upon insult.* 2 CHRONICLES 32:16

They shake their fists at God, defying the Almighty. JOB 15:25

Blasphemy is showing contempt for God or a lack of reverence for him.

No one calls on your name or pleads with you for mercy. Therefore, you have turned away from us and turned us over to our sins. ISAIAH 64:7

[Jesus said,] "Anyone who rejects me is rejecting God, who sent me." LUKE 10:16

Anyone who refuses to live by these rules is not disobeying human teaching but is rejecting God, who gives his Holy Spirit to you. 1 THESSALONIANS 4:8

Blasphemy is rejecting God and his Holy Spirit.

*Those who fight against the L*ORD *will be shattered.* 1 SAMUEL 2:10

Only fools say in their hearts, "There is no God." PSALM 14:1

Blasphemy is willful rebellion against God.

Why is blasphemy against the Holy Spirit unforgivable?

Every sin and blasphemy can be forgiven—except blasphemy against the Holy Spirit, which will never be forgiven. MATTHEW 12:31

Blasphemy against the Holy Spirit is often called the "unforgivable sin." It is unforgivable because it reflects a settled, hard-hearted attitude of defiant hostility against God. A person who has this attitude will never come to God for forgiveness; therefore, they are out of reach of his forgiveness. Forgiveness comes through the work of the Holy Spirit. If you willfully reject the help of the Holy Spirit, who convicts you of your sin and shows you your need for forgiveness, then you cannot be forgiven. If you're worried about whether you've committed the unforgivable sin, you haven't. All you have to do is ask God's Holy Spirit to forgive you, and he will.

He forgives all my sins and heals all my diseases. PSALM 103:3

*Everyone who calls on the name of the L*ORD *will be saved.* JOEL 2:32

I tell you the truth, all sin and blasphemy can be forgiven, but anyone who blasphemes the Holy Spirit will never be forgiven. This is a sin with eternal consequences. MARK 3:28-29

Nothing can ever separate us from God's love. ROMANS 8:38

No sin is too big or too terrible that God can't or won't forgive it if you ask him. God has seen it all, and he still offers everyone his complete and unconditional love. However, an attitude of defiant hostility toward God's Holy Spirit prevents you from accepting his forgiveness and pushes away your only hope of forgiveness. It reveals an attitude of unbelief and a refusal to admit sin. God does not force his forgiveness upon you; but if you want it, he will always give it. God wants a relationship with you, and that can only happen when you ask forgiveness for your rebellion against him. Only those who don't want God's forgiveness are out of its reach.

How can I be sure I have not committed blasphemy against the Holy Spirit?

[Jesus] said to the disciples, "Anyone who accepts your message is also accepting me. And anyone who rejects you is rejecting me. And anyone who rejects me is rejecting God, who sent me." LUKE 10:16

Each of you must repent of your sins and turn to God, and be baptized in the name of Jesus Christ for the forgiveness of your sins. Then you will receive the gift of the Holy Spirit. ACTS 2:38

A person who refuses to believe in God chooses to also ignore God's offer of salvation through his Son, Jesus. If you have accepted Jesus Christ as your Savior, or if you are considering God's offer of salvation, you have not committed blasphemy against his Holy Spirit. Your heart is still open to his message. Because forgiveness comes through the work of the Holy Spirit, all you need to do is ask God to forgive your sins.

Is there any hope for me if I have blasphemed the Holy Spirit?

Though your sins are like scarlet, I will make them as white as snow. Though they are red like crimson, I will make them as white as wool. ISAIAH 1:18

Hymenaeus and Alexander are two examples. [Paul] threw them out and handed them over to Satan so they might learn not to blaspheme God. 1 TIMOTHY 1:20

If you are asking this question, there may be hope for you. If, after rejecting the Holy Spirit, you are convicted in your heart to come back to God, that means you have, in fact, opened your heart ever so slightly to the whisperings of the Holy Spirit. Continue to open your heart to him, and he will accept you and welcome you back. God is not holding a grudge against you. He won't turn away a person who has a change of heart. The Holy Spirit is the only One who can give you a change of heart, so as long as you are not open to his work in you, you have no hope. Some people may need to be given over to Satan (in other words, the church stops pursuing them with God's love) so that they experience the horror and consequences of being a complete slave to sin. The only hope for such people is that they will finally listen to the gentle promptings of the Holy Spirit, recognize they've hit bottom, and cry out to God for help. And he will answer.

BLESSINGS *See also* Gifts, Giving, Provision, Rewards

Blessings have to do with giving and receiving. We are blessed when we receive godly gifts, and we bless others when we share godly gifts. We don't hear much today about blessing others, but it was a vital part of life in Bible times. To receive God's blessing means not only to enjoy innumerable gifts (life, joy, peace, abundance, children, home, good reputation, health, freedom, work, food), but in a much deeper way, being welcomed into a special relationship with God, a relationship to be affirmed and practiced. Part of this, in turn, means blessing others—sharing some of the material and spiritual blessings that God has given to us.

How can I receive God's blessings?

All praise to God, the Father of our Lord Jesus Christ, who has blessed us with every spiritual blessing in the heavenly realms because we are united with Christ. EPHESIANS 1:3

You must belong to Jesus Christ to receive God's blessings. If you want God's blessings just so you can live an easier, more comfortable life, then you don't understand the nature of God's blessings. When you belong to Christ, you understand that all you are and all you have are gifts from him, to be used to bless others. When you truly desire to serve God, you will find yourself in the middle of a rushing stream of God's blessings, to be used to refresh others.

Not one of you from this wicked generation will live to see the good land I swore to give your ancestors, except Caleb. . . . He will see this land because he has followed the LORD. DEUTERONOMY 1:35-36

Throughout the Bible, and particularly the book of Deuteronomy, we find a simple but profound principle: Obeying God brings blessings, and disobeying God brings misfortune. Be careful not to think of these blessings only in terms of material possessions. The greatest blessings are far more valuable than money or things: They come in the form of joy, family, relationships, peace of heart, spiritual gifts, and the hope of eternal life.

How has God promised to bless his people?

May the LORD bless you and protect you. May the LORD smile on you and be gracious to you. May the LORD show you his favor and give you his peace. NUMBERS 6:24-26

When you believed in Christ, he identified you as his own by giving you the Holy Spirit, whom he promised long ago. The Spirit is God's guarantee that he will give us the inheritance he promised and that he has purchased us to be his own people. EPHESIANS 1:13-14

God has said, "I will never fail you. I will never abandon you." HEBREWS 13:5

God also blesses us with mercy; without it we would fall completely into the hands of Satan, terrified beyond imagination. God blesses us with truth; with it we know God and how to receive eternal life. God blesses us with love; with it we have hope, encouragement, comfort, help, and joy.

Why is it important to thank God for my blessings?

It is good to give thanks to the LORD, . . . to proclaim your unfailing love in the morning, your faithfulness in the evening. PSALM 92:1-2

God has given you far more than you realize—all of it undeserved, all of it given freely because he loves you. Thanking God helps you become aware of his blessings and keeps you from an ungrateful attitude, which could cause you to lose out on all he has to offer. If a blessing is worth receiving, it is worth your thanksgiving.

How can I be a blessing to others?

The Holy Spirit produces this kind of fruit in our lives: love, joy, peace, patience, kindness, goodness, faithfulness, gentleness, and self-control. GALATIANS 5:22-23

As you share the fruit of the Holy Spirit with others, you will be blessed and you will be a blessing.

I long to visit you so I can bring you some spiritual gift that will help you grow strong in the Lord. When we get together, I want to encourage you in your faith, but I also want to be encouraged by yours. ROMANS 1:11-12

As you share the blessings God has given you, you bless others as well. Encouraging others with the Good News of Jesus is one of the most rewarding of God's blessings.

How do I limit God's blessings?

Because you did not trust me enough to demonstrate my holiness to the people of Israel, you will not lead them into the land I am giving them! NUMBERS 20:12

When you don't trust God, you limit the blessings he will give you.

I would have given you much, much more. Why, then, have you despised the word of the LORD and done this horrible deed? 2 SAMUEL 12:8-9

These desires give birth to sinful actions. And when sin is allowed to grow, it gives birth to death. JAMES 1:15

You limit God's blessings when you give in to temptation and willfully sin.

Should I bless my enemies?

Bless those who persecute you. Don't curse them; pray that God will bless them. ROMANS 12:14

Jesus introduced an idea that is unique to Christianity—blessing and forgiving our enemies. The natural response for us is to take revenge on our enemies. Praying for our enemies is a severe test of our devotion to Christ. Which is the greater blessing: to win our enemies over or to continue fighting with them?

What responsibilities come with God's blessings?

All must give as they are able, according to the blessings given to them by the LORD your God. DEUTERONOMY 16:17

Give as freely as you have received! MATTHEW 10:8

As God blesses you, you are to bless others. Receiving and giving go hand in hand. Be careful that you don't become so comfortable you forget God, who gave you all you have.

BODY See also Appearance, Death, Disabilities, Healing, Purity, Rest, Sickness, Stress

It is interesting that in our culture our bodies are idolized and praised, even though they are so limited and weak. Some supermodels even take out million-dollar insurance policies on their bodies! The Bible tells us that our bodies are not our own; they are the Lord's temple, the dwelling place of the Holy Spirit, "borrowed" from God. When we get them "dirty," or defile them with sin, we are ruining something that belongs to God. As with anything else we borrow, we should treat our bodies with utmost respect. Just as you would not borrow your father's brand-new car and return it scraped and dented, so also you shouldn't return to God a body wrecked by sin. You cannot separate your body from your spirit, nor does God want you to. You are to discover how your body and spirit work together to do what God has created you to do. The bodies we ultimately look forward to, which God promises we will receive when our current bodies here on earth die, are transformed bodies—both physically and spiritually.

But isn't my body my own, to do with as I choose? Don't I have the final say?

Don't you realize that your body is the temple of the Holy Spirit, who lives in you and was given to you by God? You do not belong to yourself, for God bought you with a high price. So you must honor God with your body. 1 CORINTHIANS 6:19-20

You don't own your body—God does. He paid a premium for you with the death of his own Son. Honor his sacrifice with one of your own—respect the awesomeness of your body by keeping it pure.

Don't you realize that all of you together are the temple of God and that the Spirit of God lives in you? God will destroy anyone who destroys this temple. For God's temple is holy, and you are that temple. 1 CORINTHIANS 3:16-17

You say, "I am allowed to do anything"—but not everything is good for you. And even though "I am allowed to do anything," I must not become a slave to anything. You say, "Food was made for the stomach, and the stomach for food." (This is true, though someday God will do away with both of them.) But you can't say that our bodies were made for sexual immorality. They were made for the Lord, and the Lord cares about our bodies. 1 CORINTHIANS 6:12-13

Your body was made to worship and glorify God and to fulfill the purpose for which he created you. When you do things that are not good for your body, you are breaking down the very vessel God wants to use to help accomplish his work in the world. God works through people; this means he must work through your body, not just your spirit, to get things done.

How can my body be pure? I've done some pretty impure things to my body.

Wash me clean from my guilt. Purify me from my sin. . . . Purify me from my sins, and I will be clean; wash me, and I will be whiter than snow. PSALM 51:2, 7

Don't you realize that your bodies are actually parts of Christ? 1 CORINTHIANS 6:15

Imitate God, therefore, in everything you do, because you are his dear children.
EPHESIANS 5:1

Let us go right into the presence of God with sincere hearts fully trusting him. For our guilty consciences have been sprinkled with Christ's blood to make us clean, and our bodies have been washed with pure water. HEBREWS 10:22

To have a pure body, you must start with a pure heart. God honors those who strive for pure hearts because it demonstrates a sincere commitment to be like Jesus. One of the most powerful truths Jesus taught is that when he forgives you, no matter what you have done, he sees you as pure and fully usable for his service. Now that you are forgiven and restored, strive to avoid sins that violate God's intended plan for your body, sins that include sexual immorality, drunkenness, substance abuse, self-inflicted violence, and gluttony.

When I die, will I keep this body, get a new one, or have no body at all?

Our earthly bodies are planted in the ground when we die, but they will be raised to live forever. 1 CORINTHIANS 15:42

If you live into old age, your present body will eventually become a burden to you. It will age and deteriorate, and it may become sick or disabled. You wouldn't want to live in a body like that forever—think how many problems you would accumulate over a few thousand years! The Bible teaches that in heaven God will give you a new, physical body that will never age or deteriorate, never get sick or disabled. It will also be a supernatural body. Your new body will be able to do things that it can't do now. And your new body will be perfect.

What is the body of Christ?

The human body has many parts, but the many parts make up one whole body. So it is with the body of Christ. Some of us are Jews, some are Gentiles, some are slaves, and some are free. But we have all been baptized into one body by one Spirit, and we all share the same Spirit. 1 CORINTHIANS 12:12-13

The church is his body; it is made full and complete by Christ, who fills all things everywhere with himself. EPHESIANS 1:23

You are citizens along with all of God's holy people. You are members of God's family. Together, we are his house, built on the foundation of the apostles and the prophets. And the cornerstone is Christ Jesus himself. We are carefully joined together in him, becoming a holy temple for the Lord. EPHESIANS 2:19-21

These are the gifts Christ gave to the church: the apostles, the prophets, the evangelists, and the pastors and teachers. Their responsibility is to equip God's people to do his work and build up the church, the body of Christ. EPHESIANS 4:11-12

The body of Christ simply refers to all people (past, present, and future) who have received God's forgiveness and believe in Jesus Christ as their Savior and Lord. The body of Christ is also called the church.

What is our role in the body of Christ?

After all, who is Apollos? Who is Paul? We are only God's servants through whom you believed the Good News. Each of us did the work the Lord gave us. I planted the seed in your hearts, and Apollos watered it, but it was God who made it grow. It's not important who does the planting, or who does the watering. What's important is that God makes the seed grow. . . . We are both God's workers. 1 CORINTHIANS 3:5-9)

He makes the whole body fit together perfectly. As each part does its own special work, it helps the other parts grow, so that the whole body is healthy and growing and full of love. EPHESIANS 4:16

God assigns a variety of roles to believers based on the abilities he gives them and the needs of his church. It is important for you to discover the unique gifts God has given you and how to use those gifts to serve him.

BOREDOM *See also* Apathy, Emptiness, Meaning/Meaninglessness

The dictionary defines *boredom* as being "weary with tedious dullness." This might come from doing the same thing all the time or doing work with no apparent purpose or doing nothing for too long. Many people with hectic schedules say, "I'd love to be bored for a while." But there's a difference between boredom and rest. We all need rest, but none of us need boredom. Boredom is dangerous because it signifies a lack of purpose and a lack of passion for anything meaningful. The antidote to boredom is finding something purposeful and significant to do. God has a purpose for you. Find that purpose, and you will never be bored. You can start by volunteering to help in a ministry at your church. Find a hobby that helps you develop a skill (music, crafts, sports). Then you will look forward to each day, and people will be attracted to your enthusiasm and passion for living.

Doesn't being a Christian sound boring to unbelievers?

Our great desire is that you will keep on loving others as long as life lasts, in order to make certain that what you hope for will come true. Then you will not become spiritually dull and indifferent. HEBREWS 6:11-12

Being a Christian can seem boring to people who see Christianity as a bunch of "thou shalt nots." But those who grasp what the Christian life is all about find it full and exciting. When you realize that almighty God wants to work through you to accomplish his work in the world, you will be amazed at the great things he accomplishes through you. Focus on using and developing your God-given gifts and on the eternal rewards God promises to believers, and your life will be continually exciting. If you become bored in your Christian life, it is because you are not making yourself available to God and asking him to pour his blessings onto others through you.

What are signs of boredom?

As a door swings back and forth on its hinges, so the lazy person turns over in bed.
PROVERBS 26:14

*Their days of labor are filled with pain and grief; even at night their minds cannot rest.
It is all meaningless.* ECCLESIASTES 2:23

*Let's not get tired of doing what is good. At just the right time we will reap a harvest of
blessing if we don't give up.* GALATIANS 6:9

Feelings of meaninglessness, laziness, and restlessness are all signs of boredom.

What eliminates boredom?

*Now we can rejoice in our wonderful new relationship with God because our Lord Jesus
Christ has made us friends of God.* ROMANS 5:11

God has a plan for you. Boredom disappears when you recognize his purpose for you.
When you are trying to follow Christ's example every day and asking God to do his work
through you, you will never be bored!

Is it possible to get bored doing good things for God all the time?

*Let's not get tired of doing what is good. At just the right time we will reap a harvest of
blessing if we don't give up.* GALATIANS 6:9

If doing right becomes boring, then you are doing right for the wrong reasons. Discouragement and detachment come when your motives are self-centered and not Christ-
centered.

BOUNDARIES *See also* Accountability, Self-Control

In track and field, if runners step out of their lane during a race, they are disqualified. In soc-
cer, if a player kicks the ball out-of-bounds, the other team gets the ball. In volleyball, if a
player touches a ball out-of-bounds, the other team gets a point. When it comes to sports, we
know that boundaries are necessary to keep the game fair, orderly, and under control. They
also keep people from getting hurt, and they keep the game moving forward toward a specific goal. With no boundaries, the game wouldn't make sense. It would be random and
pointless.

This same principle is true in everyday life. God gives us boundaries so that life makes
sense. When we stay within those boundaries, we have purpose and direction, and we get
hurt less. When we go out-of-bounds, we are penalized, not because God wants to punish us
but because that is the natural consequence. The world works by the rules God set in place at
Creation. We can't change them, and if we could, life wouldn't be as fulfilling—just like a
game wouldn't be good with no "out-of-bounds." Instead of seeing boundaries as negative
limitations on our freedom, try to see them as helpful. They keep life moving toward the ultimate victory God has promised to all who play the game well and live within his boundaries.
The reward for winning is more than just a trophy—it's eternal life in a perfect world.

What are God's boundaries for me?

What does the LORD your God require of you? He requires only that you fear the LORD your God, and live in a way that pleases him, and love him and serve him with all your heart and soul. And you must always obey the LORD's commands and decrees that I am giving you today for your own good. DEUTERONOMY 10:12-13

These verses sum up God's general boundaries for us. Keep within these lines, and God promises your life will be far better than if you don't. You will have purpose and direction, blessing and joy.

O people, the LORD has told you what is good, and this is what he requires of you: to do what is right, to love mercy, and to walk humbly with your God. MICAH 6:8

God's boundaries are loving restraints to keep you from falling away from him and to help you live the abundant life he offers. When you do what is right, as defined by God's Word, you "play fair" and develop a reputation of integrity. When you love mercy, you don't take advantage of others. And when you walk humbly with God, you realize that you can't take credit for your successes and that you need to rely on God and others to help you finish strong. These boundaries don't restrict you but in fact help you do well at the game of life.

Why do I need boundaries?

I have hidden your word in my heart, that I might not sin against you. PSALM 119:11

Make me walk along the path of your commands, for that is where my happiness is found. PSALM 119:35

Your commands make me wiser than my enemies, for they are my constant guide. PSALM 119:98

Guide my steps by your word, so I will not be overcome by evil. PSALM 119:133

If you've ever walked on a path in the woods, you know that the path needs to be clearly marked; if it's not, you could stray off the path and become hopelessly lost. The woods can be dangerous, and you might become afraid. God's commands and laws act as boundaries by clearly marking life's path before you. They protect you from danger and fear.

"You won't die!" the serpent replied to the woman. "God knows that your eyes will be opened as soon as you eat it, and you will be like God, knowing both good and evil." The woman was convinced. . . . She took some of the fruit and ate it. Then she gave some to her husband . . . and he ate it, too. At that moment their eyes were opened, and they suddenly felt shame. GENESIS 3:4-7

Temptation moves your focus away from God and toward your limitations. It causes you to think that stepping out-of-bounds might be better than obeying God. But just as Adam and Eve found out, too late, giving in to temptation never gives you more freedom. It just messes up your life and cuts off the blessings from God that make your life worth living.

For everything there is a season, a time for every activity under heaven.
ECCLESIASTES 3:1

God gives us the boundaries of seasons and time. These provide predictability in our life, giving us confidence to trust in his reliability.

Have you no respect for me? Why don't you tremble in my presence? I, the LORD, define the ocean's sandy shoreline as an everlasting boundary that the waters cannot cross. The waves may toss and roar, but they can never pass the boundaries I set. JEREMIAH 5:22

God provides physical boundaries in creation for your protection and your enjoyment. Fish do not swim in a desert, nor do eagles fly beneath the seas. Know your limitations, too, and your life will be more fulfilling and satisfying.

What are the benefits of God's boundaries?

The LORD God warned him, "You may freely eat the fruit of every tree in the garden— except the tree of the knowledge of good and evil. If you eat its fruit, you are sure to die."
GENESIS 2:16-17

God's boundaries are set for your own good to protect you from evil. They help you stay away from sin and its heartbreaking consequences.

Even when I walk through the darkest valley, I will not be afraid, for you are close beside me. Your rod and your staff protect and comfort me. PSALM 23:4

God's boundaries are set for your safety and comfort. They keep you from harm.

What are the consequences of failing to observe God's boundaries?

I remind you of the angels who did not stay within the limits of authority God gave them but left the place where they belonged. God has kept them securely chained in prisons of darkness, waiting for the great day of judgment. And don't forget Sodom and Gomorrah and their neighboring towns, which were filled with immorality and every kind of sexual perversion. Those cities were destroyed by fire and serve as a warning of the eternal fire of God's judgment. JUDE 1:6-7

In sports, crossing a boundary brings a penalty. Crossing God's boundaries is a matter of life and death. God judges those who refuse to observe his boundaries of right living. Like many sports, life has two sides: If you are not for God, you are against him. When you are against him, you are on the side of evil, even though you may not realize it.

[The Lord God] said to the woman, "I will sharpen the pain of your pregnancy, and in pain you will give birth. And you will desire to control your husband, but he will rule over you." And to the man he said, "Since you listened to your wife and ate from the tree whose fruit I commanded you not to eat, the ground is cursed because of you. All your life you will struggle to scratch a living from it. It will grow thorns and thistles for

you, though you will eat of its grains."... So the Lord God banished them from the Garden of Eden, and he sent Adam out to cultivate the ground from which he had been made. GENESIS 3:16-18, 23

God disciplines you when you move beyond his boundaries.

Accept the way God does things, for who can straighten what he has made crooked? ECCLESIASTES 7:13

God's boundaries are the rules of the universe, which will prevail. As the Creator, he set them up in the way creation would best function. Accepting God's boundaries will make your life happier because you can be assured that his limitations protect you and guide you toward what is best.

How can I set boundaries for myself?

Don't copy the behavior and customs of this world, but let God transform you into a new person by changing the way you think. Then you will learn to know God's will for you, which is good and pleasing and perfect. ROMANS 12:2

Start by allowing God to change the way you think. Study his Word to find out how to live as a believer and how to stay within the boundaries he has set for you.

I am saying this for your benefit, not to place restrictions on you. I want you to do whatever will help you serve the Lord best, with as few distractions as possible. 1 CORINTHIANS 7:35

Serving the Lord should be a lifelong priority. Rather than restricting you, boundaries will eliminate the distractions that can keep you from accomplishing magnificent things for God.

It might not be a matter of conscience for you, but it is for the other person.... I, too, try to please everyone in everything I do. I don't just do what is best for me; I do what is best for others so that many may be saved. 1 CORINTHIANS 10:29, 32-33

God's Word clearly states that you must live by certain rules, such as the Ten Commandments. But God also asks you to refrain from doing things that might cause others to go against their conscience, even if you feel something would be okay for you to do.

The person who strays from common sense will end up in the company of the dead. PROVERBS 21:16

Common sense is necessary in establishing personal boundaries. You can easily get into trouble when you make a decision based on impulse or emotion. When common sense screams *no*, don't do it!

When are boundaries negative?

Jesus looked at them intently and said, "Humanly speaking, it is impossible. But with God everything is possible." MATTHEW 19:26

All glory to God, who is able, through his mighty power at work within us, to accomplish infinitely more than we might ask or think. EPHESIANS 3:20

Boundaries become negative when you try to limit God. When you doubt his ability to perform a miracle in your life or to change an impossible situation, you are putting boundaries around almighty God. God can accomplish more than you can ever dare to hope for. Don't limit him with your disbelief. Nothing is impossible for him. He is ready to help you get rid of bad habits, sinful practices and desires, or anything else that is keeping you from his love and freedom.

Do not judge others, and you will not be judged. For you will be treated as you treat others. The standard you use in judging is the standard by which you will be judged. MATTHEW 7:1-2

Boundaries can be negative when you impose your boundaries on others.

BRAGGING *See also* Pride, Humility

When good things happen to us, we like to tell other people about them: a promotion at work, a new house, a new baby, a great success as a volunteer on a church project. All these things are blessings from the Lord, and often they can be shared with others. However, your attitude should be just that—one of sharing your joy with others. As with so many issues in the Christian life, your motives and attitudes determine whether something is right or wrong even more than your actions do. If you are telling others about your successes, status, material things, and other blessings to make yourself look better or more important than others, it turns into bragging. Bragging shows a need to rank yourself above others. This is a dangerous step toward thinking you don't even need God, which puts yourself above him. When you share your blessings, your goal should always be to glorify God, not yourself; otherwise it becomes bragging.

Is bragging wrong?

What gives you the right to make such a judgment? What do you have that God hasn't given you? And if everything you have is from God, why boast as though it were not a gift? 1 CORINTHIANS 4:7

Bragging is an indication that you do not have a true understanding of yourself or God. Bragging brings praise to yourself, when it's really God who deserves the praise for all he has done for you.

How long will they speak with arrogance? How long will these evil people boast? PSALM 94:4

If you are bitterly jealous and there is selfish ambition in your heart, don't cover up the truth with boasting and lying. JAMES 3:14

A braggart either thinks very highly of himself and tries to prove it, or he thinks very little of himself and tries to convince others of his worth. Either way, bragging is a sin because it is self-centered.

What often results from bragging? Why shouldn't we brag?

One night Joseph had a dream, and when he told his brothers about it, they hated him more than ever. "Listen to this dream," he said. "We were out in the field, tying up bundles of grain. Suddenly my bundle stood up, and your bundles all gathered around and bowed low before mine!" His brothers responded, "So you think you will be our king, do you? Do you actually think you will reign over us?" And they hated him all the more because of his dreams and the way he talked about them. GENESIS 37:5-8

Everyone can tell when you are bragging, and no one likes it. Bragging usually alienates people. Your bragging can actually cause others to sin because they want to avoid you so badly that they'll do almost anything to keep away from you. Joseph was eventually humbled and became a great man of God; but as a young man, his bragging caused a lot of misery for both himself and his brothers. His bragging was the key reason that his brothers got so sick of him they sold him into slavery.

They brag about their evil desires; they praise the greedy and curse the LORD.
PSALM 10:3

Bragging about your sinful thoughts and actions is an affront to God because it is sheer defiance of him. While it may amuse your friends and listeners, it proves how foolish you really are.

[Gaal shouted,] "If I were in charge here, I would get rid of Abimelech. I would say to him, 'Get some soldiers, and come out and fight!'" . . . Then Zebul turned on him and asked, "Now where is that big mouth of yours? Wasn't it you that said, 'Who is Abimelech, and why should we be his servants?' The men you mocked are right outside the city! Go out and fight them!" JUDGES 9:29, 38

Bragging is obnoxious and only makes enemies. Gaal was right that Abimelech was an evil leader, but he should not have bragged that he could easily defeat Abimelech in battle. His obnoxious bragging was overheard by the enemy and led to his own defeat. A big head leads to a big mouth, which leads to big trouble. A big mouth indicates a lack of understanding or self-confidence.

Look here, you who say, "Today or tomorrow we are going to a certain town and will stay there a year. We will do business there and make a profit." How do you know what your life will be like tomorrow? Your life is like the morning fog—it's here a little while, then it's gone. What you ought to say is, "If the Lord wants us to, we will live and do this or that." Otherwise you are boasting about your own plans, and all such boasting is evil.
JAMES 4:13-16

Braggarts have an unrealistic view of the future and are overconfident about their ability to control what lies ahead. There are many uncertainties about the future, and only God knows what it holds. Braggarts forget about God and rely on their own ability to accomplish things.

When you give to someone in need, don't do as the hypocrites do—blowing trumpets in the synagogues and streets to call attention to their acts of charity! I tell you the truth, they have received all the reward they will ever get. But when you give to someone in need, don't let your left hand know what your right hand is doing. Give your gifts in private, and your Father, who sees everything, will reward you. MATTHEW 6:2-4

Bragging shows pride, but God loves humility. When you brag, you are arranging your own rewards, whereas waiting for others to honor you shows humility. Receiving an award you ask for or give yourself isn't much of an award. But it is wonderful to receive an award presented by your peers. Even better, an award presented by the Lord lasts forever.

Can we brag about God?

This is what the LORD says: "Don't let the wise boast in their wisdom, or the powerful boast in their power, or the rich boast in their riches. But those who wish to boast should boast in this alone: that they truly know me and understand that I am the LORD who demonstrates unfailing love and who brings justice and righteousness to the earth, and that I delight in these things. I, the LORD, have spoken!" JEREMIAH 9:23-24

When you truly know God and understand how he loves you, you will want to share his goodness with others. This is not bragging; It is witnessing! It can become bragging, however, if you make it sound like God has given you more blessings than others and therefore must love you more than others.

Can we brag about others?

Let someone else praise you, not your own mouth. PROVERBS 27:2

Show them your love, and prove to all the churches that our boasting about you is justified. 2 CORINTHIANS 8:24

We proudly tell God's other churches about your endurance and faithfulness in all the persecutions and hardships you are suffering. 2 THESSALONIANS 1:4

It is good to call attention to God's work in another person's life. Praising others is not bragging; praising your role in someone else's accomplishment is bragging.

BROKENNESS *See also* Renewal, Repentance, Surrender

Brokenness is the breaking of our pride and self-sufficiency. It comes most often through circumstances that overwhelm us or through sin that makes us realize that the only way out of our mess is by God's help. Those who are open about their brokenness—such as Moses, David, and Paul—often have great influence in helping others. If you have been broken, allow God to use your experience to help others overcome their struggles.

When is brokenness good?

The LORD is close to the brokenhearted; he rescues those whose spirits are crushed. PSALM 34:18

The sacrifice you desire is a broken spirit. You will not reject a broken and repentant heart, O God. PSALM 51:17

Brokenness is good when it causes you to admit you have sinned and are in need of God's grace. God promises to draw close to you when you are brokenhearted about sin in your life.

Job scraped his skin with a piece of broken pottery as he sat among the ashes. His wife said to him, "Are you still trying to maintain your integrity? Curse God and die." JOB 2:8-9

The alternative to brokenness before God is bitterness, which leads to dissatisfaction and general irritation with life. Bitterness never allows God the opportunity to heal, for a bitter person looks inward, not upward.

I will bless those who have humble and contrite hearts, who tremble at my word. ISAIAH 66:2

Humility is a form of brokenness. It is the realization that you cannot fix your problems or control your needs. Acknowledging your dependence on God allows him to help you with all your needs.

He heals the brokenhearted and bandages their wounds. PSALM 147:3

When you are hurting the most, God comforts the most.

How can I achieve an attitude of brokenness?

[Job said to God,] "I take back everything I said, and I sit in dust and ashes to show my repentance." JOB 42:6

Brokenness comes when you understand the contrast between God's holiness and your own sinfulness, and this realization humbles your heart.

How should I respond when my heart is broken?

LORD, see my anguish! My heart is broken and my soul despairs, for I have rebelled against you. In the streets the sword kills, and at home there is only death. LAMENTATIONS 1:20

Turn to God with your hurt and ask for his help. He is the only One who can fully restore what has been broken.

BURNOUT   *See also* Balance, Busyness, Stress, Tiredness, Work

Burnout is overwhelming exhaustion and an inability to push on, brought about by stress. We all experience times of burnout, when we feel tapped out emotionally, mentally, physically, and spiritually. In our fast-paced world of "open all night" and "twenty-four-hour service," it isn't surprising that we become exhausted. Because burnout is so draining and paralyzing, we need to take care of our bodies and minds by eating right, exercising, and getting plenty of sleep and rest. One of the best ways to reduce burnout is taking time to be close to God. When we draw close to him, we can tap into his power, strength, peace, protection, and love. Doing this can help us stay strong and persevere through even the worst times of burnout.

How do I know if I am experiencing burnout?

When David and his men were in the thick of battle, David became weak and exhausted.
2 SAMUEL 21:15

If you become weak and exhausted in the middle of a long stretch of work with no end in sight, you may be experiencing burnout.

I am the only one left, and now they are trying to kill me, too. 1 KINGS 19:14

I am weary, O God; I am weary and worn out, O God. PROVERBS 30:1

What do people get in this life for all their hard work and anxiety? ECCLESIASTES 2:22

You may be experiencing burnout if you are in despair because it seems your work will never be done, or if you are in a rut and can't seem to get out.

The floodwaters are up to my neck. Deeper and deeper I sink into the mire; I can't find a foothold. PSALM 69:1-2

You may be experiencing burnout if your life feels overwhelming and even everyday tasks seem impossible.

I am overwhelmed with trouble! Haven't I had enough pain already? And now the LORD has added more! JEREMIAH 45:3

When you are burned out, you may feel bitter toward God.

What is the antidote for burnout?

The LORD is the everlasting God, the Creator of all the earth. He never grows weak or weary. No one can measure the depths of his understanding. He gives power to the weak and strength to the powerless. Even youths will become weak and tired, and young men will fall in exhaustion. But those who trust in the LORD will find new strength. They will soar high on wings like eagles. They will run and not grow weary. They will walk and not faint. ISAIAH 40:28-31

When you are weary, a key to renewal and refreshment is trusting in the Lord. This involves the patient expectation that God will give you his power and strength to persevere through life's tasks and difficulties. When you draw your strength from him, he promises to help you soar like an eagle and run like a marathoner.

Select from all the people some capable, honest men. . . . They will help you carry the load, making the task easier for you. If you follow this advice . . . then you will be able to endure the pressures. EXODUS 18:21-23

Delegate some of your workload. Delegating can ease your burden, multiply your effectiveness, and allow other people to grow.

You have six days each week for your ordinary work, but on the seventh day you must stop working. . . . It also allows your slaves and the foreigners living among you to be refreshed. EXODUS 23:12

When people are tired, their productivity decreases dramatically. Rest refreshes and energizes us to be more productive. Regular, consistent, weekly rest is an important part of avoiding burnout or recovering from it.

As [Elijah] was sleeping, an angel touched him and told him, "Get up and eat!" He looked around and there beside his head was some bread baked on hot stones and a jar of water! So he ate and drank and lay down again. Then the angel of the LORD came again and touched him and said, "Get up and eat some more, or the journey ahead will be too much for you." So he got up and ate and drank. 1 KINGS 19:5-8

Take good care of your body by exercising, resting, and eating nutritious meals. Poor nutrition and unhealthy habits invite burnout.

[Nehemiah] continued the work with even greater determination. . . . When our enemies and the surrounding nations heard about it, they . . . realized this work had been done with the help of our God. NEHEMIAH 6:9, 16

Sometimes you can't stop working, even though you feel exhausted. When you need to finish a job, pray to God for strength to keep going until you reach a stopping point or until the job is completed. You can receive the spiritual strength that only God can give when you ask him for it.

Come to me, all of you who are weary and carry heavy burdens, and I will give you rest. . . . You will find rest for your souls. MATTHEW 11:28-29

It is crucial to maintain a close fellowship with God and be restored by spending time with him. Connecting with God taps into his strength. Maybe you find it difficult to rest. You mistakenly believe that productivity requires constant activity. But sometimes you need to slow down in order to speed up. Stop awhile to let your body, mind, and spirit recover, and reset your purpose so you can be more energized and more productive when you are ready to get back to the work at hand.

It is not by force nor by strength, but by my Spirit, says the LORD of Heaven's Armies. ZECHARIAH 4:6

Recognizing your limits is essential to avoiding burnout. Maybe you are trying to do too much, and you become discouraged when nothing seems to go right. If God wants you to accomplish something, he will give you the strength to do it.

Does Jesus understand our burnout?
This High Priest of ours understands our weaknesses, for he faced all of the same testings we do, yet he did not sin. So let us come boldly to the throne of our gracious God. There we will receive his mercy, and we will find grace to help us when we need it most. HEBREWS 4:15-16

Jesus was once human like we are, experiencing the full range of emotions and struggles. Instead of condemnation, he gives mercy; instead of criticism, he offers comfort and encouragement.

BUSINESS *See also* Ambition, Employers/Employees, Leadership, Productivity, Work

Over the course of our lives, most of us will be involved with business in some way. Whether you become a successful CEO or run a home-based business, whether you work at a fast-food chain or in a Fortune 500 company, God has provided certain guidelines in the Bible that will help you manage the complexities of relationships within the workplace, the ethics of obeying a supervisor's orders versus following your conscience, the demands of time, and the stress of goals and deadlines. God has a lot to say about how we conduct ourselves in the workplace, how we can find purpose, how we can make a difference in the world, and how we can succeed. He also has a lot to say about how business can change us for good or for bad, and how it can control or corrupt us. God gives us so much advice about business because that's where so many of us spend the most productive hours of our day. Even though there is much you can't control, you can control who you are and how you react. That will affect your work far more than you realize. You will find your greatest fulfillment when you focus on filling a need and serving God as your ultimate supervisor.

Is God interested in my success in business?

She goes to inspect a field and buys it; with her earnings she plants a vineyard.
PROVERBS 31:16

God thinks highly of people who are enterprising and hardworking.

A Jew named Aquila, born in Pontus . . . recently arrived from Italy with his wife, Priscilla. . . . Paul lived and worked with them, for they were tentmakers just as he was.
ACTS 18:2-3

Paul, Aquila, and Priscilla were Christian leaders in ministry and in business. They are good examples of early Christians who used their successful business to serve God.

Try to please them all the time, not just when they are watching you. As slaves of Christ, do the will of God with all your heart. Work with enthusiasm, as though you were working for the Lord rather than for people. EPHESIANS 6:6-7

How hard you work reveals the nature of your commitment to Christ. Hard work done with excellence and integrity honors God and builds a reputation that will stick with you for a lifetime—and for eternity. Sometimes it also brings material resources that you can use for God's glory.

What principles should guide how I conduct my business?

Do not defraud or rob your neighbor. Do not make your hired workers wait until the next day to receive their pay. LEVITICUS 19:13

Be honest and fair to coworkers and employees, promptly paying them what they earn.

The LORD demands accurate scales and balances; he sets the standards for fairness.
PROVERBS 16:11

Integrity is an essential mark of a Christian. Anything less dishonors the Lord and those you lead and serve.

Whatever you do, do well. ECCLESIASTES 9:10

God calls you to pursue excellence. Excellence expresses your appreciation of the gifts God has given you and the value you place on others.

Abraham bowed low before the Hittites and said, ". . . Let me buy his cave at Machpelah, down at the end of his field. I will pay the full price in the presence of witnesses.". . . "No, my lord," he said to Abraham, "please listen to me. I will give you the field and the cave. . . ." Abraham again bowed low before the citizens of the land. . . . "No, listen to me. I will buy it from you. Let me pay the full price for the field. . . ." Ephron answered Abraham, "My lord, please listen to me. The land is worth 400 pieces of silver, but what is that between friends? . . ." So Abraham agreed to Ephron's price and paid the amount he had suggested—400 pieces of silver.
GENESIS 23:7-16

Abraham's interaction with Ephron models the kind of respect and fairness you should show others when doing business with them.

Always use honest weights and measures, so that you may enjoy a long life in the land the LORD your God is giving you. All who cheat with dishonest weights and measures are detestable to the LORD your God. DEUTERONOMY 25:15-16

God condemns cheaters who use dishonest means to become successful.

Boaz went to the town gate and took a seat there. . . . "Come over here and sit down, friend. I want to talk to you.". . . Then Boaz called ten leaders from the town and asked them to sit as witnesses. . . . "You are witnesses that today I have bought from Naomi all the property of Elimelech, Kilion, and Mahlon." RUTH 4:1-2, 9

Like Boaz, always conduct your business aboveboard and in public, with no hidden kickbacks or shady deals.

Good comes to those who lend money generously and conduct their business fairly.
PSALM 112:5

It is important to be generous in your business dealings—it is an investment that will certainly pay off later! In addition to the financial bottom line, there's also a bottom line for how to act with integrity and for how to conduct relationships.

Listen to this, you who rob the poor and trample down the needy! You can't wait for the Sabbath day to be over and the religious festivals to end so you can get back to cheating the helpless. AMOS 8:4-5

Serving God through your business during the week means that you live in harmony with what you profess on Sunday. Exploiting your workers during the week contradicts any faith you claim on Sunday.

Jesus said, "Give to Caesar what belongs to Caesar, and give to God what belongs to God." MARK 12:17

Paying taxes is an important obligation. Cheating your government is also cheating your Lord.

Don't begin until you count the cost. LUKE 14:28

Whenever you start a project or a business venture, plan ahead and make sure you can handle the costs—not only the financial costs but also the physical, relational, and spiritual as well.

Who is really in charge of my business?

Look here, you who say, "Today or tomorrow we are going to a certain town and will stay there a year. We will do business there and make a profit." How do you know what your life will be like tomorrow? Your life is like the morning fog—it's here a little while, then it's gone. What you ought to say is, "If the Lord wants us to, we will live and do this or that." JAMES 4:13-15

Whatever business ventures you pursue, remember that God is in control and that you are completely dependent on him for everything.

BUSYNESS *See also* Balance, Burnout, Priorities, Stress

We often operate under the false assumption that being busy means being productive or that resting means laziness. But you can have productive rest and unproductive activity. The Bible points out many benefits of being busy, such as earning a living, providing for your family, and advancing God's kingdom. But being too busy can damage relationships (with God and others), cause burnout, or prevent you from focusing on your real priorities. As in anything you do—whether working or resting—learn to strike a balance between work, fun, and rest so that you can be productive in all areas of life.

Does God expect me to be busy all the time?

Jesus said, "Come to me, all of you who are weary and carry heavy burdens, and I will give you rest. Take my yoke upon you. Let me teach you, because I am humble and gentle at heart, and you will find rest for your souls." MATTHEW 11:28-29

Activity itself is not a virtue; it can actually be a detriment to your spiritual life. The Lord invites you to rest and be refreshed in his care.

What are the benefits of being busy?

[A virtuous and capable wife] is energetic and strong, a hard worker. . . . She carefully watches everything in her household and suffers nothing from laziness. PROVERBS 31:17, 27

Keep busy all afternoon, for you don't know if profit will come from one activity or another—or maybe both. ECCLESIASTES 11:6

Rich harvests cannot come from lazy fingers. Fruitfulness in your life results from hard work and a lot of time. One of life's greatest challenges is learning to use your time wisely.

What are the dangers of busyness?

We are merely moving shadows, and all our busy rushing ends in nothing. We heap up wealth, not knowing who will spend it. PSALM 39:6

Never confuse activity with accomplishment. A too-full schedule may reflect a lack of wise priorities and leave you no time to enjoy the fruits of your labor.

What should I busy myself with?

I can never stop praising you; I declare your glory all day long. PSALM 71:8

Don't worry about anything; instead, pray about everything. PHILIPPIANS 4:6

You can never spend too much time praising God, thanking him, or praying!

How can I be less busy and find rest in life?

You have six days each week for your ordinary work, but on the seventh day you must stop working, even during the seasons of plowing and harvest. EXODUS 34:21

Those who live in the shelter of the Most High will find rest in the shadow of the Almighty. PSALM 91:1

God is both the model and the source of rest. Just as God rested after creation was finished, he encourages you to set aside a day of rest from your labors.

Jesus said, "Let's go off by ourselves to a quiet place and rest awhile." He said this because there were so many people coming and going that Jesus and his apostles didn't even have time to eat. MARK 6:31

Rest and renewal need to be planned into your busy schedule. You must be proactive, or all the other demands of life will dictate your schedule. God planned for work, but he also planned for rest. Keep both in balance.

Simon and the others went out to find [Jesus]. When they found him, they said, "Everyone is looking for you." But Jesus replied, "We must go on to other towns as well, and I will preach to them, too. That is why I came." MARK 1:36-38

Freeing yourself from the trap of incessant activity requires learning to say no—sometimes even to worthwhile activities.

What is the antidote to empty busyness?

Teach us to realize the brevity of life, so that we may grow in wisdom. PSALM 90:12

The key to overcoming empty busyness is to live a life that is fully productive for God. You do this by understanding his call and purpose for your life and prioritizing your activities accordingly. God empowers you to make the most of the time he gives you.

CALL OF GOD

See also Decisions, Dreams/Visions, Guidance, Holy Spirit, Purpose, Timing of God, Vision, Will of God

It is essentially human for each of us to search for our purpose, or our calling in life. We all long to be part of something bigger than ourselves. Often we wish God's call would come through an audible voice or a miraculous sign in the sky. God's call is not always to be a missionary in Africa . . . although it can be. God's call can also be to minister to the youth in your church, to care for your ailing spouse, to feed the hungry, or to volunteer at a shelter. He has given each of us special gifts and abilities. When we use those abilities to serve him and others, we are answering his call. In everything God calls us to do, we can be sure he will equip us with the heart, vision, support, and resources we need.

How do I know what my calling is?

Your word is a lamp to guide my feet and a light for my path. PSALM 119:105

The first step in knowing your calling is getting to know God better by reading his Word. As God communicates to you through the Bible, he will show you what to do and where he wants you to go.

God gave these four young men an unusual aptitude for understanding every aspect of literature and wisdom. DANIEL 1:17

God has given every individual special aptitudes and abilities. These provide the biggest clue to what God wants you to do. When he calls you to do something unique for him, he will almost always allow you to use your God-given gifts to get the job done. In the meantime, develop those special abilities and begin to use them. Then it will become apparent what God wants you to do. Always serve God and move through life in ways that utilize your primary gifts.

My life is worth nothing to me unless I use it for finishing the work assigned me by the Lord Jesus. ACTS 20:24

When God gives you a specific calling, it fills your thoughts and energies so that you have a longing to pursue it wholeheartedly.

Let God transform you into a new person by changing the way you think. Then you will learn to know God's will for you. ROMANS 12:2

When you let God transform you by the power of his Holy Spirit, he will literally begin to change the way you think so that you will know what he wants you to do.

Has God called me to do specific things?

The LORD gave me this message: "I knew you before I formed you in your mother's womb. Before you were born I set you apart and appointed you as my prophet to the nations." JEREMIAH 1:4-5

God may call you to do a certain job or to accomplish a very specific task or ministry. When he does, he will make sure you know what it is. You will feel a very strong sense of leading from him. It's up to you to respond and walk through the door of opportunity he opens.

There are different kinds of spiritual gifts, but the same Spirit is the source of them all. . . . A spiritual gift is given to each of us so we can help each other. 1 CORINTHIANS 12:4, 7

God gives each of us a spiritual gift (sometimes more than one) and a special ministry in the church where we can use those gifts to help and encourage others and to bring glory to his name. Using these specific spiritual gifts helps you fulfill the purpose for which God made you.

Each of you should remain as you were when God called you. Are you a slave? Don't let that worry you—but if you get a chance to be free, take it. And remember, if you were a slave when the Lord called you, you are now free in the Lord. And if you were free when the Lord called you, you are now a slave of Christ. God paid a high price for you, so don't be enslaved by the world. Each of you, dear brothers and sisters, should remain as you were when God first called you. 1 CORINTHIANS 7:20-24

The call to follow Jesus does not necessarily mean a call to a specific job or Christian ministry. Sometimes your call may simply be to obey God wherever you are right now.

Do everything you want to do; take it all in. But remember that you must give an account to God for everything you do. ECCLESIASTES 11:9

God gives you the freedom to follow many different roads and pursue many different activities over the course of your life, but remember that you will have to answer to him. Not everything you do is a call from God, but you are accountable to God for everything you do.

Can I lose God's call?

God's gifts and his call can never be withdrawn. ROMANS 11:29

God's call is like your family name. Even when you feel you've dishonored your family, you do not lose your name. The same principle applies when you are a member of God's family. Because you are a child of God, he has given you specific gifts, and he has called you to do certain tasks for him. If you don't use those gifts to fulfill the purpose for which he created you, then you are missing out on the best possible life he has planned for you. But as long as you have life and breath, you can answer God's call. It's never too late.

What does God provide so I can fulfill his call?

May the God of peace—who brought up from the dead our Lord Jesus, the great Shepherd of the sheep, and ratified an eternal covenant with his blood—may he equip you with all you need for doing his will. May he produce in you, through the power of Jesus Christ, every good thing that is pleasing to him. HEBREWS 13:20-21

When God calls, he equips. If you commit yourself to answering his call, the power of the resurrected Lord will enable you to fulfill it.

CARING *See also* Compassion, Friendship, Hospitality

The seeds of compassion and concern are planted in the human heart, and when need appears or tragedy strikes, those seeds quickly grow to fruition. Anyone with a sense of humanity is ready and willing to help another in need. Call it love, concern, compassion, or care—it is a willingness to reach out, provide for others in times of need, share with them, comfort them, and just be with them. But among Christians there is a heightened sense of caring. The very term *brothers and sisters in Christ* suggests a richer, deeper relationship that transcends blood relationships.

Does God care what happens to me?

I will be glad and rejoice in your unfailing love, for you have seen my troubles, and you care about the anguish of my soul. PSALM 31:7

Yes, you have been with me from birth; from my mother's womb you have cared for me. No wonder I am always praising you! PSALM 71:6

God's love for you began before you were born, continues throughout your life, and extends through eternity. Since he created you to have a relationship with him, he cares about every detail of your life. He knows all your troubles and hurts and takes care of you during them.

How does God show he cares for me?

The LORD is close to all who call on him, yes, to all who call on him in truth. He grants the desires of those who fear him; he hears their cries for help and rescues them. The LORD protects all those who love him, but he destroys the wicked. PSALM 145:18-20

If God cares so wonderfully for wildflowers that are here today and thrown into the fire tomorrow, he will certainly care for you. Why do you have so little faith? MATTHEW 6:30

Give all your worries and cares to God, for he cares about you. 1 PETER 5:7

God is always close to you, ready to help in your time of need. God's presence surrounds you, protecting you from Satan's attacks far more than you realize. God sends opportunities your way to make your life more full and satisfying. He also sends a variety of blessings your way. He promises to take your worries and cares upon himself. And he offers you eternal life in heaven, away from all hurt, pain, and sin.

How can I show others I care?

I was naked, and you gave me clothing. I was sick, and you cared for me. I was in prison, and you visited me. MATTHEW 25:36

The Samaritan soothed his wounds with olive oil and wine and bandaged them. Then he put the man on his own donkey and took him to an inn, where he took care of him. The next day he handed the innkeeper two silver coins, telling him, "Take care of this man. If his bill runs higher than this, I'll pay you the next time I'm here." LUKE 10:34-35

In the same way that God shows he cares for you by protecting you, providing for you, and preserving you, you can show care to others by doing the same for them. You can protect by being kind, helpful, and willing to reach out. You can provide by giving of your time, treasure, and talents to those in need. You can preserve by helping to maintain harmony through your words and actions. A good exercise would be to list all the ways God cares for you, then try to model this same kind of care toward others.

Where do I get the desire to care for others?

The LORD God placed the man in the Garden of Eden to tend and watch over it.
GENESIS 2:15

A caring spirit comes from the heart of God, whose very nature is to care for others. God instilled in the first person on earth the desire to care for his creation. Caring began in Eden and has been an essential part of humanity ever since.

What or whom am I responsible to care for?

You saw how the LORD your God cared for you all along the way as you traveled through the wilderness, just as a father cares for his child. DEUTERONOMY 1:31

You are responsible to care for your family.

Be kind to each other, tenderhearted, forgiving one another, just as God through Christ has forgiven you. EPHESIANS 4:32

You are responsible to care about your relationships.

Some . . . were assigned to care for the various articles used in worship. They checked them in and out to avoid any loss. 1 CHRONICLES 9:28

[Jesus said] "Get these things out of here. Stop turning my Father's house into a marketplace!" JOHN 2:16

You are responsible to care about your church.

Has the LORD redeemed you? Then speak out! Tell others he has redeemed you from your enemies. PSALM 107:2

[Jesus] told them, "Go into all the world and preach the Good News to everyone." MARK 16:15

How can they call on him to save them unless they believe in him? And how can they believe in him if they have never heard about him? And how can they hear about him unless someone tells them? ROMANS 10:14

You are responsible to care about the salvation of those who don't know Jesus.

Commit your actions to the LORD, and your plans will succeed. PROVERBS 16:3

You are responsible to care about those in need.

Pure and genuine religion in the sight of God the Father means caring for orphans and widows in their distress and refusing to let the world corrupt you. JAMES 1:27

You are responsible to care about those who are less fortunate than you.

How do we care for those we lead?

David . . . met up with the 200 men who had been left behind because they were too exhausted to go with him. They went out to meet David and his men, and David greeted them joyfully. But some evil troublemakers among David's men said, "They didn't go with us, so they can't have any of the plunder we recovered. . . ." But David said, "No, my brothers! Don't be selfish with what the LORD has given us. He has kept us safe and helped us defeat the band of raiders that attacked us. . . . We share and share alike—those who go to battle and those who guard the equipment." 1 SAMUEL 30:21-24

Good leaders care about the people they lead, not just their productivity. They also recognize and affirm everyone's different roles and abilities.

We always thank God for all of you and pray for you constantly. As we pray to our God and Father about you, we think of your faithful work, your loving deeds, and the enduring hope you have because of our Lord Jesus Christ. 1 THESSALONIANS 1:2-3

Good leaders affirm and pray for those they lead.

CAUTION/CAUTIOUSNESS   *See also* Safety, Foolishness, Risk

"Be careful crossing the street!" "Be careful driving." "Be careful, it's hot!" Just as parents warn their children about dangerous behaviors, God also warns us to be careful about our behaviors. His cautions are more along the lines of "Be careful not to let your anger control you" or "Use caution around ungodly people" or "Watch out! Don't let your thoughts lead you into sin." God gives us clear warnings in the Bible to guide us away from hurtful and destructive behaviors and toward a healthy, godly life. If we listen to his commandments and are careful to avoid temptations and wrong behaviors, we will avoid much pain and minimize the damage that sin causes in our lives. Read the caution signs from your heavenly Father, and you will be much safer as you travel through life.

What are some areas in which I should exercise caution?

Be very careful to love the LORD your God. JOSHUA 23:11

Be careful at all times to obey the decrees, regulations, instructions, and commands that he wrote for you. You must not worship other gods. 2 KINGS 17:37

Be careful then, dear brothers and sisters. Make sure that your own hearts are not evil and unbelieving, turning you away from the living God. HEBREWS 3:12

Be careful not to let anything distract you from wholehearted devotion to God, and be very cautious about anything that has the potential to damage your relationship with him.

Watch out! Be careful never to forget what you yourself have seen. DEUTERONOMY 4:9

That is the time to be careful! Beware that in your plenty you do not forget the LORD your God and disobey his commands, regulations, and decrees that I am giving you today. DEUTERONOMY 8:11

Be careful to remember everything God has done for you in the past so you don't become proud and forget to rely on him for your future.

We must listen very carefully to the truth we have heard, or we may drift away from it. HEBREWS 2:1

Be careful to focus on the truths you read in Scripture and hear from godly teachers. When you don't focus on the road as you drive, you are in danger of drifting off the road and putting your life in great danger. In the same way, when you don't focus on God's Word, you are in danger of drifting off the road that leads to a safe and happy destination.

Keep watch and pray, so that you will not give in to temptation. For the spirit is willing, but the body is weak. MARK 14:38

If you think you are standing strong, be careful not to fall. The temptations in your life are no different from what others experience. And God is faithful. He will not allow the temptation to be more than you can stand. When you are tempted, he will show you a way out so that you can endure. 1 CORINTHIANS 10:12-13

Stay alert! Watch out for your great enemy, the devil. He prowls around like a roaring lion, looking for someone to devour. 1 PETER 5:8

Be careful about temptation. Satan is constantly on the attack, trying to tempt you to sin against God. You will give in from time to time—everyone does. Exercising caution can help you be aware of when you are giving in so that you can admit it and correct it. When you throw caution to the wind, you give in to temptation at every whim; then you are in danger of being completely ineffective for God.

Guard your heart above all else, for it determines the course of your life. PROVERBS 4:23

Be careful to guard your heart because it is the center of your desires and affections. Your heart is especially vulnerable because it is easily swayed by emotion and is not always rational. If you are caught up in emotion, your heart will urge you to act on those feelings, even if those actions might lead you to destruction.

Just as the rich rule the poor, so the borrower is servant to the lender. PROVERBS 22:7

Don't love money; be satisfied with what you have. For God has said, "I will never fail you. I will never abandon you." HEBREWS 13:5

Be careful in handling your money. Money can cause damage to your relationships and compromise your values.

Plans succeed through good counsel; don't go to war without wise advice. PROVERBS 20:18

Be careful to give and receive godly counsel. When you give wrong advice, it can cause others to stumble. When you receive right advice, it makes you wiser.

The tongue is a small thing that makes grand speeches. But a tiny spark can set a great forest on fire. And the tongue is a flame of fire. . . . It can set your whole life on fire. . . . People can tame all kinds of animals, birds, reptiles, and fish, but no one can tame the tongue. It is restless and evil, full of deadly poison. JAMES 3:5-8

Be careful with your words, for they reveal your character. They have the power to build up or tear down.

What happens when I don't use caution?

Enthusiasm without knowledge is no good; haste makes mistakes. PROVERBS 19:2

A prudent person foresees danger and takes precautions. The simpleton goes blindly on and suffers the consequences. PROVERBS 22:3

Not being cautious can send you in the wrong direction, with destructive consequences.

Can I be too cautious?

Do not be afraid of the terrors of the night, nor the arrow that flies in the day. Do not dread the disease that stalks in darkness, nor the disaster that strikes at midday.
PSALM 91:5-6

When you work in a quarry, stones might fall and crush you. When you chop wood, there is danger with each stroke of your ax. ECCLESIASTES 10:9

Life is filled with risks. But those who never take any risks never succeed, never enjoy all life has to offer, and never fully experience God's plan for them. You are too cautious if you let fear control you to the point where any risk seems too great. When you move forward in obedience to God, you experience the privilege of watching him at work.

How do I balance risk and caution?

If you are afraid to attack, go down to the camp with your servant Purah. Listen to what the Midianites are saying, and you will be greatly encouraged. Then you will be eager to attack. JUDGES 7:10-11

Fear keeps you from taking risks. Caution keeps you from risking too much. The first step in balancing risk with caution is to identify what is making you afraid to take the risk, then deciding whether or not that fear is legitimate. You may be surprised at how often your fears have no basis.

The Jews who lived near the enemy came and told us again and again, "They will come from all directions and attack us!" So I placed armed guards behind the lowest parts of the wall in the exposed areas. I stationed the people to stand guard by families, armed with swords, spears, and bows. . . . We carried our weapons with us at all times, even when we went for water. NEHEMIAH 4:12-13, 23

Along with unfounded fears, you must be aware of real dangers and have a plan to deal with them if something goes wrong. Nehemiah anticipated the obstacles to his work, but that didn't stop him from working! It is good to think ahead and then continue to work diligently.

Good planning and hard work lead to prosperity, but hasty shortcuts lead to poverty. PROVERBS 21:5

You will never succeed or fulfill your dreams if you don't take the first step. Don't be afraid of making a mistake. Think about what you want to do, plan how you will accomplish it, and then move ahead!

CELEBRATION *See also* Joy, Praise, Thankfulness

When we think of celebrations, we usually think of enjoying ourselves and having a great time with others. We celebrate anniversaries, birthdays, victories, promotions, awards, milestones, marriages, the birth of a new baby. But we also celebrate special occasions such as the Lord's Supper, baptism, and other sacred events. What makes a celebration unique is that we take time out from the ordinary to honor and observe what is notable, special, or important to us. God gives us the ultimate reason to celebrate because he has rescued us from the consequences of sin and shown us the wonders of eternity. Celebration is a powerful way to increase hope because it takes the focus off our troubles and puts it on God's blessings and, ultimately, on God himself. Those who love God truly have much to celebrate!

Why should we celebrate? Is it justified?

Well done, my good and faithful servant. You have been faithful in handling this small amount, so now I will give you many more responsibilities. Let's celebrate together! MATTHEW 25:23

Task-oriented individuals often neglect opportunities to celebrate. The Bible teaches that celebration is both important and necessary. Celebration gives us the opportunity to savor the joy of work, to experience the satisfaction of accomplishment, and to enjoy the good things of creation. Celebration creates a spirit of gratitude and renews our energy for the work that still must be done.

What causes God to celebrate?

Well done, my good and faithful servant. You have been faithful in handling this small amount, so now I will give you many more responsibilities. Let's celebrate together! MATTHEW 25:23

There is joy in the presence of God's angels when even one sinner repents. LUKE 15:10

God celebrates the salvation of the lost, the defeat of sin and evil, and the daily joys and successes of his people.

The LORD your God . . . will take delight in you with gladness. . . . He will rejoice over you with joyful songs. ZEPHANIAH 3:17

God rejoices and celebrates when his people faithfully follow him and obey his commands.

What kinds of things can we celebrate?

This festival will be a happy time of celebrating with your sons and daughters . . . to honor the LORD . . . for it is he who blesses you with bountiful harvests and gives you success in all your work. DEUTERONOMY 16:14-15

Celebrate everything God gives you, including food to eat and success in your work. When you celebrate, recall God's acts of goodness, and enjoy the company of friends and fellow believers.

You must celebrate this event in this month each year after the LORD brings you into the land of the Canaanites. . . . On the seventh day you must explain to your children, "I am celebrating what the LORD did for me when I left Egypt." EXODUS 13:5, 8

Celebrate important milestones in your life or the lives of others. In celebrating milestones, especially spiritual milestones, you acknowledge God's blessings and teach your children the ultimate reason for celebration.

Come, everyone! Clap your hands! Shout to God with joyful praise! PSALM 47:1

Shout to the LORD, all the earth; break out in praise and sing for joy! . . . Make a joyful symphony before the LORD, the King! PSALM 98:4-6

Celebrate God's love for you, his blessings to you, and his promises of eternal joy and blessings in heaven by praising and worshiping him.

What are the ingredients of celebration?

Go and celebrate with a feast . . . and share gifts of food with people who have nothing prepared. This is a sacred day. . . . Don't be dejected and sad, for the joy of the LORD is your strength! NEHEMIAH 8:10

Sharing good food promotes community. God also intends joy and fun to be important parts of celebration because they lift your spirits and help you see beauty and meaning in life.

You must celebrate this event in this month each year after the LORD brings you into the land of the Canaanites. . . . On the seventh day you must explain to your children, "I am celebrating what the LORD did for me when I left Egypt." EXODUS 13:5, 8

Celebration with a purpose makes it more memorable and significant.

You must do no ordinary work on that day. LEVITICUS 23:25

Rest is an important part of celebration because it allows you time to refresh and renew your mind and body. It should take your mind off the ordinary and the routine.

David and all Israel were celebrating before God with all their might, singing songs and playing all kinds of musical instruments—lyres, harps, tambourines, cymbals, and trumpets. 1 CHRONICLES 13:8

Praise him with the tambourine and dancing; praise him with strings and flutes! Praise him with a clash of cymbals; praise him with loud clanging cymbals. Let everything that breathes sing praises to the LORD! Praise the LORD! PSALM 150:4-6

Worship is a form of celebration, and it can take many forms. Part of your worship experience should be celebrating God by praising his character and thanking him for all he has done for you.

What kind of celebration is inappropriate?

Moses saw that Aaron had let the people get completely out of control, much to the amusement of their enemies. EXODUS 32:25

You have had enough in the past of the evil things that godless people enjoy—their immorality and lust, their feasting and drunkenness and wild parties, and their terrible worship of idols. 1 PETER 4:3

Celebration that is self-centered, is indulgent, or involves sinful acts or conditions that can tempt you into sin is wrong.

Is celebration ever solemn?

The king and all Israel with him offered sacrifices to the LORD. . . . So the king and all the people of Israel dedicated the Temple of the LORD. 1 KINGS 8:62-63

Dedicating someone or something for God's use is a celebration, one that is often marked with the seriousness of commitment. These times of celebration can be just as meaningful as more joyous times of celebration.

What kinds of celebrations go on in heaven?

There is joy in the presence of God's angels when even one sinner repents. LUKE 15:10

I heard the voices of thousands and millions of angels around the throne.
REVELATION 5:11

Let us be glad and rejoice. . . . For the time has come for the wedding feast of the Lamb.
REVELATION 19:7

Heaven is filled with celebrations too wonderful for us to imagine. Angels worship God in mighty celebrations and rejoice wildly when one sinner repents. Someday we will be able to join in these heavenly events. All believers will celebrate together at the great banquet the Lord has planned.

CHALLENGES *See also* Fear, Limitations, Problems, Testing

For most of us, each day brings some kind of challenge. We may not rule a nation or run a large corporation, but every day we face tough situations, difficult people, and temptations.

Some challenges God actually sends into our lives; others he merely allows. In either case, challenges are the tools God uses to bring us greater strength and maturity. As we endure these times, we develop greater wisdom, integrity, and courage to face whatever comes our way. Challenges keep us from being too comfortable and satisfied with the status quo; they force us to follow God's leading into uncharted waters. Without God, this can be frightening; with God, it can be a great adventure. So whatever challenge you are about to face, make sure you head into it with God at your side.

Why does God allow challenges in my life?

When troubles come your way, consider it an opportunity for great joy. For you know that when your faith is tested, your endurance has a chance to grow. So let it grow, for when your endurance is fully developed, you will be perfect and complete, needing nothing.
JAMES 1:2-4

Just as it takes the rough surface of a file to sharpen and smooth the blade of a knife, so it takes rough times to sharpen you into the kind of person God can use effectively. A challenge is a tool God can use to bring you greater wisdom, more maturity to withstand the hard knocks that come your way, and the ability to cut through life's obstacles. As you meet these challenges, you gain more courage to face the next challenges that come your way.

Are any challenges too small to take to God?

Commit everything you do to the LORD. Trust him, and he will help you. PSALM 37:5

Nothing is too small for God. When you commit your plans to him, he commits himself and his infinite resources to you.

What are some of the ways God challenges me?

You must love the LORD your God with all your heart, all your soul, and all your strength.
DEUTERONOMY 6:5

If you love me, obey my commandments. JOHN 14:15

God challenges you to develop a relationship with him and to be obedient to his Word, the blueprint for your life.

This is my commandment: Love each other in the same way I have loved you.
JOHN 15:12

God challenges you to love others as much as he does.

In a world that seems opposed to God, how do I handle the challenge of keeping my faith strong?

God has given both his promise and his oath. These two things are unchangeable because it is impossible for God to lie. Therefore, we who have fled to him for refuge can have great confidence as we hold to the hope that lies before us. HEBREWS 6:18

The strength to handle challenges comes from God, for he is all-powerful. Therefore you must stay close to him through Bible study and prayer, never doubting his promises to help and strengthen you. When you face opposition, always stand your ground on the truth of God's Word. When you do, you cannot be shaken.

How do I find the strength to face my challenges?

Do not be afraid or discouraged, for the LORD will personally go ahead of you. He will be with you; he will neither fail you nor abandon you. DEUTERONOMY 31:8

I am the LORD, the God of all the peoples of the world. Is anything too hard for me? JEREMIAH 32:27

Instead of being discouraged by the size of the task, be encouraged by the limitless power of God.

What if someone dares or challenges me to do wrong?

We cannot oppose the truth, but must always stand for the truth. 2 CORINTHIANS 13:8

Sin often looks attractive and fun; if it didn't, it wouldn't tempt us. Because it is so appealing, one of your greatest challenges is to do right in the face of temptation.

What are some of life's greatest challenges?

I don't really understand myself, for I want to do what is right, but I don't do it. Instead, I do what I hate. . . . I want to do what is right, but I can't. . . . But if I do what I don't want to do, I am not really the one doing wrong; it is sin living in me that does it. I have discovered this principle of life—that when I want to do what is right, I inevitably do what is wrong. ROMANS 7:15, 18-21

The struggle of wanting to do what is right yet not being able to do it is frustrating. Because of your sinful nature, it will be an ongoing struggle within you.

Yes, we live under constant danger of death because we serve Jesus, so that the life of Jesus will be evident in our dying bodies. 2 CORINTHIANS 4:11

I have traveled on many long journeys. I have faced danger from rivers and from robbers. I have faced danger from my own people, the Jews, as well as from the Gentiles. I have faced danger in the cities, in the deserts, and on the seas. And I have faced danger from men who claim to be believers but are not. 2 CORINTHIANS 11:26

Facing dangers that threaten our physical well-being will be a challenge as long as we live on this earth.

Be strong and courageous, and do the work. Don't be afraid or discouraged, for the LORD God, my God, is with you. He will not fail you or forsake you. He will see to it that all the work related to the Temple of the LORD is finished correctly. 1 CHRONICLES 28:20

The size of a particular job, ministry, or responsibility can be a challenge because of its enormity.

How can I possibly face the challenges of today? Is there any hope?

The temptations in your life are no different from what others experience. And God is faithful. He will not allow the temptation to be more than you can stand. When you are tempted, he will show you a way out so that you can endure. 1 CORINTHIANS 10:13

God is able and available to sustain you when you are tempted to do wrong. He will not only provide a way for you to do right, he has also provided Jesus, who understands your weaknesses and temptations. Temptations come from evil sources. Victory over temptations comes from God.

O God, listen to my cry! Hear my prayer! From the ends of the earth, I cry to you for help when my heart is overwhelmed. Lead me to the towering rock of safety. PSALM 61:1-2

When troubles keep coming at you, keep going to God. Don't give up on him, for he is the only One who can ultimately give you rest from all the challenges you face.

In your strength I can crush an army; with my God I can scale any wall.
2 SAMUEL 22:30

All glory to God, who is able, through his mighty power at work within us, to accomplish infinitely more than we might ask or think. EPHESIANS 3:20

Regardless of the size of the challenge, God's strength working in you is sufficient to see you through. God will provide all that you need.

How can I challenge others?

Jonathan went to find David and encouraged him to stay strong in his faith in God.
1 SAMUEL 23:16

Encourage others to be strong in their obedience to God and to never lose hope in his promises.

You must teach these things and encourage the believers to do them. You have the authority to correct them when necessary, so don't let anyone disregard what you say.
TITUS 2:15

Speak up when you are convinced someone is teaching wrong doctrine.

Preach the word of God. Be prepared, whether the time is favorable or not. Patiently correct, rebuke, and encourage your people with good teaching. 2 TIMOTHY 4:2

Talk to others in ways that will build them up and help them grow spiritually.

How should I react when others challenge me?

Gentle words are a tree of life; a deceitful tongue crushes the spirit. PROVERBS 15:4

If you reject discipline, you only harm yourself; but if you listen to correction, you grow in understanding. PROVERBS 15:32

Listen respectfully, and respond gently and truthfully.

He did not retaliate when he was insulted, nor threaten revenge when he suffered. He left his case in the hands of God, who always judges fairly. 1 PETER 2:23

Do not get defensive or lash out. Even if the criticism is unjust, don't seek revenge.

Gently instruct those who oppose the truth. Perhaps God will change those people's hearts, and they will learn the truth. 2 TIMOTHY 2:25

If your beliefs are challenged by wrong teaching, remain strong in your commitment to God's Word. Hold fast to the truth, and keep teaching it to others. Your gentle but firm witness can pave the way for God to change hearts.

CHANCE *See also* Opportunities, Planning, Risk

When something amazing or unpredictable happens, we ask, "What are the chances?" Before a camping trip, we watch the Weather Channel and pack our rain gear because "we don't want to take any chances." Others sit at casino slot machines for hours trying to beat the slim chance of winning. Believing in luck, chance, or coincidence—whatever you want to call it—is a random, chaotic way to live. Your life drifts whichever way the wind blows.

As Christians, we know that what happens to us is more than just coincidence. Believing that God has a plan for our life and that he controls events in our life and in the world is comforting. If God is deeply involved in our lives and works to orchestrate the events in our lives, we can be confident that life has deep meaning. It is more than a random series of events that lead to the day we die, when our time is finally up. Knowing that God is in control gives us a sense of purpose and certainty about the future. Don't take the chance of believing that God isn't in control. Submit to him, and watch his plan for you unfold so that your life will be meaningful and fulfilling.

Does God control everything, or do some things happen by chance?

God said, "Let there be light," and there was light. GENESIS 1:3

The LORD is God, and he created the heavens and earth and put everything in place. He made the world to be lived in, not to be a place of empty chaos. "I am the LORD," he says, "and there is no other." ISAIAH 45:18

By faith we understand that the entire universe was formed at God's command, that what we now see did not come from anything that can be seen. HEBREWS 11:3

The Bible clearly states that God made the universe by command. We did not happen by chance but by the design of a loving Creator.

"I know the plans I have for you," says the LORD. "They are plans for good and not for disaster, to give you a future and a hope." JEREMIAH 29:11

We know that God causes everything to work together for the good of those who love God and are called according to his purpose for them. ROMANS 8:28

Though some things seem to "just happen," what determines the direction of your life is part of God's plan for you. God opens doors of opportunity, but you must walk through them. If all things happened merely by chance, it would point either to no God at all or to a God who is impersonal and detached from the human race. What a depressing and hopeless view of life that would be! However, the Bible says that God is compassionate and deeply involved in his creation, so much so that he has an eternal plan for it and for you. While you may not understand how certain life events fit into God's perfect plan, you can be confident that God is watching over your life and guiding you in a specific direction.

The wisdom we speak of is the mystery of God—his plan that was previously hidden, even though he made it for our ultimate glory before the world began. 1 CORINTHIANS 2:7

God's plan of redemption was established even before Creation.

This is God's plan: Both Gentiles and Jews who believe the Good News share equally in the riches inherited by God's children. EPHESIANS 3:6

God's plan to save humankind included a provision for all people, both Jews and Gentiles.

Does God control even chance?

Build a new cart, and find two cows that have just given birth to calves. Make sure the cows have never been yoked to a cart. Hitch the cows to the cart, but shut their calves away from them in a pen. Put the Ark of the LORD on the cart, and beside it place a chest containing the gold rats and gold tumors you are sending as a guilt offering. Then let the cows go wherever they want. If they cross the border of our land and go to Beth-shemesh, we will know it was the LORD who brought this great disaster upon us. If they don't, we will know it was not his hand that caused the plague. It came simply by chance.
1 SAMUEL 6:7-9

The Philistines were not sure if the plague was a coincidence or if it was caused by God, who was angry with them for taking the Ark of the Covenant. The Philistine leaders came up with a test to find the answer: If the cows carrying the Ark found their way back to their young, it would signal that the plague was just a coincidence. But if the cows, instead, wandered away from their calves, it would mean God was overpowering their natural instincts and therefore the plague was caused by God. There seemed to be a greater chance that the cows would follow their natural instincts and return to their calves. In this case, however, God showed his power over the laws of nature and chance.

We may throw the dice, but the LORD determines how they fall. PROVERBS 16:33

The crew cast lots to see which of them had offended the gods and caused the terrible storm. When they did this, the lots identified Jonah as the culprit. JONAH 1:7

They cast lots, and Matthias was selected to become an apostle with the other eleven. ACTS 1:26

You may try to leave your decisions or your future to chance by throwing dice or flipping a coin, but God already knows the outcome. Nothing can happen that he doesn't allow.

Often things seem like they "just happen." Where is God then?

"Where did you gather all this grain today?" Naomi asked. "Where did you work? May the LORD bless the one who helped you!" So Ruth told her mother-in-law about the man in whose field she had worked. She said, "The man I worked with today is named Boaz." "May the LORD bless him!" Naomi told her daughter-in-law. "He is showing his kindness to us as well as to your dead husband. That man is one of our closest relatives, one of our family redeemers." RUTH 2:19-20

Life had been difficult for Ruth. She had lost her husband and moved with her mother-in-law to a foreign land, where she had to work to provide for the two of them. Ruth might have felt like her life was a string of random events, but God was working behind the scenes the whole time, leading Ruth to the day when she would meet Boaz, who would later become her husband and an ancestor of the Messiah. Even when things seems disconnected or chaotic, take heart that God is working in your life, guiding you to the day when you will see how he was working for your good.

Is it wrong for me to believe in chance?

Someone may say to you, "Let's ask the mediums and those who consult the spirits of the dead. With their whisperings and mutterings, they will tell us what to do." But shouldn't people ask God for guidance? ISAIAH 8:19

Don't worry about anything; instead, pray about everything. Tell God what you need, and thank him for all he has done. Then you will experience God's peace, which exceeds anything we can understand. His peace will guard your hearts and minds as you live in Christ Jesus. PHILIPPIANS 4:6-7

Only the God of the universe can know the answers to life's hardest questions. Don't trivialize God by looking at his plans for you as nothing more than chance.

CHANGE *See also* Opportunities, Renewal, Salvation

Change is one of the great constants of life. Whether slow and gradual or swift and cataclysmic moments of trauma, change happens to everything and everyone. People change, relationships change, jobs change, technologies change—indeed, life itself can be described as a process of continual change. Some changes are positive: a new friend, a new house, a financial windfall. Others are negative: a tragic loss, a job layoff, the upheaval of natural disaster. Either way, change can be stressful. The Bible teaches two great truths about change: The first is that despite the changing world around us, God is changeless and dependable. The second is that God calls for an inner change of heart, called repentance, that produces an outward change of lifestyle, called obedience.

With all the changes in my life, how can I keep from becoming overwhelmed?

Jesus Christ is the same yesterday, today, and forever. HEBREWS 13:8

Whatever is good and perfect comes down to us from God our Father, who created all the lights in the heavens. He never changes or casts a shifting shadow. JAMES 1:17

The character of God is unchanging and thus completely reliable. This is good news because no matter how much your life changes, no matter what new situations you face, God goes with you. You can always count on his promises to help, guide, and care for you.

Heaven and earth will disappear, but my words will never disappear. MARK 13:31

The truths and advice in the Bible apply to all people in all cultures over all time. This is important because the standards for behavior found in the Word of God always apply and can be counted on to work for you every single day. As you face change, constantly turn to God's unchanging Word to maintain your perspective, to give your life a rock-solid foundation, and to provide you with direction.

When the Ishmaelites, who were Midianite traders, came by, Joseph's brothers pulled him out of the cistern and sold him to them for twenty pieces of silver. And the traders took him to Egypt. . . . Pharaoh asked his officials, "Can we find anyone else like this man so obviously filled with the spirit of God?" Then Pharaoh said to Joseph, ". . . Only I, sitting on my throne, will have a rank higher than yours. . . . I hereby put you in charge of the entire land of Egypt." GENESIS 37:28; 41:38-41

We know that God causes everything to work together for the good of those who love God and are called according to his purpose for them. ROMANS 8:28

Sometimes change seems to be for the worse. At those times, you may feel like you're going to fall apart. When such change occurs, remember that traumatic, unpredictable, or unfair changes never trump God's will. Nothing takes him by surprise. No change occurs that he does not allow and that he cannot redeem. When your carefully laid plans are changed by circumstances beyond your control, you will still find peace in obeying the call of God.

How do I change the areas in my life that need to be changed?

Repent of your sins and turn to God, so that your sins may be wiped away. ACTS 3:19

[Saul] fell to the ground and heard a voice saying to him, "Saul! Saul! Why are you persecuting me?" "Who are you, lord?" Saul asked. And the voice replied, "I am Jesus." ACTS 9:4-5

If you have not yet repented of your sins and accepted Christ as your Savior, this is the greatest change you need to make in your life. A personal encounter with Jesus Christ makes this most important change possible.

Zacchaeus stood before the Lord and said, "I will give half my wealth to the poor, Lord, and if I have cheated people on their taxes, I will give them back four times as much!" LUKE 19:8

God calls not only for a change of heart but for a change of behavior.

The seed that fell on good soil represents those who hear and accept God's word and produce a harvest of thirty, sixty, or even a hundred times as much as had been planted! MARK 4:20

The truth of God's Word produces change only when you allow it to penetrate deep into your heart. Plant it securely, and let it grow to produce a harvest of good thoughts and actions.

Don't copy the behavior and customs of this world, but let God transform you into a new person by changing the way you think. Then you will learn to know God's will for you, which is good and pleasing and perfect. ROMANS 12:2

Let the Spirit renew your thoughts and attitudes. Put on your new nature, created to be like God—truly righteous and holy. EPHESIANS 4:23-24

For real and dynamic change to occur, God has to give you a new way of thinking. He will help you focus on what is true and good and right. Then you begin to see the new you, a person who displays God's good, holy, and true character.

I am certain that God, who began the good work within you, will continue his work until it is finally finished on the day when Christ Jesus returns. PHILIPPIANS 1:6

Though we are converted in a moment of faith, the process of transformation into the likeness of Christ takes a lifetime. While it may appear slow to us, God's work in you is continuous and certain.

How do I promote positive change in others?

Don't get involved in foolish, ignorant arguments that only start fights. A servant of the Lord must not quarrel but must be kind to everyone, be able to teach, and be patient with difficult people. Gently instruct those who oppose the truth. Perhaps God will change those people's hearts, and they will learn the truth. 2 TIMOTHY 2:23-25

You will accomplish more if you don't try to change others but rather point them to God so he can do the changing.

Does God ever change?

I am the LORD, and I do not change. MALACHI 3:6

Whatever is good and perfect comes down to us from God our Father, who created all the lights in the heavens. He never changes or casts a shifting shadow. JAMES 1:17

Not only does God live forever, but his character remains unchanged forever. He is the God of eternal consistency.

How do I find the courage to face change?

Do not be afraid to go down to Egypt, for there I will make your family into a great nation. GENESIS 46:3

Change is part of God's plan for you. What you are headed to will give you joy and satisfaction beyond your expectations. Remember, the greatest advances in life come through change.

Moses again pleaded, "Lord, please! Send anyone else." EXODUS 4:13

To experience fear in the face of change is normal. To be paralyzed by fear, however, can be an indication that you doubt God's ability to care for you through life's changes.

CHARACTER *See also* Heart, Integrity, Responsibility, Values

That elusive thing called character is *who you are*—the sum total of all that distinguishes you from everyone else. Your reputation—what other people say about you—is often a good indicator of your character. If two people were talking about you, what would they say? Character is who you are, but it is also who you desire to become. Ultimately, your character is your mark on society. Those striving for good character—or better yet, godly character—are working toward moral excellence. We work hard our entire lives to become excellent in many areas, especially in careers and hobbies. Doesn't it also make sense to work hard at becoming morally excellent, to be known as someone who has developed attributes that really matter, such as integrity, kindness, love, and faithfulness?

Why does character matter?

As for human praise, we have never sought it from you or anyone else. As apostles of Christ we certainly had a right to make some demands of you, but instead we were like children among you. Or we were like a mother feeding and caring for her own children. We loved you so much that we shared with you not only God's Good News but our own lives, too. . . . You yourselves are our witnesses—and so is God—that we were devout and honest and faultless toward all of you believers. 1 THESSALONIANS 2:6-8, 10

Character gives credibility. Your personal character will either verify or nullify your life's work. Paul models how a life lived to please God honors others too.

What are the attributes of a godly character?

The Holy Spirit produces this kind of fruit in our lives: love, joy, peace, patience, kindness, goodness, faithfulness, gentleness, and self-control. GALATIANS 5:22-23

The fruits of the Spirit are some of the essential traits of a godly character.

How should being a Christian affect my character and conduct?

You are a holy people, who belong to the LORD your God. DEUTERONOMY 7:6

Whether ancient Israelites or modern-day Christians, those who are called God's people are special—holy, dedicated to the Lord, and chosen to be his own. This is a special privilege but also a special responsibility because it requires us to model the very character of God.

Obedience is better than sacrifice, and submission is better than offering the fat of rams.
1 SAMUEL 15:22

A sacrifice is offering God a gift. Obedience is offering God yourself. This is one of the clearest indications that you are committed to developing a godly character.

Will God do anything to change my character, or is it all up to me?

The Holy Spirit produces this kind of fruit in our lives: love, joy, peace, patience, kindness, goodness, faithfulness, gentleness, and self-control. GALATIANS 5:22-23

God is working in you, giving you the desire and the power to do what pleases him.
PHILIPPIANS 2:13

When you invite God into your life, you are also giving him permission to use his power to change you. He won't force change on you, but if you ask, the very power of God himself will begin a work of transformation in you that will last a lifetime. Your character and choices will see dramatic change if you allow God to do his work. When you try to change on your own, the results will be poor and you will become discouraged.

Are there things I can do to build my character?

Remember how the LORD your God led you through the wilderness for these forty years, humbling you and testing you to prove your character, and to find out whether or not you would obey his commands. DEUTERONOMY 8:2

You are not born with a godly character; it is developed through experience—by facing daily challenges and choosing wisely, by overcoming tests of adversity, by resisting temptation, and by daily committing to know God better through prayer, Bible reading, and good teaching.

We are pressed on every side by troubles, but we are not crushed. We are perplexed, but not driven to despair. 2 CORINTHIANS 4:8

I pray that your love will overflow more and more, and that you will keep on growing in knowledge and understanding. PHILIPPIANS 1:9

Developing character is like developing any other skill: You must practice. Keep on doing what is good and right, and constantly practice character traits such as kindness, generosity, compassion, and honesty. What you value most is usually what you will work hardest to attain.

How do I distinguish good character from bad character?

Even children are known by the way they act, whether their conduct is pure, and whether it is right. PROVERBS 20:11

Those who truly want to love, obey, and serve God will make their desire evident through their words and behavior. If you have these motives, you will easily recognize good and bad character in others.

Why does building character have to be so hard?

Endurance develops strength of character, and character strengthens our confident hope of salvation. ROMANS 5:4

When troubles come your way, consider it an opportunity for great joy. For you know that when your faith is tested, your endurance has a chance to grow. So let it grow, for when your endurance is fully developed, you will be perfect and complete, needing nothing. JAMES 1:2-4

One of the basic principles of life is that adversity produces strength. Your muscles grow only when stretched to their limit. Your character grows only when life's pressures push against it and test its strength. Developing strong character, therefore, is a process that takes time and constant attention. Just as your muscles will get flabby if you stop exercising, your character will get soft if you stop working at it. It is through hard work that you will achieve great accomplishment and the sense of satisfaction that goes along with it. Pain, trials, and temptation refine us so that over time we will be better equipped and more experienced to deal with them. Building your character is hard work that always pays off, both now and for eternity.

What does God promise as I grow in godly character?

We can rejoice, too, when we run into problems and trials, for we know that they help us develop endurance. And endurance develops strength of character, and character strengthens our confident hope of salvation. ROMANS 5:3-4

Let [faith] grow, for when your endurance is fully developed, you will be perfect and complete, needing nothing. JAMES 1:4

The more you grow like this, the more productive and useful you will be in your knowledge of our Lord Jesus Christ. 2 PETER 1:8

As you mature in your faith, you will become stronger and stronger, and this inner strength will give you wisdom beyond your years and a spiritual power that can help you accomplish more than you ever thought possible. As your character develops, your confidence in your salvation will increase, and the assurance of God's love will fill your soul.

CHEATING *See also* Adultery, Deceit/Deception, Honesty

Who among us has not been cheated—shortchanged, deceived, or robbed—of something we treasured? Cheating has been part of the human condition since the fall of humankind. Whether it's cheating on income taxes, tests, or a spouse, cheating is trying to gain something at someone else's expense. There appears to be a winner and a loser, but the cheater actually becomes the loser—losing character, integrity, and peace of mind. The worst kind of cheating is cheating God by shortchanging him of our resources and the time he deserves. One thing is certain—God will never cheat us!

Why does cheating matter to God?

The LORD detests the use of dishonest scales, but he delights in accurate weights.
PROVERBS 11:1

If you want God's blessing, you must live by his standards of fairness and justice. Cheating is the opposite of honesty because the motive behind it is to deceive someone else. How can anyone trust a cheater?

If you are faithful in little things, you will be faithful in large ones. But if you are dishonest in little things, you won't be honest with greater responsibilities. LUKE 16:10

Your character is revealed in the small choices you make. A little bit of cheating is cut out of the same piece of cloth as the biggest of frauds. Just as a small drop of red dye colors a large glass of clear water, a small act of deception colors your character.

The commandments say, "You must not commit adultery. You must not murder. You must not steal. You must not covet." These—and other such commandments—are summed up in this one commandment: "Love your neighbor as yourself." Love does no wrong to others, so love fulfills the requirements of God's law. ROMANS 13:9-10

Cheating is evidence that you do not love or respect the person you cheated; instead, you are thinking only of yourself.

I will not allow deceivers to serve in my house, and liars will not stay in my presence.
PSALM 101:7

When you cheat, you are actually cheating yourself of what God has planned for you.

Are some kinds of cheating worse than others?

They shamelessly cheat widows out of their property and then pretend to be pious by making long prayers in public. Because of this, they will be more severely punished.
MARK 12:40

Sin is sin, but some sin receives greater punishment from God. Cheating those who are less fortunate and then covering it up by trying to look spiritual is a double sin: first, the sin of cheating, and second, the sin of "pious" deceit. This is hypocritical, and God has strong words of warning for hypocrites.

How do I cheat God?

Should people cheat God? Yet you have cheated me! But you ask, "What do you mean? When did we ever cheat you?" You have cheated me of the tithes and offerings due to me.
MALACHI 3:8

You cheat God when you do not give him what he deserves, whether it is your money, your time, your service, or your heart.

CHURCH *See also* Body, Community, Fellowship, Worship

The church is under heavy fire these days. The news is full of tragic stories of child abuse, sexual abuse, adultery, neglect, and hedonism that tear denominations in half and dissolve congregations. Even though Satan tries to attack the church, Jesus promises us that the church will not be overcome. Despite what we hear on the news, the church is still God's house: a place of community, worship, and support for believers; a place to learn about who God is and how his followers can live out the principles of the Christian faith. God will always use the church as his divine instrument to proclaim his message of salvation and to wage battle against evil.

What is the purpose of the church? Why should I attend church?

Each day the Lord added to their fellowship those who were being saved. ACTS 2:47

The church is a gathering place for those who are saved by faith in Christ.

While Peter was in prison, the church prayed very earnestly for him. ACTS 12:5

Let us not neglect our meeting together, as some people do, but encourage one another, especially now that the day of his return is drawing near. HEBREWS 10:25

A church not only provides an organized means of preaching and teaching God's Word but also provides a chance for believers to regularly get together to strengthen, encourage, and build one another up; to pray for one another; to hold one another accountable; and to meet one another's needs. God promises to be with believers whenever they meet together.

Don't you realize that all of you together are the temple of God and that the Spirit of God lives in you? God will destroy anyone who destroys this temple. For God's temple is holy, and you are that temple. 1 CORINTHIANS 3:16-17

The church is not the physical building, but rather the believers who gather inside it. Together with other Christians and with the help of the Holy Spirit, you learn how to truly change for good and how to influence others through your changed life. The church exists in part to equip God's people to do God's work and to encourage them in their faith.

The human body has many parts, but the many parts make up one whole body. So it is with the body of Christ. Some of us are Jews, some are Gentiles, some are slaves, and some are free. But we have all been baptized into one body by one Spirit, and we all share the same Spirit. 1 CORINTHIANS 12:12-13

All believers together form God's family, but only by meeting together can they bond. The church is a place where Christians learn to work together in unity and where differences between people are reconciled by the Holy Spirit. When you meet together, you can build one another up and help one another.

"Let us be glad and rejoice, and let us give honor to him. For the time has come for the wedding feast of the Lamb, and his bride has prepared herself. She has been given the

finest of pure white linen to wear." For the fine linen represents the good deeds of God's holy people. REVELATION 19:7-8

The church is Christ's bride—a picture of the intimate fellowship that God's people will enjoy with him.

Why should I be involved in a church?
Just as our bodies have many parts and each part has a special function, so it is with Christ's body. We are many parts of one body, and we all belong to each other. ROMANS 12:4-5

God has given all believers special gifts—some are great organizers and administrators, while others are gifted musicians, teachers, or even dishwashers! When everyone in a congregation uses his or her gifts to serve, the church becomes a powerful force for good, a strong witness for Jesus, and a mighty army to combat Satan's attacks against God's people in a community. The church needs you, for the body of Christ is not complete unless you are present.

Let us not neglect our meeting together, as some people do, but encourage one another, especially now that the day of his return is drawing near. HEBREWS 10:25

Fellowship between you and other believers at church is unique because the living God is in your midst. The church brings together people who have a common perspective on life. Christian fellowship provides a place for honest sharing about the things that really matter, encouragement to stay strong in the face of temptation and persecution, and unique wisdom to deal with problems.

What kinds of things should the church do?
Jesus came and told his disciples, "I have been given all authority in heaven and on earth. Therefore, go and make disciples of all the nations, baptizing them in the name of the Father and the Son and the Holy Spirit. Teach these new disciples to obey all the commands I have given you." MATTHEW 28:18-20

One of the primary jobs of the church is to bring the Good News of salvation to those who haven't heard it and to help them become believers, baptize them, and teach them God's truth. The church is responsible for sending out missionaries, who will make God's truth known around the world.

All the believers devoted themselves to the apostles' teaching, and to fellowship, and to sharing in meals (including the Lord's Supper), and to prayer. . . . And all the believers met together in one place and shared everything they had. ACTS 2:42-44

Key functions of the church include teaching, fellowship, worship, and prayer.

Preach the word of God. Be prepared, whether the time is favorable or not. Patiently correct, rebuke, and encourage your people with good teaching. 2 TIMOTHY 4:2

The church has the special and unique role of teaching and preaching—the public proclamation of God's Word.

Take care of any widow who has no one else to care for her. 1 TIMOTHY 5:3

Are any of you sick? You should call for the elders of the church to come and pray over you, anointing you with oil in the name of the Lord. Such a prayer offered in faith will heal the sick, and the Lord will make you well. And if you have committed any sins, you will be forgiven. JAMES 5:14-15

The church should pray for its members who are facing adversity and should take special care of widows, orphans, and those in need.

What if I don't like the church I'm attending or the people in it?

Don't just pretend to love others. Really love them. . . . Take delight in honoring each other. . . . Don't be too proud to enjoy the company of ordinary people. And don't think you know it all! ROMANS 12:9-10, 16

You'll never find a perfect church or a perfect group of people—even among Christians! So don't go looking for that. Instead, make sure you are attending a church that teaches right doctrine and has a place for you to serve. Then take joy in reaching out to and loving those God has placed in your circle of influence. It's easy to like people who are likable, but you model God's love more when you serve those you find annoying.

COMFORT *See also* Caring, Compassion, Kindness, Mercy

Comfort brings relief from burdens, encouragement for the day, reassurance that we can rise above our burdens, and hope that our pain and suffering will ultimately end. Family members are often comforters. A friend who is simply there for us is perhaps the greatest source of comfort when we're wrestling with a problem, facing illness, grappling with death, or being persecuted by others. Oppressors stand above us, adversaries stand against us, but comforters stand beside us. God is our ultimate comforter, through a relationship with Jesus Christ and the Holy Spirit.

Will God comfort me in my times of distress?

Whenever they were in trouble and turned to the LORD, the God of Israel, and sought him out, they found him. 2 CHRONICLES 15:4

God's supply of comfort is always in perfect balance with your need for comfort.

He will feed his flock like a shepherd. He will carry the lambs in his arms, holding them close to his heart. He will gently lead the mother sheep with their young. ISAIAH 40:11

God has a shepherd's heart. When you are weak and discouraged, he gently carries you in his arms.

I meditate on your age-old regulations; O LORD, they comfort me. PSALM 119:52

Since God is your ultimate comfort, his Word is your greatest resource for comfort. God's Word is as close as your fingertips, and God himself is as close as your whispered prayer.

At what times does God offer me comfort?

God blesses those who mourn, for they will be comforted. MATTHEW 5:4

When you grieve.

Moses told the people, "Don't be afraid. Just stand still and watch the LORD rescue you today." EXODUS 14:13

The LORD helps the fallen and lifts those bent beneath their loads. PSALM 145:14

When you are overwhelmed.

Do not be afraid, for I am with you and will bless you. GENESIS 26:24

Even when I walk through the darkest valley, I will not be afraid, for you are close beside me. PSALM 23:4

When you are afraid.

As soon as I pray, you answer me; you encourage me by giving me strength. PSALM 138:3

When you are weak and weary.

We know that God causes everything to work together for the good of those who love God and are called according to his purpose for them. ROMANS 8:28

When you worry about the future.

How does God comfort me?

Let your unfailing love comfort me, just as you promised me, your servant. PSALM 119:76

He loves you.

We don't know what God wants us to pray for. But the Holy Spirit prays for us with groanings that cannot be expressed in words. ROMANS 8:26

He prays for you.

LORD, you know the hopes of the helpless. Surely you will hear their cries and comfort them. PSALM 10:17

He listens to you.

Your promise revives me; it comforts me in all my troubles. . . . I meditate on your age-old regulations; O LORD, they comfort me. PSALM 119:50-52

He revives you with his Word.

The LORD nurses them when they are sick and restores them to health. PSALM 41:3

He heals the brokenhearted and bandages their wounds. PSALM 147:3

He heals your body.

How can I comfort others?

Listen closely to what I am saying. That's one consolation you can give me. JOB 21:2

You can be a good listener. It is usually more important for you to listen than to talk.

"I hope I continue to please you, sir," she replied. "You have comforted me by speaking so kindly to me, even though I am not one of your workers." RUTH 2:13

You can speak kind and encouraging words.

Your love has given me much joy and comfort, my brother, for your kindness has often refreshed the hearts of God's people. PHILEMON 1:7

You can comfort others with kind actions. You can be with them in their time of need. Just being there speaks volumes about how much you care.

[God] comforts us in all our troubles so that we can comfort others. When they are troubled, we will be able to give them the same comfort God has given us. 2 CORINTHIANS 1:4

Remember the ways God has comforted you, and offer that same comfort to others. When you have experienced God's assuring love, his guiding wisdom, and his sustaining power, you are able to comfort others with understanding. The comforted become the comforter.

Will God really take time to involve himself in my little problems?

What is the price of five sparrows—two copper coins? Yet God does not forget a single one of them. And the very hairs on your head are all numbered. So don't be afraid; you are more valuable to God than a whole flock of sparrows. LUKE 12:6-7

Give all your worries and cares to God, for he cares about you. 1 PETER 5:7

God measures problems by love, not by size. It's often in the small things that you can experience God's great care. Don't look at the size of your problem; look at the greatness of God's love and concern.

What is my greatest comfort?

God loved the world so much that he gave his one and only Son, so that everyone who believes in him will not perish but have eternal life. JOHN 3:16

Those the Father has given me will come to me, and I will never reject them. JOHN 6:37

Your greatest comfort is knowing that through faith in Jesus Christ you are saved from sin and will live eternally with God. There is no sin or fear or trouble in heaven.

COMMITMENT *See also* Accountability, Perseverance, Promises

The achievement of any goal or purpose requires commitment, which means deciding to follow through with a course of action. The Bible speaks of commitment both negatively—"You must not commit any of these detestable sins" (Leviticus 18:26)—and positively—"Commit everything you do to the LORD" (Psalm 37:5). Each alternative involves making a decision, acting on that decision with a focused and sometimes costly perseverance, and then reaping the consequences or benefits of your action. Learning to commit our hearts, minds, and bodies to God is central to lives of faith. In fact, faith devoid of commitment is dead.

Why is commitment important?

The LORD leads with unfailing love and faithfulness all who keep his covenant and obey his demands. PSALM 25:10

When you are committed to following God, he will show you his will for your life—the satisfying and fulfilling goal for which he has created you.

The LORD protects those who are loyal to him. PSALM 31:23

When you are committed to God, he is committed to watching out for you and caring for you.

Wherever you go, I will go; wherever you live, I will live. Your people will be my people, and your God will be my God. RUTH 1:16

Commitment is a mark of true friendship.

Love never gives up, never loses faith, is always hopeful, and endures through every circumstance. 1 CORINTHIANS 13:7

Commitment is the evidence of love for one another.

What does it mean to be committed to God?

Jesus called out to them, "Come, follow me, and I will show you how to fish for people!" And they left their nets at once and followed him. MATTHEW 4:19-20

The commitment to follow Jesus Christ requires a decision of the mind followed by an act of the will.

Commit everything you do to the LORD. PSALM 37:5

Seek his will in all you do, and he will show you which path to take. PROVERBS 3:6

Being committed to God means that you trust him to lead you and show you what is best for you.

If you do not carry your own cross and follow me, you cannot be my disciple. But don't begin until you count the cost. LUKE 14:27-28

The commitment to follow Jesus can be costly. You might have to leave other attractive things behind.

All the people answered with one voice, "We will do everything the LORD has commanded." EXODUS 24:3

Being committed to God means that you resolve to try your best to obey all of God's Word in all areas of your life. As a human being with a sinful nature, you will never be able to achieve this goal in this life (otherwise you'd be perfect), but that should not stop you from doing your best.

If we are thrown into the blazing furnace, the God whom we serve is able to save us. . . . But even if he doesn't, we want to make it clear to you, Your Majesty, that we will never serve your gods. DANIEL 3:17-18

Being committed to God means being willing to accept the sometimes painful consequences of obedience to him. When you are committed to God, there will be others who are committed to opposing you and everything you stand for. This is the essence of spiritual warfare, and in any battle, there will be some wounds.

Give yourselves completely to God, for you were dead, but now you have new life. So use your whole body as an instrument to do what is right for the glory of God. ROMANS 6:13

Being committed to God involves more than intellectual agreement; it involves sacrificial giving of the whole self. God wants you to surrender everything you are and everything you have to him and his service.

What are my most important commitments?

Many of his disciples turned away and deserted him. Then Jesus turned to the Twelve and asked, "Are you also going to leave?" Simon Peter replied, "Lord, to whom would we go? You have the words that give eternal life. We believe, and we know you are the Holy One of God." JOHN 6:66-69

To love and honor God in all you do.

[Jesus said,] "I am giving you a new commandment: Love each other. Just as I have loved you, you should love each other. Your love for one another will prove to the world that you are my disciples." JOHN 13:34-35

To love God's people in the same way God has loved you.

[Jesus said,] "Yes, I am the vine; you are the branches. Those who remain in me, and I in them, will produce much fruit. For apart from me you can do nothing. . . . You didn't choose me. I chose you. I appointed you to go and produce lasting fruit, so that the Father will give you whatever you ask for, using my name." JOHN 15:5, 16

To serve the Lord by continuing Christ's work in the world.

Give honor to marriage, and remain faithful to one another in marriage. God will surely judge people who are immoral and those who commit adultery. HEBREWS 13:4

To love and be devoted to your spouse.

Direct your children onto the right path, and when they are older, they will not leave it. PROVERBS 22:6

To love your children, give them spiritual training, and explain the gospel of Jesus to them.

How strong is God's commitment to me?

I will be your God throughout your lifetime—until your hair is white with age. I made you, and I will care for you. I will carry you along and save you. ISAIAH 46:4

If you have put your trust in God, he has promised his total commitment to lead you and take care of you for your entire lifetime.

He gave his life to free us from every kind of sin, to cleanse us, and to make us his very own people, totally committed to doing good deeds. TITUS 2:14

God's commitment to you is so strong that he allowed his only Son to die for you. You won't have to experience the ultimate punishment for sin; instead, you will spend eternity with God.

How do I remain faithful to my commitments?

No accounting of this money was required from the construction supervisors, because they were honest and trustworthy men. 2 KINGS 12:15

They couldn't find anything to criticize or condemn. He was faithful, always responsible, and completely trustworthy. DANIEL 6:4

Live out your commitment to God by being honest and trustworthy.

If you obey the commands of the LORD your God and walk in his ways, the LORD will establish you as his holy people. DEUTERONOMY 28:9

Be faithful by obeying God's Word.

A deacon must be faithful to his wife. 1 TIMOTHY 3:12

Show your commitment by keeping your marriage vows to your spouse.

What can I do if I have broken a commitment?

If we confess our sins to him, he is faithful and just to forgive us our sins and to cleanse us from all wickedness. 1 JOHN 1:9

If you break a commitment you made to God or another person, you have broken a trust. Admit you were wrong, and ask God—as well as the other person—to forgive you. Confession and repentance help rebuild trust so your future commitments can be trusted once again.

COMMUNICATION *See also* Listening, Relationships, Words

Communication is easier today than ever before. We can communicate via cell phones, the Internet (even cell phones with Internet), fax machines, e-mail, telephones, and walkie-talkies. Why are there so many options? Because communication is important. We like to keep in touch because it is vital to the quality and success of any relationship, whether that relationship is marriage, friendship, family, or business.

The same principal applies to our relationship with God. We must find ways to communicate with him, and we must learn to listen as he communicates with us. The more time we spend communicating with God, the closer and more successful our relationship with him will be. When was the last time you felt in touch with God?

How does God communicate with me?

All Scripture is inspired by God and is useful to teach us what is true and to make us realize what is wrong in our lives. It corrects us when we are wrong and teaches us to do what is right. God uses it to prepare and equip his people to do every good work.
2 TIMOTHY 3:16-17

God communicates with you through his Word, the Bible. Read it daily to keep in touch with him.

In Christ lives all the fullness of God in a human body. COLOSSIANS 2:9

Long ago God spoke many times and in many ways to our ancestors through the prophets. And now in these final days, he has spoken to us through his Son.
HEBREWS 1:1-2

God communicates with you through his Son, Jesus Christ. Talk with him often throughout your day.

When the Father sends the Advocate as my representative—that is, the Holy Spirit— he will teach you everything and will remind you of everything I have told you.
JOHN 14:26

His Spirit joins with our spirit to affirm that we are God's children. ROMANS 8:16

God communicates with you through his Holy Spirit. Pay special attention to the way he speaks to your heart and spirit.

Even Gentiles, who do not have God's written law, show that they know his law when they instinctively obey it, even without having heard it. They demonstrate that God's law is written in their hearts, for their own conscience and thoughts either accuse them or tell them they are doing right. ROMANS 2:14-15

God communicates with you through your conscience, which is your God-given internal radar to help you know right from wrong. Always listen to your conscience. If you ignore it, it will eventually become so dull you no longer hear it.

The heavens proclaim the glory of God. The skies display his craftsmanship. Day after day they continue to speak; night after night they make him known. They speak without a sound or word; their voice is never heard. Yet their message has gone throughout the earth, and their words to all the world. PSALM 19:1-4

God communicates with you through his creation. All of nature sings about a majestic God who created rhythm and harmony in the seasons, the babbling brooks, and the crashing ocean waves. Nature shouts the power of God in the starry heavens, the roar of thunder, earthquakes, hurricanes, and the glorious snowcapped mountains. Nature also whispers about God's mind-boggling attention to detail in the wings of a butterfly, the bark of a tree, the variety of plants, and the complexity of a strand of DNA. Look for God's fingerprints, footprints, even voiceprints in his handiwork—you can't miss him.

Jesus told her, "I am the resurrection and the life. Anyone who believes in me will live, even after dying."... Then Jesus shouted, "Lazarus, come out!" And the dead man came out, his hands and feet bound in graveclothes, his face wrapped in a headcloth. Jesus told them, "Unwrap him and let him go!" JOHN 11:25, 43-44

In the past he permitted all the nations to go their own ways, but he never left them without evidence of himself and his goodness. For instance, he sends you rain and good crops and gives you food and joyful hearts. ACTS 14:16-17

God communicates through the miraculous. There are great miracles, like the resurrection of the dead, and smaller miracles, like the birth of a baby. Even everyday blessings such as food and good weather are small miracles. As you begin to recognize the everyday miracles of God all around you, you will hear him speak to you in marvelous ways.

The LORD appeared to Solomon in a dream, and God said, "What do you want? Ask, and I will give it to you!" 1 KINGS 3:5

An angel of the Lord appeared to Joseph in a dream. "Get up! Flee to Egypt with the child and his mother," the angel said. "Stay there until I tell you to return, because Herod is going to search for the child to kill him." MATTHEW 2:13

God communicates through dreams and visions. These may not be part of your everyday experience, but the Bible shows that God can use such means when he chooses to.

The angel of the LORD appeared to Manoah's wife and said, "Even though you have been unable to have children, you will soon become pregnant and give birth to a son." JUDGES 13:3

Suddenly, an angel of the Lord appeared among them, and the radiance of the Lord's glory surrounded them. They were terrified, but the angel reassured them. "Don't be afraid!" he said. "I bring you good news that will bring great joy to all people. The Savior—yes, the Messiah, the Lord—has been born today in Bethlehem, the city of David!" LUKE 2:9-11

God communicates through his angels. Perhaps you have never seen angels, but many people have seen evidence of their work. The existence of angels and their role in God's plans are clearly taught in the Bible. Angels are all around, and they are near you. It is likely that angels have played a greater role in your life than you realize.

How can I know when God is speaking to me?

As Elijah stood there, the LORD passed by, and a mighty windstorm hit the mountain. It was such a terrible blast that the rocks were torn loose, but the LORD was not in the wind.

After the wind there was an earthquake, but the LORD was not in the earthquake. And after the earthquake there was a fire, but the LORD was not in the fire. And after the fire there was the sound of a gentle whisper. When Elijah heard it, he wrapped his face in his cloak and went out and stood at the entrance of the cave. And a voice said, "What are you doing here, Elijah?" 1 KINGS 19:11-13

Good communication includes talking and listening. Prayer involves not only talking to God but also allowing God to speak to you. Only when you hear God can he make his wisdom and resources available to you. When you pray, take time to listen for his voice. Sometimes you must be still and prepared to hear God speak, to spend time in his presence without feeling the need to verbalize your prayers. Just go into his presence and listen. Be ready to hear him speak to your heart and mind. You will learn to distinguish God's voice from everything else.

Anyone who belongs to God listens gladly to the words of God. JOHN 8:47

Just as a piano is tuned against a standard tuning fork, so you become in tune with God when you compare yourself against the standards for living found in the Bible. As God communicates to you through the Bible, you will begin to discern just what he wants from you.

"Who can know the LORD's thoughts? Who knows enough to teach him?" But we understand these things, for we have the mind of Christ. 1 CORINTHIANS 2:16

When you become a Christian, the Holy Spirit helps you understand the mind of Christ. He gives you guidance, wisdom, and discernment.

How do I know God hears me?

The eyes of the LORD watch over those who do right; his ears are open to their cries for help. PSALM 34:15

We are confident that he hears us whenever we ask for anything that pleases him. And since we know he hears us when we make our requests, we also know that he will give us what we ask for. 1 JOHN 5:14-15

The God of truth, who cannot break a promise, promises that he hears you whenever you talk to him.

What does God want in my communication with him?

The LORD is close to all who call on him, yes, to all who call on him in truth. PSALM 145:18

God wants you to be sincere when you talk to him. Be honest about your motives, and talk to him because you want to, not because you are supposed to.

Let us go right into the presence of God with sincere hearts fully trusting him. For our guilty consciences have been sprinkled with Christ's blood to make us clean, and our bodies have been washed with pure water. HEBREWS 10:22

God wants you to approach him with confidence.

O God, you are my God; I earnestly search for you. . . . Your unfailing love is better than life itself; how I praise you! I will praise you as long as I live, lifting up my hands to you in prayer. You satisfy me more than the richest feast. I will praise you with songs of joy. . . . I sing for joy in the shadow of your wings. I cling to you; your strong right hand holds me securely. PSALM 63:1, 3-8

God wants you to communicate your reverence and praise. The more you know God, the more you long for him.

I urge you, first of all, to pray for all people. Ask God to help them; intercede on their behalf, and give thanks for them. 1 TIMOTHY 2:1

God wants your communication with him to include others and their needs. You aren't the only one who needs God's help!

Don't worry about anything; instead, pray about everything. Tell God what you need, and thank him for all he has done. PHILIPPIANS 4:6

God wants you to communicate with an attitude of gratitude. What are three wonderful things God has done for you today? Have you thanked him?

What is my responsibility to communicate the Good News to others?

We cannot stop telling about everything we have seen and heard. ACTS 4:20

How can they call on him to save them unless they believe in him? And how can they believe in him if they have never heard about him? And how can they hear about him unless someone tells them? And how will anyone go and tell them without being sent? That is why the Scriptures say, "How beautiful are the feet of messengers who bring good news!" ROMANS 10:14-15

God has given all believers the responsibility and the privilege of telling others about him. Share the gospel of Jesus Christ with delight and enthusiasm because it is more than just Good News—it is a matter of life and death.

How can I best communicate with others?

Oh, dear Corinthian friends! We have spoken honestly with you, and our hearts are open to you. There is no lack of love on our part, but you have withheld your love from us. I am asking you to respond as if you were my own children. Open your hearts to us! 2 CORINTHIANS 6:11-13

Be open and candid with one another, lovingly addressing issues that cause conflict. Develop a humble heart that is open to honest feedback and change.

Dear brothers and sisters, if another believer is overcome by some sin, you who are godly should gently and humbly help that person back onto the right path. GALATIANS 6:1

Pay attention to the needs and struggles of those around you. When you know that someone has a problem, especially when a fellow believer is caught in a sinful habit, get involved to show you care. Be kind and gentle, but firm. Then the lines of communication will open dramatically.

Don't use foul or abusive language. Let everything you say be good and helpful, so that your words will be an encouragement to those who hear them. EPHESIANS 4:29

Let your conversation be gracious and attractive so that you will have the right response for everyone. COLOSSIANS 4:6

Your words should be gracious, effective, good, helpful, and encouraging to others. Foul, abusive, and angry words are never good ways to communicate.

Our letters have been straightforward, and there is nothing written between the lines and nothing you can't understand. 2 CORINTHIANS 1:13

Be straightforward and clear. Don't use complicated words that show off your knowledge, and avoid using "Christianese"—religious terms that may be familiar only to Christians—when talking with new believers.

COMMUNION *See also* Fellowship

Today is your anniversary, and tonight you and your spouse are going out to dinner to celebrate. How do you spend your day? Hopefully, by preparing for your evening with your spouse! If the two of you were fighting, you would probably try to mend your relationship before going out to dinner. As the evening approaches, you would likely dress up to look your best for your spouse. You probably would buy a gift to thank your spouse for loving you and to recognize the importance of your relationship. These preparations will allow the two of you to spend time remembering and celebrating your relationship and renewing your passion for each other.

In much the same way, Communion is an anniversary dinner with God. It is important to prepare your heart before coming to the Communion ceremony, which is also called the Lord's Table or the Lord's Supper. If sin is straining your relationship with God, confess your sin and ask for forgiveness so you can present yourself as pure and clean as possible to God, your first love. As you celebrate Communion, spend time remembering all that God has done for you, and thank him for loving you enough to desire a relationship with you. Just as you set aside time on your anniversary to celebrate the love between you and your spouse, it is important to set aside time regularly to celebrate the love between you and God. Communion is one way the church helps you do this.

What is Communion?

I pass on to you what I received from the Lord himself. On the night when he was betrayed, the Lord Jesus took some bread and gave thanks to God for it. Then he broke it in pieces and said, "This is my body, which is given for you. Do this to remember me." In the same way, he took the cup of wine after supper, saying, "This cup is the new covenant between God and his people—an agreement confirmed with my blood. Do this to remember me as often as you drink it." For every time you eat this bread and drink this cup, you are announcing the Lord's death until he comes again. 1 CORINTHIANS 11:23-26

Communion is an expression of your faith in Jesus Christ. The bread symbolizes Christ's body, which was broken for you on the cross. The wine or juice symbolizes Christ's blood, which he shed for you on the cross. Through his suffering and death, Jesus took the punishment for your sins. This was necessary for you to be saved through faith in him. When you take Communion, you are demonstrating your appreciation for Christ's death.

What is the purpose of Communion?

[Jesus] took some bread and gave thanks to God for it. Then he broke it in pieces and gave it to the disciples, saying, "This is my body, which is given for you. Do this to remember me." LUKE 22:19

Remembering and reflection. Communion is a way to remember and reflect on what Jesus did for you when he died on the cross. It is a time to reflect on the truth that it was your sins that caused Jesus to die; it is a time to remember that this is not about a religious ritual but about a relationship with the One who died for you and rose again. Communion is a time to picture Christ's death and to remember his sacrifice so that you could be forgiven.

As they were eating, Jesus took some bread and blessed it. . . . And he took a cup of wine and gave thanks to God for it. MARK 14:22-23

Thanksgiving. Communion is a time to thank God for providing Jesus as the sacrifice for your sins. Jesus' death extends many benefits to you as a believer—forgiveness of sins, hope of his return, and eternal salvation. As you participate in Communion, thank God for the wonderful blessings he gives you through his Son, Jesus.

All the believers devoted themselves to the apostles' teaching, and to fellowship, and to sharing in meals (including the Lord's Supper), and to prayer. ACTS 2:42

Fellowship. Communion is meant to be shared with other believers. It is a time to remember what all believers have in common—salvation from sin. The celebration of Communion is not necessary for salvation, but the fact that Jesus instituted this sacred ceremony shows how important it is to him. It is vital for believers to get together regularly to remember and practice the truths of the Christian faith. In Communion, the members of the body of Christ are unified around the memory of what Christ has done and in the hope of what is to come.

They worshiped together at the Temple each day, met in homes for the Lord's Supper, and shared their meals with great joy and generosity—all the while praising God and enjoying the goodwill of all the people. ACTS 2:46-47

Celebration. Although the early believers no longer had Christ with them, they understood that his death and resurrection brought the hope of his return and a glorious future in heaven. Communion is a time of joyful celebration, when you can praise God for the hope of Christ's return and eternity in heaven, like the early believers did.

"The day is coming," says the LORD, *"when I will make a new covenant with the people of Israel and Judah. . . . I will put my instructions deep within them, and I will write them on their hearts. I will be their God, and they will be my people."*
JEREMIAH 31:31, 33

He is the one who mediates a new covenant between God and people, so that all who are called can receive the eternal inheritance God has promised them. For Christ died to set them free from the penalty of the sins they had committed under that first covenant.
HEBREWS 9:15

Relationship. Under the old covenant, a relationship with God was only possible through the high priest, who acted as a mediator between God and the people of Israel. But Jesus ushered in a new covenant between God and all those who believe in him. Under the new covenant, Jesus acts as the high priest so that anyone can relate directly with God. Communion is an expression of your desire for a relationship with God and an acknowledgment of God's desire to have a relationship with you because he sent his Son to die for you.

What should be my attitude when I take Communion?
Anyone who eats this bread or drinks this cup of the Lord unworthily is guilty of sinning against the body and blood of the Lord. That is why you should examine yourself before eating the bread and drinking the cup. For if you eat the bread or drink the cup without honoring the body of Christ, you are eating and drinking God's judgment upon yourself.
1 CORINTHIANS 11:27-29

Communion should not be taken lightly but rather with profound gratitude and humility before God. Paul warns believers to spend some time preparing their hearts and minds before taking the bread and the cup. Before you take Communion, pause to consider where you are in your relationship with God and with others. Examine your attitudes, and ask yourself if there are sins you have not dealt with that might be hindering your relationship with God or others. After this time of reflection, your heart will be ready to properly participate in the Lord's Supper. You will be better able to appreciate what Jesus Christ has done on your behalf.

My dear brothers and sisters, when you gather for the Lord's Supper, wait for each other. If you are really hungry, eat at home so you won't bring judgment upon yourselves when you meet together. 1 CORINTHIANS 11:33-34

Approach Communion with an attitude of sharing and rejoicing because of the spiritual bond it creates with other believers and because of what Christ has done for you.

COMMUNITY *See also* Church, Fellowship, Neighbors

We were created for community. God called Israel his chosen *people,* not his chosen *person.* Jesus commissioned the church to be one body, not a collection of individuals. Being connected with other people in loving relationships is important for living a life filled with hope. Isolating ourselves from others makes us vulnerable to discouragement and despair. When we are connected to a community of believers, we are able to worship together, support one another, and keep one another steady on God's path, even during the most difficult times.

Why is it important to meet together as a community of believers?

Each year every man in Israel must celebrate these three festivals: the Festival of Unleavened Bread, the Festival of Harvest, and the Festival of Shelters. On each of these occasions, all men must appear before the LORD your God at the place he chooses, but they must not appear before the LORD without a gift for him. DEUTERONOMY 16:16

[Jesus replied,] "You are Peter (which means 'rock'), and upon this rock I will build my church, and all the powers of hell will not conquer it." MATTHEW 16:18

We gather to celebrate the victory we have over sin and to give glory to God, remembering everything he has done for us. God established the practice of his people meeting and worshiping together. When we come together to worship, bringing our gifts and offerings, we remind one another of the God we serve.

You must call a meeting of the church. I will be present with you in spirit, and so will the power of our Lord Jesus. 1 CORINTHIANS 5:4

Because Jesus promises to be with us when we gather as a body of believers, we experience God's presence in unique and powerful ways.

Anyone with ears to hear must listen to the Spirit and understand what he is saying to the churches. REVELATION 2:29

We gather to hear the message God has for us. God speaks specifically to individual communities of believers. To some he has words of warning, and to others he has words of commendation. To some he has words of correction, and to others he has words of counsel.

All the believers lifted their voices together in prayer to God: "O Sovereign Lord, Creator of heaven and earth, the sea, and everything in them . . ." ACTS 4:24

We gather to pray. How pleased God is when his people pray together, sending a symphony of praise and thanksgiving to him!

Let us not neglect our meeting together, as some people do, but encourage one another, especially now that the day of his return is drawing near. HEBREWS 10:25

We gather to encourage, warn, and prepare one another to meet the challenges of this life and to learn how to better fellowship with the Lord. It's so easy to focus on our own needs and goals; we need others to remind us of where our true priorities lie.

What is the value of community?

To one person the Spirit gives the ability to give wise advice; to another the same Spirit gives a message of special knowledge. The same Spirit gives great faith to another, and to someone else the one Spirit gives the gift of healing. He gives one person the power to perform miracles, and another the ability to prophesy. He gives someone else the ability to discern whether a message is from the Spirit of God or from another spirit.
1 CORINTHIANS 12:8-10

A community brings together the complementary gifts, skills, and temperaments of many individuals.

All the believers were united in heart and mind. And they felt that what they owned was not their own, so they shared everything they had. ACTS 4:32

Share each other's burdens, and in this way obey the law of Christ. GALATIANS 6:2

A community shares one another's difficulties and supports one another. It provides a practical way to meet one another's needs.

Confess your sins to each other and pray for each other so that you may be healed.
JAMES 5:16

A community provides accountability and spiritual support.

How can I have a positive effect on my community?

There was a believer in Joppa named Tabitha. . . . She was always doing kind things for others and helping the poor. ACTS 9:36

Owe nothing to anyone—except for your obligation to love one another. If you love your neighbor, you will fulfill the requirements of God's law. ROMANS 13:8

Love those whom God has placed in your community. Find practical ways to be a good neighbor and help those in need.

Be careful to live properly among your unbelieving neighbors. Then even if they accuse you of doing wrong, they will see your honorable behavior, and they will give honor to God when he judges the world. 1 PETER 2:12

Live honorably within your community, especially among unbelievers. Be fair, honest, kind, and nonjudgmental.

I will be staying here at Ephesus until the Festival of Pentecost. There is a wide-open door for a great work here, although many oppose me. 1 CORINTHIANS 16:8-9

Make the most of every opportunity in these evil days. EPHESIANS 5:16

Have an open mind to whatever God wants you to do in your community. He may call you to warn others of sin, help the elderly, share your faith openly, show hospitality, or go into politics. Be prepared to walk through whatever doors of opportunity God opens.

What are some responsibilities of the Christian community?

You are the salt of the earth. But what good is salt if it has lost its flavor? Can you make it salty again? . . . You are the light of the world—like a city on a hilltop that cannot be hidden. No one lights a lamp and then puts it under a basket. Instead, a lamp is placed on a stand, where it gives light to everyone in the house. In the same way, let your good deeds shine out for all to see, so that everyone will praise your heavenly Father. MATTHEW 5:13-16

Members of the Christian community should live a lifestyle that is a witness to the community at large. The way you live will probably have the greatest effect on what people think of the church. Your actions in your neighborhood will either attract others to Christianity or repel them.

The believers in Antioch decided to send relief to the brothers and sisters in Judea, everyone giving as much as they could. ACTS 11:29

When you give generously of your personal resources, you support the work of the Christian community, which in turn ministers to others both inside and outside the community of believers.

Take care of any widow who has no one else to care for her. 1 TIMOTHY 5:3

The Christian community shows how it cares for others when it takes care of those who are alone and in need.

COMPARISONS *See also* Competition, Differences, Favoritism, Jealousy

"How do I measure up?" Most of us grapple with this question at times. Satan gets us to compare ourselves to other people, convincing us that our worth is based on how we compare to others in appearance, possessions, accomplishments, or social status. This usually leaves us feeling either inadequate and envious, or puffed up with pride. A better method of determining our worth is to look at how we measure up in God's eyes. Compared to God's standards and his holiness, we all fall short and are humbled. But when we reach out to him, he makes us holy in his eyes, even though we don't deserve it. In God's eyes, every person is valued and loved. A healthy way to live is to maintain a balance between humility over sin and exultation over God's lavish grace. God doesn't compare you to others, so neither should you. Just enjoy his grace, which has no comparison.

To what or whom should I compare myself?

All of us who have had that veil removed can see and reflect the glory of the Lord. And the Lord—who is the Spirit—makes us more and more like him as we are changed into his glorious image. 2 CORINTHIANS 3:18

You must be holy in everything you do, just as God who chose you is holy. For the Scriptures say, "You must be holy because I am holy." 1 PETER 1:15-16

Compare yourself only to the standards to which God calls his people. Does your life measure up to the kind of life God wants you to live? Are you moving toward the kind of faith and obedience God calls you to have? It's not about you and others; it's about you and God.

What kinds of comparisons should I avoid?

My dear brothers and sisters, how can you claim to have faith in our glorious Lord Jesus Christ if you favor some people over others? . . . If you give special attention and a good seat to the rich person, but you say to the poor one, "You can stand over there, or else sit on the floor"—well, doesn't this discrimination show that your judgments are guided by evil motives? JAMES 2:1, 3-4

Don't compare positions, privileges, or possessions. This only causes you to judge others and act according to wrong motives.

What are the dangers of comparing myself to others?

Peter asked Jesus, "What about him, Lord?" Jesus replied, "If I want him to remain alive until I return, what is that to you? As for you, follow me." JOHN 21:21-22

Comparing yourself to someone else takes your focus off Jesus.

We want to be like the nations around us. Our king will judge us and lead us into battle. 1 SAMUEL 8:20

Comparing what you have to what someone else has may cause you to seek something that is not necessarily good for you. You will not appreciate the blessings God has already given you.

The Pharisee stood by himself and prayed this prayer: "I thank you, God, that I am not a sinner like everyone else. . . . I'm certainly not like that tax collector!" . . . But the tax collector stood at a distance and dared not even lift his eyes to heaven as he prayed. Instead, he beat his chest in sorrow, saying, "O God, be merciful to me, for I am a sinner." I tell you, this sinner, not the Pharisee, returned home justified before God. For those who exalt themselves will be humbled, and those who humble themselves will be exalted. LUKE 18:11-14

Comparing the condition of your heart to that of someone else can lead to false righteousness and pride—you begin thinking you are better than others. On the flip side, thinking you are far worse than others can lead to shame, discouragement, and despair. God knows the real condition of your heart, and he loves you as you are. Keep focused on him, and you won't have a need to compare.

This was [the Israelite women's] song: "Saul has killed his thousands, and David his ten thousands!" This made Saul very angry. "What's this?" he said. "They credit David with ten thousands and me with only thousands. Next they'll be making him their king!" So from that time on Saul kept a jealous eye on David. 1 SAMUEL 18:7-9

Comparing yourself to someone else can lead to jealousy, which leads to anger, which eventually leads to harmful behavior. Saul's jealousy so consumed him that he later tried to kill David.

How can I avoid the dangers of comparing myself to others?

Why do you condemn another believer? Why do you look down on another believer? Remember, we will all stand before the judgment seat of God. . . . Yes, each of us will give a personal account to God. ROMANS 14:10-12

God uses his own standard to judge us. He does not compare you to others but to his own standard of love and right living. Set God and his commandments as your standard of comparison.

Examine yourselves to see if your faith is genuine. Test yourselves. Surely you know that Jesus Christ is among you; if not, you have failed the test of genuine faith. 2 CORINTHIANS 13:5

Pay careful attention to your own work, for then you will get the satisfaction of a job well done, and you won't need to compare yourself to anyone else. For we are each responsible for our own conduct. GALATIANS 6:4-5

Examine your own faith and actions. What is the attitude of your heart toward God? Are you living according to God's Word? Do you find satisfaction in doing your work well? When you remember that Jesus is among us, you have no need to compare yourself to others.

Are comparisons ever appropriate or beneficial?

What we suffer now is nothing compared to the glory he will reveal to us later. ROMANS 8:18

Everything else is worthless when compared with the infinite value of knowing Christ Jesus my Lord. For his sake I have discarded everything else, counting it all as garbage, so that I could gain Christ. PHILIPPIANS 3:8

Comparisons are appropriate when they guide you to a better understanding of God's perspectives and priorities.

Do not be like your ancestors and relatives who abandoned the LORD . . . and became an object of derision, as you yourselves can see. Do not be stubborn, as they were, but submit yourselves to the LORD. 2 CHRONICLES 30:7-8

Comparisons are beneficial when they help you learn from others' mistakes so you avoid making the same mistakes.

When you pray, don't be like the hypocrites who love to pray publicly on street corners and in the synagogues where everyone can see them. . . . But when you pray, go away by yourself, shut the door behind you, and pray to your Father in private. . . . When you pray, don't babble on and on as people of other religions do. They think their prayers are answered merely by repeating their words again and again. Don't be like them, for your Father knows exactly what you need before you ask him! MATTHEW 6:5-8

Comparisons can be helpful in learning and understanding how God wants you to live. It usually isn't helpful to compare yourself to specific individuals, but it can be helpful to study the behavior of groups of people in order to learn from them.

COMPASSION *See also* Caring, Empathy, Kindness, Mercy

When we think of someone who has compassion, we think of a person who "has a heart." Someone without compassion, on the other hand, is apathetic, unmerciful, callous, and heartless. Compassion is both an emotion (being moved with pity for someone) and an action (acting kindly toward someone in need). Jesus felt great compassion for the crowds of people who followed him, for they were desperately searching for meaning and longing to be healed from sickness (see Matthew 9:36). Jesus also had compassion on them by healing many and telling them the Good News (see Mark 6:56). Compassion is a tearing of the heart. It is deeply seated in our emotions and is expressed when we respond to someone in need. In many ways, compassion is a litmus test of our commitment and desire to love others as Christ loves us. To be Christlike is to share his compassionate feelings toward the needy, particularly those who cannot help themselves. If we are not moved by the incredible needs and hurts around us, we may develop hearts of stone, which could become too hardened to respond to God or to others.

How does God show compassion to me?

The Lord is compassionate and merciful, slow to get angry and filled with unfailing love.
PSALM 103:8

The Lord is like a father to his children, tender and compassionate to those who fear him.
PSALM 103:13

God shows his compassion to you by giving you blessings you don't deserve instead of the judgment you really deserve for your sin. He forgives you and restores you to what you were intended to be.

I still dare to hope when I remember this: The faithful love of the Lord never ends! His mercies never cease. LAMENTATIONS 3:21-22

God's compassion continuously washes over you; like wave after wave of the ocean, God's compassion washes over you endlessly.

How can I show compassion to others?

You know the generous grace of our Lord Jesus Christ. Though he was rich, yet for your sakes he became poor, so that by his poverty he could make you rich. 2 CORINTHIANS 8:9

Out of love and compassion for you, Jesus gave up his high position in heaven to come to earth and die for your sins. As a follower of Jesus, your goal is to develop that same depth of love and compassion for others: You should even be willing to give up your life for their sake.

We have studied life and found all this to be true. Listen to my counsel, and apply it to yourself. JOB 5:27

He will rescue the poor when they cry to him; he will help the oppressed, who have no one to defend them. He feels pity for the weak and the needy . . . for their lives are precious to him. PSALM 72:12-14

Moved with compassion, Jesus reached out and touched him. "I am willing," he said. "Be healed!" MARK 1:41

Show compassion to others by sharing the compassionate heart of Jesus with them. If you want to be compassionate, you must be like Jesus, who was moved by people in need and acted to help them.

COMPATIBILITY *See also* Strength, Unity

Compatibility means having things in common with other people—beliefs, interests, memories, or feelings—that help you enjoy a close relationship with them. Many of us spend so much time searching for compatibility in relationships that we ignore the call of the One with whom we are most compatible—God. God created us in his image and designed us for a relationship with him. Not only do we have many of God's characteristics built into us, but Jesus died to take away the sins that were making us incompatible with God. We also have the Holy Spirit, who helps us develop thoughts and desires that are more compatible with God's. When we ask God for forgiveness, he takes away our sins so he sees us as holy and compatible with him. Work to discover the aspects of this compatibility, and watch for positive effects in your other relationships as well.

How am I compatible with God?

God said, "Let us make human beings in our image, to be like us. They will reign over the fish in the sea, the birds in the sky, the livestock, all the wild animals on the earth, and the small animals that scurry along the ground." So God created human beings in his own image. In the image of God he created them; male and female he created them. GENESIS 1:26-27

You have the characteristics of God because God created you in his image. You cannot exercise these characteristics perfectly because of your sinful human nature, but you can feel close to God because you share the same emotions and character traits.

People who aren't spiritual can't receive these truths from God's Spirit. It all sounds foolish to them and they can't understand it, for only those who are spiritual can understand what the Spirit means. . . . But we understand these things, for we have the mind of Christ. 1 CORINTHIANS 2:14, 16

The Lord—who is the Spirit—makes us more and more like him as we are changed into his glorious image. 2 CORINTHIANS 3:18

When you become a Christian, God sends his Holy Spirit to dwell in you, giving you the desire and power to obey him. The Holy Spirit works in you to change your interests and desires to match God's. The more the Holy Spirit works in your life, the more compatible you are with God.

What does it mean to be compatible with another person?

Live in harmony with each other. Let there be no divisions in the church. Rather, be of one mind, united in thought and purpose. 1 CORINTHIANS 1:10

All of you should be of one mind. Sympathize with each other. Love each other as brothers and sisters. Be tenderhearted, and keep a humble attitude. 1 PETER 3:8

You share similar beliefs. Being "of one mind" or "united in thought and purpose" binds you together. A common purpose is perhaps the most important element of compatibility because when disagreements occur and good feelings fade, you will still be compatible because you are working toward the same purpose.

Paul left Athens and went to Corinth. There he became acquainted with a Jew named Aquila, born in Pontus, who had recently arrived from Italy with his wife, Priscilla. . . . Paul lived and worked with them, for they were tentmakers just as he was. ACTS 18:1-3

You share similar abilities. Paul shared a common skill with Priscilla and Aquila— tentmaking. This common ability lead Paul to develop a friendship and a working relationship with them. No doubt this compatibility was a springboard for encouraging and sharpening one another in the ministry of sharing the gospel.

How important is it to have compatible values in a relationship?

What harmony can there be between Christ and the devil? How can a believer be a partner with an unbeliever? 2 CORINTHIANS 6:15

Run from anything that stimulates youthful lusts. Instead, pursue righteous living, faithfulness, love, and peace. Enjoy the companionship of those who call on the Lord with pure hearts. 2 TIMOTHY 2:22

Compatibility usually means you have things in common with someone that help you feel close to that person. Sharing common interests and goals is a good thing. However, it is important to recognize the difference between compatible interests and compatible values. You can share common interests with someone who doesn't share your values, and this can get you in deep trouble. You could be drawn to someone who is fun to be around but who does not share your devotion to God and to living the Christian life. This is why it is important to pick your friends and your mate wisely, making sure your values are compatible.

What if my spouse and I are not compatible?

Since they are no longer two but one, let no one split apart what God has joined together. MATTHEW 19:6

If a Christian man has a wife who is not a believer and she is willing to continue living with him, he must not leave her. And if a Christian woman has a husband who is not a believer and he is willing to continue living with her, she must not leave him. . . . Don't you wives realize that your husbands might be saved because of you? And don't you husbands realize that your wives might be saved because of you? 1 CORINTHIANS 7:12-13, 16

Your commitment to your spouse is more important than your level of compatibility. Be careful to focus on commitment rather than compatibility, because there may in fact be people you feel more compatible with who could tempt you away from your spouse. The Bible is clear: Let no one, not even someone who seems more compatible, separate you from your spouse. You and your spouse are joined by God, so you share a bond stronger than compatibility. There are ways you can increase your compatibility—for example, by taking more interest in each other's day-to-day world.

[Adam] gave names to all the livestock, all the birds of the sky, and all the wild animals. But still there was no helper just right for him. . . . Then the LORD God made a woman from the rib, and he brought her to the man. GENESIS 2:20, 22

If you are having trouble finding areas in which you are compatible with your spouse, start with the basics. Thank God that he made men and women compatible for loving relationships with each other. How excited Adam must have been to share all the wonders of life with his new companion, Eve! What areas of your own life could you get excited about sharing with your spouse?

How can our differences make us compatible?
God called the light "day" and the darkness "night." And evening passed and morning came, marking the first day. GENESIS 1:5

Two people in a relationship often say, "We're as different as night and day." Have you ever thought about how that might be a good thing? God, in his infinite wisdom, made light and darkness work together to form one day. Both are necessary and compatible because they each facilitate life in different ways. Just as day and night are different yet compatible, you too can be compatible with people who are different from you. Embracing your differences to accomplish something significant is a wonderful picture of compatibility.

COMPETITION *See also* Ambition, Goals, Preparation, Victory

"It's a dog-eat-dog world out there." "Winner take all." "Nice guys finish last." "Move up or move over." "Winning isn't everything—it's the only thing." These are the slogans of a world driven by competition. When properly focused, competition can bring out the best in each of us. But when competition is infected with selfish ambition and sinful pride, it can destroy relationships and corrode our hearts. God's Word encourages a balanced and healthy understanding of competition.

Can competition be good?
Whatever I am now, it is all because God poured out his special favor on me—and not without results. For I have worked harder than any of the other apostles; yet it was not I but God who was working through me by his grace. 1 CORINTHIANS 15:10

Competition can drive you to improve yourself and sharpen your skills. Paul is a good example of a competitive person God used to reach people with the Good News about Jesus and to plant churches throughout the Roman world.

When does competition become a bad thing?

Abel also brought a gift—the best of the firstborn lambs from his flock. The LORD accepted Abel and his gift, but he did not accept Cain and his gift. This made Cain very angry. . . . One day Cain suggested to his brother, "Let's go out into the fields." And while they were in the field, Cain attacked his brother, Abel, and killed him. GENESIS 4:4-5, 8

Competition can lead to jealousy, anger, and bitterness when your focus is to defeat the one you are competing against rather than the larger goal you are trying to achieve.

The disciples came to Jesus and asked, "Who is greatest in the Kingdom of Heaven?" . . . He said, ". . . Anyone who becomes as humble as this little child is the greatest in the Kingdom of Heaven." MATTHEW 18:1, 3-4

Competition can create a foothold for pride and jealousy because it often leads you to compare yourself with others. Everyone has equal worth in God's eyes. When you begin to think of yourself as better than others, your competitive spirit is taking you in the wrong direction. When humility directs your competitive nature, you give everything you have to doing your best, not besting others.

Miriam and Aaron criticized Moses because he had married a Cushite woman. They said, "Has the LORD spoken only through Moses? Hasn't he spoken through us, too?" But the LORD heard them . . . [and] was very angry with them. NUMBERS 12:1-2, 9

Competition disrupts not only your relationships with others but also your relationship with God if it causes you to think you are entitled to something that someone else has. Miriam and Aaron were jealous of their brother, Moses, and were competing for his leadership position. They had an inflated view of their abilities. If you feel you are entitled to something, your competitive attitude is already misguided. You are in danger of becoming proud, which could damage important relationships.

How should I respond when tempted to compete in the wrong way?

Some are preaching out of jealousy and rivalry. But others preach about Christ with pure motives. . . . Those others do not have pure motives as they preach about Christ. They preach with selfish ambition, not sincerely, intending to make my chains more painful to me. PHILIPPIANS 1:15-17

Keep your focus on the goal of serving Christ, not on your own agenda or what others might think of you. Paul did not condemn those who were competing with him (see v. 18). Don't let the actions or opinions of others throw you off course. God will work through you—in spite of them!

COMPLACENCY *See also* Apathy, Laziness, Procrastination

Complacency is thinking too little of something that deserves more of our attention. Having a complacent attitude might mean being lazy or taking it easy when we should be hard at work, forgetting to be someplace where our full involvement is needed, taking our children or spouse for granted, underestimating the strategies of the devil, or having a casual attitude toward our awesome God. Danger—physical, social, spiritual—is on the horizon. Satan loves a complacent person because he knows that person is vulnerable to his attacks. We don't even see him coming before he strikes. Unprepared, we are hit hard and our wounds are severe. The complacent attitude that says, "Everything is fine because I'm happy and comfortable," quickly turns into a cry for help.

The Bible has strong words of warning against complacency, especially against complacency toward God and sin. We can combat complacency with preparation and purpose. When we understand how close the enemy is and what he wants to do to us, we will diligently prepare to ward off his attacks. When we understand the purpose for which God made us, we will have passion and intensity.

How can complacency lead me to sin?

Remember, it is sin to know what you ought to do and then not do it. JAMES 4:17

To know what is right and then be complacent about it or unwilling to do it is sin. God takes your actions seriously. It's not enough to avoid doing wrong. God wants you to be proactive about doing what's right.

I will search with lanterns in Jerusalem's darkest corners to punish those who sit complacent in their sins. They think the LORD will do nothing to them, either good or bad. ZEPHANIAH 1:12

God despises complacency. Complacency leads to indifference, which leads to idleness, apathy, and a lack of concern for the needs of others. Complacency stands in stark contrast to God's command to love and care for those around us.

[Delilah] tormented him with her nagging day after day until . . . Samson shared his secret with her. JUDGES 16:16-17

Complacency makes us vulnerable to Satan's strategies and temptations. Samson had become so complacent about his God-given responsibility as a leader that he gave in to Delilah's nagging and told her the secret to his strength. He thought it wouldn't matter, that everything would still be fine. Samson's complacency was a sin because he disobeyed God's command to keep the source of his strength secret. As a result, he let down his entire nation.

What must I never be complacent about?

Then you confessed, "We have sinned against the LORD! We will go into the land and fight for it, as the LORD our God has commanded us." So your men strapped on their weapons, thinking it would be easy to attack the hill country. But the LORD told me to tell you, "Do not attack, for I am not with you. If you go ahead on your own, you will be crushed by your enemies." DEUTERONOMY 1:41-42

Never be complacent about what God tells you to do or not to do. First, the Israelites would not conquer the Promised Land when God told them to (see Numbers 13:1-2,

30-33; 14:1-12). Later, God told them not to enter the land because of their sin, and they tried to go in anyway. When God says yes, move ahead. When God says no, stop.

COMPLAINING *See also* Attitude, Bitterness, Criticism, Resentment

We have all met complainers—people who like to look at the downside of every situation. Complainers always feel like they are getting a raw deal—someone else is getting something more, better, faster. Complainers express dissatisfaction with other things and people, and they also tend to be self-centered. When we complain, the focus is on ourselves. We didn't get what we wanted or deserved, or we got less than someone else. Complaining causes us to focus on what we don't have rather than on what we do have. The Bible compares complaining to a dripping faucet—it gets annoying before too long.

Is it a sin to complain?

They began to speak against God and Moses. "Why have you brought us out of Egypt to die here in the wilderness?" they complained. "There is nothing to eat here and nothing to drink. And we hate this horrible manna!" So the LORD sent poisonous snakes among the people, and many were bitten and died. NUMBERS 21:5-6

Do everything without complaining and arguing, so that no one can criticize you. Live clean, innocent lives as children of God, shining like bright lights in a world full of crooked and perverse people. PHILIPPIANS 2:14-15

Complaining is a sin because it comes from selfishness. You are coveting what you don't have. Complaining turns you into a negative, nagging person. You don't like the way things are, and you want everyone to know about it. God considered complaining a big enough sin that he punished the Israelites with poisonous snakes for it.

I am disgusted with my life. Let me complain freely. My bitter soul must complain. JOB 10:1

Complaining often reveals an attitude of bitterness.

They grumbled in their tents and refused to obey the LORD. PSALM 106:25

Complaining can lead to disobedience.

Don't speak evil against each other, dear brothers and sisters. If you criticize and judge each other, then you are criticizing and judging God's law. JAMES 4:11

Don't grumble about each other, brothers and sisters, or you will be judged. For look— the Judge is standing at the door! JAMES 5:9

Complaining about other people usually leads you to say things you will later regret. It often leads to gossip and slander.

What should I do instead of complaining?

Let everything you say be good and helpful, so that your words will be an encouragement to those who hear them. EPHESIANS 4:29

Instead of complaining about others, say something nice about them. If you can't do that, then don't say anything at all. At least if you're quiet, you can't be blamed for being negative.

Do not judge others, and you will not be judged. Do not condemn others, or it will all come back against you. Forgive others, and you will be forgiven. LUKE 6:37

Instead of complaining about the mistakes of others, forgive them as you would like to be forgiven.

To whom should I complain?

Moses heard all the families standing in the doorways of their tents whining, and the LORD *became extremely angry. Moses was also very aggravated. And Moses said to the* LORD, *"Why are you treating me, your servant, so harshly? Have mercy on me! What did I do to deserve the burden of all these people?"* NUMBERS 11:10-11

When the Israelites complained to one another, it accomplished nothing. Moses took his frustrations to God, who can solve any problem. Taking your complaints to God often changes your perspective. Learn to take your problems to the One who can do something about them.

COMPROMISE *See also* Conflict, Convictions, Fairness

She wants her way and he wants his, and neither will give in. This is a familiar story, whether between business partners, between marriage partners, between parent and child, or between any two people in any relationship. Compromise is the art of negotiation so that both sides win. When each side gives a little, both sides gain much. There is a time to compromise, and there is a time not to compromise. When God's truth, God's ways, or God's Word is on the line, we must not give in. To give up something godly or holy for something sinful or evil is a bad compromise; ultimately, you lose and Satan wins. The test of acceptable compromise is simple: Do both sides win?

When is compromise appropriate, and how do we do it effectively?

We will follow the advice given by you and by the others who respect the commands of our God. Let it be done according to the Law of God. Get up, for it is your duty to tell us how to proceed in setting things straight. EZRA 10:3-4

It is healthy to give up something for the common good when a compromise is according to the will of God and to the commands he has given in Scripture. But we must never give in if it means disobeying the Bible. It is never appropriate to compromise the will of God as revealed in Scripture.

If another believer is distressed by what you eat, you are not acting in love if you eat it. Don't let your eating ruin someone for whom Christ died. ROMANS 14:15

To maintain unity in the body of Christ or to keep others from stumbling in their faith, a Christian must be willing to change certain things. This may require compromising personal preferences, but never Christian convictions.

When is compromise inappropriate?

Do not let sin control the way you live; do not give in to sinful desires. ROMANS 6:12

Compromise is inappropriate when it causes you to sin in any way or when it causes others to sin.

Saul admitted to Samuel, "Yes, I have sinned. I have disobeyed your instructions and the LORD's command, for I was afraid of the people and did what they demanded."
1 SAMUEL 15:24

Dear friend, don't let this bad example influence you. Follow only what is good.
3 JOHN 1:11

Compromise is inappropriate when it is motivated by peer pressure or following the bad example of others.

One day Samson went to the Philistine town of Gaza and spent the night with a prostitute. JUDGES 16:1

Trading your integrity and your values for an act of pleasure is a terrible compromise. Trading the freedom of a godly life for slavery to sin is an incredibly foolish choice. If you make these kinds of compromises a way of life, you risk your life on earth as well as your eternal future.

How do we avoid compromising our convictions?

Daniel was determined not to defile himself by eating the food and wine given to them by the king. He asked . . . for permission not to eat these unacceptable foods. . . . "Please test us for ten days on a diet of vegetables and water," Daniel said. . . . The attendant agreed to Daniel's suggestion. DANIEL 1:8, 12-14

Never be afraid to take a stand for what you know is right and true, but do so in a respectful manner. You may be surprised how often other people will admire you for sticking to your beliefs, even if they disagree with them. But if you meet resistance, you must not compromise by going against God's Word.

I have a few complaints against you. You tolerate some among you whose teaching is like that of Balaam, who showed Balak how to trip up the people of Israel. He taught them to sin by . . . committing sexual sin. REVELATION 2:14

Don't allow compromise to dull your sensitivity to sin. A little sin every once in a while can lead to a life defined by sin.

Delilah pouted, "How can you tell me, 'I love you,' when you don't share your secrets with me? . . ." She tormented him with her nagging day after day until . . . Samson shared his secret with her. JUDGES 16:15-17

You are most likely to compromise in areas where you are spiritually weak. Learn to recognize where you are vulnerable so that you can be prepared when the temptation to compromise comes.

How should I respond when I am tempted to compromise God's ways?

You will be successful if you carefully obey the decrees and regulations that the LORD gave to Israel through Moses. Be strong and courageous; do not be afraid or lose heart!
1 CHRONICLES 22:13

Careful obedience backed by strength and courage will help you resist temptation and remain steadfast in God's ways.

The temptations in your life are no different from what others experience. And God is faithful. He will not allow the temptation to be more than you can stand. When you are tempted, he will show you a way out so that you can endure. 1 CORINTHIANS 10:13

Put on all of God's armor so that you will be able to stand firm against all strategies of the devil. EPHESIANS 6:11

Never compromise your Christian convictions. When you are tempted to do so, the only appropriate response is to resist, which sometimes means literally walking or running away. God promises to give you the strength to resist compromise.

CONFESSION *See also* Apology, Forgiveness, Repentance

Confession can either acknowledge our guilt or profess our allegiance to Christ. Confession reveals what is within—sin or faith. When we acknowledge the ugliness of sin, it can be embarrassing and even painful. Ironically, many people find it equally embarrassing to reveal their faith. Perhaps this comes from not wanting to let others see deep into our lives or from being vulnerable to ridicule. But confession of sin is a necessary part of knowing God and being freed from sin; confession of our faith acknowledges our being identified with Christ.

What is involved in true confession?

If my people who are called by my name will humble themselves and pray and seek my face and turn from their wicked ways, I will hear from heaven and will forgive their sins and restore their land. 2 CHRONICLES 7:14

I recognize my rebellion; it haunts me day and night. Against you, and you alone, have I sinned; I have done what is evil in your sight. . . . The sacrifice you desire is a broken spirit. You will not reject a broken and repentant heart, O God. PSALM 51:3-4, 17

Sorrow for your sin, humility before God, seeking God and his forgiveness, turning to God in prayer, turning away from sin—these are ingredients of confession to God.

Praise the LORD! I will thank the LORD with all my heart as I meet with his godly people.
PSALM 111:1

If you confess with your mouth that Jesus is Lord and believe in your heart that God raised him from the dead, you will be saved. ROMANS 10:9

Confession includes praising God for his mercy and for his desire to forgive you. Confession also includes gladly acknowledging Jesus as Lord and publicly claiming allegiance to him.

Does God truly forgive my sin when I confess it to him?

If we confess our sins to him, he is faithful and just to forgive us our sins and to cleanse us from all wickedness. 1 JOHN 1:9

God promises to forgive your sins when you confess them, and he always keeps his promises. You must recognize and admit your sins to God so he can forgive them. Confession indicates your desire to have your sins forgiven. If you have no desire to have your sins forgiven, God will not force his forgiveness on you.

People who conceal their sins will not prosper, but if they confess and turn from them, they will receive mercy. PROVERBS 28:13

Confession paves the way for God to work in you. Confession wipes the slate clean so that you can be reconciled to God and have another chance to live for him.

In addition to forgiveness, what are other benefits of confession?

Finally, I confessed all my sins to you and stopped trying to hide my guilt. I said to myself, "I will confess my rebellion to the LORD." And you forgave me! All my guilt is gone. PSALM 32:5

God removes your guilt.

Restore to me the joy of your salvation, and make me willing to obey you. PSALM 51:12

God restores your joy and willing obedience.

Confess your sins to each other and pray for each other so that you may be healed. JAMES 5:16

God transforms you from the inside out.

When is it appropriate to confess my sins to others?

Give the following instructions to the people of Israel: If any of the people . . . betray the LORD by doing wrong to another person, they are guilty. They must confess their sin and make full restitution for what they have done. NUMBERS 5:6-7

I will go home to my father and say, "Father, I have sinned against both heaven and you." LUKE 15:18

When you have wronged others and need their forgiveness, confess your sin to them. Confessing your sin to others is a necessary step in seeking reconciliation.

CONFIDENCE *See also* Affirmation, Approval, Faith, Hope, Trust

Confidence is expressed in many different ways. We can be confident in ourselves or our abilities, confident that something will happen, confident about certain facts (including salvation), confident in God's promises. We can also take someone into our confidence. Confidence can lead you down one of two paths: to cockiness, which results in pride and boasting, or to inner assurance, which results in healthy self-esteem and sure conviction of where you are going. In the Bible, the word for *confidence* is sometimes translated *boldness*. With Christ by our side, we boldly set forth to do his work, and we are confident that we can do anything within his will. Our ultimate confidence comes from trusting that God's Word is true. If we are sure of that, then we can endure any trials we face here on earth, and we can know all the blessings that await us in heaven.

Where do I get my confidence?

The LORD is my light and my salvation—so why should I be afraid? The LORD is my fortress, protecting me from danger, so why should I tremble? PSALM 27:1

The LORD keeps watch over you as you come and go, both now and forever. PSALM 121:8

Many great athletes say that the real contest in sports is mental, not physical. It's the same way in your spiritual life. Your confidence comes not from your physical circumstances (for example, how you look or what you achieve), but from the inner assurance that God is by your side, making his wisdom and power available to you daily and working out his plan for your life.

There is more than enough room in my Father's home. If this were not so, would I have told you that I am going to prepare a place for you? When everything is ready, I will come and get you. JOHN 14:2-3

I have told you all this so that you may have peace in me. Here on earth you will have many trials and sorrows. But take heart, because I have overcome the world. JOHN 16:33

Confidence comes from knowing with certainty that your eternal future is secured. When you know that this life isn't all there is, you don't need to fear what happens to you here on earth.

See how very much our Father loves us, for he calls us his children. 1 JOHN 3:1

Confidence comes from knowing that God loves you unconditionally. Any sin you commit or have committed cannot cause God to love you any less.

God has given us different gifts for doing certain things well. ROMANS 12:6

There are different kinds of spiritual gifts, but the same Spirit is the source of them all. There are different kinds of service, but we serve the same Lord. God works in different ways, but it is the same God who does the work in all of us. 1 CORINTHIANS 12:4-6

Confidence comes from recognizing and exercising the gifts and abilities God has given you. If you have no confidence in yourself, you fail to recognize that God has given you these special abilities and the opportunities to use them.

How can I have confidence in the face of life's greatest hardships?

Give all your worries and cares to God, for he cares about you. 1 PETER 5:7

You can have confidence even during the hardest times because God knows your troubles and cares about you.

I am convinced that nothing can ever separate us from God's love. Neither death nor life, neither angels nor demons, neither our fears for today nor our worries about tomorrow— not even the powers of hell can separate us from God's love. No power in the sky above or in the earth below—indeed, nothing in all creation will ever be able to separate us from the love of God that is revealed in Christ Jesus our Lord. ROMANS 8:38-39

God assures you that even the powers of hell cannot keep his love away from you. You can have confidence that God is with you, even in your most difficult times.

I can do everything through Christ, who gives me strength. PHILIPPIANS 4:13

Life has its ups and downs, and material comforts come and go. But no matter what situation you find yourself in, God promises to give you the help and strength you need. You can be confident that his love for you will never change.

What should I do when I lose confidence in God?

If only I knew where to find God, I would go to his court. JOB 23:3

When tragedy strikes, your first thought might be, *Where is God?* Nagging doubts cause you to question whether he still loves you. When you lose the confidence that he is with you and cares about you, you are in danger of pushing him away and separating yourself from your only real hope. In moments of crisis, immediately move toward God, not away from him, and you will gain both comfort and perspective.

Faith is the confidence that what we hope for will actually happen; it gives us assurance about things we cannot see. HEBREWS 11:1

Faith is the confident assurance that what you believe is really going to happen. When you begin to lose confidence in God, go right to his promises in the Bible. As you take confidence from the ones he has already fulfilled, you will develop greater faith that his promises about the future will be fulfilled.

What's the difference between healthy confidence and unhealthy pride?

I know that my Redeemer lives. JOB 19:25

Healthy confidence is a realization and an assurance that God loves you, that he has given you talents and gifts, that he wants you to use those gifts for him, and that he has given you salvation and eternal life in heaven. This gives you complete certainty that your life can have meaning, now and forever.

When he had become powerful, he also became proud, which led to his downfall.
2 CHRONICLES 26:16

Unhealthy pride results when arrogance and cockiness are substituted for healthy confidence. Thinking you can make it without God and failing to seek his help are the warning signs that confidence has turned to pride.

CONFLICT *See also* Confrontation, Revenge, Reconciliation

Two grown men stand toe-to-toe, faces red, veins standing out on their necks, both shouting at each other. "I was safe!" "You were out!" "Safe!" "Out!" When a ball player disagrees with an umpire's call, sometimes a spectacular argument begins. Since people have differing opinions on everything from politics to sports to religion, conflict seems to be a given in human relationships. The Bible is not silent on the issue of conflict, and it does not condemn all conflict as sinful. According to the Bible, there is nothing inherently wrong with conflict. Moses, David, Paul, even Jesus all found themselves in conflict with others. Disagreements happen. But the manner in which we are to resolve our conflicts is extremely important. Conflict can become the catalyst for greater understanding and deeper relationships, or it can bring anger, bitterness, and broken relationships.

What causes conflict?

Absalom . . . stole the hearts of all the people of Israel . . . and the conspiracy gained momentum. 2 SAMUEL 15:6, 12

You want what you don't have, so you scheme and kill to get it. You are jealous of what others have, but you can't get it, so you fight and wage war to take it away from them.
JAMES 4:2

Conflict begins when you aren't getting what you want but you are determined to get it. You want someone's behavior to change, you want your way, you want to win, you want a particular material thing, you want someone's loyalty—the list goes on and on. When someone else isn't willing to give you what you want, you find yourself in conflict, which can lead to all-out war.

Barnabas . . . wanted to take along John Mark. But Paul disagreed strongly. . . . Their disagreement was so sharp that they separated. ACTS 15:37-39

Conflict begins when people with opposing viewpoints are not willing to find common ground. Sometimes differences of opinion are so strong that no resolution is possible, and a parting of ways is necessary.

What sorrow awaits you teachers of religious law and you Pharisees. Hypocrites! For you are careful to tithe even the tiniest income from your herb gardens, but you ignore the more important aspects of the law—justice, mercy, and faith. You should tithe, yes, but do not neglect the more important things. Blind guides! You strain your water so you won't accidentally swallow a gnat, but you swallow a camel! MATTHEW 23:23-24

There are times when you must not ignore wrong attitudes or behavior. In those situations, you might actually initiate conflict in order to speak for truth and justice. Jesus confronted the Pharisees not only for their hypocritical behavior but also because of their destructive influence as teachers and leaders.

How does God want me to respond to conflict?

Dear friends, never take revenge. Leave that to the righteous anger of God. . . . Instead, "If your enemies are hungry, feed them. If they are thirsty, give them something to drink. In doing this, you will heap burning coals of shame on their heads." Don't let evil conquer you, but conquer evil by doing good. ROMANS 12:19-21

Peace lies in the power of love, not the love of power. Followers of Christ know better than to take revenge into their own hands. They know that fighting according to the world's ways brings even greater problems. Instead, we are to practice the principle of paradox: bless our enemies, give to those who threaten us, and feed those who would take our food. When we respond in this way, God's power is unleashed in the situation. Only his power can solve conflict that from a human standpoint could never be solved.

What are some ways to resolve conflict?

Abram said to Lot, "Let's not allow this conflict to come between us or our herdsmen. . . . Take your choice of any section of the land you want, and we will separate." GENESIS 13:8-9

Isaac's men then dug another well, but again there was a dispute over it. . . . Isaac moved on and dug another well. This time there was no dispute over it. GENESIS 26:21-22

Solving conflict takes initiative; someone must make the first move. It also requires humility, persistence, and a greater desire for peace than for personal victory.

A servant of the Lord must not quarrel but must be kind to everyone . . . and be patient with difficult people. Gently instruct those who oppose the truth. 2 TIMOTHY 2:24-25

When someone disagrees with what you are saying, maintain a gracious, gentle, and patient attitude instead of becoming angry and defensive.

How do I deal with the inner conflict between my sinful nature and my new nature in Christ?

Any kingdom divided by civil war is doomed. A town or family splintered by feuding will fall apart. MATTHEW 12:25

I know that nothing good lives in me, that is, in my sinful nature. I want to do what is right, but I can't. I want to do what is good, but I don't. . . . Thank God! The answer is in Jesus Christ our Lord. So you see how it is: In my mind I really want to obey God's law, but because of my sinful nature I am a slave to sin. ROMANS 7:18-19, 25

The Spirit gives us desires that are the opposite of what the sinful nature desires. . . . The Holy Spirit produces this kind of fruit in our lives: love, joy, peace, patience, kindness, goodness, faithfulness, gentleness, and self-control. GALATIANS 5:17, 22-23

When you become a Christian, a new conflict begins inside you that will be a lifelong battle: what you want versus what God wants. Fortunately, you also have the Holy Spirit living in you, and he gives you the tools you need to fight your sinful nature. Over time, he will replace your conflict with peace, anger with patience, rage with gentleness, and sinful thoughts and actions with self-control. While all Christians must recognize the battle over sin that constantly rages within us, we must not become desensitized to it; it is a fight we must win at all costs. If we allow Satan to command any area of our lives, he will defeat us.

Should Christians take their conflicts to court?
If another believer sins against you, go privately and point out the offense. MATTHEW 18:15

When one of you has a dispute with another believer, how dare you file a lawsuit and ask a secular court to decide the matter instead of taking it to other believers! . . . Even to have such lawsuits with one another is a defeat for you. Why not just accept the injustice and leave it at that? 1 CORINTHIANS 6:1, 7

Jesus lays out a step-by-step process for how Christians should deal with conflict. The first step is one-on-one communication, not suing. The Bible says that lawsuits among Christians are to be avoided, even if that means you must accept injustice. You might have to give up your rights in order to resolve a conflict.

CONFORMITY *See also* Acceptance, Compromise, Peer Pressure
A potter shapes a lump of clay into an object of his design. The pliable material conforms to his idea of how it should look and function. Culture does the same thing to people. It has a way of molding us and conforming us to its way of looking, thinking, and behaving. Unfortunately, our culture's values and morals rarely reflect God's values and morals, so when we conform to it, we no longer reflect God. The Christian's task is to conform to Jesus' way of thinking and acting, even when it goes against culture. Jesus wants to break the old mold and shape us into new people.

Can we conform to God and still hold on to old habits?
The man replied, "I've obeyed all these commandments since I was young." When Jesus heard his answer, he said, "There is still one thing you haven't done. Sell all your possessions and give the money to the poor, and you will have treasure in heaven. Then come, follow me." But when the man heard this he became very sad, for he was very rich. LUKE 18:21-23

It is very difficult to let go of the things of this world that distract you from following Jesus. Conforming to his standards is hard work and requires much effort from you, but it brings you freedom from sin and gives you eternal rewards far greater than you could imagine.

CONFRONTATION *See also* Conflict, Criticism, Discipline

We usually think of confrontation as negative and something to avoid. Confrontation usually involves harsh disagreement, arguing, and a clash of opinions. Being confronted or confronting someone else is awkward and tense. These feelings make it seem like confrontation is a bad thing, but the Bible tells us that confrontation can be good and helpful. Jesus himself was confrontational when important issues were at stake. He confronted the Pharisees about their arrogance, and he confronted his disciples about their lack of faith. The role of confrontation is not to criticize but to teach and correct. When you confront others lovingly and gently, it can be a valuable tool to bring them back to Christ and his way of living.

Why is it important to confront others when they've done something wrong?

Take no part in the worthless deeds of evil and darkness; instead, expose them.
EPHESIANS 5:11

Evil and wickedness must be confronted. Left unchecked, they will grow until they overpower the person who is involved in them.

Nathan said to David, "You are that man! ... You have despised [the LORD] by taking Uriah's wife to be your own...." Then David confessed to Nathan, "I have sinned against the LORD." 2 SAMUEL 12:7, 10, 13

If another believer sins, rebuke that person; then if there is repentance, forgive.
LUKE 17:3

Confronting someone who does wrong may lead the person to repent and reconcile with God and others.

How do I effectively confront others?

A servant of the Lord must not quarrel but must be kind to everyone, be able to teach, and be patient with difficult people. Gently instruct those who oppose the truth. Perhaps God will change those people's hearts, and they will learn the truth.
2 TIMOTHY 2:24-25

The way you confront someone is as important as what you say. Consider how you would want someone to speak to you. Confront the person in private, without quarreling or anger. Approach the issue gently with kindness and patience. Then let God change the person's heart.

God has not given us a spirit of fear and timidity, but of power, love, and self-discipline.
2 TIMOTHY 1:7

If confrontation is necessary, ask God to give you the power, love, and self-discipline to say what you must.

CONFUSION *See also* Distractions, Frustration, Spiritual Warfare

Confusion is a mixture of uncertainty and chaos. It is more than not knowing what to do; turmoil is added to the mix. Thus, it is common to hear the phrase "I'm all mixed up" at those times. We are confused when our mind is in turmoil, when we're all mixed up, when we don't even know where to begin to sort out a problem. And since we live in such a complex and fast-moving world, we can be confused a lot! To get rid of the confusion and make sense of things, we have to start with some facts, with some things we know to be true, because truth doesn't change. We can count on that. And the more we can count on something, the less confused we'll be. So we must find a rock-solid starting place where our mind won't be tossed about, a place where all the mixed-up pieces will be put in order for us. That place is the Bible because it comes from the mind of God, who established truth.

The more time you spend reading the wisdom of God, the more you gain God's perspective. And God's perspective makes life less confusing. You learn why he created you, what purpose he has for you, where your life is headed, and what your future will be. Life is less confusing when you realize God truly is in control. He doesn't manipulate you or order you around, but rather he assures you that this world is not random and chaotic. If the world were only random chaos, life would be meaningless, and everyone would be hopelessly confused. But because God is in control and has established basic truths that never change, there are things you can always count on. Instead of a life of uncertainty and chaos, you can live a life of purpose that will make a difference for all eternity. How wonderful to know that when life is confusing, you have something certain and true to hold on to!

What causes confusion?

People who aren't spiritual can't receive these truths from God's Spirit. It all sounds foolish to them and they can't understand it, for only those who are spiritual can understand what the Spirit means. 1 CORINTHIANS 2:14

Wherever there is jealousy and selfish ambition, there you will find disorder and evil of every kind. JAMES 3:16

Confusion is often the direct result of not knowing God. People who don't know God and his truth are tossed about by whatever ideas seem good at the time. The line between right and wrong, between good and bad, is not clear.

This is what King Sennacherib of Assyria says: What are you trusting in that makes you think you can survive my siege of Jerusalem? . . . What makes you think your God can rescue you from me? 2 CHRONICLES 32:10, 14

You are being fooled by those who deliberately twist the truth concerning Christ. GALATIANS 1:7

Confusion can be caused by evil. Satan tries to confuse God's followers into thinking that God cannot or will not help them.

[The LORD said,] "Come, let's go down and confuse the people with different languages. Then they won't be able to understand each other." In that way, the LORD scattered them all over the world, and they stopped building the city. GENESIS 11:7-8

The LORD your God will hand them over to you. He will throw them into complete confusion until they are destroyed. DEUTERONOMY 7:23

God can stir up confusion as a means of judgment or as a way to deliver his people from oppression or protect them from impending danger.

How should I respond when I'm confused about God?

This change of plans greatly upset Jonah, and he became very angry. So he complained to the LORD about it: "Didn't I say before I left home that you would do this, LORD? That is why I ran away to Tarshish! I knew that you are a merciful and compassionate God, slow to get angry and filled with unfailing love. You are eager to turn back from destroying people." JONAH 4:1-2

Jonah was confused about the mercy God showed to the people of Nineveh. When you expect God to act in a certain way, you might be confused when he does something different. His ways are not your ways. Your heart may be confused because you are out of tune with God. Examine yourself to see where you stand with him.

This salvation was something even the prophets wanted to know more about when they prophesied about this gracious salvation prepared for you. 1 PETER 1:10

God's prophets preached his message of salvation even though they didn't understand everything about it. Respond in obedience to God regardless of how little you understand his ways. Just as you don't need to know everything about plumbing to take a bath, you don't need to know everything about God to follow him. Just trust what he says.

I will climb up to my watchtower and stand at my guardpost. There I will wait to see what the LORD says and how he will answer my complaint. HABAKKUK 2:1

Wait for God to answer your prayers. Don't be confused when he does not answer immediately. Realize that how and when he answers is always in your best interest because he created you for a purpose. The timing of an answer to prayer may be as significant as the answer itself.

The world is a confusing place. What can I do to be less confused?

If you need wisdom, ask our generous God, and he will give it to you. He will not rebuke you for asking. JAMES 1:5

Seeing life through limited human vision can bring confusion and frustration. Ask God to help you view life from his perspective. He does not resent your asking; in fact, he longs to grant your request.

How sweet your words taste to me; they are sweeter than honey. Your commandments give me understanding; no wonder I hate every false way of life. Your word is a lamp to guide my feet and a light for my path. PSALM 119:103-105

All Scripture is inspired by God and is useful to teach us what is true and to make us realize what is wrong in our lives. It corrects us when we are wrong and teaches us to do what is right. 2 TIMOTHY 3:16

Confusion comes when you waver or when you are uncertain which road to take. You will be even more confused if you don't know what you are looking for at the end of the road. But if you let God's Word be your compass for life, you will at least be certain about what roads *not* to take. Don't be surprised if you are feeling confused when you have neglected reading your Bible. It contains the wisdom you need to deal with any situation. Through the Word of God, you discover the mind of God.

The Holy Spirit helps us in our weakness . . . for the Spirit pleads for us believers in harmony with God's own will. ROMANS 8:26-27

His Spirit searches out everything and shows us God's deep secrets. . . . When we tell you these things, we do not use words that come from human wisdom. Instead, we speak words given to us by the Spirit, using the Spirit's words to explain spiritual truths. 1 CORINTHIANS 2:10, 13

Be sensitive to the Holy Spirit, who lives in you as a believer and gives you wisdom, discernment, and guidance. This amazing gift of God's own presence within you helps lessen your confusion. Don't neglect this gift! The more you are sensitive to the words and promptings of the Holy Spirit, the closer you will be to God and the more life will make sense. And when your confusion and turmoil are so great you don't even know how to express it to God, the Holy Spirit prays for you.

Obey your spiritual leaders, and do what they say. HEBREWS 13:17

Listen to wise teaching. You will gain understanding and learn what to do.

CONSCIENCE *See also* Discernment, Thoughts, Truth, Wisdom

Conscience is that little voice inside us that helps us determine right from wrong. It is God's gift to us to keep us sensitive to his moral code. But we must use the gift. If we don't listen to and obey our conscience, we will reach a point where we no longer hear it. Or it could malfunction if not properly cared for. It could become a flawed judge, condemning us too harshly or letting us off too easily. Our conscience will function effectively only when we stay close to God, spend time in his Word, and make an effort to understand ourselves and our own tendencies toward right and wrong. If your conscience is working faithfully, you will have a strong inner voice of accountability telling you to do what is right. If you have trouble doing the right thing or if you find yourself unmoved by evil, it could indicate that your conscience has become dulled or inactive. Let God sharpen and resensitize your conscience through his Word. Then your conscience will speak in harmony with God's voice.

Where does my conscience come from? What does it do?

Through everything God made, [people] can clearly see his invisible qualities—his eternal power and divine nature. ROMANS 1:20

When God created humans, he made them with an innate knowledge of himself. Conscience is the God-given instinct deep inside you that guides you in knowing right from wrong. It helps you understand if you are in line with God's will and God's Word.

Speaking among themselves, they said, "Clearly we are being punished because of what we did to Joseph long ago. We saw his anguish when he pleaded for his life, but we wouldn't listen." GENESIS 42:21

Your conscience testifies against you, pointing out your sin and bringing a sense of guilt upon you. It urges you to deal with the guilt by righting the wrong. It is essential to listen to and obey your conscience, or else it will become dull and useless.

How do I keep a clear conscience?

I always try to maintain a clear conscience before God and all people. ACTS 24:16

Keeping a clear conscience is the best way to keep away from sin. The reverse is also true: Keeping away from sin is the best way to keep a clear conscience. When you sin, your conscience has a reason to convict you. When you avoid sin, you actively nurture your conscience and keep it clear.

My conscience is clear, but that doesn't prove I'm right. It is the Lord himself who will examine me and decide. 1 CORINTHIANS 4:4

Conscience is not always an unbiased judge. You can persuade your conscience that all is well when it really isn't. You can buy off your conscience in a sense. But you can't buy off God. He is the only truly unbiased judge. So make sure your thoughts and actions, as well as your conscience, are in line with God's Word.

Can you lose your conscience?

A murderer's tormented conscience will drive him into the grave. Don't protect him! PROVERBS 28:17

You can't lose your conscience, but you can become so dulled to its voice that you don't or can't hear it. The conscience is like a muscle; it must be exercised and developed. Even if you don't exercise it, the muscle is still there. Those who have done horrible deeds still have a conscience. But over time they have learned to tune it out, allowing them to commit heinous deeds. Without conscience, a person feels free to do whatever he or she wants.

CONSEQUENCES *See also* Accountability, Decisions, Obedience, Sin

A gun fires, a bullet is sent, and a person in its path dies. That death is the consequence of someone pulling the trigger of a loaded gun. Similarly, words are spoken that may wound someone. The wounds are the consequence of damaging words. Other words are spoken and a person accepts Christ. That too is a consequence of words, but words that serve God. Before you act or speak, think, *What will the consequences of my actions be?*

What are the consequences of sin?

The wages of sin is death, but the free gift of God is eternal life through Christ Jesus our Lord. ROMANS 6:23

The final consequence of sin is death. All people will die a physical death, but those who do not accept God's free gift of salvation will also be eternally separated from God.

[The woman] took some of the fruit and ate it. Then she gave some to her husband, who was with her, and he ate it, too. GENESIS 3:6

Even a seemingly small sin must be looked at for what it is: disobedience to God. One of the realities of sin is that its effects spread, like a ripple in a pond. The consequences of your actions go far beyond yourself.

The wicked . . . dig a deep pit to trap others, then fall into it themselves. The trouble they make for others backfires on them. The violence they plan falls on their own heads. PSALM 7:14-16

This is what the LORD says: "I will reward your evil with evil; you won't be able to pull your neck out of the noose." MICAH 2:3

Don't be misled—you cannot mock the justice of God. You will always harvest what you plant. GALATIANS 6:7

You pay the price for your actions. God does not prevent you from acting foolishly, but he allows you to experience the consequences of your foolishness.

To [Adam] he said, "Since you listened to your wife and ate from the tree whose fruit I commanded you not to eat, the ground is cursed because of you. All your life you will struggle to scratch a living from it." GENESIS 3:17

Hardship and difficulty are consequences of sin.

Does sin always have negative consequences?

This is the reply of the Holy One of Israel: "Because you despise what I tell you and trust instead in oppression and lies, calamity will come upon you suddenly—like a bulging wall that bursts and falls. In an instant it will collapse and come crashing down." ISAIAH 30:12-13

They must bear the consequences for their sins, says the Sovereign LORD. EZEKIEL 44:12

Sin is wrong, so it always produces bad consequences. Sometimes it may seem that you have avoided any consequences, but they will come, sooner or later.

On the judgment day, fire will reveal what kind of work each builder has done. The fire will show if a person's work has any value. If the work survives, that builder will receive a reward. But if the work is burned up, the builder will suffer great loss. The builder will be saved, but like someone barely escaping through a wall of flames. 1 CORINTHIANS 3:13-15

Some of the consequences of sin will not be felt until the final Day of Judgment, but even those who have salvation through Jesus Christ will feel the consequences of their sin.

Do I ever suffer the consequences of another person's sin, or does another person suffer the consequences of my sin?

When Adam sinned, sin entered the world. Adam's sin brought death, so death spread to everyone, for everyone sinned. ROMANS 5:12

Everyone still suffers the consequences of Adam's sin. You too have sinned and deserve the same punishment as Adam.

Joshua said to Achan, "Why have you brought trouble on us?" JOSHUA 7:25

Sin always affects others, even innocent people. The most extreme example is murder. The victim's family suffer more than the punished murderer. Your sinful actions affect more people than just yourself. Beware of the temptation to rationalize your sins by saying they are too small or too personal to hurt anyone but you.

Can forgiveness stop sin's consequences?

David confessed to Nathan, "I have sinned against the LORD." Nathan replied, "Yes, but the LORD has forgiven you. . . . Nevertheless . . . your child will die." 2 SAMUEL 12:13-14

The Kingdom of Heaven will be like ten bridesmaids who took their lamps and went to meet the bridegroom. Five of them were foolish, and five were wise. The five who were foolish didn't take enough olive oil for their lamps. . . . Then the five foolish ones asked the others, "Please give us some of your oil because our lamps are going out." But the others replied, "We don't have enough for all of us. Go to a shop and buy some for yourselves." But while they were gone to buy oil, the bridegroom came. Then those who were ready went in with him to the marriage feast, and the door was locked. MATTHEW 25:1-3, 8-10

The consequences of sin are often irreversible. Even though God forgives you, he may not eliminate the consequences of your wrongdoing. He allows the natural consequences of your actions. These consequences should be a powerful reminder for you when you face temptation again.

Can there also be positive consequences to my actions?

If we are faithful to the end, trusting God just as firmly as when we first believed, we will share in all that belongs to Christ. HEBREWS 3:14

When you accept Jesus Christ as Savior and live faithfully for him, you will experience the positive consequences of heavenly rewards and eternal life.

How joyful are those who fear the LORD—all who follow his ways! PSALM 128:1

Anyone who wants to come to him must believe that God exists and that he rewards those who sincerely seek him. HEBREWS 11:6

A life focused on God brings joy to God and many blessings to you. The more you trust and obey God, the more you will experience the blessings he gives.

CONSISTENCY *See also* Balance, Faithfulness, Perseverance

Consistency means living in harmony with character. It means there is a uniformity and trustworthiness surrounding our actions and beliefs. Consistency also means sequential faithfulness—what you do today is in harmony with what you will do tomorrow. Someone can anticipate your future actions by how you act today and how you acted yesterday. The challenge is to be consistently faithful in ways that are pleasing to God and helpful to others. The Bible also calls us to be consistent in our obedience to God, our faithfulness and love toward others, and our growth to maturity in the faith. Consistency in the Christian life is closely tied to the discipline of developing godly character.

What does consistent living look like?

If you are wise and understand God's ways, prove it by living an honorable life, doing good works with the humility that comes from wisdom. JAMES 3:13

A consistent life is characterized by an inward understanding of God's ways and the outward good works that result.

Jesus Christ is the same yesterday, today, and forever. HEBREWS 13:8

Jesus is the role model for consistency in beliefs, character, and actions.

How can I possibly obey all of God's commandments consistently?

Be careful to obey all the commands I am giving you today. DEUTERONOMY 8:1

We can be sure that we know him if we obey his commandments. 1 JOHN 2:3

The rule for perfect living is to obey all of God's commandments. But no one is perfect; everyone sins. That's why Jesus Christ died and rose again—to forgive your sins. The key is to attempt to obey all of God's commandments, realizing that sometimes you will fail. When you do fail, consistently seek Jesus and his forgiveness.

Does it really make a difference to others if I live a consistent life or not?

Then people who are not Christians will respect the way you live. 1 THESSALONIANS 4:12

You yourself must be an example to them by doing good works of every kind. Let everything you do reflect the integrity and seriousness of your teaching. TITUS 2:7

People may not accept your faith, but if your lifestyle is consistently kind and helpful, they will be more likely to trust and admire you.

I will keep on obeying your instructions forever and ever. PSALM 119:44

Keep on doing what is right, and trust your lives to the God who created you, for he will never fail you. 1 PETER 4:19

When you drift away from consistent obedience to God, you lose your eternal perspective of why obedience is so important. Your daily choices become more selfish, and you slide into being cynical and dissatisfied with your life.

How do I develop more consistency in my walk with God?

O people, the LORD has told you what is good, and this is what he requires of you: to do what is right, to love mercy, and to walk humbly with your God. MICAH 6:8

When you obey my commandments, you remain in my love. . . . I have told you these things so that you will be filled with my joy. Yes, your joy will overflow! JOHN 15:10-11

Develop a desire to obey God. He knows that because of your sinful nature, you won't always obey him. What he wants is your desire to obey, because that is the evidence that you love and respect him and that you believe his way is best.

CONTENTMENT *See also* Joy, Peace, Satisfaction, Trust

Contentment is among life's most elusive qualities. The answer to "How much is enough?" always seems to be "Just a little bit more." Yet the Bible holds up contentment as a central and attainable characteristic of the Christian life. We should be contented people, at peace with God, our neighbors, our family, and ourselves. That kind of contentment brings a sense of serenity, gratefulness, happiness, and pleasure. Contentment in this sense means to accept that what we have is enough. But we should be careful not to be so content that we become complacent and no longer strive for anything, particularly godliness. We become so comfortable that we do not feel the need for God. We also need to be careful that in our contentment we don't neglect the fight against injustice, poverty, and evil. Make it your daily quest to find the contentment that pleases God.

How can I find contentment, regardless of life's circumstances?

True godliness with contentment is itself great wealth. After all, we brought nothing with us when we came into the world, and we can't take anything with us when we leave it.
1 TIMOTHY 6:6-7

Contentment begins with realizing your eternal destiny. It isn't what you have, but where you are headed. When you realize that there is something greater than your time here on earth, you approach your life differently.

Satisfy us each morning with your unfailing love, so we may sing for joy to the end of our lives. PSALM 90:14

Contentment comes from the assurance that God loves you unconditionally. Nothing you do can make him love you more, and nothing you do can make him love you less.

I take pleasure in my weaknesses, and in the insults, hardships, persecutions, and troubles that I suffer for Christ. 2 CORINTHIANS 12:10

I have learned how to be content with whatever I have. I know how to live on almost nothing or with everything. I have learned the secret of living in every situation, whether it is with a full stomach or empty, with plenty or little. For I can do everything through Christ, who gives me strength. PHILIPPIANS 4:11-13

When your contentment depends on things going your way, you will become unhappy when things don't. When your contentment comes from watching Jesus meet your needs, you will be secure and happy because he never fails you. He teaches you to discern between the things that really matter and the things that are just distractions.

You cannot become my disciple without giving up everything you own. LUKE 14:33

Contentment comes out of a willingness to give up everything for God. That is when you are truly free to rest in the peace and security God offers. Contentment does not come from how much you have but from what you do for God with what you have.

Are there any risks of being content?
When you had eaten and were satisfied, you became proud and forgot me. HOSEA 13:6

When contentment leads to complacency, you are in trouble. Enjoying God's blessings should lead you to seek him, not forget him; to thank him, not ignore him. Your faith is at risk when you find your ultimate contentment in things that fail the test of eternity—possessions, wealth, food, career, social position. When these things are gone, your contentment fades too. Ultimate contentment comes only through your relationship with the Lord, who never fails.

CONTROL *See also* Holy Spirit, Power, Self-Control

Have you ever been late for an appointment because you were stuck in traffic? Have you ever gone on a long-awaited vacation only to have it rain every day? Have you ever been left unemployed because of a company buyout or restructuring? We all face situations that are beyond our control. The Bible teaches that even when we find ourselves in unpredictable, uncontrollable, and frustrating circumstances, there is one thing we can control: our reaction to the situation. We can choose to trust God to work in our lives to bring order, hope, and peace out of chaos.

Our world seems so out of control. How can people still say God is in control?
[Christ] existed before anything else, and he holds all creation together. COLOSSIANS 1:17

In the beginning, Lord, you laid the foundation of the earth and made the heavens with your hands. HEBREWS 1:10

God was powerful enough to create the earth, the planets, and all the heavens, so we can trust that God has ultimate control over the universe. If God released his control over the earth and if the forces of nature (gravity, for example) ceased to function, the world would end in a moment.

[Christ] is far above any ruler or authority or power or leader or anything else—not only in this world but also in the world to come. God has put all things under the authority of Christ and has made him head over all things for the benefit of the church. EPHESIANS 1:21-22

Jesus has God's power, which is far greater than any powers in this out-of-control world. By this power, he gives all of his followers eternal life and brings all things under his sovereign control.

How can I learn to have more self-control?

If we could control our tongues, we would be perfect and could also control ourselves in every other way. JAMES 3:2

Become more aware of what you say, and begin to speak more carefully. If you can control your tongue, you can take control of most other aspects of your life.

Supplement your faith with a generous provision of moral excellence, and moral excellence with knowledge, and knowledge with self-control, and self-control with patient endurance, and patient endurance with godliness. . . . The more you grow like this, the more productive and useful you will be in your knowledge of our Lord Jesus Christ. 2 PETER 1:5-8

Self-control, like so many character traits of the Christian, comes only by intentional effort and discipline. It is also connected to other character traits. In other words, if you want to develop self-control, you must develop other traits like morality, patience, and godliness.

All athletes are disciplined in their training. They do it to win a prize that will fade away, but we do it for an eternal prize. 1 CORINTHIANS 9:25

Godly habits—such as reading God's Word, praying, and giving your time and money to serve God and others—give you spiritual stamina, purpose, and direction for your life. This helps you keep your eyes on your goal—the eternal prize of living forever with God in heaven.

Does the Bible give any advice for dealing with controlling people?

Jacob . . . told [Rachel's] father, "I'll work for you for seven years if you'll give me Rachel, your younger daughter, as my wife." "Agreed!" Laban replied. . . . Finally, the time came for him to marry her. . . . So Laban invited everyone in the neighborhood and prepared a wedding feast. But that night, when it was dark, Laban took Leah to Jacob. GENESIS 29:18-23

Laban manipulated Jacob for many years. Jacob finally broke free from Laban's control through a combination of confrontation, negotiation, and patience. You can read the full story in Genesis 29–31. Through it all, God continually blessed Jacob.

Diotrephes, who loves to be the leader, refuses to have anything to do with us. When I come, I will report some of the things he is doing and the evil accusations he is making against us. 3 JOHN 1:9-10

Diotrephes was a church leader who refused to welcome and support traveling teachers who came through town. He was afraid that these teachers would confront him over some of his wrong teachings in the church. Diotrephes wanted to control his congregation. As John advises, we are to confront those who control others for selfish reasons. Never sacrifice the truth or the good of the whole church for one selfish and controlling person. But remember that any confrontation must be handled with love (see Ephesians 4:15).

Is it possible to exercise control without being controlling?

Now listen! Today I am giving you a choice between life and death, between prosperity and disaster. For I command you this day to love the LORD your God and to keep his commands. . . . If you do this, you will live and multiply, and the LORD your God will bless you and the land you are about to enter and occupy. But if your heart turns away and you refuse to listen, and if you are drawn away to serve and worship other gods, then I warn you now that you will certainly be destroyed. DEUTERONOMY 30:15-18

Moses did all he could to persuade the people to live by God's commands, but in the end he knew that the choice was theirs. If you are a leader in any capacity—parent, teacher, supervisor, church elder, board member—you have the responsibility to lead by doing and saying everything you can to persuade others to move in the right direction. This is a good example of being in control without being controlling.

When it was clear that we couldn't persuade him, we gave up and said, "The Lord's will be done." ACTS 21:14

After you have done your best, you must let go and trust God to complete the work he asked you to start.

CONVICTIONS *See also* Accountability, Integrity, Truth, Values

Conviction is more than just belief; it is commitment to a belief. What you think, say, and do shows the level of your conviction. For example, when you believe Jesus Christ is who he claims to be, out of this belief should come the conviction to live by his teachings. Convictions prepare us to effectively live a life of faith and to defend our faith when necessary. The word *conviction* can also refer to the work of the Holy Spirit in our heart, telling us what is right and wrong. Without the Holy Spirit's conviction, we would be unprepared to face temptation and would easily give in when confronted by someone with stronger convictions. Convictions hold us steady on the path of life and help us to live faithfully and act out our belief in God in practical ways. Keep your convictions strong, and your life will be a great story of faith in God.

What are some basic convictions I must have to effectively live out my faith?

God loved the world so much that he gave his one and only Son, so that everyone who believes in him will not perish but have eternal life. JOHN 3:16

If you confess with your mouth that Jesus is Lord and believe in your heart that God raised him from the dead, you will be saved. ROMANS 10:9

If we confess our sins to him, he is faithful and just to forgive us our sins and to cleanse us from all wickedness. 1 JOHN 1:9

That if I am truly sorry for my sins and confess them to God, and if I believe that God's Son, Jesus, died for me and took upon himself the punishment for my sin, then God forgives me and gives me the gift of salvation. The moment I accept this gift, the Holy Spirit enters my life and begins transforming me into a new person on the inside. Then I know that my life is different.

God has given both his promise and his oath. These two things are unchangeable because it is impossible for God to lie. Therefore, we who have fled to him for refuge can have great confidence. HEBREWS 6:18

That God always keeps his promises.

God gave the people all these instructions: "I am the LORD your God, who rescued you from the land of Egypt, the place of your slavery. You must not have any other god but me." EXODUS 20:1-3

That God must have first priority in my life.

You must continue to believe this truth and stand firmly in it. Don't drift away from the assurance you received when you heard the Good News. COLOSSIANS 1:23

All Scripture is inspired by God and is useful to teach us what is true and to make us realize what is wrong in our lives. It corrects us when we are wrong and teaches us to do what is right. 2 TIMOTHY 3:16

That the Bible was written by God and reveals God's truth for all matters of faith and life.

I am convinced that nothing can ever separate us from God's love. Neither death nor life, neither angels nor demons, neither our fears for today nor our worries about tomorrow—not even the powers of hell can separate us from God's love. No power in the sky above or in the earth below—indeed, nothing in all creation will ever be able to separate us from the love of God that is revealed in Christ Jesus our Lord. ROMANS 8:38-39

That nothing can separate me from God's love.

I am praying to you because I know you will answer, O God. Bend down and listen as I pray. PSALM 17:6

That God hears and answers prayer.

I know that you can do anything, and no one can stop you. JOB 42:2

I know the greatness of the LORD—that our Lord is greater than any other god. PSALM 135:5

That no one is greater than God. He is sovereign and all-powerful.

Why is it important to have godly convictions?

You may believe there's nothing wrong with what you are doing, but keep it between yourself and God. Blessed are those who don't feel guilty for doing something they have decided is right. But if you have doubts about whether or not you should eat something, you are sinning if you go ahead and do it. For you are not following your convictions. If you do anything you believe is not right, you are sinning. ROMANS 14:22-23

Convictions can keep you from sinning.

I lavish unfailing love for a thousand generations on those who love me and obey my commands. EXODUS 20:6

Convictions help you experience more of God's blessing.

God gave these four young men an unusual aptitude for understanding every aspect of literature and wisdom. And God gave Daniel the special ability to interpret the meanings of visions and dreams. . . . Whenever the king consulted them in any matter requiring wisdom and balanced judgment, he found them ten times more capable than any of the magicians and enchanters in his entire kingdom. DANIEL 1:17, 20

Convictions bring wisdom as a reward.

We will be mature in the Lord, measuring up to the full and complete standard of Christ. Then we will no longer be immature like children. We won't be tossed and blown about by every wind of new teaching. We will not be influenced when people try to trick us with lies so clever they sound like the truth. Instead, we will speak the truth in love, growing in every way more and more like Christ, who is the head of his body, the church. EPHESIANS 4:13-15

Convictions help you become more like Christ.

How can I develop stronger convictions?

He guards the paths of the just and protects those who are faithful to him. Then you will understand what is right, just, and fair, and you will find the right way to go. PROVERBS 2:8-9

Let the Holy Spirit guide your lives. Then you won't be doing what your sinful nature craves. The sinful nature wants to do evil, which is just the opposite of what the Spirit wants. And the Spirit gives us desires that are the opposite of what the sinful nature desires. GALATIANS 5:16-17

Every day you are faced with many decisions between right and wrong, good and bad, God's way and the way of the world. Practice choosing God's way. Be tenacious about not letting Satan take over any territory in your heart. Be committed to winning even the little battles.

Listen to me, you who know right from wrong, you who cherish my law in your hearts. Do not be afraid of people's scorn, nor fear their insults. ISAIAH 51:7

Be committed to knowing God's Word so that you can obey it. Do not be intimidated when others make fun of you for living by the principles of Scripture. Your convictions will be rewarded by God.

The godly offer good counsel; they teach right from wrong. PSALM 37:30

Seek advice from godly people who have demonstrated wisdom. They can encourage and motivate you to hold fast to your convictions.

How do I live out my convictions?

Shadrach, Meshach, and Abednego replied, "O Nebuchadnezzar, we do not need to defend ourselves before you. If we are thrown into the blazing furnace, the God whom we serve is able to save us. He will rescue us from your power, Your Majesty. But even if he doesn't, we want to make it clear to you, Your Majesty, that we will never serve your gods or worship the gold statue you have set up." DANIEL 3:16-18

Peter and the apostles replied, "We must obey God rather than any human authority." ACTS 5:29

You live out your convictions by never compromising your conscience and by keeping God as your main focus.

Daniel was determined not to defile himself by eating the food and wine given to them by the king. He asked the chief of staff for permission not to eat these unacceptable foods. DANIEL 1:8

You live out your convictions by respectfully negotiating so that you do not have to compromise your values.

If another believer is distressed by what you eat, you are not acting in love if you eat it. Don't let your eating ruin someone for whom Christ died. ROMANS 14:15

You live out your convictions by discerning between personal preferences and Christian convictions.

What is the difference between having convictions and being stubborn?

Again and again the LORD had sent his prophets and seers to warn both Israel and Judah. . . . But the Israelites would not listen. They were as stubborn as their ancestors who had refused to believe in the LORD their God. They rejected his decrees and the covenant he had made with their ancestors, and they despised all his warnings. They worshiped worthless idols, so they became worthless themselves. 2 KINGS 17:13-15

Because the Sovereign LORD helps me, I will not be disgraced. Therefore, I have set my face like a stone, determined to do his will. And I know that I will not be put to shame.
ISAIAH 50:7

Conviction is living according to God's Word. Stubbornness is refusing to listen to God's Word or godly people.

COPING *See also* Challenges, Overcoming, Patience, Stress, Trouble

Life is stressful. Every day, new challenges and pressures come our way. Hard times are inevitable. Sometimes we wonder if we can cope with it all. Family, friends, work, church, money, conflict, emotions, stress—life can be overwhelming. How do we manage all this and continue to live and function in a healthy way? Coping is the manner in which we deal with life. We can't control much of what comes our way, but we can control how we respond to it and to whom we go for help. The proper perspective is crucial. God offers a unique perspective on coping with life. Along with his perspective, he offers strength and wisdom that you cannot find anywhere else. How you view the challenges of life, and how much you rely on God, will determine how well you cope.

How do I cope when life becomes overwhelming?

The LORD helps the fallen and lifts those bent beneath their loads. PSALM 145:14

All praise to God, the Father of our Lord Jesus Christ. God is our merciful Father and the source of all comfort. 2 CORINTHIANS 1:3

These verses tell us two important truths: (1) God notices when you are overloaded and overwhelmed, and (2) he provides an extra measure of mercy, comfort, and help to those who need it most. When you are overwhelmed, don't shut God out; let him help you.

Give your burdens to the LORD, and he will take care of you. PSALM 55:22

Give all your worries and cares to God, for he cares about you. 1 PETER 5:7

When you are overwhelmed with problems and the worry that comes along with them, you must not become so discouraged that you no longer think God can help you. Don't ever quit believing that God cares about you and will help you through your problems. If you give up on God, you will cut off your greatest source of help.

Why am I discouraged? Why is my heart so sad? I will put my hope in God! I will praise him again—my Savior and my God! PSALM 42:5-6

I will keep on hoping for your help; I will praise you more and more. PSALM 71:14

The act of praising God in the midst of adversity helps you cope because it keeps you focused on what you need most: hope, confidence, and God himself, who has promised an end to all adversity and a future where joy and peace will reign forever.

How do I cope when life's demands seem impossible?

Nothing is impossible with God. LUKE 1:37

I can do everything through Christ, who gives me strength. PHILIPPIANS 4:13

Sometimes God will do the impossible in your life simply to show you he is there. Expect it, and don't miss it when he does it. What seems impossible for you is never impossible for God.

You're going to wear yourself out—and the people, too. This job is too heavy a burden for you to handle all by yourself. . . . But select from all the people some capable, honest men who fear God and hate bribes. Appoint them as leaders over groups of one thousand, one hundred, fifty, and ten. . . . They will help you carry the load, making the task easier for you. If you follow this advice, and if God commands you to do so, then you will be able to endure the pressures, and all these people will go home in peace.
EXODUS 18:18, 21-24

Don't try to keep your problems to yourself. Seek God's help in prayer first, then share your burden with wise and godly people you can trust. Many times, godly advice may provide a workable solution you had not considered. God's wisdom may flow to you through godly counselors.

My dear brothers and sisters, be strong and immovable. Always work enthusiastically for the Lord, for you know that nothing you do for the Lord is ever useless.
1 CORINTHIANS 15:58

Attitude is an important part of coping because it affects motivation. Never give up, fight your battles with courage, and maintain a positive attitude based on these facts: The God of the universe created you, loves you, and has offered you the assurance of eternal life. God is working for you, not against you. Remind yourself of that every day, and watch how that affects your attitude and ability to cope in a positive way.

How can I cope when others fail or hurt me?

Don't put your trust in mere humans. They are as frail as breath. What good are they?
ISAIAH 2:22

Realize that everyone is human. Even those closest to you cannot be perfect and will let you down. We all have the capacity to hurt one another. Instead of being surprised when this happens, be understanding and ready to forgive.

Don't say, "I will get even for this wrong." Wait for the LORD to handle the matter.
PROVERBS 20:22

Don't repay evil for evil. Don't retaliate with insults when people insult you. Instead, pay them back with a blessing. That is what God has called you to do, and he will bless you for it. 1 PETER 3:9

Wait for the Lord to take care of matters his way. Respond with a blessing rather than retaliation. Evil is best overcome with goodness, not with more evil.

May integrity and honesty protect me, for I put my hope in you. PSALM 25:21

When your heart is right with God and you value and live by his principles, you will be much better equipped to cope when others mistreat you. You will better understand why bad things happen to you and how to cope with them.

How can I cope with my insecurities?

How precious are your thoughts about me, O God. PSALM 139:17

What is the price of two sparrows—one copper coin? But not a single sparrow can fall to the ground without your Father knowing it. And the very hairs on your head are all numbered. So don't be afraid; you are more valuable to God than a whole flock of sparrows. MATTHEW 10:29-31

Remind yourself how valuable you are to God.

Do not be afraid or discouraged, for the LORD will personally go ahead of you. He will be with you; he will neither fail you nor abandon you. DEUTERONOMY 31:8

Be aware of God's presence in your life. Take courage that he is by your side, helping you through all things.

How can I help others cope?

Listen closely to what I am saying. That's one consolation you can give me. JOB 21:2

Learn to distinguish between those who are just complaining and those who are truly struggling. Tune your ears to hear the inner cry of people who are hurting. Sometimes what they need most is someone who will simply listen.

When I am with those who are weak, I share their weakness, for I want to bring the weak to Christ. Yes, I try to find common ground with everyone, doing everything I can to save some. 1 CORINTHIANS 9:22

Empathize with others. A sympathetic heart recognizes other people's problems; an empathetic heart shares the hurts and helps bring hope and healing to those people. Remember the tough times you have experienced—they give you the insight and patience to help others through their tough times.

Let everything you say be good and helpful, so that your words will be an encouragement to those who hear them. EPHESIANS 4:29

Speak words that are encouraging, fitting, and helpful.

Our people must learn to do good by meeting the urgent needs of others; then they will not be unproductive. TITUS 3:14

Be practical in meeting others' needs. Don't just feel bad for them—help them.

COURAGE *See also* Convictions, Overcoming, Spiritual Warfare

Courage is acting on what we know is right and good, daring to do what we should. Fear paralyzes; courage releases us to move forward. It renders fear ineffective. It gives us the confident assurance that we can succeed. Christians have an extra resource—God's promise to help in time of need. This gives us boldness to face any situation that comes our way. Sometimes the most courageous thing to do is run away from a situation, if that will bring about the greatest good. The Bible also speaks of the courage to stand firm against evil, to remain strong in our faith, to resist temptation, and to do the right thing. The more we learn to rely on God, the more courageous we will become.

Where do I get the courage to keep going when life seems too hard or obstacles too big?

The LORD your God . . . is with you! DEUTERONOMY 20:1

Be strong and courageous! Do not be afraid or discouraged. For the LORD your God is with you wherever you go. JOSHUA 1:9

The LORD is my light and my salvation—so why should I be afraid? PSALM 27:1

True courage comes from understanding that God is stronger than your biggest problem or strongest enemy and that he wants to use his power to help you. Courage is not confidence in your own strength, which is misplaced confidence, but confidence well placed in God's strength. Fear comes from feeling alone against a great threat. Courage comes from knowing God is beside you, helping you fight against the threat. To stay courageous, focus more on God's presence and less on your problems.

Two of the men who had explored the land, Joshua son of Nun and Caleb son of Jephunneh, tore their clothing. They said to all the people of Israel, "The land we traveled through and explored is a wonderful land! . . . Don't be afraid of the people of the land. They are only helpless prey to us! They have no protection, but the LORD is with us! Don't be afraid of them!" NUMBERS 14:6-9

You can't completely escape fear, but you can learn to manage it so that it doesn't control you. Joshua and Caleb had courage because of the promise that God was greater than any enemy or problem they faced.

Will God take away the things that frighten me?

All the believers lifted their voices together in prayer to God: ". . . O Lord, hear their threats, and give us, your servants, great boldness. . . . Stretch out your hand with healing power; may miraculous signs and wonders be done through the name of your holy servant Jesus." After this prayer, the meeting place shook, and they were all filled with the Holy Spirit. Then they preached the word of God with boldness. ACTS 4:24, 29-31

The early church was constantly threatened by religious persecution. The believers did not pray for the threats to end but for the courage to face them. Sometimes God will remove the things that frighten you. But often the Holy Spirit gives you the boldness to turn threats into opportunities for spiritual growth and sharing your faith.

Having hope will give you courage. You will be protected and will rest in safety. JOB 11:18

Hope helps you see beyond your immediate crisis. It is through faith and hope that we accept Christ as Savior and place our eternal future in his hands. If God took away everything that frightened you, there would be no need for hope in your life.

How do I find the courage to face death?

Dear friends, don't be afraid of those who want to kill your body; they cannot do any more to you after that. LUKE 12:4

Realize that eternal life begins the moment you die.

Death is swallowed up in victory. 1 CORINTHIANS 15:54

Be assured that Jesus has won the victory over death. Jesus' death and resurrection proves he has the power to give you life after death if you believe in him.

Are there consequences for lacking courage?

[Pilate] announced his verdict. ". . . I . . . find him innocent. . . ." But the mob shouted louder and louder, demanding that Jesus be crucified, and their voices prevailed. LUKE 23:14, 23

Standing up for what is right may get you in trouble with ungodly people. Failing to stand up for what is right can get you in trouble with God.

COVETING *See also* Desires, Greed, Jealousy, Lust, Seduction

Coveting is a form of greed. It is a burning desire to have someone or something for selfish gratification. It is wanting what does not belong to us or what we cannot or should not have. Seeing others who have something more (or better) lights a fire in us. If it is not controlled, this fire blazes into obsession and lust. It tempts us to think, *Why can't I have a home like that? a spouse like that? a bank account like that?* Coveting is a sin because we are seeking contentment in things other than God. It is ironic that we so wholeheartedly pursue money, possessions, even relationships, when in reality they don't bring contentment.

What is the difference between wanting and coveting?

Give me an understanding heart so that I can . . . know the difference between right and wrong. 1 KINGS 3:9

Don't be greedy, for a greedy person is an idolater. COLOSSIANS 3:5

You want what you don't have, so you scheme and kill to get it. You are jealous of what others have, but you can't get it, so you fight and wage war to take it away from them. Yet you don't have what you want because you don't ask God for it. JAMES 4:2

The difference between wanting and coveting is motivation. Wanting something is not always bad. You want to love your children and provide food and shelter for them. You want to please your spouse. You want to obey God. You want to enjoy the life God has given you. But when wanting becomes selfish or self-serving, it turns to coveting. Ask yourself why you want something. Examine the feelings you have when you think about it. If you want something and you can't stop thinking about it or if you want something just to have it or hoard it or if you want something because someone else has it or if you want something that makes you look better than someone else, you are probably beginning to covet. If you are tempted to do wrong to get something, if you feel like you deserve it, if you feel unhappy not having it, or if you are jealous that someone else has it—then you are coveting.

What are the consequences of coveting?

As [David] looked out over the city, he noticed a woman of unusual beauty taking a bath. He sent someone to find out who she was. . . . Then David sent messengers to get her; and when she came to the palace, he slept with her. . . . Then Nathan said to David . . . "This is what the LORD says: Because of what you have done, I will cause your own household to rebel against you." 2 SAMUEL 11:2-4; 12:7, 11

Greed causes fighting; trusting the LORD leads to prosperity. PROVERBS 28:25

Coveting can cause you to stop thinking rationally. You may become obsessed with getting what you want, even if it means taking it from someone else. The consequences of coveting come in many forms, but they always damage your relationship with others and with God.

Just as Death and Destruction are never satisfied, so human desire is never satisfied. PROVERBS 27:20

The perpetual quest for what you cannot have leaves a growing, consuming emptiness that is never filled. Coveting is a cycle of dissatisfaction, a never-ending drive for just one more thing. The consequence of coveting is that you will never be satisfied with what you have.

[Sinners] set an ambush for themselves; they are trying to get themselves killed. Such is the fate of all who are greedy for money; it robs them of life. PROVERBS 1:18-19

People who long to be rich fall into temptation and are trapped by many foolish and harmful desires that plunge them into ruin and destruction. For the love of money is the root of all kinds of evil. And some people, craving money, have wandered from the true faith and pierced themselves with many sorrows. 1 TIMOTHY 6:9-10

Coveting reorders your priorities. It moves God down the list from his rightful spot at the top. And the less you have your eyes on God, the more you will be tempted to neglect and disobey him. After a while, you won't even notice how far you've moved away from him.

How does coveting affect my relationships?

Wherever there is jealousy and selfish ambition, there you will find disorder and evil of every kind. JAMES 3:16

Coveting brings disorder to relationships. It causes jealousy and promotes selfishness. It is really the opposite of love, because coveting wants to take from others, while love wants to give to others. Love binds relationships together, while coveting rips them apart.

Greed brings grief to the whole family, but those who hate bribes will live.
PROVERBS 15:27

Coveting can bring grief to those close to you, like your family members, for it leads you into sinful behavior. Coveting occurs because you are dissatisfied, and dissatisfaction leads to disunity in relationships.

How can I avoid coveting?

I know how to live on almost nothing or with everything. I have learned the secret of living in every situation, whether it is with a full stomach or empty, with plenty or little.
PHILIPPIANS 4:12

By his divine power, God has given us everything we need for living a godly life. We have received all of this by coming to know him, the one who called us to himself by means of his marvelous glory and excellence. And because of his glory and excellence, he has given us great and precious promises. These are the promises that enable you to share his divine nature and escape the world's corruption caused by human desires.
2 PETER 1:3-4

Make your relationship with God your number one priority. The more you focus on God, the less you will focus on the things of this world that tempt you to covet. The more you see life from God's perspective, the less important material gains will be.

Give me an eagerness for your laws rather than a love for money! PSALM 119:36

Pray for an eager spirit to study and obey God's Word, for the Word of God gives you the right perspective on money and possessions.

Don't love money; be satisfied with what you have. For God has said, "I will never fail you. I will never abandon you." HEBREWS 13:5

Fight the temptation to think that more money will solve your problems.

One of the angels ordered, "Run for your lives! And don't look back or stop anywhere in the valley!" GENESIS 19:17

Run from anything that stimulates youthful lusts. Instead, pursue righteous living, faithfulness, love, and peace. 2 TIMOTHY 2:22

Don't keep looking at the things that stir covetous feelings in you. When you start to covet something, run the other way! Quickly get your mind onto something else.

[The godly] delight in the law of the LORD, meditating on it day and night.
PSALM 1:2

Clothe yourself with the presence of the Lord Jesus Christ. And don't let yourself think about ways to indulge your evil desires. ROMANS 13:14

Fix your thoughts on what is true, and honorable, and right, and pure, and lovely, and admirable. Think about things that are excellent and worthy of praise. PHILIPPIANS 4:8

What you think about affects what you do. Don't spend time dwelling on what you can't or shouldn't have. Don't allow your mind to go there. Do something to get your mind on more worthy and important things. Sometimes it is helpful to practice doing without something important to you. You could try fasting, for example. It strengthens your self-control and gives you the confidence that you can stay away from something you are beginning to covet.

Let us not neglect our meeting together, as some people do, but encourage one another, especially now that the day of his return is drawing near. HEBREWS 10:25

Get busy with God's people to do God's work.

Seek the Kingdom of God above all else, and live righteously, and he will give you everything you need. MATTHEW 6:33

Make a list of what you actually need—not what you want. Then enjoy watching God satisfy your needs.

The commandments say, "You must not commit adultery. You must not murder. You must not steal. You must not covet." These—and other such commandments—are summed up in this one commandment: "Love your neighbor as yourself." ROMANS 13:9

Don't look out only for your own interests, but take an interest in others, too. PHILIPPIANS 2:4

Practice the art and discipline of loving others. When you genuinely love others, it is harder to covet because you want what is best for someone else, not just yourself.

CRISIS *See also* Coping, Pain, Panic, Tragedy

A crisis is a major problem that needs immediate attention. Sometimes a crisis accompanies a long stretch of hard times, and sometimes it strikes unexpectedly. During times of crisis, it's common to experience disbelief, panic, grief, loss of hope, and even anger. Sometimes a crisis is a random natural occurrence, such as a tornado or a flood. Other times a crisis is caused by poor decisions, such as talking on the phone while trying to switch lanes on a busy highway. There are also times when a crisis is caused by someone else's actions. No matter the cause or the magnitude of the crisis, the one we go to for help is the key to effectively dealing with it. Any crisis can raise questions about the presence of God and his role in the situation. The answers you find to those questions will determine how well you cope when your life seems to be falling apart.

What are some possible reasons for crisis in my life?

The LORD hurled a powerful wind over the sea, causing a violent storm that threatened to break the ship apart. JONAH 1:4

Jonah experienced a crisis because he ran away from God. Those around him were affected by the crisis, too, because of Jonah's sin. A crisis you are experiencing can affect others because of your sin. And your crisis could be the result of someone else's sin.

A prudent person foresees danger and takes precautions. The simpleton goes blindly on and suffers the consequences. PROVERBS 27:12

Sometimes a crisis is the result of poor decisions.

A severe famine struck the land of Canaan, forcing Abram to go down to Egypt, where he lived as a foreigner. GENESIS 12:10

People can never predict when hard times might come. Like fish in a net or birds in a trap, people are caught by sudden tragedy. ECCLESIASTES 9:12

Sometimes a crisis comes for no apparent reason. It's no one's fault. It's just a part of living in this fallen world.

By means of their suffering, [God] rescues those who suffer. For he gets their attention through adversity. JOB 36:15

I myself will punish you for your sinfulness, says the LORD. JEREMIAH 21:14

Sometimes God allows a crisis in your life to get your attention.

Where is God in my time of crisis?

He lifted me out of the pit of despair, out of the mud and the mire. He set my feet on solid ground and steadied me as I walked along. PSALM 40:2

I sank down to the very roots of the mountains. I was imprisoned in the earth, whose gates lock shut forever. But you, O LORD my God, snatched me from the jaws of death! JONAH 2:6

You need not pray for God to be with you in times of crisis—he is already there. Instead, pray that you will recognize his presence and have the humility and discernment to accept his help.

I have told you all this so that you may have peace in me. Here on earth you will have many trials and sorrows. But take heart, because I have overcome the world. JOHN 16:33

God does not say he will always prevent crises in your life; we live in a sinful world where terrible things happen. But God does promise to always be there with you and for you, helping you through any crisis. And he promises to help you find peace and hope in any crisis.

How should I respond to crisis?

Have mercy on me, O God, have mercy! I look to you for protection. I will hide beneath the shadow of your wings until the danger passes by. PSALM 57:1

When a crisis leaves you vulnerable and exposed, seek the merciful protective covering of the Lord himself.

From the depths of despair, O LORD, I call for your help. PSALM 130:1

Before you reach the end of your rope, call on the Lord. Your weakness gives opportunity for his strength. Your crises are opportunities for God to restore and heal you.

The LORD is my strength and shield. I trust him with all my heart. He helps me, and my heart is filled with joy. I burst out in songs of thanksgiving. PSALM 28:7

As pressure and stress bear down on me, I find joy in your commands. PSALM 119:143

When crises threaten to overwhelm you, God's Word is a firm foundation to help you keep your feet on the ground.

Messengers came and told Jehoshaphat, "A vast army from Edom is marching against you from beyond the Dead Sea."... Jehoshaphat stood before the community of Judah and Jerusalem in front of the new courtyard at the Temple of the LORD. He prayed, "... O our God, won't you stop them? We are powerless against this mighty army that is about to attack us. We do not know what to do, but we are looking to you for help." 2 CHRONICLES 20:2, 5-6, 12

Times of crisis are times of testing. Jehoshaphat faced three attacking armies without the military resources to rebuff them. He turned to prayer as a first response rather than a last resort, and God delivered him and his people in a remarkable way. Crisis becomes a means for God to reveal his care and his power on your behalf.

What are some blessings that can come from my times of crisis?

The sailors were awestruck by the LORD's great power, and they offered him a sacrifice and vowed to serve him. JONAH 1:16

Sometimes a crisis helps you—and others—see God more clearly.

We can rejoice, too, when we run into problems and trials, for we know that they help us develop endurance. And endurance develops strength of character, and character strengthens our confident hope of salvation. ROMANS 5:3-4

Times of crisis can strengthen your character. They may be times when God's transforming power touches you most deeply.

Be truly glad. There is wonderful joy ahead, even though you have to endure many trials for a little while. These trials will show that your faith is genuine. 1 PETER 1:6-7

Times of crisis test and strengthen your faith. Ask God for the endurance to hold on to him so that you do not fall into the pit of despair or backslide into sin. Look forward to the joy that awaits on the other side of the trial.

These trials make you partners with Christ in his suffering. 1 PETER 4:13

Times of crisis help you identify with the suffering that Jesus endured for your sake.

How can I help others in their times of crisis?

Never abandon a friend—either yours or your father's. PROVERBS 27:10

When I am with those who are weak, I share their weakness, for I want to bring the weak to Christ. Yes, I try to find common ground with everyone, doing everything I can to save some. 1 CORINTHIANS 9:22

When others face crises, you need to be there with them. The power of your personal presence may comfort them more than the eloquence of your words.

CRITICISM *See also* Accusations, Confrontation, Judging Others

There is a time and place for healthy criticism, such as when someone clearly needs correction and would be hurt without it. At such times, criticism can be healing and redemptive if it is constructive. But too often criticism focuses only on the negative without equal appreciation for the positive. Many times when we criticize others, we demean, degrade, or humiliate them. Depreciating another to make a point or to make ourselves look better is wrong. It does much more damage than good, particularly when the criticism robs others of their sense of personal worth.

Why should we be careful about criticizing others?

Why do you condemn another believer? Why do you look down on another believer? Remember, we will all stand before the judgment seat of God. ROMANS 14:10

Don't speak evil against each other, dear brothers and sisters. If you criticize and judge each other, then you are criticizing and judging God's law. But your job is to obey the law, not to judge whether it applies to you. JAMES 4:11

Constructive criticism can be a welcome gift if given in the spirit of love. But when you offer criticism that ridicules, demeans, or judges someone, it has at least four harmful consequences: (1) You tear down the other person's self-esteem, making that person feel ashamed and worthless; (2) you damage your own reputation, making yourself look mean and merciless; (3) you damage your ability to offer helpful advice because you've made someone defensive; and (4) you bring greater judgment on yourself from God, who detests it when you hurt others.

How can I offer criticism appropriately?

First get rid of the log in your own eye; then you will see well enough to deal with the speck in your friend's eye. MATTHEW 7:5

Before criticizing someone else, take an inventory of your own sins and shortcomings so that you can approach the person with understanding and humility.

[Love] does not demand its own way. It is not irritable, and it keeps no record of being wronged. 1 CORINTHIANS 13:5

Constructive criticism is always offered in love, to build up another person. It addresses a specific need, not a long list of shortcomings or character flaws.

How should I respond to criticism? How do I evaluate whether it is constructive or destructive?

A wise person stays calm when insulted. An honest witness tells the truth; a false witness tells lies. Some people make cutting remarks, but the words of the wise bring healing.
PROVERBS 12:16-18

Better to be criticized by a wise person than to be praised by a fool. ECCLESIASTES 7:5

Stay calm and don't lash back. Measure criticism according to the character of the person who is giving it. Evaluate whether the criticism is coming from a person with a reputation for truth or for lies. Ask yourself if the criticism is meant to heal or to hurt.

My conscience is clear, but that doesn't prove I'm right. It is the Lord himself who will examine me and decide. 1 CORINTHIANS 4:4

Always work to maintain a clear conscience by being honest and trustworthy. This allows you to shrug off criticism you know is unjustified.

Be happy when you are insulted for being a Christian, for then the glorious Spirit of God rests upon you. 1 PETER 4:14

Consider it a privilege to be criticized for your faith in God. God has special blessings for those who patiently endure this kind of criticism.

If you listen to constructive criticism, you will be at home among the wise.
PROVERBS 15:31

Don't reject truthful information that could help you grow. This requires a great deal of humility, because accepting criticism is a hard thing to do. Sometimes it's painful to hear the truth, but it's worse to continue in harmful behaviors.

How should I respond to unjust criticism?

A gentle answer deflects anger, but harsh words make tempers flare. PROVERBS 15:1

When you are unjustly criticized, respond gently with the truth. Getting angry and defensive will only make the criticism seem true.

[Pilate] took Jesus back into the headquarters again and asked him, "Where are you from?" But Jesus gave no answer. "Why don't you talk to me?" Pilate demanded. "Don't you realize that I have the power to release you or crucify you?" JOHN 19:9-10

Silence is often a good response to criticism. Intentional silence can express strength and communicate your desire to avoid conflict. A second strategy is simply to state what you believe is the truth concerning your position.

Obviously, I'm not trying to win the approval of people, but of God. If pleasing people were my goal, I would not be Christ's servant. GALATIANS 1:10

Criticism from other people loses much of its power when you focus on pleasing God more than pleasing others.

CULTS *See also* Idolatry, Worship

A cult is any group that incorporates mind control in its practices for the purpose of deceiving, influencing, or governing its followers. Many kinds of groups can be cults, including those that are religious, political, athletic, philosophical, or racial. Most cults have the following common elements:

- Mind control, or brainwashing
- A charismatic, self-appointed leader who exerts totalitarian control over the group's members in order to indoctrinate them
- Attempts to separate members from anything not associated with the cult, often accomplished by living communally, completely separating themselves from society
- A fanatical focus on the complete authority and worship of the leader. Cult members are taught not to question the teachings, practices, or ideas of the leader. Almost every cult revolves around a self-centered and self-seeking person.
- An emphasis on withholding truth from nonmembers and being secretive and evasive when questioned by people outside the group

Cults have an "us versus them" mentality, which works deceptively to maintain the loyalty of its members. The more the group's members fear the outside world, the more likely they will be to stay within the fold of the cult. In stark contrast to cults, Christianity welcomes all people and encourages its followers to test its truths openly to see how well the Word of God applies to all people, cultures, and times. Christian churches discourage the idolizing of any pastor or leader. God alone is to be worshiped and obeyed. And rather than spending all their efforts serving a self-appointed leader, Christians are called to spend their time serving others.

What is a cult?

When the judge died, the people returned to their corrupt ways, behaving worse than those who had lived before them. They went after other gods, serving and worshiping them. And they refused to give up their evil practices and stubborn ways. JUDGES 2:19

A cult is a group of people who have their own religion and offer their wholehearted worship and devotion to something or someone other than God. Cults tend to be very isolationist and possessive. They often practice bizarre rituals and follow a religious system instituted by a person with an engaging personality. All these practices run contrary to what God has established in the Bible.

How can I tell if an organization is a cult?

Beware of false prophets who come disguised as harmless sheep but are really vicious wolves. You can identify them by their fruit, that is, by the way they act. Can you pick grapes from thornbushes, or figs from thistles? A good tree produces good fruit, and a bad tree produces bad fruit. MATTHEW 7:15-17

You must compare the teachings of a group of people with the teachings of the Bible. That's why it is so important to read and know the Bible. If a group's teachings are contrary to what is found in God's Word, then you may be dealing with a cult.

If you confess with your mouth that Jesus is Lord and believe in your heart that God raised him from the dead, you will be saved. ROMANS 10:9

Cults do not teach that faith in Jesus Christ as Savior and forgiveness of sins through him is the only way to heaven.

We are all in agreement—we administrators, officials, high officers, advisers, and governors—that the king should make a law that will be strictly enforced. Give orders that for the next thirty days any person who prays to anyone, divine or human—except to you, Your Majesty—will be thrown into the den of lions. DANIEL 6:7

There are danger signs that can warn you that a group is a cult. Although Daniel wasn't facing a cult, he was facing the cultlike devotion of people who were opposed to God and wanted to divert worship away from him. Cults do the same thing.

Can God forgive me for having been involved in a cult?

I have swept away your sins like a cloud. I have scattered your offenses like the morning mist. Oh, return to me, for I have paid the price to set you free. ISAIAH 44:22

If we confess our sins to him, he is faithful and just to forgive us our sins and to cleanse us from all wickedness. 1 JOHN 1:9

God longs for all people to turn to him, no matter what sins they have committed. He forgives all your sins when you sincerely ask him.

CULTURE *See also* Heritage, Neighbors, Peer Pressure, Prejudice

The weather affects our lives every day: Temperature, precipitation, wind, and other factors affect what we choose to wear and even what we will do on a given day. The weather can also affect our attitudes. If it is dark and gloomy, we might feel depressed and weary. If it is a brilliant, sunny day, we might feel energetic and joyful. Adjusting to the changing weather is something we do without stopping to think about it too much.

Like the weather, our culture also affects us every day—far more than we might realize or be willing to admit. Although we don't watch a "culture forecast" on TV, our culture affects what we do far more than the weather forecast. Culture plays a subtle but important role in influencing our values, beliefs, and actions. Our culture takes on a personality of its own, pressuring us to conform and fit in, challenging what we believe, and even shaming us into compliance. Cold weather may influence us to put on a coat, but it is the culture that tells us which coat is stylish. The changing weather of our culture permeates our entire worldview and affects our attitudes, thoughts, feelings, desires, and faith. We must be aware of how our culture affects who we are and what we believe. Ask yourself, What's the cultural weather like today? How does it affect me? How should I respond?

How does culture affect me?

The king ordered Ashpenaz, his chief of staff, to bring to the palace some of the young men of Judah's royal family . . . who had been brought to Babylon as captives. "Select

only strong, healthy, and good-looking young men," he said. . . . "Train these young men in the language and literature of Babylon." The king assigned them a daily ration of food and wine from his own kitchens. . . . But Daniel was determined not to defile himself by eating the food and wine given to them by the king.
DANIEL 1:3-5, 8

King Nebuchadnezzar wanted Daniel and his friends to adapt to Babylonian culture. They were chosen based on what the Babylonians valued in young men: strength, health, attractiveness, and intellect. They were to be taught the language, literature, and customs of the land. They were instructed to eat what the Babylonians ate, and they were to be trained to act as Babylonians. They were even given Babylonian names in order to literally change their identities. We are not slaves in a foreign land, but the influence of culture has not changed much: What you learn in school or on the job, what you read, the movies you see, what you eat, how you dress, how you act, what you value and desire, and even your name are by-products of our culture. You may not think about how culture affects your life, but it does. Its influence is subtle yet powerful. Daniel and his friends carefully chose where they could conform and where they could not, what was worth fighting for and what was not. We must do the same. When culture tells you to compromise your faith or to live in a way that goes against God's commands, then you must draw the line.

Don't copy the behavior and customs of this world, but let God transform you into a new person by changing the way you think. Then you will learn to know God's will for you, which is good and pleasing and perfect. ROMANS 12:2

Culture affects your worldview, perhaps so much that you don't even think about it. As a result, you may be copying ungodly behaviors without even realizing it. To follow God's will, you have to know what it is by becoming familiar with God's Word. Christians become transformed people by allowing God to challenge their worldview and change the way they think about the culture.

There must be heirs for the survivors so that an entire tribe of Israel is not wiped out.
JUDGES 21:17

With God as our witness, and in the sight of all Israel—the LORD's assembly—I give you this charge. Be careful to obey all the commands of the LORD your God, so that you may continue to possess this good land and leave it to your children as a permanent inheritance. 1 CHRONICLES 28:8

Our Christian culture affects our identity on a group level and gives us a sense of belonging. The Israelites were instructed to be immersed in their culture so they could pass on their rich cultural heritage to their children. A Christian cultural heritage helps you understand where you came from and where you are going. Don't just conform to this culture; get involved and contribute to it so that the next generation can set its hope on God and remember the miracles he did for your generation.

How do I follow God in an immoral culture?

But Joseph refused. "Look," he told her, "my master trusts me with everything in his entire household. . . . How could I do such a wicked thing? It would be a great sin against God."
GENESIS 39:8-9

Refuse to give in to what the Bible says is wrong.

While the Israelites were camped at Acacia Grove, some of the men defiled themselves by having sexual relations with local Moabite women. These women invited them to attend sacrifices to their gods, so the Israelites feasted with them and worshiped the gods of Moab. NUMBERS 25:1-2

The Israelites were easily influenced by some of the sinful practices of the surrounding culture. The strength of your faith may be revealed by how easily you are influenced by your culture. What kind of example have you been exhibiting to others? A good role model influences others for good rather than being easily influenced by evil.

Though it is against the law, I will go in to see the king. If I must die, I must die.
ESTHER 4:16

Esther was only a young Jewish girl, but God put her in a position of great influence in order to save her people. You can influence culture far more than you realize. Persist in obeying God and doing right, and you will influence the culture you live in.

You must not make for yourself an idol of any kind or an image of anything.
EXODUS 20:4

In our Western culture, it's hard to imagine bowing down to statues of wood or stone, but we have our own idols that lead us away from God. An idol is anything that takes God's place in our hearts. It could be money, convenience, hobbies, the computer, our reputation, beauty, celebrities, or success. You must remove anything that has taken God's place in your life. These are usually the things that culture says you must have. What idol are you tempted to worship? Don't let the culture convince you it is more important than your relationship with God.

The world would love you as one of its own if you belonged to it, but you are no longer part of the world. I chose you to come out of the world, so it hates you. Do you remember what I told you? "A slave is not greater than the master." Since they persecuted me, naturally they will persecute you. JOHN 15:19-20

Bless those who persecute you. Don't curse them; pray that God will bless them. . . . Never pay back evil with more evil. . . . Instead, "If your enemies are hungry, feed them. If they are thirsty, give them something to drink. In doing this, you will heap burning coals of shame on their heads." Don't let evil conquer you, but conquer evil by doing good.
ROMANS 12:14, 17, 20-21

Jesus tells his followers that following him rather than the culture will mean being misunderstood and possibly even mocked and persecuted. God's message is countercultural. When you follow his ways—by praying for your enemies or giving your money to help others, for example—it will not make sense according to culture's standards. As a result, you can expect some ridicule and opposition. But that won't always be the norm. In God's future culture of heaven, goodness and righteousness will be the norm.

The LORD observed the extent of human wickedness on the earth, and he . . . was sorry he had ever made them and put them on the earth. It broke his heart. And the LORD said, "I will wipe this human race I have created from the face of the earth. . . ." But Noah found favor with the LORD. GENESIS 6:5-8

Consistent obedience to God's commandments will set you apart from an immoral culture. Sometimes you might feel as though you are alone in your obedience to God. You might feel like everyone is laughing at you. However, just because no one else is doing what you're doing doesn't mean you're wrong. Remain faithful, as Noah did. Obey God's commands, and find confidence in your relationship with him.

What does it mean to be in the world but not of the world?

They had followed the practices of the pagan nations the LORD had driven from the land ahead of them, as well as the practices the kings of Israel had introduced. 2 KINGS 17:8

The people of Israel were given laws and rules to set them apart from the surrounding pagan cultures. But instead of influencing the cultures around them for God, they allowed those cultures to influence them against God. As a Christian, you should be aware of your culture and the cultural values and practices that are not godly. Determine to be a godly influence on your culture instead of letting it be an ungodly influence on you.

I know and am convinced on the authority of the Lord Jesus that no food, in and of itself, is wrong to eat. But if someone believes it is wrong, then for that person it is wrong. And if another believer is distressed by what you eat, you are not acting in love if you eat it. Don't let your eating ruin someone for whom Christ died. Then you will not be criticized for doing something you believe is good. For the Kingdom of God is not a matter of what we eat or drink, but of living a life of goodness and peace and joy in the Holy Spirit. If you serve Christ with this attitude, you will please God, and others will approve of you, too. So then, let us aim for harmony in the church and try to build each other up. ROMANS 14:14-19

In Paul's day, there was a debate among believers as to whether it was acceptable to eat meat from animals that had been sacrificed to idols. Although Paul and the non-Jewish believers thought it was acceptable, they agreed not to eat the meat because it offended the Jewish Christians. Paul's point is that many things of this world—certain food and drink, and certain customs—are not wrong in and of themselves. It's what you choose to do with these things that can become right or wrong. Nuclear energy isn't inherently wrong. It can be used to power homes and provide light, but it can also be used to build bombs. Wine isn't inherently wrong, but it can also lead to drunkenness. Being in the world but not of the world means to claim certain things for Christ and to use those things not as the world would but in a way that serves others and brings glory to God.

You gave [human beings] charge of everything you made, putting all things under their authority—the flocks and the herds and all the wild animals, the birds in the sky, the fish in the sea, and everything that swims the ocean currents. O LORD, our Lord, your majestic name fills the earth! PSALM 8:6-9

People who don't believe in Christ are both in the world and of the world. They are of the world because they have no purpose or future beyond this life. They become chained to the things the culture says offer security. The world—the culture—is all they've got. The messages and values taught by the culture are the highest authority they know. On the other hand, believers in Christ live in the world—the culture—like everyone else, but they are not enslaved by it because they know it offers a false promise of security. So Christians are not of the culture because they know that life on earth is just a part of eternity. They are not enslaved by culture because their belief in Christ—not anything they are or have in this world—gives them eternal value. They are free to use all that God has given them to influence the culture and to invest their lives in the eternal future, not the present.

You are the light of the world—like a city on a hilltop that cannot be hidden. No one lights a lamp and then puts it under a basket. Instead, a lamp is placed on a stand, where it gives light to everyone in the house. In the same way, let your good deeds shine out for all to see, so that everyone will praise your heavenly Father. MATTHEW 5:14-16

[Jesus said,] "I'm not asking you to take them out of the world, but to keep them safe from the evil one. They do not belong to this world any more than I do. Make them holy by your truth. . . . Just as you sent me into the world, I am sending them into the world." JOHN 17:15-18

There are two equal but opposite dangers that believers encounter regarding the world: full acceptance of the culture and its ways, or complete rejection of the culture. Jesus teaches several principles about the world: God loves the world and sent his Son to redeem all who believe (see John 3:16); the world hates Jesus and therefore hates Jesus' followers (see John 15:18); the world is a place of trouble and tribulation, not only because of the normal trials of life but because of intentional persecution of Jesus' followers (see John 16:33). So Jesus' followers have a complex relationship with the culture; it is both a place of mission and a place of danger. Either absorption by the culture or isolation from the culture would violate Jesus' intention for you. You are to learn to live in the world and to enjoy the good things of God's creation (see 1 Timothy 4:4) without being controlled by your desires or compromised by the world's pressures (see 1 John 2:15-17). You are also to see the world as your mission field.

DATING *See also* Relationships, Romance, Sex/Sexuality, Singleness

Dating can be fun and exciting when you meet someone special. As you spend more time together, romance often blossoms. At first glance, dating seems like a great way to develop a relationship with a member of the opposite sex. How else can you get to know someone you are attracted to? But for a Christian, dating can also bring confusion. There are many questions to consider: Is it wrong to date someone who is not a Christian? Is it wrong to date at all? How much physical contact is okay?

The Bible does not answer these questions specifically. But the Bible does tell us not to marry a non-Christian, to stay away from sexual sin, and to guard our hearts from anything that leads to sexual immorality. The Bible is full of wisdom that can help us approach dating in a pure and godly way. When we seek to honor God in our relationships, our perspective on dating changes. We stop asking how close we can get to the boundaries and start asking how close this relationship can get us to God.

Is there a right or wrong way to date?

You must not intermarry with them. Do not let your daughters and sons marry their sons and daughters, for they will lead your children away from me to worship other gods.
DEUTERONOMY 7:3-4

Don't team up with those who are unbelievers. 2 CORINTHIANS 6:14

There are many warnings in the Bible about marrying someone who is not a Christian. The issue is not intolerance or religious superiority; it's about your first love. The most important priority in the life of a Christian is love for God and obedience to him. It affects everything you are and do, and it determines your eternal future. If the person you marry, the one with whom you will spend most of your life, does not believe in God, it will be difficult to keep God as your first priority. What if your spouse asks you, through words or actions, to compromise your faith? What if your spouse grows jealous of your loyalty to God? What if your spouse begins to oppose your faith? The Bible says that by marrying an unbeliever you set yourself up for being drawn away from God. While it is not necessarily wrong to date someone who is an unbeliever, you must be aware that it could lead to a more serious relationship, which could then lead to the kind of marriage God warns against.

What kinds of boundaries should I set up in my dating relationships?

Pray for us, for our conscience is clear and we want to live honorably in everything we do.
HEBREWS 13:18

It is essential to set boundaries and guidelines for your dating relationships before you get involved with anyone. Your boundaries should be based on the principles for relationships and marriage that God has created and laid out in the Bible. You should have guidelines that cover issues like appropriate physical touch, appropriate topics to discuss, treating someone with respect and honor, pure speech, and building a spiritual basis for the relationship. When you are committed to staying within your boundaries, you are building the foundation for a healthy relationship, and you can end each date with a clear conscience.

A beautiful woman who lacks discretion is like a gold ring in a pig's snout.
PROVERBS 11:22

Charm is deceptive, and beauty does not last; but a woman who fears the LORD will be greatly praised. PROVERBS 31:30

Good judgment is vital to making good decisions. This is especially true when making decisions about dating. Beauty and lust have clouded people's judgment since the beginning of time. If you are dating someone who is pushing you to engage in activities that are not in line with God's guidelines for relationships, don't allow your judgment to be clouded. Good judgment calls you to set up clear boundaries and make godly decisions (which might include ending the relationship) so that you will not be led to compromise your relationship with God.

God's will is for you to be holy, so stay away from all sexual sin. Then each of you will control his own body and live in holiness and honor—not in lustful passion.
1 THESSALONIANS 4:3-5

Guard against physical intimacy in a dating relationship. Such intimacy should be reserved only for marriage because it is a picture of the purity and devotion that we strive for in our relationship with God.

DEATH *See also* Aging/Old Age, Grief, Eternity, Resurrection

Death always seems to get the last word. No matter what we do to extend our lives, death inevitably catches up with us. Why are we afraid to die? Why do we try so hard to preserve our lives? Perhaps because of fear of the unknown. On this side of death, at least we know the rules of how things work, even if we don't like them. We know what things bring us happiness and pleasure. But what kind of existence—if any—do we have after our bodies die? The uncertainty creates fear and despair in many people.

The Bible has a great deal to say about death—and what is on the other side of it. When you believe God's Word, you can have great hope instead of fear and despair. Jesus died for our sins and rose from the dead, showing us he has triumphed over death. All who trust in him will share in that victory over death! There are two kinds of death—the end of life here on earth, and the missed opportunity to live in heaven with God forever. To die physically is to leave our earthly body and our earthly relationships. To die spiritually is to be eternally separated from God and his people in heaven. When Christians die physically, we gain a greater life as we take up eternal residence in heaven with God. It may not be pleasant to think of dying physically, but it is devastating to think of missing heaven forever.

Is death really the end?

Jesus told her, "I am the resurrection and the life. Anyone who believes in me will live, even after dying. Everyone who lives in me and believes in me will never ever die."
JOHN 11:25-26

When our dying bodies have been transformed into bodies that will never die, this Scripture will be fulfilled: "Death is swallowed up in victory. O death, where is your victory? O death, where is your sting?" 1 CORINTHIANS 15:54-55

For those who believe in Jesus as their Savior, death is only the beginning of an eternity of unspeakable joy in the presence of the Lord and other believers.

There is more than enough room in my Father's home. JOHN 14:2

Though death is a great unknown, Jesus Christ has gone before you. He is preparing a glorious place for you to stay. If you know and love Jesus, you can be confident that your room is ready and waiting.

What will happen to me when I die?

Let me reveal to you a wonderful secret. We will not all die, but we will all be transformed! 1 CORINTHIANS 15:51

We want you to know what will happen to the believers who have died so you will not grieve like people who have no hope. . . . When Jesus returns, God will bring back with him the believers who have died. 1 THESSALONIANS 4:13-14

What an adventure awaits those who love Jesus Christ! A Christian who dies will meet God and live with him forever in heaven. Our bodies will be totally transformed into bodies that will never again be subjected to sin, pain, and the limitations of this world.

Christ lives within you, so even though your body will die because of sin, the Spirit gives you life because you have been made right with God. ROMANS 8:10

When the trumpet sounds, those who have died will be raised to live forever. And we who are living will also be transformed. 1 CORINTHIANS 15:52

When you give Jesus Christ control of your life, you receive the gift of eternal life. This does not prevent the death of your earthly body, but it does guarantee that God will give you a new body in which your spirit will continue to live forever in heaven, where there is no aging or sickness or death.

How do I get eternal life?

God loved the world so much that he gave his one and only Son, so that everyone who believes in him will not perish but have eternal life. JOHN 3:16

Believing in Jesus is the only way to guarantee eternal life in heaven after you die. It is wise to examine your heart and make sure that you truly believe in him and his saving power.

What about people who haven't put their faith in Jesus? Is there any hope for them when they die?

[The other criminal] said, "Jesus, remember me when you come into your Kingdom." And Jesus replied, "I assure you, today you will be with me in paradise." LUKE 23:42-43

Just as the man on the cross next to Jesus expressed his faith in the moments before his death, so anyone can receive Jesus' assurance of eternal life, even at the last minute. Therefore, since you do not know a person's every thought, there is always hope that someone who appears to be an unbeliever will turn to the Lord in the last minutes of life.

How can I be certain that there is eternal life?

[Jesus] was buried, and he was raised from the dead on the third day, just as the Scriptures said. He was seen by Peter and then by the Twelve. After that, he was seen by more than 500 of his followers at one time. 1 CORINTHIANS 15:4-6

The resurrection of Jesus is not religious lore. The biblical record mentions eyewitnesses to the risen Jesus as well as others who interviewed the eyewitnesses. Historical investigation confirms the fact of the Resurrection. This assures you that there is eternal life.

In fact, Christ has been raised from the dead. He is the first of a great harvest of all who have died. 1 CORINTHIANS 15:20

Jesus' resurrection guarantees the resurrection of all those who believe he died and rose from the dead to forgive their sin.

Is fear of dying a bad thing?

Teach us to realize the brevity of life, so that we may grow in wisdom. PSALM 90:12

Since you have been raised to new life with Christ, set your sights on the realities of heaven. . . . Think about the things of heaven. COLOSSIANS 3:1-2

Fear of the unknown is natural, but obsession with dying is not healthy. Fear of dying can be a good thing when it draws you closer to God and causes you to make every day count for him. It is helpful to think of death as a beginning, not an end. For a believer, it is your entrance into eternal life with God.

For to me, living means living for Christ, and dying is even better. PHILIPPIANS 1:21

Fear of dying may indicate a weak relationship with God, a misunderstanding of heaven, a lack of eternal perspective, or a lack of trust in God's promises. When you are at peace with God, you will not fear death. Take time to learn about heaven from the Bible. Trust God's assurances of eternal life, and apply yourself to knowing and serving God. The more real God is to you, the less fearsome death will be.

DEBT *See also* Materialism, Money, Stewardship

Being in debt is not a sin, but it can lead to sin if we are not careful to manage it properly. God calls us to be responsible with our money—how we spend it, lend it, repay it, and give it.

When we go into debt, for whatever reason, we are accepting an obligation to repay that debt in a timely manner. Debt is an important issue because why we go into debt and how we repay debt affect so many other areas of life. If we get too far into debt, it can be a symptom of irresponsibility, carelessness, or covetousness. Before going into debt, be honest with yourself about why you want to spend the money. What are your real motives? Make sure it's not about just trying to keep up a lifestyle that is beyond your means. Make sure you're not trying to prove something. Trying to live beyond our means will almost always get us in trouble. It can also show that we are not content with what God has given us. A good model for responsibly handling money is to give God ten percent of what we earn, save another ten percent, and live contentedly on the rest. This will usually prevent serious debt problems. When we see our money as a gift from God rather than just the fruit of our own labor, it can help us to spend more carefully.

Why should I be cautious about debt?

Just as the rich rule the poor, so the borrower is servant to the lender. PROVERBS 22:7

No one can serve two masters. For you will hate one and love the other; you will be devoted to one and despise the other. You cannot serve both God and money. MATTHEW 6:24

Debt can cause you to be "owned" by those to whom you owe. Debt can make money your master rather than God.

How should I handle my debts?

The wicked borrow and never repay, but the godly are generous givers. PSALM 37:21

To take out a loan and not repay it is wrong; to give generously pleases God.

Give to everyone what you owe them: Pay your taxes and government fees to those who collect them, and give respect and honor to those who are in authority. ROMANS 13:7

Pay your debts in a timely manner because it is important to honor your commitments. Having a home mortgage or car loan isn't wrong, but when payments are due, you should pay them on time. Owing money to someone else is a responsibility not to be taken lightly.

Don't agree to guarantee another person's debt or put up security for someone else. If you can't pay it, even your bed will be snatched from under you. PROVERBS 22:26-27

If you cosign a note, be absolutely sure you can repay the entire debt if the other person defaults on the loan. Otherwise you will put yourself, your business, or even your family at risk.

How did Jesus pay the debt for my sins?

God presented Jesus as the sacrifice for sin. People are made right with God when they believe that Jesus sacrificed his life, shedding his blood. This sacrifice shows that God was being fair when he held back and did not punish those who sinned in times past. ROMANS 3:25

Since we have been made right in God's sight by the blood of Christ, he will certainly save us from God's condemnation. . . . So now we can rejoice in our wonderful new relationship with God because our Lord Jesus Christ has made us friends of God. ROMANS 5:9-11

Your sins left you with a debt to God so great that you could never repay it on your own. But Jesus Christ paid your debt through his death on the cross, making you right with God and pure in his sight. The punishment you were supposed to pay for your sins was paid by Jesus. He cleared your debt; now you owe nothing. When you trust in Jesus, God mercifully forgives the debt of your sin and invites you to share in all the rich blessings he has prepared for you in heaven.

DECEIT/DECEPTION *See also* Hypocrisy, Lying, Manipulation

To deceive is to cover up the truth, twist the facts, send someone in the wrong direction, or make things seem different from the way they really are. Telling only half the truth is also a form of deception. What makes deception especially hurtful is that it isn't just a mistake or an oversight; it is a calculated plan to mislead someone or a deliberate attempt to get someone to believe a lie. Deception breaks the bond of trust that is necessary to human relationships. Without trust, relationships deteriorate. Since God created us for relationship with himself and others, it is easy to understand why God hates deception. God is truth; deception is lies. The two will always be opposed to each other. The good news is that because God is truth, he will never deceive you. You can believe and count on everything he says.

How can I know when I'm being deceived?

Delilah said to Samson, "Please tell me what makes you so strong and what it would take to tie you up securely." JUDGES 16:6

When your conscience tells you no and your desire tells you yes, can you still hear and follow your conscience? Delilah's beauty and promise of sexual pleasure convinced Samson that she was sincere. Samson was the spiritual leader of Israel, yet he was spending the evening in the home of an ungodly woman who was tempting him to sexual immorality. What had happened to his conscience? When you make a practice of not listening to your conscience, soon you will hardly hear it. Then you will be extremely vulnerable to deception. Don't put yourself in a position where you can no longer hear or follow your conscience.

The people of Berea . . . searched the Scriptures day after day to see if Paul and Silas were teaching the truth. ACTS 17:11

If someone is trying to convince you to do something that contradicts Scripture, you can be sure it is wrong. Know the Bible well enough to discern when someone is deceiving you.

The tree was beautiful and its fruit looked delicious, and she wanted the wisdom it would give her. GENESIS 3:6

If something seems too good to be true, it could indicate that you are being deceived. Sometimes it is for real, but if it sounds too good to be true, it probably is.

Evil people and impostors will flourish. They will deceive others and will themselves be deceived. 2 TIMOTHY 3:13

There will be false teachers among you. They will cleverly teach destructive heresies and even deny the Master who bought them. In this way, they will bring sudden destruction. 2 PETER 2:1

As long as Satan has power to deceive, he will. People who are deceived by Satan will in turn try to deceive you. The worst kind of deceiver is the false teacher, who appears to give good advice but really wants to lead you down a path of destruction.

Do I deceive myself?

The human heart is the most deceitful of all things. JEREMIAH 17:9

Don't be misled—you cannot mock the justice of God. You will always harvest what you plant. GALATIANS 6:7

You deceive yourself when you think you can get away with sin. You deceive yourself when you think you can ignore God and still receive his blessings.

Stop deceiving yourselves. If you think you are wise by this world's standards, you need to become a fool to be truly wise. 1 CORINTHIANS 3:18

You deceive yourself when you live as though this world is all there is.

Is deception always wrong?

Do not deceive or cheat one another. LEVITICUS 19:11

Don't lie to each other, for you have stripped off your old sinful nature and all its wicked deeds. COLOSSIANS 3:9

God commands us not to lie. It is always wrong to deceive.

[Jesus] never sinned, nor ever deceived anyone. 1 PETER 2:22

Jesus never lied or deceived anyone. He is our model for right and wrong.

Rahab had hidden the two men, but she replied, "Yes, the men were here earlier, but I didn't know where they were from. They left the town at dusk, as the gates were about to close. I don't know where they went. If you hurry, you can probably catch up with them." (Actually, she had taken them up to the roof and hidden them beneath bundles of flax....) JOSHUA 2:4-6

It was by faith that Rahab the prostitute was not destroyed with the people in her city who refused to obey God. For she had given a friendly welcome to the spies. HEBREWS 11:31

There are times in Scripture when a person lies to protect another from harm, as Rahab did for Israel's spies. Some Bible scholars say that people who ask questions with the sole purpose of harming others forfeit their right to be told the truth, especially during a time of war. During war, you cannot aid the enemy just because someone asks you to. Since the only goal of the king's soldiers was to capture and eventually kill the Israelite spies, they gave up their right to be told the truth. You shouldn't avoid deception by betraying innocent people. Another viewpoint, however, is that God never needs, wants, or asks us to sin, even to accomplish his will. Rahab had to think quickly, and lying was the only thing that came to mind. While Scripture does not explicitly condemn Rahab for her lie, it does make clear that lying is wrong (see Exodus 20:16; Leviticus 19:11; Proverbs 6:16-17; 12:22; 24:28). But God was merciful and continued with his plan despite Rahab's lie. While Rahab's act may have been wrong, depending on your viewpoint, her motives were good (to save God's people). The Bible commends her faith but not her deception.

DECISIONS *See also* Discernment, Guidance, Planning, Wisdom

Making a decision means arriving at a solution that ends uncertainty. It is choosing between options—some big, some little, some good, some bad. We make hundreds if not thousands of decisions each day, some as small as choosing between chocolate or vanilla ice cream and some as big as whom to marry, what job to take, or where to live. But the most important decision you'll ever make is what you will do about Jesus. If you choose to believe that he is who he says he is and you decide to give him control of your life, then your life on earth and your eternal destiny will be radically changed. If you decide to accept Jesus as God's Son, it will affect all the other decisions you make.

What must I do to make good decisions?

You know what [God] wants; you know what is right because you have been taught his law. ROMANS 2:18

Start by making the basic decision to do what the Bible says is right and avoid what the Bible says is wrong. You can't make complicated decisions if you haven't practiced the fundamental ones. For example, if you make the basic decision to consistently tell the truth, it will be easier to turn down a tantalizing job opportunity that would require you to be dishonest to get ahead.

Show me the right path, O LORD; point out the road for me to follow. PSALM 25:4

Trust in the LORD with all your heart; do not depend on your own understanding. Seek his will in all you do, and he will show you which path to take. PROVERBS 3:5-6

Follow God's direction. God's Word shows you how to stay on God's path. Decide not to do anything that will take you away from it, or you'll soon be in danger of getting hopelessly lost.

Jesus went up on a mountain to pray, and he prayed to God all night. At daybreak he called together all of his disciples and chose twelve of them to be apostles. LUKE 6:12-13

Follow Jesus' example—don't make a decision without asking for God's help first. Saturate your life with prayer. Talking with God calms your spirit and clears your mind so you are able to hear his counsel.

The godly offer good counsel; they teach right from wrong. PSALM 37:30

Intelligent people are always ready to learn. Their ears are open for knowledge.
PROVERBS 18:15

Listen to the advice of godly people and carefully consider it as you make a decision.

What do you benefit if you gain the whole world but lose your own soul? Is anything worth more than your soul? MATTHEW 16:26

Resist the temptation to make choices out of a desire for personal satisfaction. Such ambition could lead you to make some very bad decisions.

How does God help me make decisions?
If you need wisdom, ask our generous God, and he will give it to you. He will not rebuke you for asking. JAMES 1:5

Some people fear that they are bothering God with their problems. Nothing could be further from the truth. God is looking for ways to help you because he loves you. Your commitment to him releases the resources he has available for you.

The Holy Spirit helps us in our weakness. For example, we don't know what God wants us to pray for. But the Holy Spirit prays for us with groanings that cannot be expressed in words. ROMANS 8:26

When you are overwhelmed, confused, or uncertain, do not hesitate to pray. In fact, these are the best times to pray because the Holy Spirit helps us best in our weakness. Describe your situation to God, and trust him to prescribe the solution.

How do I know if I've made a good decision?
Help us, O God of our salvation! Help us for the glory of your name. PSALM 79:9

You know you've made a good decision when it honors God.

The Holy Spirit produces this kind of fruit in our lives: love, joy, peace, patience, kindness, goodness, faithfulness, gentleness, and self-control. GALATIANS 5:22-23

You know you've made a good decision when it produces good results.

We know that God causes everything to work together for the good of those who love God and are called according to his purpose for them. ROMANS 8:28

Even if you don't always make the best decisions, God has the power to turn your poor choices into good results.

What is the danger of indecision?
You see and recognize what is right but refuse to act on it. You hear with your ears, but you don't really listen. ISAIAH 42:20

Indecision is really a decision. When you procrastinate making decisions, you forfeit your control over the direction your life will take, and you are at the mercy of the decisions made by others.

If you refuse to serve the LORD, then choose today whom you will serve. Would you prefer the gods your ancestors served beyond the Euphrates? Or will it be the gods of the Amorites in whose land you now live? But as for me and my family, we will serve the LORD. JOSHUA 24:15

Indecision regarding matters of faith can slowly but surely draw you away from God. If you do not decide for God, you are actually deciding against him.

How can I be more decisive?
Do not waver, for a person with divided loyalty is as unsettled as a wave of the sea that is blown and tossed by the wind. Such people should not expect to receive anything from the Lord. Their loyalty is divided between God and the world, and they are unstable in everything they do. JAMES 1:6-8

When you ask God to give you wisdom, perspective, and a desire to obey him, he promises to do it. The more you get know God through prayer and reading the Bible, the more you know what he wants you to do. You can be more decisive when faced with choices because God's will for you is more obvious.

Because the Sovereign LORD helps me, I will not be disgraced. Therefore, I have set my face like a stone, determined to do his will. And I know that I will not be put to shame. ISAIAH 50:7

You should move ahead decisively when you know the right thing to do, you are certain it is what God wants you to do, it does not contradict God's Word, and it does not use improper methods (such as deception) to accomplish something good. Do the right thing the right way, and you will never regret your decision.

It was by faith that Abraham obeyed when God called him to leave home and go to another land that God would give him as his inheritance. He went without knowing where he was going. HEBREWS 11:8

Having faith in God will help you be decisive because you know he holds the future. You don't have to know exactly where you are going when you are going with God.

How is my character revealed in my decisions?
Lot took a long look at the fertile plains of the Jordan Valley. . . . The whole area was well watered everywhere. . . . (This was before the LORD destroyed Sodom and Gomorrah.) Lot chose for himself the whole Jordan Valley . . . and parted company with his uncle Abram. GENESIS 13:10-11

Lot's choice showed his selfishness. He chose the best land for himself, even though he knew he would be moving into an area known for its evil. Your decisions determine your actions, and together they show what is in your heart.

Should I "put out a fleece"?

Gideon said to God, ". . . This time let the fleece remain dry while the ground around it is wet with dew." JUDGES 6:39

"Putting out a fleece" is a phrase that comes from the biblical story of Gideon. It means that you ask God to show you a sign of your own choosing to confirm that you are making the right decision. Great caution must be exercised if you put out a fleece because you limit the options of a God who has unlimited options. It is also dangerous because you might blame God if the decision doesn't go the way you wanted. Don't try to force God to act within your limited range of options. Let him show you the best decision from his unlimited options.

DENIAL *See also* Avoidance/Avoiding, Excuses, Rejection

Denial occurs when we refuse to acknowledge or accept something. For example, when a loved one becomes seriously ill, someone may go into denial, refusing to believe or accept that the person is really sick. Denial is also common in people who have addictions when they refuse to acknowledge their dependency or accept responsibility for their actions. Denial is most dangerous when we refuse to acknowledge God or accept what Jesus Christ has done for us. When we deny God, we turn our backs on him. The Bible makes it clear that if we deny God, he will deny us in heaven. Don't let denial harden your heart to the truth of God's message. Acknowledge God, accept his grace, and open yourself up to the healing and blessings that are found only in him.

What does it mean to deny God?

Yes, they knew God, but they wouldn't worship him as God or even give him thanks. And they began to think up foolish ideas of what God was like. As a result, their minds became dark and confused. ROMANS 1:21

Refusing to acknowledge God's authority over your life or your need to accept Jesus Christ as Savior is to deny God.

The king sent Jehudi to get the scroll [God's Word]. . . . Each time Jehudi finished reading three or four columns, the king took a knife and cut off that section of the scroll. He then threw it into the fire . . . until the whole scroll was burned up. Neither the king nor his attendants showed any signs of fear or repentance at what they heard. Even when [others] begged the king not to burn the scroll, he wouldn't listen. JEREMIAH 36:21, 23-25

Refusing to consider that the Bible is God's Word and the ultimate source of truth is to deny God.

A servant girl . . . said to [Peter], "You were one of those with Jesus the Galilean." But Peter denied it in front of everyone. "I don't know what you're talking about," he said. MATTHEW 26:69-70

Being ashamed of Jesus is to deny him.

Such people claim they know God, but they deny him by the way they live. TITUS 1:16

Saying that you know God and then living as though you don't is to deny him.

What are the consequences of denying God?

You can enter God's Kingdom only through the narrow gate. The highway to hell is broad, and its gate is wide for the many who choose that way. MATTHEW 7:13

Jesus told him, "I am the way, the truth, and the life. No one can come to the Father except through me." JOHN 14:6

Denying God is choosing not to have a relationship with him. You cannot enter heaven if you don't have a relationship with God through his Son, Jesus.

Everyone who acknowledges me publicly here on earth, I will also acknowledge before my Father in heaven. But everyone who denies me here on earth, I will also deny before my Father in heaven. MATTHEW 10:32-33

If we deny him, he will deny us. 2 TIMOTHY 2:12

Those who deny Jesus face the awful consequence of having Jesus deny them before God on the Day of Judgment.

Is denial ever a good thing? What kinds of denial does God call me to?

Those who belong to Christ Jesus have nailed the passions and desires of their sinful nature to his cross and crucified them there. GALATIANS 5:24

God calls you to exercise restraint and self-discipline in the way you live. You must give up some things to prevent yourself from giving up on God.

Wash yourselves and be clean! Get your sins out of my sight. Give up your evil ways. ISAIAH 1:16

Get rid of all evil behavior. Be done with all deceit, hypocrisy, jealousy, and all unkind speech. 1 PETER 2:1

You need to deny yourself the pleasure of living in sin. Recognize that sin may bring you great pleasure in the short term, but it will bring great pain and consequences for eternity.

You cannot become my disciple without giving up everything you own. LUKE 14:33

Everything else is worthless when compared with the infinite value of knowing Christ Jesus my Lord. For his sake I have discarded everything else, counting it all as garbage, so that I could gain Christ. PHILIPPIANS 3:8

Are you willing to give up everything for Jesus? He loves that kind of attitude in his followers.

DEPRESSION *See also* Discouragement, Loneliness, Spiritual Dryness

Sooner or later most of us experience some form of depression. It can develop slowly, like the approach of an all-day rain. It can overwhelm us suddenly, like an avalanche of darkness. It can be the result of a failure or loss, or it can invade our minds for no discernible reason. The Bible records the stories of several people who experienced a range of depression. Parts of Scripture were written by people in the midst of depression. The good news is that God does not regard depression as sin, nor does he take it lightly. Rather, he responds to those who suffer the darkness of depression with great tenderness, understanding, and compassion.

What causes depression? How am I vulnerable to it?

Day and night I have only tears for food, while my enemies continually taunt me, saying, "Where is this God of yours?" My heart is breaking as I remember how it used to be: I walked among the crowds of worshipers, leading a great procession to the house of God, singing for joy and giving thanks amid the sound of a great celebration! Why am I discouraged? Why is my heart so sad? PSALM 42:3-5

Depression often comes from looking backward at what you have lost.

I don't really understand myself, for I want to do what is right, but I don't do it. Instead, I do what I hate. . . . I love God's law with all my heart. But there is another power within me that is at war with my mind. . . . Oh, what a miserable person I am! Who will free me from this life that is dominated by sin and death? ROMANS 7:15, 22-24

Depression can occur when you realize how wide the gap is between the ideal you strive for and the reality you see within and around you.

[Jesus] became anguished and distressed. He told them, "My soul is crushed with grief to the point of death. Stay here and keep watch with me." MATTHEW 26:37-38

Depression can come when God asks you to do an extraordinarily hard task and you realize what you may have to suffer to do it.

The Spirit of the LORD had left Saul, and the LORD sent a tormenting spirit that filled him with depression and fear. 1 SAMUEL 16:14

When you neglect the Lord to the point where he can no longer get your attention, he may neglect you for a while. Depression can easily move into the vacant room in your heart. The further you move from God, the less hope you have of receiving the joy of his blessings.

Hope deferred makes the heart sick. PROVERBS 13:12

A heart without hope is a heart headed for depression.

This is the case of a man who is all alone, without a child or a brother, yet who works hard to gain as much wealth as he can. But then he asks himself, "Who am I working for? Why am I giving up so much pleasure now?" It is all so meaningless and depressing. ECCLESIASTES 4:8

If you spend your life pursuing meaningless things, you may become depressed when you recognize that what you have has little lasting value.

Does God care when I feel depressed? How does he bring healing?

The LORD is close to the brokenhearted; he rescues those whose spirits are crushed.
PSALM 34:18

God blesses those who mourn, for they will be comforted. MATTHEW 5:4

God isn't disappointed by your depression or emotional struggles. On the contrary, he feels a special closeness to you. You can actually experience even more of God's presence in times of brokenness.

From the depths of despair, O LORD, I call for your help. PSALM 130:1

There is no depression so deep that God is not present with you. Even if you don't feel his presence, he has not abandoned you. Allow yourself to cry out to God in prayer even from the darkest pit of despair. He wants to help you. You don't have to wallow in the darkness if you allow God's comforting light to enter your soul.

He was despised and rejected—a man of sorrows, acquainted with deepest grief.
ISAIAH 53:3

Remember that Jesus understands the pain of human life. He suffered all that you have suffered and more.

Jesus said, "Come to me, all of you who are weary and carry heavy burdens, and I will give you rest." MATTHEW 11:28

Jesus cares deeply for the weary and provides comfort, love, and rest.

No power in the sky above or in the earth below—indeed, nothing in all creation will ever be able to separate us from the love of God that is revealed in Christ Jesus our Lord.
ROMANS 8:39

Not even the worst depression can separate you from the love Jesus has for you and wants to lavish on you. Don't push him away. He knows all that has happened and what you are going through, and he loves you with a greater love than you could ever imagine.

What can I do when I'm depressed? How can I recover?

As [Elijah] was sleeping, an angel touched him and told him, "Get up and eat!" . . . So he ate and drank and lay down again. Then the angel of the LORD came again and . . . said, "Get up and eat some more." . . . The food gave him enough strength to travel forty days and forty nights to Mount Sinai. . . . The LORD said to him, "What are you doing here, Elijah?" Elijah replied, "I have zealously served the LORD God Almighty. But the people of Israel have broken their covenant with you, torn down your altars, and killed every one of your prophets. I am the only one left, and now they are trying to kill me, too." . . . Then the LORD told him, "Go back the same way you came. . . . I will preserve 7,000 others in Israel who have never bowed down to Baal or kissed him!" 1 KINGS 19:5-10, 15, 18

Recovery from depression involves a number of factors, illustrated in Elijah's experience. To begin the process, you need to care for your body with good rest and nutrition. Then you need to re-engage with God. Elijah was first cared for physically, and then God gave him a fresh vision as well as specific direction for his next steps.

[Jesus] said to Peter, "Couldn't you watch with me even one hour? Keep watch and pray, so that you will not give in to temptation. For the spirit is willing, but the body is weak!" Then Jesus left them a second time and prayed, "My Father! If this cup cannot be taken away unless I drink it, your will be done." . . . He went to pray a third time, saying the same things again. MATTHEW 26:40-44

Jesus shows us that earnest, candid, persistent prayer is the way to surrender to God's will for you. This surrender usually lifts you from depression to the joy of knowing that you are now doing what you were created to do.

Why am I discouraged? Why is my heart so sad? I will put my hope in God! I will praise him again—my Savior and my God! Now I am deeply discouraged, but I will remember you. PSALM 42:5-6

Depression can be a time for soul-searching. You may become even more discouraged if you concentrate on unpleasant or overwhelming circumstances, but when you ask the questions the psalmist asked, then your focus changes to God, who can help you through any circumstance. He will stay with you until he finally rescues you from your last discouraging moment. Praise God for how he has rescued his people in the past, and praise him for how he will rescue you now and in the future.

We praise God for the glorious grace he has poured out on us who belong to his dear Son. EPHESIANS 1:6

When you praise the Lord, it lifts your mood. It is a deliberate act of obedience that is hard to do when you are down, but it produces almost immediate results. Praise the Lord for his unfailing, unconditional love for you. Praise him for the gifts of salvation and eternal life. Praise him for all the good you see around you. Praise him for his promise to help you through your depression.

Those who listen to instruction will prosper; those who trust the LORD will be joyful. PROVERBS 16:20

Trusting in the Lord's presence in your life is the best way to overcome depression. But God often works through other people, so with his guidance you may also need to seek medical or psychological help, which he can use to heal you. Let God use others to help you.

I have told you these things so that you will be filled with my joy. Yes, your joy will overflow! JOHN 15:11

When you are depressed, you are vulnerable to temptations, the lies of Satan, and being distracted from God's promises and power. The Bible will help you recognize these things for what they are. As you read God's Word, your perspective will begin to change. Develop the habit of seeking God and counting on his Word, and you will find the encouragement you need.

Can any good come out of my depression?

Don't be dejected and sad, for the joy of the LORD is your strength! NEHEMIAH 8:10

Those who plant in tears will harvest with shouts of joy. PSALM 126:5

My power works best in weakness. 2 CORINTHIANS 12:9

When you are weak, you are more receptive to the Lord's strength. When everything is going your way, it's easy to overlook God's hand in your life. As God works through your weakness, however, you learn to depend more on him and recognize and be grateful for the good work that only he can accomplish in you.

Jesus said, "Come to me, all of you who are weary and carry heavy burdens, and I will give you rest." MATTHEW 11:28

God can use your depression to get you to slow down and rest long enough to be with him. As you come to him in prayer and Bible reading, you welcome the Holy Spirit to do his work of comfort, transformation, and encouragement—often in ways you cannot explain.

How can I help someone who is depressed?

[Job said,] "I have heard all this before. What miserable comforters you are! . . . But if it were me, I would encourage you. I would try to take away your grief." JOB 16:2, 5

Singing cheerful songs to a person with a heavy heart is like taking someone's coat in cold weather or pouring vinegar in a wound. PROVERBS 25:20

The best way to help someone who is down is to model the gentle, caring love of Christ. Those dealing with depression need comfort and understanding, not advice and lectures. You can help someone who is depressed by your quiet presence, your love, and your encouragement. Telling people to snap out of it or minimizing their pain with false cheeriness will just make them feel worse.

DESIRES *See also* Ambition, Emotions, Motives, Purpose

All of us are created with desires. Our desires can be healthy or unhealthy, godly or ungodly, casual or intense. We can desire something simple, like a home-cooked meal, or we can develop a burning passion for a cause or a relationship that eventually consumes us. Some desires can even drive a person to violence or crime to satisfy them.

The Bible tells us to develop a desire for the Lord. It is good and holy to desire God, to long to know him personally, and to come to love him deeply. It is also good and holy to desire our mates in marriage, to long to provide the best for our families, to hunger to share Christ with others, and to make God's Word known. Control your desires, tame them as you would tame a wild animal, and direct them down a path that honors God.

Is it okay to want something?

The LORD appeared to Solomon in a dream, and God said, "What do you want? Ask, and I will give it to you!" 1 KINGS 3:5

Hope deferred makes the heart sick, but a dream fulfilled is a tree of life. PROVERBS 13:12

God gave you desires as a means of expressing yourself. Desire is good and healthy when directed toward proper objects: those which are good and right and God-honoring. A particular desire can be either right or wrong, depending upon your motives and the object of your desire. For example, the desire to love a member of the opposite sex, if directed toward your spouse, is healthy and right. But if you are married, that same desire directed toward someone who is not your spouse is adultery. The desire to lead an organization is healthy if your motive is to serve others, but it is wrong if your motive is to have the power to control others.

I desire [God] more than anything on earth. PSALM 73:25

LORD, we show our trust in you by obeying your laws; our heart's desire is to glorify your name. ISAIAH 26:8

Your greatest desire must be for a relationship with God because that will influence all your other desires.

How do I know if my desires are right or wrong?

Samson told his father, "Get her for me! She looks good to me." JUDGES 14:3

When you take only yourself into account, your desires are selfish and wrong. You become so obsessed with what you want that you forget to ask if it is what God wants for you, if it's actually good for you, or if it would harm others.

You are still controlled by your sinful nature. You are jealous of one another and quarrel with each other. Doesn't that prove you are controlled by your sinful nature? Aren't you living like people of the world? 1 CORINTHIANS 3:3

Fix your thoughts on what is true, and honorable, and right, and pure, and lovely, and admirable. PHILIPPIANS 4:8

Desiring sin is always wrong. Make sure the object of your desire is good, is consistent with God's Word, and is not harmful to others.

How do evil desires grow in me?

The serpent . . . asked the woman, "Did God really say you must not eat the fruit from any of the trees in the garden?" GENESIS 3:1

You want what you don't have, so you scheme and kill to get it. You are jealous of what others have, but you can't get it, so you fight and wage war to take it away from them. Yet you don't have what you want because you don't ask God for it. And even when you ask, you don't get it because your motives are all wrong—you want only what will give you pleasure. JAMES 4:2-3

The seed of an evil desire is planted quietly, without fanfare or drums, without malice or evil intent—you simply take a step away from God. With the second and third steps away from God, the poisonous fruit of desire or lust begins to grow until you cannot control it.

How can I resist evil desires?

If you are wise and understand God's ways, prove it by living an honorable life, doing good works with the humility that comes from wisdom. JAMES 3:13

Keep yourself busy with good deeds.

Don't let us yield to temptation, but rescue us from the evil one. MATTHEW 6:13

Pray that good desires will overcome bad ones.

Josiah removed all detestable idols. 2 CHRONICLES 34:33

Take away the source of temptation.

Think about the things of heaven. COLOSSIANS 3:2

Fill your mind with thoughts of God and things that honor him.

Plans go wrong for lack of advice; many advisers bring success. PROVERBS 15:22

Find a godly person who is willing to help you. Everyone needs someone who will encourage them and hold them accountable.

Can God change the desires of my heart?

I will give you a new heart, and I will put a new spirit in you. I will take out your stony, stubborn heart and give you a tender, responsive heart. EZEKIEL 36:26

When you give control of your life to God, he gives you a new heart, a new nature, and a new desire to please him.

God stirred the hearts of the priests and Levites . . . to go to Jerusalem to rebuild the Temple of the LORD. EZRA 1:5

God stirs your heart with right desires. It is up to you to act upon them.

Is it wrong to desire my husband or wife sexually?

I am my lover's, and he claims me as his own. SONG OF SONGS 7:10

God has built a fire in the hearts of men and women to desire each other sexually. It is a natural, beautiful, God-given gift. But outside God's plan of marriage, this fire can blaze up and devour a person. Passion that is not controlled within the bounds of marriage is destructive and leads to broken relationships with others and with God.

DIFFERENCES *See also* Diversity, Judging Others, Teamwork

Why did God make everyone so different? Because it is through our uniqueness that we can truly make a difference and do something significant. The Bible tells us that God made each of us with a unique set of abilities and gifts so that we can benefit the church and advance his kingdom in the world. We can feel significant and worthwhile when we exercise those God-given abilities. God also wants us to learn how to use our differences to work effectively with others. Teamwork goes better when everyone understands how his or her unique contributions are essential to the overall goal. The church should be the ultimate example of different people coming together and working in harmony to accomplish many great things. Too often, though, we let our differences cause confusion, conflict, and tension. We feel misunderstood. We feel like our part should be more important. One of our greatest challenges is to remember why God made us different and then focus on how those differences can help us work together. We must not allow our differences to set us against one another; instead they should bring us together to accomplish more than we could have accomplished on our own.

How should I handle differences with others?

You, too, must show love to foreigners, for you yourselves were once foreigners in the land of Egypt. DEUTERONOMY 10:19

Love those who are different from you, whether the difference is race, skin color, personality, status, or political viewpoint. It's easier to focus on things you have in common with others when you truly love them. The strongest friendships are often between people who recognize and appreciate each other's differences.

How wonderful and pleasant it is when brothers live together in harmony! For harmony is as precious as the anointing oil. . . . Harmony is as refreshing as the dew. PSALM 133:1-3

Live in harmony despite your differences. In the church, God wants believers to function together in unity. When Christians use their differences to work in harmony with one another, the church becomes a healing and refreshing balm to the community.

Christ himself has brought peace to us. He united Jews and Gentiles into one people when, in his own body on the cross, he broke down the wall of hostility that separated us. EPHESIANS 2:14

Make every effort to keep yourselves united in the Spirit, binding yourselves together with peace. EPHESIANS 4:3

God puts very different people together in the church, but he unites them through the Holy Spirit. The Holy Spirit shows you how you can be different without being hostile. Learn to appreciate and admire the differences in others.

Can our differences make us better?

As iron sharpens iron, so a friend sharpens a friend. PROVERBS 27:17

We are many parts of [Christ's] body, and we all belong to each other. In his grace, God has given us different gifts for doing certain things well. So if God has given you the ability to prophesy, speak out with as much faith as God has given you. If your gift is serving others, serve them well. If you are a teacher, teach well. ROMANS 12:5-7

Just as all kinds of instruments make the music of an orchestra better, so people with different gifts and perspectives make any team better. God often puts very different people together in a marriage, too, so that their gifts can complement each other. It is usually through diversity that the most progress is made. If everyone always thought the same thing, the status quo would never change, and not much would get done.

DIGNITY *See also* Acceptance, Respect, Worth/Worthiness

Dignity is the quality of worth and significance that every human being was given when created in the image of God. God values every person he has created. Dignity has two angles—recognizing our own worth before God, and recognizing that same worth in others. Unfortunately, our sinful human nature causes us to rank everyone from important to insignificant. But a proper view of dignity motivates us to fulfill God's purpose for ourselves while also helping others find and achieve God's purpose for them. This causes us to respect others and build them up rather than rank them below us. When we realize how much God esteems us, the opinions of others matter less.

What is dignity, and where do we get it?

God created human beings in his own image. In the image of God he created them; male and female he created them. GENESIS 1:27

You made [human beings] only a little lower than God and crowned them with glory and honor. PSALM 8:5

The LORD speaks—the one who formed me in my mother's womb to be his servant, who commissioned me to bring Israel back to him. The LORD has honored me, and my God has given me strength. ISAIAH 49:5

Dignity is understanding who God made you to be—a human being who bears his image. In the eyes of the Creator, you have great worth and value and have been made for a special purpose. Your dignity comes not from what others think about you, but from the fact that God chose to create you. Lasting dignity comes from honoring your Creator.

What is the evidence of dignity in my life?

Those were the days when I went to the city gate and took my place among the honored leaders. The young stepped aside when they saw me, and even the aged rose in respect at my coming. The princes stood in silence and put their hands over their mouths. The highest officials of the city stood quietly, holding their tongues in respect. JOB 29:7-10

Teach the older men to exercise self-control, to be worthy of respect, and to live wisely. They must have sound faith and be filled with love and patience. TITUS 2:2

You show dignity when you reflect the image of God, your source of dignity. When you behave respectably, have self-control and a strong faith, and are loving and patient, you exhibit dignity.

How can I live with dignity?

Humble yourselves before the Lord, and he will lift you up in honor. JAMES 4:10

Recognize that God created you and is the source of your dignity.

My child, never forget the things I have taught you. Store my commands in your heart. If you do this, you will live many years, and your life will be satisfying. . . . Then you will find favor with both God and people, and you will earn a good reputation. Trust in the LORD with all your heart; do not depend on your own understanding. PROVERBS 3:1-2, 4-5

Obey God's Word, which communicates and defines dignity.

Imitate God, therefore, in everything you do, because you are his dear children. Live a life filled with love, following the example of Christ. He loved us and offered himself as a sacrifice for us, a pleasing aroma to God. EPHESIANS 5:1-2

Pursue love for others, which is the expression of dignity.

Be careful to live properly among your unbelieving neighbors. Then even if they accuse you of doing wrong, they will see your honorable behavior, and they will give honor to God when he judges the world. 1 PETER 2:12

Behave honorably to provide an incentive for others to desire greater dignity.

Pray for us, for our conscience is clear and we want to live honorably in everything we do. HEBREWS 13:18

Maintain a clear conscience, the result of living with dignity.

Choose a good reputation over great riches; being held in high esteem is better than silver or gold. PROVERBS 22:1

Develop a good reputation, the reward of dignity.

How do I acknowledge the dignity of others?

Honor your father and mother. Love your neighbor as yourself. MATTHEW 19:19

Give to everyone what you owe them: Pay your taxes and government fees to those who collect them, and give respect and honor to those who are in authority. ROMANS 13:7

Showing respect and honor for others acknowledges that they are people created in God's image.

Slaves, obey your earthly masters with deep respect and fear. Serve them sincerely as you would serve Christ. EPHESIANS 6:5

Obeying those in authority acknowledges their role and responsibility to lead you.

Moses went out to meet his father-in-law. He bowed low and kissed him. They asked about each other's welfare and then went into Moses' tent. EXODUS 18:7

Warmly accepting others acknowledges their worth and your desire to treat them as equals.

Welcome [Phoebe] in the Lord as one who is worthy of honor among God's people. Help her in whatever she needs, for she has been helpful to many, and especially to me. ROMANS 16:2

Meeting others' needs acknowledges that they are important.

DISABILITIES *See also* Challenges, Limitations, Strengths

Many people go through life with the special challenge of having a physical, mental, emotional, or other kind of disability. Yet these disabilities by no means negate the fact that they are loved and valued by God, who has a unique purpose for everyone. In one sense, we are all born with a severe disability that affects our physical, mental, and spiritual capacities—sin. Every day we face the enormous challenge of overcoming our sinful nature so it does not control our actions, thoughts, and desires. Despite our best efforts, sin still limits us. Instead of making us discouraged, this should help us to be more sensitive to people with more visible types of disabilities. The Bible gives us many examples of how to relate to those who are disabled. We make a great mistake when we set them aside as less than human, when we fail to engage them in our lives, or when we believe we can't learn from them. God sees value in each of his children and offers everyone the opportunity to experience his healing, mercy, and salvation.

Does God care about people with disabilities?

I will not forget the blind and lame. JEREMIAH 31:8

God's compassionate purposes have always included people with disabilities. God loves every person equally, regardless of limitations.

[Jesus] told John's disciples, "Go back to John and tell him what you have seen and heard—the blind see, the lame walk, the lepers are cured, the deaf hear, the dead are raised to life, and the Good News is being preached to the poor." LUKE 7:22

Throughout his earthly ministry, Jesus demonstrated special concern for those with disabilities. Jesus' concern for people with disabilities was not limited to a feeling in his heart; he also reached out to them with help and healing.

When [your God] comes, he will open the eyes of the blind and unplug the ears of the deaf. The lame will leap like a deer, and those who cannot speak will sing for joy! ISAIAH 35:5-6

When Jesus returns and the earth is made perfect, all those with disabilities will be healed.

Can God use people with disabilities?

NOTICE WHAT LARGE LETTERS I USE AS I WRITE THESE CLOSING WORDS IN MY OWN HANDWRITING. GALATIANS 6:11

The apostle Paul may have had a serious vision problem, yet the Lord was pleased to use him in mighty ways. Never use your limitations as an excuse not to serve God.

Ruth replied, "Don't ask me to leave you and turn back. Wherever you go, I will go; wherever you live, I will live. Your people will be my people, and your God will be my God." RUTH 1:16

Ruth had two significant social disabilities—she was a foreigner and a widow. Yet she is a model of loyalty, and she became an ancestor of the Messiah.

A spiritual gift is given to each of us so we can help each other. 1 CORINTHIANS 12:7

God has given every Christian—including those with disabilities—a spiritual gift for the purpose of serving others.

How should I treat the disabled?

David asked, "Is anyone in Saul's family still alive—anyone to whom I can show kindness for Jonathan's sake?" . . . Ziba replied, "Yes, one of Jonathan's sons is still alive. He is crippled in both feet." . . . "Don't be afraid!" David said [to Mephibosheth]. "I intend to show kindness to you . . . , and you will eat here with me at the king's table!" . . . And from that time on, Mephibosheth ate regularly at David's table, like one of the king's own sons.
2 SAMUEL 9:1, 3, 7, 11

Invite them into your home to eat at your table. Treat them like you would treat any guest.

A man with leprosy approached [Jesus] and knelt before him. "Lord," the man said, "if you are willing, you can heal me and make me clean." Jesus reached out and touched him. "I am willing," he said. "Be healed!" And instantly the leprosy disappeared. MATTHEW 8:2-3

[Jesus] saw a woman who had been crippled by an evil spirit. She had been bent double for eighteen years and was unable to stand up straight. When Jesus saw her, he called her over and said, "Dear woman, you are healed of your sickness!" Then he touched her, and instantly she could stand straight. How she praised God! LUKE 13:11-13

Offer whatever friendship, encouragement, and healing that you can.

DISAPPOINTMENT See also Discouragement, Sadness, Encouragement

Disappointment in some form haunts us almost every day. Perhaps we didn't get everything done that we wanted to, or someone hurt us or let us down, or we let someone else down, or things just didn't go our way. We've all felt like we are not good enough. When disappointment comes, we are at an important crossroads, even though we don't always realize it. We can condemn ourselves, ask the "what if" or "if only" questions that lead to regret, or play the blame game so someone else is always at fault. If we go down those roads, disappointment can quickly lead to discouragement, depression, anger, shame, or bitterness. If disappointment dominates our thoughts, we become negative, sad, grumpy people. But if we see disappointment as an opportunity to learn and grow, or if we choose to focus on what we have and not what we missed, then disappointment can be put into perspective. The truth is, life is full of disappointment. We often disappoint God by our sins. Yet God doesn't want us to dwell on what could have been; rather we should focus on what can be. He is the God of hope. He sent his Son, Jesus, to take the punishment for our disappointing behavior so that we could stand before him as more than good enough. We can be holy in his eyes. The next time you're feeling disappointed, remember everything you already have, determine to use your disappointment for growth, and be happy that you have the approval of the One who really matters.

What disappoints God?

The LORD observed the extent of human wickedness on the earth, and he saw that every-thing they thought or imagined was consistently and totally evil. So the LORD was sorry he had ever made them and put them on the earth. It broke his heart. GENESIS 6:5-6

Wickedness and evil of any kind disappoint God.

Who made God angry for forty years? Wasn't it the people who sinned, whose corpses lay in the wilderness? And to whom was God speaking when he took an oath that they would never enter his rest? Wasn't it the people who disobeyed him? HEBREWS 3:17-18

Sin disappoints God.

"When you give blind animals as sacrifices, isn't that wrong? And isn't it wrong to offer animals that are crippled and diseased? . . . I am not pleased with you," says the LORD of Heaven's Armies, "and I will not accept your offerings." MALACHI 1:8-10

Giving God less than your best disappoints him.

Soldiers don't get tied up in the affairs of civilian life, for then they cannot please the officer who enlisted them. 2 TIMOTHY 2:4

Letting other things in your life overshadow your commitment to God disappoints him.

What should I do if I feel disappointed with God?

Moses went back to the LORD and protested. EXODUS 5:22

Take it to God in prayer, and try to understand his ways.

Martha said to Jesus, "Lord, if only you had been here, my brother would not have died." JOHN 11:21

Be honest with God about your thoughts and feelings. He knows them anyway, so why try to hide them?

Three different times I begged the Lord to take it away. Each time he said, "My grace is all you need. My power works best in weakness." So now I am glad to boast about my weaknesses, so that the power of Christ can work through me. . . . For when I am weak, then I am strong. 2 CORINTHIANS 12:8-10

Wrestle with the question of why God won't just take away your pain. Ask him what he plans to do through your weakness. It is through this struggle that you can discover your purpose in life.

How should I deal with life's disappointments?

O God, you are my God; I earnestly search for you. My soul thirsts for you; my whole body longs for you. PSALM 63:1

Move toward God, not away from him. Running from the One who can help you will only lead to more disappointment.

[Jesus] said to Simon, "Now go out where it is deeper, and let down your nets to catch some fish." "Master," Simon replied, "we worked hard all last night and didn't catch a thing. But if you say so, I'll let the nets down again." LUKE 5:4-5

Listen to the Lord and trust his Word, even when it seems unreasonable. God's Word often gives advice that seems opposite of what you've been taught by others. When you follow God's advice, you will find solutions for your disappointment.

We know that God causes everything to work together for the good of those who love God and are called according to his purpose for them. ROMANS 8:28

Believe that God is working in your life to use both the good and the bad for a greater purpose. Nothing that happens to you is meaningless. Disappointment turns into hope as you watch God redeem your current adversity.

Is there a way to avoid or minimize disappointment?

You hoped for rich harvests, but they were poor. And when you brought your harvest home, I blew it away. Why? Because my house lies in ruins, says the LORD of Heaven's Armies, while all of you are busy building your own fine houses. HAGGAI 1:9

Put God first. Give him the best minutes of your day, the first part of your money, the highest priority in your life. By doing this, you will learn what is truly important and discover the rewards and satisfaction of having a relationship with the God who created you and loves you.

They cried out to you and were saved. They trusted in you and were never disgraced. PSALM 22:5

Sometimes the most obvious truths are the hardest to live out; they are so simple to grasp yet so hard to master. One of the most obvious truths in a Christian's life is that God's way is best. If you live by the principles given by God himself in Scripture, you will face less disappointment because you will suffer fewer consequences from sinful actions. It's hard to discipline yourself to be in God's Word regularly, let alone follow it. But it's much harder to deal with the disappointment that comes from sin's consequences.

Let's not get tired of doing what is good. At just the right time we will reap a harvest of blessing if we don't give up. GALATIANS 6:9

Good deeds can become disappointing when others don't seem to notice or appreciate them. Good work can be disappointing when you don't see it making a difference. But anything good you do has immense value, both for you and for others. Don't let disappointment keep you from doing good, if for no other reason than to enjoy the blessings God will reward you with when you meet him face-to-face.

We have a priceless inheritance—an inheritance that is kept in heaven for you, pure and undefiled, beyond the reach of change and decay. . . . So be truly glad. There is wonderful joy ahead, even though you have to endure many trials for a little while.
1 PETER 1:4-6

Just as focusing on a fixed point in the distance helps you travel in a straighter line, focusing on the eternal horizon will lead you to live forever with Jesus where there is no pain or sorrow or suffering. As you move straight toward your eternal goal, you will be able to put life's disappointments in perspective.

DISCERNMENT *See also* Decisions, Holy Spirit, Listening, Wisdom

Discernment is the process of training yourself to distinguish between right and wrong by disciplining your conscience, mind, senses, and body. Recognizing the difference between right and wrong is a developed skill. When we grow and mature in our faith, we are able to recognize temptation before it has engulfed us. We can also learn to recognize truth from falsehood. Knowing the Scriptures helps us discern false teaching when someone is using a passage of Scripture incorrectly. When we have trained ourselves to detect right from wrong and practice discernment, we can avoid the pitfalls and confusion that so many people fall into. Life works better because you are living the way God intended.

What is discernment?

Solid food is for those who are mature, who through training have the skill to recognize the difference between right and wrong. HEBREWS 5:14

I am writing to you not because you don't know the truth but because you know the difference between truth and lies. 1 JOHN 2:21

Discernment is the ability to differentiate between right and wrong, true and false, good and bad, important and trivial, godly and ungodly. Discernment helps you interpret issues properly and understand the motives of those pushing a certain agenda. Discernment shows you the way through the maze of options you face. Like the sun that burns away the fog, discernment cuts through confusion and distractions and brings clarity to your life.

Fear of the LORD is the foundation of wisdom. Knowledge of the Holy One results in good judgment. PROVERBS 9:10

Discernment is a stepping-stone to wisdom. It enables you to see behind the facades that mask truth. Whereas the devil is the father of lies, God is the source of all truth, and he gives discernment to those who seek it.

Why is it important to be discerning?

The LORD looks down from heaven on the entire human race; he looks to see if anyone is truly wise, if anyone seeks God. PSALM 14:2

God gives special attention to those who are trying to discern his truth.

Getting wisdom is the wisest thing you can do! And whatever else you do, develop good judgment. PROVERBS 4:7

Discernment is a high priority and a valuable compass for daily living. It points you to God's wisdom rather than to human foolishness.

Dear friends, do not believe everyone who claims to speak by the Spirit. You must test them to see if the spirit they have comes from God. For there are many false prophets in the world. This is how we know if they have the Spirit of God: If a person claiming to be a prophet acknowledges that Jesus Christ came in a real body, that person has the Spirit of God. But if someone claims to be a prophet and does not acknowledge the truth about Jesus, that person is not from God. 1 JOHN 4:1-3

Discernment tunes your ear to God's message rather than to false teaching.

Don't lose sight of common sense and discernment. Hang on to them, for they will refresh your soul. They are like jewels on a necklace. They keep you safe on your way, and your feet will not stumble. PROVERBS 3:21-23

Discernment enhances the quality of your life. Godly wisdom and understanding keep you from tripping over the lies and deceptions Satan throws at you.

How can I become more discerning?

Your commandments give me understanding; no wonder I hate every false way of life. PSALM 119:104

God is the source of truth and wisdom. The more you read and study his Word, the more discerning you will become.

We have received God's Spirit (not the world's spirit), so we can know the wonderful things God has freely given us. When we tell you these things, we do not use words that come from human wisdom. Instead, we speak words given to us by the Spirit, using the Spirit's words to explain spiritual truths. . . . Only those who are spiritual can understand what the Spirit means. Those who are spiritual can evaluate all things . . . for we have the mind of Christ. 1 CORINTHIANS 2:12-16

The Holy Spirit, who is called the Advocate in Scripture, promises to guide you to recognize God's truth. The more you know the Holy Spirit and allow yourself to be guided by him, the more discerning you will become.

Don't copy the behavior and customs of this world, but let God transform you into a new person by changing the way you think. Then you will learn to know God's will for you, which is good and pleasing and perfect. ROMANS 12:2

The more you try to mirror the mind of Christ, the more discerning you will become.

What are some characteristics of discerning people?
The wisdom from above is first of all pure. It is also peace loving, gentle at all times, and willing to yield to others. It is full of mercy and good deeds. It shows no favoritism and is always sincere. JAMES 3:17

Discerning people demonstrate peace, love and gentleness, mercy and goodness—characteristics that come from God.

If you punish a mocker, the simpleminded will learn a lesson; if you correct the wise, they will be all the wiser. PROVERBS 19:25

Discerning people listen to counsel and learn from reproof.

Let the wise listen to these proverbs and become even wiser. Let those with understanding receive guidance PROVERBS 1:5

Intelligent people are always ready to learn. Their ears are open for knowledge. PROVERBS 18:15

Discerning people grow in wisdom as they listen to God.

What are some of the benefits of discernment?
Oh, the joys of those who do not follow the advice of the wicked. . . . They are like trees planted along the riverbank, bearing fruit each season. Their leaves never wither, and they prosper in all they do. PSALM 1:1-3

Discernment helps you become spiritually mature as you grasp God's truth more clearly and better understand his plan for you.

The king appointed Daniel to a high position and gave him many valuable gifts. He made Daniel ruler over the whole province of Babylon, as well as chief over all his wise men. DANIEL 2:48

Those with discernment often rise to leadership.

With their words, the godless destroy their friends, but knowledge will rescue the righteous. PROVERBS 11:9

A house is built by wisdom and becomes strong through good sense. PROVERBS 24:3

Discernment is healthy for relationships.

I will teach you wisdom's ways and lead you in straight paths. When you walk, you won't be held back; when you run, you won't stumble. PROVERBS 4:11-12

Wisdom will multiply your days and add years to your life. PROVERBS 9:11

Discernment leads to a blessed, full life because it protects you from harmful decisions that could lead to disastrous consequences.

DISCIPLINE *See also* Confrontation, Leadership, Spiritual Disciplines

Ask someone what discipline is, and you will likely hear the word *punishment*. But that is only a small part of the Bible's concept of discipline. Discipline in the Bible is more goal oriented—it is intended to help and motivate someone to walk in a closer relationship with God. We tend to think of discipline in a negative way—keeping someone in line or stopping bad behavior. But the true heart of discipline is positive—discipling others and helping people become followers, particularly followers of Christ. The emphasis is on loving guidance and teaching.

What are the benefits of discipline?

I used to wander off until you disciplined me; but now I closely follow your word.
PSALM 119:67

Discipline can keep you following God's Word, which will save you much grief and heartache.

Their command is a lamp and their instruction a light; their corrective discipline is the way to life. PROVERBS 6:23

No discipline is enjoyable while it is happening—it's painful! But afterward there will be a peaceful harvest of right living for those who are trained in this way. HEBREWS 12:11

God's way is the best way to live. But a life of joy, satisfaction, and purpose doesn't just happen; it takes a plan. Discipline keeps you on track—it is the light that helps you see the plan so you don't forget it.

What is the purpose of discipline?

Just as a parent disciplines a child, the LORD your God disciplines you for your own good.
DEUTERONOMY 8:5

My child, don't reject the LORD's discipline, and don't be upset when he corrects you. For the LORD corrects those he loves, just as a father corrects a child in whom he delights.
PROVERBS 3:11-12

The goals of discipline are guidance, teaching, and preventing harm to yourself and others, which in turn promote healthy relationships. Sin always damages your relationship with God and others because sin is selfish. God's discipline is an act of love to keep you from damaging your most important relationships and to help you become the person he created you to be. He wants to prevent you from becoming an immature, selfish person. On your own, you tend to move away from God and toward sin. God's discipline reminds you why a relationship with him is best. Disciplining children should have the same motive. Discipline in love builds character, but punishment in anger can destroy a person's sense of self-worth.

To learn, you must love discipline; it is stupid to hate correction. PROVERBS 12:1

Discipline is essential to developing skill, maturity, and character.

These are the proverbs of Solomon, David's son, king of Israel. . . . Their purpose is to teach people to live disciplined and successful lives, to help them do what is right, just, and fair. PROVERBS 1:1, 3

The biblical concept of discipline is summarized in the introduction to the book of Proverbs. As Solomon wrote Proverbs to disciple his people—to teach them how to live, to act, and to be just and fair—so God wrote his Word to disciple you in the way he wants you to live.

How does God discipline his children?

As you endure this divine discipline, remember that God is treating you as his own children. Who ever heard of a child who is never disciplined by its father? HEBREWS 12:7

He disciplines you as a loving father.

I know, O LORD, that your regulations are fair; you disciplined me because I needed it. PSALM 119:75

He disciplines you when you need it.

Lord, your discipline is good, for it leads to life and health. You restore my health and allow me to live! ISAIAH 38:16

He disciplines you when you need restoration.

When we are judged by the Lord, we are being disciplined so that we will not be condemned along with the world. 1 CORINTHIANS 11:32

He disciplines you to keep you from being condemned.

How should I discipline my children?

Those who spare the rod of discipline hate their children. Those who love their children care enough to discipline them. PROVERBS 13:24

Discipline your children with love. Discipline is about relationships, not rules. It is about safety, not retaliation. Your goal is restoration, not revenge; teaching and redeeming trust, not taunting.

Discipline your children while there is hope. Otherwise you will ruin their lives. PROVERBS 19:18

Discipline your children when they need it—before it is too late. Proper discipline puts your children back on the right path. If someone wanders off a path, it's much easier to get back on it if it's just a few feet away. But if someone is far off the path, it's very difficult to find the way back. That person is in danger.

Fathers, do not aggravate your children, or they will become discouraged. COLOSSIANS 3:21

Discipline your children without causing discouragement. Discipline will bring conflict—your kids will probably get mad at you. But constant nagging that might communicate they are never good enough attacks their sense of value and worth instead of focusing on the problem at hand.

Our earthly fathers disciplined us for a few years, doing the best they knew how. But God's discipline is always good for us, so that we might share in his holiness. HEBREWS 12:10

Discipline your children with godly wisdom. Every parent will make some mistakes when disciplining their children. Since God's discipline is always best, we need to constantly seek his wisdom. Remember, God's wisdom comes from his Word and from godly people who know his Word and practice good discipline.

Could my troubles actually be God's discipline?

My child, don't reject the LORD's discipline, and don't be upset when he corrects you. For the LORD corrects those he loves. PROVERBS 3:11-12

No one can tell [Jerusalem] anything; it refuses all correction. It does not trust in the LORD or draw near to its God. ZEPHANIAH 3:2

Like Jerusalem in the time of Zephaniah, if you stubbornly refuse to listen to God or anyone else, you might be refusing the correction that could help you. When you get to that point, you are rebelling against God, and the only thing that will get your attention is his discipline. Stay open to God's correction in your life, trusting the direction he gives you through his Word and your brothers and sisters in Christ. Be careful, however, not to immediately assume that your trouble or someone else's trouble is God's discipline. If you are sincerely trying to follow him as best you can, there is likely another reason for your struggles.

How should discipline in the church be handled?

If another believer sins against you, go privately and point out the offense. If the other person listens and confesses it, you have won that person back. But if you are unsuccessful, take one or two others with you and go back again, so that everything you say may be confirmed by two or three witnesses. If the person still refuses to listen, take your case to the church. Then if he or she won't accept the church's decision, treat that person as a pagan or a corrupt tax collector. MATTHEW 18:15-17

If you have an issue with another believer—for example, you are convinced he or she has sinned against you or has fallen into a sinful habit—then follow the advice Jesus gives here. Remember that the goal of discipline is not to judge or condemn but to reconcile yourself with the other person so you can live in harmony. As difficult as this may be, it is better than the alternative that often occurs: cutting off the relationship due to anger or resentment, seeking revenge, or gossiping about the other person. None of these are healthy for you or the church.

If people are causing divisions among you, give a first and second warning. After that, have nothing more to do with them. TITUS 3:10

If a person continues in flagrant sin after repeated warnings, or if he or she is causing division in the church and refuses to stop, then it is appropriate to expel that person from the fellowship.

The man who caused all the trouble hurt all of you more than he hurt me. Most of you opposed him, and that was punishment enough. Now . . . it is time to forgive and comfort him. 2 CORINTHIANS 2:5-7

If a person repents after the church gives united disapproval, forgiveness and comfort are in order. Don't shut out someone who is genuinely repentant.

DISCOURAGEMENT See also Depression, Disappointment, Failure

Discouragement settles in when we are facing a problem or task that seems overwhelming, if not impossible; when we've really messed up and feel embarrassed or ashamed; when we work our hardest at something and still fail; when important relationships are strained; or when we have expectations for greatness, but our limitations won't let us achieve our goal. Many great people in the Bible faced discouragement. Moses felt discouraged as a leader when the Israelites couldn't get along. Job was deeply discouraged when he lost everything despite his faithfulness to the Lord. When we are discouraged, we can be in danger of giving up—on God, friends, family, job, even hope itself. It feels like everyone's against us and nobody cares. What was most important to us begins to seem trivial. Worst of all, we can't see the way back to joy and happiness. At this low point, we can either sink deeper in the mire of discouragement or begin to climb our way back out of it. The opposite of discouragement is encouragement; it is the antidote you need when you are down. God is your greatest encourager. Seek his help first. Then find others who can help you put things in perspective, face whatever brought you down, and plan the steps to recovery. When you begin to see a way out, your hope will return, and over time your joy will return as well.

What causes discouragement?

I almost lost my footing. My feet were slipping. . . . For I envied the proud when I saw them prosper despite their wickedness. PSALM 73:2-3

Discouragement can come when you stop looking at what God has given you and focus on the prosperity of others.

"I have had enough, LORD," [Elijah] said. "Take my life, for I am no better than my ancestors." 1 KINGS 19:4

Discouragement often comes after a great spiritual experience. Elijah had just been part of a huge miracle that proved God was greater than the gods of the false prophets. Despite that spiritual high, Elijah became exhausted and vulnerable when his life was threatened by Queen Jezebel, a mere human being.

Moses heard all the families standing in the doorways of their tents whining, and the LORD became extremely angry. Moses was also very aggravated. And Moses said to the LORD,

"Why are you treating me, your servant, so harshly? Have mercy on me! What did I do to deserve the burden of all these people? . . . The load is far too heavy! If this is how you intend to treat me, just go ahead and kill me. Do me a favor and spare me this misery!" NUMBERS 11:10-11, 14-15

Discouragement can come when you are overwhelmed by the constant demands and problems of others. You can even reach a point when your response to others is almost irrational.

As for my companion, he betrayed his friends; he broke his promises. His words are as smooth as butter, but in his heart is war. His words are as soothing as lotion, but underneath are daggers! PSALM 55:20-21

Discouragement comes when those closest to you turn against you.

Who is adequate for such a task as this? 2 CORINTHIANS 2:16

Discouragement comes when you feel that you can't get the job done; you're just not up to the task.

We think you ought to know . . . about the trouble we went through. . . . We were crushed and overwhelmed beyond our ability to endure, and we thought we would never live through it. In fact, we expected to die. 2 CORINTHIANS 1:8-9

Discouragement can come from the crushing burdens and heartbreaks of life.

How does God help me when I am discouraged?

Be strong and courageous! Do not be afraid or discouraged. For the LORD your God is with you wherever you go. JOSHUA 1:9

You can be encouraged because God is with you.

If the world hates you, remember that it hated me first. JOHN 15:18

You can be encouraged because Jesus has been through what you are going through.

I lie in the dust; revive me by your word. . . . I weep with sorrow; encourage me by your word. PSALM 119:25, 28

You can be encouraged when you listen to God speak through his Word.

He gives power to the weak and strength to the powerless. Even youths will become weak and tired, and young men will fall in exhaustion. But those who trust in the LORD will find new strength. They will soar high on wings like eagles. They will run and not grow weary. They will walk and not faint. ISAIAH 40:29-31

You can be encouraged when you receive God's power and strength.

Each one of you will put to flight a thousand of the enemy, for the LORD your God fights for you, just as he has promised. JOSHUA 23:10

You can be encouraged when God defends you.

May our Lord Jesus Christ himself and God our Father, who loved us and by his grace gave us eternal comfort and a wonderful hope, comfort you and strengthen you in every good thing you do and say. 2 THESSALONIANS 2:16-17

You can be encouraged when God comforts you.

As soon as I pray, you answer me; you encourage me by giving me strength. PSALM 138:3

You can be encouraged when God answers your prayers.

I am convinced that nothing can ever separate us from God's love. Neither death nor life, neither angels nor demons, neither our fears for today nor our worries about tomorrow—not even the powers of hell can separate us from God's love. No power in the sky above or in the earth below—indeed, nothing in all creation will ever be able to separate us from the love of God that is revealed in Christ Jesus our Lord. ROMANS 8:38-39

You can be encouraged by the assurance of God's love.

How should I respond to feelings of discouragement?

When the Egyptians oppressed and humiliated us by making us their slaves, we cried out to the LORD, the God of our ancestors. He heard our cries. DEUTERONOMY 26:6-7

When Hezekiah heard this, he turned his face to the wall and prayed to the LORD. ISAIAH 38:2

Turn to God in prayer, and he will lift you up. Prayer moves you into the presence of God, where you can be honest with him and share your burdens with him.

Job stood up and tore his robe in grief. . . . He said, "I came naked from my mother's womb, and I will be naked when I leave. The LORD gave me what I had, and the LORD has taken it away. Praise the name of the LORD!" In all of this, Job did not sin by blaming God. JOB 1:20-22

Humble yourselves before the Lord, and he will lift you up in honor. JAMES 4:10

Acknowledge God's sovereignty and how much you need his help.

I am deeply discouraged, but I will remember you. . . . But each day the LORD pours his unfailing love upon me, and through each night I sing his songs, praying to God who gives me life. . . . Why am I discouraged? Why is my heart so sad? I will put my hope in God! I will praise him again—my Savior and my God! PSALM 42:6-8, 11

Trust God's promise that he will bring good out of the bad. Let him teach you something important even from your discouragement. Never separate yourself from the One who can give you the most help.

Give your burdens to the LORD, and he will take care of you. PSALM 55:22

Let God carry your burdens when they are too heavy. This doesn't mean he will solve all your problems or take them away—that will happen only in heaven. But for now, God does promise to give you wisdom, strength, comfort, and the discernment to deal with your problems.

The LORD of Heaven's Armies says: All this may seem impossible to you now, a small remnant of God's people. But is it impossible for me? says the LORD of Heaven's Armies. ZECHARIAH 8:6

Let God do the impossible!

Stay alert! Watch out for your great enemy, the devil. He prowls around like a roaring lion, looking for someone to devour. Stand firm against him, and be strong in your faith. Remember that your Christian brothers and sisters all over the world are going through the same kind of suffering you are. 1 PETER 5:8-9

Recognize your own vulnerability to Satan's attacks and commit to standing firm against him.

Because of my imprisonment, most of the believers here have gained confidence and boldly speak God's message without fear. PHILIPPIANS 1:14

Look for opportunities to turn your discouraging situation into an encouraging testimony.

The one who endures to the end will be saved. MATTHEW 24:13

Think of all the hostility he endured from sinful people; then you won't become weary and give up. HEBREWS 12:3

If you give in to discouragement, you are defeated. Never give up—hold tight to God's promise of ultimate victory.

How can we help others who are feeling discouraged?

Jonathan went to find David and encouraged him to stay strong in his faith in God. 1 SAMUEL 23:16

Encourage them to stay close to God and focus on building their relationship with him.

"[The king of Assyria] may have a great army, but they are merely men. We have the LORD our God to help us and to fight our battles for us!" Hezekiah's words greatly encouraged the people. 2 CHRONICLES 32:8

Remind them of what God can do and wants to do for them. Encourage them with hope for the future.

A cheerful look brings joy to the heart; good news makes for good health. PROVERBS 15:30

Share an encouraging smile with them.

DISTRACTIONS *See also* Priorities, Procrastination, Temptation

When we get in a car, we usually have a destination in mind and the goal of getting there safely. On the way, however, there are lots of things that demand our attention: traffic signals, other cars, pedestrians, the radio, the kids in the backseat, the cell phone. All these things can distract us from our purpose of getting safely to our destination. Sometimes these distractions can cause us to lose control and end up in an accident.

Distractions interrupt every part of our lives, including our spiritual life. As Christians, we have a purpose: to be in a personal relationship with God and live that out in our daily lives. Many things distract us from doing that. God's enemies—that is, Satan and his demons—work hard to distract us. They try everything to get our minds off God and onto sin. It's called temptation. If they can turn our heads for even a minute, they put us in danger of swerving off the path of righteousness. Many other things distract us from our spiritual walk with God—our busyness, our "stuff," our problems, even the good things in our lives. If we are aware of these distractions, we can try to minimize them so we stay on course as we follow God. Think about some of the distractions that keep you from focusing on the road God wants you to take. How can you minimize them?

What is the danger of distractions?

Peter called to him, "Lord, if it's really you, tell me to come to you, walking on the water." "Yes, come," Jesus said. So Peter went over the side of the boat and walked on the water toward Jesus. But when he saw the strong wind and the waves, he was terrified and began to sink. "Save me, Lord!" he shouted. Jesus immediately reached out and grabbed him. "You have so little faith," Jesus said. "Why did you doubt me?" MATTHEW 14:28-31

Distractions take your focus off Jesus. You can be in the middle of doing great things, but if you take your eyes off Jesus for even a moment, you might begin to sink.

How can God use distractions?

One day Moses was tending the flock of his father-in-law, Jethro. . . . There the angel of the LORD appeared to him in a blazing fire from the middle of a bush. Moses stared in amazement. Though the bush was engulfed in flames, it didn't burn up. . . . "Why isn't that bush burning up? I must go see it." When the LORD saw Moses coming to take a closer look, God called to him from the middle of the bush. EXODUS 3:1-4

Moses was just doing his ordinary job on an ordinary day. God used a burning bush—definitely a distraction—to get Moses' attention. God had a much bigger job that he wanted Moses to accomplish.

As he was approaching Damascus . . . a light from heaven suddenly shone down around him. He fell to the ground and heard a voice saying to him, "Saul! Saul! Why are you persecuting me?" ACTS 9:3-4

God sometimes uses distractions to get you to stop thinking about what you think is right and start thinking about what he says is right. Saul (later called Paul) sincerely believed that persecuting Christians was the right thing to do—he thought God was pleased with his actions. God had to get his attention with a dramatic distraction that changed the course of his whole life (and the lives of many others!). The more stubborn and passionate you are, the more dramatic God may have to be to get your attention.

How do I deal with distractions?

One day some parents brought their children to Jesus so he could lay his hands on them and pray for them. But the disciples scolded the parents for bothering him. But Jesus said, "Let the children come to me. Don't stop them!" MATTHEW 19:13-14

As Jesus was starting out on his way to Jerusalem, a man came running up to him, knelt down, and asked, "Good Teacher, what must I do to inherit eternal life?" MARK 10:17

Distractions bombarded Jesus all the time. But he didn't see them as distractions; he saw them as opportunities to save the lost and to help someone in need. A distraction can become a divine opportunity to show someone the love and care of God. Sometimes God interrupts you for good reason. Don't miss a chance to help the people God brings to you.

Don't copy the behavior and customs of this world, but let God transform you into a new person by changing the way you think. Then you will learn to know God's will for you, which is good and pleasing and perfect. ROMANS 12:2

Mark out a straight path for your feet so that those who are weak and lame will not fall but become strong. HEBREWS 12:13

Some distractions are clearly bad for you because they take your focus off what you should be doing. You need to discern between a distraction that should refocus your attention and one that should not. If a distraction is mainly about you (it tempts you to do wrong or to shirk a commitment), then it is not a good thing. If a distraction is mainly about others (it allows you to help someone in deep need or it provides a teachable moment), then it is a good thing. If you set clear goals for how you will serve God and manage your day and then you focus on those goals, you will be less likely to get sidetracked by harmful distractions.

Select seven men who are well respected and are full of the Spirit and wisdom. We will give them this responsibility. Then we apostles can spend our time in prayer and teaching the word. ACTS 6:3-4

Stay focused on what you do well, and learn to delegate tasks that others can do as well as or better than you.

No, dear brothers and sisters, I have not achieved [perfection], but I focus on this one thing: Forgetting the past and looking forward to what lies ahead. PHILIPPIANS 3:13

Don't let your past distract you. Focus your energies on what you can do now and in the future for God and for others.

Our lives are in his hands, and he keeps our feet from stumbling. PSALM 66:9

Keep your eyes fixed on the Lord. If you don't stay focused on God, you let down your guard and make it easier for Satan and the world to distract your heart and mind.

DIVERSITY *See also* Differences, Equality, Prejudice, Unity

On a football team, diversity is just as essential as teamwork. The team needs blockers, wide receivers, running backs, a quarterback. Without players of different sizes and skills, the team cannot play the game well. The same is true in business: A company needs a variety of people with diverse skills—in accounting, sales, production, administration, shipping, and managing. The church is no different. It cannot function well unless there are preachers, teachers, custodians, administrators, musicians, decorators, and evangelists. Diversity is everywhere. We are diverse in skin color, ethnicity, religion, looks, skills, abilities, interests, personalities. Diversity demonstrates God's creativity in making us, and it can contribute to effective teamwork. Too often, however, diversity causes prejudice and hatred because we want others to be just like us.

The Bible tells us that diversity should be celebrated and embraced because God created us to be different in order to accomplish the variety of work that needs to be done. Although we are diverse, God created us all in his image. Men and women, rich and poor, slave and free—all have equal value in God's eyes, although all have different roles and gifts. We are unique in our individuality, but equal in our value. This is diversity at its best, welding differing backgrounds, racial origins, educational levels, and social positions into one team to accomplish the work God has given us. In Christ, diversity can contribute to unity of ministry and purpose.

Can diversity be consistent with equality?

There are different kinds of spiritual gifts, but the same Spirit is the source of them all. There are different kinds of service, but we serve the same Lord. God works in different ways, but it is the same God who does the work in all of us. . . . The human body has many parts, but the many parts make up one whole body. So it is with the body of Christ. . . . Our bodies have many parts, and God has put each part just where he wants it.
1 CORINTHIANS 12:4-6, 12, 18

Being equal does not mean we are identical. Diversity is part of God's plan for us today and for eternity. In God's eyes, we are all equal even though we are not all alike.

With so much diversity, how is unity possible?

There will be one flock with one shepherd. JOHN 10:16

We are many parts of one body, and we all belong to each other. ROMANS 12:5

There is one body and one Spirit. EPHESIANS 4:4

God is the creator of true unity. The presence of the Holy Spirit in the church brings unity and peace to any group of people.

DIVORCE *See also* Marriage, Reconciliation, Relationships

At the heart of divorce is the deterioration of a marriage relationship. One spouse (or both) fails to honor the other as someone of great worth. Christians have divided opinions on the issues of divorce and remarriage after divorce. Some feel strongly that a divorced person cannot remarry without committing adultery; others feel just as strongly that God's grace can cover even the sin of divorce, thus allowing for a new start. Somewhere in between are those who recognize the practicality of remarriage, especially for single parents who struggle to earn a living and raise children without a helpmate. A biblical perspective on divorce may be more helpful when we focus on how to prevent it rather than how to define and condemn it. We all see the painful consequences of divorce and the ripple effect of hurt that affects all divorced people as well as their families.

What does the Bible say about divorce?

You cry out, "Why doesn't the LORD accept my worship?" I'll tell you why! Because the LORD witnessed the vows you and your wife made when you were young. But you have been unfaithful to her. . . . Didn't the LORD make you one with your wife? In body and spirit you are his. . . . So guard your heart; remain loyal to the wife of your youth. . . . "For I hate divorce!" says the LORD. MALACHI 2:14-16

God sees divorce as wrong because it breaks a binding commitment that a man and a woman made before him. He was a witness at the wedding. Divorce tears apart what God bound together into one seamless piece. Divorce involves a conscious decision by one or both spouses to break this sacred commitment.

Some Pharisees came and tried to trap him with this question: "Should a man be allowed to divorce his wife for just any reason?" MATTHEW 19:3

The Christian wife brings holiness to her marriage, and the Christian husband brings holiness to his marriage. 1 CORINTHIANS 7:14

Both the Old Testament and New Testament acknowledge the reality of divorce (see Deuteronomy 24:1-4; Malachi 2:14-16; Matthew 5:31-32; 1 Corinthians 7:10-11). Despite people's best intentions and efforts, even among believers, divorce sometimes happens. But the fact that sin is powerful and inevitable is not an excuse for divorce or the actions that lead to it. Divorce is always wrong, just like every other sin. But another fact is also clear: Every sin can be forgiven. If you are divorced, you do not have to forfeit joy and blessing for the rest of your life. God restores sinners, no matter what the sin. When you recognize your sin, are truly sorry for it, confess it to God, and commit to living more like Jesus, he allows you to move on. He forgets your sin. Be careful, however, not to use God's grace as a loophole for divorce. The expectation of forgiveness does not excuse sinful motives. But remember that God's grace can cover any sin.

What are some ways to prevent divorce?

As the church submits to Christ, so you wives should submit to your husbands in everything. For husbands, this means love your wives, just as Christ loved the church. EPHESIANS 5:24-25

Encourage each other and build each other up. 1 THESSALONIANS 5:11

Couples who love each other with the kind of self-giving love Jesus showed when he died for us, couples who seek to please one another, and couples who encourage and build each other up are the couples who will likely remain together in a happy marriage. The formula may sound simple, but the fulfillment takes some doing! Don't let anyone convince you that love should be easy. Sin is easy; love is hard work because it requires you to think about the other person more than yourself. But loving and serving others brings far greater rewards than just living for yourself.

How do I deal with the bitterness I feel from divorce?

When you are praying, first forgive anyone you are holding a grudge against, so that your Father in heaven will forgive your sins, too. MARK 11:25

Get rid of all bitterness . . . forgiving one another, just as God through Christ has forgiven you. EPHESIANS 4:31-32

Look after each other so that none of you fails to receive the grace of God. Watch out that no poisonous root of bitterness grows up to trouble you, corrupting many. HEBREWS 12:15

If you are a victim of divorce, you may have been hurt badly, you may have been treated unjustly, or you may have been humiliated. But if you allow bitterness to fester and grow, it will overshadow all you do and render you useless for effectively serving God. Only forgiveness can get rid of bitterness. Then God's Holy Spirit can continue to work in your life and help you start over.

How can I forgive someone who has hurt me so deeply?

Make allowance for each other's faults, and forgive anyone who offends you. Remember, the Lord forgave you, so you must forgive others. COLOSSIANS 3:13

All of you should be of one mind. Sympathize with each other. Love each other as brothers and sisters. Be tenderhearted, and keep a humble attitude. Don't repay evil for evil. Don't retaliate with insults when people insult you. Instead, pay them back with a blessing. That is what God has called you to do, and he will bless you for it. 1 PETER 3:8-9

As Christians, we must strive to be more and more like Jesus. Therefore, you must do what he would do—and he would forgive. This may be the hardest thing you will ever have to do. Not only that, but you will still have to live with the painful consequences of divorce. Forgiveness is not easy, but it is necessary in order to move on. It also demonstrates that love, not bitterness or hatred, rules your heart.

Will God forgive me if I do get divorced?

He forgives all my sins. PSALM 103:3

May you have the power to understand . . . how wide, how long, how high, and how deep his love is. EPHESIANS 3:18

If we confess our sins to him, he is faithful and just to forgive us our sins and to cleanse us from all wickedness. 1 JOHN 1:9

No sin is beyond God's forgiveness, and you are never beyond the extent of God's all-encompassing love. No matter what happens to you, God can restore you to wholeness. On the other hand, God's forgiveness should not motivate you to get divorced or prevent you from doing the hard work of trying to restore the broken relationship with your spouse. God grants forgiveness to those who are sincere and are truly sorry for what they've done. If you approach divorce with selfish motives and a hard heart, you are not being sincere with God.

How can I love again?

He has told us about the love for others that the Holy Spirit has given you. COLOSSIANS 1:8

May the Lord make your love for one another and for all people grow and overflow, just as our love for you overflows. 1 THESSALONIANS 3:12

God himself has taught you to love one another. 1 THESSALONIANS 4:9

After divorce, trust is broken, and it may be hard to allow yourself to love again. But God is love, and his Spirit still lives in you. Allow God's healing love to wash over you. When you bask in his unconditional love, he heals you enough to love again. The more you appreciate and understand just how much God still loves you, regardless of what you have done or what others have done to you, the more his love will overflow from you to others.

DOUBT *See also* Convictions, Faith, Trust, Worry

To doubt is to be uncertain or undecided, to hesitate, or to consider something unlikely. It is an inclination toward unbelief. We doubt when we don't have enough information or enough faith to convince us that something is true. Doubts can be minor, such as uncertainty about the accuracy of a newspaper report, or major, such as a lack of faith in the claims of the Bible. Doubt requires resolution, for when we doubt, we have no clear direction. Until our doubt is resolved, it nags at us and causes us to feel anxious and disquieted. Working through our doubts, however, can be good for us when we end up with stronger convictions and beliefs.

Is it a sin to doubt God?

When doubts filled my mind, your comfort gave me renewed hope and cheer. PSALM 94:19

John the Baptist, who was in prison, heard about all the things the Messiah was doing. So he sent his disciples to ask Jesus, "Are you the Messiah we've been expecting, or should we keep looking for someone else?" MATTHEW 11:2-3

King David, John the Baptist, and many other biblical heroes struggled with doubt. God doesn't mind doubt as long as you are seeking him in the midst of it. Doubt can become sin if it leads you away from God to skepticism, cynicism, or hard-heartedness. But doubt is a blessing when your honest searching leads you back to God and greater faith in him.

"Did God really say you must not eat the fruit from any of the trees in the garden? . . . You won't die!" the serpent replied to the woman. GENESIS 3:1, 4

One of Satan's tactics is to get you to doubt God's goodness. Satan tries to make you forget all that God has given you and focus instead on what you don't have.

When I have doubts, does it mean I have less faith?

Abram replied, "O Sovereign LORD, how can I be sure that I will actually possess [this land]?" GENESIS 15:8

Many people in the Bible whom we consider to be pillars of the faith had times of doubt. This doesn't mean they had less faith, but their faith was being challenged in a new way. When you have moments of doubt, you are probably in new territory. Allow your doubts to move you closer to God, not further away from him. As you do, you will find the strength to trust God, and your faith will grow even stronger.

What should I do when I find myself doubting God?

The father instantly cried out, "I do believe, but help me overcome my unbelief!" MARK 9:24

Be candid and honest about your doubts. Pray that God will give you the confident faith you need.

Don't be afraid of them! Just remember what the LORD your God did to Pharaoh and to all the land of Egypt. DEUTERONOMY 7:18

[Jesus] said, "Why are you arguing about having no bread? . . . Don't you remember anything at all? When I fed the 5,000 with five loaves of bread, how many baskets of leftovers did you pick up afterward?" MARK 8:17-19

When you are struggling with doubt, take time to remember all the ways God has worked, both in the Bible and in your own life. As you recall God's track record, you will grow more confident that he will work in your present situation as well.

I will climb up to my watchtower and stand at my guardpost. There I will wait to see what the LORD says and how he will answer my complaint. HABAKKUK 2:1

Be patient. Let God answer your questions on his schedule, not yours. Don't throw away your faith just because God doesn't resolve your doubt immediately.

Encourage each other and build each other up, just as you are already doing. 1 THESSALONIANS 5:11

When you are wrestling with doubt, keep attending church, and stay close to other Christians. Resist the temptation to isolate yourself, for that will only weaken your faith more.

Does my doubt keep God from helping me?

Jesus immediately reached out and grabbed [Peter]. "You have so little faith," Jesus said. "Why did you doubt me?" MATTHEW 14:31

When Peter was walking on the water toward Jesus, he was overcome by doubt. But Jesus did not punish Peter or let him drown. He saved him. Doubt can be the place where you begin to admit your weaknesses and grow in your faith. Let your doubts drive you to the Word of God and draw you into a deeper relationship with him.

DREAMS/VISIONS *See also* Discernment, Guidance, Vision

You wake up in a cold sweat, a terrifying and vivid dream still swirling in your head. Was it a message from God, a reaction to a recent event, or just a normal part of sleep? We know from scientific studies that every human being dreams while sleeping. (When a dream comes to a person while they are awake, it is called a vision.) Dreaming seems to be the mind's way of sorting through life's events and stresses. But is it possible that some dreams are God's way of telling you something? The Bible tells several stories of God communicating to people through dreams. It was clear to the dreamer that God had spoken, and the unfolding of future events verified the accuracy of the dream. Because of this, we can assume that God could still choose to communicate to us through dreams. He might use a dream to motivate us to action, to warn us, or to change our attitude about something. Many people today are certain that God has communicated to them through dreams. But since dreams and visions are so mysterious in nature, it is hard to know whether or not they are from God. You should exercise great care when trying to determine if God is telling you something in a dream. Although it is certainly possible for God to communicate to us in dreams, it is important to realize that most dreams are not of supernatural origin.

Does God still speak to people through dreams?

"In the last days," God says, "I will pour out my Spirit upon all people. Your sons and daughters will prophesy. Your young men will see visions, and your old men will dream dreams." ACTS 2:17

The phrase "last days" means the time leading up to the return of Jesus Christ. Some scholars believe that "last days" refers to the entire time between Christ's first and second comings, which of course includes our present time. Others believe it refers only to the few years prior to Christ's return and his final judgment. Regardless of which interpretation is correct, this verse clearly indicates that God has not finished communicating to his people through dreams.

Why would God communicate to me in a dream?

That night Paul had a vision: A man from Macedonia in northern Greece was standing there, pleading with him, "Come over to Macedonia and help us!" So we decided to leave for Macedonia at once, having concluded that God was calling us to preach the Good News there. ACTS 16:9-10

God could use a dream when he needs a special way to get your attention, perhaps when he wants to give you specific directions. The Holy Spirit had kept Paul and his companions from going to Asia or Bithynia (see Acts 16:6-7). They were probably confused as to where they were to go to preach the Good News. It was clear from this vision that the Holy Spirit was guiding them to Macedonia, where they would be most productive in the Lord's work.

As [Jacob] slept, he dreamed of a stairway. . . . At the top of the stairway stood the LORD, and he said, "I am the LORD, the God of your grandfather Abraham, and the God of your father, Isaac. The ground you are lying on belongs to you. I am giving it to you and your descendants. Your descendants will be as numerous as the dust of the earth! . . . I will not leave you until I have finished giving you everything I have promised you." GENESIS 28:12-15

God could use a dream to encourage you, as he did Jacob, and remind you of his presence and his promises. Jacob's dream contained no new revelation from God, but it confirmed important knowledge.

How can I know if a dream or vision is from God?
Plans go wrong for lack of advice; many advisers bring success. PROVERBS 15:22

You should consult wise and mature believers to help you interpret a dream. Even then, only time will tell if it is truly from the Lord.

All Scripture is inspired by God and is useful to teach us what is true and to make us realize what is wrong in our lives. It corrects us when we are wrong and teaches us to do what is right. 2 TIMOTHY 3:16

The Word of God is authoritative. No dream from God would ever contradict the clear teaching and intent of the Scriptures. No dream should be given the same authority as the Word of God or should be considered a new word from God. Thus, a dream can only confirm what you know from God's Word to be true or untrue.

DRINKING/DRUNKENNESS *See also* Abstinence, Addiction, Temptation

The difference between having a drink and becoming drunk is a matter of control. Drinking becomes a problem when we get drunk or lose control of what we say or do. Any drinking that impairs your thinking or your behavior is wrong. When drinking dominates your thoughts, dictates your schedule, or becomes an essential part of your day, then you have lost control to the power of alcohol. The Bible teaches us that self-control is one of the ingredients of right living. When we sacrifice self-control for self-indulgence, we sacrifice our safety, our reputation, our relationships with others, and our relationship with God. If you struggle with drinking (or know someone who does), it is critical to get help. You are letting alcohol control you. However, God promises that when we recognize our problems and ask him to control our thoughts and actions, he will give us the strength and power we need to resist temptation and regain control of our lives.

Is it wrong for Christians to drink?
If what I eat causes another believer to sin, I will never eat meat again as long as I live— for I don't want to cause another believer to stumble. 1 CORINTHIANS 8:13

Don't be drunk with wine, because that will ruin your life. Instead, be filled with the Holy Spirit. EPHESIANS 5:18

The Bible does not say that having a drink is wrong, but it clearly says that being drunk is. The Bible also encourages you to abstain from drinking in front of others if it might cause them to stumble in their faith. It is more important to help others grow in their walk with the Lord than to try to show that drinking does not hurt your own walk with the Lord.

"The time will come," says the LORD, "when the grain and grapes will grow faster than they can be harvested. Then the terraced vineyards on the hills of Israel will drip with sweet wine!" AMOS 9:13

After supper he took another cup of wine and said, "This cup is the new covenant between God and his people—an agreement confirmed with my blood, which is poured out as a sacrifice for you." LUKE 22:20

Don't drink only water. You ought to drink a little wine for the sake of your stomach because you are sick so often. 1 TIMOTHY 5:23

Both Jesus and Paul drank wine and gave it to others to drink. If it was absolutely wrong (like adultery, for example), they would have abstained and likely would have taught against it. The Bible also talks about drinking wine on the new earth after Jesus returns to live among us.

When does drinking become wrong?
The people got up early the next morning to sacrifice burnt offerings and peace offerings. After this, they celebrated with feasting and drinking, and they indulged in pagan revelry. EXODUS 32:6

Who has anguish? Who has sorrow? Who is always fighting? Who is always complaining? Who has unnecessary bruises? Who has bloodshot eyes? It is the one who spends long hours in the taverns, trying out new drinks. Don't gaze at the wine, seeing how red it is, how it sparkles in the cup, how smoothly it goes down. For in the end it bites like a poisonous snake; it stings like a viper. PROVERBS 23:29-32

Drinking becomes wrong when it leads to drunkenness, when it influences your thoughts or actions, when it causes others to stumble, or when it causes you to disobey and dishonor God.

I'm addicted to alcohol. Can God help me?
The temptations in your life are no different from what others experience. And God is faithful. He will not allow the temptation to be more than you can stand. When you are tempted, he will show you a way out so that you can endure. 1 CORINTHIANS 10:13

Anyone who belongs to Christ has become a new person. The old life is gone; a new life has begun! 2 CORINTHIANS 5:17

God can and does help anyone who is trapped by an addiction when that person confesses the sin, calls upon him for help, and follows his ways. God helps by showing you how to rely on the power of the Holy Spirit, by showing you the principles of self-control found in his Word, and by guiding you to other believers and counselors who can help you combat your addiction.

DRUGS *See also* Addiction, Habits, Self-Control, Temptation

Although the Bible does not talk about drugs in the sense that we talk about them today, it has a lot to say about behavior that is dangerous, addictive, and harmful to our bodies. God makes it clear that our bodies are not our own to do with them whatever we want; they belong to him. Putting anything into our bodies that could potentially harm them is wrong—it not only harms us, but it impairs our ability to have a relationship with God. It jeopardizes our safety and the safety of others. The Bible also teaches that wasteful behavior is foolish and unproductive, not to mention that it sets a bad example for others who look up to us. Everything we have—time, money, talent, resources, relationships, physical and emotional well-being—is entrusted to us by God. Whenever we abuse those gifts or use them for self-gratification, we are being selfish, wasteful, and disobedient to God. Drug addiction never affects just you; it affects everyone around you. Despite all this, the Bible also says that God offers hope, help, forgiveness, and recovery to those who are addicted to drugs.

Does the Bible say anything about drugs?

You say, "I am allowed to do anything"—but not everything is good for you. And even though "I am allowed to do anything," I must not become a slave to anything. . . . Our bodies . . . were made for the Lord, and the Lord cares about our bodies.
1 CORINTHIANS 6:12-13

Don't you realize that your body is the temple of the Holy Spirit, who lives in you and was given to you by God? You do not belong to yourself, for God bought you with a high price. So you must honor God with your body. 1 CORINTHIANS 6:19-20

Whether you eat or drink, or whatever you do, do it all for the glory of God.
1 CORINTHIANS 10:31

The Bible doesn't specifically mention the kind of drug addiction we're familiar with today, but it does address the problem of putting things into your body that harm it and impair your ability to function. Taking drugs to get high is a cheap substitute for the true joy that comes from being filled with and controlled by the Holy Spirit. When the Holy Spirit controls your life, your joy is authentic and contagious.

Some say that anything in moderation is okay. Can't that apply to drugs too?

They promise freedom, but they themselves are slaves of sin and corruption. For you are a slave to whatever controls you. 2 PETER 2:19

Whatever has control over you is your master. If God is your master, he will raise you up and encourage you, but drugs will only tear you down and make you a slave to their addictive power. Some things are not good for you, even in moderation.

EMOTIONS *See also* Attitude, Self-Control, Thoughts

Emotions are a gift from God. They are evidence that we are made in God's image, for the Bible shows us that God displays the whole range of emotions, from anger to love to zeal. But like any gift from God, we can misuse our emotions. Instead of a blessing, emotions can become a curse. Emotions come from the heart, where there is a desperate battle going on between our old sinful nature and our new nature in Christ. Our new nature in Christ helps us use our emotions to reflect the character of God, which helps us love people in healthy ways. Our sinful nature, however, tries to get us to redirect and lose control of our emotions so we lapse into behavior that is harmful to ourselves and others. For example, love can be a powerful force for good when it motivates us to care for someone in need. But it can be a powerful force for evil if we allow it to turn into lust or jealous rage. We must learn to control our emotions and direct them in ways that are productive and not destructive. The issue isn't an emotion itself, but what that emotion leads us to do.

Is it okay to show my emotions?

A funeral procession was coming out as [Jesus] approached the village gate. The young man who had died was a widow's only son, and a large crowd from the village was with her. When the Lord saw her, his heart overflowed with compassion. "Don't cry!" he said. LUKE 7:12-13

Jesus made a whip from some ropes and chased them all out of the Temple. He . . . scattered the money changers' coins over the floor, and turned over their tables. . . . He told them, "Get these things out of here. Stop turning my Father's house into a marketplace!" JOHN 2:15-16

When Jesus saw her weeping and saw the other people wailing with her, a deep anger welled up within him, and he was deeply troubled. JOHN 11:33

Jesus often showed his emotions. Letting others see your emotions shows how deeply you care.

He told them, "My soul is crushed with grief to the point of death. Stay here and keep watch with me." MATTHEW 26:38

Jesus was honest with his disciples about his deep emotions. You should also feel free to be open with trusted friends.

The king was overcome with emotion. He went up to the room over the gateway and burst into tears. 2 SAMUEL 18:33

It is not a sign of weakness to display your emotions. Rather, it is a sign of your humanity and an important component of your emotional health.

How can I best handle my emotions?

Guard your heart above all else, for it determines the course of your life. PROVERBS 4:23

The Bible says that "the human heart is the most deceitful of all things, and desperately wicked" (Jeremiah 17:9). Your heart is the center of the battle between your sinful nature and your new nature as a believer. It is also the center of your emotions. In other words, your emotions are constantly tainted by your sinful nature. This should make you cautious about trusting your emotions, because Satan wants you to think that your sinful feelings are always right. Guarding your heart means not allowing bad influences in. To effectively guard your heart, you must fill it with God's Word, which comes from God's heart so it is good and perfect.

I cannot keep from speaking. I must express my anguish. JOB 7:11

Keep an open dialogue with God and with others you trust so you are not covering up your emotions. Share your feelings with a few godly confidants so they can hold you accountable when you get off track and also so they can help you redirect your emotions from unhealthy expressions to healthy ones.

Many of the older priests, Levites, and other leaders who had seen the first Temple wept aloud when they saw the new Temple's foundation. The others, however, were shouting for joy. The joyful shouting and weeping mingled together in a loud noise that could be heard far in the distance. EZRA 3:12-13

A single event can produce multiple emotions. Try to understand that the feelings of others may be quite different from yours, even over the same event. Don't try to force others to feel the way you do, and don't be pressured to feel the same way others do.

I will give you a new heart, and I will put a new spirit in you. I will take out your stony, stubborn heart and give you a tender, responsive heart. EZEKIEL 36:26

When you let Christ control you, he will direct your emotions into healthy behavior.

Supplement your faith with a generous provision of . . . self-control, and self-control with patient endurance, and patient endurance with godliness. 2 PETER 1:5-6

It's hard to keep your emotions from controlling you (worrying too much, getting caught up in doing the wrong thing, letting anger get out of control). Don't deny your emotions, but don't let them control you or cause you to sin. Use the emotions God has given you to deepen your relationship with him, whether they are feelings of sorrow or joy, anguish or peace, anger or love, doubt or gratitude.

How can I keep emotions from controlling my actions?

When Haman saw that Mordecai would not bow down or show him respect, he was filled with rage. He had learned of Mordecai's nationality, so he decided it was not enough to lay hands on Mordecai alone. Instead, he looked for a way to destroy all the Jews throughout the entire empire of Xerxes. ESTHER 3:5-6

People with understanding control their anger; a hot temper shows great foolishness. PROVERBS 14:29

"Don't sin by letting anger control you." Don't let the sun go down while you are still angry, for anger gives a foothold to the devil. EPHESIANS 4:26-27

Some emotions, like anger, can quickly get out of control and cause you to do things you never intended. Don't let anger fester because it can overcome you. Deal promptly and rationally with the situation that caused you to be angry.

Get rid of all bitterness, rage, anger, harsh words, and slander, as well as all types of evil behavior. Instead, be kind to each other, tenderhearted, forgiving one another, just as God through Christ has forgiven you. EPHESIANS 4:31-32

Forgiving others who have wronged you keeps your emotions from becoming negative, bitter, or resentful.

He will rescue the poor when they cry to him; he will help the oppressed, who have no one to defend them. He feels pity for the weak and the needy . . . for their lives are precious to him. PSALM 72:12-14

Jesus replied, "'You must love the Lord your God with all your heart, all your soul, and all your mind.' This is the first and greatest commandment. A second is equally important: 'Love your neighbor as yourself.'" MATTHEW 22:37-39

Moved with compassion, Jesus reached out and touched him. . . . "Be healed!" MARK 1:41

There are times when you want your emotions to control your actions. It is good when they move you to do good things for others. When you are moved by compassion, act on that emotion by helping someone in need. When you are moved by your love for God, act on it by loving your neighbor as yourself.

The Philistines arrived and spread out across the valley of Rephaim. So David asked the LORD, "Should I go out to fight the Philistines?" 2 SAMUEL 5:18-19

They have made God's law their own, so they will never slip from his path. PSALM 37:31

Before you act on your emotions, check God's Word to make sure that what you plan to do is appropriate. Sometimes emotions can trick you. They move you to take an action that you think is good, but you later find out it was harmful to you or others. Before you act, check Scripture to see if what you want to do is in line with God's way. This can save you a lot of grief down the road.

How do I experience life's most positive emotions?

Letting your sinful nature control your mind leads to death. But letting the Spirit control your mind leads to life and peace. ROMANS 8:6

The Holy Spirit produces this kind of fruit in our lives: love, joy, peace, patience, kindness, goodness, faithfulness, gentleness, and self-control. GALATIANS 5:22-23

Life's most positive and healthy emotions are the fruit of the Spirit of God. The more you let the Holy Spirit control you, the less your sinful nature controls you. Then you will experience the benefits of godly living.

EMPATHY *See also* Caring, Compassion, Kindness, Respect

Empathy is more than feeling bad for someone who is going through a hard time. It is more than feeling glad for someone who experiences a success. Empathy is allowing yourself to feel the same emotions that another person feels. It's more like crawling inside another and experiencing that person's pain or joy. Empathy is a wonderful skill to develop because it allows us to gain a unique understanding of what another person is experiencing. It helps us find the best way to offer comfort and support. Empathy is one way to fulfill God's commandment to love one another. It is only when we truly seek to understand one another that we will be able to show love to one another.

How is God empathetic toward me?

In all their suffering [the Lord] also suffered, and he personally rescued them. In his love and mercy he redeemed them. He lifted them up and carried them through all the years. ISAIAH 63:9

We have a great High Priest who has entered heaven, Jesus the Son of God. . . . This High Priest of ours understands our weaknesses, for he faced all of the same testings we do, yet he did not sin. HEBREWS 4:14-15

God sent his Son, Jesus, to earth as a human being in order to fully experience the human condition. You can never say that God doesn't understand your hurt and pain, for Jesus suffered great hurt and pain. His heart breaks when your heart breaks. God created the full range of human emotions, and he has experienced the full range of human emotions. He understands your weaknesses, your fears, and your joys. But even more than that, God's empathy for you moved him to allow you to experience eternal joy, free from all pain and suffering, through faith in Jesus.

How can I be more empathetic?

God is our merciful Father and the source of all comfort. He comforts us in all our troubles so that we can comfort others. When they are troubled, we will be able to give them the same comfort God has given us. 2 CORINTHIANS 1:3-4

The more you experience the empathy of God, who is the source of all mercy and comfort, the more you will be able to show empathy to others.

Is there any encouragement from belonging to Christ? Any comfort from his love? Any fellowship together in the Spirit? Are your hearts tender and compassionate? PHILIPPIANS 2:1

You were cleansed from your sins when you obeyed the truth, so now you must show sincere love to each other as brothers and sisters. Love each other deeply with all your heart. 1 PETER 1:22

Let's not merely say that we love each other; let us show the truth by our actions. 1 JOHN 3:18

The more you realize your desperate need for God's mercy, the more you will understand the importance of showing mercy to others. As you recognize your own need for God's compassion, you should be moved to act with compassion toward others.

Share each other's burdens, and in this way obey the law of Christ. GALATIANS 6:2

Empathy involves vulnerability. To be empathetic, you must open yourself to sharing someone's pain.

Be happy with those who are happy, and weep with those who weep. ROMANS 12:15

Remember those in prison, as if you were there yourself. Remember also those being mistreated, as if you felt their pain in your own bodies. HEBREWS 13:3

Being empathetic is more than just being concerned about others' troubles; it is feeling what they are going through just as if you were experiencing them yourself.

Do to others as you would like them to do to you. LUKE 6:31

You can minister to others in ways you would like to be ministered to. When you don't know what to do, ask yourself what you would want someone to do for you in that situation.

EMPLOYERS/EMPLOYEES *See also* Authority, Business, Leadership, Work

Sometimes it feels like we need a degree in psychology to understand all the complexities of life on the job. One of the most complex issues at work is learning how to manage others while satisfying your boss. We have to juggle submission and authority, compromise and service. We struggle with hiring and firing, motivating and disciplining. The Bible has a surprising amount to say about employer-employee relationships. This advice will help you function more effectively in the workplace. The Bible is an important on-the-job manual for everyone who is employed.

How should an employer treat his or her employees?

Do not make your hired workers wait until the next day to receive their pay. LEVITICUS 19:13

Never take advantage of poor and destitute laborers. . . . You must pay them their wages. . . . If you don't, they might cry out to the LORD against you, and it would be counted against you as sin. DEUTERONOMY 24:14-15

Employers should always pay their workers fair wages, and do it promptly, because God expects fairness.

Boaz arrived from Bethlehem and greeted the harvesters. "The LORD be with you!" he said. "The LORD bless you!" the harvesters replied. RUTH 2:4

Employers can bless their workers by encouraging them and showing appreciation for what they are doing.

Masters, treat your slaves in the same way. Don't threaten them; remember, you both have the same Master in heaven, and he has no favorites. EPHESIANS 6:9

Though this passage speaks of master-slave relationships, the same principle applies to employers. Employers should not intimidate or threaten because they will ultimately have to answer to God for their conduct.

How should an employee respond to his or her employer?

No accounting of this money was required from the construction supervisors, because they were honest and trustworthy men. 2 KINGS 12:15

If you are faithful in little things, you will be faithful in large ones. LUKE 16:10

Employees should be completely faithful and honest in their work.

Lazy people irritate their employers, like vinegar to the teeth or smoke in the eyes. PROVERBS 10:26

Employees should work hard for their employers.

If your boss is angry at you, don't quit! A quiet spirit can overcome even great mistakes. ECCLESIASTES 10:4

Even if an employer is critical and overbearing, an employee should continue to do his or her best and strive to please God. At work, you represent God even more than you represent your company.

"What should we do?" asked some soldiers. John replied, "Don't extort money or make false accusations. And be content with your pay." LUKE 3:14

Employees should expect only what they originally agreed to. But being content with your current situation doesn't mean you can't take on more responsibility and authority; what it does mean is working hard and well and doing your best so that after work you can rest with a clear conscience.

EMPTINESS *See also* Loss, Meaning/Meaninglessness, Spiritual Dryness

Your car coughs, sputters, and finally stops miles from town—your gas tank is empty. A hiker drinks the last few drops of water from his canteen—there is nothing left, and he's miles from camp. A husband buries his young wife, wondering how he can go on and how he can raise his little children by himself—his heart feels empty. When a thing is empty—whether a gas tank, a canteen, or something else—either it's not going to work or it's not going to satisfy. But when a person is empty, motivation, meaning, and purpose are lost. There seems to be no reason to go on. Many things can cause us to feel empty—the death of a loved one, failure to get a promotion, the end of a friendship, being ignored or rejected. These feelings all have one thing in common: some kind of loss. Loss empties our emotional tank. We've used up our reserves, and now we're hungry and thirsty, looking for something to fill and satisfy us.

It is said that nature abhors a vacuum. The same can be said of people. When our hearts are empty, we try to fill them with something, anything—even if it's evil and destructive. That is the moment Satan waits for. He is always ready to move into an empty heart, to deceive us into thinking that what he offers can satisfy. Merely getting rid of the bad leaves us empty and open to even worse sin (see Luke 11:24-26). But when our hearts are filled with the love, truth, and goodness of God, through the presence of the Holy Spirit, there is little room for evil to enter. It is only through being filled with God's Spirit that meaning, purpose, and satisfaction are restored. Since God made you for a specific purpose, you will find true meaning only when you fill your soul with him.

Why does life sometimes seem so empty?

Don't go back to worshiping worthless idols that cannot help or rescue you—they are totally useless! 1 SAMUEL 12:21

They are all foolish, worthless things. All your idols are as empty as the wind. ISAIAH 41:29

Feelings of emptiness come when God is not filling you. This happens when something else becomes more important than him. God created you to have a relationship with him. When you push the Creator into a corner of your heart, you leave a big, empty space.

This is what the LORD of Heaven's Armies says: Look at what's happening to you! You have planted much but harvest little. You eat but are not satisfied. You drink but are still thirsty. You put on clothes but cannot keep warm. Your wages disappear as though you were putting them in pockets filled with holes! . . . Why? Because my house lies in ruins, says the LORD of Heaven's Armies, while all of you are busy building your own fine houses. HAGGAI 1:5-6, 9

Feelings of emptiness come when you confuse accomplishment with purpose. You may accomplish much, but it feels empty and meaningless if there is no eternal purpose behind it.

If I gave everything I have to the poor and even sacrificed my body, I could boast about it; but if I didn't love others, I would have gained nothing. 1 CORINTHIANS 13:3

Feelings of emptiness come when you live without loving. Nothing feels more empty than life without love.

Just as Death and Destruction are never satisfied, so human desire is never satisfied. PROVERBS 27:20

Feelings of emptiness come when seeking pleasure is your top priority. Pleasure feels good, but only for a short time. The more you seek pleasure, the more you need to be satisfied. The satisfaction is short-lived, lasting only until you need your next "fix." Then you are caught in a meaningless cycle.

Endless crowds stand around him, but then another generation grows up and rejects him, too. So it is all meaningless—like chasing the wind. ECCLESIASTES 4:16

Feelings of emptiness come when you seek popularity. People are fickle, and today's praises can turn into tomorrow's mocking.

How do I fill the emptiness inside me?

Don't you realize that your body is the temple of the Holy Spirit, who lives in you and was given to you by God? You do not belong to yourself, for God bought you with a high price. So you must honor God with your body. 1 CORINTHIANS 6:19-20

God is working in you, giving you the desire and the power to do what pleases him.
PHILIPPIANS 2:13

God created you to function best when you are filled with his Spirit. Only God can fill the emptiness inside you because he created you with a longing for him. When you invite him into your life, you will find true satisfaction and fulfillment.

When an evil spirit leaves a person, it goes into the desert, seeking rest but finding none. Then it says, "I will return to the person I came from." So it returns and finds its former home empty, swept, and in order. Then the spirit finds seven other spirits more evil than itself, and they all enter the person and live there.
MATTHEW 12:43-45

May you experience the love of Christ, though it is too great to understand fully. Then you will be made complete with all the fullness of life and power that comes from God.
EPHESIANS 3:19

When you accept God's gift of salvation and believe in Jesus Christ as Savior, you are filled with his Holy Spirit. The presence of God is within you, along with his love, help, encouragement, peace, and comfort. If you are not filled with God's Holy Spirit, your heart is like an empty home, waiting to be occupied by someone else. Satan is looking for empty hearts to fill with his presence.

Jesus replied, "Anyone who drinks this water will soon become thirsty again. But those who drink the water I give will never be thirsty again. It becomes a fresh, bubbling spring within them, giving them eternal life." JOHN 4:13-14

The thief's purpose is to steal and kill and destroy. [Jesus'] purpose is to give them a rich and satisfying life. JOHN 10:10

You experience life to the fullest when you are engaged in a relationship with Jesus Christ, who gives you blessings here on earth and the promise of eternal life with him in heaven.

Where can I find real meaning and purpose in life?

Don't be so concerned about perishable things like food. Spend your energy seeking the eternal life that the Son of Man can give you. JOHN 6:27

You find true meaning and purpose in life when you choose to follow God's way on earth.

Live happily with the woman you love through all the meaningless days of life that God has given you under the sun. The wife God gives you is your reward for all your earthly toil. ECCLESIASTES 9:9

You find meaning and purpose in life as you enjoy relationships with the people God has placed in your life.

Be strong and immovable. Always work enthusiastically for the Lord, for you know that nothing you do for the Lord is ever useless. 1 CORINTHIANS 15:58

You find meaning and purpose in life when God uses you to accomplish the work for which he created you.

ENCOURAGEMENT *See also* Affirmation, Comfort, Sharing, Support

When our strength fails and we grow weary and discouraged, we need someone to come alongside us, show us understanding, cheer us up, and inspire us to keep going. When bills pile up and money runs short, we need someone to help us, not tell us how we messed up. When friends or family turn against us, we need a good comforter. Encouragers help us regain commitment, resolve, and motivation. They inspire us with courage and hope. They help us love and live again. Encouragers give a beautiful gift, often a spiritual gift, when they bring renewal through their encouragement.

How does God encourage me?

Jesus turned around, and when he saw her he said, "Daughter, be encouraged! Your faith has made you well." And the woman was healed at that moment. MATTHEW 9:22

He heals your wounds and renews your faith.

[Elijah] went on alone into the wilderness, traveling all day. He sat down under a solitary broom tree and prayed that he might die. "I have had enough, LORD," he said. . . . But as he was sleeping, an angel touched him and told him, "Get up and eat!" He looked around and there beside his head was some bread baked on hot stones and a jar of water! 1 KINGS 19:4-6

He meets your needs so that you can continue to do good work for him.

As soon as I pray, you answer me; you encourage me by giving me strength. PSALM 138:3

He responds when you talk to him and gives you strength when you are weak.

I lie in the dust; revive me by your word. . . . I weep with sorrow; encourage me by your word. PSALM 119:25, 28

Such things were written in the Scriptures long ago to teach us. And the Scriptures give us hope and encouragement as we wait patiently for God's promises to be fulfilled. ROMANS 15:4

He revives you and gives you hope as you read his written Word.

How can I be an encouragement to others?

Jonathan went to find David and encouraged him to stay strong in his faith in God. 1 SAMUEL 23:16

Through your words and example, you can inspire others to stay close to God.

Don't use foul or abusive language. Let everything you say be good and helpful, so that your words will be an encouragement to those who hear them. EPHESIANS 4:29

Try to find something encouraging and helpful to say to whomever God might put in your path.

[An elder] must have a strong belief in the trustworthy message he was taught; then he will be able to encourage others with wholesome teaching and show those who oppose it where they are wrong. TITUS 1:9

Share with others what you've learned from God's Word.

A cheerful look brings joy to the heart; good news makes for good health. PROVERBS 15:30

Smile at others!

Haggai and Zechariah son of Iddo prophesied to the Jews in Judah and Jerusalem. They prophesied in the name of the God of Israel who was over them. Zerubbabel . . . responded by starting again to rebuild the Temple of God in Jerusalem. EZRA 5:1-2

Encourage people to get involved in serving God in some practical way.

I appeal to you to show kindness to my child, Onesimus. . . . Onesimus hasn't been of much use to you in the past, but now he is very useful to both of us. PHILEMON 1:10-11

Show others that you trust them.

I am certain that God, who began the good work within you, will continue his work until it is finally finished. PHILIPPIANS 1:6

Remind others of what God wants to do for them and through them.

ENDURANCE *See also* Commitment, Faithfulness, Perseverance

Endurance is often compared to running a marathon, a grueling race that covers more than twenty-six miles and seems like it takes a lifetime to finish! The goal in a marathon is to run the race well, to endure all the challenges along the way, and to finish strong and receive the rewards that come with finishing. Those who finish near the top get tangible rewards (trophies and cash), but all who finish earn the deeper, more lasting reward of immense satisfaction that comes from enduring and completing one of the toughest races on earth.

Life is like a marathon. Endurance is necessary to complete the journey well. And there are tangible rewards for finishing strong—an inheritance to pass to future generations, a reputation others can follow, a legacy. But the greatest reward for finishing life well is the prize of eternal life with God. Rewards are given to all who have faith in Jesus Christ and who endure the challenges of this life—persecution, ridicule, and temptations. Just as the marathoner must train hard and build up endurance to run the race and finish it well, so Christians must train and build up endurance to live a life of faith in Jesus and stay strong to the end. When we develop endurance, we will not collapse during the race but can push on toward the goal of becoming more and more like Jesus until we cross the finish line into heaven and receive all the eternal rewards he has promised.

How do I develop endurance?

Put on every piece of God's armor so you will be able to resist the enemy in the time of evil. Then after the battle you will still be standing firm. EPHESIANS 6:13

God has provided you with a wide variety of spiritual armor and weapons that can help you endure attacks from the enemy. You must put them on and learn how to use them. God's Word shows you how.

Let us run with endurance the race God has set before us. We do this by keeping our eyes on Jesus, the champion who initiates and perfects our faith. Because of the joy awaiting him, he endured the cross, disregarding its shame. Now he is seated in the place of honor beside God's throne. Think of all the hostility he endured from sinful people; then you won't become weary and give up. HEBREWS 12:1-3

You have the example of Jesus as your model for endurance. The next time you are tempted to give up, remember what Jesus endured for you.

Since we are surrounded by such a huge crowd of witnesses to the life of faith, let us strip off every weight that slows us down, especially the sin that so easily trips us up. HEBREWS 12:1

Be persistent about getting rid of sin, which drags you down and keeps you from enduring.

[The] vision is for a future time. It describes the end, and it will be fulfilled. If it seems slow in coming, wait patiently, for it will surely take place. It will not be delayed. HABAKKUK 2:3

Maintain an eternal perspective. Remember that in this life you will face many problems, but in the life to come, all your problems will be gone forever. This hope gives you endurance to go on.

What are the benefits of endurance?

We give great honor to those who endure under suffering. For instance, you know about Job, a man of great endurance. You can see how the Lord was kind to him at the end, for the Lord is full of tenderness and mercy. JAMES 5:11

God is pleased with you when you do what you know is right and patiently endure unfair treatment. 1 PETER 2:19

Endurance pleases God because it honors him and reveals his plan for you.

Be very glad—for these trials make you partners with Christ in his suffering, so that you will have the wonderful joy of seeing his glory when it is revealed to all the world. 1 PETER 4:13

Endurance makes you a partner with Christ in his suffering and in his glory.

Make every effort to respond to God's promises. Supplement your faith with a generous provision of moral excellence, and moral excellence with knowledge, and knowledge with self-control, and self-control with patient endurance, and patient endurance with godliness, and godliness with brotherly affection, and brotherly affection with love for everyone. 2 PETER 1:5-7

Endurance in your faith produces all kinds of good character traits. Endurance is like the fire that purifies precious metals and hardens valuable pottery. It cleanses, clarifies, and solidifies your faith. Living through the trials and tests of life allows you to discover the riches of your faith and develop godly character.

When we are weighed down with troubles, it is for your comfort and salvation! For when we ourselves are comforted, we will certainly comfort you. Then you can patiently endure the same things we suffer. 2 CORINTHIANS 1:6

Endurance encourages others to follow your example.

If I already believe in Jesus, why do I have to endure?

If we are faithful to the end, trusting God just as firmly as when we first believed, we will share in all that belongs to Christ. HEBREWS 3:14

Endurance is essential for Jesus' followers. Though you have the promise of eternal life, you also live in a fallen world that is out to compromise and destroy your faith. God promises that those who endure in their faith will not only survive, they will reign with Christ forever!

Where do I find the strength to keep going when I'm tempted to give up?

Let's not get tired of doing what is good. At just the right time we will reap a harvest of blessing. GALATIANS 6:9

When you feel like quitting, it is a sign that you are focusing too much on this life, not the life you will live for eternity if you endure. Endurance comes from keeping your thoughts on God's promises for the future, not the problems of the moment.

I am certain that God, who began the good work within you, will continue his work until it is finally finished on the day when Christ Jesus returns. PHILIPPIANS 1:6

I can do everything through Christ, who gives me strength. PHILIPPIANS 4:13

You cannot endure by your strength alone. God is at work in your life. He gives you the strength to keep going when you are exhausted and the faith to keep believing when you are discouraged.

In what areas should I develop endurance?

Be strong and very courageous. Be careful to obey all the instructions Moses gave you. Do not deviate from them, turning either to the right or to the left. Then you will be successful in everything you do. JOSHUA 1:7

In obeying God's Word. For you to grow in your faith and develop endurance, obedience needs to be consistent, not just when you feel like it.

I rise early, before the sun is up; I cry out for help and put my hope in your words. I stay awake through the night, thinking about your promise. PSALM 119:147-148

In seeking God's will and direction every day. Walking with God daily shows that your faith is real and has a lasting effect on your life.

We work wearily with our own hands to earn our living. We bless those who curse us. We are patient with those who abuse us. 1 CORINTHIANS 4:12

In responding to difficult people. As you deal with people who make your life more difficult, it is important to endure with patience, grace, and kindness. The only way to win people over is by patiently modeling the love of Christ to them.

Be truly glad. There is wonderful joy ahead, even though you have to endure many trials for a little while. These trials will show that your faith is genuine. It is being tested as fire tests and purifies gold. 1 PETER 1:6-7

In suffering through adversity. A life of faith will often bring persecution, hardship, and unique problems. Endurance through such times demonstrates that your faith is strong and genuine and can withstand any difficult test.

ENEMIES *See also* Evil, Persecution, Revenge, Spiritual Warfare

An enemy is someone who opposes you. He or she may dislike or even hate you for something you've done or for something you stand for. Whether our enemies are hostile nations or playground bullies, the Bible gives specific instructions for how to deal with them. No matter who our enemies are or how they've wronged us, Jesus tells us not to seek revenge but to love them and pray for them. That doesn't mean we should be a doormat and let them trample us, nor should we behave like them. Jesus himself stood against his enemies. He tells us to keep their best interests in mind and treat them as we want to be treated. When we find it hard to love our enemies, remember that we were all once enemies of Jesus before we believed in him. Yet he still showed his love for us by dying on the cross for our sin so that we could live forever with him.

Where can I turn when I feel overwhelmed by those who are against me?

You hold me safe beyond the reach of my enemies; you save me from violent opponents. PSALM 18:48

I, yes I, am the one who comforts you. So why are you afraid of mere humans, who wither like the grass and disappear? ISAIAH 51:12

Seek God's protection. He is strong where you are weak. He is your haven of safety when you are vulnerable and under attack. Be encouraged that you have the very power and presence of God defending you. Although your enemies may think they have you trapped, they underestimate the power of the One you serve.

Lead me in the right path, O LORD, or my enemies will conquer me. Make your way plain for me to follow. PSALM 5:8

Follow God's direction. You may be out of options, but he is the God of unlimited resources. Only he can show you the way to victory.

What does it mean to love my enemies?

You have heard the law that says, 'Love your neighbor' and hate your enemy. But I say, love your enemies! Pray for those who persecute you! MATTHEW 5:43-44

Don't repay evil for evil. Don't retaliate with insults when people insult you. Instead, pay them back with a blessing. That is what God has called you to do, and he will bless you for it. 1 PETER 3:9

Showing love to your enemies seems unreasonable—unless you realize that you were once an enemy of God until he forgave you. When you love your enemies, you see them as Christ does—people in need of grace. Getting to that point takes prayer. When you pray for someone, you can't help but feel compassion for them. This is how you can refrain from retaliating when someone hurts you, and this is how God can turn an enemy into a friend.

Love your enemies! Do good to those who hate you. Bless those who curse you. Pray for those who hurt you. If someone slaps you on one cheek, offer the other cheek also. If someone demands your coat, offer your shirt also. LUKE 6:27-29

Never take revenge. Leave that to the righteous anger of God. For the Scriptures say, "I will take revenge; I will pay them back," says the LORD. ROMANS 12:19

Respond to your enemies with forgiveness, no matter what they try to do. You should pray for them as well as show them kindness. Your words should be gentle. Your attitude should not be one of revenge or ill will. This is what Jesus would do, and this is what sets you apart from the rest of the world.

He was oppressed and treated harshly, yet he never said a word. ISAIAH 53:7

Don't repay evil for evil. 1 PETER 3:9

Sometimes your best response to opposition is no outward response at all, but simply to pray. If you repay evil for evil, you stoop to fighting on your enemies' terms and cut yourself off from God's righteous power. No matter how much opposition you experience, continue to do right and trust God.

Is it possible to turn an enemy into a friend?

I used to believe that I ought to do everything I could to oppose the very name of Jesus the Nazarene. Indeed, I did just that in Jerusalem. Authorized by the leading priests, I caused many believers there to be sent to prison. And I cast my vote against them when they were condemned to death. Many times I had them punished in the synagogues to get them to curse Jesus. I was so violently opposed to them that I even chased them down in foreign cities. ACTS 26:9-11

All they knew was that people were saying, "The one who used to persecute us is now preaching the very faith he tried to destroy!" GALATIANS 1:23

Every day, enemies of God become believers in God! It is a mystery why God seems to overwhelm some enemies until they turn to his side, as he did with Saul, and he seems to allow other enemies to continue to oppose him. But there are believers all around the world who once actively opposed God, God's people, and God's way of living.

Be careful to live properly among your unbelieving neighbors. Then even if they accuse you of doing wrong, they will see your honorable behavior, and they will give honor to God when he judges the world. 1 PETER 2:12

There is nothing more powerful and effective than an enemy who has become a friend. With love, forgiveness, prayer, and kind words, you will be able to turn some of your enemies into your friends.

How can my enemies defeat me?

Delilah pouted, "How can you tell me, 'I love you,' when you don't share your secrets with me?" . . . She tormented him with her nagging day after day until he was sick to death of it. Finally, Samson shared his secret with her. JUDGES 16:15-17

Do not let sin control the way you live; do not give in to sinful desires. ROMANS 6:12

Don't let this bad example influence you. Follow only what is good. 3 JOHN 1:11

The crafty Philistines knew they couldn't match Samson's brute strength, so they aimed at his weakness—seductive women. Temptation always strikes at your weak spot. "How can you say you love me?" Delilah whined, and Samson gave in. Your weak spots are those areas you refuse to give over to God. They are the joints in your spiritual armor at which the enemy takes aim, the areas in which you compromise your convictions for a few moments of pleasure. It is in those areas of weakness that you must ask God for the most help so he can cover your vulnerable spots with his strength. You must understand your weaknesses so you can arm yourself against Satan's attacks.

Are there really spiritual enemies—powers of darkness— trying to get me?

[The man] said, "Don't be afraid, Daniel. Since the first day you began to pray for understanding and to humble yourself before your God, your request has been heard in heaven. I have come in answer to your prayer. But for twenty-one days the spirit prince of the kingdom of Persia blocked my way. Then Michael, one of the archangels, came to help me." DANIEL 10:12-13

Jesus was led by the Spirit into the wilderness to be tempted there by the devil. MATTHEW 4:1

The Bible clearly teaches that human beings are involved in a spiritual battle, and faith in Jesus puts you right in the middle of it. You are in a battle for your very soul. You must recognize this fact and arm yourself, or you will be defeated.

We are not fighting against flesh-and-blood enemies, but against evil rulers and authorities of the unseen world, against mighty powers in this dark world, and against evil spirits in the heavenly places. EPHESIANS 6:12

The world offers only a craving for physical pleasure, a craving for everything we see, and pride in our achievements and possessions. These are not from the Father, but are from this [evil] world. 1 JOHN 2:16

Satan is alive and active, and his legions of demons are always on the attack. A battle rages in the spiritual realm—a battle you can't see, but one you will experience if you seek to serve God. You need God's power to stand strong and keep temptation from overcoming you. Since you do not always know or understand the evil that is threatening you, you need God's power to give you strength to face an unknown enemy. Have peace that God has already won the battle over death and has the power to save you.

In what ways does God do battle for me?

The LORD is a warrior; Yahweh is his name! EXODUS 15:3

This is what the LORD says: Do not be afraid! Don't be discouraged by this mighty army, for the battle is not yours, but God's. 2 CHRONICLES 20:15

The LORD will march forth like a mighty hero; he will come out like a warrior, full of fury. He will shout his battle cry and crush all his enemies. ISAIAH 42:13

Put on every piece of God's armor. EPHESIANS 6:13

Satan always defies God and wears down believers until they are led into sin. This gives him pleasure and greater power over the earth. But God is a warrior. A battle rages in the spiritual realm, and as a believer, you are right in the thick of it. God is always ready to fight on your behalf, always ready to come to your defense. He provides you with armor so that you can fight alongside him (see Ephesians 6:10-18). But you must join God in the battle, or you will be vulnerable and helpless to withstand the enemy. If you join with God, you are guaranteed victory.

ENVIRONMENT *See also* Stewardship

Fundamental to any understanding of God is that he is the Creator of everything in nature. Just as a human artist expresses his or her personality through creativity, so God has expressed his infinite glory and his character through Creation. The Bible teaches that because our environment is an expression of the person and nature of God, it is to be treated with deep respect. While it is clear that we are not to worship nature, we do show our love and respect for the Creator when we care for his creation.

What does the Bible say about the environment and my responsibility for it?

God blessed them and said, "Be fruitful and multiply. Fill the earth and govern it. Reign over the fish in the sea, the birds in the sky, and all the animals that scurry along the ground." GENESIS 1:28

The LORD God placed the man in the Garden of Eden to tend and watch over it. GENESIS 2:15

Human beings were created to share responsibility for the earth by being good stewards of God's creation. The first assignment God gave to Adam was to tend and care for the Garden of Eden, and he expects us to care for our little corners of the earth as well.

When you are attacking a town and the war drags on, you must not cut down the trees with your axes. . . . Are the trees your enemies, that you should attack them? DEUTERONOMY 20:19

Even in times of war, God is concerned about the needless destruction of the environment.

The land must have a year of complete rest. LEVITICUS 25:5

God's instructions for the people of Israel to let farmland rest every seventh year allowed for the conservation of good, productive land.

Let the fields and their crops burst out with joy! Let the trees of the forest rustle with praise before the LORD. PSALM 96:12-13

God created nature to proclaim his glory. You should do all you can to preserve this testimony for God.

EQUALITY *See also* Acceptance, Diversity, Fairness, Worth/Worthiness

One of the most encouraging messages of the Bible is that all people have equal value in God's eyes. How tragic that human beings have so completely abused this principle. In government, at work, and even in families, we tend to size up our place in the proverbial pecking order. Almost every great human tragedy, from war to slavery, has occurred because one group of people felt superior to another. We mix up the distinction between equality and roles. While we all have equal value, we do not have equal roles. God established families, government, and places of employment to function best with a leader. Leadership is vital to order, productivity, and teamwork. The problem comes when leaders abuse their authority. They start acting as though their superior position gives them superior value. When we fail to see others as equal in value, injustice and evil get the upper hand, and we devalue their worth in God's eyes. Justice and fairness begin with seeing everyone as equal in worth before God. Being a child of God outranks any other position or status.

Does God view all people equally?

God created human beings in his own image. In the image of God he created them; male and female he created them. GENESIS 1:27

The rich and poor have this in common: The LORD made them both. PROVERBS 22:2

All people are created by God, in the image of God. Therefore, all people have equal value in the eyes of God.

God loved the world so much that he gave his one and only Son, so that everyone who believes in him will not perish but have eternal life. JOHN 3:16

Adam's one sin brings condemnation for everyone, but Christ's one act of righteousness brings a right relationship with God and new life for everyone. ROMANS 5:18

God's salvation is available to everyone.

Remember that the heavenly Father to whom you pray has no favorites. He will judge or reward you according to what you do. So you must live in reverent fear of him during your time as "foreigners in the land." 1 PETER 1:17

God will determine punishments and rewards as he judges each person equally and individually.

How is there equality among believers?

There is no longer Jew or Gentile, slave or free, male and female. For you are all one in Christ Jesus. GALATIANS 3:28

Faith in Jesus unites all believers as equals.

How should there be equality in my relationships?

Do not judge others, and you will not be judged. For you will be treated as you treat others. The standard you use in judging is the standard by which you will be judged. MATTHEW 7:1-2

Be careful not to judge other people. You may not know all the facts of their circumstances. Just as you would not want others to constantly assess and evaluate you, refrain from doing so to others.

You husbands must give honor to your wives. Treat your wife with understanding as you live together. She may be weaker than you are, but she is your equal partner in God's gift of new life. 1 PETER 3:7

Husbands and wives are created equal. Although God has assigned different roles and responsibilities to husbands and wives, both have equal value and are worthy of equal honor.

ETERNITY *See also* Heaven, Hell, Presence of God, Rewards, Salvation

King Solomon wrote in the book of Ecclesiastes that God has planted eternity in the human heart (see Ecclesiastes 3:11). This means that we innately know there is more than just this life. Something we were made for is still missing. Because we are created in God's image, we have eternal value, and nothing but the eternal God can truly satisfy us. He has built into us a restless yearning for the kind of perfect world that can be found only in heaven. He gives us a glimpse of that world through nature, art, and relationships. Someday he will restore the earth to the perfection it had at Creation, and eternity will be a never-ending exploration of its beauty. Even more wonderful, we will have a perfect relationship with God for all eternity.

How should my hope of eternal life affect the way I live now?

Then [Jesus] told them a story: "A rich man had a fertile farm that produced fine crops. He said to himself, 'What should I do? I don't have room for all my crops.' Then he said, 'I know! I'll tear down my barns and build bigger ones. . . . And I'll sit back and say to myself, "My friend, you have enough stored away for years to come. Now take it easy! Eat, drink, and be merry!"' But God said to him, 'You fool! You will die this very night. Then who will get everything you worked for?'" LUKE 12:16-20

No eye has seen, no ear has heard, and no mind has imagined what God has prepared for those who love him. 1 CORINTHIANS 2:9

If the rewards of this earthly life were the only thing to live for, then a "why bother" attitude would be understandable. But there are two reasons why this perspective is mistaken: First, when you try to obey God, you put yourself in position to enjoy life the way it is meant to be enjoyed: Your relationships are more faithful, your life is full of integrity, and your conscience is clear. Second, this life is not all there is. The Bible is very clear that those who trust Jesus Christ for forgiveness of sin receive the promise of eternal life. Your faithfulness in this life may or may not result in material prosperity, but your rewards in heaven will be more than you could ever imagine.

If any of you wants to be my follower, you must turn from your selfish ways, take up your cross, and follow me. If you try to hang on to your life, you will lose it. But if you give up your life for my sake and for the sake of the Good News, you will save it. MARK 8:34-35

Those who belong to Christ Jesus have nailed the passions and desires of their sinful nature to his cross and crucified them there. GALATIANS 5:24

When you are absolutely convinced that Jesus died on the cross to spare you from eternal punishment and give you the free gift of eternal life, then the troubles of this world are put in perspective. You know that your future—for all eternity—is secure. This gives you peace no matter what happens in this life, and it changes the way you react to the troubles and trials life throws your way. Your sinful nature no longer controls you; you are free to live as God wants you to live.

Jesus told her, "I am the resurrection and the life. Anyone who believes in me will live, even after dying." JOHN 11:25

Be thankful in all circumstances, for this is God's will for you who belong to Christ Jesus. 1 THESSALONIANS 5:18

You shouldn't be too elated when earthly things go well, nor too distressed when they fail, because you know that even the best of this life is just a shadow of what is to come.

EUTHANASIA See also Death, Suicide, Timing of God, Worth/Worthiness

The debate about euthanasia often turns into a battle of human rights. In the midst of terminal suffering, is it more humane to preserve life or end it? When we seek answers to such questions, we must ask what the Creator of life says about the value of life in such circumstances. God makes it clear in his Word that purposefully ending a human life is an enormous responsibility with huge implications. It is a serious action to take someone's life in self-defense or time of war. It is even more serious to play God and decide that the quality of someone's life is no longer good enough to make living worthwhile. When considering the issue of euthanasia, think about these questions: Would God say that this person's life has no more value? Can anyone say beyond a shadow of a doubt that God's plan and purpose for this person is complete?

Why is euthanasia wrong?

You made me; you created me. PSALM 119:73

You made all the delicate, inner parts of my body and knit me together in my mother's womb. PSALM 139:13

I knew you before I formed you in your mother's womb. Before you were born I set you apart and appointed you as my prophet to the nations. JEREMIAH 1:5

God created you as a unique individual, and he has a perfect plan for your life. It is he who breathed life into you and he alone who has the right to decide when your life should end. Taking someone's life, even out of compassion, is playing God—it is assuming that a mere human being knows best when someone else's life should end. Taking away God's gift of life demonstrates a lack of respect for his ability to be involved in that person's life.

You must not murder. EXODUS 20:13

Rescue those who are unjustly sentenced to die; save them as they stagger to their death. Don't excuse yourself by saying, "Look, we didn't know." For God understands all hearts, and he sees you. He who guards your soul knows you knew. He will repay all people as their actions deserve. PROVERBS 24:11-12

It's not hard to justify almost any action, whether it is right or wrong. For example, isn't it better for a penniless father to steal food than to let his child die of starvation? Isn't it better to "pull the plug" on an elderly woman whose body is wracked with cancer than let her suffer? How you justify your own actions or someone else's actions depends upon what you value. If you value the idea that a person should not have to endure great pain near the end of life, then you can justify a lethal injection. But if you value God's sovereignty, you know that he has a purpose for everyone's life. Until God decides to end someone's life, it still has value.

Don't I have the final say over what happens to me?

You say, "I am allowed to do anything"—but not everything is good for you. And even though "I am allowed to do anything," I must not become a slave to anything. . . . Our bodies . . . were made for the Lord, and the Lord cares about our bodies. 1 CORINTHIANS 6:12-13

Your life was given to you for the purpose of glorifying God. His Holy Spirit lives in your body. When you do things that are not good for your body or that destroy your body, you are breaking down the temple where God dwells.

EVIL See also Enemies, Hell, Sin, Spiritual Warfare

Since the fall of humankind, the earth has not known a time without the influence of evil. We face an enemy far more powerful than any human foe. That enemy is Satan, the very embodiment of evil. His goal is to overcome good with evil, in your life and in the world. Although we cannot see Satan and his demons, we can see the destruction they cause in people's lives. Satan uses all sorts of tactics to try to take us prisoner for the side of evil. But God has given us very powerful spiritual weapons and armor to fight against the forces of evil (see Ephesians 6:10-18). If you want to be a mighty warrior and consistently overcome evil attacks, you must learn to use these weapons!

What is the goal of evil?

He will defy the Most High and oppress the holy people of the Most High. DANIEL 7:25

The goal of evil is to wear down believers until they are led into sin. This gives Satan pleasure and greater power over the earth and its people. He wants to get you to spend eternity with him instead of with God.

Where does evil come from?

You were the model of perfection. . . . You were in Eden, the garden of God. . . . I ordained and anointed you as the mighty angelic guardian. . . . You were blameless in all you did from the day you were created until the day evil was found in you . . . and you sinned. So I banished you in disgrace. . . . I expelled you, O mighty guardian. . . . I threw you to the ground. EZEKIEL 28:12-17

Evil began in the heart of Satan, once a mighty angel in heaven. When he sinned against God, he was expelled from heaven and now roams the earth, tempting people to sin.

Everyone has sinned; we all fall short of God's glorious standard. ROMANS 3:23

I know that nothing good lives in me, that is, in my sinful nature. I want to do what is right, but I can't. I want to do what is good, but I don't. I don't want to do what is wrong, but I do it anyway. ROMANS 7:18-19

Since Satan first convinced Adam and Eve to sin, all people have been born with a sinful nature. We are all literally infected with a spiritual disease that causes us to sin—to go our own way instead of God's way. We know this is true because no one has ever lived a perfect life (except Jesus, God's Son). So while we can work to sin less and to keep sin from controlling us, we can never—on this earth—eliminate sin altogether.

The human heart is the most deceitful of all things, and desperately wicked. Who really knows how bad it is? JEREMIAH 17:9

Your own heart, polluted by sin and selfishness, can be the source for evil thoughts and actions.

We are not fighting against flesh-and-blood enemies, but against evil rulers and authorities of the unseen world, against mighty powers in this dark world, and against evil spirits in the heavenly places. EPHESIANS 6:12

Cosmic forces of evil, led by Satan, are engaged in a deadly rebellion against God and against you personally if you claim allegiance to God.

If God is good, why does he let people do evil things?

The LORD God placed the man in the Garden of Eden to tend and watch over it. But the LORD God warned him, "You may freely eat the fruit of every tree in the garden—except the tree of the knowledge of good and evil. If you eat its fruit, you are sure to die." GENESIS 2:15-17

Genuine love requires the freedom to choose. From the beginning, God desired a loving relationship with us, so he gave us this freedom of choice. The alternative would have been robots, not humans. But with the ability to make choices comes the possibility of choosing your own way over God's way. Your own way always leads to sin, which breaks God's heart. Evil still exists, and evil people continue to do evil things, but you can choose to do right. And when you do, God is greatly pleased.

Why do people often seem to get away with evil?

Why are the wicked so prosperous? Why are evil people so happy? . . . Your name is on their lips, but you are far from their hearts. JEREMIAH 12:1-2

A day of anger is coming, when God's righteous judgment will be revealed. He will judge everyone according to what they have done. . . . He will pour out his anger and wrath on those who live for themselves, who refuse to obey the truth and instead live lives of wickedness. There will be trouble and calamity for everyone who keeps on doing what is evil. ROMANS 2:5-6, 8-9

Sometimes it seems that evil people do anything they want, and not only do they get away with it, they seem to flourish. God has promised, however, that in his time everyone will be judged, evil will be exposed, and the righteous will prevail. If righteousness always prevailed on earth, then people wouldn't be following God for the right reasons—they would follow God only to have an easy life. God doesn't promise the absence of evil on this earth. In fact, he warns that evil is pervasive and powerful. But God promises to help you stand against evil. When you do, you will receive the reward of eternal life with God in heaven, where at last there will be no more evil.

How can I combat and confront evil?

Hold up the shield of faith to stop the fiery arrows of the devil. EPHESIANS 6:16

The Spirit who lives in you is greater than the spirit who lives in the world. 1 JOHN 4:4

Every child of God defeats this evil world, and we achieve this victory through our faith. 1 JOHN 5:4

Your first line of defense is to draw strength from God, who is more powerful than your problems and your enemies. Your faith in God is like a shield that protects you from the temptations and afflictions hurled at you every day. Without a strong faith, the weapons of Satan and your enemies would find your vulnerabilities and defeat you. Even when life seems overwhelming, hold tightly to your faith like a shield, and you will be able to withstand the evil forces that come at you. Rejoice in the knowledge that God has already won the victory.

The temptations in your life are no different from what others experience. And God is faithful. He will not allow the temptation to be more than you can stand. When you are tempted, he will show you a way out so that you can endure. 1 CORINTHIANS 10:13

Don't give in to temptation. Sin separates you from God and puts you in the clutches of the enemy. Giving in to temptation puts you right in the middle of the road, where evil hurtles toward you at high speed. The next time you find yourself confronted with evil, get off the road of temptation before the consequences of sin run you over. God has promised to give you the strength to resist temptation.

Clothe yourself with the presence of the Lord Jesus Christ. And don't let yourself think about ways to indulge your evil desires. ROMANS 13:14

Surrender yourself to Christ's control. Don't put yourself in situations where you know your resolve for righteousness will be tested. The closer you are to Christ, the harder it is to be caught in the snare of evil.

Be strong in the Lord and in his mighty power. Put on all of God's armor so that you will be able to stand firm against all strategies of the devil. EPHESIANS 6:10-11

Your own strength is insufficient to combat evil. With the armor God gives you in his Word, however, you can find the strength and protection to win the battle.

The devil took [Jesus] to the holy city, Jerusalem, to the highest point of the Temple, and said, "If you are the Son of God, jump off! For the Scriptures say, 'He will order his angels to protect you. And they will hold you up with their hands so you won't even hurt your foot on a stone.'" Jesus responded, "The Scriptures also say, 'You must not test the Lord your God.'" MATTHEW 4:5-7

The devil has less power than you think. The devil can tempt you, but he cannot coerce you. You can resist the devil as Jesus did—by responding to the lies of temptation with the truth of God's Word.

You belong to God. . . . You have already won a victory . . . because the Spirit who lives in you is greater than the spirit who lives in the world. 1 JOHN 4:4

You must never forget that the Holy Spirit is great enough to overcome any threat against you.

When the Spirit of truth comes, he will guide you into all truth. He will not speak on his own but will tell you what he has heard. He will tell you about the future. JOHN 16:13

When you believe the truths taught in God's Word and live them out, you will have the upper hand in any battle against evil. You must be loyal to God and ask him for help. When you do this, he will give you discernment as well as protection against Satan and his demons, who are fighting even now for your very soul. The Word of God and the power of the Holy Spirit are the resources you need to overcome evil. Stand strong and confident in your faith, and be confident that God will help you fight and win your battles against evil.

It often seems like evil is winning the war. Is it?
Here on earth you will have many trials and sorrows. But take heart, because I have overcome the world. JOHN 16:33

It will appear at times that evil has the upper hand. But the Lord's power is supreme, and he wins the final victory.

The devil, who had deceived them, was thrown into the fiery lake of burning sulfur, joining the beast and the false prophet. There they will be tormented day and night forever and ever. REVELATION 20:10

He will wipe every tear from their eyes, and there will be no more death or sorrow or crying or pain. All these things are gone forever. REVELATION 21:4

When Jesus returns to usher in eternity, he will eradicate evil forever. No matter how bleak things may seem now, when you put your faith in Jesus Christ, you are on the winning side!

EVOLUTION

How did the earth come into existence? Where did the stars and planets come from? When did life begin? Have human beings always existed, or did we evolve and mutate from simpler life forms over millions of years? Many scientists have used the theory of evolution to answer these questions about origins—how things began and how they got to where they are now. The word *evolution* can be defined simply as something changing over time, and few people can argue with this broad definition. For example, there is no question that human beings from different ethnic groups look quite different from others; therefore, if we believe all people came from Adam and Eve, we also have to admit there has been a certain evolution of races and colors and sizes of people. There is no doubt that things and people change over time. These changes are minor but often obvious. The Bible has no argument with this kind of evolution. However, *evolution* is also defined as a process whereby all life, including human life, developed from inorganic matter by entirely natural means. In this definition, evolution involves major changes. Not only can characteristics within a species change (such as the height or skin color of a human, or the length of a finch's bill), but one species can actually change into another species (monkeys can turn into humans). This not only stretches logic and plausibility, it also directly contradicts the teachings of Scripture. When evolution walks out onto this limb, it gets into serious scientific and theological trouble.

God created human beings for the primary purpose of having an eternal relationship with them. He isn't interested in such a relationship with amoebas or snakes, with rocks or apes. He desires a relationship with humans, whom he created in his image with his characteristics. He didn't create a monkey so that it could become a person over time. He created a person with whom he can have a relationship. Once we come to grips with this profound reality, "evolution"—the process of change—can become a positive issue: We can focus on becoming all God wants us to be.

If things did not evolve, how did the earth and life on the earth come into existence?

In the beginning God created the heavens and the earth. GENESIS 1:1

More and more, scientific discoveries are supporting Creation as told in the Bible. Interestingly, the discoveries of modern astrophysicists have confirmed that the universe had a finite beginning. Scientists now point to strong evidence that all matter came into existence in one unimaginably powerful explosion of energy. Scientists often refer to this as the Big Bang. Unfortunately, most scientists won't acknowledge the source of this great beginning, even though the Bible makes it crystal clear. If the universe had a beginning, it stands to reason there must have been a creator. Something cannot come from nothing. The Bible teaches that God is eternal—that is, he exists outside of space and time. He chose to create the universe and its inhabitants as an expression of his love. God not only began life but continues to express his love to his creation through the gift of his Son, Jesus Christ, in order to have a personal relationship with humankind (see John 3:16).

God made all sorts of wild animals, livestock, and small animals, each able to produce offspring of the same kind. And God saw that it was good. Then God said, "Let us make human beings in our image, to be like us." GENESIS 1:25-26

The Bible clearly states that God made the heavens, the earth, and all that inhabits the earth (see Genesis 1:1–2:1). Plants, animals, and human beings may be different in certain characteristics and functions than they were many thousands of years ago, but a plant is still a plant and a human being is still a human being.

God created human beings in his own image. In the image of God he created them; male and female he created them. GENESIS 1:27

The LORD God formed the man from the dust of the ground. He breathed the breath of life into the man's nostrils, and the man became a living person. GENESIS 2:7

He is the Creator of everything that exists, including his people. JEREMIAH 51:19

God created human beings. Scripture makes a clear distinction between animals and human beings: Unlike animals, humans have the very spirit of God breathed into them, which gives them an eternal soul.

What does the natural world tell us about God?

God said, "Let there be light."... Then God said, "Let the land sprout with vegetation— every sort of seed-bearing plant, and trees that grow seed-bearing fruit."... Then God said, "Let lights appear in the sky to separate the day from the night. Let them mark off the seasons, days, and years."... Then God said, "Let the waters swarm with fish and other life. Let the skies be filled with birds of every kind."... Then God said, "Let the earth produce every sort of animal."... Then God said, "Let us make human beings." GENESIS 1:3, 11, 14, 20, 24-26

The enormity of the universe—now believed to contain at least one hundred billion galaxies, each with one hundred billion stars—reveals a God who is powerful. The complexity of life—the hundreds of amino acids needed to form a protein molecule, and the hundreds of protein molecules needed to form one cell, and the miraculous double-helix DNA molecule that encodes all the information necessary for living cells to be maintained and reproduced—all point to a God who is intelligent beyond human understanding. The multitude of forces, elements, and precise conditions necessary for life to exist on earth point not to a cosmic accident, but to a God who deliberately created the world, and created it for a reason—to enter into a relationship with his created beings. Creation speaks of a God who is both infinitely powerful and infinitely loving.

EXCELLENCE *See also* Abilities, Holiness, Perfection, Righteousness

Excellence is a new and higher standard. Not only do we admire and appreciate the characteristics that bring about excellence (hard work, skill, persistence, vision, knowledge, caring), but we also admire and appreciate the end result of excellence (beauty, quality, functionality, victory, teamwork, inspiration). Excellence goes beyond expectations—and it is rare for something to exceed expectations. God is the standard for excellence. He wants us to pursue excellence because doing so shows that we care about doing things right, that we care about helping people to the best of our ability. Pursuing excellence helps others experience excellence, giving them a glimpse of God and inspiring them to pursue excellence themselves. God initiated excellence in the beauty of his creation, and we are called to perpetuate it. We do this first by striving to accomplish God's purpose in our lives to the best of our ability. Our lives reach for excellence when we consistently strive to model ourselves after Jesus Christ, who was perfect, and when we go about the work he has called us to do. We'll never be perfect in this life, but as we work toward that goal, we will model excellence to those around us.

Where did excellence have its origin?

God looked over all he had made, and he saw that it was very good! GENESIS 1:31

The splendor of God's pristine creation before the fall into sin was excellence in its purest form. Not only was the end product excellent, but it was excellent in every detail. The glory of the Creator was reflected in the excellence of his creation.

Yes, there will be an abundance of flowers and singing and joy! The deserts will become as green as the mountains of Lebanon, as lovely as Mount Carmel or the plain of Sharon. There the LORD will display his glory, the splendor of our God. ISAIAH 35:2

All nature praises its Creator and displays a beauty of symmetry that surpasses expectations.

Why does God encourage excellence?

God looked over all he had made, and he saw that it was very good! GENESIS 1:31

You were created in God's image, so your work should be modeled after God's work. When God created the earth, he lavished his energy and creativity on it. Every detail was given his full attention.

I run with purpose in every step. I am not just shadowboxing. 1 CORINTHIANS 9:26

Excellence in the Christian life is an indication that you are striving to be like Christ, who was excellent in every way.

Sing your praise to the LORD with the harp, with the harp and melodious song. PSALM 98:5

Excellence is an act of worship.

How can I pursue excellence?

The LORD has filled Bezalel with the Spirit of God, giving him . . . expertise in all kinds of crafts. EXODUS 35:31

Recognize the gifts and talents God has given you, and use them to the best of your ability.

These men had an excellent reputation, and it was their job to make honest distributions to their fellow Levites. NEHEMIAH 13:13

Work hard to be someone with an excellent reputation who can be trusted with responsibility.

The LORD said to me, ". . . Take careful notice. Use your eyes and ears, and listen to everything I tell you." EZEKIEL 44:5

Follow the example of those who are going to inherit God's promises because of their faith and endurance. HEBREWS 6:12

Carefully watch the example of others as they pursue excellence—or even as they settle for mediocrity. Learn from the good examples, and avoid the bad ones.

What kind of life excels more than any other?

You should earnestly desire the most helpful gifts. But now let me show you a way of life that is best of all. 1 CORINTHIANS 12:31

This "best of all" statement introduces the great love chapter of the Bible—1 Corinthians 13. Of all the excellent things to pursue, love is the best. Loving God and other people produces a life of excellence because true love excels at helping others strive for perfection.

EXCUSES See also Assumptions, Blame, Denial, Lying

An excuse is a way to justify certain behavior. There are legitimate excuses ("I couldn't meet with you because I was sick"), and there are poor excuses ("He dared me to steal it"). Poor excuses try to rationalize improper behavior. When we find ourselves blaming others for our actions or lying to preserve our "integrity," excuses get us into trouble. It is far better in the long run to admit we've done wrong, seek forgiveness, and move forward.

What are some examples of poor excuses in the Bible?

The man replied, "It was the woman you gave me who gave me the fruit, and I ate it." GENESIS 3:12

Adam, the first man, made the first excuse. He ate the forbidden fruit, but he blamed Eve for offering it to him. He even indirectly blamed God for giving him "the woman." Then Eve blamed the serpent for convincing her to eat the fruit. Both tried to excuse their actions by blaming someone else. People started making excuses after the very first sin!

I told them, "Whoever has gold jewelry, take it off." When they brought it to me, I simply threw it into the fire—and out came this calf! EXODUS 32:24

Aaron's lame excuse for making an idol—something expressly condemned by God—was that it just happened! We often do the same thing, blaming our sin on circumstances beyond our control. But the Bible clearly says you are completely accountable for all your actions (see Romans 14:12; Revelation 20:12).

"It's true that the army spared the best of the sheep, goats, and cattle," Saul admitted. "But they are going to sacrifice them to the LORD your God. We have destroyed everything else." 1 SAMUEL 15:15

Saul tried to justify disobeying God's orders with the excuse that he did it in order to do a good thing. His life was a story of one excuse after another. Finally, he ran out of excuses and lost his kingdom (see 1 Samuel 15:26) because he simply wouldn't own up to his mistakes and admit when he was wrong.

How does God respond when I make excuses for my sin?

One day Cain suggested to his brother, "Let's go out into the fields." And while they were in the field, Cain attacked his brother, Abel, and killed him. . . . The LORD said, "What

have you done? Listen! Your brother's blood cries out to me from the ground! Now you are cursed and banished from the ground, which has swallowed your brother's blood."
GENESIS 4:8-11

Excuses for sin will not be overlooked by God. You can't hide from him, so don't bother trying. You are only setting yourself up for future judgment.

The heavenly Father . . . will judge or reward you according to what you do. So you must live in reverent fear of him during your time as "foreigners in the land." 1 PETER 1:17

Sooner or later you must learn to stop making excuses for your actions and start being responsible for what you do. Excuses are a cover-up, an attempt to make you look good when you haven't done good. Taking responsibility for your actions is the only way to stop the excuses.

Can anyone be excused for not accepting the Lord?

At the name of Jesus every knee should bow, in heaven and on earth and under the earth, and every tongue confess that Jesus Christ is Lord. PHILIPPIANS 2:10-11

People have all kinds of excuses for avoiding God—being too busy, procrastinating, blaming God for their hardships, not wanting to give up their favorite vices, or even not knowing where to begin. Do you think those excuses will hold up when you see God face-to-face?

Ever since the world was created, people have seen the earth and sky. Through everything God made, they can clearly see his invisible qualities—his eternal power and divine nature. So they have no excuse for not knowing God. ROMANS 1:20

Everyone has seen the testimony of nature, God's work, which the Bible says clearly reveals the hand of an almighty Creator. That alone witnesses to his presence and power. People who fail to come to terms with God are really without excuse.

F

FAILURE *See also* Limitations, Mistakes, Shame

To fail is to fall short, to not measure up, to feel reduced in stature, to disappoint, to break down, to fall, to not reach your goal or fulfill your purpose, to lack success. No wonder we are so afraid of failure! When it comes to failure, we must decide by whose rules we are playing. Would you rather be a success as a businessperson and a failure as a parent, or vice versa? Would you rather be successful in the world's eyes or in God's eyes? Now is the time to decide what standards of failure and success you will live by.

What is failure in God's eyes?

The LORD passed in front of Moses, calling out, "Yahweh! The LORD! The God of compassion and mercy! I am slow to anger and filled with unfailing love and faithfulness. I lavish unfailing love to a thousand generations. I forgive iniquity, rebellion, and sin. But I do not excuse the guilty." EXODUS 34:6-7

"I will put you on trial. . . . I will speak against those who cheat employees of their wages, who oppress widows and orphans, or who deprive the foreigners living among you of justice, for these people do not fear me," says the LORD of Heaven's Armies. MALACHI 3:5

Failure in God's eyes is not living the way he created you to live. God gave you the gift of life and created you to have a relationship with him. Your greatest failure would be to reject that life and the God who gave it to you.

How can I keep from failing?

Anyone who hears my teaching and doesn't obey it is foolish, like a person who builds a house on sand. When the rains and floods come and the winds beat against that house, it will collapse with a mighty crash. MATTHEW 7:26-27

Failure results when you disobey God's Word. The Bible is God's instruction manual for how life should work. It is the foundation that will keep your life from falling apart. You can prevent much failure by reading the Bible and building your life on its principles.

Joshua cried out, "Oh, Sovereign LORD, why did you bring us across the Jordan River if you are going to let the Amorites kill us?" . . . But the LORD said to Joshua, "Get up! Why are you lying on your face like this? Israel has sinned and broken my covenant! . . . That is why the Israelites are running from their enemies in defeat." JOSHUA 7:7, 10-12

At first you may not understand the true cause of failure. Joshua learned that the real cause of his failure was not a faulty battle plan but a greedy soldier whose deception brought disaster on the army as well as the rest of the people (read the whole story in Joshua chapter 7). This insight, however, only came to Joshua as he sought God's direction and counsel in assessing the failure. Don't underestimate God's desire and ability to show you when a spiritual problem has caused you to fail.

Plans go wrong for lack of advice; many advisers bring success. PROVERBS 15:22

Good advice helps prevent failure. A concert of wise counsel makes good music for success.

When I have failed, how do I get past it? How can I turn my failures into successes?

The godly may trip seven times, but they will get up again. PROVERBS 24:16

When you fail, you must get up again. Many of life's inspiring success stories come from people who failed many times but never gave up. Most important, never give up on your relationship with God, who promises you the ultimate success of eternal life.

This High Priest of ours understands our weaknesses. . . . So let us come boldly to the throne of our gracious God . . . [to] find grace to help us when we need it most. HEBREWS 4:15-16

Realize that God's work is not limited by your failures. He does not reject you in your weakness but rather embraces you so that you can receive strength to be all he intended you to be. When failure drives you into the arms of God, then it is actually a success.

Our earthly fathers disciplined us for a few years, doing the best they knew how. But God's discipline is always good for us, so that we might share in his holiness. No discipline is enjoyable while it is happening—it's painful! But afterward there will be a peaceful harvest of right living for those who are trained in this way. HEBREWS 12:10-11

Failure doesn't determine your identity or your worth; it is simply feedback on how you are doing. Because God has adopted you as his child, he uses your failure to train you, to reveal his love, and to hone your character. Failure is not a dead end. In Christ it becomes the doorway to positive and lasting change.

All glory to God, who is able to keep you from falling away and will bring you with great joy into his glorious presence without a single fault. All glory to him who alone is God, our Savior through Jesus Christ our Lord. All glory, majesty, power, and authority are his before all time, and in the present, and beyond all time! JUDE 1:24-25

Train yourself to live by God's definition of failure and success. The world defines success as an abundance of achievements and possessions, and failure as a lack of those things. God defines success as obedience to him, which results in love, godly character, godly living, salvation, and eternal life in heaven. God defines failure as rejecting him. When you live by God's definition of success, your failures will only be temporary.

Will God ever fail me?

The faithful love of the LORD never ends! His mercies never cease. LAMENTATIONS 3:22

You can always depend on God's love.

If we are unfaithful, he remains faithful, for he cannot deny who he is. 2 TIMOTHY 2:13

You can always depend on God's faithfulness.

Look up to the skies above, and gaze down on the earth below. For the skies will disappear like smoke, and the earth will wear out like a piece of clothing. The people of the earth will die like flies, but my salvation lasts forever. My righteous rule will never end! ISAIAH 51:6

You can always depend on God's gift of salvation and his eternal righteous rule.

Teach these new disciples to obey all the commands I have given you. And be sure of this: I am with you always, even to the end of the age. MATTHEW 28:20

You can always depend on God's presence.

The rain and snow come down from the heavens and stay on the ground to water the earth. They cause the grain to grow, producing seed for the farmer and bread for the hungry. It is the same with my word. I send it out, and it always produces fruit. It will accomplish all I want it to, and it will prosper everywhere I send it. ISAIAH 55:10-11

You can always depend on God's Word to be true.

FAIRNESS *See also* Equality, Justice, Sharing

Fairness is not the same as equality. Although we all have equal value in God's eyes, he doesn't give us all the same circumstances, the same talents, the same job, the same kind of family, or the same environment in which to live. Since we are all unique individuals, he treats us differently in order to bring each of us to him. But he loves us all equally, and he desires the same salvation for us all. Likewise, treating others with fairness involves weighing the circumstances and doing what is best for the people in that situation. We may not be able to treat others equally, but we do need to treat them with fairness, and we should strive to love and value everyone equally.

What is the goal of fairness?

The LORD gives righteousness and justice to all who are treated unfairly. PSALM 103:6

The LORD has told you what is good, and this is what he requires of you: to do what is right, to love mercy, and to walk humbly with your God. MICAH 6:8

Do to others whatever you would like them to do to you. MATTHEW 7:12

Fairness is treating all people with the same standard of love and justice. You make sure that goodness prevails, regardless of the advantages or disadvantages to you personally. Fairness is simply acting with no other motive than to do the right thing.

How can I treat others fairly?

When you are called to testify in a dispute, do not be swayed by the crowd to twist justice. And do not slant your testimony in favor of a person just because that person is poor. EXODUS 23:2-3

Try your best not to show favoritism. When you're asked to tell the truth in order to settle a dispute, tell it accurately and without bias. Avoid the temptation to hurt someone who doesn't deserve it. Also avoid the temptation to help a friend by withholding or distorting the truth.

Those who are honest and fair, who refuse to profit by fraud, who stay far away from bribes, who refuse to listen to those who plot murder, who shut their eyes to all enticement to do wrong—these are the ones who will dwell on high. ISAIAH 33:15-16

Anticipating the complete fairness that will govern life in eternity can motivate you to model that perfect standard here in this life.

Tell the truth to each other. Render verdicts in your courts that are just and that lead to peace. ZECHARIAH 8:16

The more you tell the truth and treat others fairly, the more you experience peace of mind and heart, and the easier it is to see each person as an equal.

How should I respond when life isn't fair?

You say, "The Lord isn't doing what's right!" Listen to me, O people of Israel. Am I the one not doing what's right, or is it you? EZEKIEL 18:25

Don't blame God for the consequences of your actions.

He will judge the world with justice and rule the nations with fairness. PSALM 9:8

His government and its peace will never end. He will rule with fairness and justice. ISAIAH 9:7

Recognize that God will ultimately triumph with justice and fairness.

The LORD loves justice, and he will never abandon the godly. He will keep them safe forever. PSALM 37:28

Your final vindication will be through God's efforts, not your own.

FAITH *See also* Faithfulness, Hope, Salvation, Trust

Faith is more than just believing; it is trusting our very lives to what we believe. For example, we may believe that someone can walk across a deep gorge on a tightrope. But are we willing to trust that person to carry us across? Faith would say yes. Faith in God means that we are willing to trust him with our very lives. We are willing to follow his guidelines for living as outlined in the Bible because we have the conviction that his will is best for us. We are even willing to endure ridicule and persecution for our faith because we are so sure that God is who he says he is and will keep his promises about salvation and eternal life in heaven.

Faith seems so complicated; how can I ever get it?

Jesus overheard them and said to Jairus, "Don't be afraid. Just have faith." MARK 5:36

Too often we make faith difficult, but that wasn't what Jesus intended. Faith isn't complicated. It is simply trusting Jesus to do what he has promised.

I have calmed and quieted myself, like a weaned child who no longer cries for its mother's milk. Yes, like a weaned child is my soul within me. PSALM 131:2

It is not hard for little children to have faith. They simply believe with calm assurance that their parents will provide and protect them. You can have this same uncomplicated trust in God.

Why should I have faith in God?

I tell you the truth, those who listen to my message and believe in God who sent me have eternal life. JOHN 5:24

According to God's own words, faith in him is the only way to heaven. It is the only doorway to eternal life. The One who created heaven clearly tells us how to get there.

Faith is the confidence that what we hope for will actually happen. HEBREWS 11:1

Faith gives you hope. When the world seems to be a crazy, mixed-up place, believers can be absolutely confident that one day Jesus will come and make it right again. Your faith in his promise to do that someday will allow you to keep going today.

How can I strengthen my faith?

The LORD had said to Abram, "Leave your native country."... So Abram departed as the LORD had instructed. GENESIS 12:1, 4

Like a muscle, faith gets stronger the more you exercise it. When you do what God asks you to do and see him bless you as a result of your obedience, your faith grows stronger. Then the next time God calls you to do something, you will have more confidence to move ahead without hesitation.

I honor and love your commands. I meditate on your decrees.... Your decrees have been the theme of my songs wherever I have lived. PSALM 119:48, 54

Faith is grounded in God's Word. Your faith will grow stronger as you study the Bible and reflect on the truths about who God is, his guidelines for your life, and how he wants to use you to do his work on earth.

[Jesus] said to Thomas, "Put your finger here, and look at my hands. Put your hand into the wound in my side. Don't be faithless any longer. Believe!" "My Lord and my God!" Thomas exclaimed. Then Jesus told him, "You believe because you have seen me. Blessed are those who believe without seeing me." JOHN 20:27-29

The people's minds were hardened, and to this day whenever the old covenant is being read, the same veil covers their minds so they cannot understand the truth. And this veil can be removed only by believing in Christ. 2 CORINTHIANS 3:14

The strongest faith is not one based on physical senses but on spiritual conviction. Although we cannot see the spiritual side of this world, it is very real. Your faith will become stronger the more you allow the Holy Spirit to strengthen your "spiritual vision," so that you can see the results of God working in your life and in the lives of those around you.

How much faith must I have?

I tell you the truth, if you had faith even as small as a mustard seed, you could say to this mountain, "Move from here to there," and it would move. Nothing would be impossible.
MATTHEW 17:20

Jesus says that faith is not a matter of size or quantity. It is not the size of your faith but the size of the one in whom you believe that makes the difference. You do not have to have great faith in God; rather, you have faith in a great God.

How does faith in God affect my life?

God, with undeserved kindness, declares that we are righteous. . . . People are made right with God when they believe that Jesus sacrificed his life, shedding his blood. ROMANS 3:24-25

Faith is your lifeline to God. Sin has broken any relationship with God, because a holy God cannot live with unholy people. But the simple act of faith, when you accept Jesus as Savior and ask him to forgive your sins, makes you righteous in God's sight.

You will keep in perfect peace all who trust in you. ISAIAH 26:3

Faith in God frees you from the pressures, priorities, and perspectives of this world. It brings peace of mind and heart because it links you to God's peace and power. Faith that God is sovereign gives you the peaceful assurance that he is in control.

The Holy Spirit produces this kind of fruit in our lives: love, joy, peace, patience, kindness, goodness, faithfulness, gentleness, and self-control. GALATIANS 5:22-23

Faith is inviting God's Holy Spirit to live in you. It is not just an act of the mind; it also taps you into the very resources of God so that you have the power to live in an entirely new way. When God himself is living within you, your life is dramatically changed.

How can I pass on my faith to the next generation?

The Israelites served the LORD throughout the lifetime of Joshua and the leaders who outlived him—those who had seen all the great things the LORD had done for Israel. . . . After that generation died, another generation grew up who did not acknowledge the LORD or remember the mighty things he had done for Israel. JUDGES 2:7, 10

One generation's devotion to God does not guarantee the next generation's devotion to God. But one generation can leave a legacy of faithfulness. To encourage the next generation, you must get involved with those younger than you, share with them your own stories of God's faithfulness, and live in a way that shows them your faith in action.

FAITHFULNESS *See also* Commitment, Loyalty, Perseverance, Trust

"You can count on me." "I will never let you down." What wonderful expressions of faithfulness! A husband and wife vow on their wedding day to be faithful to each other, to be devoted and committed to each other, and to stay together no matter what. Throughout the Bible, God holds faithfulness as one of his foundational qualities. Nothing builds our sense of security like the faithfulness of another person. And nothing builds our confidence in our eternal security like the faithfulness of God.

Why should I be faithful?

Oh, the joys of those who do not follow the advice of the wicked, or stand around with sinners, or join in with mockers. But they delight in the law of the LORD, meditating on it day and night. They are like trees planted along the riverbank, bearing fruit each season. Their leaves never wither, and they prosper in all they do. PSALM 1:1-3

Faithfulness determines the quality of your character, which affects the quality of your life. Faithfulness brings vitality and productivity.

If we are faithful to the end . . . we will share in all that belongs to Christ. HEBREWS 3:14

Faithfulness brings eternal rewards.

How do I develop faithfulness?

No accounting of this money was required from the construction supervisors, because they were honest and trustworthy men. 2 KINGS 12:15

The other administrators and high officers . . . couldn't find anything to criticize or condemn. [Daniel] was faithful, always responsible, and completely trustworthy. DANIEL 6:4

You develop faithfulness by being honest and trustworthy.

If you obey the commands of the LORD your God and walk in his ways, the LORD will establish you as his holy people as he swore he would do. DEUTERONOMY 28:9

You develop faithfulness by obeying God's Word, which teaches you about the faithfulness of God.

A deacon must be faithful to his wife. 1 TIMOTHY 3:12

You develop faithfulness by keeping your promises and commitments, no matter what.

How is God faithful to me?

Praise the Lord. . . . He has sent us a mighty Savior from the royal line of his servant David, just as he promised through his holy prophets long ago. LUKE 1:68-70

God will do . . . what he says, and he has invited you into partnership with his Son, Jesus Christ our Lord. 1 CORINTHIANS 1:9

God faithfully does what he says he will do. As you read the Bible, you will discover myriads of promises God has already fulfilled. When you read the promises concerning the future, you can count on God's faithfulness to fulfill them because he has proved he always does just what he says.

The LORD will answer when I call to him. PSALM 4:3

When you call on God, he faithfully answers. His answer isn't always what you want to hear, but it is always what is best for you.

The love of the LORD remains forever with those who fear him. His salvation extends to the children's children of those who are faithful to his covenant, of those who obey his commandments! PSALM 103:17-18

Jesus Christ is the same yesterday, today, and forever. HEBREWS 13:8

Those who look to God know what the future looks like and have the assurance of peace and security. God is not subject to whims or unpredictable mood swings. Your greatest hope is in God's unchanging character and his unwavering love for you. You can count on God to remain faithful to all generations, for all time, and for all eternity.

What are the rewards of faithfulness?

The LORD rewarded me for doing right. He has seen my innocence. To the faithful you show yourself faithful; to those with integrity you show integrity. To the pure you show yourself pure, but to the wicked you show yourself hostile. 2 SAMUEL 22:25-27

Faithful people know God more deeply, and they experience and appreciate his grace more fully.

A faithful, sensible servant is one to whom the master can give the responsibility of managing his other household servants and feeding them. If the master returns and finds that the servant has done a good job, there will be a reward. I tell you the truth, the master will put that servant in charge of all he owns. MATTHEW 24:45-47

Faithfulness in small things brings opportunities for greater things.

On the judgment day, fire will reveal what kind of work each builder has done. The fire will show if a person's work has any value. If the work survives, that builder will receive a reward. But if the work is burned up, the builder will suffer great loss. The builder will be saved, but like someone barely escaping through a wall of flames. 1 CORINTHIANS 3:13-15

While all who believe in Jesus Christ will inherit eternal life, you can receive additional rewards and blessings based on your obedience in this life. Those who are faithful with what they are given here will receive even greater blessings in heaven.

FALSE PROPHETS/TEACHERS   *See also* Compromise, Idolatry, Motives

The Bible describes a true prophet of God as someone who accurately teaches and preaches the truths of Scripture, who tells others the truth even if it's unpopular, who sincerely tries to serve others, who is more interested in the welfare of others than self, and whose life is marked by humility. False prophets are just the opposite. Most of them are motivated by all the wrong reasons and usually promote themselves rather than God. False prophets are common and can be found in almost any church or community. They are dangerous because they give the church a bad reputation, using eloquence, greed, power, and control to convince others they know the way to God. They do this all for personal gain. Most false prophets are calculating—they want to get people to follow them for their own personal advantage. Some false teachers, however, are just confused. They want to accurately teach God's Word, but either they are careless in checking their ideas against Scripture or they make an honest mistake. You can tell these false teachers from the others because they are willing to change their message when confronted.

We must be very discerning when trying to decide whether someone is a false prophet. Even godly teachers will sometimes make mistakes or errors in judgment when teaching from God's Word; no one is perfect, and no one perfectly knows God and his Word. We must be careful not to attack our leaders when they say something we don't agree with or when they make a mistake in their teaching. False prophets and teachers make wrong teaching a habit and try to justify sinful lifestyle choices. When we are well versed in what the Bible says, we will be better able to recognize those who teach false and harmful messages while claiming they are from God.

How do I recognize a false prophet?

Suppose there are prophets among you or those who dream dreams about the future, and they promise you signs or miracles, and the predicted signs or miracles occur. If they then say, "Come, let us worship other gods"—gods you have not known before—do not listen to them. The LORD your God is testing you to see if you truly love him with all your heart and soul. Serve only the LORD your God and fear him alone. Obey his commands, listen to his voice, and cling to him. DEUTERONOMY 13:1-4

A false prophet will ultimately try to get you to worship other gods. A god can be whatever you worship—whatever takes the greatest priority in your life. It can be a person, an object, a hobby, a career, or a certain kind of lifestyle. A false prophet will talk more about himself or about other things than about God. Some false prophets have a great deal of spiritual power. Don't be deceived by that, for Satan also has spiritual power and gives it to those who serve him. Make sure that any spiritual power or vision from your leaders points you to God and doesn't contradict anything in his Word.

There were also false prophets in Israel, just as there will be false teachers among you. They will cleverly teach destructive heresies. 2 PETER 2:1

A false prophet will teach heresy, which is any message that contradicts the truth taught in the Bible.

In Christ lives all the fullness of God in a human body. COLOSSIANS 2:9

Do not believe everyone who claims to speak by the Spirit. You must test them to see if the spirit they have comes from God. For there are many false prophets in the world. This is how we know if they have the Spirit of God: If a person claiming to be a prophet acknowledges that Jesus Christ came in a real body, that person has the Spirit of God. But if someone claims to be a prophet and does not acknowledge the truth about Jesus, that person is not from God. 1 JOHN 4:1-3

A false prophet will not acknowledge that Jesus was fully God and also fully man when he came to earth. This is an essential doctrine of the Christian faith. God, in the form of Jesus, had to be fully man in order to experience the human life and yet live without sin. He had to be fully God so he could take our sins on himself, die in our place, and rise from the dead to show his power over death and give us the hope of eternal life. A false prophet or teacher will say either that Jesus was just a good man or that he was only divine and never became a man.

False teachers, like vicious wolves, will come in. . . . Even some men from your own group will rise up and distort the truth in order to draw a following. ACTS 20:29-30

A false prophet always tries to gain a following. He is more concerned about popularity than accurately teaching the Scriptures. He may distort the truth of Scripture to convince you that he has some secret or special knowledge from God.

Evil prophets deceive my people by saying, "All is peaceful" when there is no peace at all! It's as if the people have built a flimsy wall, and these prophets are trying to reinforce it by covering it with whitewash! EZEKIEL 13:10

False prophets make you believe all is well with your soul and your life, lulling you into a false sense of security. True prophets will show you how things really are, revealing your sin so that you can be restored to peace with God.

Suppose a prophet full of lies would say to you, "I'll preach to you the joys of wine and alcohol!" That's just the kind of prophet you would like! MICAH 2:11

False prophets and teachers encourage you to use to excess what is good, causing you to sin. And false teachers often point to the passages in the Bible that talk only about freedom and ignore the passages that talk about self-discipline.

Why is false teaching so deceptive and dangerous?

Evil people and impostors will flourish. They will deceive others and will themselves be deceived. 2 TIMOTHY 3:13

As long as Satan has power to deceive, he will use false teachers to deceive you. False teachers are the worst kind of deceiver because they appear to be concerned for your welfare but actually want to lead you down the path to destruction.

Those who insist on circumcision for salvation . . . are turning whole families away from the truth by their false teaching. TITUS 1:10-11

False teaching is dangerous because it can lead to the spiritual destruction of families as well as individuals.

Stop those whose teaching is contrary to the truth. Don't let them waste their time in endless discussion of myths and spiritual pedigrees. These things only lead to meaningless speculations, which don't help people live a life of faith in God. 1 TIMOTHY 1:3-4

False teachers embroil the church in irrelevant disputes and discussions. They get people sidetracked from important spiritual discussions and living a life of faith.

How can I keep from being deceived by false teaching?

The gatekeeper opens the gate for him, and the sheep recognize his voice and come to him. . . . After he has gathered his own flock, he walks ahead of them, and they follow him because they know his voice. They won't follow a stranger; they will run from him because they don't know his voice. JOHN 10:3-5

Jesus says that when you really know someone, you can instantly recognize his or her voice. You can pick it out in a crowd because it is distinct and you are familiar with it. As you spend time studying God's Word and getting to know him better in prayer, you will get to know his voice. Then when you hear others preaching or teaching, you will be able to recognize whether what they say is consistent with what Jesus says.

If you explain these things to the brothers and sisters, Timothy, you will be a worthy servant of Christ Jesus, one who is nourished by the message of faith and the good teaching you have followed. 1 TIMOTHY 4:6

The only way for believers to stand their ground is to be spiritually fit. Are you consistently exposing yourself to solid teaching, or are you leaving your spiritual formation to chance?

Don't let anyone capture you with empty philosophies and high-sounding nonsense that come from human thinking and from the spiritual powers of this world, rather than from Christ. COLOSSIANS 2:8

By knowing God and his truth we are able to recognize the devil and his evil nonsense.

How should I respond to false prophets and teachers?

The people of Berea were more open-minded than those in Thessalonica, and they listened eagerly to Paul's message. They searched the Scriptures day after day to see if Paul and Silas were teaching the truth. ACTS 17:11

Do not believe everyone who claims to speak by the Spirit. You must test them to see if the spirit they have comes from God. 1 JOHN 4:1

Don't be afraid to test those you think may be false teachers. Ask them questions to see if they believe in the foundational truths about Jesus and the Scriptures. Search the Scriptures yourself to see if what they say is consistent with what God says.

If another believer sins, rebuke that person; then if there is repentance, forgive. LUKE 17:3

Those who insist on circumcision for salvation . . . are turning whole families away from the truth by their false teaching. . . . So reprimand them sternly to make them strong in the faith. TITUS 1:10-13

Don't be afraid to confront false teachers. If you don't, maybe no one will, and their teaching could lead many astray.

All Scripture is inspired by God and is useful to teach us what is true and to make us realize what is wrong in our lives. It corrects us when we are wrong and teaches us to do what is right. God uses it to prepare and equip his people to do every good work.
2 TIMOTHY 3:16-17

Know the Bible inside and out. Then you will know if someone's teaching is wrong.

FAMILY *See also* Adoption, Heritage, Marriage, Parents/Parenting

The family is one of the greatest expressions of God's design for human relationships. There is no greater institution, no better social organization to effect positive change in the world than the family. There is no better place to learn the essential principles of life than the family. And nowhere can the truths of God's Word be more effectively taught and modeled than in the family. Conversely, there is no institution and no social group with more power and ability to destroy a person than the family. Physical abuse, verbal abuse, and neglect suffered within a family can damage the emotional well-being of a child well into adulthood and often for a lifetime. When parents fail to teach spiritual truths to their children, they directly affect the children's relationship with God and with other people. Family is the environment that shapes a child's entire life.

How does the Bible define family?

The LORD God made a woman from the rib, and he brought her to the man. "At last!" the man exclaimed. "This one is bone from my bone, and flesh from my flesh!"... This explains why a man leaves his father and mother and is joined to his wife, and the two are united into one. GENESIS 2:22-24

You are citizens along with all of God's holy people. You are members of God's family.
EPHESIANS 2:19

The Bible talks about both an earthly family (made up of husband, wife, and children) and the family of God (which includes all believers in Jesus Christ).

All Israel was listed in the genealogical records in The Book of the Kings of Israel.
1 CHRONICLES 9:1

The Bible lists several genealogies, all recorded by family units. This shows the family as central and fundamental to the development of people and of nations.

As for me and my family, we will serve the LORD. JOSHUA 24:15

The family is one of God's greatest resources for effecting change in individuals as well as communities. This change is directly related to the family's spiritual commitment and zeal.

How does God care for my family?

Children are a gift from the LORD; they are a reward from him. Children born to a young man are like arrows in a warrior's hands. How joyful is the man whose quiver is full of them! PSALM 127:3-5

Family was God's idea, so be assured that he cares deeply about your family and wants it to be a source of blessing, security, and encouragement to you. When you recognize God as the leader of your family and embrace his principles of love and caring, you invite him into your family, and his blessings will follow.

My Spirit will not leave them, and neither will these words I have given you. They will be on your lips and on the lips of your children and your children's children forever. ISAIAH 59:21

Peter replied, "Each of you must repent of your sins and turn to God, and be baptized in the name of Jesus Christ for the forgiveness of your sins. Then you will receive the gift of the Holy Spirit. This promise is to you, and to your children." ACTS 2:38-39

Too often we think in individualistic terms. But God cares about groups of people too, especially families, because a group of people that are passionate about God can have an enormous effect on a neighborhood or a community. So pray not just for the individuals in your family but for your family as a whole, knowing that God wants to use them to accomplish great things for him.

What are my responsibilities to my family?

You must commit yourselves wholeheartedly to these commands that I am giving you today. Repeat them again and again to your children. Talk about them when you are at home. DEUTERONOMY 6:6-7

Direct your children onto the right path, and when they are older, they will not leave it. PROVERBS 22:6

To give them spiritual training.

God loved the world so much that he gave his one and only Son, so that everyone who believes in him will not perish but have eternal life. JOHN 3:16

To clearly explain how they can receive salvation and eternal life in Jesus Christ.

You can tell your children and grandchildren about how I made a mockery of the Egyptians and about the signs I displayed among them—and so you will know that I am the LORD. EXODUS 10:2

I remember your genuine faith, for you share the faith that first filled your grandmother Lois and your mother, Eunice. 2 TIMOTHY 1:5

To share spiritual experiences—stories of how God has worked in your life—and remind your family of their spiritual heritage.

All of you should be of one mind. Sympathize with each other. Love each other as brothers and sisters. Be tenderhearted, and keep a humble attitude. 1 PETER 3:8

To be an example of Christ's love and to extend mercy to one another. Just as God loves you and shows you mercy, even when you don't deserve it, you must care for your family the same way, even when they don't deserve it. Love unconditionally, even when you are not loved in return. Sometimes that is the only way to restore damaged relationships.

FASTING *See also* Abstinence, Spiritual Disciplines, Surrender

Fasting is intentionally abstaining from something (usually food) in order to more fully communicate with God. Fasting sharpens your mind and brings more focus, commitment, and passion to your prayers. Fasting is making an extra effort to show God you are serious about communicating with him.

Why should I fast?

Jesus, full of the Holy Spirit, returned from the Jordan River. He was led by the Spirit in the wilderness, where he was tempted by the devil for forty days. Jesus ate nothing all that time and became very hungry.... Then Jesus returned to Galilee, filled with the Holy Spirit's power. LUKE 4:1-2, 14

Fasting can help you develop a more immediate sense of God's presence. Some have described fasting as praying with the body.

Jehoshaphat was terrified by this news and begged the LORD for guidance. He also ordered everyone in Judah to begin fasting. 2 CHRONICLES 20:3

Fasting helps you become more focused on the Lord so you can better receive his guidance.

When is it appropriate to fast?

They mourned and wept and fasted all day for Saul and his son Jonathan, and for the LORD's army and the nation of Israel, because they had died by the sword that day. 2 SAMUEL 1:12

David had refused to eat anything on the day of the funeral. 2 SAMUEL 3:35

In times of mourning.

As news of the king's decree [to destroy the Jews] reached all the provinces, there was great mourning among the Jews. They fasted, wept, and wailed, and many people lay in burlap and ashes. ESTHER 4:3

In times of crisis.

Ezra ... spent the night there without eating or drinking anything. He was still in mourning because of the unfaithfulness of the returned exiles. EZRA 10:6

In times of intercession for others' sins.

Paul and Barnabas also appointed elders in every church. With prayer and fasting, they turned the elders over to the care of the Lord, in whom they had put their trust. ACTS 14:23

In times of dedication.

David begged God to spare the child. He went without food and lay all night on the bare ground. 2 SAMUEL 12:16

In times of illness.

The people of Nineveh believed God's message, and from the greatest to the least, they declared a fast and put on burlap to show their sorrow. JONAH 3:5

In times of repentance.

What are some guidelines for fasting? How should I fast?
"We have fasted before you!" they say. "Why aren't you impressed? We have been very hard on ourselves, and you don't even notice it!" "I will tell you why!" I respond. "It's because you are fasting to please yourselves. Even while you fast, you keep oppressing your workers. What good is fasting when you keep on fighting and quarreling? . . . Is this what you call fasting? Do you really think this will please the LORD?" ISAIAH 58:3-5

The key to fasting is not the act or ritual itself, but the condition of your heart and your motives. It is not what you do but why you do it. You must truly want to hear from God and be prepared to act on what you hear.

When you fast, don't make it obvious, as the hypocrites do, for they try to look miserable and disheveled so people will admire them for their fasting. I tell you the truth, that is the only reward they will ever get. But when you fast, comb your hair and wash your face. Then no one will notice that you are fasting, except your Father, who knows what you do in private. And your Father, who sees everything, will reward you. MATTHEW 6:16-18

Fasting, like prayer, is not a public performance but a personal and private aspect of your relationship with God.

FAVORITISM *See also* Comparisons, Fairness, Judging Others
Everyone has favorites. There's nothing wrong with having a favorite food, hobby, sports team, piece of clothing, game, or TV show. Most of us have favorite friends. Having favorites is normal and expected. Favoritism becomes an issue, however, if we show partiality to others when we should be treating them equally. In a family, children want to be treated fairly and loved equally. At work, employees expect to be treated by the same standards and have an equal chance to succeed. We may enjoy being around one of our children more than the others, but if we play favorites, the others will feel jealousy, hurt, anger, and resentment. On a spiritual level, God treats all his children equally. Everyone has the opportunity for salvation, eternal life, and rewards in heaven. Everyone has personal access to God. Everyone receives undeserved mercy. The Bible gives us insights about when favoritism might be appropriate and when it will cause grief and heartache.

Does God play favorites?
God is an honest judge. PSALM 7:11

If God gave everyone what is deserved, no one would make it to heaven, for the Bible says that all people have sinned against him and deserve eternal punishment (see Romans 3:23; 6:23). Not only is God gracious for offering everyone a way to heaven, he is merciful in giving it for free. All you need to do is accept it.

The fastest runner doesn't always win the race, and the strongest warrior doesn't always win the battle. The wise sometimes go hungry, and the skillful are not necessarily wealthy. ECCLESIASTES 9:11

Everyone who believes in [God] will not perish but have eternal life. JOHN 3:16

God does not promise equality here on earth, but he does promise that all people have equal opportunity for eternal life in heaven. Everyone receives eternal life the same way—through simple faith in Jesus Christ. When you arrive in heaven, everything will be fair.

When is favoritism wrong?

I instructed the judges, "You must hear the cases of your fellow Israelites and the foreigners living among you. Be perfectly fair in your decisions and impartial in your judgments. Hear the cases of those who are poor as well as those who are rich." DEUTERONOMY 1:16-17

Favoritism is wrong when we judge people by the law or by established rules. If people can't trust the law to be impartial, chaos and deception will reign.

If you give special attention and a good seat to the rich person, but you say to the poor one, "You can stand over there, or else sit on the floor"—well, doesn't this discrimination show that your judgments are guided by evil motives? . . . Yes indeed, it is good when you obey the royal law as found in the Scriptures: "Love your neighbor as yourself." But if you favor some people over others, you are committing a sin. You are guilty of breaking the law. JAMES 2:3-4, 8-9

Jesus came to rescue the poor, the sick, and the downtrodden. If you show favoritism to those who are healthy, rich, and happy, you are completely missing the point of the gospel. You should be equally happy to serve all of God's people, regardless of their social or economic status.

Fathers, do not provoke your children to anger by the way you treat them. Rather, bring them up with the discipline and instruction that comes from the Lord. EPHESIANS 6:4

The Bible teaches that parents are to avoid making their children angry by the way they treat them. Parents should show the same unconditional love to all their children. Our heavenly Father loves all people equally and unconditionally, and we should follow his example.

Is it wrong to have a favorite child?

Isaac loved Esau because he enjoyed eating the wild game Esau brought home, but Rebekah loved Jacob. GENESIS 25:28

Jacob loved Joseph more than any of his other children because Joseph had been born to him in his old age. GENESIS 37:3

Isaac openly favored Esau, while Rebekah favored Jacob. Jacob's favoritism toward Joseph was obvious by his actions. The result of their favoritism was deceit, pain, and broken relationships. Although it is easy to say that we should love everyone equally, especially those in our own families, some personalities connect more naturally and some children are more lovable. Parents must learn to minimize the effects of favoritism by recognizing their personal bias and making an effort to treat each individual in the same loving manner. The human family should be a model of God's family: God the Father shows us, his children, unconditional love. God does not play favorites, and neither should we.

FEAR *See also* Enemies, Evil, Terrorism, Tragedy, Courage

Fear is real and natural. But sometimes the fear itself is more real than the thing we fear. Fear may leave us unsettled, insecure, and doubting our self-worth. It can cause sleep problems or health problems. Fear makes us worry about tomorrow or even if there will be a tomorrow. The Christian does not need to live in fear, however. The Bible tells us how to avoid it, how to live with it, and what we can learn from it.

What can I do when I am overcome with fear?

Be strong and courageous! Do not be afraid and do not panic. . . . For the LORD your God will personally go ahead of you. He will neither fail you nor abandon you. DEUTERONOMY 31:6

Remind yourself that God is always with you. Your situation may be genuinely threatening, but God has not abandoned you. He promises to stay with you always. Even in life-threatening situations, God does not leave you; instead, if you were to die, he ushers you into his very presence.

All praise to God, the Father of our Lord Jesus Christ, who has blessed us with every spiritual blessing in the heavenly realms. EPHESIANS 1:3

Remind yourself that no enemy or adversity can take away your most important blessings—the forgiveness God gives you, your relationship with him, and your eternal salvation. These remain secure even when your world falls apart.

Don't worry about anything; instead, pray about everything. Tell God what you need, and thank him for all he has done. Then you will experience God's peace, which exceeds anything we can understand. His peace will guard your hearts and minds as you live in Christ Jesus. PHILIPPIANS 4:6-7

Pray with a thankful heart, asking God to give you what you need in order to deal with your fear. Then he will give you his peace. Peace is not the absence of fear but the conquest of fear.

The LORD is my light and my salvation—so why should I be afraid? The LORD is my fortress, protecting me from danger, so why should I tremble? When evil people come to devour me, when my enemies and foes attack me, they will stumble and fall. Though a mighty army surrounds me, my heart will not be afraid. Even if I am attacked, I will remain confident. PSALM 27:1-3

The Scriptures remind you not to focus on the mere mortals who threaten or intimidate you, but rather on your Creator, who loves you. God is for you. Instead of fearing others, face them with courage and confidence because you know their limitations are no match for God's power.

God has not given us a spirit of fear and timidity, but of power, love, and self-discipline. 2 TIMOTHY 1:7

Debilitating fear is not from the Lord. When you are overcome by it, you can call upon the Holy Spirit to give you the power to face your enemies, the strength to overcome evil with good, and the discipline to persevere through your trials. Your fear can be an opportunity for you to develop greater faith.

What does it mean to fear God?

Doesn't his majesty terrify you? Doesn't your fear of him overwhelm you? JOB 13:11

Let the whole world fear the LORD, and let everyone stand in awe of him. PSALM 33:8

How joyful are those who fear the LORD—all who follow his ways! PSALM 128:1

Fearing God is not the same as being afraid of God. Being afraid of someone drives you away from them. Fearing God means being awed by his power and goodness. This draws you closer to him and to the blessings he gives. Fear of God is like the respect you have for a beloved teacher, coach, parent, or mentor—it motivates you to do your best and avoid doing anything that would offend God or provoke his displeasure. You fear him because of his awesome power; you love God because he blesses you with it.

Serve the LORD with reverent fear, and rejoice with trembling. PSALM 2:11

Because God is so great and mighty and because he holds the power of life and death in his hands, you should have a healthy, reverent fear of him. A healthy fear of God is recognizing what he could do if he gave you what you deserved. But rejoice that he gives you mercy and forgiveness instead! A healthy fear should drive you to God for forgiveness and give you perspective about your relationship with him.

FELLOWSHIP *See also* Church, Community, Friendship, Hospitality

One of the primary reasons God created people was to enjoy fellowship with them. He also created us with certain needs that can be met only through relationships. For Christians, fellowship is deeper than just friendly camaraderie. True fellowship is built on the shared belief that through Jesus' death and resurrection we are forgiven. This not only allows us to have fellowship with God but shapes our fellowship with other believers. Whether in our relationship with God or others, true fellowship requires a desire to enjoy one another's company, an investment of time, focused attention, and practical service. Christians can enthusiastically enjoy fellowship on earth with the added hope of continuing their relationships forever in heaven.

Why do I need the fellowship of other believers?

When he arrived and saw this evidence of God's blessing, he was filled with joy, and he encouraged the believers to stay true to the Lord. ACTS 11:23

We are many parts of one body, and we all belong to each other. ROMANS 12:5

Teach and counsel each other with all the wisdom he gives. Sing psalms and hymns and spiritual songs to God with thankful hearts. COLOSSIANS 3:16

God created you for relationship. You cannot grow as a believer by yourself, without other Christians around you. Fellowship with other believers is necessary to keep you accountable, to help you learn God's Word correctly, to pray for one another's needs, to encourage one another, and to help you mature in your faith.

How does my relationship with God affect the way I fellowship with others?

Where two or three gather together as my followers, I am there among them.
MATTHEW 18:20

I want to encourage you in your faith, but I also want to be encouraged by yours.
ROMANS 1:12

Confess your sins to each other and pray for each other so that you may be healed.
JAMES 5:16

Fellowship among believers, at church or in small groups, is unique because the living God is in their midst. Christians have a common perspective on life because they know their sins have been forgiven, and this affects their freedom and their future. Christian fellowship provides a place for honest sharing about things that really matter, for encouragement to stay strong in the face of temptation and persecution, and for supernatural help in dealing with problems.

All the believers were united in heart and mind. And they felt that what they owned was not their own, so they shared everything they had. The apostles testified powerfully to the resurrection of the Lord Jesus, and God's great blessing was upon them all. There were no needy people among them, because those who owned land or houses would sell them and bring the money to the apostles to give to those in need. ACTS 4:32-35

God's love for you should move you to share your resources with others. This practical expression of love unleashes God's power and empowers your witness to the world.

What does God promise when I make godly fellowship a priority?

If we are living in the light, as God is in the light, then we have fellowship with each other, and the blood of Jesus, his Son, cleanses us from all sin. 1 JOHN 1:7

God blesses Christian fellowship. You will experience God more fully when you live open and truthful relationships with others.

All of you should be of one mind. Sympathize with each other. Love each other as brothers and sisters. Be tenderhearted, and keep a humble attitude. Don't repay evil for evil. Don't retaliate with insults when people insult you. Instead, pay them back with a blessing. That is what God has called you to do, and he will bless you for it. 1 PETER 3:8-9

Your spiritual well-being will be enhanced by the quality of your relationships. God promises to help you as you help those he loves.

What if I just don't like some other Christians?
Don't just pretend to love others. Really love them. . . . Take delight in honoring each other. . . . Don't be too proud to enjoy the company of ordinary people. And don't think you know it all! ROMANS 12:9-10, 16

Since we are living by the Spirit, let us follow the Spirit's leading in every part of our lives. Let us not become conceited, or provoke one another, or be jealous of one another. GALATIANS 5:25-26

Be humble, thinking of others as better than yourselves. PHILIPPIANS 2:3

It's easy to like people who are likable, but we model God's love more when we serve those who are annoying. You'll never find a perfect church, and you'll never find a perfect group of people—even among Christians. Instead, take joy in reaching out and loving those God has placed in your sphere of influence. You may be surprised at how the power of God can bring the most unlikely people together as friends. When you reach out to others in love, your heart is also changed.

FOLLOWING *See also* Character, Commitment, Reputation

We are all followers in some way, as we can see in our daily choices. We follow diets, exercise programs, and fashion trends. We follow role models, friends, and other people we admire. We spend our free time following TV shows, sports teams, and the stock market. But your most important choice is spiritual—will you follow God? Choosing to follow God is a wise choice because he created us and knows what's best for us. When we make the choice to follow God, we can make other choices about who or what to follow using God's wisdom and vision for our lives.

How can I know if I am following after the wrong people or things?
Be very careful never to make a treaty with the people who live in the land where you are going. If you do, you will follow their evil ways and be trapped. EXODUS 34:12

God specifically directed this command to the Israelites when they were establishing their own country and had not yet had any diplomatic experience. This is still an important principle for us today. If you find yourself compromising what is right in order to please those around you, then you are following after the wrong things.

If sinners entice you, turn your back on them! They may say, "Come and join us."...
Don't go along with them! Stay far away from their paths. PROVERBS 1:10-11, 15

If you spend a lot of time with people who encourage you to do what you know is wrong, you are in danger of following the wrong path.

What does it mean to follow Jesus?

Calling the crowd to join his disciples, [Jesus] said, "If any of you wants to be my follower, you must turn from your selfish ways, take up your cross, and follow me." MARK 8:34

As soon as [Simon Peter, James, and John] landed, they left everything and followed Jesus. LUKE 5:11

Following Jesus means more than acknowledging him as Savior. It means reorienting your life so that no matter what you do, you do it in service to him. For example, you may work in sales, but if you follow Jesus, you view your job as a way to supply people's needs with fairness and integrity.

My sheep listen to my voice; I know them, and they follow me. JOHN 10:27

Being a disciple of Jesus is a matter of following him with a willing heart. He will bless you not because of your ability but because of your availability.

Let your good deeds shine out for all to see, so that everyone will praise your heavenly Father. MATTHEW 5:16

When you follow Jesus, make sure others can truly see that you follow him. They will want to follow Jesus too if they like what they see.

Why is following God so hard sometimes?

When troubles come your way, consider it an opportunity for great joy. For you know that when your faith is tested, your endurance has a chance to grow. So let it grow, for when your endurance is fully developed, you will be perfect and complete, needing nothing.
JAMES 1:2-4

Following God doesn't make life easy. In fact, the more important a task is, the more Satan will throw roadblocks in your way. If you know God is leading you in a certain direction, don't give up just because the going gets tough. If anything, those obstacles could be a sign that you are headed in the right direction. Move forward boldly with your eyes fixed on God. Your faith will be strengthened as you obey him in your daily choices and life decisions. Then you will be able to step out in faith wherever God calls you.

FOOLISHNESS *See also* Excuses, Meaning/Meaninglessness, Risk, Wisdom

Foolishness is lacking sense, good judgment, or discretion. It is failing to use your God-given faculties to make smart decisions. Foolishness can be a momentary lapse or a lifetime of thoughtlessness. The ultimate act of foolishness is ignoring God. People who neglect to be proactive about their relationship with God not only stumble through life but have no hope for an eternal future in heaven. The best resource to combat foolishness is God's Word, which gives wisdom and guidance.

What does foolish behavior look like?

Doing wrong is fun for a fool, but living wisely brings pleasure to the sensible.
PROVERBS 10:23

"My people are foolish and do not know me," says the LORD. "They are stupid children who have no understanding. They are clever enough at doing wrong, but they have no idea how to do right!" JEREMIAH 4:22

Fools have lost the proper perspective on right and wrong, truth and falsehood. Fools have no anchor of absolute truth in God and, therefore, drift through life seeking truth in random places.

Anyone who listens to my teaching and follows it is wise, like a person who builds a house on solid rock. Though the rain comes in torrents and the floodwaters rise and the winds beat against that house, it won't collapse because it is built on bedrock. But anyone who hears my teaching and doesn't obey it is foolish, like a person who builds a house on sand. When the rains and floods come and the winds beat against that house, it will collapse with a mighty crash. MATTHEW 7:24-27

Fools ignore God's Word and therefore ignore the advice that can guide them safely through life.

A person is a fool to store up earthly wealth but not have a rich relationship with God.
LUKE 12:21

Fools have misplaced priorities, putting the most value on what matters least.

Be careful how you live. Don't live like fools, but like those who are wise. Make the most of every opportunity in these evil days. Don't act thoughtlessly, but understand what the Lord wants you to do. EPHESIANS 5:15-17

Fools act thoughtlessly and with no regard for the future.

The Lord said to him, "You Pharisees are so careful to clean the outside of the cup and the dish, but inside you are filthy—full of greed and wickedness! Fools! Didn't God make the inside as well as the outside?" LUKE 11:39-40

Fools are hypocrites. On the outside, they try to convince themselves and others that they are good, but on the inside, they are full of sin and deceit.

A hard worker has plenty of food, but a person who chases fantasies has no sense.
PROVERBS 12:11

Fools are lazy. They waste time and don't understand the meaning of hard work. They don't recognize that something produces something, and nothing produces nothing.

What are the consequences of foolishness?

[The mockers, simpletons, and fools] hated knowledge and chose not to fear the LORD. They rejected my advice and paid no attention when I corrected them. Therefore, they must eat the bitter fruit of living their own way, choking on their own schemes. For simpletons turn away from me—to death. Fools are destroyed by their own complacency. But all who listen to me will live in peace, untroubled by fear of harm. PROVERBS 1:29-33

Foolishness leads to complacency about God. Ultimately it leads to destruction.

The wise can see where they are going, but fools walk in the dark. ECCLESIASTES 2:14

People who aren't spiritual can't receive these truths from God's Spirit. It all sounds foolish to them and they can't understand it, for only those who are spiritual can understand what the Spirit means. 1 CORINTHIANS 2:14

Foolishness brings confusion: Wisdom sounds wrong and foolishness sounds right.

As a dog returns to its vomit, so a fool repeats his foolishness. PROVERBS 26:11

Foolish behavior can turn into a repetitive cycle and even become addictive.

How can I be wise instead of foolish?

Fear of the LORD is the foundation of true knowledge, but fools despise wisdom and discipline. PROVERBS 1:7

When you honor and respect God, you acknowledge his ultimate power and authority over all things. Wise people understand their relationship to God.

Stop deceiving yourselves. If you think you are wise by this world's standards, you need to become a fool to be truly wise. For the wisdom of this world is foolishness to God. 1 CORINTHIANS 3:18-19

Live according to God's standard of wisdom, not the world's. Make sure you use the right measuring stick for wisdom and foolishness.

What sorrow awaits you teachers of religious law and you Pharisees. Hypocrites! For you are careful to tithe even the tiniest income from your herb gardens, but you ignore the more important aspects of the law—justice, mercy, and faith. You should tithe, yes, but do not neglect the more important things. Blind guides! You strain your water so you won't accidentally swallow a gnat, but you swallow a camel! MATTHEW 23:23-24

Align your priorities with God's. What is most important to God must be most important to you, or you will miss the things of greatest value.

A youngster's heart is filled with foolishness, but physical discipline will drive it far away. PROVERBS 22:15

Discipline yourself and accept discipline from others. Discipline keeps you from wandering off the right path.

FORGIVENESS
See also Grace, Reconciliation, Repentance, Salvation

The Bible commands us to forgive others when they have wronged us and to seek forgiveness when we have wronged others. When we do this, we follow the example of God, who extends to us the ultimate forgiveness—pardon for our sins. Forgiveness is the pathway to freedom. When God forgives you, you are freed from guilt and restored to fellowship with him. When you forgive someone who has wronged you, you are freed from the bitterness and resentment that can saturate your soul like toxic waste. When you receive forgiveness from someone else, you are freed from indebtedness to them. Receiving God's forgiveness and forgiving others are at the core of what it means to be a Christian.

What does it mean to be forgiven?

Though your sins are like scarlet, I will make them as white as snow. Though they are red like crimson, I will make them as white as wool. ISAIAH 1:18

You are holy and blameless as you stand before him without a single fault. COLOSSIANS 1:22

Forgiveness means that God looks at you as though you had never sinned. When you receive his forgiveness, you are blameless before him. God doesn't just sweep your sins under the carpet; instead, he completely washes them away.

Oh, what joy for those whose disobedience is forgiven, whose sins are put out of sight. ROMANS 4:7

You were dead because of your sins and because your sinful nature was not yet cut away. Then God made you alive with Christ, for he forgave all our sins. COLOSSIANS 2:13

Forgiveness gives you great joy because you have been freed from the heavy weight of guilt. You are no longer a slave to your sinful nature.

God showed how much he loved us by sending his one and only Son into the world so that we might have eternal life through him. This is real love—not that we loved God, but that he loved us and sent his Son as a sacrifice to take away our sins. 1 JOHN 4:9-10

Forgiveness through Jesus is the only way you can have the assurance of eternal life in heaven.

I've done some pretty awful things. How can God forgive me?

This is my blood, which confirms the covenant between God and his people. It is poured out as a sacrifice to forgive the sins of many. MATTHEW 26:28

Jesus died so that God's forgiveness would be freely available to you. Jesus took the punishment you deserve. He paid your debt in full. All you need to do is ask him to forgive you.

If we claim we have no sin, we are only fooling ourselves and not living in the truth. But if we confess our sins to him, he is faithful and just to forgive us our sins and to cleanse us from all wickedness. 1 JOHN 1:8-9

Confessing your sin is the first step in receiving forgiveness. When you confess your sins, you agree with God that you have done something wrong. Because Jesus Christ died for your sins, God accepts your confession and forgives you. There is nothing more you must do. Don't allow lingering feelings of shame to persuade you otherwise.

Against you, and you alone, have I sinned; I have done what is evil in your sight. PSALM 51:4

Realize that God is the one who has ultimately been wronged by your sin, so he is the one you first need to ask for forgiveness.

The sacrifice you desire is a broken spirit. You will not reject a broken and repentant heart, O God. PSALM 51:17

God is more ready to forgive than you may be to repent. A broken and humble heart is the quickest way to receive forgiveness, which restores spiritual wholeness.

How can I forgive someone who has hurt me deeply?

When you are praying, first forgive anyone you are holding a grudge against, so that your Father in heaven will forgive your sins, too. MARK 11:25

You will receive God's forgiveness only when you are willing to forgive others who have wronged you. Being unwilling to forgive shows that you have not understood or benefited from God's forgiveness.

Be kind to each other, tenderhearted, forgiving one another, just as God through Christ has forgiven you. EPHESIANS 4:32

God's forgiveness provides the motivation and the model for forgiving others. If God has forgiven you though you have wronged him, how can you refuse to forgive someone who has wronged you? Your forgiveness, like God's, should be a gift of grace; it should be free to the recipient even though it may be costly to the giver.

Jesus said, "Father, forgive them, for they don't know what they are doing." LUKE 23:34

Jesus forgave even those who mocked and killed him. In the same way, be more concerned about your offenders and their relationship with God than about nursing your own grudges and self-pity.

Love your enemies! Pray for those who persecute you! MATTHEW 5:44

Forgiveness means praying for those who hate and hurt you. This releases you from the destructive emotions of anger, bitterness, and revenge.

Don't repay evil for evil. Don't retaliate with insults when people insult you. Instead, pay them back with a blessing. That is what God has called you to do, and he will bless you for it. 1 PETER 3:9

When people say hurtful things to you or about you, God wants you to respond by blessing them.

Even if [a] person wrongs you seven times a day and each time turns again and asks forgiveness, you must forgive. LUKE 17:4

Just as love does not have a limit, neither does forgiveness.

Is there a limit to how much God will forgive me?

"Come now, let's settle this," says the LORD. "Though your sins are like scarlet, I will make them as white as snow. Though they are red like crimson, I will make them as white as wool." ISAIAH 1:18

No matter how sinful and disobedient you have been, you can receive God's forgiveness by turning to him in repentance.

The Kingdom of Heaven can be compared to a king who decided to bring his accounts up to date. . . . One of his debtors was brought in who owed him millions of dollars. He couldn't pay. . . . His master was filled with pity for him, and he released him and forgave his debt. MATTHEW 18:23-25, 27

God is merciful toward you, even though your debt is great.

He is so rich in kindness and grace that he purchased our freedom with the blood of his Son and forgave our sins. EPHESIANS 1:7

God will forgive all your sins because Christ has already paid the penalty for every sin by his death.

FRIENDSHIP *See also* Acceptance, Relationships, Respect, Trust

How many friends do you have? Who are they? If you are like most people, your friends range from casual acquaintances to those for whom you would die. Sometimes friends are closer than brothers or sisters. Friends share affection, companionship, confidences, consideration, devotion, esteem, faithfulness, fellowship, harmony, helpfulness, loyalty, partnership, support, sympathy, trust, and understanding. Friends are special. God created us for relationships with one another and especially with him. Our friendship with God should be the model for all our other friendships.

Can I truly be friends with God?

Inside the Tent of Meeting, the LORD would speak to Moses face to face, as one speaks to a friend. EXODUS 33:11

The LORD is a friend to those who fear him. He teaches them his covenant. PSALM 25:14

God saw Moses as his friend. As you develop your relationship with God, you develop a friendship with him. He is your Lord, but he also desires to be your friend.

What is the mark of true friendship?

Jonathan made a solemn pact with David, because he loved him as he loved himself.
1 SAMUEL 18:3

A friend is always loyal, and a brother is born to help in time of need.
PROVERBS 17:17

Loyalty and commitment are the marks of true friendship. These traits hold friendships together despite changing circumstances.

How can I show devotion to my friends?

Jonathan made David reaffirm his vow of friendship again, for Jonathan loved David as he loved himself. 1 SAMUEL 20:17

Loving a friend as much as you love yourself demonstrates your devotion.

If someone has enough money to live well and sees a brother or sister in need but shows no compassion—how can God's love be in that person? Dear children, let's not merely say that we love each other; let us show the truth by our actions. Our actions will show that we belong to the truth, so we will be confident when we stand before God.
1 JOHN 3:17-19

Your actions are an outward demonstration of your devotion. Taking care of the needs of others is a good way to show affection. You can show devotion by eagerly listening to someone. Listening honors and respects the other person.

What should I do when I'm having trouble making friends?

King Hiram of Tyre had always been a loyal friend of David. When Hiram learned that David's son Solomon was the new king of Israel, he sent ambassadors to congratulate him. 1 KINGS 5:1

Do to others whatever you would like them to do to you. MATTHEW 7:12

Everyone wants to have good friends, but few are willing to invest the time and effort necessary to build such relationships. You may not make friends quickly and easily, but you can build strong, lasting friendships over time. It might help you to consider the qualities you desire in a good friend, then work to develop those qualities in your own life.

I no longer call you slaves. . . . Now you are my friends. JOHN 15:15

I will never fail you. I will never abandon you. HEBREWS 13:5

Remember that God is your constant friend, and he will never leave you. Keep showing God's love to others, and they will be drawn to you.

Be kind to each other, tenderhearted, forgiving one another, just as God through Christ has forgiven you. EPHESIANS 4:32

Acts of kindness and generosity attract others to you.

Does the Bible offer any guidelines for male-female friendships?

Love is patient and kind. Love is not jealous. . . . It does not demand its own way.
1 CORINTHIANS 13:4-5

Paul's timeless description of Christian love is the standard of conduct that should mark all relationships.

[Lydia] was baptized along with other members of her household, and she asked us to be her guests. "If you agree that I am a true believer in the Lord," she said, "come and stay at my home." And she urged us until we agreed. ACTS 16:15

Paul . . . said good-bye to the brothers and sisters. . . . Then he set sail for Syria, taking Priscilla and Aquila with him. ACTS 18:18

Talk to younger men as you would to your own brothers. Treat . . . younger women with all purity as you would your own sisters. 1 TIMOTHY 5:1-2

The best way to keep your friendships pure is to treat your friends like brothers and sisters. Paul gave women such as Lydia and Priscilla this kind of respect. You can do the same by training yourself to focus on your friend's heart and by encouraging him or her to grow closer to Christ.

Anyone who even looks at a woman with lust in his eye has already committed adultery with her in his heart. MATTHEW 5:28

Let there be no sexual immorality, impurity, or greed among you. EPHESIANS 5:3

In dramatic contrast to our culture, Jesus calls you to a high standard of sexual purity in thought as well as in action.

FRUSTRATION *See also* Confusion, Distractions, Problems, Stress

Frustration has many faces—you may feel baffled, rejected, crippled, defeated, disappointed, dissatisfied, neutralized, undermined, or inhibited. Frustration thwarts and confuses you, making you feel like you are so close to your goals and yet so far away. The Bible says that frustrations are a part of living in this sinful world. Sin and evil so often seem to frustrate good. But God offers us the bigger picture: Frustrations are temporary obstacles that can be overcome, not by eliminating them but by persevering through them.

Why should I anticipate frustration?

To [Adam] he said, " . . . The ground is cursed because of you. All your life you will struggle to scratch a living from it. It will grow thorns and thistles for you, though you will eat of its grains. By the sweat of your brow will you have food to eat until you return to the ground from which you were made." GENESIS 3:17-19

Frustration is ultimately the consequence of sin—things just don't go the way we want them to. While you wouldn't welcome frustration, you shouldn't be surprised by it. We live in a fallen world with fallen people; therefore, you can expect obstacles and frustrations in all forms. When you realize and accept that frustration is part of everyday life, you are better prepared to handle it in a positive way.

Why do I get frustrated?

You will plant crops but not harvest them. You will press your olives but not get enough oil to anoint yourselves. You will trample the grapes but get no juice to make your wine.
MICAH 6:15

Sometimes you can become frustrated when your hard work doesn't pay off.

Even when you ask, you don't get it because your motives are all wrong—you want only what will give you pleasure. JAMES 4:3

At times you may feel frustrated when you expect certain answers to your prayers, but they never come. You may not see the bigger picture of why it appears God isn't answering you.

Why, then, did you deliver me from my mother's womb? Why didn't you let me die at birth? JOB 10:18

Pain and suffering bring frustration.

How should I respond to frustration?

People may be right in their own eyes, but the LORD examines their heart.
PROVERBS 21:2

Examining the source of your frustration helps you know how to deal with it. There is a big difference between being frustrated in your quest to do good and being frustrated because you are not getting your way. Each frustration must be dealt with differently.

Moses cried out to the LORD, "What should I do with these people?" EXODUS 17:4

Recognize that some of your problems don't have a human solution. You must take them to God.

G

GAMBLING *See also* Addiction, Debt, Money, Stewardship

Everyone likes a little luck, especially when it involves money. Whether it's winning a sweepstakes or finding a hundred-dollar bill on the sidewalk, good luck makes us feel like someone is watching out for us. It's intoxicating. It makes us feel like things are going our way for once. Gambling is one way people try to find that luck, to experience the thrill of receiving something big and unexpected. The Bible doesn't say much about gambling specifically, but it has a lot to say about money, the dangers of addiction, and good stewardship of our resources—all issues related to gambling. It's hard to argue that betting ten dollars in a game of poker is any worse than spending ten dollars on movie tickets or at the county fair to try to win a prize. But the real issue comes down to heart and motives. Those who gamble to get rich quick often struggle with laziness and greed, character traits the Bible calls sin. Those who can't stop gambling are addicted to it, and whatever we are addicted to becomes our master and god. Gambling is dangerous because it takes a person's focus off God and leads to behavior that is destructive. Those who are addicted to gambling put themselves and their families at risk. When we take matters into our own hands to experience the thrill of the unexpected, we often take the wrong route, with harmful consequences. God wants us to experience those intoxicating feelings of receiving something wonderful and unexpected, and he will send them our way. But if we're focused on fabricating them ourselves, we miss the spectacular things God gives us.

Are there any examples of gambling in the Bible?

After they had nailed him to the cross, the soldiers gambled for his clothes by throwing dice. MATTHEW 27:35

The soldiers who crucified Jesus gambled to see who would get his clothes.

What should I know about gambling?

[Sinners] set an ambush for themselves; they are trying to get themselves killed. Such is the fate of all who are greedy for money; it robs them of life. PROVERBS 1:18-19

Greedy people try to get rich quick but don't realize they're headed for poverty. PROVERBS 28:22

Gambling is rooted in the hope of getting rich quick, but it often ends in poverty. Gambling almost always increases your debts, while careful spending and saving reduce your debts. Gambling sets you up for a loss because the odds are against you. When you work hard and save, you set yourself up for success.

Like a partridge that hatches eggs she has not laid, so are those who get their wealth by unjust means. At midlife they will lose their riches; in the end, they will become poor old fools. JEREMIAH 17:11

What do you benefit if you gain the whole world but lose your own soul? Is anything worth more than your soul? MATTHEW 16:26

Gambling is foolish because you lose more than you gain. If gambling interferes with a relationship with God, you could even lose your soul.

The earnings of the godly enhance their lives, but evil people squander their money on sin. PROVERBS 10:16

Gambling squanders the resources God has given you. On the other hand, giving and saving are the result of hard work and careful habits, and they enhance your life.

No one can serve two masters. For you will hate one and love the other; you will be devoted to one and despise the other. You cannot serve both God and money. LUKE 16:13

People who long to be rich fall into temptation and are trapped by many foolish and harmful desires that plunge them into ruin and destruction. For the love of money is the root of all kinds of evil. And some people, craving money, have wandered from the true faith and pierced themselves with many sorrows. 1 TIMOTHY 6:9-10

You are a slave to whatever controls you. 2 PETER 2:19

Gambling is highly addictive. It has the power to totally consume you, to take control of your life, and to draw you away from God.

GENEROSITY *See also* Giving, Sharing, Stewardship, Tithing

Who is more generous—a billionaire who gives one million dollars to his church or a struggling single mom who gives one hundred dollars? If you already have a lot of money, does that mean you are not generous? Jesus says we can't know the answer to these questions without knowing the heart of the giver. The Bible doesn't focus on how much money a person has, but rather on how generous that person is with it. One thing is clear: What we do with our money reveals what we care about most. Jesus says, "Wherever your treasure is, there the desires of your heart will also be" (Matthew 6:21). It's not what we have, but what we do with what we have that is significant—whether it's money, time, or talents. Generosity is both a spiritual gift and a spiritual discipline. To some, generosity comes easy; others must work hard at it. But none of us can afford to neglect it. Generosity is an important character trait because it is the opposite of selfishness. Selfishness promotes greed, stinginess, envy, and hard-heartedness—all traits that destroy relationships. On the other hand, generosity promotes giving, trust, mercy, and putting the needs of others above your own—all traits that build relationships. When we realize that everything we have is a gift from a generous God, it motivates us to share our material possessions more freely. God is the ultimate model of generosity because he sacrificed his beloved Son so we could enjoy salvation and eternal life and all the blessings and rewards that go with them. This ultimate gift is free; all we need to do is accept God's generosity.

What is generosity?

If there are any poor Israelites in your towns when you arrive in the land the LORD your God is giving you, do not be hard-hearted or tightfisted toward them. Instead, be generous and lend them whatever they need. DEUTERONOMY 15:7-8

Don't forget to do good and to share with those in need. These are the sacrifices that please God. HEBREWS 13:16

Generosity is sharing with someone in need.

All must give as they are able, according to the blessings given to them by the LORD your God. DEUTERONOMY 16:17

Generosity involves sharing your blessings.

They gave not only what they could afford, but far more. And they did it of their own free will. 2 CORINTHIANS 8:3

You must each decide in your heart how much to give. And don't give reluctantly or in response to pressure. "For God loves a person who gives cheerfully." 2 CORINTHIANS 9:7

Generosity is not just what you give but the attitude with which you give it.

In what ways has God shown generosity toward me?

There is a great difference between Adam's sin and God's gracious gift. For the sin of this one man, Adam, brought death to many. But even greater is God's wonderful grace and his gift of forgiveness to many through this other man, Jesus Christ. ROMANS 5:15

[The] Lord . . . gives generously to all who call on him. ROMANS 10:12

God generously offers you the gift of life forever in a perfect world. All you have to do is accept it. If God were not generous and compassionate, he might have made his followers work for their salvation, or he might have given only a privileged few the chance to get into heaven. But he offers the same gift to everyone.

[God] generously poured out the Spirit upon us through Jesus Christ our Savior. TITUS 3:6

God also generously gives the Holy Spirit to all who believe in him. God doesn't provide his presence just to the super righteous or the giants of the faith. He provides his presence to everyone who chooses to believe in him.

Dear brothers and sisters, regarding your question about the special abilities the Spirit gives us. . . . A spiritual gift is given to each of us so we can help each other. 1 CORINTHIANS 12:1, 7

God gives every person special abilities, and he gives every believer unique spiritual gifts.

What are the benefits of generosity?

You will be enriched in every way so that you can always be generous. And when we take your gifts to those who need them, they will thank God. So two good things will result from this ministry of giving—the needs of the believers in Jerusalem will be met, and they will joyfully express their thanks to God. As a result of your ministry, they will give glory to God. For your generosity to them and to all believers will prove that you are obedient to the Good News of Christ. And they will pray for you with deep affection because of the overflowing grace God has given to you. 2 CORINTHIANS 9:11-14

Generosity glorifies God and enriches your life. Others will thank God and honor him as their needs are met, and many will pray for you.

God has given each of you a gift. . . . Use them well to serve one another. 1 PETER 4:10

The more generous you are with others, the more God's generosity flows through you.

Remember the words of the Lord Jesus: "It is more blessed to give than to receive." ACTS 20:35

Keeping something may please you, but giving provides you the joy of pleasing God and the satisfaction of helping others.

How do I know if I'm giving enough to my church?

While Jesus was in the Temple, he watched the rich people dropping their gifts in the collection box. Then a poor widow came by and dropped in two small coins. "I tell you the truth," Jesus said, "this poor widow has given more than all the rest of them. For they have given a tiny part of their surplus, but she, poor as she is, has given everything she has." LUKE 21:1-4

Jesus describes God's standard for gauging generosity: The degree of sacrifice matters more than the amount of the gift. Millionaire philanthropists whose high-dollar gifts never alter their lifestyle may be less generous in God's eyes than the struggling single parent who foregoes a needed pair of shoes in order to give. God looks for the willing heart, not the extravagant amount. God looks for what giving does in your life, not just what it will accomplish for his kingdom. Does your giving cause you to do without something significant? Can you honestly say you give sacrificially? That kind of giving reveals true generosity.

GENTLENESS *See also* Compassion, Kindness, Mercy, Sensitivity

In a world full of violence, the concept of gentleness is rare but needed. There is peace in the heart of a gentle person that soothes the hearts of those around him or her. People look for gentleness in a potential marriage partner. Businesspeople appreciate a gentle spirit in the office. Church meetings run more smoothly when conducted in a spirit of gentleness. Jesus was gentle. Did this rob him of authority? No. True leaders can be gentle because their power is under control. The Bible calls us to be gentle in our dealings with others, not only because it is kind and right but because it models a characteristic of Christ.

How is God gentle?

After the earthquake there was a fire, but the LORD was not in the fire. And after the fire there was the sound of a gentle whisper. 1 KINGS 19:12

Although God has the power of the universe at his fingertips, he often speaks most eloquently in whispers.

The LORD is like a father to his children, tender and compassionate to those who fear him. For he knows how weak we are; he remembers we are only dust. PSALM 103:13-14

God is loving and gentle because he knows it will draw us to him.

How did Jesus demonstrate gentleness?

Jesus said, "Come to me, all of you who are weary and carry heavy burdens, and I will give you rest. Take my yoke upon you. Let me teach you, because I am humble and gentle at heart, and you will find rest for your souls." MATTHEW 11:28-29

Jesus saw the huge crowd as he stepped from the boat, and he had compassion on them because they were like sheep without a shepherd. So he began teaching them many things. MARK 6:34

You can see the gentle heart of Jesus when the Bible describes him as a shepherd and as a teacher who had compassion for crowds of hurting people, lifting their heavy burdens. Jesus provides the best example of gentleness.

What does gentleness accomplish?

Jacob went on ahead. As he approached his brother, he bowed to the ground seven times before him. Then Esau ran to meet him and embraced him, threw his arms around his neck, and kissed him. And they both wept. . . . Jacob [said,] . . . "What a relief to see your friendly smile. It is like seeing the face of God!" GENESIS 33:3-4, 10

A friendly smile given in a tense moment is a gentle reminder of your love and support.

If another believer is overcome by some sin, you who are godly should gently and humbly help that person back onto the right path. GALATIANS 6:1

When you need to confront someone about sin, a gentle approach is usually most effective. A gentle approach shows you care about the person; harshness shows you care only about the behavior.

A servant of the Lord must not quarrel but must be kind to everyone, be able to teach, and be patient with difficult people. Gently instruct those who oppose the truth. Perhaps God will change those people's hearts, and they will learn the truth. 2 TIMOTHY 2:24-25

When teaching God's Word, gentleness and patience help you get your message across.

A gentle answer deflects anger, but harsh words make tempers flare. . . . Gentle words are a tree of life. PROVERBS 15:1, 4

A gentle response to an angry person or comment will keep an argument from getting out of control.

Clothe yourselves with tenderhearted mercy, kindness, humility, gentleness, and patience. Make allowance for each other's faults, and forgive anyone who offends you. COLOSSIANS 3:12-13

Gentleness opens the door to forgiveness.

GIFTS *See also* Abilities, Call of God, Generosity, Giving

We give gifts as a symbol of our love, commitment, and care for others. When we find the perfect gift for friends or loved ones, it gives us great joy to see them use and delight in it. Similarly, God handpicks special gifts for each one of us, and he takes great delight when we use those gifts responsibly and for his glory. The gifts God gives us are a symbol of his deep, personal, and attentive love and commitment to each one of us. We can use these gifts for our personal enjoyment, as with a hobby, and we can use them to serve others. Some of God's gifts are spiritual gifts. We never use up these spiritual gifts; rather, the more we use them, the more they grow and allow us to make a unique contribution in our sphere of influence. Just as you thank someone who has given you a special gift, be sure to express your thanks to God for the special gifts he has given to you.

What are some of the gifts God gives to me?

God loved the world so much that he gave his one and only Son, so that everyone who believes in him will not perish but have eternal life. JOHN 3:16

The greatest gift God gives you is his Son. Through his Son, Jesus, he also gives you the gift of eternal life.

If you sinful people know how to give good gifts to your children, how much more will your heavenly Father give the Holy Spirit to those who ask him. LUKE 11:13

[God] has identified us as his own by placing the Holy Spirit in our hearts as the first installment that guarantees everything he has promised us. 2 CORINTHIANS 1:22

God gives you his Holy Spirit. The Holy Spirit gives you wisdom, insight, comfort, advice, spiritual gifts, and the very power of God.

All praise to God, the Father of our Lord Jesus Christ, who has blessed us with every spiritual blessing in the heavenly realms because we are united with Christ. EPHESIANS 1:3

God gives you special spiritual blessings when you belong to Christ.

Whatever is good and perfect comes down to us from God our Father, who created all the lights in the heavens. He never changes or casts a shifting shadow. JAMES 1:17

God gives you everything you have that is good and perfect. He does not give you bad things.

How does God give?

[Christ Jesus] gave his life to purchase freedom for everyone. 1 TIMOTHY 2:6

God gives sacrificially. He gave his Son, who then gave his life in order to give you eternal life.

You know the generous grace of our Lord Jesus Christ. Though he was rich, yet for your sakes he became poor, so that by his poverty he could make you rich. 2 CORINTHIANS 8:9

God gives unselfishly. He shares everything he has with you.

God will generously provide all you need. Then you will always have everything you need and plenty left over to share with others. 2 CORINTHIANS 9:8

God gives generously and abundantly. His gifts go even beyond what you need.

Rejoice, you people of Jerusalem! Rejoice in the LORD your God! For the rain he sends demonstrates his faithfulness. Once more the autumn rains will come, as well as the rains of spring. The threshing floors will again be piled high with grain, and the presses will overflow with new wine and olive oil. JOEL 2:23-24

God gives faithfully. He never begrudges any good thing to his children.

It is the one and only Spirit who distributes all these gifts. He alone decides which gift each person should have. 1 CORINTHIANS 12:11

God gives personally. He plans gifts according to your abilities and your character.

What are some gifts I can give to God?

You must love the LORD your God with all your heart, all your soul, and all your strength. DEUTERONOMY 6:5

You can give God your undivided devotion. You cannot truly love God with only part of your heart.

The sacrifice you desire is a broken spirit. You will not reject a broken and repentant heart, O God. PSALM 51:17

You can give God your humbled spirit and repentant heart.

Samuel replied, "What is more pleasing to the LORD: your burnt offerings and sacrifices or your obedience to his voice? Listen! Obedience is better than sacrifice, and submission is better than offering the fat of rams." 1 SAMUEL 15:22

You can give God your obedience. When you obey him, you give him the gift of yourself for his use. This shows God your commitment and devotion to him.

While [Jesus] was eating, a woman came in with a beautiful alabaster jar of expensive perfume and poured it over his head. The disciples were indignant when they saw this. "What a waste!" they said. "It could have been sold for a high price and the money given to the poor." But Jesus, aware of this, replied, "Why criticize this woman for doing such a good thing to me?" MATTHEW 26:7-10

You can give God your lavish worship.

On the first day of each week, you should each put aside a portion of the money you have earned. 1 CORINTHIANS 16:2

You can give God your first and your best.

What are some gifts I can give to others?

Love is patient and kind. Love is not jealous or boastful or proud or rude. It does not demand its own way. It is not irritable, and it keeps no record of being wronged. It does

not rejoice about injustice but rejoices whenever the truth wins out. Love never gives up, never loses faith, is always hopeful, and endures through every circumstance.
1 CORINTHIANS 13:4-7

You can give others the gift of love.

If you forgive those who sin against you, your heavenly Father will forgive you.
MATTHEW 6:14

You can give others the gift of forgiveness.

You are being faithful to God when you care for the traveling teachers who pass through, even though they are strangers to you. They have told the church here of your loving friendship. Please continue providing for such teachers in a manner that pleases God.
3 JOHN 1:5-6

You can give others the gifts of hospitality and friendship.

The Scriptures say, "They share freely and give generously to the poor. Their good deeds will be remembered forever." 2 CORINTHIANS 9:9

You can give of your money, service, and other resources to meet others' needs.

How do God's gifts help the church?

Just as our bodies have many parts and each part has a special function, so it is with Christ's body. We are many parts of one body, and we all belong to each other. In his grace, God has given us different gifts for doing certain things well. ROMANS 12:4-6

God has given every believer certain gifts. Some of us are great organizers and administrators, while others are gifted musicians, teachers, even dishwashers! When all those in a congregation use their gifts to serve, the church becomes a powerful force for good, a strong witness for Jesus, and a mighty army to combat Satan's attacks.

How should I receive gifts from others?

Ten lepers stood at a distance, crying out, "Jesus, Master, have mercy on us!" . . . One of them, when he saw that he was healed, came back to Jesus, shouting, "Praise God!" He fell to the ground at Jesus' feet, thanking him for what he had done. LUKE 17:12-16

Accept gifts with thanks and appreciation.

[God] took notice of his lowly servant girl, and from now on all generations will call me blessed. LUKE 1:48

Accept gifts with humility; don't expect them as if you deserve them.

GIVING *See also* Generosity, Sharing, Stewardship, Tithing

Giving is sharing something you have—possessions, time, or talents, for example—with someone else. More important, giving is sharing yourself. Giving is a remarkable concept, originating in the heart of a giving God who pours forth more blessings on his people than we expect or deserve. The gift of life, the gift of love, the gift of salvation, the gift of eternity in heaven—all these are priceless. The possessions we have may be a tangible result of how we have invested our time, energy, and talents. But who we are—our character—is a result of how we have invested ourselves with God and others. One of the greatest promises of the Bible is that the more we give, the more we receive—not necessarily in material possessions, but in spiritual and eternal rewards.

Why should I give?

"Bring all the tithes into the storehouse so there will be enough food in my Temple. If you do," says the LORD of Heaven's Armies, "I will open the windows of heaven for you. I will pour out a blessing so great you won't have enough room to take it in! Try it! Put me to the test!" MALACHI 3:10

You should give back to God because God commands it.

As you harvest your crops, bring the very best of the first harvest to the house of the LORD your God. EXODUS 23:19

You should give your best to God because it demonstrates that he is first in your life.

Everything we have has come from you, and we give you only what you first gave us! 1 CHRONICLES 29:14

You should give because it reminds you that the things you have are gifts from God.

When we take your gifts to those who need them, they will thank God. 2 CORINTHIANS 9:11

You should give to others so that God will be glorified.

Give freely and become more wealthy; be stingy and lose everything. The generous will prosper; those who refresh others will themselves be refreshed. PROVERBS 11:24-25

You should not give in order to get more, but your personal resources often grow as you give. This may occur because the qualities that make you generous also make you responsible and trustworthy. Or God may entrust more to you so that you will channel more of his blessings into this world.

How does giving to others affect my own life?

Remember the words of the Lord Jesus: "It is more blessed to give than to receive." ACTS 20:35

Giving allows you to experience the joy of pleasing God and the satisfaction of helping others.

Give, and you will receive. Your gift will return to you in full—pressed down, shaken together to make room for more, running over, and poured into your lap. The amount you give will determine the amount you get back. LUKE 6:38

While you should not give in order to receive more, God has promised to bless you in response to your giving. Those who trust him find that they always have what they need when they really need it.

If you give even a cup of cold water to one of the least of my followers, you will surely be rewarded. MATTHEW 10:42

The simplest gifts often bring the most sacred rewards. No gift is too small, no act of kindness too insignificant, to be noticed by the Lord.

But I'm barely making it myself. What if I don't seem to have enough to give?

Honor the LORD with . . . the best part of everything you produce. Then he will fill your barns with grain. PROVERBS 3:9-10

Whoever gives to the poor will lack nothing. PROVERBS 28:27

God promises to provide for you when you give back to him.

God will generously provide all you need. Then you will always have everything you need and plenty left over to share with others. 2 CORINTHIANS 9:8

It's easy to think you would be happy if you had just a little more. The secret of happiness, however, is learning to be content with what you have, whether it is much or little, and learning to live abundantly even with little (see Philippians 4:11-12).

GOALS *See also* Decisions, Planning, Priorities, Purpose, Vision

When a ship sets out on a long voyage at sea, the captain needs to plot the course. He must choose the route, set the schedule, determine the places to stop, and assign the responsibilities for each crew member. By planning ahead and setting attainable goals, the captain ensures that the ship will stay on track and arrive at its destination in a safe and timely manner. The same principle is true for our lives. Setting attainable goals is necessary to give us a destination and a plan for getting there. Without goals, we wander aimlessly through life. When we allow God to be our captain and plot our life's journey according to his plan for us, then we will stay on track and arrive safely at our ultimate destination—heaven.

Why are goals important?

The LORD had said to Abram, "Leave your native country, your relatives, and your father's family, and go to the land that I will show you. I will make you into a great nation. I will bless you and make you famous, and you will be a blessing to others." GENESIS 12:1-2

God's goals set the agenda for your life. God's promise to Abram gave him such a strong purpose and direction that he risked everything to pursue it.

Even the Son of Man came not to be served but to serve others and to give his life as a ransom for many. MARK 10:45

A goal keeps you focused on your primary mission and determines how you conduct your life. Jesus' goal of giving his life for all people shaped the way he lived every day, guiding his interaction with others.

I don't have the strength to endure. I have nothing to live for. JOB 6:11

Goals give you a reason to keep going.

Preaching the Good News is not something I can boast about. I am compelled by God to do it. How terrible for me if I didn't preach the Good News! 1 CORINTHIANS 9:16

Goals are motivating.

How can I pursue my goals?

My ambition has always been to preach the Good News where the name of Christ has never been heard, rather than where a church has already been started by someone else. ROMANS 15:20

Don't quit; you will be able to achieve far more than you thought possible. Paul was an older man when he wrote this, but he was still driven by this basic goal, which would eventually carry him as far as Spain.

I run with purpose in every step. I am not just shadowboxing. 1 CORINTHIANS 9:26

I focus on this one thing: Forgetting the past and looking forward to what lies ahead, I press on to reach the end of the race and receive the heavenly prize for which God, through Christ Jesus, is calling us. PHILIPPIANS 3:13-14

Keep your eyes on the target, and resist the temptation to get sidetracked. Stay focused on your primary goals in order to be most effective and make significant progress.

Let love be your highest goal! 1 CORINTHIANS 14:1

Don't walk over others to achieve your goals. Loving others should always be your highest goal.

What kinds of goals does God want me to have?

Go and make disciples of all the nations, baptizing them in the name of the Father and the Son and the Holy Spirit. Teach these new disciples to obey all the commands I have given you. MATTHEW 28:19-20

Jesus' ultimate goal for his followers is to share his Good News with all people everywhere.

Let us aim for harmony in the church and try to build each other up. ROMANS 14:19

You should make it your goal to foster harmony and love among other Christians.

If you want to be a friend of the world, you make yourself an enemy of God. JAMES 4:4

Love God, not the pleasures of the world.

Our goal is to please him. 2 CORINTHIANS 5:9

Whatever you do, your goal should be to please God.

GOSSIP *See also* Assumptions, Judging Others, Motives

Let's admit it: Gossip is often fun. The Bible calls rumors "dainty morsels" (Proverbs 18:8). Everyone loves to be in on the latest news. But the very people with whom you gossip may also gossip about you. Gossip separates friends, reveals people's secrets, and causes much hurt. Gossip is a sin, and it should be avoided. Gossip unjustly robs another person of his or her reputation. Worse, gossip often does this with half-lies, half-truths, insinuations, or a combination of these. We can stop a conversation that turns to gossip by changing the subject or saying something kind about the person others are gossiping about. If you don't add fuel, the fire will eventually go out.

Why is gossip so bad?

Do not spread slanderous gossip among your people. LEVITICUS 19:16

Do not judge others, and you will not be judged. MATTHEW 7:1

Gossip is a sin that God commands us to avoid. It puts you in the position of judging others. In a court of law, rumors and opinions are not allowed because they might unjustly sway the opinion of the jury. The same is true when we turn our living rooms into courtrooms where we sit as judge and jury, allowing rumors and opinions to color and often damage the reputation of others who have no chance to defend themselves.

Rumors are dainty morsels that sink deep into one's heart. PROVERBS 18:8

Gossip hurts others. It also destroys your credibility if the gossip proves to be false.

If you claim to be religious but don't control your tongue, you are fooling yourself, and your religion is worthless. JAMES 1:26

What comes out of your mouth shows what is in your heart. Your words show what kind of person you really are. Gossip, criticism, flattery, lying, and profanity are not only unkind but are heart problems, as well. Being more careful with your words isn't enough. You need a change of heart—then good, kind, and healing words will follow.

How do I stop gossip?

Fire goes out without wood, and quarrels disappear when gossip stops. PROVERBS 26:20

Stop the chain of gossip with you! When you hear gossip, you can do something about it—you can decide not to spread it any further.

You must examine the facts carefully. DEUTERONOMY 13:14

If you are concerned about something you've heard, look carefully into the matter before you assume that what you have been told is true. Go to the source and get the facts straight.

Do to others whatever you would like them to do to you. MATTHEW 7:12

The Golden Rule can also be applied to your speech: Talk about others in the same way you would like them to talk about you.

Whatever you do or say, do it as a representative of the Lord Jesus, giving thanks through him to God the Father. COLOSSIANS 3:17

If you are tempted to gossip, ask yourself, *Does the person I'm talking to need to know this? Is it true, accurate, and helpful?*

GRACE *See also* Compassion, Forgiveness, Mercy

Grace is undeserved favor. It is mercy given when we don't expect it or deserve it. The Bible tells us God extends his grace by offering us salvation—eternal life with him—for free! We don't have to do anything to earn it. In fact, we can't earn it or buy it. We simply accept it by believing that Jesus, God's Son, died for our sins so we don't have to. God's ultimate act of grace is our example for extending grace to others. We are to be quick to forgive, hasty to extend kindness, generous in love—even when others don't deserve it. Grace is a tangible expression of love.

What is grace? How can I receive it?

The wages of sin is death, but the free gift of God is eternal life through Christ Jesus our Lord. ROMANS 6:23

God saved you by his grace when you believed. And you can't take credit for this; it is a gift from God. Salvation is not a reward for the good things we have done, so none of us can boast about it. EPHESIANS 2:8-9

Grace is a big favor you do for someone without expecting anything in return. When the Bible says you are saved by grace, it means that God has done you the biggest favor of all—he has pardoned you from the death sentence you deserved because of your sin. You do not have to earn God's grace or work your way to heaven. Because of God's grace, you are forgiven and restored to full fellowship with God. Like the gift of life itself, you cannot take credit for it—any more than a baby can brag about being born! The fact that this is God's gift and not the product of your own effort gives you great comfort, security, and hope. You must accept grace like a gift, or you can't enjoy its benefits.

Let us come boldly to the throne of our gracious God. There we will receive his mercy, and we will find grace to help us when we need it most. HEBREWS 4:16

You may freely approach God at any time, and he will freely give you his mercy and grace.

How does grace affect my daily life?

Sin is no longer your master, for you no longer live under the requirements of the law. Instead, you live under the freedom of God's grace. ROMANS 6:14

God's grace forgives the penalty of sin and breaks the power of sin over your life. The Holy Spirit gives you the desire to please God and the spiritual wisdom to discern the truth and pursue it.

After starting your Christian lives in the Spirit, why are you now trying to become perfect by your own human effort? GALATIANS 3:3

We are God's masterpiece. He has created us anew in Christ Jesus, so we can do the good things he planned for us long ago. EPHESIANS 2:10

You need to continually remind yourself that God's approval of you is because of his grace alone. It is not because of what you do or don't do, but because he loves you and has forgiven all your sins. God created you to do good works by his grace at work within you.

How does grace affect my view of God?
The LORD is compassionate and merciful, slow to get angry and filled with unfailing love. PSALM 103:8

If you believe God is always angry with you, you will be defensive, fearful, or antagonistic toward him. But when you believe the depth of his love and grace toward you, you live with the joy of being forgiven and knowing you will live forever with him in heaven. You no longer fear God's retribution, but you seek him out for relationship with him.

How should I respond to God's grace?
I am certain that God, who began the good work within you, will continue his work until it is finally finished on the day when Christ Jesus returns. PHILIPPIANS 1:6

When you understand God's grace, you will desire to grow more like Jesus.

You know the generous grace of our Lord Jesus Christ. Though he was rich, yet for your sakes he became poor, so that by his poverty he could make you rich. 2 CORINTHIANS 8:9

Grace involves sacrifice. Respond to God's grace by following Jesus' example of sacrifice.

We make this plea, not because we deserve help, but because of your mercy. DANIEL 9:18

Recognizing and accepting God's grace takes humility. The more you realize how much you need God's grace, the more you realize you don't deserve it—which is exactly why you need it!

GREED *See also* Ambition, Coveting, Lust, Materialism

Greed is similar to lust; it's a burning desire to have something for personal gratification, and we're willing to do almost anything to get it. If greed is left unchecked, the desire will destroy us and those around us. Greed is a hunger that can never be fully satisfied. The more stuff we get, the more we want. Then we want more . . . and more . . . and more. Greed can overpower us, moving us to seek things we know aren't even good for us. Greed will often get us what we want, but usually at great cost. Why? Because at the heart of greed is selfish pleasure at the expense of others. We may think our plans are so clever ("What a great deal I just made!"), yet we jeopardize relationships in the process—including our relationship with God. More is never enough when we seek things that never truly satisfy.

What can greed do to me?

Some people are always greedy for more, but the godly love to give! PROVERBS 21:26

Like greedy dogs, they are never satisfied . . . all following their own path and intent on personal gain. ISAIAH 56:11

Greed can so consume you that you become blind to others' needs. It is at the opposite end of the spectrum from generosity, giving, and graciousness.

Be stingy and lose everything. PROVERBS 11:24

The more obsessed you are with having more, the greater the odds that you will wind up with less.

How can I resist becoming greedy?

Looking at the man, Jesus felt genuine love for him. "There is still one thing you haven't done," he told him. "Go and sell all your possessions and give the money to the poor, and you will have treasure in heaven. Then come, follow me." At this the man's face fell, and he went away sad, for he had many possessions. MARK 10:21-22

Ask yourself, *How tightly do I hold on to what I have?* If Jesus gave you the same advice that he gave this rich young man, could you do it?

I came naked from my mother's womb, and I will be naked when I leave. The LORD gave me what I had, and the LORD has taken it away. JOB 1:21

Don't store up treasures here on earth. . . . Store your treasures in heaven. . . . Wherever your treasure is, there the desires of your heart will also be. MATTHEW 6:19-21

Ask yourself, *Who really owns my things?* Remind yourself that everything comes from the hand of God, and therefore everything you have is God's. This changes your perspective on your possessions.

Think about the things of heaven, not the things of earth. For you died to this life, and your real life is hidden with Christ in God. COLOSSIANS 3:2-3

Ask yourself, *What do I think about most?* Redirect your focus from material things that don't last to things that last forever—your relationship with God and with others.

GRIEF *See also* Brokenness, Loneliness, Loss, Suffering

Grief brings suffering, anxiety, confusion, restlessness, pain, heartache, and usually plenty of tears. Grief is like a stabbing pain. It tortures your soul and robs you of the joy of living. But the Bible assures us that even when we go through the darkest times of grief, God is with us, giving comfort and hope.

How do I get over my grief?

The king was overcome with emotion. He went up to the room over the gateway and burst into tears. And as he went, he cried, "O my son Absalom!"
2 SAMUEL 18:33

Recognize that grieving is necessary and important. You need the freedom to grieve. It is an important part of healing because it allows you to release the emotional pressure of your sorrow.

When Sarah was 127 years old, she died. . . . Abraham mourned and wept for her. . . . He said to the Hittite elders, . . . "Please sell me a piece of land so I can give my wife a proper burial." GENESIS 23:1-4

Participate in the process of grieving. Take time to mourn, but also become involved in the necessary steps to bring closure to your loss. You grieve because you have had a positive experience—what you lost was important to you. Being involved in the process of grieving is a way of honoring what was meaningful.

[God] will wipe every tear from their eyes, and there will be no more death or sorrow or crying or pain. All these things are gone forever. REVELATION 21:4

Take comfort in the fact that there will be no more grief in heaven.

In what ways does God minister to me in my grief?

Even when I walk through the darkest valley, I will not be afraid, for you are close beside me. Your rod and your staff protect and comfort me. PSALM 23:4

God blesses those who mourn, for they will be comforted. MATTHEW 5:4

God ministers to you through his comforting presence.

I weep with sorrow; encourage me by your word. . . . Your promise revives me; it comforts me in all my troubles. . . . I meditate on your age-old regulations; O LORD, they comfort me. PSALM 119:28, 50-52

God ministers to you through his Word.

The Holy Spirit helps us in our weakness. For example, we don't know what God wants us to pray for. But the Holy Spirit prays for us with groanings that cannot be expressed in words. ROMANS 8:26

God ministers to you through his Spirit. When you don't even know what to pray, the Holy Spirit will pray for you.

God, who encourages those who are discouraged, encouraged us by the arrival of Titus.
2 CORINTHIANS 7:6

God ministers to you through other people in your life. When you need encouragement, God will bring friends and counselors.

He will wipe every tear from their eyes, and there will be no more death or sorrow or crying or pain. All these things are gone forever. REVELATION 21:4

God ministers to you through his promise of eternity with him, free of all grief. When you lose perspective, ask God to show you a glimpse of eternity.

How can God use my grief for good?

I am glad I sent [that letter], not because it hurt you, but because the pain caused you to repent and change your ways. 2 CORINTHIANS 7:9

God can use sorrow in your life to help you turn away from sin and seek salvation. Your times of grief can lead to confession, repentance, and a restored relationship with God. When grief leaves your soul empty, God can fill it with more than you ever dreamed.

I cry out, ". . . Everything I had hoped for from the LORD is lost!" The thought of my suffering and homelessness is bitter beyond words. I will never forget this awful time, as I grieve over my loss. Yet I still dare to hope when I remember this: The faithful love of the LORD never ends! His mercies never cease. Great is his faithfulness; his mercies begin afresh each morning. I say to myself, "The LORD is my inheritance; therefore, I will hope in him!" The LORD is good to those who depend on him, to those who search for him. LAMENTATIONS 3:18-25

Grief can renew your hope in God. In your grief, hold on to the knowledge that the "faithful love of the LORD never ends!"

You have turned my mourning into joyful dancing. You have taken away my clothes of mourning and clothed me with joy, that I might sing praises to you and not be silent. O LORD my God, I will give you thanks forever! PSALM 30:11-12

Grief can lead to a time of praise and thanksgiving to God.

How did Jesus handle grief?

Jesus saw the huge crowd as he stepped from the boat, and he had compassion on them and healed their sick. MATTHEW 14:14

[Jesus] told them, "My soul is crushed with grief to the point of death. Stay here and keep watch with me." MARK 14:34

Jesus expressed his emotions honestly. At times Jesus needed to be alone with his grief, and at times he sought others to share in his grief. He did not let his circumstances or his feelings diminish his dedication to God. Jesus remained focused and continued to serve.

How can I help others who are grieving?

Singing cheerful songs to a person with a heavy heart is like taking someone's coat in cold weather or pouring vinegar in a wound. PROVERBS 25:20

Be happy with those who are happy, and weep with those who weep. ROMANS 12:15

Give your attention, sympathy, and comfort to the grieving. Pretending that the pain is not there is like rubbing salt in a wound. It is difficult to be with someone who is grieving, but you don't need to come up with the right words to make it all go away—you can't. Your concern and your presence will help a grieving person more than your words.

My life seeps away. Depression haunts my days. JOB 30:16

A broken heart crushes the spirit. PROVERBS 15:13

A broken spirit saps a person's strength. PROVERBS 17:22

Be aware of the toll that grief takes on a person's spirit, mind, and body. Your awareness will lead to sympathy. Your sympathy will lead to soothing the wounded, and that will lead to healing.

I have heard all this before. What miserable comforters you are! JOB 16:2

How can your empty clichés comfort me? All your explanations are lies! JOB 21:34

Be careful with the words you use to those who are grieving. Explanations and clichés are rarely comforting. Instead, grieving people urgently need love, sympathy, and the power of your presence. Sometimes the best comfort you can give is just to be there.

GUIDANCE *See also* Decisions, Discernment, Will of God, Wisdom

When traveling to a new destination, we often seek the advice of someone who has been there, who knows the lay of the land, the best sites to see, and even the places to avoid. As we travel through life, it is important to have a close relationship with the ultimate guide—Jesus Christ. He knows where we've been and what will happen in the future. When we seek his advice, he points us to places of unimaginable beauty, joy, and peace, and he also helps us avoid the dangerous spots. God promises to be our constant guide in this journey called life, leading us through the dark valleys and in the mountaintop experiences, bringing us to that place of eternal peace and rest we long for.

How can I be sure God will guide me?

The LORD directs the steps of the godly. He delights in every detail of their lives. PSALM 37:23

God does indeed care about you and is watching over you, as he promises in his Word. He knows everything about your life, and he helps you follow his path for you.

"I know the plans I have for you," says the LORD. "They are plans for good and not for disaster, to give you a future and a hope." JEREMIAH 29:11

God is always seeking the best for you. When you are close to God, he is always ready to direct you to what is best for you.

How can I experience God's guidance?

Trust in the LORD with all your heart; do not depend on your own understanding. Seek his will in all you do, and he will show you which path to take. PROVERBS 3:5-6

The first step in receiving guidance is knowing where to put your trust. Travelers rely on an accurate map when they don't know where they are going. A critically ill person relies on a medical expert who knows the proper treatment. In the same way, the believer realizes his own spiritual limitations and relies on God's Word in matters of faith. You do not understand all the complexities of life, but the Lord does. You must trust him to guide you.

Keep on asking, and you will receive what you ask for. Keep on seeking, and you will find. Keep on knocking, and the door will be opened to you. For everyone who asks, receives. Everyone who seeks, finds. And to everyone who knocks, the door will be opened.
MATTHEW 7:7-8

God invites you to pray—to go directly to him—to seek his guidance. The Lord expects you to take responsibility for seeking and following his direction.

If God's will is going to happen anyway, why do I need guidance?

The LORD said to Moses, "Why are you crying out to me? Tell the people to get moving!"
EXODUS 14:15

You guide me with your counsel, leading me to a glorious destiny. PSALM 73:24

Seek his will in all you do, and he will show you which path to take. PROVERBS 3:6

What you do still makes a difference. Your choices determine whether or not you participate in God's will. God's work will get done, if not by you then by someone else. But if you want to participate in accomplishing God's will and his work, you can't just sit back and let it happen. Seek his guidance first, and then make a decision to move ahead. If you ask God for guidance, your choices will usually be in line with his will, and you will be involved in his work.

Will God tell me what is in my future?

The LORD says, "I will guide you along the best pathway for your life. I will advise you and watch over you." PSALM 32:8

Your word is a lamp to guide my feet and a light for my path. PSALM 119:105

The LORD will work out his plans for my life—for your faithful love, O LORD, endures forever. PSALM 138:8

If we could see our future, we'd become either scared of the hard times ahead or proud about our accomplishments. Instead, God's guidance is less like a searchlight that brightens the whole horizon and more like a flashlight that illuminates just enough of the path ahead to show you where to take the next few steps. God has a definite plan for you—never doubt that. But he doesn't usually reveal it all at once. He wants you to learn to trust him each step of the way.

GUILT See also Forgiveness, Regrets, Repentance, Shame

We've all felt guilty about something we've done wrong. Guilt is a God-given mechanism that alerts us when we've sinned. Sometimes we aren't even aware we've done something wrong until the feeling of guilt creeps up. Other times we feel stronger guilt than the deed actually warrants. Ignoring guilt is dangerous because we can eventually tune it out and begin to feel too comfortable with sin. The best way to deal with guilt is to confess our sin to God and ask for forgiveness. If we've sinned against another person, we need to confess to him or her as well. Forgiveness is the only cleansing agent that can remove both the sin and the guilt.

In what ways am I guilty?

Everyone has sinned; we all fall short of God's glorious standard. ROMANS 3:23

The person who keeps all of the laws except one is as guilty as a person who has broken all of God's laws. JAMES 2:10

The magnitude of guilt may change with the magnitude of sin, but guilt is always present with sin. Every human being is guilty of sin.

Remember, it is sin to know what you ought to do and then not do it. JAMES 4:17

The guilt of sin comes not only from doing wrong things; it also comes from not doing right things.

How can I be free from guilt?

Cleanse me from these hidden faults. Keep your servant from deliberate sins! Don't let them control me. Then I will be free of guilt. PSALM 19:12-13

If we confess our sins to him, he is faithful and just to forgive us our sins and to cleanse us from all wickedness. 1 JOHN 1:9

Guilt is the consequence of wrongdoing. You can be free from guilt by avoiding sin as much as possible and confessing any sins to God. Don't let guilty feelings keep you from talking to God; prayer is your only means of confessing to him and restoring your relationship with him.

Acknowledge your guilt. Admit that you rebelled against the LORD your God. JEREMIAH 3:13

There is a high cost to acknowledging guilt and admitting sin, but there's an even higher cost if you don't. Humbly admitting your guilt is much less painful in the long run. You can't deal with your guilt if you deny that you have any.

This is the message of Good News for the people of Israel—that there is peace with God through Jesus Christ, who is Lord of all. ACTS 10:36

Everyone who believes in him is declared right with God—something the law of Moses could never do. ACTS 13:39

I am not ashamed of this Good News about Christ. It is the power of God at work, saving everyone who believes. . . . This Good News tells us how God makes us right in his sight. ROMANS 1:16-17

Everyone has been declared guilty of sin. But God offers everyone the most amazing gift—life with him forever in heaven, where all is good and perfect. It sounds too good to be true, but that is God's Good News. And all you have to do is believe it by accepting the truth that Jesus died for your sins. When you do, your guilt is gone completely, and your life is so changed you'll gratefully follow Jesus and live the way he asks his believers to live. Anyone who can free you from a death sentence is worth following. God doesn't want you to feel guilty about being free; he wants you to enjoy your freedom and make the most of it.

How do I handle feelings of guilt that linger even after I confess my sin?

Purify me from my sins, and I will be clean; wash me, and I will be whiter than snow.
PSALM 51:7

Trust God's truth, not your fickle, fluctuating feelings. Your guilt may really be shame or regret over what you have done, or the lingering consequences of your actions. Embrace God's promise of forgiveness, which cleanses you from shame and regret.

He forgives all my sins and heals all my diseases. . . . He does not punish us for all our sins; he does not deal harshly with us, as we deserve. PSALM 103:3, 10

All sin . . . can be forgiven. MARK 3:28

When God forgives you, he looks at you as though you have never sinned. When you receive his forgiveness, you are blameless before him. If you have confessed your sin, don't go through another day burdened by the weight of unnecessary guilt.

HABITS See also Addiction, Consistency, Priorities, Self-Control

A habit is a usual pattern of behavior. Most people have both good habits and bad habits. The question is, which kind of habits prevail? We think of bad habits as things like smoking, drinking too much, or biting your nails. But spreading gossip, complaining, backbiting, or worry can become bad habits too. Bad habits and can hurt us—and others—physically and emotionally. Good habits, on the other hand, can be of great value. Exercise and good nutrition are healthy habits. The habits of prayer and reading the Bible have amazing, positive results. We can also make witnessing about Jesus a habit. The Bible has much to say about habits—those that will benefit us for a lifetime (and beyond), and those that are bound to destroy us.

What are some bad habits the Bible talks about?

"All right, go ahead," Pharaoh replied. "I will let you go.". . . But Pharaoh again became stubborn and refused to let the people go. EXODUS 8:28, 32

Pharaoh developed a bad habit of lying to get what he wanted.

The people began to complain about their hardship. NUMBERS 11:1

The Israelites developed a bad habit of complaining. Chronic complaining can quickly turn into bitterness.

[The younger widows] will learn to be lazy and will spend their time gossiping.
1 TIMOTHY 5:13

Too much time and too little to do can be fertile ground for bad habits. Idleness makes it easy to develop the bad habit of gossiping.

Stop bringing me your meaningless gifts; the incense of your offerings disgusts me! As for your celebrations of the new moon and the Sabbath and your special days for fasting— they are all sinful and false. I want no more of your pious meetings. ISAIAH 1:13

The people of Israel love their rituals of sacrifice, but to me their sacrifices are all meaningless. I will hold my people accountable for their sins, and I will punish them.
HOSEA 8:13

Religious rituals without true faith are bad habits. Make sure you haven't created habits of worship that God doesn't consider to be worship at all.

How can God help me deal with bad habits?

I don't really understand myself, for I want to do what is right, but I don't do it. Instead, I do what I hate. ROMANS 7:15

One of the best ways to deal with bad habits is to recognize them for what they are and confess them honestly. Paul knew that he could not kick the habit of sin completely. But he did know that he could make progress every day with God's help. In the same way, you may have to give up a habit in phases, one step at a time.

Those who are dominated by the sinful nature think about sinful things, but those who are controlled by the Holy Spirit think about things that please the Spirit. ROMANS 8:5

God has given you the Holy Spirit to help make you holy. While victory does not come immediately, you will progress as you submit your mind and heart to the love, wisdom, and truth of God's Spirit living in you.

Do not let sin control the way you live; do not give in to sinful desires. Do not let any part of your body become an instrument of evil to serve sin. Instead, give yourselves completely to God, for you were dead, but now you have new life. ROMANS 6:12-13

One of Satan's lies is that you are a victim who has no power to resist the powerful influences around you. The world teaches you that heredity, environment, and circumstances excuse you from responsibility. But God is more powerful than anything that seeks to control you. Call upon God's power through prayer and the support of the Holy Spirit and fellow believers. Then God will break the chains that hold you, and he will set you free.

What are some good habits to cultivate?

Let us not neglect our meeting together, as some people do. HEBREWS 10:25

Meeting together with other believers is a good habit because it provides necessary support and fellowship, it develops the habit of group Bible study, it keeps you busy when you might otherwise be slipping into bad habits, and it offers accountability.

The LORD is my strength and shield. I trust him with all my heart. . . . I burst out in songs of thanksgiving. PSALM 28:7

As a young boy, David developed the habit of talking to God, singing songs about him, and writing psalms. This helped him trust and follow God all his life.

Train yourself to be godly. . . . "Physical training is good, but training for godliness is much better, promising benefits in this life and in the life to come." 1 TIMOTHY 4:7-8

Good habits—such as reading God's Word, praying, and giving your time and money in service to God and others—give you spiritual stamina, purpose, and direction. These habits also help you keep your eyes on the ultimate goal of eternal life.

How can I pass on good habits to my family?

Be an example to all believers in what you say, in the way you live, in your love, your faith, and your purity. 1 TIMOTHY 4:12

When you make God part of your daily life, you will be a godly example to others. Children readily learn by example. Hopefully they see more good habits in their parents than bad.

You must commit yourselves wholeheartedly to these commands that I am giving you today. Repeat them again and again to your children. Talk about them when you are at home and when you are on the road, when you are going to bed and when you are getting up. DEUTERONOMY 6:6-7

Be purposeful in teaching good habits to your children. Explain why you follow God and how you have seen him work in your life. Make it a habit to pass on a godly heritage.

HAPPINESS *See also* Celebration, Contentment, Joy, Pleasure

Happiness can be experienced in two ways: It can be a reaction to a pleasurable and satisfying experience, or it can be a state of well-being and contentment. The first kind of happiness is temporary and lasts only for the duration of the happy event. The second kind of happiness is deeper and more continuous. It bubbles up in spite of unhappy circumstances. This kind of inner joy can only come from knowing and obeying God. Only he can bring continuous joy, even during the hard times of life.

Where can I find real and lasting happiness?

Joyful are those who have the God of Israel as their helper, whose hope is in the LORD their God. PSALM 146:5

The Lord himself is the source of true happiness. The more you love him, know him, walk with him, and become like him, the greater your happiness will be.

How joyful are those who fear the LORD and delight in obeying his commands. PSALM 112:1

It may seem ironic that the more you fear the Lord, the happier you will be. But the Bible says that fear of the Lord (respecting him so much you want to listen to what he says) is the way to wisdom. Wisdom helps you make good choices that bring happiness and avoid harmful choices that bring misery.

I know the LORD is always with me. . . . No wonder my heart is glad, and I rejoice. PSALM 16:8-9

Happiness is based on God's presence within you, which brings contentment and confidence in the face of hardship.

How beautiful on the mountains are the feet of the messenger who brings good news, the good news of peace and salvation, the news that the God of Israel reigns! ISAIAH 52:7

The Good News of Jesus brings joy and happiness when you develop a relationship with him. And there is an added measure of happiness when you share this news with others.

How can I be happy in the midst of difficult circumstances?

Don't be surprised at the fiery trials you are going through, as if something strange were happening to you. Instead, be very glad—for these trials make you partners with Christ in his suffering, so that you will have the wonderful joy of seeing his glory when it is revealed to all the world. 1 PETER 4:12-13

God promises a greater reward for those who endure difficult circumstances because of their faith. Temporary suffering will be replaced by a greater joy that lasts forever. Anticipating these rewards makes us happier even in the midst of adversity.

When all you owned was taken from you, you accepted it with joy. You knew there were better things waiting for you that will last forever. HEBREWS 10:34

Hope in God's promises of eternal life can make you happy because you know that what you are presently going through will one day come to an end.

The apostles left the high council rejoicing that God had counted them worthy to suffer disgrace for the name of Jesus. ACTS 5:41

When you live in such a way that even your suffering brings honor to Jesus, he will give you a special place of honor that will bring you a deep sense of joy.

How can I make God happy?
The LORD your God will delight in you if you obey his voice and keep the commands and decrees written in this Book of Instruction, and if you turn to the LORD your God with all your heart and soul. DEUTERONOMY 30:10

Can finite, sinful human beings truly bring joy and delight to the Lord, the Creator of the universe? God says yes. He created you because he wants to have a relationship with you and to delight in being with you. God is most delighted when you love him wholeheartedly and show it by obeying him.

How can I bring happiness to others?
Love each other with genuine affection, and take delight in honoring each other. ROMANS 12:10

Treating others with God's love will bring them happiness. Just as God is the wellspring of true happiness, so you are his conduit of that happiness to others.

HATRED *See also* Anger, Revenge, Sin, Terrorism
Is it wrong to hate? That depends on the object of our hatred. We should never hate another person, because every person is a unique creation of God and has an eternal soul that can be redeemed. But we should certainly hate anything that tries to tempt us away from God or that opposes God altogether. Foul language, perversion, crime, violence, evil, even gossip are things to hate. We are to love the sinner but hate the sin. Be careful not to let your hatred of sinful actions lead you to judge and hate the person who commits them.

What causes unhealthy hatred?
Haman was a happy man as he left the banquet! But when he saw Mordecai sitting at the palace gate, not standing up or trembling nervously before him, Haman became furious. ESTHER 5:9

When you follow the desires of your sinful nature, the results are very clear: sexual immorality, impurity, lustful pleasures. GALATIANS 5:19

Hatred comes from allowing your own sinful nature to overcome you. For example, Haman hated Mordecai because Mordecai refused to bow down before him. This petty jealousy, a hunger for recognition, drove Haman to violent hatred that could not be satisfied unless Mordecai was dead. Such consuming hatred can lead to violent thoughts or actions.

How do I let go of hatred?

A gentle answer deflects anger, but harsh words make tempers flare. PROVERBS 15:1

Cultivate a gentle spirit to help manage your anger. Anger leads to bitterness, which leads to hatred.

Get rid of all bitterness, rage, anger, harsh words, and slander, as well as all types of evil behavior. Instead, be kind to each other, tenderhearted, forgiving one another.
EPHESIANS 4:31-32

The more you work at being tenderhearted, the easier it will be to forgive others. It's hard to continue to hate someone you've forgiven.

If someone says, "I love God," but hates a Christian brother or sister, that person is a liar; for if we don't love people we can see, how can we love God, whom we cannot see?
1 JOHN 4:20

Nurturing your love for God will increase your love for others. Love will overcome your hatred.

Can following Jesus cause others to hate me?

The world hates them because they do not belong to the world, just as I do not belong to the world. JOHN 17:14

It is no shame to suffer for being a Christian. 1 PETER 4:16

Following Jesus may cause some people to hate you. Those who love sin hate those who are against sin. If you take a stand against sin, expect opposition.

What can I do if someone hates me?

If you are presenting a sacrifice at the altar in the Temple and you suddenly remember that someone has something against you, leave your sacrifice there at the altar. Go and be reconciled to that person. Then come and offer your sacrifice to God. MATTHEW 5:23-24

Examine yourself honestly and search for anything you have said or done that might have made the other person angry. If you find something, confess it to the other person and ask for forgiveness.

If your enemies are hungry, feed them. If they are thirsty, give them something to drink. In doing this, you will heap burning coals of shame on their heads. ROMANS 12:20

Continue to act in a loving way toward someone who shows hatred toward you—but don't subject yourself to further harm. Your attitude of love may influence the other person to change his or her attitude toward you.

The earnest prayer of a righteous person has great power and produces wonderful results. JAMES 5:16

Pray for the other person. You can't change a person's heart, but God can.

HEALING *See also* Body, Disabilities, Hope, Miracles, Rest

Sickness can strike us in a variety of ways. It can affect our body, mind, emotions, and spirit. When our body is sick, we may struggle with the ability to move, work, serve, and sometimes just function. Some people fight mental disorders and emotional turmoil. And we all suffer from spiritual sickness: sin. We long for healing at various times in our lives—for relief from a common cold or a life-threatening disease, for deliverance from confusion or depression, for release from spiritual corruption. God wants to heal us, and he welcomes our pleas for restoration.

Does God heal me?

I am the LORD who heals you. EXODUS 15:26

God is not bound by the limitations of this world. He can intervene to overcome any threat to your life, including illness and disease—physical, mental, emotional, or spiritual.

"Lord," he said, "if you are willing, you can heal me and make me clean." Jesus reached out and touched him. "I am willing," he said. "Be healed!" LUKE 5:12-13

Jesus is willing and able to heal you. You are not bothering God when you pray for healing; you are expressing your faith and trust in him. Jesus may not heal all of your illnesses in this life, but he does perform a great act of healing in you every day when he forgives your sins.

How does God heal?

Isaiah said, "Make an ointment from figs." So Hezekiah's servants spread the ointment over the boil, and Hezekiah recovered! 2 KINGS 20:7

Through physicians and medicine.

I will never forget your commandments, for by them you give me life. PSALM 119:93

Through his words and commands.

Jesus met a man with an advanced case of leprosy. . . . "Lord," he said, "if you are willing, you can heal me and make me clean." Jesus reached out and touched him. . . . "Be healed!" And instantly the leprosy disappeared. LUKE 5:12-13

Through miracles.

Esau hated Jacob. . . . [Years later] Esau ran to meet him and embraced him, threw his arms around his neck, and kissed him. And they both wept. GENESIS 27:41; 33:4

Through time.

[Jesus] was pierced for our rebellion, crushed for our sins. He was beaten so we could be whole. He was whipped so we could be healed. ISAIAH 53:5

Through Christ. His death brings you life; his wounds bring you healing. By taking upon himself the punishment you deserved for your sin, he sets you free.

[Jesus] will wipe every tear from their eyes, and there will be no more death or sorrow or crying or pain. All these things are gone forever. REVELATION 21:4

Through his promise of heaven. There you will receive complete healing.

How can I seek God's healing?

Are any of you sick? You should call for the elders of the church to come and pray over you, anointing you with oil in the name of the Lord. Such a prayer offered in faith will heal the sick, and the Lord will make you well. And if you have committed any sins, you will be forgiven. JAMES 5:14-15

The Lord often uses others to give you his gifts—including healing. He has given authority to church leaders to be vessels for this special work. While you may not feel worthy or capable, pray for healing for one another out of obedience to God.

When I refused to confess my sin, my body wasted away, and I groaned all day long. Day and night your hand of discipline was heavy on me. My strength evaporated like water in the summer heat. Finally, I confessed all my sins to you and stopped trying to hide my guilt. I said to myself, "I will confess my rebellion to the LORD." And you forgave me! All my guilt is gone. PSALM 32:3-5

Sin can literally make you sick. Healing can come if you repent of your sin and receive God's forgiveness.

Why doesn't God always heal people?

[The Lord] said, "My grace is all you need. My power works best in weakness." 2 CORINTHIANS 12:9

We do not know why God heals some people but not others, at some times but not at other times. But we do know that God's power is magnified through our weaknesses and infirmities when we allow him to work within us. If you have been praying to be healed or for a loved one to be healed, and God has not done it, trust that he has something even greater that he wants to accomplish through the illness.

How should I respond when I'm not healed?

You guide me with your counsel, leading me to a glorious destiny. Whom have I in heaven but you? I desire you more than anything on earth. My health may fail, and my spirit may grow weak, but God remains the strength of my heart; he is mine forever. PSALM 73:24-26

Whether or not God chooses to heal you physically, you have the unspeakably miraculous gift of knowing him personally. The promise of your ultimate healing and eternal life with God in heaven are your greatest sources of comfort and hope.

HEART *See also* Attitude, Emotions, Presence of God, Thoughts

The human heart is a vital organ that pumps blood and oxygenates the body. When the heart doesn't function properly, the body doesn't function properly. Doctors urge us to exercise and eat nutritious food to keep our heart fit and healthy. In the Bible, the heart is also considered to be the center of thought and feeling. It is so important that God cautions us to guard it above all else because it filters everything that happens to us and around us. When we neglect our heart, it becomes filthy and clogged with all kinds of foulness that settles inside us—bitterness, rage, impure thoughts. A dirty heart can no longer tell the good from the harmful. But when we keep our heart pure and clean, it can block the toxins of sinful desires and thoughts that will destroy us. Guarding our heart is the best prescription for a happy and healthy life.

What kind of heart does God desire for me?

Never before had there been a king like Josiah, who turned to the Lord with all his heart and soul and strength, obeying all the laws of Moses. 2 KINGS 23:25

God desires a devoted, obedient heart.

I know, my God, that you examine our hearts and rejoice when you find integrity there. You know I have done all this with good motives, and I have watched your people offer their gifts willingly and joyously. 1 CHRONICLES 29:17

God desires a heart of integrity.

You desire honesty from the womb, teaching me wisdom even there. . . . Create in me a clean heart, O God. Renew a loyal spirit within me. . . . The sacrifice you desire is a broken spirit. You will not reject a broken and repentant heart, O God. PSALM 51:6, 10, 17

God desires an honest, clean, repentant heart.

How can my heart be the kind God desires?

I will give you a new heart, and I will put a new spirit in you. I will take out your stony, stubborn heart and give you a tender, responsive heart. EZEKIEL 36:26

Only God can give you the heart he desires you to have.

When the Lord saw their change of heart, he gave this message to Shemaiah: "Since the people have humbled themselves, I will not completely destroy them and will soon give them some relief." 2 CHRONICLES 12:7

Develop an attitude of humility. Only when you are humble can your heart begin to change.

Put all your rebellion behind you, and find yourselves a new heart and a new spirit.
EZEKIEL 18:31

Get rid of any sinful habit or lifestyle. Practice obeying God's Word, and you will see your heart change for the better.

Just think how much more the blood of Christ will purify our consciences from sinful deeds so that we can worship the living God. For by the power of the eternal Spirit, Christ offered himself to God as a perfect sacrifice for our sins. HEBREWS 9:14

When you believe that Jesus died for your sins, he forgives you and purifies your heart.

How do I guard and protect my heart?

Guard your heart above all else, for it determines the course of your life. PROVERBS 4:23

Christ will make his home in your hearts as you trust in him. Your roots will grow down into God's love and keep you strong. EPHESIANS 3:17

Keep away from anything that might take God's place in your hearts. 1 JOHN 5:21

Keep God at the center of your heart to prevent anything else from controlling it.

Listen and be wise: Keep your heart on the right course. PROVERBS 23:19

The purpose of a guardrail on a dangerous curve is not to inhibit your freedom to drive but to save your life! The guardrail is a sign of security and safety, not an obstacle to flying. In the same way, you need a guardrail as you travel through life, not to inhibit your freedom but to keep your life from going out of control. Your heart determines where you go because it controls your passions and emotions. If you don't guard your heart with God's Word and stay focused on the road God wants you to travel, you may have a terrible accident when temptations distract you.

How do I get my heart to long for God?

Jesus replied, "The most important commandment is this: 'Listen, O Israel! The LORD our God is the one and only LORD. And you must love the LORD your God with all your heart, all your soul, all your mind, and all your strength.'" MARK 12:29-30

Wherever your treasure is, there the desires of your heart will also be. LUKE 12:34

When God is the center of your life, your relationship with him will be your highest priority. You will long to spend time in prayer and reading the Bible, your thoughts will often turn to God, you will want to please him, and you will want to obey him. The more you love God, the more your heart will long to be closer to his.

HEAVEN *See also* Angels, Eternity, Resurrection, Salvation

People often have misguided ideas about heaven: that it consists of departed souls eternally playing harps in comfy cloud-chairs, or that they get to do anything they want. Perhaps the most tragic misconception is that heaven is the place where everyone goes when they die—or at least everyone who has lived a "good" life. The Bible presents a picture of heaven as the glorious, awesome home of God. And the Bible is also very specific about who will—and who will not—live there.

Is there really a heaven?

There is more than enough room in my Father's home. If this were not so, would I have told you that I am going to prepare a place for you? JOHN 14:2

We know that when this earthly tent we live in is taken down (that is, when we die and leave this earthly body), we will have a house in heaven. 2 CORINTHIANS 5:1

Not only is there a heaven, but Jesus is making preparations for your arrival. Heaven is described most often in terms of being your home. It is not a paradise you will simply visit as on a vacation, but it is an eternal dwelling place where you will live in joyful fellowship with your heavenly Father and his family.

In the beginning God created the heavens and the earth. . . . Then God looked over all he had made, and he saw that it was very good! GENESIS 1:1, 31

We are looking forward to the new heavens and new earth he has promised, a world filled with God's righteousness. 2 PETER 3:13

God originally created earth to be heaven—the place where he lived with humankind and walked and talked with them side by side. Sin changed all that; it separated us from God and corrupted the earth. But God originally conceived of a heavenly paradise that is a very physical place, with trees and plants, mountains and waterfalls, fruits and vegetables. The Bible consistently refers to the new heaven—the place where we will be reunited with God—as the new earth. The place where we will live forever with God will be very similar to the place we live now. If God said the original earth he created was "very good," then the new earth he is preparing for us will be similar and familiar to us.

What is heaven like?

Look! I am creating new heavens and a new earth, and no one will even think about the old ones anymore. ISAIAH 65:17

He will take our weak mortal bodies and change them into glorious bodies like his own. PHILIPPIANS 3:21

They will see his face, and his name will be written on their foreheads. And there will be no night there—no need for lamps or sun—for the Lord God will shine on them. And they will reign forever and ever. REVELATION 22:4-5

Heaven is far beyond anything you can imagine. In heaven you will live forever with God. Everything will be perfect and glorious. God will give you a new body, and you will be able to talk face-to-face with the Lord himself. The best this world has to offer can't even compare with the glory to come!

We will be like him, for we will see him as he really is. 1 JOHN 3:2

He will wipe every tear from their eyes, and there will be no more death or sorrow or crying or pain. All these things are gone forever. REVELATION 21:4

You will be like Christ in heaven. You will not be equal to him in power and authority, but you will be like him in character and perfection, for there will be no sin in those who are welcomed into heaven. In heaven you will never hurt, cry, have pain, or experience sorrow. Evil will be gone forever.

How can I be sure I will go to heaven?

God loved the world so much that he gave his one and only Son, so that everyone who believes in him will not perish but have eternal life. JOHN 3:16

If you believe Jesus died to take the punishment for your sins, and you recognize that only he can forgive you, the Bible promises you will go to heaven. You cannot earn your way to heaven; it is God's gift to those who give their allegiance to Jesus.

Because God's children are human beings—made of flesh and blood—the Son also became flesh and blood. For only as a human being could he die, and only by dying could he break the power of the devil, who had the power of death. Only in this way could he set free all who have lived their lives as slaves to the fear of dying. HEBREWS 2:14-15

God sent his Son, Jesus, to die—to take the punishment for sin that we deserve. If he had only died, it wouldn't be enough. But he rose from the dead, proving that he alone has power over death. The only One who has ever defied death promises the same victory to all who follow him.

Our earthly bodies are planted in the ground when we die, but they will be raised to live forever. 1 CORINTHIANS 15:42

Faith in Jesus is meaningless if it does not last. Jesus' resurrection was the essential aspect of God's plan to allow you to spend eternity with him. Because Jesus was raised from the dead with a new body, you can be assured that he has power over death. You too will be resurrected one day with a new body and live forever with him in heaven.

How does my knowing about heaven affect my life now?

Our present troubles are small and won't last very long. Yet they produce for us a glory that vastly outweighs them and will last forever! 2 CORINTHIANS 4:17

As a heaven-bound follower of Jesus, try to put heaven and earth in perspective. Here on earth, you will probably live for less than a hundred years. In heaven, a hundred million years will just be the beginning. Yet God determined that how we live during our short time on earth will prepare us for heaven. This gives purpose to your life, perspective on your troubles, and anticipation for the unique role God has planned for you in eternity.

Does the Bible really claim there is only one way to heaven?

Jesus told him, "I am the way, the truth, and the life. No one can come to the Father except through me." JOHN 14:6

Jesus is the only way to heaven. You may want to buy your way in, work your way in, or think your way in. But the Bible is clear—Jesus Christ provides the only way in. Believing this truth and gratefully accepting it is the only way to get to life's most important destination.

HELL *See also* Death, Evil, Judgment, Punishment

The greatest misconception about hell is that it doesn't exist. Just as we believe scientists when they tell us there is such a thing as gravity, so should we believe God when he tells us there is such a place as hell. Many people wonder how a merciful and caring God could send people to such a terrible place. The truth is that God doesn't send anyone to hell; people choose to go there by their own rebellion, and God honors their choice. The Bible is clear: Sin is rebellion against God, and rebels can't live in a kingdom without causing chaos. The only way to avoid hell is to surrender to God and change from a rebel to a servant. Then he forgives us and lets us enter and live in his kingdom forever. At the end of time, each of us will be judged for the choice we've made. Although God desperately wishes that no one should live in hell, he respects us enough to let us choose.

Is there really a place called hell?

You can enter God's Kingdom only through the narrow gate. The highway to hell is broad, and its gate is wide for the many who choose that way. MATTHEW 7:13

At the end of the world . . . the angels will come and separate the wicked people from the righteous, throwing the wicked into the fiery furnace, where there will be weeping and gnashing of teeth. MATTHEW 13:49-50

The Bible leaves no doubt that hell is a very real place.

What is hell like?

[A] rich man . . . died and was buried, and his soul went to the place of the dead. There, in torment, he saw Abraham in the far distance with Lazarus at his side. The rich man shouted, "Father Abraham, have some pity! Send Lazarus over here to dip the tip of his finger in water and cool my tongue. I am in anguish in these flames." LUKE 16:22-24

God did not spare even the angels who sinned. He threw them into hell, in gloomy pits of darkness. 2 PETER 2:4

Both the beast and his false prophet were thrown alive into the fiery lake of burning sulfur. REVELATION 19:20

The Bible compares hell to a burning fire, a dark and gloomy place where everyone is forever separated from God and all that is good. Some people think that it will be fun, like a never-ending bawdy party. On the contrary, the Bible alludes to hell as a lonely place where people are isolated from relationships. And while eternity is hard for us to imagine, there will be no end to hell.

Who will be sent to hell?

The Lord is coming . . . to execute judgment on the people of the world. He will convict every person of all the ungodly things they have done and for all the insults that ungodly sinners have spoken against him. JUDE 1:14-15

Anyone whose name was not found recorded in the Book of Life was thrown into the lake of fire. REVELATION 20:15

Any person who has not claimed allegiance to Jesus Christ as Lord will spend eternity in hell. Many people will be surprised on Judgment Day to find that living good lives and being successful did not secure their place in heaven. You can argue that it is not fair, that any good person shouldn't go to hell, but God is fair and gives an open invitation to everyone. He then honors your choice. You can't decide where people spend eternity; all you can decide is if God is telling the truth.

How can I be assured that I am not going to hell?

God loved the world so much that he gave his one and only Son, so that everyone who believes in him will not perish but have eternal life. JOHN 3:16

If you confess with your mouth that Jesus is Lord and believe in your heart that God raised him from the dead, you will be saved. ROMANS 10:9

There is only one way to be certain that you will not go to hell: You must confess your sin to Jesus and believe he is your personal Savior. By taking this step, you secure your place in heaven, and you no longer have to fear hell.

HELP *See also* Caring, Encouragement, Kindness, Support

All of us have limitations—areas of weakness, feelings of inadequacy, a lack of skill or knowledge. Sometimes we just don't know what to do or how to do it. Sometimes a crisis strikes, and we just can't handle it by ourselves. We need help. Despite our culture's admiration of the strong, independent spirit, no one can really survive alone. That's why God created us to be in relationship with other people. Part of relationship is giving and receiving help. We need help to get things done. We need help to restore relationships. We need help to develop our skills. We need help thinking through problems. We need help to say "I'm sorry." God wants to help us too. He is our ultimate helper, for he is wiser, stronger, and more loving than we and our human helpers are. We should seek the help of both God and others, and we should offer help to those in need.

In what ways does God help me?

Whenever they were in trouble and turned to the LORD, the God of Israel, and sought him out, they found him. 2 CHRONICLES 15:4

God helps you by always being available. God is present to help you whenever you call out to him. Prayer is the lifeline that connects you to God for daily help.

God . . . will supply all your needs from his glorious riches, which have been given to us in Christ Jesus. PHILIPPIANS 4:19

God helps you by providing resources to meet your needs. God has a full supply house and a ready supply system that are free for the asking.

The LORD is my strength and shield. I trust him with all my heart. He helps me, and my heart is filled with joy. I burst out in songs of thanksgiving. PSALM 28:7

God helps you by giving you strength to face any crisis. He protects you and gives you spiritual victory.

Right behind you a voice will say, "This is the way you should go," whether to the right or to the left. ISAIAH 30:21

God helps you by giving you his Holy Spirit. The Spirit gives you an extra measure of wisdom and discernment.

In what ways can I help others?

If someone has enough money to live well and sees a brother or sister in need but shows no compassion—how can God's love be in that person? 1 JOHN 3:17

You can help others by sharing your abundance with those who have less. Be open to the promptings of the Holy Spirit. Look for opportunities that may be God asking you to be his helper.

Paul had a vision: A man from Macedonia in northern Greece was standing there, pleading with him, "Come over to Macedonia and help us!" ACTS 16:9

Tell others the Good News of Jesus, giving them an opportunity to experience salvation and eternal life.

Feed and shepherd God's flock—his church, purchased with his own blood—over which the Holy Spirit has appointed you as elders. ACTS 20:28

You can help other believers grow spiritually.

When God's people are in need, be ready to help them. Always be eager to practice hospitality. ROMANS 12:13

You can help others by showing hospitality.

Two people are better off than one, for they can help each other succeed. If one person falls, the other can reach out and help. But someone who falls alone is in real trouble. ECCLESIASTES 4:9-10

You can help others by being available. When people try to do everything themselves, they are limited by their weaknesses. But when you depend on each other for help, you compensate for each other's weaknesses with your strengths.

HERITAGE *See also* Past, Reputation

Our heritage helps us understand who we are by reminding us of where we come from. It also gives us a sense of purpose and direction for where we are heading. Usually our heritage is passed down to us from our older relatives. Our heritage might be as simple as family traditions, our hair color, or a special skill. Sometimes it is bigger, like an inheritance. All of us have a heritage—the collection of the character and personality of the ancestors who have gone before us.

There is another kind of heritage that everyone can become a part of. We can all receive the spiritual heritage that comes from the family of God, which has spanned the centuries since the beginning of time. We can tap into the spiritual writings and wisdom of those who have faithfully served God in the past. We can also tap into the very presence and power of God himself in the form of the Holy Spirit, who existed at the dawn of time. All those who claim allegiance to Jesus Christ are God's children, and to each of us who love, obey, and honor him, he promises to start his own spiritual heritage through us. Unlike any other heritage, this one will last for eternity.

What is my heritage as a child of God?

Because we are united with Christ, we have received an inheritance from God, for he chose us in advance, and he makes everything work out according to his plan. . . . The Spirit is God's guarantee that he will give us the inheritance he promised and that he has purchased us to be his own people. . . . I pray that your hearts will be flooded with light so that you can understand the confident hope he has given to those he called—his holy people who are his rich and glorious inheritance.
EPHESIANS 1:11, 14, 18

The spiritual legacy of Christ—his plan from the beginning to come to earth and die for your sins—gives you the opportunity for a wonderful future with a lavish inheritance beyond your wildest dreams. All you have to do is allow him to adopt you into his family.

The LORD says, "I will rescue those who love me. I will protect those who trust in my name. When they call on me, I will answer; I will be with them in trouble. I will rescue and honor them. I will reward them with a long life and give them my salvation."
PSALM 91:14-16

You have an ongoing relationship with God, today and forever. Your relationship with God is personal, not merely a philosophical recognition of him. His love is the core of that personal relationship.

Since we are surrounded by such a huge crowd of witnesses to the life of faith, let us strip off every weight that slows us down, especially the sin that so easily trips us up. And let us run with endurance the race God has set before us. HEBREWS 12:1

Our faithful predecessors are part of our spiritual heritage. Their legacy of faith shows God's faithfulness and work in the lives of his people for generations.

What is the value of a strong spiritual heritage?

O LORD, you alone are my hope. I've trusted you, O LORD, from childhood. Yes, you have been with me from birth; from my mother's womb you have cared for me. No wonder I am always praising you! . . . O God, you have taught me from my earliest childhood, and I constantly tell others about the wonderful things you do. PSALM 71:5-6, 17

Your spiritual heritage can serve as a foundation and inspiration for further spiritual growth.

O God, we have heard it with our own ears—our ancestors have told us of all you did in their day, in days long ago. . . . It was not their own strong arm that gave them victory. It was your right hand and strong arm and the blinding light from your face that helped them, for you loved them. PSALM 44:1, 3

Your spiritual heritage reminds you to give God credit for your successes.

We will not hide these truths from our children; we will tell the next generation about the glorious deeds of the LORD, about his power and his mighty wonders. . . . He commanded our ancestors to teach them to their children, so the next generation might know them— even the children not yet born—and they in turn will teach their own children. So each generation should set its hope anew on God, not forgetting his glorious miracles and obeying his commands. PSALM 78:4-7

Your spiritual heritage can foster your personal hope in God and encourage you to obey him.

How can I pass on a spiritual heritage?

Praise the LORD! How joyful are those who fear the LORD and delight in obeying his commands. Their children will be successful everywhere; an entire generation of godly people will be blessed. They themselves will be wealthy, and their good deeds will last forever. PSALM 112:1-3

Direct your children onto the right path, and when they are older, they will not leave it. PROVERBS 22:6

You can live your life exemplifying faith, obedience, and integrity. Those who watch and respect you will follow in your footsteps.

He brought them out and asked, "Sirs, what must I do to be saved?" ACTS 16:30

You can encourage others in your family to experience a personal relationship with God, beginning with salvation through Jesus Christ.

Many sacrifices were offered on that joyous day, for God had given the people cause for great joy. The women and children also participated in the celebration, and the joy of the people of Jerusalem could be heard far away. NEHEMIAH 12:43

Worship God together as a family. The joy of united worship echoes far into the future.

HOLINESS *See also* Perfection, Purity, Righteousness, Salvation

Holiness is much more than the absence of sin; it is the practice of righteousness, purity, and godliness. Holiness means being wholly dedicated and devoted to God, distinct and separate from the world, committed to right living and purity. When we become Christians, God makes us holy by forgiving our sins. He looks at us as though we have never sinned. But while he sees us as holy, we have not perfected holiness. We must still strive each day to be more like Jesus. Only when we get to heaven will we be completely holy.

How is God holy?

"Who is able to stand in the presence of the LORD, this holy God?" they cried out.
1 SAMUEL 6:20

God is completely separate from sin and evil. He is perfect and has no sin in him.

The Son of Man will send his angels, and they will remove from his Kingdom everything that causes sin and all who do evil. MATTHEW 13:41

God's holiness will not tolerate evil in his eternal Kingdom.

[The seraphim] were calling out to each other, "Holy, holy, holy is the LORD of Heaven's Armies! The whole earth is filled with his glory!" ISAIAH 6:3

God's holiness is so glorious it not only fills heaven but is reflected in nature on earth.

The Sovereign LORD has sworn . . . by his holiness. AMOS 4:2

When God makes a promise, his holiness ensures that he will always do what he says.

What does it mean to be holy and live a holy life?

I am writing . . . to you who have been called by God to be his own holy people. He made you holy by means of Christ Jesus, just as he did for all people everywhere who call on the name of our Lord Jesus Christ. 1 CORINTHIANS 1:2

All who believe in Jesus Christ and have their sins forgiven are made holy.

Christ made us right with God; he made us pure and holy, and he freed us from sin. 1 CORINTHIANS 1:30

You were cleansed; you were made holy; you were made right with God. 1 CORINTHIANS 6:11

You become holy not by good deeds but by what Jesus did for you, cleansing you from sin through his forgiveness.

[Christ] gave up his life for [the church] to make her holy and clean . . . to present her to himself as a glorious church without a spot or wrinkle or any other blemish. EPHESIANS 5:25-27

To be holy means that God looks at you as though you have never sinned.

Our High Priest offered himself to God as a single sacrifice for sins. . . . By that one offering he forever made perfect those who are being made holy. HEBREWS 10:12, 14

Holiness here on earth is not perfection; it is striving for purity. However, God promises that believers will one day be perfectly holy in heaven.

How can I be more holy?

I, the LORD, am holy, and I make you holy. LEVITICUS 21:8

Give your bodies to God because of all he has done for you. Let them be a living and holy sacrifice—the kind he will find acceptable. This is truly the way to worship him. Don't copy the behavior and customs of this world, but let God transform you into a new person by changing the way you think. Then you will learn to know God's will for you, which is good and pleasing and perfect. ROMANS 12:1-2

When you ask God's Holy Spirit to control your thoughts and behavior, the Lord will change your life from the inside out. He will renew your mind and give you the spiritual insight to see what God wants you to do and how to live it out.

Make them holy by your truth; teach them your word, which is truth. JOHN 17:17

Your holiness develops as you learn the truth of God's Word.

You must be holy because I, the LORD your God, am holy. LEVITICUS 19:2

Sin and holiness cannot coexist. If you want an intimate relationship with God, you must strive to be holy as he is holy.

HOLY SPIRIT *See also* Discernment, Guidance, Presence of God

Who is the Holy Spirit? God is three persons in one—the Father, the Son, and the Holy Spirit. God became a human being in Jesus so that Jesus could die for our sins. Jesus rose from the dead to offer salvation to all people through spiritual renewal and rebirth. When Jesus ascended into heaven, his physical presence left the earth, but he promised to send the Holy Spirit so that his spiritual presence would still be among humankind (see Luke 24:49). The Holy Spirit first became available to all believers at Pentecost (see Acts 2). In the Old Testament, the Holy Spirit empowered specific individuals for specific purposes; but now all believers have the power of the Holy Spirit available to them.

When do I receive the Holy Spirit?

When you believed in Christ, he identified you as his own by giving you the Holy Spirit, whom he promised long ago. The Spirit is God's guarantee that he will give us the inheritance he promised and that he has purchased us to be his own people. He did this so we would praise and glorify him. EPHESIANS 1:13-14

God gives you the Holy Spirit when you believe in Jesus Christ. In fact, it is through the promptings of the Holy Spirit that you are able to believe in Christ.

What you see was predicted long ago by the prophet Joel: "In the last days," God says, "I will pour out my Spirit upon all people. Your sons and daughters will prophesy. Your young men will see visions, and your old men will dream dreams. In those days I will pour out my Spirit even on my servants—men and women alike—and they will prophesy." ACTS 2:16-18

The gift of the Holy Spirit was not made available to all people until Jesus Christ was resurrected and ascended into heaven. Peter's preaching at Pentecost marked the dramatic outpouring of the Spirit, fulfilling the prophecies of old.

[Jesus said,] "You will receive power when the Holy Spirit comes upon you. And you will be my witnesses, telling people about me everywhere—in Jerusalem, throughout Judea, in Samaria, and to the ends of the earth." ACTS 1:8

The Lord gives you an extra measure of the Holy Spirit whenever you need special power and courage to witness for him.

How does the Holy Spirit help me?

We have received God's Spirit (not the world's spirit), so we can know the wonderful things God has freely given us. 1 CORINTHIANS 2:12

The Holy Spirit helps you recognize the blessings God gives you.

Let the Holy Spirit guide your lives. Then you won't be doing what your sinful nature craves. GALATIANS 5:16

The Holy Spirit convicts you of sin. He helps you discern right from wrong, good from bad, and God's way from the way of the world. The Holy Spirit shows you how to live a life that pleases God.

The Holy Spirit helps us in our weakness. For example, we don't know what God wants us to pray for. But the Holy Spirit prays for us with groanings that cannot be expressed in words. ROMANS 8:26

The Holy Spirit helps you pray. You can take great comfort and confidence in the fact that your prayers—as inadequate as they may seem—are heard, understood, and responded to through the loving intercession of the Holy Spirit.

[God's] Spirit joins with our spirit to affirm that we are God's children. ROMANS 8:16

The Holy Spirit fills you with the assurance that you are a child of God, saved from sin.

HOMOSEXUALITY *See also* Sex/Sexuality, Tolerance

Homosexual activity is consistently forbidden in Scripture (see Genesis 19; Romans 1:24-27; 1 Corinthians 6:9-10) because it violates the nature of sexual relationships that God established at Creation, which are to be fulfilled only in the marriage relationship of a man and a woman (see Genesis 2:18-24). While some assert that God creates people as homosexuals, it would be contrary to God's nature to create a person in direct violation of his own standards. Homosexuality is not a condition to be celebrated but a temptation to be controlled. Homosexual desire is a consequence of fallen human nature. As such, we must respond to it like any other temptation or sin. Any desire that violates God's laws must be controlled. The Lord promises hope for those who want to break free from sexual sin (see 1 Corinthians 6:11; 10:13; 2 Corinthians 5:17). The adage to love the sinner while hating the sin applies to the homosexual as well.

Is homosexuality wrong?

Do not practice homosexuality, having sex with another man as with a woman. It is a detestable sin. LEVITICUS 18:22

God views the practice of homosexuality as a sin because it violates the boundaries of sexual relationships that he established. At the very beginning of time, God created the perfect union between a man and a woman.

How can a person overcome homosexual feelings?

The temptations in your life are no different from what others experience. And God is faithful. He will not allow the temptation to be more than you can stand. When you are tempted, he will show you a way out so that you can endure. 1 CORINTHIANS 10:13

Remember, it is sin to know what you ought to do and then not do it. JAMES 4:17

A person can overcome homosexual feelings in the same way that a person can overcome any sinful temptation—by looking to God for help, resolving to stand firm, and avoiding tempting situations.

Can God forgive me for my homosexual behavior?

Let us come boldly to the throne of our gracious God. There we will receive his mercy, and we will find grace to help us when we need it most. HEBREWS 4:16

I will forgive their wickedness, and I will never again remember their sins. HEBREWS 8:12

If we confess our sins to him, he is faithful and just to forgive us our sins and to cleanse us from all wickedness. 1 JOHN 1:9

When you confess your sin to God, he not only forgives you but gives you a new outlook on life. He will change your heart and make you a new person, free from the imprisonment of your past sins.

HONESTY *See also* Integrity, Promises, Reputation, Truth

Honesty creates trust, and trust is the basis of all relationships. God wants us to be completely honest—with him, with others, and with yourself. Our success does not honor God if we cheat or damage others to get ahead. When we are honest in all details of our life, we experience these distinct advantages: (1) a clear conscience, (2) the trust and respect of others, and (3) God's blessing. Make the decision to be honest in all areas of life.

Why is it so important to be honest?

Who may climb the mountain of the LORD? Who may stand in his holy place? Only those whose hands and hearts are pure, who . . . never tell lies. PSALM 24:3-4

To live in God's presence requires honesty. Honesty shows purity, integrity, and a desire to do what is true and right.

The LORD demands accurate scales and balances; he sets the standards for fairness. PROVERBS 16:11

God expects you to be honest.

If you are dishonest in little things, you won't be honest with greater responsibilities. LUKE 16:10

Your level of honesty demonstrates the quality of your character.

Does honesty always mean telling everything I know?

Let your conversation be gracious. COLOSSIANS 4:6

Honesty should not be confused with gossip. Just because you know something doesn't mean you have to tell everyone about it. Honesty also involves integrity—making sure that what you say is helpful and builds others up rather than tears them down. The person who thinks before speaking is the wisest. It is not deceitful to withhold information that others don't need to know, unless of course you are under oath in a court of law.

What are the benefits of honesty?

The LORD detests lying lips, but he delights in those who tell the truth. PROVERBS 12:22

The LORD detests double standards; he is not pleased by dishonest scales. PROVERBS 20:23

Honesty is essential for truth, justice, and trust in all relationships. Truth is revealed and justice carried out only when people are honest. If you can't trust friends and family members to be honest, your relationships will crumble because of distrust and deceit.

Who may worship in your sanctuary, LORD? Who may enter your presence on your holy hill? Those who lead blameless lives and do what is right, speaking the truth from sincere hearts. PSALM 15:1-2

Honesty is necessary in your relationship with God. Dishonesty is a sin and keeps you from a close relationship with him.

You desire honesty from the womb, teaching me wisdom even there. PSALM 51:6

Honesty prepares you to learn God's ways. The definition of dishonesty is avoiding what it true. Since God is truth, you cannot learn his ways if you are in the habit of being dishonest.

Look at those who are honest and good, for a wonderful future awaits those who love peace. PSALM 37:37

Striving for honesty helps you enjoy life because you can live at peace with God and yourself.

How should I show my honesty?

Search me, O God, and know my heart; test me and know my anxious thoughts. PSALM 139:23

It matters very little how I might be evaluated by you or by any human authority. I don't even trust my own judgment on this point. My conscience is clear, but that doesn't prove I'm right. It is the Lord himself who will examine me and decide. 1 CORINTHIANS 4:3-4

You must honestly evaluate yourself, trying to see yourself as God and others see you.

The other administrators and high officers began searching for some fault in the way Daniel was handling government affairs, but they couldn't find anything to criticize or condemn. He was faithful, always responsible, and completely trustworthy. DANIEL 6:4

Stop telling lies. Let us tell our neighbors the truth, for we are all parts of the same body. EPHESIANS 4:25

You must be honest in all your life choices, for it reflects who you are as a Christian.

HOPE *See also* Eternity, Promises, Resurrection, Trust

For a prisoner on death row, a pardon offers hope of freedom. For the spiritual prisoner who is on death row because of the consequences of sin, God offers ultimate hope by forgiving that person's sins so he or she can be with him in heaven forever. When life seems impossible, God brings eternal hope. Hope is essential to our ability to persevere through the tough times. Without hope, we give up. Hope requires only one thing—trust in the one who brings real hope.

What is my hope? Where does hope come from?

LORD, where do I put my hope? My only hope is in you. PSALM 39:7

O Lord, you alone are my hope. I've trusted you, O LORD, from childhood. PSALM 71:5

The Lord himself is the source of greatest hope. Only when you trust him with your future can hope begin to grow, because he created you with a great future in mind.

Through Christ you have come to trust in God. And you have placed your faith and hope in God because he raised Christ from the dead and gave him great glory. 1 PETER 1:21

The Resurrection, the greatest event in history, is the foundation of hope. It should affect how you live each day.

We live with great expectation, and we have a priceless inheritance—an inheritance that is kept in heaven for you, pure and undefiled, beyond the reach of change and decay. . . .

So be truly glad. There is wonderful joy ahead, even though you have to endure many trials for a little while. 1 PETER 1:3-4, 6

Just as focusing on a fixed point in the distance helps you travel in a straighter line, Jesus' followers fix their eyes on the eternal horizon, knowing they will live with him forever in heaven, where there is no pain or sorrow or suffering. As you move straight toward your eternal goal, your hope for eternity makes you better able to endure the discomforts and even the tragedies of daily life.

How can I cultivate stronger hope?

Do not snatch your word of truth from me, for your regulations are my only hope.... May all who fear you find in me a cause for joy, for I have put my hope in your word.... I am worn out waiting for your rescue, but I have put my hope in your word.... You are my refuge and my shield; your word is my source of hope.... I rise early, before the sun is up; I cry out for help and put my hope in your words. PSALM 119:43, 74, 81, 114, 147

Each day you can read God's Word and have your hope renewed and reinforced. His Word will never fail to lift you up.

All glory to God, who is able, through his mighty power at work within us, to accomplish infinitely more than we might ask or think. Glory to him in the church and in Christ Jesus through all generations forever and ever! EPHESIANS 3:20-21

Most people hope too little in God, expecting too little from him. If you remind yourself of the amazing things God has already done, you will know that you have reason to believe the sovereign Lord of the universe wants to bless you more abundantly than you can imagine.

What can I do when things seem hopeless?

Hannah was in deep anguish, crying bitterly as she prayed to the LORD. 1 SAMUEL 1:10

You can pray. In the midst of Hannah's hopelessness, she prayed to God, knowing that if any hope were to be found, she would find it in him.

The jailer put them into the inner dungeon and clamped their feet in the stocks. Around midnight Paul and Silas were praying and singing hymns to God, and the other prisoners were listening. ACTS 16:24-25

You can worship. Paul and Silas were on death row for preaching about Jesus, yet in this hopeless situation they sang praises to God. Why? Because they had an eternal perspective.

How can I have hope when times are tough?

Let us hold tightly without wavering to the hope we affirm, for God can be trusted to keep his promise. HEBREWS 10:23

When everything else is falling apart, cling to the fact that God keeps his word. Your hope is rooted in God's integrity and faithfulness.

[Jesus said,] "I have told you all this so that you may have peace in me. Here on earth you will have many trials and sorrows. But take heart, because I have overcome the world."
JOHN 16:33

Your troubles do not surprise God and should not surprise you. Trouble is a fact of life in this fallen world. Your focus should be on Jesus, who experienced all your troubles and shows you how to have peace in spite of them.

*Joyful are those who have the God of Israel as their helper, whose hope is in the L*ORD *their God. He made heaven and earth, the sea, and everything in them. He keeps every promise forever. He gives justice to the oppressed and food to the hungry. The L*ORD *frees the prisoners. The L*ORD *opens the eyes of the blind. The L*ORD *lifts up those who are weighed down.* PSALM 146:5-8

Your hope is rooted in the wonderful acts of God in creation and history. The Bible assures you that God is able to deliver you from any and every difficult circumstance. He will either deliver you from it or bring you through it—for his glory and your joy.

How can I keep hoping when God doesn't seem to act?
O Lord, you alone are my hope. PSALM 71:5

Who but God controls the future? Who but God has a home for you that is eternal? Who but God forgives your sins? Who but God can give you a life that lasts forever? No wonder he is our hope!

We were given this hope when we were saved. (If we already have something, we don't need to hope for it. . . .) ROMANS 8:24

Hope, by definition, is expecting something that has not yet occurred. Once hope is fulfilled, there's no need for hope anymore. Thus, an important part of hope is waiting patiently for God to work. God's timing is perfect.

HOSPITALITY *See also* Caring, Generosity, Kindness, Neighbors

In Bible times, hospitality was not merely a gracious act, it was a necessity. There were no motels or hotels as we know them, only a very few crude inns that had no bathrooms, bedrooms, or restaurants. Strangers were to be treated as guests, and the host was expected not only to house them but also to feed and protect them. Hospitality was known as the love of strangers. We no longer practice this kind of hospitality today, and we have developed an unfortunate distrust of strangers. But we are still to be hospitable—that is, graciously receiving others into our homes, feeding them, sometimes housing them, always making them feel welcome. God gives the ultimate hospitality, for he has promised to receive everyone who trusts him into his eternal home in heaven.

What does it mean to be hospitable?
Cheerfully share your home with those who need a meal or a place to stay. 1 PETER 4:9

The basics of good hospitality—inviting others into your home and offering them something to eat and drink—are simple acts of kindness that almost anyone can do.

As Jesus and the disciples continued on their way to Jerusalem, they came to a certain village where a woman named Martha welcomed him into her home. Her sister, Mary, sat at the Lord's feet, listening to what he taught. But Martha was distracted by the big dinner she was preparing. She came to Jesus and said, "Lord, doesn't it seem unfair to you that my sister just sits here while I do all the work? Tell her to come and help me." But the Lord said to her, "My dear Martha, you are worried and upset over all these details! There is only one thing worth being concerned about. Mary has discovered it, and it will not be taken away from her." LUKE 10:38-42

Don't be intimidated by hospitality, thinking you must prepare big meals and clean the house. The Bible mentions both elaborate feasts (see Genesis 18:1-8; 2 Samuel 3:20) and spontaneous get-togethers (see Acts 10:23). Just share generously and enjoy the people you are with. The most important part of hospitality is sharing yourself and your Lord with others.

To whom should I be hospitable?
When God's people are in need, be ready to help them. Always be eager to practice hospitality. ROMANS 12:13

Other believers.

You are being faithful to God when you care for the traveling teachers who pass through, even though they are strangers to you. 3 JOHN 1:5

God's workers—those in ministry.

Don't forget to show hospitality to strangers, for some who have done this have entertained angels without realizing it! HEBREWS 13:2

Strangers.

Share your food with the hungry, and give shelter to the homeless. Give clothes to those who need them, and do not hide from relatives who need your help. ISAIAH 58:7

The hungry, poor, and needy—including your relatives.

[Jesus] turned to his host. "When you put on a luncheon or a banquet," he said, "don't invite your friends, brothers, relatives, and rich neighbors. For they will invite you back, and that will be your only reward. Instead, invite the poor, the crippled, the lame, and the blind. Then at the resurrection of the righteous, God will reward you for inviting those who could not repay you." LUKE 14:12-14

Those who cannot repay you.

How can I make my home a place of hospitality?
One day Elisha went to the town of Shunem. A wealthy woman lived there, and she urged him to come to her home for a meal. After that, whenever he passed that way, he would

stop there for something to eat. She said to her husband, "I am sure this man who stops in from time to time is a holy man of God. Let's build a small room for him on the roof and furnish it with a bed, a table, a chair, and a lamp. Then he will have a place to stay whenever he comes by." 2 KINGS 4:8-10

Please prepare a guest room for me, for I am hoping that God will answer your prayers and let me return to you soon. PHILEMON 1:22

You can host others in your home, thoughtfully preparing for their needs.

As soon as Laban heard that his nephew Jacob had arrived, he ran out to meet him. He embraced and kissed him and brought him home. GENESIS 29:13

You can give others a warm welcome to your home.

Christ will make his home in your hearts as you trust in him. Your roots will grow down into God's love and keep you strong. EPHESIANS 3:17

I stand at the door and knock. If you hear my voice and open the door, I will come in, and we will share a meal together as friends. REVELATION 3:20

When you open your heart's door to Jesus and invite him into your life, you show him your personal hospitality. Jesus knocks at the door of your heart and home, wanting to come in and fellowship with you. Invite him in with enthusiasm!

I was hungry, and you fed me. I was thirsty, and you gave me a drink. I was a stranger, and you invited me into your home. I was naked, and you gave me clothing. I was sick, and you cared for me. I was in prison, and you visited me. . . . And the King will say, "I tell you the truth, when you did it to one of the least of these my brothers and sisters, you were doing it to me!" MATTHEW 25:35-36, 40

When you are hospitable to others who need help, you show hospitality to Christ, for this is what he would do.

HUMILIATION *See also* Humility, Shame, Vulnerability

Sometimes our own actions cause us to be humiliated, and sometimes we are humiliated by others. When we bring humiliation upon ourselves, it goes deeper than just embarrassment. We feel embarrassment when we do something, usually by accident, that is out of character and makes us feel self-conscious and distressed. But we experience humiliation when we do something that utterly destroys our self-respect and dignity. For example, if we're caught stealing, we are humiliated in front of our peers and family, feeling ashamed for what we have done. Humiliation usually brings feelings of guilt or shame because it reveals how sin has degraded our integrity. When others try to humiliate us, their objective is the same—to bring us shame, even if it is not justified. We can usually recover quickly from embarrassment, but it often takes much longer to recover from humiliation. If our enemies can humiliate us, they can render us useless for a long time. No one likes to be humiliated, but it can be a springboard for spiritual repentance and restoration because it forces us to go to the only one who can offer complete forgiveness and restore our reputation. God promises to make us as clean as newly fallen snow and turn our humiliation into an opportunity to love, restore, and raise us up again.

What causes humiliation?

They will be humbled, and all will be brought low—do not forgive them. ISAIAH 2:9

O LORD, we and our kings, princes, and ancestors are covered with shame because we have sinned against you. DANIEL 9:8

When you disobey God, you walk out of his presence into the shadows of shame and humiliation. Sin is humiliating because it degrades you, making you unfit to be in God's presence. You realize you have let God down.

You rescue the humble, but you humiliate the proud. PSALM 18:27

Pride ends in humiliation, while humility brings honor. PROVERBS 29:23

When you are proud, you seek to elevate yourself, but in reality pride actually degrades you in the eyes of God and others. On Judgment Day, the proud will be humiliated when they realize how low they have really fallen in God's eyes.

If you ignore criticism, you will end in poverty and disgrace; if you accept correction, you will be honored. PROVERBS 13:18

Ignoring constructive criticism can be humiliating when you realize your mistake.

We can't escape the constant humiliation; shame is written across our faces. PSALM 44:15

Humiliation can perpetuate itself, so deal with its causes before it consumes you.

How can I overcome humiliation?

No one who trusts in you will ever be disgraced, but disgrace comes to those who try to deceive others. . . . Protect me! Rescue my life from them! Do not let me be disgraced, for in you I take refuge. PSALM 25:3, 20

Those who look to him for help will be radiant with joy; no shadow of shame will darken their faces. PSALM 34:5

Humility is the first step toward overcoming humiliation. Humility comes when you recognize your need for God and then acknowledge how he meets your needs.

Oh, that my actions would consistently reflect your decrees! Then I will not be ashamed when I compare my life with your commands. . . . I cling to your laws. LORD, don't let me be put to shame! . . . May I be blameless in keeping your decrees; then I will never be ashamed. PSALM 119:5-6, 31, 80

Obedience to God's Word and his ways helps you overcome and avoid actions that cause humiliation.

Never let loyalty and kindness leave you! Tie them around your neck as a reminder. Write them deep within your heart. Then you will find favor with both God and people, and you will earn a good reputation. PROVERBS 3:3-4

Choose a good reputation over great riches; being held in high esteem is better than silver or gold. PROVERBS 22:1

A good reputation helps you recover from humiliation.

Peter said, "Man, I don't know what you are talking about." And immediately, while he was still speaking, the rooster crowed. At that moment the Lord turned and looked at Peter. Suddenly, the Lord's words flashed through Peter's mind: "Before the rooster crows tomorrow morning, you will deny three times that you even know me." And Peter left the courtyard, weeping bitterly. LUKE 22:60-62

After breakfast Jesus asked Simon Peter, "Simon son of John, do you love me more than these?" "Yes, Lord," Peter replied, "you know I love you." "Then feed my lambs," Jesus told him. JOHN 21:15

Peter was ashamed of himself for denying his Lord, but Jesus forgave Peter completely. Had Peter not accepted Jesus' forgiveness, he would have been paralyzed by his humiliation and would not have been fit for further service to God. You must accept forgiveness to move past humiliation.

What can I learn from humiliation?

I prayed, "O my God, I am utterly ashamed; I blush to lift up my face to you. For our sins are piled higher than our heads, and our guilt has reached to the heavens." EZRA 9:6

I recognize my rebellion; it haunts me day and night. PSALM 51:3

The young man became so hungry that even the pods he was feeding the pigs looked good to him. But no one gave him anything. LUKE 15:16

When you finally realize the damaging and humiliating effects of your sins, you have two choices: You can either continue in your downward cycle, or you can reach up to God by confessing your sins and repenting of them. Only through confession and repentance can your humiliation be washed away.

Hezekiah humbled himself and repented of his pride, as did the people of Jerusalem. So the LORD's anger did not fall on them during Hezekiah's lifetime. 2 CHRONICLES 32:26

Humiliation can lead to seeking and receiving God's mercy and forgiveness.

Israel's vine has been stripped of branches, but [the LORD] will restore its splendor. NAHUM 2:2

Restoration and refreshment can follow humiliation. Sometimes you must be broken to be made whole; you must be wounded to be healed; you must become nothing to become something.

Joseph, her fiancé, was a good man and did not want to disgrace her publicly, so he decided to break the engagement quietly. As he considered this, an angel of the Lord appeared to him in a dream. "Joseph, son of David," the angel said, "do not be afraid to take Mary as your wife.". . . When Joseph woke up, he did as the angel of the Lord commanded and took Mary as his wife. But he did not have sexual relations with her until her son was born. And Joseph named him Jesus. MATTHEW 1:19-20, 24-25

Humiliation can lead to trust and obedience. Sometimes you may not learn to trust and obey until difficulties force you to.

Pride leads to disgrace, but with humility comes wisdom. PROVERBS 11:2

I am not writing these things to shame you, but to warn you as my beloved children. 1 CORINTHIANS 4:14

Instruction, understanding, and wisdom should be part of your journey to overcome humiliation.

HUMILITY *See also* Submission, Vulnerability, Worth/Worthiness

Humility is the honest recognition of our worth as God sees us. It is the delicate balance between humbly recognizing our sin and knowing how much God loves and values us. Pride elevates us above others and often above God himself. But just as unacceptable as pride is degrading our sense of self-worth because it denies the value God placed upon us when he created us in his image and when he sent his Son to die for us. Jesus did not die for worthless objects or creatures but for people he loves very much—and those people have great value in God's eyes. To see ourselves as God sees us is our goal.

What is true humility?

Anyone who becomes as humble as this little child is the greatest in the Kingdom of Heaven. MATTHEW 18:4

Humility is childlike. It is an attitude of total trust in a great God, and its effects reach into the Kingdom of Heaven. By contrast, pride is actually weakness, for it reaches no further than your own ego.

Jacob prayed, "O God . . . you promised me, 'I will treat you kindly.' I am not worthy of all the unfailing love and faithfulness you have shown to me, your servant." GENESIS 32:9-10

Humility is not thinking too highly of yourself. Jacob realized that he was not worthy of all he had received from God. Humility comes when you recognize your need for God and then acknowledge how he provides for you.

As the Scriptures say, "God opposes the proud but favors the humble." So humble yourselves before God. . . . Let there be tears for what you have done. . . . Humble yourselves before the Lord, and he will lift you up in honor. JAMES 4:6-7, 9-10

Humility involves a willingness to admit and confess sin. Whereas pride gives the devil the key to your heart, humility gives God the key. Instead of pride, you need the humility that comes from godly sorrow for sin. Openly admit that you need God, and seek his forgiveness. A proud person cannot do this.

[Believers] must not slander anyone and must avoid quarreling. Instead, they should be gentle and show true humility to everyone. TITUS 3:2

Humility is being gentle and amicable to all.

How was Jesus humble?

The time came for [Mary's] baby to be born. She gave birth to her first child, [Jesus]. She wrapped him snugly in strips of cloth and laid him in a manger, because there was no lodging available for them. LUKE 2:6-7

God wanted Jesus to have a humble birth to show that his offer of salvation is for everyone, regardless of race or class or socioeconomic position.

Though he was God, [Christ] did not think of equality with God as something to cling to. Instead, he gave up his divine privileges; he took the humble position of a slave and was born as a human being. When he appeared in human form, he humbled himself in obedience to God and died a criminal's death on a cross. PHILIPPIANS 2:6-8

[Jesus] was given a position "a little lower than the angels"; and because he suffered death for us, he is now "crowned with glory and honor." Yes, by God's grace, Jesus tasted death for everyone. HEBREWS 2:9

Jesus had all the glory and honor of sitting at God's right hand, but he gave that up to die a criminal's death so that you could be saved from eternal punishment and have eternal life with him.

Take my yoke upon you. Let me teach you, because I am humble and gentle at heart, and you will find rest for your souls. MATTHEW 11:29

Jesus is the ultimate example of gentleness and humility. His way of dealing with and teaching people demonstrates true humility. If you study the life of Jesus, you will understand true humility.

How do I become humble?

Remember how the LORD your God led you through the wilderness for these forty years, humbling you and testing you to prove your character. . . . He did it to teach you that people do not live by bread alone; rather, we live by every word that comes from the mouth of the LORD. DEUTERONOMY 8:2-3

Humility comes when you recognize that you need God, and then you watch him meet your needs!

Sympathize with each other. Love each other as brothers and sisters. Be tenderhearted, and keep a humble attitude. 1 PETER 3:8

Humility comes from developing sympathetic and tender hearts toward others.

Don't be selfish; don't try to impress others. Be humble, thinking of others as better than yourselves. PHILIPPIANS 2:3

Humility comes from thinking of others' welfare before thinking about yourself.

How does God respond to the humble?

If my people who are called by my name will humble themselves and pray and seek my face and turn from their wicked ways, I will hear from heaven. 2 CHRONICLES 7:14

Humble yourselves under the mighty power of God, and at the right time he will lift you up in honor. 1 PETER 5:6

God honors the humble and acknowledges their prayers. When you come to God in humility, your prayers will be more aligned with his plans for you because you have taken the important step of recognizing that he is sovereign.

He leads the humble in doing right, teaching them his way. PSALM 25:9

God leads and teaches the humble. Humility means acknowledging your proper place before the Lord. When you humbly worship him, he will lead you and teach you the right way to live.

The LORD delights in his people; he crowns the humble with victory. PSALM 149:4

God takes delight in the humble and offers them victory.

The humble will see their God at work and be glad. Let all who seek God's help be encouraged. PSALM 69:32

God gives joy to the humble. Humility opens your eyes so you can see God at work in your life.

Though the LORD is great, he cares for the humble, but he keeps his distance from the proud. PSALM 138:6

God takes care of the humble.

How can humility help me in times of trouble?

[The man] said, "Don't be afraid, Daniel. Since the first day you began to pray for understanding and to humble yourself before your God, your request has been heard in heaven. I have come in answer to your prayer." DANIEL 10:12

Pride can keep you from seeking the help you need. Humility gives you the wisdom and courage to admit your needs in any situation. You won't get help—from God or others—if you can't admit you have a problem.

HURTS/HURTING *See also* Brokenness, Pain, Problems, Suffering

No human being has ever lived a life free from personal hurt and pain. Adversity, suffering, sickness, tragedy, persecution, opposition, anger, bitterness, disappointment—all these things and more attack us from every direction and hurt us, often deeply. Sometimes we hurt because of circumstances beyond our control—an illness or the death of a loved one. But most often hurt comes from relationships with those around us. Expectations aren't met, the wrong words are spoken or the right words not spoken, and disappointment moves down into the heart, where it turns into discouragement and hurt. The reality is that we are all imperfect and can never fully satisfy even those we love the most. We will hurt others, and they will hurt us.

When we wrestle with our daily hurts, it is helpful to keep two things in mind. First, Jesus' model of unconditional love shows us we should avoid intentionally hurting others. Second, we must practice the art of forgiveness. Whether we need to apologize for hurting someone or forgive someone who has hurt us, true forgiveness is the best antidote for melting away the feelings of hurt and experiencing the joy of restoration. We must remember that God is the One we've hurt the most, but he has already offered us his complete forgiveness and desires to fully restore our relationship with him. When we are hurt by a friend, loved one, or even a stranger, it reminds us to seek a more perfect relationship with the One who will never hurt or disappoint us.

When I've been hurt, how can I find healing?

The king was overcome with emotion. He went up to the room over the gateway and burst into tears. And as he went, he cried, "O my son Absalom! My son, my son Absalom! If only I had died instead of you! O Absalom, my son, my son." 2 SAMUEL 18:33

I wrote that letter in great anguish, with a troubled heart and many tears. I didn't want to grieve you, but I wanted to let you know how much love I have for you. 2 CORINTHIANS 2:4

You need to express your hurt—privately to God or to a friend, or even publicly. Unexpressed hurt can fester inside you, driving you toward unhealthy emotions like depression or bitterness.

I weep with sorrow; encourage me by your word. . . . Your promise revives me; it comforts me in all my troubles. . . . I meditate on your age-old regulations; O LORD, they comfort me. . . . If your instructions hadn't sustained me with joy, I would have died in my misery. PSALM 119:28, 50-52, 92

Look to God's Word as a source of comfort and healing. The words of the Bible are from God himself, and they bring healing for your hurts.

You have turned my mourning into joyful dancing. You have taken away my clothes of mourning and clothed me with joy. PSALM 30:11

We believers also groan, even though we have the Holy Spirit within us as a foretaste of future glory, for we long for our bodies to be released from sin and suffering. We, too, wait with eager hope for the day when God will give us our full rights as his adopted children, including the new bodies he has promised us. ROMANS 8:23

God does not promise believers a life free from pain and suffering. But as a Christian, you have a relationship with God, who helps you through your hurts, comforts you despite your hurts, and sometimes miraculously heals your hurts. Most important, you have a God who will one day take away all of your hurts when you arrive at heaven. Whatever pain you are experiencing is temporary; it will end, perhaps here on earth, but certainly in eternity.

Esau ran to meet him and embraced him, threw his arms around his neck, and kissed him. And they both wept. GENESIS 33:4

Forgiveness is like a miracle medicine to heal your brokenness. Accept it gladly.

How can God use my hurt for his glory?

[God] said, "My grace is all you need. My power works best in weakness." So now I am glad to boast about my weaknesses, so that the power of Christ can work through me. 2 CORINTHIANS 12:9

God can use your weakness and pain to reveal his strength and power. It is often through pain that you most vividly experience God's work in your life.

We don't look at the troubles we can see now; rather, we fix our gaze on things that cannot be seen. For the things we see now will soon be gone, but the things we cannot see will last forever. 2 CORINTHIANS 4:18

You suffered along with those who were thrown into jail, and when all you owned was taken from you, you accepted it with joy. You knew there were better things waiting for you that will last forever. HEBREWS 10:34

God can use your pain to help you gain an eternal perspective and a new way of looking at your circumstances.

Trials will show that your faith is genuine. It is being tested as fire tests and purifies gold—though your faith is far more precious than mere gold. So when your faith remains strong through many trials, it will bring you much praise and glory and honor on the day when Jesus Christ is revealed to the whole world. 1 PETER 1:7

Hurtful situations can strengthen your faith, develop your endurance, and mold your character.

I am glad I sent [the letter], not because it hurt you, but because the pain caused you to repent and change your ways. It was the kind of sorrow God wants his people to have, so you were not harmed by us in any way. 2 CORINTHIANS 7:9

God can use painful situations to bring about personal remorse and a change of heart to help you make the right choices in the future.

How should I respond to those who hurt me?

If you forgive those who sin against you, your heavenly Father will forgive you. But if you refuse to forgive others, your Father will not forgive your sins.
MATTHEW 6:14-15

Peter came to him and asked, "Lord, how often should I forgive someone who sins against me? Seven times?" "No, not seven times," Jesus replied, "but seventy times seven!"
MATTHEW 18:21-22

Jesus said, "Father, forgive them, for they don't know what they are doing." And the soldiers gambled for his clothes by throwing dice. LUKE 23:34

Forgiveness is not an option; it is a command. It is necessary for your own health and your relationship with God. Jesus gave you the perfect example of forgiveness. Forgiveness doesn't mean you say that the hurt doesn't exist or that it doesn't matter, nor does it make everything all right. Forgiveness allows you to let go of the hurt and let God deal with the one who hurt you. Forgiveness sets you free and allows you to move on with your life. It's not always easy, but forgiving others who have hurt you is the healthiest thing you can do for yourself.

Don't say, "I will get even for this wrong." Wait for the LORD to handle the matter.
PROVERBS 20:22

Don't repay evil for evil. Don't retaliate with insults when people insult you. Instead, pay them back with a blessing. That is what God has called you to do, and he will bless you for it. 1 PETER 3:9

Wait for the Lord to take care of things his way. God wants you to respond with love and blessing rather than retaliation.

Make allowance for each other's faults, and forgive anyone who offends you. Remember, the Lord forgave you, so you must forgive others. COLOSSIANS 3:13

You can sometimes avoid being hurt by being less sensitive to others' faults, offenses, and wrongs. It helps to remember that we're all human.

How can I help people who are hurting?

My life seeps away. Depression haunts my days. JOB 30:16

A glad heart makes a happy face; a broken heart crushes the spirit.
PROVERBS 15:13

A cheerful heart is good medicine, but a broken spirit saps a person's strength.
PROVERBS 17:22

Be aware of the effects of hurt on a person's spirit, mind, and body. Awareness leads to sympathy, sympathy leads to empathy, empathy leads to helping, and helping leads to healing.

He comforts us in all our troubles so that we can comfort others. When they are troubled, we will be able to give them the same comfort God has given us. 2 CORINTHIANS 1:4

Share your experiences of God's comfort. God's healing in you may bring hope and healing to others.

I have heard all this before. What miserable comforters you are! JOB 16:2

Be careful with the words you offer to the brokenhearted. Explanations and clichés are rarely comforting. Offer those who are hurting your love, sympathy, and your presence. Sometimes the best comfort you can give is to just be there.

All his brothers, sisters, and former friends came and feasted with him in his home. And they consoled him and comforted him because of all the trials the LORD had brought against him. And each of them brought him a gift of money and a gold ring. JOB 42:11

Support your own family and friends. Family life should be a safe haven in a hurting world. The family should be both a healing clinic and a training camp where you learn to cope with and conquer hurtful influences.

HYPOCRISY *See also* Deceit/Deception, Motives, Honesty

Hypocrisy is like a mirage in the desert sands. To a lonely traveler, a mirage gives the appearance of a pool of water—cool, pure, life-giving. A closer look, however, reveals nothing but dry ground. God hates hypocrisy because it is like a religious mirage. It gives the appearance of purity and integrity on the outside when the heart is really spiritually dry and deceptive. Hypocrisy is pretending to be who you aren't. Spiritual hypocrisy is pretending to be a godly person, but with selfish motives. A hypocrite tries to look pious to others in order to gain something—a certain reputation, a business connection, or a position of influence in the church or community. Hypocrisy is a form of lying and deception because it parades to the world a false sense of who God is and what he desires for our lives. Hypocrisy is fueled by pride and selfishness. What God wants is sincerity and honesty, and that is fueled by humility.

What does God think about hypocrisy?

God says to the wicked: "Why bother reciting my decrees and pretending to obey my covenant? For you refuse my discipline and treat my words like trash." PSALM 50:16-17

God is angry when people pretend to be good in order to gain something for themselves. God has chosen to do his work through people, so when people pretend to do good things for God but their deception shows through, it gives God a bad name.

I hate all your show and pretense—the hypocrisy of your religious festivals and solemn assemblies. AMOS 5:21

God hates religious hypocrisy because it demonstrates a heart that is selfish rather than sincere.

The Lord says, "These people say they are mine. They honor me with their lips, but their hearts are far from me. And their worship of me is nothing but man-made rules learned by rote." ISAIAH 29:13

God sees through people's hypocrisy; he cannot be fooled.

How do I avoid being a hypocrite?

If you are presenting a sacrifice at the altar in the Temple and you suddenly remember that someone has something against you, leave your sacrifice there at the altar. Go and be reconciled to that person. Then come and offer your sacrifice to God. MATTHEW 5:23-24

Take care of any wrong in your life before worshiping God publicly.

The wisdom from above is first of all pure. . . . It is full of mercy and good deeds. It shows no favoritism and is always sincere. JAMES 3:17

You need God's Spirit to give you wisdom and true sincerity.

If we confess our sins to him, he is faithful and just to forgive us our sins and to cleanse us from all wickedness. 1 JOHN 1:9

We can be sure that we know him if we obey his commandments. If someone claims, "I know God," but doesn't obey God's commandments, that person is a liar and is not living in the truth. 1 JOHN 2:3-4

Confession without a change of behavior is a spiritual charade. It is hypocrisy to confess your sin and then deliberately continue it. It's easy to glibly ask God for forgiveness with no real repentance. Don't cheerfully claim God's promise in 1 John 1:9 without going on to read 1 John 2:3-4. Such confession is ineffective. It is an attempt to escape punishment without really pleasing God.

How should I respond when others are hypocritical?

I do not spend time with liars or go along with hypocrites. PSALM 26:4

Don't spend lots of time with obviously hypocritical people because it is so easy to pick up their habits.

When Peter came to Antioch, I had to oppose him to his face, for what he did was very wrong. GALATIANS 2:11

When your brothers and sisters in Christ are acting hypocritically, confrontation may be necessary.

I,J,K

IDOLATRY *See also* Affection, Cults, Desires, Worship

An idol is anything or anyone that draws the affection and devotion of our hearts away from God. When we look at idolatry using that definition, it suddenly becomes just as relevant as it was thousands of years ago when people worshiped statues of wood and stone. While we can't imagine bowing down to inanimate objects, we have our own idols that lead us away from God—money, convenience, hobbies, reputation, beauty, celebrities, success—these can all be idols if they become more important to us than God, if we find ourselves thinking about them far more than we think about God. Things that prevent us from keeping God at the center of our lives need to be removed. How? We might have to quit a hobby or remove something from our home. What idol are you in danger of bowing down to worship? What has a higher priority to you than God?

What is idolatry?

God gave the people all these instructions: "I am the LORD your God, who rescued you from the land of Egypt, the place of your slavery. You must not have any other god but me. You must not make for yourself an idol of any kind or an image of anything in the heavens or on the earth or in the sea. You must not bow down to them or worship them, for I, the LORD your God, am a jealous God who will not tolerate your affection for any other gods." EXODUS 20:1-5

Idolatry is worshiping anything or anyone other than God himself.

Aaron took the gold, melted it down, and molded it into the shape of a calf. When the people saw it, they exclaimed, "O Israel, these are the gods who brought you out of the land of Egypt!" EXODUS 32:4

Idolatry is shaping God into the image of what you want him to be and trying to make him do what you want rather than doing what he wants.

Wherever your treasure is, there the desires of your heart will also be.
LUKE 12:34

Idolatry is allowing something else to become more important than God. When you attach supreme value to something, whether it is a person, possession, money, power, or education, it becomes a god that controls your life. When you give God the supreme value in your life, he will occupy your thoughts and will shape your character (see Philippians 4:8).

What kinds of idols do people worship today?

Yes, they knew God, but they wouldn't worship him as God or even give him thanks. . . . Instead of worshiping the glorious, ever-living God . . . they worshiped and served the things God created instead of the Creator himself. ROMANS 1:21-25

Many people worship parts of creation rather than God himself, the Creator.

Manasseh . . . practiced sorcery, divination, and witchcraft, and he consulted with mediums and psychics. He did much that was evil in the LORD's sight, arousing his anger. 2 CHRONICLES 33:6

Some people worship spiritual powers who are not from God.

As Peter entered his home, Cornelius fell at his feet and worshiped him. But Peter pulled him up and said, "Stand up! I'm a human being just like you!" ACTS 10:25-26

When the crowd saw what Paul had done, they shouted in their local dialect, "These men are gods in human form!" ACTS 14:11

Many people make the mistake of worshiping celebrities and other impressive figures.

How do I turn my heart back to God if I realize I've been worshiping an idol?

Joshua said, "Destroy the idols among you, and turn your hearts to the LORD." . . . The people said to Joshua, "We will serve the LORD our God. We will obey him alone." JOSHUA 24:23-24

The first step to turning your heart to God is turning away from idols. Idols are often tangible and tempting (hobbies, gadgets, television, work, etc.) and can occupy much of your time. When these distractions consistently pull you away from God to the point where you no longer know him as you should, they become idols. Try giving up some of your "distractions" for a while and try to draw closer to God with this extra time. It might not feel good at first giving up something you love to do. But replacing it with a relationship with God will feel better than anything you can imagine.

IMPOSSIBLE *See also* Doubt, Faith, Limitations, Miracles

The Bible is filled with seemingly impossible stories: A flood covers the earth, a sea is divided so people can walk through, the sun keeps shining until a battle can be won, a man survives three days in the belly of a fish, a virgin gives birth to a baby boy. To the person who does not believe in God or the authority of the Bible, these stories defy logic. But those who believe in the Creator of all things also believe that he can alter what he has created; he can break into natural law and cause something supernatural. In order for us to experience the impossible and recognize it for what it is, we need faith. Faith opens up a new dimension and we understand that what we see is not all there is. Suddenly, we can recognize the "impossible" things God does for his people because we believe that anything is possible for him. Learn to recognize and appreciate the "impossible" things God does for you and around you each day: experiencing unexpected forgiveness or healing for the body and heart, appreciating the intricate systems of the human body, being amazed at the exact conditions needed to support life on earth, or rejoicing in the birth of a baby. The more you see the "impossible" acts of God with eyes of faith, the stronger your faith in God will become.

Can God really do the impossible?

This is what the LORD of Heaven's Armies says: "All this may seem impossible to you now, a small remnant of God's people. But is it impossible for me?" ZECHARIAH 8:6

Jesus took the five loaves and two fish, looked up toward heaven, and blessed them. . . . About 5,000 men were fed that day! MATTHEW 14:19-21

Jesus looked at them intently and said, "Humanly speaking, it is impossible. But with God everything is possible." MATTHEW 19:26

There should be no doubt that God specializes in doing what seems impossible from a human perspective. The end of your abilities is the beginning of his. The God who spoke all of creation into being can do miracles for you. But you must believe he can, and that he wants to.

How do I deal with impossible situations?

"What do you mean, 'If I can'?" Jesus asked. "Anything is possible if a person believes." MARK 9:23

It was by faith that even Sarah was able to have a child, though she was barren and was too old. She believed that God would keep his promise. HEBREWS 11:11

Place your faith and hope in God. Trust that God can do the impossible and wants to work in your life. But even if he chooses not to, believe that he is the only one who can.

David . . . picked up five smooth stones from a stream and put them into his shepherd's bag. Then, armed only with his shepherd's staff and sling, he started across the valley to fight the Philistine. . . . Reaching into his shepherd's bag and taking out a stone, he hurled it with his sling and hit the Philistine in the forehead. The stone sank in, and Goliath stumbled and fell face down on the ground. So David triumphed over the Philistine with only a sling and a stone, for he had no sword. 1 SAMUEL 17:39-40, 49-50

Daniel [said], "There are no wise men, enchanters, magicians, or fortune-tellers who can reveal the king's secret. But there is a God in heaven who reveals secrets, and he has shown King Nebuchadnezzar what will happen in the future. Now I will tell you your dream and the visions you saw as you lay on your bed." DANIEL 2:27-28

In each of these situations, God's people had to deal with impossible circumstances. What was common in each situation was: (1) open communication with God by acknowledging the impossible, and (2) obedience to God's response, whether it meant waiting or moving forward. God often uses what he has already given us to accomplish the impossible, for example, a sling shot and an ability to discern dreams.

How does God use impossible situations to accomplish his will?

The LORD said to Moses, "Has my arm lost its power? Now you will see whether or not my word comes true!" NUMBERS 11:23

Even when there was no reason for hope, Abraham kept hoping—believing that he would become the father of many nations. For God had said to him, "That's how many descendants you will have!" ROMANS 4:18

God does the impossible to remind you he is God and you are not. When you have seen God do the impossible in the past, you can trust him more fully with your future.

The LORD said to Moses, "Return to Pharaoh and make your demands again. I have made him and his officials stubborn so I can display my miraculous signs among them." EXODUS 10:1

God does the impossible to display his character and unlimited power.

Worship only the LORD, who brought you out of Egypt with great strength and a powerful arm. Bow down to him alone, and offer sacrifices only to him. 2 KINGS 17:36

Come and see what our God has done, what awesome miracles he performs for people! PSALM 66:5

God does the impossible to draw people to him.

INFERTILITY *See also* Adoption, Coping, Grief

It seems unfair that some couples who long to have children are unable to, while some women get pregnant who don't want children. It is sad to see couples who so desperately want children of their own and can't conceive. We want to cry out to God, "Why? It's not fair! It doesn't make sense—they would be such great parents." To discover that the children we have planned for and dreamed about will not exist is similar to experiencing the death of a loved one. We make painful changes in plans and re-evaluate expectations for the future. Sometimes there is just no good explanation for why things happen. The answer won't be found in the *why*, but it can be found in the *who*. As your heavenly Father, God understands your loss because he grieves over every lost son and daughter who decides not to be part of his family. When we remember how deeply he loves us, we can take comfort that someday we will not only have the answers, but we will enjoy being part of a family that will bring immense joy and happiness for eternity.

How can I have an attitude of hope if I am childless?

I wait quietly before God, for my victory comes from him. . . . Let all that I am wait quietly before God, for my hope is in him. . . . O my people, trust in him at all times. Pour out your heart to him, for God is our refuge. PSALM 62:1, 5, 8

Your hope and trust must be in God, the Creator of life. He wants you to pour your heart out to him and to seek what is best from him. He is a refuge for you in your time of pain, suffering, loss, and sorrow. These are not empty platitudes, but the answer to finding peace.

How can I help those who are childless?

Isaac pleaded with the LORD on behalf of his wife, because she was unable to have children. The LORD answered Isaac's prayer, and Rebekah became pregnant with twins. GENESIS 25:21

Pray to God on their behalf.

"Why are you crying, Hannah?" Elkanah would ask. "Why aren't you eating? Why be downhearted just because you have no children? You have me—isn't that better than having ten sons?" 1 SAMUEL 1:8

Listen with understanding and don't minimize the hurt of childlessness. The greatest eloquence of sympathy is sometimes listening without saying anything.

Wicked people are broken like a tree in the storm. They cheat the woman who has no son to help her. They refuse to help the needy widow. JOB 24:20-21

Look for ways to be of practical assistance to families without children, especially as the husband and wife age. Perhaps God wants you to fill in the gaps with time and friendship.

How can I deal with the tensions infertility seems to cause?

When Rachel saw that she wasn't having any children for Jacob, she became jealous of her sister. She pleaded with Jacob, "Give me children, or I'll die!" Then Jacob became furious with Rachel. "Am I God?" he asked. "He's the one who has kept you from having children!" GENESIS 30:1-2

There are three things that are never satisfied—no, four that never say, "Enough!": the grave, the barren womb, the thirsty desert, the blazing fire. PROVERBS 30:15-16

Why does God permit his loved ones to suffer pain, such as the pain of being unable to bear children? Why can't he just give a child to parents who want one so badly? The real answer is that nobody knows. What is known is that we live in a fallen world where life doesn't always go the way we had hoped. For reasons we do not fully understand, God does not always allow us to have what we desire. Maybe it's because he has a different plan. Or maybe it is simply because life is dealing a hard blow. When we get to heaven, we will find out. But for now we must trust that God is in control, loves us, and is with us in our heartache.

Those who trust in the LORD will find new strength. They will soar high on wings like eagles. They will run and not grow weary. They will walk and not faint. ISAIAH 40:31

Don't worry about anything; instead, pray about everything. Tell God what you need, and thank him for all he has done. Then you will experience God's peace, which exceeds anything we can understand. His peace will guard your hearts and minds as you live in Christ Jesus. PHILIPPIANS 4:6-7

God's love for you is greater than anything you could ever imagine. Relying on his strength and love for you will help you begin to deal with the pain and tension caused by not being able to bear children.

How can I accept God's timing?

Sarai, Abram's wife, had not been able to bear children. . . . [Later, she] became pregnant, and she gave birth to a son for Abraham in his old age. This happened at just the time God had said it would. GENESIS 16:1; 21:2

The LORD is good to those who depend on him, to those who search for him. So it is good to wait quietly for salvation from the LORD. LAMENTATIONS 3:25-26

Sometimes God says yes when you pray. Sometimes he says no. Sometimes he wants you to wait. And sometimes you simply have to leave your life to God's control, even when you don't always understand his ways. Rushing ahead may get you what you think is best, but waiting for God's timing will get you God's best for you, which is always better.

Is it wrong to continue to plead to God for children?

Isaac pleaded with the LORD on behalf of his wife, because she was unable to have children. The LORD answered Isaac's prayer, and Rebekah became pregnant with twins. GENESIS 25:21

Listen to my voice in the morning, LORD. Each morning I bring my requests to you and wait expectantly. PSALM 5:3

As long as you believe in miracles, pray. As long as you believe in God, pray. Then let God be God. Even when you're short on hope, pray. Let him do what he knows is best.

INTEGRITY *See also* Character, Honesty, Reputation, Truth, Values

Integrity is essentially the unity between our character and the character of God. This union results in greater purity of heart, mind, and actions, and reflects the heart, mind, and actions of Jesus. Integrity is also a process. Just as pure gold is the result of a refining process that purifies the metal and tests it with fire, the process of living with integrity is refining. We are tested daily to see how pure we are within. If, in our testing, the Lord finds our hearts and actions becoming increasingly pure, then we are striving for integrity and are living more and more in union with God.

What is integrity?

The LORD has told you what is good, and this is what he requires of you: to do what is right, to love mercy, and to walk humbly with your God. MICAH 6:8

Integrity is character and conduct in harmony with God and his Word.

Who may worship in your sanctuary, LORD? Who may enter your presence on your holy hill? Those who lead blameless lives and do what is right, speaking the truth from sincere hearts. . . . Such people will stand firm forever. PSALM 15:1-2, 5

Integrity means living a life that is consistent in belief and behavior, in words and deeds. Your integrity is reflected in your relationships with God and with other people.

The LORD asked Satan, "Have you noticed my servant Job? He is the finest man in all the earth. He is blameless—a man of complete integrity. He fears God and stays away from evil. And he has maintained his integrity, even though you urged me to harm him without cause." JOB 2:3

Honesty guides good people; dishonesty destroys treacherous people. . . . The godly are directed by honesty; the wicked fall beneath their load of sin. PROVERBS 11:3-5

Integrity is the guiding principle of life and relationships and is directed by honesty.

Why is integrity important?

I know, my God, that you examine our hearts and rejoice when you find integrity there. You know I have done all this with good motives, and I have watched your people offer their gifts willingly and joyously. 1 CHRONICLES 29:17

Integrity pleases God.

May integrity and honesty protect me, for I put my hope in you. PSALM 25:21

For those who are righteous, the way is not steep and rough. You are a God who does what is right, and you smooth out the path ahead of them. ISAIAH 26:7

Integrity allows you to continue uninterrupted fellowship with God and helps you to live under his protection and guidance. When you lack integrity, you are exposed to all kinds of sin and harm, especially the disintegration of your character.

Who may climb the mountain of the LORD? Who may stand in his holy place? Only those whose hands and hearts are pure, who do not worship idols and never tell lies. They will receive the LORD's blessing and have a right relationship with God their savior. PSALM 24:3-5

The godly walk with integrity; blessed are their children who follow them. PROVERBS 20:7

Not only does God bless you when you live your life with integrity, but future generations will benefit as well.

How can I develop integrity in my own life?

My child, listen to what I say, and treasure my commands. Tune your ears to wisdom, and concentrate on understanding. . . . Then you will understand what it means to fear the LORD, and you will gain knowledge of God. . . . You will understand what is right, just, and fair, and you will find the right way to go. PROVERBS 2:1-2, 5, 9

Concentrate on learning wisdom from God. The more you understand what is just, right, and fair to him, the more you will develop integrity.

If you are faithful in little things, you will be faithful in large ones. But if you are dishonest in little things, you won't be honest with greater responsibilities. LUKE 16:10

We reject all shameful deeds and underhanded methods. We don't try to trick anyone or distort the word of God. We tell the truth before God, and all who are honest know this. 2 CORINTHIANS 4:2

Consistently live an honest life in all your dealings with people—even when you are in the minority. It is not enough to possess integrity; you must practice it.

The purpose of my instruction is that all believers would be filled with love that comes from a pure heart, a clear conscience, and genuine faith. 1 TIMOTHY 1:5

Be an example to all believers in what you say, in the way you live, in your love, your faith, and your purity. 1 TIMOTHY 4:12

If you keep yourself pure, you will be a special utensil for honorable use. Your life will be clean, and you will be ready for the Master to use you for every good work.
2 TIMOTHY 2:21

Those who want to be used for godly purposes commit themselves to a life of integrity.

What tests integrity?

Declare me innocent, O LORD, for I have acted with integrity; I have trusted in the LORD without wavering. Put me on trial, LORD, and cross-examine me. Test my motives and my heart. For I am always aware of your unfailing love, and I have lived according to your truth. PSALM 26:1-3

God gives the ultimate test—he examines your life for integrity.

Joseph refused [the advances of Potiphar's wife]. "Look," he told her, "my master trusts me with everything in his entire household. No one here has more authority than I do. He has held back nothing from me except you, because you are his wife. How could I do such a wicked thing? It would be a great sin against God." She kept putting pressure on Joseph day after day, but he refused to sleep with her, and he kept out of her way as much as possible. One day, however, no one else was around when he went in to do his work. She came and grabbed him by his cloak, demanding, "Come on, sleep with me!" Joseph tore himself away, but he left his cloak in her hand as he ran from the house. GENESIS 39:8-12

You must never twist justice or show partiality. Never accept a bribe, for bribes blind the eyes of the wise and corrupt the decisions of the godly. DEUTERONOMY 16:19

If you are faithful in little things, you will be faithful in large ones. But if you are dishonest in little things, you won't be honest with greater responsibilities. And if you are untrustworthy about worldly wealth, who will trust you with the true riches of heaven?
LUKE 16:10-11

Living in any culture with its temptations, evils, and sinful pleasures will test your integrity. You are often torn between two loves, two worlds, and can be easily distracted from living with integrity by a society that doesn't care much about truth and righteousness.

How does God respond to my commitment to integrity?

The LORD rewarded me for doing right. He has seen my innocence. To the faithful you show yourself faithful; to those with integrity you show integrity. PSALM 18:24-25

This psalmist isn't boasting in his accomplishment, but thanking God for giving him the power and direction to live according to God's ways. This passage represents the same promise for you. God will empower your obedience.

Be careful to live properly among your unbelieving neighbors. Then even if they accuse you of doing wrong, they will see your honorable behavior, and they will give honor to God when he judges the world. 1 PETER 2:12

Your integrity may not bring immediate rewards, but it will one day be recognized and commended by God.

INTIMACY *See also* Humility, Marriage, Sex/Sexuality, Vulnerability

Heart to heart, mind to mind, soul to soul—this is intimacy. There is relational intimacy, where two people become soul mates, free to openly share all of their burdens, fears, and joys with each other. Then there is physical intimacy, reserved only for marriage, where a man and woman, through their physical relationship, reach new heights of vulnerability that allow them to communicate at the deepest level. And finally there is intimacy with God, where we learn to understand the very heart of God. As we do this, all other intimacy takes on new and even greater meaning. God created us for intimacy; we are lonely people longing for relationship. The risks are worth the rewards.

What does it mean to have intimacy with God?

"When that day comes," says the LORD, "you will call me 'my husband' instead of 'my master.' . . . I will make you my wife forever, showing you righteousness and justice, unfailing love and compassion. I will be faithful to you and make you mine, and you will finally know me as the LORD." HOSEA 2:16, 19-20

God is the source of love, the only one who could create us with the ability to love. Therefore, no one knows as much about love as God does. Intimacy with God means experiencing his love to the fullest and returning that love to him. The love he communicates is completely loyal, trusting, and honest. God created marriage to illustrate what an intimate relationship with him should look like.

See how very much our Father loves us, for he calls us his children, and that is what we are! 1 JOHN 3:1

God reaches out to you, offering an intimate relationship—as intimate as husband and wife or parent and child, a commitment that is forever, a love relationship beyond all others.

The LORD your God is living among you. . . . He will rejoice over you with joyful songs. ZEPHANIAH 3:17

The Lord God, Creator of the universe, sings songs about you! What a portrait of a loving, intimate God.

I am with you, and I will protect you wherever you go. One day I will bring you back to this land. I will not leave you until I have finished giving you everything I have promised you. GENESIS 28:15

Be sure of this: I am with you always, even to the end of the age. MATTHEW 28:20

The Lord is with you, as close as you want him, as long as you let him, until the end of life. These are vows of permanent intimacy.

What must I do to experience an intimate relationship with God?

Enoch lived 365 years, walking in close fellowship with God. Then one day he disappeared, because God took him. GENESIS 5:23-24

Walk with God—daily and consistently.

My heart has heard [the Lord] say, "Come and talk with me." And my heart responds, "LORD, I am coming." PSALM 27:8

The LORD is close to all who call on him, yes, to all who call on him in truth. PSALM 145:18

Talk with God—daily and consistently.

You must worship no other gods, for the LORD, whose very name is Jealous, is a God who is jealous about his relationship with you. EXODUS 34:14

Worship God only—daily and consistently.

Noah was a righteous man, the only blameless person living on earth at the time, and he walked in close fellowship with God. GENESIS 6:9

Live the way God wants you to live.

Come close to God, and God will come close to you. Wash your hands, you sinners; purify your hearts. JAMES 4:8

Stay close to God and purify your heart before him.

Jesus replied, "You must love the LORD your God with all your heart, all your soul, and all your mind." MATTHEW 22:37

Love God completely.

What is the basis for true and lasting intimacy in marriage?

Drink water from your own well—share your love only with your wife. . . . May you always be captivated by her love. PROVERBS 5:15, 19

The husband should fulfill his wife's sexual needs, and the wife should fulfill her husband's needs. 1 CORINTHIANS 7:3

As the church submits to Christ, so you wives should submit to your husbands in everything. For husbands, this means love your wives, just as Christ loved the church. He gave up his life for her. EPHESIANS 5:24-25

True and lasting intimacy in marriage is based upon the following: (1) faithfulness; (2) rejoicing in each other; (3) satisfying each other in love and sexuality; (4) accepting each other as a blessing from the Lord; (5) recognizing the great value of one's mate; (6) recognizing how much spouses can truly bring delight and satisfaction to each other; (7) living happily with each other; (8) talking together about the Lord and spiritual things; (9) giving thanks to the Lord together; (10) submitting to each other; and (11) loving each other as passionately as Christ loved the church and died for it.

J

JEALOUSY *See also* Comparisons, Coveting, Desires, Greed, Selfishness

Jealousy is one of the most common emotions, and can be one of the most dangerous. We're jealous of those who have better houses, nicer cars, more vacation time, more attractive spouses, happier families, more talents. Jealousy is an emotion of passion and when uncontrolled, it leads to hatred. When allowed to go that far, it can drive an inflamed person to kill, as Cain killed Abel. Short of that, relationships have been destroyed, families broken, and businesses poisoned through jealousy. Learning to recognize and deal with feelings of jealousy before they overwhelm us is essential.

What does it mean that God is "a jealous God"?

You must not make for yourself an idol of any kind. . . . You must not bow down to them or worship them, for I, the LORD your God, am a jealous God who will not tolerate your affection for any other gods. EXODUS 20:4-5

We usually think of jealousy only in negative terms. But jealousy has two definitions. One has to do with being envious of others. But jealousy can also mean "a demand for complete devotion." In this respect, a husband and wife are supposed to be "jealous" for each other, expecting that they will share their most intimate love with no one else. Likewise, God is "jealous" for the undivided devotion of his people. When people give their honor, praise, and love to other things, God is jealous that the honor due him has been squandered elsewhere. The positive side of jealousy is guarding against losing the love most important to you. Because God deserves all of your honor, praise, and love, your worship of him alone is an honest recognition of what he deserves.

God . . . is jealous about his relationship with you. EXODUS 34:14

They have roused my jealousy by worshiping things that are not God. DEUTERONOMY 32:21

God's jealousy is not petty but springs from deep love and a desire for your best interests. Jealousy understood like this is essential to trust in any relationship. Divided loyalties (between God and your "idols") only harm your relationship with him and therefore harm what is best for you.

How can jealousy affect my life? What can jealousy lead to?

The people of Ephraim mobilized an army and crossed over the Jordan River to Zaphon. They sent this message to Jephthah: "Why didn't you call for us to help you fight against the Ammonites? We are going to burn down your house with you in it!" JUDGES 12:1

Jealousy makes enemies of friends. The twelve tribes of Israel were once friends and brothers, united in the common cause of building a nation under God. When the tribe of Ephraim didn't get to participate in a big victory, they threatened to burn down the houses of their countrymen. This sounds like school children on the playground rather than grown men and women uniting against evil. Don't let jealousy and pettiness drive a wedge between you and your friends.

The LORD accepted Abel and his gift, but he did not accept Cain and his gift. This made Cain very angry.... While they were in the field, Cain attacked his brother, Abel, and killed him. GENESIS 4:4-5, 8

Saul kept a jealous eye on David.... The very next day ... [Saul] began to rave in his house like a madman. David was playing the harp, as he did each day. But Saul had a spear in his hand, and he suddenly hurled it at David, intending to pin him to the wall. 1 SAMUEL 18:9-11

Jealousy for attention or affection can drive a person to extreme action, even seeking to harm or kill others. Saul's jealousy of David consumed him to the point where he could think of nothing else and became ineffective for God. Envy and jealousy destroy not only the person who feels them, but often leads that person to attack those who are the objects of the envy and jealousy. While you may not attack a person with a spear as Saul did, you may use sharp words and piercing comments which can be just as dangerous.

How can we deal with jealousy?

When Rachel saw that she wasn't having any children for Jacob, she became jealous of her sister. GENESIS 30:1

Instead of enjoying the favor and love of her husband, Rachel focused on her inability to give Jacob children. She became jealous of her sister, Leah. The cure for jealousy is being thankful and enjoying what you do have instead of focusing on what you don't have.

Should you be jealous because I am kind to others? MATTHEW 20:15

Jealousy reveals selfishness. We want for ourselves what someone else has. Jealousy shows a smallness of heart that resents the blessings and joy of others. The inability to rejoice in another's success or good fortune limits your own capacity for joy. The cure for jealousy is gratitude.

Jesus said this to let [Peter] know by what kind of death he would glorify God.... Peter turned around and saw behind them the disciple Jesus loved.... Peter asked Jesus, "What about him, Lord?" Jesus replied, "If I want him to remain alive until I return, what is that to you? As for you, follow me." JOHN 21:19-22

When Peter heard Jesus' prophecy of his death, he wondered what would happen to the other disciple (John). Jesus made it clear that Peter was to pay attention to his own concerns, not those of others. In many situations you may be tempted to compare your lot in life with another's. Jesus sternly rebukes this attitude. It shows discontent with God's plan and stirs dissent among people. Instead, keep your focus on God and accept that his will for you is best.

JOY *See also* Confidence, Hope, Praise, Satisfaction

Joy happens in two ways. There is the joy that is a reaction to happy events (which is temporary), and there is the joy that happens in spite of circumstances (which is strong and lasting). This strong and lasting joy can only happen by following God and living with his attitudes toward life. Happiness based on events is a good part of life, but if that is all we can count on, we constantly have to create happy events to keep us upbeat. Those who know the joy that comes from God don't need perpetual events to keep them happy. They learn how to develop inner joy in spite of circumstances, because they know that no matter what happens, God offers hope and promise.

What is joy?

You will show me the way of life, granting me the joy of your presence and the pleasures of living with you forever. PSALM 16:11

Let the godly rejoice. Let them be glad in God's presence. Let them be filled with joy. PSALM 68:3

Since we have been made right in God's sight by faith, we have peace with God because of what Jesus Christ our Lord has done for us. Because of our faith, Christ has brought us into this place of undeserved privilege where we now stand, and we confidently and joyfully look forward to sharing God's glory. ROMANS 5:1-2

Joy is the celebration of walking with God. It is an inner happiness that lasts despite the circumstances around you because it is based on a relationship with Jesus Christ. It is peace with God. It is realizing how privileged you are to know Jesus as Savior, to have your sins forgiven, to be friends with God Almighty, and to be certain you will live forever with him in heaven. It is experiencing the dramatic change that occurs in your life when you allow the Holy Spirit to control your heart and thoughts.

Where does joy come from?

Joyful are those who have the God of Israel as their helper, whose hope is in the LORD their God. PSALM 146:5

The Lord himself is the wellspring of true joy. The more you love him, know him, walk with him, and become like him, the greater your joy. You will find lasting joy in heaven, but you can experience great joy now from walking with God.

The joy of the LORD is your strength! NEHEMIAH 8:10

The LORD your God is living among you. He is a mighty savior. He will take delight in you with gladness. With his love, he will calm all your fears. He will rejoice over you with joyful songs. ZEPHANIAH 3:17

Joy springs from God's love, which is not dependent on circumstances or on your performance. When you realize just how great his love for you really is, you are far less vulnerable to the depression and despair that come from problems and disappointments.

[God himself] will wipe every tear from their eyes, and there will be no more death or sorrow or crying or pain. REVELATION 21:4

Joy is rooted in the certainty of heaven, where you will be fully and finally liberated from the trials and troubles of life.

How can I more fully experience joy?

Let us run with endurance the race set before us. We do this by keeping our eyes on Jesus. . . . Because of the joy awaiting him, he endured the cross, disregarding its shame. HEBREWS 12:1-2

Keep your eyes on Jesus. Following him leads to the greatest joy you will ever experience.

All who seek the LORD will praise him. Their hearts will rejoice with everlasting joy. PSALM 22:26

May all who search for you be filled with joy and gladness in you. May those who love your salvation repeatedly shout, "The LORD is great!" PSALM 40:16

Actively pursue God as the priority of your life. The more you know God, the Creator of joy, the more you will know joy!

Those who look to him for help will be radiant with joy; no shadow of shame will darken their faces. . . . Taste and see that the LORD is good. Oh, the joys of those who take refuge in him! PSALM 34:5, 8

I am convinced that I will remain alive so I can continue to help all of you grow and experience the joy of your faith. PHILIPPIANS 1:25

A growing faith and trust in God is vital to experiencing joy in every situation. Joy overflows from the fullness of your faith and trust in the Lord.

The Holy Spirit produces this kind of fruit in our lives: love, joy, peace, patience, kindness, goodness, faithfulness, gentleness, and self-control. GALATIANS 5:22-23

The presence of the Holy Spirit in your life produces joy. He guides you and advises you to make decisions that will bring you greater joy.

You have been faithful in handling this small amount. . . . Let's celebrate together! MATTHEW 25:21

Serving God well brings a deep sense of satisfaction, which is an occasion for joy.

[The believers] worshiped together at the Temple each day, met in homes for the Lord's Supper, and shared their meals with great joy and generosity. ACTS 2:46

Stay in touch with other believers because joy overflows from others who know God.

How can I be joyful in hard times?

Don't be surprised at the fiery trials you are going through, as if something strange were happening to you. Instead, be very glad—for . . . you will have the wonderful joy of seeing his glory. 1 PETER 4:12-13

Difficult circumstances help you better understand what Jesus went through for you. If Jesus suffered to give you the greatest gift of all—eternal life—then you should joyfully suffer for him and faithfully proclaim his message despite the suffering it might cause you. When you suffer for him, it helps you appreciate his suffering for you.

When all you owned was taken from you, you accepted it with joy. You knew there were better things waiting for you that will last forever. HEBREWS 10:34

Hope in God's promises of eternal life give you joy because you know the hardships you are presently going through will one day end.

The apostles left the high council rejoicing that God had counted them worthy to suffer disgrace for the name of Jesus. ACTS 5:41

Doing something significant for God, even though you may suffer for it, brings great joy because you know that God is working through you to accomplish something important for his kingdom. You experience joy when you know that God is pleased with you and that your work for him will bring a reward in heaven.

Even though the fig trees have no blossoms, and there are no grapes on the vines; even though the olive crop fails, and the fields lie empty and barren; even though the flocks die in the fields, and the cattle barns are empty, yet I will rejoice in the LORD! I will be joyful in the God of my salvation! HABAKKUK 3:17-18

Joy is a choice. You may not realize it, but most of the time you choose your moods and your attitudes. God's promises of what you can have now and what awaits you in the future are the basis for choosing joy no matter what you face.

I will be glad and rejoice in your unfailing love, for you have seen my troubles, and you care about the anguish of my soul. PSALM 31:7

I am convinced that nothing can ever separate us from God's love. ROMANS 8:38

Joy is the celebration of your friendship with God. Feelings and circumstances need not prevail; even in times of trouble and anguish, you can experience joy because of God's unfailing love for you.

What brings God joy?

He led me to a place of safety; he rescued me because he delights in me. PSALM 18:19

The LORD's delight is in those who fear him, those who put their hope in his unfailing love. PSALM 147:11

God literally delights in having a relationship with his people. It breaks his heart when people he creates rebel against him or don't want to bother with him.

JUDGING OTHERS *See also* Assumptions, Comparisons, Prejudice

Passing judgment on others is second nature to most of us. We see a child acting up and condemn the parent for poor discipline. We look at a person's hairstyle or clothing and immediately label them. Someone speaks up for what he believes and we instantly categorize him. The problem with judging others is that we see the person's words and actions through a negative filter in our mind. Our perspective narrows to include only their faults when really, it should be broad enough to include their goodness, too. The Bible warns us against judging others. When we judge others, we assume we know their thoughts and motives and are qualified to pronounce judgment. In reality, only God can know a person's heart. Before we jump to conclusions about someone, it helps to remember hurts we've experienced when others wrongfully judged us. This will broaden our perspective toward people, ridding us of the negative filter that defiles their reputation. Seeing others as Jesus sees them, as God's children worthy of love and kindness, will replace judgment with mercy.

What does God think of judging others?

Don't make judgments about anyone ahead of time—before the Lord returns. For he will bring our darkest secrets to light and will reveal our private motives. Then God will give to each one whatever praise is due. 1 CORINTHIANS 4:5

Be very slow to judge others, because only God is capable of judging perfectly every time. Once you've formed an opinion about someone it's difficult to change it. If you've incorrectly formed a bad opinion about someone, you may think negatively about that person for years, damaging the possibility of any relationship.

You may think you can condemn such people, but you are just as bad, and you have no excuse! When you say they are wicked and should be punished, you are condemning yourself, for you who judge others do these very same things. ROMANS 2:1

When you condemn others for their sin, God sees your hypocrisy if you haven't first carefully considered your own sins.

The LORD said to Samuel, "Don't judge by his appearance or height, for I have rejected him. The LORD doesn't see things the way you see them. People judge by outward appearance, but the LORD looks at the heart." 1 SAMUEL 16:7

God doesn't want you to make judgments based on outward appearance.

Do not twist justice in legal matters by favoring the poor or being partial to the rich and powerful. Always judge people fairly. LEVITICUS 19:15

When you have to make a judgment, do so with fairness and integrity.

What are the consequences of judging others?

You will be treated as you treat others. The standard you use in judging is the standard by which you will be judged. MATTHEW 7:2

Do not judge others, and you will not be judged. Do not condemn others, or it will all come back against you. Forgive others, and you will be forgiven. LUKE 6:37

You will be judged by the same standard you use, so it's better to be merciful and forgiving than harsh and critical.

What's the difference between judging others and offering constructive criticism?

Make allowance for each other's faults, and forgive anyone who offends you. Remember, the Lord forgave you, so you must forgive others. COLOSSIANS 3:13

Don't speak evil against each other, dear brothers and sisters. If you criticize and judge each other, then you are criticizing and judging God's law. But your job is to obey the law, not to judge whether it applies to you. JAMES 4:11

One coach berates a player publicly for a mistake made in the game. Another coach waits until the game is over and addresses the player privately with instruction about how to avoid making the same mistake again. While no one likes criticism—even when it is constructive—you sometimes need it. But it is much easier to receive criticism when it is offered gently and in love rather than harshly and to humiliate. To judge someone is to criticize with no effort to see that person succeed or improve. To offer constructive criticism is to invest in another for the purpose of building a relationship and helping that person become the person God created him or her to be.

JUDGMENT *See also* Justice, Mercy, Punishment, Rewards

Most of us have a hard time with the concept that God will one day judge us; that our secret lives will be revealed and our sins brought to light. The Bible makes it clear that faith in Jesus Christ will be rewarded with eternal life in heaven and those who did not put their faith in Jesus will face eternal separation from him. The knowledge of this future judgment should cause us to carefully consider our standing with God, as well as our actions toward our fellow human beings. God, in his kindness, has given us his Word to show us how to live in a way that will please him, and in his patience, he has given us time to repent from our sins and turn to him. How wonderful that he doesn't slay us the first time we sin, but he loves us enough to allow us time to turn from our sinful way of life and begin walking with his Son, Jesus. In the end, no excuses will be accepted, but if you take advantage of God's kindness and patience today and each day, your judgment will be favorable and God will welcome you into his eternal kingdom.

How will I be able to face the judgment of God?

Since we have been made right in God's sight by the blood of Christ, he will certainly save us from God's condemnation. For since our friendship with God was restored by the death of his Son while we were still his enemies, we will certainly be saved through the life of his Son. ROMANS 5:9-10

One of the hardest things to accept, yet one of the most important, is that we don't make the rules for how life really works. God does. His rules say that sin deserves eternal death and that everyone has sinned. Your hope is based on the fact that Jesus Christ stood in your place for the judgment you deserved for your sin. God no longer looks at you as an enemy, but as a friend—even as his own child.

There is no condemnation for those who belong to Christ Jesus. And because you belong to him, the power of the life-giving Spirit has freed you from the power of sin that leads to death. ROMANS 8:1-2

Jesus Christ has saved you from the threat of condemnation and death.

Should I be afraid of facing God's judgment?

He will judge the world with justice and rule the nations with fairness. PSALM 9:8

Nothing evil will be allowed to enter, nor anyone who practices shameful idolatry and dishonesty—but only those whose names are written in the Lamb's Book of Life. REVELATION 21:27

The final event of history is a two-fold judgment: (1) God will judge all people who have ever lived to determine whether they should enter heaven or hell. This is based solely on their allegiance to and faith in God. This is the judgment you must be afraid of if you have not accepted Jesus Christ as your Savior and asked him to forgive your sins. (2) God will judge the deeds of all those who enter heaven and give rewards based on those deeds. This second judgment does not determine whether or not you get into heaven, but what rewards you receive when you get there. How do you think you will be judged?

How does the future judgment affect my life now?

God loved the world so much that he gave his one and only Son, so that everyone who believes in him will not perish but have eternal life. JOHN 3:16

Can anything ever separate us from Christ's love? ROMANS 8:35

This is real love—not that we loved God, but that he loved us and sent his Son as a sacrifice to take away our sins. 1 JOHN 4:10

You can know for certain of God's great love for you because he allowed his Son to die in your place, to take the punishment for your sin so that you can be free from eternal judgment. Think of it: He sent his Son to die for you so that you could live forever with him. No wonder John wrote, "This is real love."

On the judgment day, fire will reveal what kind of work each builder has done. The fire will show if a person's work has any value. If the work survives, that builder will receive a reward. But if the work is burned up, the builder will suffer great loss. The builder will be saved, but like someone barely escaping through a wall of flames.
1 CORINTHIANS 3:13-15

The promise of salvation does not eliminate your responsibility to live rightly now. God has given you all that is necessary to lead a meaningful, spiritually productive life. You ignore his promises and provisions at great risk.

JUSTICE *See also* Accountability, Consequences, Fairness

When others wrong us, we cry out for justice. When we wrong God, we cry out for mercy. Fortunately, God is merciful. But if we don't accept his merciful gift of salvation, we are subject to his justice, the punishment of eternal death and separation from him. Until God sets up his eternal kingdom, where perfect justice prevails, justice will continue to be needed here on earth—both God's justice to urge us toward his kingdom, and law and order to keep anarchy from ruling. When administering justice, we should also keep God's example of mercy in mind. While justice provides law and order, mercy provides hope and forgiveness—God's formula for restoration.

Is God always fair and just?

O LORD, God of Israel, you are just. EZRA 9:15

God will use this persecution to show his justice. . . . In his justice he will pay back those who persecute you. 2 THESSALONIANS 1:5-6

When you are burdened with trouble, it is tempting to think God is not fair or just. How can he allow a Christian to suffer when so many unbelievers down the street are prospering? But God has made it clear in the Bible that justice and fairness, while always right, will often be perverted in this life by selfish people. The Bible also makes it clear that justice will not be twisted forever. True justice will one day prevail, forever, for those who follow God.

Why should I strive for justice?

You must not pass along false rumors. You must not cooperate with evil people. . . . Do not slant your testimony. EXODUS 23:1-3

I want to see a mighty flood of justice. AMOS 5:24

God is just. Those who follow him try to be more and more like him each day, developing a desire for justice in all situations.

At last everyone will say, "There truly is a reward for those who live for God; surely there is a God who judges justly here on earth." PSALM 58:11

The dead were judged according to what they had done. REVELATION 20:12

God rewards those who seek after justice.

The city writhes in chaos; every home is locked to keep out intruders. ISAIAH 24:10

Outwardly you look like righteous people, but inwardly your hearts are filled with hypocrisy and lawlessness. MATTHEW 23:28

I appeal to you, dear brothers and sisters, by the authority of our Lord Jesus Christ, to live in harmony with each other. Let there be no divisions in the church. Rather, be of one mind, united in thought and purpose. 1 CORINTHIANS 1:10

Without justice chaos and evil will reign. Justice is essential to living in peace.

The world seems so unjust. Will God's justice really prevail?

[The Lord] is coming! He is coming to judge the earth. He will judge the world with justice, and the nations with his truth. PSALM 96:13

Complete justice will occur only when Jesus returns. But make no mistake: This is his solemn promise and it is certain.

May your Kingdom come soon. May your will be done on earth, as it is in heaven. MATTHEW 6:10

Through the work of his church, God's kingdom is advancing in the world now. Though complete justice will come only in the future, you can—and must—work for justice in your own spheres of influence.

How can I work effectively for justice?

Uphold the rights of the oppressed and the destitute. PSALM 82:3

Speak out against injustice.

There is joy for those who deal justly with others and always do what is right. PSALM 106:3

Be just and fair to all. Do what is right and good. ISAIAH 56:1

Persist in doing what is right. Don't become unjust yourself.

Don't say, "I will get even for this wrong." Wait for the LORD to handle the matter. PROVERBS 20:22

Don't repay evil with evil. Work for justice without a vengeful spirit.

How do God's justice and mercy relate to each other?

The LORD said to Moses, . . . "Designate cities of refuge to which people can flee if they have killed someone accidentally." NUMBERS 35:9-11

"I'm in a desperate situation!" David replied to Gad. "But let us fall into the hands of the LORD, for his mercy is great. Do not let me fall into human hands." 2 SAMUEL 24:14

The wages of sin is death, but the free gift of God is eternal life through Christ Jesus our Lord. ROMANS 6:23

God is just in that he very clearly tells you what sin is and what its consequences will be. All people are treated equally. God is merciful in that he offers a way for you to be spared the punishment you deserve for your sin. You would be much worse off if you always got the justice you deserved. Justice is getting what you deserve. Grace is getting what you don't deserve—forgiveness for your sins and friendship with God.

You have heard the law that says, "Love your neighbor" and hate your enemy. But [Jesus said], love your enemies! MATTHEW 5:43-44

Justice punishes evil, crime, and wrongdoing. Mercy forgives the sinner. Jesus sets a new standard for mercy. One of the hardest things you can do is forgive someone who has wronged you. But it is only through forgiveness that you can be free of the bitterness of injustice. Your mercy may be exactly what someone needs to understand God's mercy.

KINDNESS *See also* Help, Hospitality, Support, Thoughtfulness

Kindness is the sign of a loving heart, one of the greatest of all virtues. A kind person is pleasant, good, gracious—always appreciated. There's a lot of talk these days about "random acts of kindness." Maybe this is because we live in a society starved for good deeds. God is our model for kindness. The kindest act ever committed was when God sent his own Son, Jesus, to die on the cross for our sins so that we might live forever in heaven. God also showers us with kindness each day, sending sunshine and rain, food and provisions, family and friends, comfort and encouragement, boundless love and wisdom.

How does God show kindness to me?

The LORD is merciful and compassionate, slow to get angry and filled with unfailing love. . . . The LORD is righteous in everything he does; he is filled with kindness. PSALM 145:8, 17

Since it is through God's kindness, then it is not by their good works. For in that case, God's grace would not be what it really is—free and undeserved. ROMANS 11:6

God gives you mercy, even though you don't deserve it. He is patient with you and doesn't lash out when you do something wrong. He loves you compassionately and unconditionally. God didn't just create kindness, he is kindness itself. Everything he does for you is an act of kindness to help you become all he created you to be.

God, with undeserved kindness, declares that we are righteous. He did this through Christ Jesus when he freed us from the penalty for our sins. ROMANS 3:24-25

[God] raised us from the dead along with Christ and seated us with him in the heavenly realms because we are united with Christ Jesus. So God can point to us in all future ages as examples of the incredible wealth of his grace and kindness toward us, as shown in all he has done for us who are united with Christ Jesus. EPHESIANS 2:6-7

When God our Savior revealed his kindness and love, he saved us, not because of the righteous things we had done, but because of his mercy. He washed away our sins. TITUS 3:4-5

God forgives your sins and offers you salvation—a guarantee of living forever with him in heaven. If God were not kind, you would get the punishment you deserve. Since he is kind, you get the forgiveness you don't deserve.

[God] never left them without evidence of himself and his goodness. For instance, he sends you rain and good crops and gives you food and joyful hearts. ACTS 14:17

In God's kindness, he meets your needs. God's kindness has hands and feet, not merely talk.

Why should I be kind to others?

This is what the LORD of Heaven's Armies says: Judge fairly, and show mercy and kindness to one another. ZECHARIAH 7:9

Be kind to each other, tenderhearted, forgiving one another, just as God through Christ has forgiven you. EPHESIANS 4:32

Be kind because God has been kind to you and asks you to pass it on to others. It is a way to show others Jesus' love. When you discover how wonderful kindness is, you will want to share it with others.

The King will say to those on his right, "Come, you who are blessed by my Father, inherit the Kingdom prepared for you from the creation of the world. For I was hungry, and you fed me. I was thirsty, and you gave me a drink. I was a stranger, and you invited me into your home. I was naked, and you gave me clothing. I was sick, and you cared for me. I was in prison, and you visited me." MATTHEW 25:34-36

Love your enemies! Do good to them. Lend to them without expecting to be repaid. Then your reward from heaven will be very great, and you will truly be acting as children of the Most High, for he is kind to those who are unthankful and wicked. LUKE 6:35

God rewards kindness because it demonstrates unconditional love. Kindness is not motivated by reward, but you are rewarded for your kindness.

How should I show kindness to others?

Never let loyalty and kindness leave you! Tie them around your neck as a reminder. Write them deep within your heart. PROVERBS 3:3

There was a believer in Joppa named Tabitha (which in Greek is Dorcas). She was always doing kind things for others and helping the poor. ACTS 9:36

True kindness is not a single act but a lifestyle. Begin showing kindness in the small things you do and say until you are truly kind in all situations.

Jesus [told this] story: "A Jewish man was traveling on a trip from Jerusalem to Jericho, and he was attacked by bandits. They stripped him of his clothes, beat him up, and left him half dead beside the road. . . . A despised Samaritan came along, and when he saw the man, he felt compassion for him. Going over to him, the Samaritan soothed his wounds." LUKE 10:30, 33-34

Kindness does not look the other way and ignore the needy, but is attentive to and responds sensitively to the needs of others.

The people of the island were very kind to us. It was cold and rainy, so they built a fire on the shore to welcome us. ACTS 28:2

Whenever we have the opportunity, we should do good to everyone—especially to those in the family of faith. GALATIANS 6:10

Kindness looks for opportunities to help, such as times of trouble and hardship.

Be kind to each other, tenderhearted, forgiving one another, just as God through Christ has forgiven you. EPHESIANS 4:32

Kindness is forgiving others.

I want you to know . . . what God in his kindness has done through the churches in Macedonia. They are being tested by many troubles, and they are very poor. But they are also filled with abundant joy, which has overflowed in rich generosity. For I can testify that they gave not only what they could afford, but far more. And they did it of their own free will. 2 CORINTHIANS 8:1-3

Kindness is generously sharing what you have with others.

Don't forget to show hospitality to strangers, for some who have done this have entertained angels without realizing it! HEBREWS 13:2

Kindness is helping those you don't know who need your help.

If you give even a cup of cold water to one of the least of my followers, you will surely be rewarded. MATTHEW 10:42

Your acts of kindness do not need to be major, award-winning events. God sees and rewards every act of kindness.

Where do I find the desire to be kind?

Since God chose you to be the holy people he loves, you must clothe yourselves with tenderhearted mercy, kindness, humility, gentleness, and patience. COLOSSIANS 3:12

Kindness to others is a response to the kindness that overflows from your relationship with God.

The Holy Spirit produces this kind of fruit in our lives: . . . kindness. GALATIANS 5:22

Kindness is planted in you by the Holy Spirit.

God can point to us in all future ages as examples of the incredible wealth of his grace and kindness toward us, as shown in all he has done for us who are united with Christ Jesus. EPHESIANS 2:7

Kindness is a response to the amazing kindness Jesus has shown to you.

KNOWLEDGE/LEARNING *See also* Discernment, Thoughts, Wisdom

We live in a culture driven by the acquisition of information. Finding information is easy, but what we do with that knowledge is what counts. Knowing a lot isn't helpful if we don't use it for something good. The same principle applies to the Christian life. We can know a lot about the Bible. We can know the difference between right and wrong. We can know Bible history and theology. But if we don't apply this knowledge to make a difference in our lives and the lives of others, then everything we know goes to waste. The book of Proverbs in the Bible declares that the fear of the Lord is the beginning of knowledge, meaning that our understanding of information and of the world should initially pass through the filter of what God knows. Since God is omniscient and knows how everything works, we can respect the accuracy and the authority of his input. We "fear the Lord" when we respect what he says in his Word. Through prayer we learn wisdom—the godly application of our knowledge.

Why is knowledge so important?

Wisdom will enter your heart, and knowledge will fill you with joy. PROVERBS 2:10

Using the wisdom God has given you helps you apply what you know and saves you from choosing many wrong paths.

What is the most important thing I can know?

Fear of the LORD is the foundation of true knowledge, but fools despise wisdom and discipline. PROVERBS 1:7

[Mockers and fools] hated knowledge and chose not to fear the LORD. They rejected my advice and paid no attention when I corrected them. Therefore, they must eat the bitter fruit of living their own way. PROVERBS 1:29-31

Learn to fear the Lord. This is not the cowering kind of fear, but a healthy respect for who God is, why he created you, and what he wants you to accomplish.

How can knowledge be harmful?

You felt secure in your wickedness. "No one sees me," you said. But your "wisdom" and "knowledge" have led you astray, and you said, "I am the only one, and there is no other." So disaster will overtake you. ISAIAH 47:10-11

Knowledge is harmful when it leads you to think you no longer need God. If you think you can rely on your own smarts to make it through this life, you will be deeply disappointed when you get to the end.

Because of your superior knowledge, a weak believer for whom Christ died will be destroyed. 1 CORINTHIANS 8:11

Sometimes it is easy to complicate the simplicity of the message of the Bible with all the doctrine you may know. If you are a learned student of the Bible, be careful not to let your head knowledge of the Bible get in the way of the heart message of the Bible. This can be a stumbling block to newer Christians if you make them think being a Christian is more about what you know than how you live.

LAZINESS *See also* Apathy, Complacency, Neglect, Work

There is a great distinction between laziness and rest: honest, hard work. Rest after hard or strenuous work, after productivity and progress, is a good thing. But resting without doing any work is laziness. Shortcuts, cutting corners, and ignoring responsibilities are all forms of laziness. Laziness is in direct opposition to God's desire for people to live productive and rewarding lives. God tells us to be active: Love others, care for our families, serve in our church, earn a living, help the poor and weak, feed the hungry, be examples of his truth, tell others about him. Laziness, on the other hand, is wasteful, destructive, neglectful, and careless and leads to nothing because it invests nothing. Lazy people think it feels good to do nothing, but it feels better to see your work make a difference in the lives of others. Enthusiastic work for the Lord is the pathway to blessings and progress.

Is it a sin to be lazy?

Sodom's sins were pride, gluttony, and laziness. EZEKIEL 16:49

We hear that some of you are living idle lives, refusing to work and meddling in other people's business. 2 THESSALONIANS 3:11

Laziness is often overlooked as sin. We tend to think of sin as doing something we shouldn't; but sin is also neglecting to do what we should. Laziness is a sin because it wastes your God-given talents and ability to work, it wastes the time God has given you on earth, and it wastes opportunities to serve God and others. Laziness selfishly expects others to provide for you, and opens the door to temptation with your idle time. Laziness is transformed by purpose. Purpose requires courage to have the discipline to say no to those distractions that keep you from your purpose.

What are the consequences of laziness?

Lazy people are soon poor. PROVERBS 10:4

Lazy people want much but get little, but those who work hard will prosper.
PROVERBS 13:4

A lazy person's way is blocked with briers. PROVERBS 15:19

Laziness will bring trouble into a life. Those who work hard are alert and prepare for coming troubles. But those who are lazy are always at risk because they can neither see trouble coming nor prepare for it. It is much more satisfying to work hard and make progress toward a better life than to be lazy and get nowhere.

Work hard and become a leader; be lazy and become a slave. PROVERBS 12:24

The lazy lose control of their lives and destinies.

Despite their desires, the lazy will come to ruin, for their hands refuse to work. Some people are always greedy for more, but the godly love to give! PROVERBS 21:25-26

Desire without action produces frustration and futility. The irony of laziness is that it heightens unmet desires yet fails to motivate people to action.

Those too lazy to plow in the right season will have no food at the harvest.
PROVERBS 20:4

*I walked by the field of a lazy person, the vineyard of one with no common sense.
I saw that it was overgrown with nettles. It was covered with weeds, and its walls
were broken down. Then, as I looked and thought about it, I learned this lesson:
A little extra sleep, a little more slumber, a little folding of the hands to rest—then
poverty will pounce on you like a bandit; scarcity will attack you like an armed robber.*
PROVERBS 24:30-34

Laziness is as easy to slip into as any bad habit. Giving in little by little turns into a lifestyle over time. Then the lazy will have to live with the consequences of their lifestyle: hunger, poverty, disorder, and purposelessness.

How can I cultivate responsibility instead of laziness in myself and others?

*Take a lesson from the ants, you lazybones. Learn from their ways and become wise!
Though they have no prince or governor or ruler to make them work, they labor hard all
summer, gathering food for the winter.* PROVERBS 6:6-8

Observe the progress of those who are successful. What motivates them? How do they fight laziness? How can you apply these lessons in your life? How can you use what you've learned to motivate others?

How can I overcome laziness?

*The godly offer good counsel; they teach right from wrong. They have made God's law
their own, so they will never slip from his path.* PSALM 37:30-31

Fools think their own way is right, but the wise listen to others. PROVERBS 12:15

*To one person the Spirit gives the ability to give wise advice; to another the same Spirit
gives a message of special knowledge.* 1 CORINTHIANS 12:8

Most people truly want to live a life of purpose. If you have a habit of being lazy, or if others accuse you of being lazy, there may be other issues that are the root cause of it. You may be dealing with depression, or there may be a medical reason. Seek help from a counselor as well as a doctor. God has given you special abilities and spiritual gifts. Listen to those who can help you.

LEADERSHIP *See also* Authority, Mentoring, Vision, Wisdom

Leadership comes in many forms and levels. It is sometimes defined as the ability to create in others the desire to follow. People tend to follow men and women who know where they are going and why. Whenever others follow your direction or your way of thinking, you are in a leadership role. Therefore, leaders need to know what they believe and why. As a Christian leader, you are a witness, one who shows others how to follow Christ as you follow the leadership of God.

What are some keys to effective leadership?

[Moses said to the Israelites,] "You are such a heavy load to carry! How can I deal with all your problems and bickering? Choose some well-respected men from each tribe who are known for their wisdom and understanding, and I will appoint them as your leaders." DEUTERONOMY 1:12-13

Good leaders delegate responsibilities to trustworthy subordinates.

Jesus told them, "In this world the kings and great men lord it over their people, yet they are called 'friends of the people.' But among you it will be different. Those who are the greatest among you should take the lowest rank, and the leader should be like a servant." LUKE 22:25-26

Good leaders lead by serving, not by ordering others around.

David said to God, "I have sinned greatly by taking this census." 1 CHRONICLES 21:8

Good leaders accept responsibility for their actions.

[Daniel] prayed three times a day, just as he had always done. DANIEL 6:10

Good leaders maintain good habits.

[John the Baptist said of Jesus,] "He must become greater and greater, and I must become less and less." JOHN 3:30

Good leaders do not emphasize themselves.

Listen, you leaders of Israel! You are supposed to know right from wrong. MICAH 3:1

Good leaders are dedicated to doing what is right.

Let us stop going over the basic teachings about Christ again and again. Let us go on instead and become mature in our understanding. HEBREWS 6:1

Good leaders demonstrate maturity and wisdom.

Fools think their own way is right, but the wise listen to others. PROVERBS 12:15

Good leaders have others who hold them accountable.

What are the primary characteristics of a spiritual leader?

An elder must be a man whose life is above reproach. He must be faithful to his wife. He must exercise self-control, live wisely, and have a good reputation. He must enjoy having guests in his home, and he must be able to teach. He must not be a heavy drinker or be violent. He must be gentle, not quarrelsome, and not love money. He must manage his own family well, having children who respect and obey him. . . . An elder must not be a new believer, because he might become proud, and the devil would cause him to fall. Also, people outside the church must speak well of him so that he will not be disgraced and fall into the devil's trap. 1 TIMOTHY 3:2-7

An elder must live a blameless life. TITUS 1:7

Paul lists numerous characteristics for church leaders. The primary characteristic is consistency between what they believe and how they live. Leaders apply the truth of God's Word to every aspect of life. This is what is meant by *integrity*—the integration of faith and life. This can be seen in four primary areas. Leaders are maturing in (1) personal spirituality, exhibiting a vibrant faith in Jesus Christ and ministering out of the overflow of knowing God more and more deeply; (2) emotional maturity, exercising self-control in anger, conflict, ambition, finances, and substance use (such as alcohol); (3) relational responsibility in valuing people, especially their family relationships, and as gracious hosts; and (4) ministry competency, being knowledgeable and skilled in communicating God's truth and care to others. These high standards do not mean that spiritual leaders are faultless, but that they are committed to bearing the fruit of faith in all of life.

How can leaders make good decisions?

Fear of the LORD is the foundation of true knowledge, but fools despise wisdom and discipline. PROVERBS 1:7

Trust in the LORD with all your heart; do not depend on your own understanding. Seek his will in all you do, and he will show you which path to take. PROVERBS 3:5-6

Good leaders begin all decisions with humility and reverence for God to whom they are ultimately accountable.

Rehoboam rejected the advice of the older men and instead asked the opinion of the young men who had grown up with him and were now his advisers. 1 KINGS 12:8

Leaders will have many people offering them advice. If you, as a leader, consistently reject the advice of wise counselors, like Rehoboam did, you will probably make foolish decisions. But if you listen to advice and weigh it carefully, you are more likely to make good choices.

Jesus went up on a mountain to pray, and he prayed to God all night. At daybreak he called together all of his disciples and chose twelve of them to be apostles. LUKE 6:12-13

Leaders need to saturate their decisions with prayer. This is especially true in decisions concerning the selection and care for those with whom you work most closely.

Show me the right path, O LORD; point out the road for me to follow. PSALM 25:4

Your laws please me; they give me wise advice. PSALM 119:24

Knowing Scripture and gleaning its wisdom gives you clear direction in your decision making and provides you with the discernment you need to make healthy choices. A right decision is one that is consistent with the principles of truth found in God's Word.

What does it mean to be a servant leader?

You must have the same attitude that Christ Jesus had. . . . He gave up his divine privileges. . . . In human form, he humbled himself in obedience. PHILIPPIANS 2:5-8

Jesus revolutionizes our understanding of leadership by teaching "downward mobility." In a most striking picture of servanthood, Jesus humbles himself through obedience. By performing the task of a slave, Jesus models how far we are to go in serving one another.

Mary responded, "I am the Lord's servant. May everything you have said about me come true." LUKE 1:38

The essence of servant leadership is doing what God asks you to do.

When Jesus heard them, he stopped and called, "What do you want me to do for you?" "Lord," they said, "we want to see!" Jesus felt sorry for them and touched their eyes. MATTHEW 20:32-34

Servant leaders listen and respond to the needs of those around them.

Whoever wants to be a leader among you must be your servant, and whoever wants to be first among you must be the slave of everyone else. MARK 10:43-44

You must learn to follow before you can learn to lead.

What can we learn from Jesus as a leader?

[Jesus] appointed twelve of them and called them his apostles. They were to accompany him, and he would send them out to preach. MARK 3:14

[Jesus] called his twelve disciples together and began sending them out two by two. MARK 6:7

Leaders develop teams which create community. They share responsibilities and work through tough issues, gaining strength from mutual encouragement and accountability. Leaders know that differing gifts, attitudes, and experiences of team members complement each other and provide balance and support in practical ways.

Jesus was led by the Spirit into the wilderness to be tempted there by the devil. For forty days and forty nights he fasted and became very hungry. During that time the devil came and said to him, "If you are the Son of God, tell these stones to become loaves of bread." But Jesus told him, "No! The Scriptures say, 'People do not live by bread alone, but by every word that comes from the mouth of God.'" MATTHEW 4:1-4

Which of you can truthfully accuse me of sin? JOHN 8:46

Leaders practice what they preach. They resist temptation and lead lives that are above reproach. They also live a lifestyle consistent with the standards they expect of others.

Jesus called his twelve disciples together and gave them authority to cast out evil spirits and to heal every kind of disease and illness. MATTHEW 10:1

Jesus used many similar stories and illustrations to teach the people as much as they could understand. In fact, in his public ministry he never taught without using parables; but afterward, when he was alone with his disciples, he explained everything to them. MARK 4:33-34

Leaders equip and release those they lead. They provide them with the necessary wisdom and experience, then let go and allow them to take responsibility for the tasks.

Even the Son of Man came not to be served but to serve others and to give his life as a ransom for many. MARK 10:45

Leaders have a clear sense of mission and dedicate themselves to fulfilling that mission.

Go and make disciples of all the nations, baptizing them in the name of the Father and the Son and the Holy Spirit. Teach these new disciples to obey all the commands I have given you. And be sure of this: I am with you always, even to the end of the age. MATTHEW 28:19-20

Leaders cast a specific vision for those they lead.

If any of you wants to be my follower, you must turn from your selfish ways, take up your cross daily, and follow me. If you try to hang on to your life, you will lose it. But if you give up your life for my sake, you will save it. And what do you benefit if you gain the whole world but are yourself lost or destroyed? LUKE 9:23-25

Leaders expect the most from those they lead and push them to give their best efforts.

Jesus knew that his hour had come to leave this world and return to his Father. He had loved his disciples during his ministry on earth, and now he loved them to the very end. . . . So he got up from the table, took off his robe, wrapped a towel around his waist, and poured water into a basin. Then he began to wash the disciples' feet, drying them with the towel he had around him. JOHN 13:1, 4-5

Leaders serve those they lead in practical, sacrificial, humbling ways.

LIMITATIONS *See also* Challenges, Disabilities

As kids we may have dreamed of being able to fly like a bird or having X-ray vision. As adults, these fantasies remind us of our limitations as humans. And the more we age, the more we understand the limits of our bodies as it becomes harder to do the things that were once easy—running, walking up the stairs, reading small print. We also face emotional limitations, for example, traumatic events that send us into shock. Many times difficult circumstances drain us emotionally and cause depression, anxiety, or apathy. In God's unlimited knowledge he created us with limitations, not to discourage us, but to help us realize our utter need for him. It is in our weakness that God's strength shines. And when we accomplish something great despite our limitations, it is obvious that God was working through us and he deserves the credit. Jesus tells us that what is humanly impossible is possible with God. Next time life makes you aware of your limitations, instead of being discouraged, see it as an opportunity for God's power to defy your limitations.

Does God have any limitations?

O LORD, you have examined my heart and know everything about me. You know when I sit down or stand up. You know my thoughts even when I'm far away. You see me when

I travel and when I rest at home. You know everything I do. You know what I am going to say even before I say it, LORD. You go before me and follow me. You place your hand of blessing on my head. Such knowledge is too wonderful for me, too great for me to understand! PSALM 139:1-6

No one can measure the depths of his understanding. ISAIAH 40:28

God's knowledge has no limit. He is omniscient. He knows even your secret thoughts.

The LORD said to Moses, "Has my arm lost its power? Now you will see whether or not my word comes true!" NUMBERS 11:23

Have you never heard? Have you never understood? The LORD is the everlasting God, the Creator of all the earth. He never grows weak or weary. ISAIAH 40:28

Jesus looked at them intently and said, "Humanly speaking, it is impossible. But with God everything is possible." MATTHEW 19:26

God's power and strength have no limit. He is omnipotent. No problem is too difficult for him to solve.

I can never escape from your Spirit! I can never get away from your presence! If I go up to heaven, you are there; if I go down to the grave, you are there. If I ride the wings of the morning, if I dwell by the farthest oceans, even there your hand will guide me, and your strength will support me. PSALM 139:7-10

God's presence has no limit. He is omnipresent. No place is too far away from God.

He does great things too marvelous to understand. He performs countless miracles. JOB 9:10

[God] has planted eternity in the human heart, but even so, people cannot see the whole scope of God's work from beginning to end. ECCLESIASTES 3:11

A vast crowd brought to him people who were lame, blind, crippled, those who couldn't speak, and many others. They laid them before Jesus, and he healed them all. MATTHEW 15:30

God's abilities have no limit. His plans cannot be stopped. There is no miracle too awesome for him to perform.

Even perfection has its limits, but your commands have no limit. PSALM 119:96

I send [my word] out, and it always produces fruit. It will accomplish all I want it to, and it will prosper everywhere I send it. ISAIAH 55:11

God's Word has no limit. You can never master all it has to offer you.

"Come now, let's settle this," says the LORD. "Though your sins are like scarlet, I will make them as white as snow. Though they are red like crimson, I will make them as white as wool." ISAIAH 1:18

He is so rich in kindness and grace that he purchased our freedom with the blood of his Son and forgave our sins. EPHESIANS 1:7

God's forgiveness has no limit. There is no sin too awful for him to forgive.

How can God use my limitations?

Asa cried out to the LORD his God, "O LORD, no one but you can help the powerless against the mighty! Help us, O LORD our God, for we trust in you alone. It is in your name that we have come against this vast horde. O LORD, you are our God; do not let mere men prevail against you!" 2 CHRONICLES 14:11

Your limitations can point you to God for help and guidance. When God works through your weaknesses, you know it is his power and not your own efforts. This is when you will most clearly see him.

Peter saw his opportunity and addressed the crowd. "People of Israel," he said, "what is so surprising about this? And why stare at us as though we had made this man walk by our own power or godliness? For it is the God of Abraham, Isaac, and Jacob—the God of all our ancestors—who has brought glory to his servant Jesus by doing this." ACTS 3:12-13

God can use your limitations as a testimony of his existence and involvement in your life. Peter didn't take the credit for healing a man. Instead, he highlighted God's power by giving God the credit for this miracle.

This High Priest of ours understands our weaknesses, for he faced all of the same testings we do, yet he did not sin. So let us come boldly to the throne of our gracious God. There we will receive his mercy, and we will find grace to help us when we need it most. HEBREWS 4:15-16

God's work is not limited by your failures. He doesn't reject you in your weakness but embraces you so that you can receive strength to be all he intends you to be. The seeds of success are often planted in the soil of failure.

I was given a thorn in my flesh, a messenger from Satan to torment me and keep me from becoming proud. 2 CORINTHIANS 12:7

Don't let anyone think less of you because you are young. 1 TIMOTHY 4:12

The apostle Paul had his "thorn in the flesh." Timothy faced challenges because he was young. Yet God used them—and many other biblical heroes—despite their limitations. And God will use you, too, if you move forward in faith.

How do I respond to my limitations?

I am nothing—how could I ever find the answers? I will cover my mouth with my hand. JOB 40:4

Job replied to the LORD: "I know that you can do anything, and no one can stop you. You asked, 'Who is this that questions my wisdom with such ignorance?' It is I—and I was talking about things I knew nothing about, things far too wonderful for me." JOB 42:1-3

Acknowledge your limitations to God, while remembering that he is limitless. The contrast of your weakness with God's strength and power will convince you of your utter dependence on him. The first step to overcoming any problem is to recognize that the problem exists. If you can't recognize your limitations, you can never begin to overcome them.

The Lord turned to [Gideon] and said, "Go with the strength you have, and rescue Israel from the Midianites. I am sending you!" "But Lord," Gideon replied, "how can I rescue Israel? My clan is the weakest in the whole tribe of Manasseh, and I am the least in my entire family!" The Lord said to him, "I will be with you. And you will destroy the Midianites as if you were fighting against one man." JUDGES 6:14-16

Your limitations are not an excuse to stop serving God. "I can't" is not acceptable, because "he can." Always be aware of your weaknesses, but be ready to experience God's power through them.

Two people are better off than one, for they can help each other succeed. If one person falls, the other can reach out and help. But someone who falls alone is in real trouble. ECCLESIASTES 4:9-10

Recognize your own limitations and the importance of letting others help you. You were not made to go it alone. Wisdom is the recognition of your own inadequacies. Foolishness is thinking you have none. God often helps you through the caring help of others.

Are there good limitations that I should impose on myself?

Don't copy the behavior and customs of this world, but let God transform you into a new person by changing the way you think. Then you will learn to know God's will for you, which is good and pleasing and perfect. ROMANS 12:2

We will not boast about things done outside our area of authority. We will boast only about what has happened within the boundaries of the work God has given us, which includes our working with you. 2 CORINTHIANS 10:13

God gives you some limitations to keep you safe. Study his Word to find out how to live as a believer, and how to be transformed by his power and presence. His Word provides the proper boundaries for living. To avoid his Word is to ignore the boundaries God has set for you, not to restrict you, but to free you from slavery to sin.

What does the Lord your God require of you? He requires only that you fear the Lord your God, and live in a way that pleases him, and love him and serve him with all your heart and soul. And you must always obey the Lord's commands and decrees . . . for your own good. DEUTERONOMY 10:12-13

Sin whispers to the wicked, deep within their hearts. They have no fear of God at all. PSALM 36:1

God's limitations on you are his loving restraints to keep you from falling away from him. His boundaries call you to right living, to show mercy to others, and to have a relationship with him. The limitations he places on you are motivated by love and designed for your blessing. Obey God out of love and respect so you can experience the blessings of a relationship with him. Fewer limitations might tempt you to think you have no need for God. A healthy knowledge of your limitations gives you a healthy dose of humility and prompts respect for the only One who is limitless.

LISTENING *See also* Communication, Discernment, Wisdom

We hear so much, but we tend to listen to so little. Our relationships are built on the degree to which we listen and accept what we hear. For example, as a father reads his newspaper, his child comes with an urgent request. After a few "uh-huhs" from the father, it is apparent to the child that the father hears but isn't listening. How often throughout the Scriptures God's people heard him speak but refused to listen, refused to acknowledge what he said, and refused to obey and act upon it. Listen! Listen to wise counsel from others. Listen to God. Listen and learn.

Why is listening so important?

My child, listen to what I say. . . . Then you will understand what is right, just, and fair, and you will find the right way to go. PROVERBS 2:1, 9

Listening to God is essential to making good decisions. When you truly listen to the Holy Spirit and to God's commands, you will have the guidance you need to make wise choices.

Listen to me! For I have important things to tell you. PROVERBS 8:6

Listening keeps you from being closed-minded. It gives you the opportunity to hear a variety of ideas from many different sources. The more you listen, the better your chances of hearing an excellent nugget of wisdom. God's truth is found in God's Word, but the application of it is often found through the advice and experience of others.

Moses listened to his father-in-law's advice and followed his suggestions. EXODUS 18:24

Listening shows that you respect others. It honors their words. You feel affirmed when you've been listened to.

How can I be a good listener?

"What have you done?" Joseph demanded. GENESIS 44:15

Listening involves asking questions. Joseph wanted to listen to how his brothers answered this question because their answer would reveal whether their hearts had changed.

The heart of the godly thinks carefully before speaking. PROVERBS 15:28

Listening often involves saying less and carefully choosing your words.

Why should I listen to God?

Come and listen to my counsel. I'll share my heart with you and make you wise. PROVERBS 1:23

Listen to me. . . . I alone am God, the First and the Last. ISAIAH 48:12

Let those who are wise understand these things. Let those with discernment listen carefully. The paths of the LORD are true and right, and righteous people live by walking in them. HOSEA 14:9

Listening to God makes you wise because he is the source of all wisdom and knowledge.

Listen closely, Israel, and be careful to obey. Then all will go well with you.
DEUTERONOMY 6:3

Listening opens the pipeline to God's blessings. Only when you truly listen to God will you know how to receive his blessings. Don't miss them by refusing to listen.

Listen to me, for all who follow my ways are joyful. PROVERBS 8:32

Listening to God brings lasting joy. Following his ways is like following a pathway of peace, but you must listen for his directions to stay on course!

How can I better listen to God? How can I improve?

Listen to my voice in the morning, LORD. Each morning I bring my requests to you and wait expectantly. PSALM 5:3

Come to God regularly and wait expectantly. God always answers; are you patient enough to listen?

Be still, and know that I am God! PSALM 46:10

Find times to be quiet and meditate so you will know the voice of God when he speaks.

Pay attention to how you hear. To those who listen to my teaching, more understanding will be given. But for those who are not listening, even what they think they understand will be taken away from them. LUKE 8:18

Always pay attention to the many ways in which God can speak to you. Don't miss an opportunity for a lesson from the Master Teacher. The more you listen to God, the more you will hear. But if you close your ears and your heart to God, even what you think you know will prove to be nothing in the end.

After the earthquake there was a fire, but the LORD was not in the fire. And after the fire there was the sound of a gentle whisper. 1 KINGS 19:12

Recognize that God sometimes speaks to you in quietness. God's power and greatness are often displayed in his gentleness and control. Listen for him to speak to you personally in quiet times.

Does God really listen when I pray?

Because he bends down to listen, I will pray as long as I have breath! PSALM 116:2

Listen! The LORD's arm is not too weak to save you, nor is his ear too deaf to hear you call. ISAIAH 59:1

We are confident that he hears us whenever we ask for anything that pleases him. And since we know he hears us when we make our requests, we also know that he will give us what we ask for. 1 JOHN 5:14-15

God hears every prayer, listens carefully, and answers. His answer may be yes, no, or wait, not now. And his answers are always best for you.

Because of your sins, he has turned away and will not listen anymore. ISAIAH 59:2

"Since they refused to listen when I called to them, I would not listen when they called to me," says the LORD of Heaven's Armies. ZECHARIAH 7:13

When you persist in your sinful way of life and turn away from God, he will not listen to your requests because they will all come from selfish motives. If you are not sincere when you come to God in prayer, your prayers are meaningless.

LONELINESS *See also* Abandonment, Emptiness, Loss, Pain, Rejection

In the dark hours of the night you wrestle with God and with your feelings, for you feel desperately alone, rejected. Perhaps a best friend deserted you. The marriage you hoped for never happened. Or the one you did marry wants another. Your child has turned against you, or your parents and friends don't seem to care. Ironically, you can feel equally lonely on a crowded city street or in a busy airport. But God's message to the lonely is, "Don't be afraid, for I am with you" (Isaiah 41:10).

The LORD God said, "It is not good for the man to be alone. I will make a helper who is just right for him." GENESIS 2:18

God did not intend for you to be lonely. On the contrary, it was God who recognized Adam's need for companionship. He gave Adam the task of naming the animals so that Adam could recognize his own need for a human companion. It was then that God created woman.

David bowed three times to Jonathan with his face to the ground. Both of them were in tears as they embraced each other and said good-bye, especially David. 1 SAMUEL 20:41

Their disagreement was so sharp that they separated. Barnabas took John Mark with him and sailed for Cyprus. ACTS 15:39

After we were separated from you for a little while (though our hearts never left you), we tried very hard to come back because of our intense longing to see you again. 1 THESSALONIANS 2:17

You live in a sinful, fallen world. Therefore, you will often be separated from friends and family for various reasons. Sometimes you are lonely because you have hurt those you care about and they have left you. Sometimes your friends stop being your friends for reasons you don't understand. And sometimes you have to say good-bye when a friend moves away. God doesn't want you to be lonely, but he allows people's actions in this life to take their natural course. In each of these circumstances, he promises to help you learn from it and he promises never to leave you, always supplying you with comfort and strength when you ask.

How can God help me with my loneliness?

Even when I walk through the darkest valley . . . you are close beside me. PSALM 23:4

The mountains may move and the hills disappear, but even then my faithful love for you will remain. ISAIAH 54:10

Recognize that you are not unlovable or deficient just because you are lonely. You have value because God made you, loves you, and promises never to leave you.

Elijah replied, "I have zealously served the LORD God Almighty. But the people of Israel have broken their covenant with you, torn down your altars, and killed every one of your prophets. I am the only one left, and now they are trying to kill me, too." 1 KINGS 19:10

If you are suffering in a manner that pleases God, keep on doing what is right, and trust your lives to the God who created you, for he will never fail you. 1 PETER 4:19

Sometimes you may feel alone in your stand for Christ. Take comfort in knowing that there are others who are equally committed and that God rewards your bold commitment to him.

We are many parts of one body, and we all belong to each other. ROMANS 12:5

Let us not neglect our meeting together, as some people do, but encourage one another, especially now that the day of his return is drawing near. HEBREWS 10:25

The best way to avoid loneliness is to get together with other believers. Get involved in a local church. Get busy with God's people doing God's work.

Don't be afraid, for I am with you. Don't be discouraged, for I am your God. I will strengthen you and help you. I will hold you up with my victorious right hand. ISAIAH 41:10

Loneliness can cause you to be afraid. But knowing that God is with you and fighting for you can calm your fears.

How can I help those who are lonely?

Pure and genuine religion in the sight of God the Father means caring for orphans and widows. JAMES 1:27

You are being faithful to God when you care for the traveling teachers who pass through. 3 JOHN 1:5

Invite lonely people into your home or visit them and befriend them. Often in caring for those who are lonely, your need for company will be met as well.

LOSS *See also* Brokenness, Emptiness, Grief, Suffering, Hope

All people have the common experience of suffering loss. Whether it's the loss of a favorite possession, a job, a friend to a move, or the ultimate loss of a loved one to death, loss hurts. Jesus understands the grief of loss. While he lived on earth, he lost his close friend Lazarus to death, he lost the respect of his own village and siblings, he lost the devotion of his friends

Thomas and Peter, and he lost the loyalty of his disciple Judas. He understands loss and showed us how to deal with it.

How do I deal with loss in my life?

Jesus wept. JOHN 11:35

Don't deny your loss. The tears of Jesus at Lazarus's death validate your tears of grief.

The Egyptians mourned [Joseph's] death for seventy days. GENESIS 50:3

Grief is a process that should not be denied or hurried. The rituals of wakes, visitations, funerals, and memorial services all help you move through stages of grief. If your loss does not involve death (such as in the case of a friend moving away, a damaged relationship, or the loss of a good job), you still need to allow yourself to grieve to bring healing to your hurt soul.

Job stood up and tore his robe in grief. . . . He said, . . . "The Lord gave me what I had, and the Lord has taken it away." JOB 1:20-21

Losses always bring pain. Recognizing and expressing our pain is not wrong or sinful, but rather is a healthy expression of how God created us.

You suffered along with those who were thrown into jail, and when all you owned was taken from you, you accepted it with joy. You knew there were better things waiting for you that will last forever. HEBREWS 10:34

It is important to allow yourself to grieve, but there is a time for grieving to end. As a Christian, you have the comfort of knowing that one day you will be with God in heaven where all grief will be gone forever.

I feel like I've lost everything. Where can I turn?

The Lord is close to the brokenhearted; he rescues those whose spirits are crushed. PSALM 34:18

Turn to God in times of loss, for he alone can give you hope.

I weep with sorrow; encourage me by your word. PSALM 119:28

Turn to God's Word in times of loss, for there you will find God's encouragement.

He comforts us in all our troubles so that we can comfort others. When they are troubled, we will be able to give them the same comfort God has given us. 2 CORINTHIANS 1:4

Turn to godly people in times of loss, for they can give you God's comfort.

How can God help me survive life's losses?

He heals the brokenhearted and bandages their wounds. PSALM 147:3

Though he brings grief, he also shows compassion because of the greatness of his unfailing love. LAMENTATIONS 3:32

God blesses those who mourn, for they will be comforted. MATTHEW 5:4

In times of loss, God fills you with his blessings—comfort, joy, songs of praise, thanksgiving, and mercy. When you cry out for someone to touch you, God will hold you close.

Are there any losses that are for my good?

I once thought these things were valuable, but now I consider them worthless because of what Christ has done. PHILIPPIANS 3:7

To know the power of Christ in your life you must be willing to lose all your self-importance and pride.

Put to death the sinful, earthly things lurking within you. COLOSSIANS 3:5

When you give your heart and life to Christ, you must treat your old life as if it were dead and gone!

[The Lord said], "I will take back the ripened grain and new wine I generously provided each harvest season. I will take away the wool and linen clothing I gave her to cover her nakedness. . . . But then I will win her back once again. I will lead her into the desert and speak tenderly to her there." HOSEA 2:9, 14

Sometimes God takes away things in your life that have taken his place in your heart. These losses help you realign your priorities with God's and remind you that your greatest gain is the eternal inheritance he has promised.

What can I never lose?

Be sure of this: I am with you always, even to the end of the age. MATTHEW 28:20

I am convinced that nothing can ever separate us from God's love. Neither death nor life, neither angels nor demons, neither our fears for today nor our worries about tomorrow—not even the powers of hell can separate us from God's love. No power in the sky above or in the earth below—indeed, nothing in all creation will ever be able to separate us from the love of God that is revealed in Christ Jesus our Lord. ROMANS 8:38-39

When you trust in the Lord, you will never lose his love, his presence, and his promise of salvation—the three greatest gifts to see you through life's difficulties and give you hope.

LOVE *See also* Commitment, Grace, Intimacy, Worship

A healthy definition of love is crucial to understanding the central message of the Bible. According to the Bible, love is not confined to sexuality, nor is it primarily a feeling at all. The Bible teaches that love is a commitment. As a commitment, love is not dependent on good feelings, but rather on a consistent and courageous decision to extend oneself for the well-being of another. That commitment then produces good feelings, not the other way around. Jesus is the perfect demonstration of God's unconditional love for us because he gave his life to save us.

What is love?

Love is patient and kind. Love is not jealous or boastful or proud or rude. It does not demand its own way. It is not irritable, and it keeps no record of being wronged. It does not rejoice about injustice but rejoices whenever the truth wins out. Love never gives up, never loses faith, is always hopeful, and endures through every circumstance.
1 CORINTHIANS 13:4-7

These famous verses about love are some of the most eloquent and accurate descriptions of love ever written. Love is a commitment and a choice of conduct that produces powerful feelings. If you practice the qualities and behaviors described in these verses, you will experience satisfaction and fulfillment beyond imagination.

There is no greater love than to lay down one's life for one's friends. JOHN 15:13

Love is willing to sacrifice for the good of others, even to death.

Why does love matter?

God created human beings in his own image. In the image of God he created them; male and female he created them. Then God blessed them. GENESIS 1:27-28

I am giving you a new commandment: Love each other. Just as I have loved you, you should love each other. JOHN 13:34

Love matters because it matters to God. Since people are created in God's image, we are called to honor others with respect and with words and conduct that value them. Love does not mean that you will necessarily feel affection for all people, but that you are committed to the way of valuing others as they are valued by God.

If I could speak all the languages of earth and of angels, but didn't love others, I would only be a noisy gong or a clanging cymbal. If I had the gift of prophecy, and if I understood all of God's secret plans and possessed all knowledge, and if I had such faith that I could move mountains, but didn't love others, I would be nothing. If I gave everything I have to the poor and even sacrificed my body, I could boast about it; but if I didn't love others, I would have gained nothing. 1 CORINTHIANS 13:1-3

Talents, accomplishments, and even sacrifices that are governed by any purpose or motive other than love will amount to nothing of eternal value.

Does God really love me? How can I know?

God loved the world so much that he gave his one and only Son, so that everyone who believes in him will not perish but have eternal life. JOHN 3:16

God showed how much he loved us by sending his one and only Son into the world so that we might have eternal life through him. This is real love. 1 JOHN 4:9-10

God loves you so much he sent his son, Jesus, to earth to die for you. Jesus took the punishment you deserve for your sins. His forgiveness is so complete that it is as though you never sinned at all. His love for you can never be changed or broken.

We know how dearly God loves us, because he has given us the Holy Spirit to fill our hearts with his love. ROMANS 5:5

The Holy Spirit's presence in your heart shows God's love for you because he is always with you, always helping you, always showing you the best way to live.

How can I accept God's love?

"No," Peter protested, "you will never ever wash my feet!" Jesus replied, "Unless I wash you, you won't belong to me." JOHN 13:8

You begin to accept God's love when you put aside your pride and self-sufficiency.

Let the children come to me. Don't stop them! For the Kingdom of God belongs to those who are like these children. LUKE 18:16

Jesus encourages you to learn to receive his love with the same kind of trust a little child shows. Receiving God's love is an act of simple faith.

I will be faithful to you and make you mine, and you will finally know me as the LORD. HOSEA 2:20

God's love is absolutely faithful. You will know the benefits and security of that love when you commit yourself to faithfulness as well. Nurturing your relationship with God through worship, Bible reading, and prayer will help you grow more confident in God's faithful love.

Why should I love God?

Love the LORD your God, walk in all his ways, obey his commands, hold firmly to him, and serve him. JOSHUA 22:5

Jesus replied, "The most important commandment is this: . . . 'You must love the LORD your God with all your heart, all your soul, all your mind, and all your strength.'" MARK 12:29-30

God wants you to love him, not for his benefit, but for yours. He does, however, require that your love for him is complete—all your heart, soul, mind, and strength.

See how very much our Father loves us. 1 JOHN 3:1

Love God because he loves you and desires a relationship with you more than anything else.

Remain in my love. . . . I have told you these things so that you will be filled with my joy. Yes, your joy will overflow! JOHN 15:10-11

Love God because doing so will bring overflowing joy to your life.

How should I show my love to God?

Those who accept my commandments and obey them are the ones who love me. JOHN 14:21

Love God by obeying him and respecting his commandments.

I will sing your praises among the nations. For your unfailing love is higher than the heavens. Your faithfulness reaches to the clouds. PSALM 108:3-4

I was glad when they said to me, "Let us go to the house of the LORD." PSALM 122:1

Love God by worshiping him and praising him for his love to you.

If you give even a cup of cold water to one of the least of my followers, you will surely be rewarded. MATTHEW 10:42

Do you love me? . . . Feed my sheep. JOHN 21:15-17

He will not forget . . . how you have shown your love to him by caring for other believers. HEBREWS 6:10

Show love to needy people whom God loves.

How can I love people I don't even like? How can I learn to love the unlovely?
We love each other because he loved us first. 1 JOHN 4:19

As you reflect on God's love for you and receive it for yourself, you will grow in your ability to love those you do not like. When you learn to love the unlovable, you have developed the ability to see others as Jesus does.

I am giving you a new commandment: Love each other. Just as I have loved you, you should love each other. Your love for one another will prove to the world that you are my disciples. JOHN 13:34-35

If we love each other, God lives in us, and his love is brought to full expression in us. 1 JOHN 4:12

Being a Christian comes with certain expectations, and one of them is that you will love others. Loving others is proof that you belong to Christ.

If your enemies are hungry, feed them. If they are thirsty, give them something to drink. ROMANS 12:20

Even if you don't like certain people, you can still choose to do tangible acts of love for them.

Don't think you are better than you really are. Be honest in your evaluation of yourselves. ROMANS 12:3

Before you are too quick to dislike or dismiss someone, remember that you too have qualities that others may find unattractive.

LOYALTY See also Commitment, Faithfulness, Friendship
Loyalty can be defined as a highly personal form of commitment. Loyalty says, "No matter what happens around us or between us there is no fear, doubt, or hurt that can make me turn

my back on you." When loyalty is present, a relationship is secure and solid. When it is not, we live in insecurity and fear. The Bible teaches that loyalty is part of the character of God himself. He expresses his loyalty by refusing to give up on us no matter how we disappoint him with our sin. We express our loyalty to God through obedience to his Word.

Why is loyalty important?

The LORD leads with unfailing love and faithfulness all who keep his covenant and obey his demands. PSALM 25:10

Loyalty in a relationship is essential to maintain integrity and effectiveness. Without loyalty, other people become dispensable and are not valued as persons. And loyalty to God keeps the pipeline of his blessings open to you.

Wherever you go, I will go; wherever you live, I will live. Your people will be my people, and your God will be my God. RUTH 1:16

Loyalty is the mark of true friendship.

Love never gives up, never loses faith, is always hopeful, and endures through every circumstance. 1 CORINTHIANS 13:7

Loyalty is love in action.

What are the benefits of loyalty?

Saul listened to Jonathan and vowed, "As surely as the LORD lives, David will not be killed." 1 SAMUEL 19:6

Loyalty not only brings the satisfaction of commitment to a relationship, but may also bring practical benefits such as protection and care for your welfare. Jonathan's loyalty to David was instrumental in saving David's life on more than one occasion. (See 1 Samuel 14–19.)

Barnabas agreed and wanted to take along John Mark. But Paul disagreed strongly, since John Mark had deserted them in Pamphylia and had not continued with them in their work. Their disagreement was so sharp that they separated. Barnabas took John Mark with him and sailed for Cyprus. ACTS 15:37-39

Loyalty can keep the relationship alive so that you can help in restoring one who has failed. Barnabas's persistent loyalty to John Mark made it possible for John Mark to have another opportunity to "prove himself"—and he did (see Colossians 4:10).

Does loyalty have limits?

No one can serve two masters. For you will hate one and love the other; you will be devoted to one and despise the other. You cannot serve both God and money. LUKE 16:13

Loyalty, by definition, is undeviating commitment. If you claim loyalty to God, you cannot also claim loyalty to anything that takes priority over God.

Some of you are saying, "I am a follower of Paul." Others are saying, "I follow Apollos," or "I follow Peter." 1 CORINTHIANS 1:12

No matter how charismatic or powerful an individual church leader may be, Christians must always remember their ultimate loyalty is to Jesus alone.

I fully expect and hope that I will . . . continue to be bold for Christ. PHILIPPIANS 1:20

Your loyalty to Jesus should know no limit.

LUST *See also* Ambition, Coveting, Desires, Greed

We can lust after many things (power, status, material possessions), but lust most often refers to sexual greed. Healthy sexual desire is not sin, for we are created by God to enjoy sexual pleasure within the boundaries of committed marriage (see Genesis 2:23-25). But when that desire is fueled by selfishness, it becomes lust. Lust views another person as merely an object of sexual pleasure and disregards God's standard for the meaning and purpose of sexual behavior. Lust at its extreme becomes jealous and violent when it pushes someone to do anything to get what they want. Most of us don't reach this extreme, but we must be aware of the harm that lust leads to.

If lust does not involve actual physical behavior, why is it wrong?

Guard your heart above all else, for it determines the course of your life. PROVERBS 4:23

Once lust is allowed to take up residence in your mind, it tends to consume your thoughts, and eventually your actions.

He had 700 wives of royal birth and 300 concubines. And in fact, they did turn his heart away from the LORD. 1 KINGS 11:3

Because lust is a sin, dwelling on it or consistently giving in to it will negatively change your behavior and turn your heart from God. Solomon's lust eventually led not only to promiscuity but a rejection of God.

It is what comes from inside that defiles you. For from within, out of a person's heart, come evil thoughts, sexual immorality, theft, murder, adultery, greed, wickedness, deceit, lustful desires, envy, slander, pride, and foolishness. MARK 7:20-22

Your actions don't just come from your mind; they come from your heart. They tell you the condition of your heart because every action begins as a thought. Left unchecked, wrong thoughts will eventually result in wrong actions. If you continue to think about having sex with someone who is not your spouse, your heart will begin to convince your mind that what you want to do is okay. The Bible says that the heart is "desperately wicked" (Jeremiah 17:9). In other words, don't trust your emotions to tell you what is right and good. Trust God's Word, for it comes from God's heart, which is good and perfect.

What is the difference between lust and love?

Amnon wouldn't listen to her, and since he was stronger than she was, he raped her.
2 SAMUEL 13:14

Love gives time after time and never takes that which is not offered. Lust takes what it wants regardless of the other's needs or desires.

Love is patient and kind. . . . It does not demand its own way. 1 CORINTHIANS 13:4-5

Love is patient and kind. Lust is impatient and rude.

How can I keep my desires from becoming lustful?

Anyone who even looks at a woman with lust has already committed adultery with her in his heart. MATTHEW 5:28

You can prevent lust from taking root in your mind by avoiding that "second look."

Fix your thoughts on what is true, and honorable, and right, and pure, and lovely, and admirable. PHILIPPIANS 4:8

When you fill your heart and mind with what is pure and good, lust finds no place to dwell.

Oh, how beautiful you are! How pleasing, my love, how full of delights!
SONG OF SONGS 7:6

When you focus your desires on your spouse, lust for others has less room to grow. Make sure, however, the desires for your mate are pure and healthy.

LYING *See also* Deceit/Deception, Hypocrisy, Honesty

Lying is deceiving someone. It can be direct—"I didn't touch that cake" (as you swallow the last bite)—or it can be indirect, such as telling only part of the truth when it benefits you to do so. But to fall short of truth, in any way, is to lie. Pilate asked, "What is truth?" (John 18:38). He had the answer to his question—Jesus—standing before him, in person. "I am the way, the truth and the life," Jesus said on another occasion (John 14:6). Think of it! Jesus not only tells the truth, he is truth. We cannot follow the God of truth while we persistently tell lies—even "small" ones. Determine to tell the truth in all matters of life, big or small.

Why do I lie?

[Ananias] brought part of the money to the apostles, claiming it was the full amount. With his wife's consent, he kept the rest. ACTS 5:2

To make yourself look good. In truth, people are most respected when they own up to their mistakes and hold their ground when others find their views unpopular. Lying always makes you look bad when it comes to light.

The LORD asked Cain, "Where is your brother? Where is Abel?" "I don't know," Cain responded. "Am I my brother's guardian?" GENESIS 4:9

To avoid trouble and punishment. Lying tries to shift the blame away from you, but this solution is only temporary and often brings greater punishment when the truth is discovered.

[Abraham said to Sarai,] "When the Egyptians see you, they will say, 'This is his wife. Let's kill him; then we can have her!' So please tell them you are my sister. Then they will spare my life and treat me well because of their interest in you." GENESIS 12:12-13

Sarah was afraid, so she denied it, saying, "I didn't laugh." But the LORD said, "No, you did laugh." GENESIS 18:15

To calm fear, which is a result of a lack of faith. Lying sugarcoats fears, but when the heat of testing melts the coating, you are still left with the same old fears.

It is what comes from inside that defiles you. For from within, out of a person's heart, come evil thoughts, sexual immorality, theft, murder, adultery, greed, wickedness, deceit, lustful desires, envy, slander, pride, and foolishness. MARK 7:20-22

[Jesus said to some of the Jews,] "For you are the children of your father the devil, and you love to do the evil things he does. . . . There is no truth in him. When he lies, it is consistent with his character; for he is a liar and the father of lies." JOHN 8:44

The bottom-line reason for lying is that we are all born with a sinful nature, and therefore we are prone to sin.

Why is it so important to tell the truth?

If you are faithful in little things, you will be faithful in large ones. But if you are dishonest in little things, you won't be honest with greater responsibilities. LUKE 16:10

God shows his anger from heaven against all sinful, wicked people who suppress the truth by their wickedness. ROMANS 1:18

Telling the truth is the litmus test to see if you are trying to model your life after the God of truth. Telling the truth is the only way to have trust in a relationship. Telling the truth is commanded by God.

Jesus told [Thomas], "I am the way, the truth, and the life. No one can come to the Father except through me." JOHN 14:6

Lying is in opposition to God. Truth always speaks what is right and good. Lying always seeks to cover up the truth.

What does God think about lying?

I hate and abhor all falsehood. PSALM 119:163

There are six things the LORD hates—no, seven things he detests: haughty eyes, a lying tongue. PROVERBS 6:16-17

God is truth, so he is completely opposed to lies.

God is not a man, so he does not lie. He is not human, so he does not change his mind. Has he ever spoken and failed to act? Has he ever promised and not carried it through?
NUMBERS 23:19

God does not tolerate deception because it violates his character.

What should my attitude be regarding lying?

The godly hate lies. PROVERBS 13:5

Don't lie to each other, for you have stripped off your old sinful nature and all its wicked deeds. COLOSSIANS 3:9

God commands you to be an example of his truthfulness. Truth lived out is even more convincing than truth spoken. You should hate lies because they are part of the old sinful nature you had before you became a Christian.

Help me never to tell a lie. PROVERBS 30:8

You should live by the priority of truth in your daily choices.

Declare me innocent, O God! Defend me against these ungodly people. Rescue me from these unjust liars. PSALM 43:1

Rescue me, O LORD, from liars and from all deceitful people. PSALM 120:2

Pray for God's protection and deliverance from the effect of others' deceit.

How can I know when someone is lying to me?

Watch out for people who cause divisions and upset people's faith by teaching things contrary to what you have been taught. Stay away from them. Such people are not serving Christ our Lord; they are serving their own personal interests. By smooth talk and glowing words they deceive innocent people. ROMANS 16:17-18

All Scripture is inspired by God and is useful to teach us what is true and to make us realize what is wrong in our lives. It corrects us when we are wrong and teaches us to do what is right. 2 TIMOTHY 3:16

Test what you hear using God's Word. Truth is always in harmony with God and his Word.

Smooth words may hide a wicked heart, just as a pretty glaze covers a clay pot. People may cover their hatred with pleasant words, but they're deceiving you. They pretend to be kind, but don't believe them. Their hearts are full of many evils. While their hatred may be concealed by trickery, their wrongdoing will be exposed in public. PROVERBS 26:23-26

Test a speaker's words by the speaker's life. Are his or her words and lifestyle in harmony?

M

MANIPULATION *See also* Control, Deceit/Deception, Power

Manipulation occurs when we deceive or control others to get what we want. People become a means to an end, tools to service our self-centered desires. Manipulation shows itself in forms of bribery, flattery, deception, cheating, seduction, lying, and taking advantage of others. We also try to manipulate God when we tell him that we'll do something for him if he shows us a sign or miracle ("I'll do that for you only if you do this for me"). When we see our needs and wants as top priority, we begin to feel entitled—that we're in control—and thus think others exist to serve us. The Bible is clear that God hates lies and deception, but manipulation breaks God's greatest commandment—to love others as he loves us. Love and manipulation cannot coexist.

How can I recognize manipulation in myself and in others?

[Teachers of religious law] shamelessly cheat widows out of their property and then pretend to be pious by making long prayers in public. Because of this, they will be more severely punished. MARK 12:40

Hypocrisy—when what you say doesn't match what you do—is a form of manipulation. You pretend to be a better person than you really are in order to get something you really want. If you need to put on a facade for others, chances are you are being manipulative.

[Our enemies] were just trying to intimidate us, imagining that they could discourage us and stop the work. . . . And Tobiah kept sending threatening letters to intimidate me. NEHEMIAH 6:9, 19

Intimidation is a form of manipulation. When manipulators can't entice, they may try to intimidate or pressure you into submission.

Those false teachers are so eager to win your favor, but their intentions are not good. They are trying to shut you off from me so that you will pay attention only to them. GALATIANS 4:17

Isolation is often a form of manipulation. Be careful when someone tries to isolate you from other people or from Christian influence. It may be an attempt to control you. You need discernment to help you recognize the manipulation.

Samson's wife came to him in tears and said, "You don't love me; you hate me! You have given my people a riddle, but you haven't told me the answer." "I haven't even given the answer to my father or mother," he replied. "Why should I tell you?" So she cried whenever she was with him and kept it up for the rest of the celebration. At last, on the seventh day he told her the answer because she was tormenting him with her nagging. Then she explained the riddle to the young men. JUDGES 14:16-17

Emotional pressure, nagging, and guilt are often used to manipulate. If you use these as your weapons, you are guilty of manipulation. Instead, trade them for self-control, encouragement, and forgiveness.

She seduced him with her pretty speech and enticed him with her flattery. PROVERBS 7:21

Such people are not serving Christ our Lord; they are serving their own personal interests. By smooth talk and glowing words they deceive innocent people. ROMANS 16:18

Flattery is often used to manipulate. Sometimes it is difficult to tell the difference between a sincere compliment and a false one. That is why we tend to be so vulnerable to flattery in the disguise of a compliment.

How does manipulation affect my relationships?

Isaac said to Jacob, "Come closer so I can touch you and make sure that you really are Esau."... When Isaac caught the smell of his clothes, he was finally convinced, and he blessed his son.... Almost before Jacob had left his father, Esau returned from his hunt. Esau prepared a delicious meal and brought it to his father.... Isaac began to tremble uncontrollably and said, "Then who just served me wild game? I have already eaten it, and I blessed him just before you came. And yes, that blessing must stand!" When Esau heard his father's words, he let out a loud and bitter cry. "Oh my father, what about me? Bless me, too!" he begged. But Isaac said, "Your brother was here, and he tricked me. He has taken away your blessing." GENESIS 27:21, 27, 30-35

When Jacob woke up in the morning—it was Leah! "What have you done to me?" Jacob raged at Laban. "I worked seven years for Rachel! Why have you tricked me?" GENESIS 29:25

The selfishness and dishonesty so often involved in manipulation are directly opposed to the self-giving love and the trust necessary for maintaining and deepening relationships. Long-lasting healthy relationships are nurtured in love, not manipulation.

What is the danger in manipulation? What are the consequences of manipulation?

Disgrace comes to those who try to deceive others. PSALM 25:3

I will not allow deceivers to serve in my house, and liars will not stay in my presence. PSALM 101:7

The LORD preserves those with knowledge, but he ruins the plans of the treacherous. PROVERBS 22:12

God hates cheating and deceitfulness, two primary forms of manipulation. These ungodly actions run across the "grain" of God's character. Those who practice manipulation cannot expect God's blessings.

Wealth created by a lying tongue is a vanishing mist and a deadly trap. PROVERBS 21:6

Like a partridge that hatches eggs she has not laid, so are those who get their wealth by unjust means. At midlife they will lose their riches; in the end, they will become poor old fools. JEREMIAH 17:11

Dishonest gain is temporary. The "fool's gold" of wealth gained by manipulation may have a momentary sweetness, but it has an eternal bitterness.

If you set a trap for others, you will get caught in it yourself. If you roll a boulder down on others, it will crush you instead. PROVERBS 26:27

They all fool and defraud each other; no one tells the truth. With practiced tongues they tell lies; they wear themselves out with all their sinning. JEREMIAH 9:5

Manipulators deceive themselves in the long run by thinking that putting themselves first wins the game of life. Manipulation is ultimately self-destruction.

How can I avoid being manipulated by others?

[The king of the north] will flatter and win over those who have violated the covenant. But the people who know their God will be strong and will resist him. DANIEL 11:32

Don't let anyone capture you with empty philosophies and high-sounding nonsense that come from human thinking and from the spiritual powers of this world, rather than from Christ. COLOSSIANS 2:8

Do not believe everyone who claims to speak by the Spirit. You must test them to see if the spirit they have comes from God. 1 JOHN 4:1

Wouldn't it be nice to know everyone's motives before they talked to you? While that is just a dream, there are ways to discern people's motives. The Bible is the ultimate manual for understanding human character. The more you know God and his Word, the more you will be able to recognize real character in others, helping you discern whether people are trying to help or manipulate you.

Does God manipulate me into obeying him?

Truly, God will not do wrong. The Almighty will not twist justice. JOB 34:12

[Christ] never sinned, nor ever deceived anyone. 1 PETER 2:22

God does not manipulate his people because God's nature would not permit this. He is holy, just, perfect, and all-powerful. He gives people the choice to obey and do his will, or disobey and suffer the consequences. The choice is ultimately yours, but he may sometimes motivate you by showing you the benefits of the right choice.

God is working in you, giving you the desire and the power to do what pleases him. PHILIPPIANS 2:13

May the God of peace—who brought up from the dead our Lord Jesus . . . equip you with all you need for doing his will. May he produce in you, through the power of Jesus Christ, every good thing that is pleasing to him. HEBREWS 13:20-21

You obey God when you have a desire to obey him. You do his will when he equips you to do his will. You are not like a puppet on a string, manipulated by a divine puppeteer, but rather motivated to put your life in line with God because that is what is best for you.

MARRIAGE *See also* Commitment, Family, Intimacy, Love, Relationships

"I now pronounce you man and wife," the minister says. The bride and groom look lovingly into each other's eyes. Family, friends, even casual acquaintances feel like cheering. Two people have found each other, pledged to a lifetime of commitment, vowing to be devoted and loving, and promising never to leave or forsake each other. Vows of faithfulness are the bedrock of a successful marriage. Through those vows two people, in a miraculous way, become one. Then begins a lifetime of working together, worshiping together, playing together, loving together, raising children together, building a home together, and solving problems together. God's loving relationship with his people is so similar to the marriage relationship that he uses human marriage to illustrate his covenant with his people in the Old Testament and Christ's love for the church in the New Testament.

Why did God establish marriage?

The LORD God said, "It is not good for the man to be alone. I will make a helper who is just right for him." GENESIS 2:18

God created marriage for companionship. After creating Adam, God knew this man needed a companion, another human who could walk side by side with him on life's journey.

God blessed them and said, "Be fruitful and multiply. Fill the earth and govern it." GENESIS 1:28

Didn't the LORD make you one with your wife? In body and spirit you are his. And what does he want? Godly children from your union. MALACHI 2:15

God created marriage as the best environment for raising children. Marriage was designed to help children learn about love by being born into a loving relationship. How tragic when parents fail to model Christ's love for their children.

The Scriptures say, "A man leaves his father and mother and is joined to his wife, and the two are united into one." This is a great mystery, but it is an illustration of the way Christ and the church are one. EPHESIANS 5:31-32

God created marriage as a symbol of the relationship between Jesus Christ and the church. A marriage under God should teach the couple much about how God relates to his people.

What are the keys to a happy, strong marriage?

Choose today whom you will serve. . . . But as for me and my family, we will serve the LORD. JOSHUA 24:15

Can two people walk together without agreeing on the direction? AMOS 3:3

A united purpose to serve the Lord is one key to a strong marriage. If you want to take a walk with someone, you must decide together on the direction. If you want to walk through life with your spouse, you must decide together which direction you want to go—toward the ways of God or away from him.

Drink water from your own well—share your love only with your wife. PROVERBS 5:15

Give honor to marriage, and remain faithful to one another in marriage. God will surely judge people who are immoral and those who commit adultery. HEBREWS 13:4

Faithfulness to your spouse is another key to a strong and happy marriage. Without faithfulness there is no real trust or intimacy.

Since they are no longer two but one, let no one split apart what God has joined together. MATTHEW 19:6

Commitment to stay together no matter what is essential for a strong and lasting relationship. If you leave open the option for splitting up someday, chances are you will. If you don't see breaking up as an option, you will be committed to making your marriage work in all circumstances. This commitment joins you together in pursuing and accomplishing united lifelong goals.

We must not just please ourselves. We should help others do what is right and build them up in the Lord. ROMANS 15:1-2

Self-sacrifice is essential to a strong marriage. This means thinking of your spouse's needs and interests first. Who wouldn't want to be in a relationship where someone is always meeting your needs?

May God . . . help you live in complete harmony with each other, as is fitting for followers of Christ Jesus. Then all of you can join together with one voice, giving praise and glory to God. ROMANS 15:5-6

Understand each other's differences and celebrate them. This fosters respect for each other and turns differences that would normally annoy or distract you into unique strengths that interest and help you.

Our letters have been straightforward, and there is nothing written between the lines and nothing you can't understand. 2 CORINTHIANS 1:13

Let your conversation be gracious and attractive so that you will have the right response for everyone. COLOSSIANS 4:6

Communication is necessary in a strong and happy marriage. Since mind reading is only possible for God, talk to your spouse and keep the lines of communication open, even when the conversation is awkward or hard. Instead of making each other guess, be honest. This will build trust and comfort into your relationship.

Kiss me and kiss me again, for your love is sweeter than wine. . . . The king has brought me into his bedroom. . . . My lover is like a sachet of myrrh lying between my breasts. SONG OF SONGS 1:2, 4, 13

A healthy sex life is important for a strong and happy marriage because it allows you to express intimacy and vulnerability in a way unique to any other relationship. It is a way you can share special closeness that demonstrates your complete openness to each other.

This is what sets marriage apart as a committed relationship like no other, and makes it a symbol of our relationship with God.

Love will last forever! 1 CORINTHIANS 13:8

Love is the greatest key to a strong and happy marriage. Love for your spouse should be the driving force behind all that you do and say.

How can I show my affection for my spouse?
Reward her for all she has done. Let her deeds publicly declare her praise.
PROVERBS 31:31

He escorts me to the banquet hall; it's obvious how much he loves me.
SONG OF SONGS 2:4

Come, my love, let us go out to the fields and spend the night among the wildflowers.
SONG OF SONGS 7:11

Let others know how much you appreciate your spouse. Sometimes your spouse may enjoy hearing it from others, but not as much as hearing it from you.

The king is lying on his couch, enchanted by the fragrance of my perfume.
SONG OF SONGS 1:12

Look for ways to please each other. People experience love in different ways. Scent seemed to be one way that Solomon experienced love or pleasure. Ask your spouse what pleases him or her most and make an effort to help your mate experience that with you.

How should a husband treat his wife and a wife treat her husband?
Live happily with the woman you love through all the meaningless days of life that God has given you under the sun. The wife God gives you is your reward for all your earthly toil. ECCLESIASTES 9:9

Husbands . . . love your wives, just as Christ loved the church. He gave up his life for her.
EPHESIANS 5:25

You husbands must give honor to your wives. Treat your wife with understanding as you live together. She may be weaker than you are, but she is your equal partner in God's gift of new life. Treat her as you should so your prayers will not be hindered. 1 PETER 3:7

A husband should love his wife sacrificially, with the depth of love that Christ showed when he died for all people.

Her husband can trust her, and she will greatly enrich his life. She brings him good, not harm, all the days of her life. PROVERBS 31:11-12

For wives, this means submit to your husbands as to the Lord. . . . As the church submits to Christ, so you wives should submit to your husbands in everything. EPHESIANS 5:22-24

A wife should love her husband sacrificially, helping and supporting him, believing in him and submitting to him as he submits in Christlike love to her (see Ephesians 5:21).

What does the Bible say about selecting a marriage partner? Why should I be careful about whom I marry?

The LORD had clearly instructed the people of Israel, "You must not marry them, because they will turn your hearts to their gods." Yet Solomon insisted on loving them anyway.
1 KINGS 11:2

The person you marry can build you up or destroy you. The Bible encourages you not to marry someone who is an unbeliever because it is too easy for that person to tempt you away from your faith. But if you marry a believer, you still must be sure you are marrying for the right reasons.

Don't team up with those who are unbelievers. How can righteousness be a partner with wickedness? How can light live with darkness? 2 CORINTHIANS 6:14

God intends marriage to last for life because that is a beautiful picture of how lasting your relationship with him should be. When someone is your partner for life, it is so important for that person to share your commitment to God so that together you can serve him with all your heart. Otherwise, you will spend too much time negotiating with your spouse how your faith should affect your life, when you should be just living it out freely.

What if I have already married an unbeliever? Should we stay together?

If a Christian man has a wife who is not a believer and she is willing to continue living with him, he must not leave her. And if a Christian woman has a husband who is not a believer and he is willing to continue living with her, she must not leave him.
1 CORINTHIANS 7:12-13

Don't leave your spouse just because he or she isn't a Christian. If possible, win your spouse to Christ with your love. But if that doesn't happen, continue to love your mate as Christ loved everyone, sacrificially and unselfishly. Take your situation to God and ask him to draw your spouse to him. Also, pray that your faith will grow stronger so that you will not be tempted to fall away.

Is marriage God's will for everyone?

Some are born as eunuchs, some have been made eunuchs by others, and some choose not to marry for the sake of the Kingdom of Heaven. Let anyone accept this who can.
MATTHEW 19:12

God gives to some the gift of marriage, and to others the gift of singleness. So I say to those who aren't married and to widows—it's better to stay unmarried, just as I am. But if they can't control themselves, they should go ahead and marry. It's better to marry than to burn with lust. 1 CORINTHIANS 7:7-9

God created marriage and called it good (see Genesis 1:27-31). But the Bible also makes it clear that marriage is not for everyone. Sometimes, because of certain cultural, personal, or spiritual reasons, marriage is best avoided.

MATERIALISM *See also* Ambition, Greed, Money, Generosity, Stewardship

Because people have an enormous passion for wanting more, materialism has great power to turn us away from the Lord. It's not the things themselves, but our focus on acquiring and managing them that begins to consume all our time and push God out of the picture. We must constantly assess what's most valuable. Investing money for the future is important, but investing in God's work and in the lives of others pays dividends for eternity. Our monetary investments become worthless when we die, because the old cliché is true—you can't take it with you. So we must focus on the spiritual investments we make. The love of material things becomes a death trap because our possessions chain us to this earth. Our only hope of escape is to keep an eternal perspective, to realize that real wealth is not in earthly possessions but in our relationship with God.

What is the relationship between materialism and contentment?

Trust in your money and down you go! PROVERBS 11:28

Teach those who are rich in this world not to be proud and not to trust in their money, which is so unreliable. Their trust should be in God, who richly gives us all we need for our enjoyment. 1 TIMOTHY 6:17

Money and possessions can easily deceive you into thinking, "If only I had a little more, I would be content." Nothing could be further from the truth. Always wanting a bit more is a result of a materialistic attitude which always leads to discontent. Contentment is not how much material wealth you have, but how much spiritual wealth you have. If you look to money to make you feel content, you will always be disappointed.

Why should I avoid a lifestyle of materialism?

You must burn their idols in fire, and you must not covet the silver or gold that covers them. You must not take it or it will become a trap to you. DEUTERONOMY 7:25

Wherever your treasure is, there the desires of your heart will also be. MATTHEW 6:21

Materialism has great power to turn you away from God. It's not the things themselves, but the focus on acquiring and managing them that steals your focus from God.

Those who love money will never have enough. How meaningless to think that wealth brings true happiness! ECCLESIASTES 5:10

Material things never bring the happiness they promise.

Don't store up treasures here on earth, where moths eat them and rust destroys them, and where thieves break in and steal. MATTHEW 6:19

Material things are temporary. The newness wears off quickly and things break, making your efforts to acquire them a waste of time.

All too quickly the message is crowded out by the worries of this life, the lure of wealth, and the desire for other things, so no fruit is produced. MARK 4:19

Materialism makes you spiritually lazy. It is difficult to be depending on Christ when you feel like you don't need him.

How do I make sure I'm not becoming too materialistic?

Don't worry about your personal belongings, for the best of all the land of Egypt is yours.
GENESIS 45:20

I focus on this one thing: Forgetting the past and looking forward to what lies ahead, I press on to reach the end of the race and receive the heavenly prize for which God, through Christ Jesus, is calling us. PHILIPPIANS 3:13-14

Try to worry less about what you have, and start thinking more about what God wants you to become. Start investing more energy in your eternal purpose where real contentment is found.

I came naked from my mother's womb, and I will be naked when I leave. The LORD gave me what I had, and the LORD has taken it away. Praise the name of the LORD! JOB 1:21

Remember that everything comes from the hand of God, and everything belongs to him. To avoid materialism, decide to use your material things for the Kingdom of God by serving him with them. For example, a computer can be used to view pornography or to write a Sunday school lesson. It is not necessarily the material things that are wrong, but how you use them. Use your possessions to serve Christ and your focus will shift from entitlement to gratefulness, from getting to giving, and from your desires to God's desires.

You have given me greater joy than those who have abundant harvests of grain and new wine. PSALM 4:7

Joy and satisfaction come from a relationship with God and his people; you can't have a relationship with possessions. Most of your good memories involve warm moments with others, relational investments you've made, or times spent with other people. You will cherish those memories more than memories of what you owned or didn't own.

Store your treasures in heaven, where moths and rust cannot destroy, and thieves do not break in and steal. MATTHEW 6:20

Think about the things of heaven, not the things of earth. For you died to this life, and your real life is hidden with Christ in God. COLOSSIANS 3:2-3

Redirect your focus from material things which don't last to things that do—your relationship with God and with others, and God's Word.

Use your worldly resources to benefit others and make friends. Then, when your earthly possessions are gone, they will welcome you to an eternal home. LUKE 16:9

Focus your efforts on helping others rather than on acquiring more. True satisfaction is found in meeting a genuine need for another person.

MATURITY *See also* Character, Responsibility, Wisdom

Spiritual growth is like physical growth—you start small and grow one day at a time. In order to grow, you need nourishment. Spiritually, you mature in the faith by challenging your mind to study God's Word (ask questions about it and seek answers), by prayer, by the counsel of other believers, and by life's experiences. Look at each day as a building block, and before you know it, you will be on your way to spiritual maturity.

How can I reach the maturity I desire in life? Who can mentor me along the way?

The LORD says, "I will guide you along the best pathway for your life." PSALM 32:8

I am certain that God, who began the good work within you, will continue his work until it is finally finished. PHILIPPIANS 1:6

If you need wisdom, ask our generous God, and he will give it to you. He will not rebuke you for asking. JAMES 1:5

Reading the Bible and praying to God are the first and most important steps toward maturity. Because God is the source of all wisdom, he is the ultimate example of maturity. You should model your life after Jesus and seek wisdom from the source.

After the death of Moses the LORD's servant, the LORD spoke to Joshua son of Nun, Moses' assistant. He said, "Moses my servant is dead. Therefore, the time has come for you to lead these people, the Israelites, across the Jordan River into the land I am giving them." JOSHUA 1:1-2

A good spiritual mentor can help you grow and mature in your faith, as well as in everyday life. Look for a person who is several stages ahead of you in life, who has weathered many experiences and who exemplifies godliness. Ask them to help you learn how to become a mature Christian.

I couldn't talk to you as I would to spiritual people. . . . I had to feed you with milk, not with solid food. 1 CORINTHIANS 3:1-2

When I was a child, I spoke and thought and reasoned as a child. But when I grew up, I put away childish things. 1 CORINTHIANS 13:11

Let us stop going over the basic teachings about Christ again and again. Let us go on instead and become mature in our understanding. HEBREWS 6:1

When someone first becomes a Christian, he or she is like a child, immature in the faith. But as with physical growth, we grow up, one day at a time, gaining wisdom and maturity.

What are some secrets to reaching maturity?

Run to win! All athletes are disciplined in their training. They do it to win a prize that will fade away, but we do it for an eternal prize. 1 CORINTHIANS 9:24-25

To reach spiritual maturity, you must discipline yourself like an athlete. Athletes excel as they exercise and push the boundaries of their physical capabilities. When you give as much emphasis to spiritual discipline, you will experience a deepening faith and a maturity in the way you approach life.

What can keep me from maturing? What should I avoid?

It's your sins that have cut you off from God. Because of your sins, he has turned away and will not listen anymore. ISAIAH 59:2

Soldiers don't get tied up in the affairs of civilian life, for then they cannot please the officer who enlisted them. 2 TIMOTHY 2:4

The roadblocks you will encounter on the road to maturity will be in the form of temptations that will entice you to get off the road and discourage you to the point of giving up. When you allow yourself to get sidetracked by temptation, you will lose sight of what is truly important. Just as a child acts upon immediate desires, temptation causes sin which makes you spiritually immature in some way. True maturity is recognizing and resisting the temptations that try to slow down your journey toward the goals God has set for you.

MEANING/MEANINGLESSNESS   *See also* Eternity, Joy, Purpose

A primary cause of despair is the conviction that life is ultimately meaningless. Why keep trying if it really doesn't matter? Conversely, a sense that our life has meaning gives us energy, purpose, and resilience, even in the midst of trials. The Bible talks often about the deepest reasons for our existence, supplying compelling incentive to persevere and overcome to reach a future that is well worth the effort.

Why does it sometimes seem that life lacks meaning?

The same destiny ultimately awaits everyone, whether righteous or wicked, good or bad, . . . religious or irreligious. ECCLESIASTES 9:2

The inevitability of death can make life seem meaningless if you believe there is nothing beyond it.

The wise and the foolish both die. . . . In the days to come, both will be forgotten. ECCLESIASTES 2:16

The fact that the dead are often forgotten can make our own accomplishments feel meaningless.

How do you know what your life will be like tomorrow? Your life is like the morning fog—it's here a little while, then it's gone. JAMES 4:14

The brevity of life can make it seem meaningless.

Endless crowds stand around [one leader], but then another generation grows up and rejects him, too. So it is all meaningless—like chasing the wind. ECCLESIASTES 4:16

The fleeting nature of worldly success can make life seem meaningless.

Those who love money will never have enough. How meaningless to think that wealth brings true happiness! ECCLESIASTES 5:10

Centering your life on money and possessions leads to a sense of meaninglessness. Wanting more is an endless cycle. With this attitude, there is never enough.

Good people are often treated as though they were wicked, and wicked people are often treated as though they were good. This is so meaningless! ECCLESIASTES 8:14

The injustices of this world can make life seem meaningless, because if you believe this life is all there is, then for some people, justice is never served.

Why do even the most important things often seem empty?

It is useless for you to work so hard from early morning until late at night, anxiously working for food to eat; for God gives rest to his loved ones. PSALM 127:2

As I looked at everything I had worked so hard to accomplish, it was all so meaningless—like chasing the wind. . . . So I gave up in despair, questioning the value of all my hard work in this world. . . . What do people get in this life for all their hard work and anxiety? . . . It is all meaningless. ECCLESIASTES 2:11, 20-23

Human effort alone will feel meaningless without the perspective of knowing your work has lasting and eternal value.

The wisdom of this world is foolishness to God. As the Scriptures say, "He traps the wise in the snare of their own cleverness." And again, "The LORD knows the thoughts of the wise; he knows they are worthless." 1 CORINTHIANS 3:19-20

The Gentiles . . . are hopelessly confused. Their minds are full of darkness; they wander far from the life God gives because they have closed their minds and hardened their hearts against him. EPHESIANS 4:17-18

Human thought alone will feel meaningless without an eternal perspective.

"We have all heard of the pride of Moab, for his pride is very great. We know of his lofty pride, his arrogance, and his haughty heart. I know about his insolence," says the LORD, "but his boasts are empty—as empty as his deeds." JEREMIAH 48:29-30

His mighty arm has done tremendous things! He has scattered the proud and haughty ones. He has brought down princes from their thrones and exalted the humble. LUKE 1:51-52

Human attitudes that focus on self, like pride, greed, and selfishness, are meaningless.

Listen to this, you pleasure-loving kingdom, living at ease and feeling secure. You say, "I am the only one, and there is no other. I will never be a widow or lose my children." Well, . . . calamities will come upon you. ISAIAH 47:8-9

Dependence on self and independence from God are meaningless.

What brings meaning to my life? What will make my life count?

God said, "Let us make human beings in our image, to be like us. They will reign over the fish in the sea, the birds in the sky, the livestock, all the wild animals on the earth, and the small animals that scurry along the ground." GENESIS 1:26

Everything comes from [the Lord] and exists by his power and is intended for his glory. All glory to him forever! ROMANS 11:36

God, as your Creator, gives you value. You are made in his image for his glory, and his very breath gives you life.

You will show me the way of life, granting me the joy of your presence and the pleasures of living with you forever. PSALM 16:11

I pray that your love will overflow more and more, and that you will keep on growing in knowledge and understanding. For I want you to understand what really matters, so that you may live pure and blameless lives until the day of Christ's return. PHILIPPIANS 1:9-10

A personal, growing relationship with Jesus Christ today and for eternity gives life meaning. He created you for a purpose, and the better you know him, the clearer his purpose for you will become.

Jesus called out to [Peter and Andrew], "Come, follow me, and I will show you how to fish for people!" MATTHEW 4:19

The old life is gone; a new life has begun! All of this is a gift from God, who brought us back to himself through Christ. And God has given us this task of reconciling people to him. 2 CORINTHIANS 5:17-18

You are called to participate in God's work in the world and have a positive effect on others.

Jesus told [Martha], "I am the resurrection and the life. Anyone who believes in me will live, even after dying. Everyone who lives in me and believes in me will never ever die." JOHN 11:25-26

The fact that death is not the end for Jesus' followers invests your life with eternal significance. Knowing there is life after death gives you true perspective on what you do here and now.

Our purpose is to please God, not people. He alone examines the motives of our hearts. 1 THESSALONIANS 2:4

If you keep yourself pure, you will be a special utensil for honorable use. Your life will be clean, and you will be ready for the Master to use you for every good work. 2 TIMOTHY 2:21

Pleasing God by obeying him and doing his will prepares you to be used by God to accomplish his purposes for your life.

My life is worth nothing to me unless I use it for finishing the work assigned me by the Lord Jesus—the work of telling others the Good News about the wonderful grace of God.
ACTS 20:24

Of all the important work on earth, what is more important than sharing God with others?

How can I understand the meaning of my life more fully?

Cry out for insight, and ask for understanding. Search for them as you would for silver; seek them like hidden treasures. PROVERBS 2:3-4

Getting wisdom is the wisest thing you can do! PROVERBS 4:7

Understanding the deep truths of life doesn't just happen. You have to search for them. You won't stumble onto insight, understanding, and wisdom. You find them only when you pursue God.

Your commandments give me understanding; no wonder I hate every false way of life.
PSALM 119:104

Studying the Bible provides insight into your life's meaning and keeps you from being deceived by harmful lies and empty promises.

I cry out to God Most High, to God who will fulfill his purpose for me. PSALM 57:2

Pray, asking God to reveal his truth to you and to fulfill his purpose in you. God will not fail to use you for his purpose if you give yourself to him completely.

Is religion ever meaningless?

Don't go back to worshiping worthless idols that cannot help or rescue you—they are totally useless! 1 SAMUEL 12:21

Their gods are like helpless scarecrows in a cucumber field! They cannot speak, and they need to be carried because they cannot walk. Do not be afraid of such gods, for they can neither harm you nor do you any good. JEREMIAH 10:5

If religion involves worshiping anyone or anything other than the one, true, living God, it is meaningless.

Household gods give worthless advice, fortune-tellers predict only lies, and interpreters of dreams pronounce falsehoods that give no comfort. So my people are wandering like lost sheep; they are attacked because they have no shepherd. ZECHARIAH 10:2

A quest to know the future apart from the God who controls the future is meaningless.

The people of Israel love their rituals of sacrifice, but to me their sacrifices are all meaningless. I will hold my people accountable for their sins, and I will punish them.
HOSEA 8:13

These people honor me with their lips, but their hearts are far from me. Their worship is a farce, for they teach man-made ideas as commands from God. MATTHEW 15:8-9

Religious observances or rituals without true faith are meaningless. They are only superstitious habits.

Jesus told this story to some who had great confidence in their own righteousness and scorned everyone else: "Two men went to the Temple to pray. One was a Pharisee, and the other was a despised tax collector. The Pharisee stood by himself and prayed this prayer: 'I thank you, God, that I am not a sinner like everyone else. For I don't cheat, I don't sin, and I don't commit adultery. I'm certainly not like that tax collector! I fast twice a week, and I give you a tenth of my income.' But the tax collector stood at a distance and dared not even lift his eyes to heaven as he prayed. Instead, he beat his chest in sorrow, saying, 'O God, be merciful to me, for I am a sinner.' I tell you, this sinner, not the Pharisee, returned home justified before God. For those who exalt themselves will be humbled, and those who humble themselves will be exalted." LUKE 18:9-14

Prayer without honesty and humility is meaningless. It is not the prayer itself that gets God's attention, but the condition of the heart and the attitude behind it.

[Jesus said,] "I am the vine; you are the branches. Those who remain in me, and I in them, will produce much fruit. For apart from me you can do nothing." JOHN 15:5

Command [everyone] in God's presence to stop fighting over words. Such arguments are useless, and they can ruin those who hear them. 2 TIMOTHY 2:14

How foolish! Can't you see that faith without good deeds is useless? JAMES 2:20

Christian service without God is meaningless because apart from him we can do nothing of lasting value.

Anyone who hears my teaching and doesn't obey it is foolish, like a person who builds a house on sand. When the rains and floods come and the winds beat against that house, it will collapse with a mighty crash. MATTHEW 7:26-27

Don't just listen to God's word. You must do what it says. Otherwise, you are only fooling yourselves. JAMES 1:22

Not responding to God's Word is foolish. There's no hope to have a meaningful life when you don't listen to the one who made you.

MEDITATION *See also* Listening, Prayer, Spiritual Disciplines

Meditation is setting aside time to intentionally think about God, talk to him, and listen to him. When we make the time to really listen to God, we remove ourselves from the distractions and noise of the world around us and move within range of his voice. We prepare ourselves to learn and to have our desires molded into what God desires. As a result, we change and our thoughts and our actions fall more in line with his commands. Meditation goes beyond the study of God to communion with him that ultimately leads to godly actions.

How can meditating help me in my spiritual walk?

You must commit yourselves wholeheartedly to these commands that I am giving you today. . . . Tie [these commands] to your hands and wear them on your forehead as reminders. Write them on the doorposts of your house and on your gates.
DEUTERONOMY 6:6, 8-9

Moses instructed the people to remember God's Word every day and tell family and friends of God's past help and blessings. Each day would then strengthen, not dim, their love and commitment to God, encouraging them to be even more faithful to obey him. When you meditate on God's Word you remember who he is and what he has done. You remember him as the one who helps you fight and win in life's battles. Remember God first thing in the morning and fall asleep with him on your mind. Meditate on God as the source of the hope you think you've lost. Think about him with a thankful heart when you have plenty, for you will need him when you have little. Meditate on him and his great love for you. Weave him into the fabric of your life so you, your children, and your grandchildren will be trained to love God with a grateful heart all of your days. Then your spiritual walk will be strong and focused.

How do I meditate?

I wait quietly before God, for my victory comes from him. . . . Let all that I am wait quietly before God, for my hope is in him. PSALM 62:1, 5

Meditation involves thinking about God quietly and intently, with confidence that he will hear you and you will hear him.

[The righteous] delight in the law of the LORD, meditating on it day and night. PSALM 1:2

Oh, how I love your instructions! I think about them all day long. PSALM 119:97

Meditation involves taking the time to read God's Word and consider it. He often speaks to your heart as you read the words he has written for you.

I will bless the LORD who guides me; even at night my heart instructs me. PSALM 16:7

Meditation involves setting aside time to seek God's guidance and instruction.

What should I think about when I meditate?

O God, we meditate on your unfailing love as we worship in your Temple. PSALM 48:9

Think about God's unfailing love for you.

I recall all you have done, O LORD; I remember your wonderful deeds of long ago. They are constantly in my thoughts. I cannot stop thinking about your mighty works. PSALM 77:11-12

Think about all God has done for you.

I will meditate on your majestic, glorious splendor and your wonderful miracles.
PSALM 145:5

Think about God's majestic, glorious splendor and praise him for it.

Those who are dominated by the sinful nature think about sinful things, but those who are controlled by the Holy Spirit think about things that please the Spirit. ROMANS 8:5

Think about the Holy Spirit, what pleases him, and how you can allow yourself to be used by him.

Fix your thoughts on what is true, and honorable, and right, and pure, and lovely, and admirable. Think about things that are excellent and worthy of praise. PHILIPPIANS 4:8

Think about things that are true, honorable, right, pure, lovely, admirable, excellent, and worthy of praise.

MENTORING *See also* Advice, Example, Friendship, Wisdom

A mentoring relationship has the specific purpose of teaching and learning. As Christians, we have a responsibility to teach younger generations the lessons and values of Jesus Christ. Good mentors commit to building a relationship with someone younger or with less life experience. Through this relationship, a mentor shares wisdom, life experiences, and support in hopes of helping their mentoree learn and grow. Similarly, Christ sent us the Holy Spirit as our ultimate spiritual mentor. It is through the Holy Spirit that Christ helps us build a relationship with God and guides us into wisdom, maturity, and understanding.

What is mentoring? How does a leader mentor?

Moses and his assistant Joshua set out, and Moses climbed up the mountain of God. EXODUS 24:13

Inside the Tent of Meeting, the LORD would speak to Moses face to face, as one speaks to a friend. Afterward Moses would return to the camp, but the young man who assisted him, Joshua son of Nun, would remain behind in the Tent of Meeting. EXODUS 33:11

After the death of Moses the LORD's servant, the LORD spoke to Joshua son of Nun, Moses' assistant. He said, "Moses my servant is dead. Therefore, the time has come for you to lead these people, the Israelites, across the Jordan River into the land I am giving them." JOSHUA 1:1-2

Mentoring is more than just teaching; it is sharing life together. Moses and Joshua are examples of effective mentoring. First, Moses oversaw Joshua's active involvement in the work. Second, Moses welcomed Joshua into his own spiritual arena, even allowing Joshua to be with him during his most significant experiences with God. Then, when Moses died, it was clear that Joshua was prepared to assume responsibility as a faithful, fully equipped, credible leader.

You have heard me teach things that have been confirmed by many reliable witnesses. Now teach these truths to other trustworthy people who will be able to pass them on to others. 2 TIMOTHY 2:2

Mentors should have multiple generations in mind. Paul instructs Timothy to think not only about those he is teaching, but also about those they will eventually teach. From

Paul to Timothy, from Timothy to his students, then to their students represents four generations! Such long-range vision for changing lives is imperative for mentors who want to make a lasting impact.

Why is mentoring important?

As for you, Titus, promote the kind of living that reflects wholesome teaching. Teach the older men to exercise self-control, to be worthy of respect, and to live wisely. . . . Similarly, teach the older women to live in a way that honors God. . . . These older women must train the younger women to love their husbands and their children, to live wisely and be pure, to work in their homes, to do good, and to be submissive to their husbands. . . . In the same way, encourage the young men to live wisely. And you yourself must be an example to them by doing good works of every kind. TITUS 2:1-7

Mentoring those who are younger and less experienced can help them learn how to cope with the daily pressures and problems in life with integrity and godliness.

Anoint Jehu son of Nimshi to be king of Israel, and anoint Elisha son of Shaphat from the town of Abel-meholah to replace you as my prophet. 1 KINGS 19:16

Elijah said to Elisha, "Stay here, for the Lord has told me to go to Bethel." But Elisha replied, "As surely as the Lord lives and you yourself live, I will never leave you!" So they went down together to Bethel. 2 KINGS 2:1-2

Elijah said to Elisha, "Tell me what I can do for you before I am taken away." And Elisha replied, "Please let me inherit a double share of your spirit and become your successor." 2 KINGS 2:9

No one will live forever, but the work of the Lord continues from generation to generation. Mentoring ensures the continuation of God's work from one generation to the next. The Lord instructed Elijah to prepare his successor Elisha over an extended time. Elisha was loyal to Elijah to the very end. By then, Elisha was eager to assume his place in God's work.

Should I have a spiritual mentor?

Jehoiada made a covenant between the Lord and [King Joash] and the people that they would be the Lord's people. He also made a covenant between the king and the people. 2 KINGS 11:17

Jehoiada's guidance made King Joash's rule successful. When Jehoiada died, instead of finding another godly advisor and confidante, Joash tried—and failed—to govern well on his own (see 2 Chronicles 24:2, 17-18). A mentor—sometimes called a spiritual director or discipler—is a mature believer who will keep you accountable and supply wise guidance and encouragement. Meeting regularly and being completely honest with your mentor are essential to being effectively guided. Mentorship is God's method for spiritual maturation. God provided Elijah for Elisha, Barnabas for Paul, and Paul for Timothy (see 1 Kings 19:19-21; Acts 9:26-27; 16:1-3). Don't make Joash's mistake; invite someone to be your mentor.

MERCY *See also* Compassion, Empathy, Forgiveness, Grace

Mercy is compassion poured out on needy people. But the mercy of God, which he expects us to model, goes one step further. God's mercy is undeserved favor. Even though we don't deserve mercy, he still extends it to us. Our sin and rebellion against God deserve his punishment; but instead he offers us forgiveness and eternal life. Just as God is merciful toward us despite our sin, we should extend mercy toward those who have wronged us.

What is mercy?

The LORD is compassionate and merciful, slow to get angry and filled with unfailing love. He will not constantly accuse us, nor remain angry forever. He does not punish us for all our sins; he does not deal harshly with us, as we deserve. PSALM 103:8-10

Mercy is more than exemption from the punishment you deserve for your sins. It is receiving an undeserved gift—salvation being the greatest undeserved gift of all. Mercy is experiencing favor with Almighty God when he forgives your sins and gives you the opportunity to receive eternal life if you believe in him.

What is the source of mercy?

The LORD passed in front of Moses, calling out, "Yahweh! The LORD! The God of compassion and mercy! I am slow to anger and filled with unfailing love and faithfulness." EXODUS 34:6

God is our merciful Father and the source of all comfort. 2 CORINTHIANS 1:3

Let us come boldly to the throne of our gracious God. There we will receive his mercy, and we will find grace to help us when we need it most. HEBREWS 4:16

God is the source of mercy. The mercy you show others is a reflection of his mercy. When you are merciful, you reveal godliness, for all mercy originates with God.

To whom does God show mercy?

God blesses those who are merciful, for they will be shown mercy. MATTHEW 5:7

God promises his mercy to those who extend mercy to others. Offer mercy and you will receive mercy.

The LORD your God will be merciful only if you listen to his voice and keep all his commands that I am giving you today. DEUTERONOMY 13:18

God is merciful to those with sincere hearts, who respect and honor him. Mercy is a reward for faithful obedience.

He does not punish us for all our sins; he does not deal harshly with us, as we deserve. PSALM 103:10

God offers mercy to sinners. No one deserves God's mercy and yet he gives it gladly. Thank God for his patience and mercy and receive it gratefully.

God said to Moses, "I will show mercy to anyone I choose, and I will show compassion to anyone I choose." So it is God who decides to show mercy. We can neither choose it nor work for it. ROMANS 9:15-16

Ultimately, God chooses who will receive his mercy. You cannot earn it. You are, literally, at his mercy.

Why does God show me mercy?

Lead me in the right path, O LORD, or my enemies will conquer me. Make your way plain for me to follow. PSALM 5:8

To guide you along the right path for your life and to keep your enemies from defeating you.

I will be glad and rejoice in your unfailing love. PSALM 31:7

Each morning I will sing with joy about your unfailing love. PSALM 59:16

To give you joy.

You, O LORD, are a God of compassion and mercy, slow to get angry and filled with unfailing love and faithfulness. PSALM 86:15

To demonstrate his deep and unfailing love for you.

How does God show me mercy?

He forgives all my sins. . . . He redeems me from death. . . . He fills my life with good things. PSALM 103:3-5

God showers numerous acts of mercy on you each day. Anything good in your life is from God's merciful hand.

Unfailing love and faithfulness make atonement for sin. PROVERBS 16:6

God is so rich in mercy, and he loved us so much, that even though we were dead because of our sins, he gave us life. EPHESIANS 2:4-5

God shows you mercy by being slow to get angry over your sins, by offering you eternal life and salvation, and by showing you unfailing love no matter what you have done against him.

When God our Savior revealed his kindness and love, he saved us, not because of the righteous things we had done, but because of his mercy. He washed away our sins, giving us a new birth and new life through the Holy Spirit. He generously poured out the Spirit upon us through Jesus Christ our Savior. Because of his grace he declared us righteous and gave us confidence that we will inherit eternal life. TITUS 3:4-7

By God's love you were given the free gift of salvation even though you didn't deserve it. Because of God's mercy, you have forgiveness and freedom from guilt. Because of God's grace, you have been blessed beyond your wildest dreams because you have secured a perfect life for all eternity in heaven.

How can I show mercy?

Shouldn't you have mercy on your fellow servant, just as I had mercy on you?
MATTHEW 18:33

Be merciful to others even when they don't deserve it.

O people, the LORD has told you what is good, and this is what he requires of you: to do what is right, to love mercy, and to walk humbly with your God. MICAH 6:8

When you obey God sincerely, your life will overflow with merciful acts.

This is what the LORD of Heaven's Armies says: Judge fairly, and show mercy and kindness to one another. ZECHARIAH 7:9

You can show mercy by judging fairly and honestly, and showing kindness to others.

The wisdom from above is first of all pure. It is also peace loving, gentle at all times, and willing to yield to others. It is full of mercy and good deeds. It shows no favoritism and is always sincere. JAMES 3:17

Merciful actions are the result of wisdom from God. Ask God for his wisdom so you can know how to share his mercy with others.

MIRACLES *See also* Healing, Resurrection, Impossible

It is hard to imagine, in our time, the parting of the Red Sea, or the sun and moon standing still in the sky. The miracles of God recorded in the Bible can seem like ancient myths if we fail to recognize God's intervention in our lives today. Just as Pharaoh was blind to God's miracles performed right before his eyes through Moses, we too can blind ourselves from God's miracles, failing to notice the mighty work he is doing all around us. When we look for God he shows himself in miraculous ways: in the birth of a baby, a new cure for a deadly disease, an awesome sunset, or the restoration of a hopeless relationship. Yes, we have a miracle-working God. The Lord is able—and willing—to do the impossible in order to help us do his work. This means that no situation is hopeless. Thus God encourages us to pray big prayers and never lose hope.

What are miracles?

The apostles stayed there a long time, preaching boldly about the grace of the Lord. And the Lord proved their message was true by giving them power to do miraculous signs and wonders. ACTS 14:3

God confirmed the message by giving signs and wonders and various miracles and gifts of the Holy Spirit whenever he chose. HEBREWS 2:4

Miracles are supernatural events that point people to God. They are visible signs of God's power, authority, presence, and love for his people. They help you know him, encourage believers to keep going, rescue you, are always about his kingdom work, and help you see his hand in your life.

Pharaoh called in his own wise men and sorcerers. . . . They threw down their staffs, which also became serpents! But then Aaron's staff swallowed up their staffs.
EXODUS 7:11-12

[The man of lawlessness] will come to do the work of Satan with counterfeit power and signs and miracles. 2 THESSALONIANS 2:9

It is important to note that not all miracles are from God. Satan and his demons have the ability to perform miracles, although they do not have the same power as God. You can tell when miracles are not from God because the person who performs them will do so only to destroy, to promote himself or his own interests, or to lead people away from God.

How does God use miracles?

He rescues and saves his people; he performs miraculous signs and wonders in the heavens and on earth. He has rescued Daniel from the power of the lions. DANIEL 6:27

The LORD [says], "I will do mighty miracles for you, like those I did when I rescued you from slavery in Egypt." MICAH 7:15

Sometimes God uses miracles to rescue you.

The LORD said to Moses, "Return to Pharaoh and make your demands again. I have made him and his officials stubborn so I can display my miraculous signs among them." EXODUS 10:1

Sometimes God uses miracles to show his power.

Jesus told [the concerned father], "Go back home. Your son will live!" And the man believed what Jesus said and started home. While the man was on his way, some of his servants met him with the news that his son was alive and well. He asked them when the boy had begun to get better, and they replied, "Yesterday afternoon at one o'clock his fever suddenly disappeared!" Then the father realized that that was the very time Jesus had told him, "Your son will live." And he and his entire household believed in Jesus. JOHN 4:50-53

Sometimes God uses miracles to help you believe in him.

Jesus saw the huge crowd as he stepped from the boat, and he had compassion on them and healed their sick. MATTHEW 14:14

Sometimes God uses miracles to show his compassion for you.

Jesus met a man with an advanced case of leprosy. When the man saw Jesus, he bowed with his face to the ground, begging to be healed. "Lord," he said, "if you are willing, you can heal me and make me clean." Jesus reached out and touched him. "I am willing," he said. "Be healed!" And instantly the leprosy disappeared. LUKE 5:12-13

Sometimes God uses miracles to heal you.

Jesus told the servants, "Fill the jars with water.". . . He said, "Now dip some out, and take it to the master of ceremonies.". . . When the master of ceremonies tasted the water that was now wine, . . . he called the bridegroom over. "A host always serves the best wine first," he said. "Then, when everyone has had a lot to drink, he brings out the less expensive wine. But you have kept the best until now!" JOHN 2:7-10

Sometimes God uses miracles to help you.

How should I respond when God performs miracles in my life?

All of [Jesus'] followers began to shout and sing as they walked along, praising God for all the wonderful miracles they had seen. LUKE 19:37

You should offer praise and thanksgiving to him.

I will praise you, LORD, with all my heart; I will tell of all the marvelous things you have done. PSALM 9:1

You can best show your gratitude to God by telling others what God has done for you and giving him all the credit.

Is there something wrong with me if I pray for a miracle and God doesn't grant one?

I am sending him because he has been longing to see you, and he was very distressed that you heard he was ill. And he certainly was ill; in fact, he almost died.
PHILIPPIANS 2:26-27

[Paul] left Trophimus sick at Miletus. 2 TIMOTHY 4:20

God occasionally used Paul to perform miraculous healings. Yet in these passages Paul describes the illnesses of two companions where there was no miracle. But Paul blames neither himself nor God. Rather, Paul seems to acknowledge that there are times when God, for his own good purposes, chooses not to perform miracles.

Give thanks to the LORD, for he is good! His faithful love endures forever. PSALM 107:1

Although you might ask God for a miracle, only God knows when he is about to perform one. But you can know that God's love for you is eternal and unchanging. You can therefore trust that God is doing a good work in your life even when he doesn't give you exactly what you pray for. The miracle of God's love for sinners is the greatest miracle of all and one that you can experience every day.

What keeps me from seeing more miracles in my life?

When Aaron raised his hand and struck the ground with his staff, gnats infested the entire land. . . . All the dust in the land of Egypt turned into gnats. Pharaoh's magicians tried to do the same thing with their secret arts, but this time they failed. . . . "This is the finger of God!" the magicians exclaimed to Pharaoh. But Pharaoh's heart remained hard. He wouldn't listen to them, just as the LORD had predicted. EXODUS 8:17-19

You won't see a miracle if you are too stubborn to believe a miracle can happen today, or that God won't perform one on your behalf. Even Pharaoh's magicians saw this miracle as an act of God, but Pharoah was too stubborn to admit it. He convinced himself this couldn't be from the hand of God. When you get rid of pride and stubbornness, you will be surprised to see how much God is doing in your life that you never noticed before.

Who can list the glorious miracles of the LORD? Who can ever praise him enough?
PSALM 106:2

Maybe you think a miracle is always a dramatic event like a dead person coming back to life. But miracles are happening all around you that are supernatural occurrences, maybe not as dramatic as the parting of the Red Sea, but no less powerful. The birth of a baby, healing of an illness, the rebirth of the earth in spring, salvation by faith alone, the work of love and forgiveness to change someone, hearing the specific call of God in your life. These are just a few. If you think you've never seen a miracle, look closer. They are happening all around you.

MISTAKES *See also* Consequences, Failure, Sin

Although burning the breakfast toast is a mistake, it is trivial and leaves no lasting consequences. On the other hand, a doctor who misreads a chart and removes a kidney instead of an appendix has made a mistake of considerably greater implications. We all make mistakes. When we think of the word *mistake*, we usually think of making an error by accident. We didn't mean to do it. While that is often the case, mistakes can also be intentional and sinful. And sometimes mistakes can be the natural consequence of careless or sinful actions. The Bible is full of stories about people who made mistakes, both trivial and catastrophic. However, the most fatal mistake we can make is turning away from God. It is a mistake that carries the consequence of eternal death.

What are some of the biggest mistakes I can make?

When the crowd saw what Paul had done, they shouted in their local dialect, "These men are gods in human form!" They decided that Barnabas was the Greek god Zeus and that Paul was Hermes. ACTS 14:11-12

Worshiping anyone or anything other than God is a mistake.

We have stopped evaluating others from a human point of view. At one time we thought of Christ merely from a human point of view. How differently we know him now!
2 CORINTHIANS 5:16

Ignoring, neglecting, or refusing to acknowledge Jesus as God is a mistake with eternal consequences.

The LORD's light penetrates the human spirit, exposing every hidden motive.
PROVERBS 20:27

"Can anyone hide from me in a secret place? Am I not everywhere in all the heavens and earth?" says the LORD. JEREMIAH 23:24

Nothing in all creation is hidden from God. Everything is naked and exposed before his eyes, and he is the one to whom we are accountable. HEBREWS 4:13

To think God doesn't see sin or overlooks it is a mistake.

[God asked Adam,] "Have you eaten from the tree whose fruit I commanded you not to eat?" The man replied, "It was the woman you gave me who gave me the fruit."... "The serpent deceived me," [the woman] replied. "That's why I ate it." GENESIS 3:11-13

Sarai said to Abram, "This is all your fault! I put my servant into your arms, but now that she's pregnant she treats me with contempt." GENESIS 16:5

People ruin their lives by their own foolishness and then are angry at the LORD. PROVERBS 19:3

Not taking responsibility for your own actions is a big mistake. It causes more mistakes with increasingly harder consequences as time goes on.

Jonah got up and went in the opposite direction to get away from the LORD. JONAH 1:3

Running away from God is a futile mistake. Wherever you try to go, he's already there.

What can I learn from my mistakes?

After looking in all directions to make sure no one was watching, Moses killed the Egyptian and hid the body in the sand. EXODUS 2:12

Everyone, even the most godly leaders, makes mistakes. Moses, one of the Bible's most godly leaders, made several immature and terrible mistakes. When you make a mistake, it is essential to admit it, then turn to God and others for help and forgiveness.

Whoever stubbornly refuses to accept criticism will suddenly be destroyed beyond recovery. PROVERBS 29:1

If you are told you have made a mistake, consider the source and the substance of the criticism, then listen and learn for the future.

We all make many mistakes. For if we could control our tongues, we would be perfect and could also control ourselves in every other way. JAMES 3:2

One of the most common mistakes is saying something you later regret. Practice thinking about the consequences of your words before you open your mouth.

How can I avoid making mistakes?

I will teach you hidden lessons from our past—stories we have heard and known, stories our ancestors handed down to us. We will not hide these truths from our children; we will tell the next generation about the glorious deeds of the LORD, about his power and his mighty wonders. PSALM 78:2-4

Who will hear these lessons from the past and see the ruin that awaits you in the future?
ISAIAH 42:23

Reviewing your past helps you avoid making the same mistakes. You can learn from your history to make better choices.

I have hidden your word in my heart, that I might not sin against you. PSALM 119:11

God's Word is full of wisdom. Knowing God's Word gives guidance that helps you avoid making mistakes. The Bible is not an advice column, but the wisdom of Almighty God.

Without wise leadership, a nation falls; there is safety in having many advisers.
PROVERBS 11:14

Godly counsel helps you avoid mistakes. When in doubt, ask a wise person who follows God for advice and help.

It was by faith that Abraham obeyed when God called him to leave home and go to another land that God would give him as his inheritance. He went without knowing where he was going.... It was by faith that Moses left the land of Egypt, not fearing the king's anger. He kept right on going because he kept his eyes on the one who is invisible.
HEBREWS 11:8, 27

Faith in God keeps you close to him. The closer you are to God, the easier it is to hear his voice to guide your actions, which makes you much more likely to make good choices. Without God's guidance you will make far more mistakes.

People with understanding control their anger; a hot temper shows great foolishness.
PROVERBS 14:29

We all make many mistakes. For if we could control our tongues, we would be perfect and could also control ourselves in every other way. JAMES 3:2

Think before speaking and acting, and you will avoid mistakes. Mistakes are made when you speak or behave impulsively.

Is there hope for me, even with all the mistakes I've made?

Abram believed the LORD, and the LORD counted him as righteous because of his faith.
GENESIS 15:6

Abram made many mistakes. So how could God call him "righteous"? Despite his bad choices, Abram believed and trusted in God. It was faith, not perfection, that made him right in God's eyes. This same principle is true for you, too. Rather than measuring your goodness, God is looking for your faith and your willingness to follow him.

When the Aramean chariot commanders saw Jehoshaphat in his royal robes, they went after him. "There is the king of Israel!" they shouted. But Jehoshaphat called out, and ... God helped him by turning the attackers away from him. As soon as the chariot commanders realized he was not the king of Israel, they stopped chasing him. 2 CHRONICLES 18:31-32

God still helped Jehoshaphat even though he made the mistake of ignoring the warnings of the prophet Micaiah. God will help you even in the midst of your mistakes, if you ask him.

"I don't even know the man," [Peter] said. MATTHEW 26:72

Jesus restored Peter to fellowship and used him to build the early church, even after his most painful mistake of outright denial. Following Jesus means allowing him to forgive your mistakes and help you work toward a better future.

When I make a big mistake, how do I move on?

"Why are you so angry?" the LORD asked Cain. "Why do you look so dejected? You will be accepted if you do what is right. But if you refuse to do what is right, then watch out! Sin is crouching at the door, eager to control you. But you must subdue it and be its master." GENESIS 4:6-7

Begin by admitting your mistakes and sins so you are open to forgiveness and restoration of your relationships.

If we confess our sins to him, he is faithful and just to forgive us our sins and to cleanse us from all wickedness. 1 JOHN 1:9

Receive God's forgiveness. He wants to give it as much as you need to receive it.

Confess your sins to each other and pray for each other so that you may be healed. The earnest prayer of a righteous person has great power and produces wonderful results. JAMES 5:16

Ask for others' forgiveness when needed and receive their forgiveness when it's extended.

Since we are surrounded by such a huge crowd of witnesses to the life of faith, let us strip off every weight that slows us down, especially the sin that so easily trips us up. And let us run with endurance the race God has set before us. HEBREWS 12:1

Focus forward! Once forgiven, don't linger on your mistakes. The door of the future is too small for the baggage of your past to fit through. Let it go and walk through the doorway to your future.

MODESTY *See also* Appearance, Dignity, Humility, Simplicity

Modesty is more than just dressing appropriately; it is living appropriately with self-control, avoiding wrong and indecent behavior, and serving others with grace and kindness. Modesty understands what is and is not appropriate Christian behavior. Modest people live humbly without drawing attention to themselves in inappropriate ways, and aspire to simplicity rather than ostentation. Modesty focuses on inner beauty, which is reflected in outward appearance and behavior. As followers of Christ, we are called to set an appropriate example in what we say, what we do, and even how we look.

I want women to be modest in their appearance. They should wear decent and appropriate clothing and not draw attention to themselves. 1 TIMOTHY 2:9

Be careful to live properly among your unbelieving neighbors. Then even if they accuse you of doing wrong, they will see your honorable behavior, and they will give honor to God when he judges the world. 1 PETER 2:12

Godly modesty is maintaining a standard of appropriateness that cannot be criticized and keeps you from being a stumbling block to others. It is keeping faith, love, and holiness in harmony with your appearance. Modesty frees you from focusing excessive time and attention on yourself and worrying about how you appear to others.

Don't you realize that your body is the temple of the Holy Spirit, who lives in you and was given to you by God? You do not belong to yourself. 1 CORINTHIANS 6:19

Don't be concerned about the outward beauty of fancy hairstyles, expensive jewelry, or beautiful clothes. You should clothe yourselves instead with the beauty that comes from within, the unfading beauty of a gentle and quiet spirit, which is so precious to God. 1 PETER 3:3-4

Modesty focuses on inward beauty, the kind of beauty that remains strong and youthful long after your body turns old and frail.

How should I show modesty in my behavior?

Because we belong to the day, we must live decent lives for all to see. Don't participate in the darkness of wild parties and drunkenness, or in sexual promiscuity and immoral living, or in quarreling and jealousy. ROMANS 13:13

We are instructed to turn from godless living and sinful pleasures. We should live in this evil world with wisdom, righteousness, and devotion to God. TITUS 2:12

If you have committed yourself to following Jesus, your behavior should reflect his as much as possible. You can show modesty by avoiding wrong and indecent behavior and by serving others with grace and kindness.

Does being modest mean I shouldn't try to look nice?

Go ahead. Eat your food with joy, and drink your wine with a happy heart, for God approves of this! Wear fine clothes, with a splash of cologne! ECCLESIASTES 9:7-8

When you fast, comb your hair and wash your face. MATTHEW 6:17

Whatever you do or say, do it as a representative of the Lord Jesus, giving thanks through him to God the Father. COLOSSIANS 3:17

You should not be obsessed with your physical appearance, but neither should you ignore it. How you present yourself is, in part, a reflection of who you are and plays a role in your ability to interact with others. Your body is the house in which the Holy Spirit dwells, so you should keep up the place in which he lives. The more you keep yourself fit, the more energy you will have to serve him. Keeping your body clean and pleasant-looking provides more opportunities to become involved in others' lives and influence them with the good news of Jesus. However, dressing in a provocative way that tempts someone of the opposite sex or distracts others from seeing Jesus in you is immodest and inappropriate.

Can I show modesty and still have fun?

Go and celebrate with a feast . . . and share gifts of food with people who have nothing prepared. This is a sacred day. . . . Don't be dejected and sad, for the joy of the LORD is your strength! NEHEMIAH 8:10

The life of the godly is full of light and joy, but the light of the wicked will be snuffed out. PROVERBS 13:9

You have been faithful in handling this small amount. . . . Let's celebrate together! MATTHEW 25:21

Modesty is not about a lack of emotions, fun, or celebration. Joy, fun, and celebration, as God intended, are important parts of Christian faith because they lift your spirits and help you see the beauty and meaning in life. However, even in celebration, your appearance and conduct should not be provocative or inappropriate.

MONEY *See also* Debt, Generosity, Materialism, Stewardship, Tithing

Money is neither good nor bad, but simply a neutral medium of exchange. Throughout the Bible we read about money being earned, borrowed, and spent. However, money has come to represent wealth, power, and status. As such, it has a tendency to wield extraordinary power and control over our lives. The Bible warns us about the love of money. Then it is not neutral, but sinful. Jesus goes so far as to identify money as a potential rival to God (see Matthew 6:24). The Bible consistently teaches that money—like natural resources, material goods, or time itself—is ours to be used for the glory of God, not to take the place of God and distract us from doing his work.

What is a proper perspective toward money?

Wherever your treasure is, there the desires of your heart will also be. MATTHEW 6:21

The Bible mentions many wealthy people who loved God while saying nothing negative about the amount of wealth they owned (Abraham, David, Joseph of Arimathea, Lydia). Scripture doesn't focus on how much money you can or cannot have, but rather on what you do with it. Jesus made one thing clear: Wherever your money goes, your heart will follow after it. So work hard and succeed without guilt; but make sure to work just as hard at finding ways to please God with your money.

The LORD is my shepherd; I have all that I need. PSALM 23:1

Those who love money will never have enough. How meaningless to think that wealth brings true happiness! ECCLESIASTES 5:10

Money can cultivate a dangerous craving—the more you have, the more you want. It is a vicious cycle that never has a satisfactory conclusion. Keep reminding yourself that God must be first in your life and that money cannot satisfy your deepest needs.

Give me an eagerness for your laws rather than a love for money! PSALM 119:36

Don't love money; be satisfied with what you have. HEBREWS 13:5

Money is not the root of all evil; the love of it is!

[God] did all this so you would never say to yourself, "I have achieved this wealth with my own strength and energy." Remember the LORD your God. He is the one who gives you power to be successful. DEUTERONOMY 8:17-18

Wealth and prosperity should not be your goals, nor are they definitive signs of God's blessing—many who are poor are rich in other ways. Prosperity, when given by God, is to be received with gratitude and humility, and it is to be shared with gracious hospitality and generosity.

Trust in your money and down you go! PROVERBS 11:28

Too often we buy things to fill a void or a need in our lives. The Bible points to a way to acquire a deep and lasting happiness that always satisfies.

How can I best handle my money?

If someone has enough money to live well and sees a brother or sister in need but shows no compassion—how can God's love be in that person? 1 JOHN 3:17

Consistent and generous giving is one of the most effective ways to keep you from being greedy with your money. When your giving meets needs in the lives of others, you will find much deeper satisfaction than if you had spent the money on yourself.

Honor the LORD with your wealth and with the best part of everything you produce. Then he will fill your barns with grain. PROVERBS 3:9-10

"Bring all the tithes into the storehouse. . . . If you do," says the LORD of Heaven's Armies, "I will open the windows of heaven for you. I will pour out a blessing so great you won't have enough room to take it in! Try it! Put me to the test!" MALACHI 3:10

Instead of viewing money as yours, to use as you wish, see it as God's, to use as he wishes. Giving back to God the first part of everything you receive will help you maintain this perspective.

Fools spend whatever they get. PROVERBS 21:20

Give, and you will receive. LUKE 6:38

Properly handling money requires good stewardship in earning, giving, spending, and saving your money. God understands the importance of providing for the needs of your family and the future. But he also expects you to use your money generously to help others.

Teach those who are rich in this world not to be proud and not to trust in their money, which is so unreliable. Their trust should be in God, who richly gives us all we need for our enjoyment. Tell them to use their money to do good. They should be rich in good works and generous to those in need, always being ready to share with others. 1 TIMOTHY 6:17-18

You will be held accountable for how you use the money God has entrusted to you. Therefore you should use it in ways that honor God and help others. If you have children, teach them God's principles about earning money, giving generously, saving regularly, and spending responsibly. You should be motivated by knowing the link between how you use your money on earth and the corresponding rewards in heaven.

Why don't I ever seem to have enough?

A party gives laughter, wine gives happiness, and money gives everything!
ECCLESIASTES 10:19

It's human nature to believe that if you just had more money, you could be happier and fix almost any problem. But when you get more, you will want even more, and you will never seem to have enough.

Why spend your money on food that does not give you strength? ISAIAH 55:2

Review your finances. You might be surprised at how much you are spending on frivolous things you don't really need.

The LORD sent this message . . . "Why are you living in luxurious houses while my house lies in ruins?" HAGGAI 1:3-4

When you're not managing your money by God's priorities, you will feel as though you never have enough. God's priorities first ask: "Where can I help?" not, "What can I get?"

Beware! Guard against every kind of greed. Life is not measured by how much you own.
LUKE 12:15

You may be depending on your money to bring security. But this is false thinking. Your money is never secure on earth and can disappear suddenly. Only in heaven are your treasures completely secure.

Is debt a sin?

One of [the king's] debtors was brought in who owed him millions of dollars.
MATTHEW 18:24

In teaching on forgiveness, Jesus used this parable that seems to assume the lending or borrowing of money is not itself sinful.

Just as the rich rule the poor, so the borrower is servant to the lender. PROVERBS 22:7

Although borrowing money is not, in itself, sinful, you must be careful and wise when you borrow so you don't become a slave to debt. It is usually wise to avoid borrowing money unless you must.

Owe nothing to anyone. ROMANS 13:8

Although incurring debt may not be sinful, the failure to repay a debt is.

Will God provide for my financial needs?

Don't worry . . . saying, "What will we eat? What will we drink? What will we wear?"
These things dominate the thoughts of unbelievers, but your heavenly Father already
knows all your needs. Seek the Kingdom of God above all else, and live righteously, and
he will give you everything you need. MATTHEW 6:31-33

God knows your true needs and promises to supply them fully. Worry puts you in danger of denying, dismissing, or even not noticing God's love and care. You can overcome anxiety by reminding yourself how much God loves and cares for you.

I have learned how to be content with whatever I have. . . . I have learned the secret
of living in every situation. PHILIPPIANS 4:11-12

This same God who takes care of me will supply all your needs from his glorious riches,
which have been given to us in Christ Jesus. PHILIPPIANS 4:19

God promises to supply all of your needs, but the problem comes when your definition of "need" is different from God's. Studying God's Word will help you discover what God considers to be important to a fulfilling life.

What are the benefits of using my money as God directs?

The one who plants generously will get a generous crop. . . . "God loves a person
who gives cheerfully." And God will generously provide all you need. Then you will
always have everything you need and plenty left over to share with others.
2 CORINTHIANS 9:6-8

You should not give in order to get, but you might indeed receive when you give. When you are generous toward others, God is generous toward you.

Give freely and become more wealthy; be stingy and lose everything.
PROVERBS 11:24

God often blesses those who use money as a tool for his purposes. Those who hoard their money, using it only for themselves, never have enough.

Teach those who are rich in this world not to be proud and not to trust in their money,
which is so unreliable. Their trust should be in God. . . . Tell them to use their money to
do good. They should be rich in good works and generous to those in need, always being
ready to share with others. By doing this they will be storing up their treasure as a good
foundation for the future. 1 TIMOTHY 6:17-19

The only lasting investment comes from trusting God and investing in helping others. Money can be a tool for blessing or a trap for deception. Use the resources God has given you to do good for others.

MOTIVES *See also* Convictions, Decisions, Integrity

One person may give a thousand dollars to charity in order to earn a tax break; another may do it to win political favor; still another may act out of deep compassion for the poor. The same act can be set in motion by very different motives. The Bible teaches that God is more interested in our motives than in our behavior because eventually selfish and sinful motives produce selfish and sinful behavior.

As long as I do the right thing, what difference do my motives make?

I know, my God, that you examine our hearts and rejoice when you find integrity there. You know I have done all this with good motives, and I have watched your people offer their gifts willingly and joyously. 1 CHRONICLES 29:17

The sacrifice of an evil person is detestable, especially when it is offered with wrong motives. PROVERBS 21:27

Your motives are very important to God. The condition of your heart is essential to the condition of your relationship with God.

The LORD accepted Abel and his gift, but he did not accept Cain and his gift. GENESIS 4:4

It is quite likely that Cain's sacrifice was regarded as inappropriate because his motives were impure. When your motives are selfish, even seemingly right behavior can be seen as inappropriate.

Don't do your good deeds publicly, to be admired by others, for you will lose the reward from your Father in heaven. MATTHEW 6:1

Even when you ask, you don't get it because your motives are all wrong—you want only what will give you pleasure. JAMES 4:3

Wrong motives can hinder your prayers when selfishness rules your requests.

How can I have purer motives?

May the words of my mouth and the meditation of my heart be pleasing to you, O LORD, my rock and my redeemer. PSALM 19:14

My conscience is clear, but that doesn't prove I'm right. It is the Lord himself who will examine me and decide. 1 CORINTHIANS 4:4

Start by asking God to change the way you think by changing your heart. Ask him to reveal to you any area in which your motives are less than pure.

Learn to know the God of your ancestors intimately. Worship and serve him with your whole heart and a willing mind. For the LORD sees every heart and knows every plan and thought. 1 CHRONICLES 28:9

Your attitude toward God is a good indicator of your motives toward others. If you are halfhearted in the way you approach your relationship with God, chances are your motives toward others may be halfhearted and self-centered too.

We keep on praying for you, asking our God to enable you to live a life worthy of his call. May he give you the power to accomplish all the good things your faith prompts you to do. 2 THESSALONIANS 1:11

Welcome it when God tests your motives. This gives you an opportunity to grow.

People may be right in their own eyes, but the LORD examines their heart. PROVERBS 21:2

Before you do something, remember that God is as interested in your motives as he is in your actions.

What are some wrong motives?

Jealousy and selfishness are not God's kind of wisdom. Such things are earthly, unspiritual, and demonic. JAMES 3:15

If you let jealousy motivate you, your actions will be selfish and hurtful.

Saul thought, "I'll send [David] out against the Philistines and let them kill him rather than doing it myself." 1 SAMUEL 18:17

The words of the godly are a life-giving fountain; the words of the wicked conceal violent intentions. PROVERBS 10:11

If you are motivated to harm someone, you are being overcome by evil desires.

[The Israelites] come pretending to be sincere and sit before you. They listen to your words, but they have no intention of doing what you say. Their mouths are full of lustful words, and their hearts seek only after money. EZEKIEL 33:31

If your motives are not sincere and you are just trying to improve your position by pretending to be close to God, he is displeased.

Watch out! Don't do your good deeds publicly, to be admired by others, for you will lose the reward from your Father in heaven. MATTHEW 6:1

You shouldn't do good in order to be admired by people—you should do it to please God alone.

What are some right motives?

Tell the people of Israel to bring me their sacred offerings. Accept the contributions from all whose hearts are moved to offer them. EXODUS 25:2

He will delight in obeying the LORD. ISAIAH 11:3

To serve God simply because you want to.

Elijah said to Elisha, "Tell me what I can do for you before I am taken away." And Elisha replied, "Please let me inherit a double share of your spirit and become your successor." 2 KINGS 2:9

To follow the example of a godly person because you want to live a more godly life.

Give me the wisdom and knowledge to lead them properly, for who could possibly govern this great people of yours? 2 CHRONICLES 1:10

To grow in wisdom and knowledge in order to serve God more effectively.

A third time [Jesus] asked him, "Simon son of John, do you love me?" Peter . . . said, "Lord, you know everything. You know that I love you." Jesus said, "Then feed my sheep." JOHN 21:17

To help others out of love for Jesus, not out of a desire for personal praise or as a way to impress God.

Pay careful attention to your own work, for then you will get the satisfaction of a job well done, and you won't need to compare yourself to anyone else. GALATIANS 6:4

To do the right thing because it is right, not because it will benefit you or impress others.

MUSIC *See also* Abilities, Praise, Worship

Music is one of the most powerful and influential forms of expression, for it touches a part of us that words alone cannot reach. Singing, playing an instrument, or listening to any kind of music can unlock feelings and emotions deep within us and help us understand and express thoughts we could not otherwise. Music often defines what an entire culture is thinking and feeling, and it can even prompt change in a culture. In fact, generations are often defined by the music that was written by its people. Without music, we would miss a large part of communication that is important to acknowledge and express. But like so many things, music is a God-given gift that can be used for good or for harm. It can be used to honor God and point people to him, or it can dishonor God and move people to actions that are wrong and inappropriate. Music may be the most powerful language of our day, so we must work at understanding it.

Does God like music? Is he honored by it?

Write down the words of this song, and teach it to the people of Israel. Help them learn it. DEUTERONOMY 31:19

In this verse, God was telling Moses to write down his words in the form of a song. God himself was the lyricist.

The trumpeters and singers performed together in unison to praise and give thanks to the LORD. Accompanied by trumpets, cymbals, and other instruments, they raised their voices and praised the LORD with these words: "He is good! His faithful love endures forever!" At that moment a thick cloud filled the Temple of the LORD. The priests could not continue their service because of the cloud, for the glorious presence of the LORD filled the Temple of God. 2 CHRONICLES 5:13-14

God likes music and is certainly honored by musical worship. He came with his powerful presence and entered the newly constructed Temple during a time of musical worship.

For the LORD your God is living among you. . . . He will rejoice over you with joyful songs.
ZEPHANIAH 3:17

God created music—he himself sings!

Praise the LORD! How good to sing praises to our God! How delightful and how fitting!
PSALM 147:1

God delights when you use music to praise him.

What role does music play in worship?

David . . . appointed men . . . to proclaim God's messages to the accompaniment of lyres, harps, and cymbals. . . . Their responsibilities included the playing of cymbals, harps, and lyres at the house of God. . . . They and their families were all trained in making music before the LORD, and each of them—288 in all—was an accomplished musician.
1 CHRONICLES 25:1, 6-7

Throughout Scripture, music was used to worship the Lord. The fact that King David appointed so many musicians and singers to serve in the Temple testifies to the importance of music in worship. Through the beauty and harmony of music, we testify to the glory and majesty of God, and we express our thanks and praise for our Creator and Provider.

Moses and the people of Israel sang this song to the LORD: "I will sing to the LORD, for he has triumphed gloriously; he has hurled both horse and rider into the sea. The LORD is my strength and my song; he has given me victory. This is my God, and I will praise him—my father's God, and I will exalt him!" EXODUS 15:1-2

After God's mighty victory over the Egyptians, Moses, Miriam, and other Israelites composed a song of praise and worship to the Lord. Music played a central role in Israel's worship and has continued to play a central role in Christian worship. In addition to the joy of singing praise to God, songs are a powerful tool for teaching and remembering the truths of God. Often, worship causes music to well up within you, and music often causes worship to well up within you.

Sing! Beat the tambourine. Play the sweet lyre and the harp. Blow the ram's horn at new moon, and again at full moon to call a festival! For this is required by the decrees of Israel; it is a regulation of the God of Jacob. PSALM 81:2-4

David saw music as a required form of worship.

Praise him with a blast of the ram's horn; praise him with the lyre and harp! Praise him with the tambourine and dancing; praise him with strings and flutes! Praise him with a clash of cymbals; praise him with loud clanging cymbals. PSALM 150:3-5

Let the message about Christ, in all its richness, fill your lives. . . . Sing psalms and hymns and spiritual songs to God with thankful hearts. COLOSSIANS 3:16

Music energizes our praise of God.

What musical instruments are appropriate in a worship service?

For the dedication of the new wall of Jerusalem, the Levites throughout the land were asked to come to Jerusalem to assist in the ceremonies. They were to take part in the joyous occasion with their songs of thanksgiving and with the music of cymbals, harps, and lyres. . . . We went together with the trumpet-playing priests . . . and the singers. . . . They played and sang loudly under the direction of Jezrahiah the choir director.
NEHEMIAH 12:27, 41-42

Any instruments that help people praise God! The priests and Levites used percussion, strings, and brass. Psalm 150 expands this list. The question is not which instruments are appropriate for worship. The question, rather, is how can we most effectively energize a worshiping congregation to exalt the Lord "loudly" (Nehemiah 12:42). The Bible puts far more emphasis on exuberant praise to God than on what instruments are appropriate to offer the praise.

N,O

NEEDS *See also* Help, Provision, Responsibility, Satisfaction

All humans have basic needs that must be met in order to survive: food, water, shelter, and love. Needs are different from "wants" in that when our needs are met, we can be content and satisfied. Wants, even when fulfilled, can often leave us unsatisfied, discontent, and desiring more. Wants are not always negative but when they oppose God's desires they can become fuel for the fires of jealousy, covetousness, deceit, materialism, or other sins that result when we become obsessed with getting what we want. Our needs can often allow God to show his power and provision through us and teach us that God is sufficient. Learning to recognize the difference between needs and wants allows us to find contentment in living by God's sustaining power and provision.

What do I really need?

God blesses those who are poor and realize their need for him, for the Kingdom of Heaven is theirs. MATTHEW 5:3

> You need God—his love, his presence, his promise of eternal life.

[Jesus] is the kind of high priest we need because he is holy and blameless, unstained by sin. HEBREWS 7:26

> You need Jesus—his mercy, his forgiveness, and his salvation.

The apostles said to the Lord, "Show us how to increase our faith." LUKE 17:5
Hold up the shield of faith to stop the fiery arrows of the devil. EPHESIANS 6:16

> You need faith to stand firm in the face of temptation.

If you need wisdom, ask our generous God, and he will give it to you. He will not rebuke you for asking. JAMES 1:5

> You need God's wisdom so that you will do what is right, what is appropriate, and what is pleasing to him.

[The Lord] said, "My grace is all you need. My power works best in weakness." 2 CORINTHIANS 12:9

> You need God's strength to help you in times of weakness.

I know, O LORD, that your regulations are fair; you disciplined me because I needed it. PSALM 119:75

> You need the Lord's discipline to keep you following his ways.

So it is with Christ's body. We are many parts of one body, and we all belong to each other. ROMANS 12:5

> You need other Christians to encourage you and serve with you.

Does God really care about my daily needs?

I will be your God throughout your lifetime—until your hair is white with age. I made you, and I will care for you. ISAIAH 46:4

God will generously provide all you need. Then you will always have everything you need and plenty left over to share with others. 2 CORINTHIANS 9:8

You must learn to distinguish between wants and needs. When you understand what you truly need and see how God provides, you will realize how much he truly cares for you. God doesn't promise to give you a lot of possessions, but he does promise to help you possess the character traits that reflect his nature so that you can accomplish his plan for you. He doesn't promise to preserve your physical life, but he does promise to keep your soul for all eternity if you've pledged your allegiance to him.

The Lord is my shepherd; I have all that I need. PSALM 23:1

You have God's promise to love you and care for you. Just as a shepherd loves and cares for each one of his sheep, God loves and cares for you.

How do I keep clear distinctions between needs and wants?

I have learned how to be content with whatever I have. I know how to live on almost nothing or with everything. I have learned the secret of living in every situation, whether it is with a full stomach or empty, with plenty or little. PHILIPPIANS 4:11-12

If we have enough food and clothing, let us be content. 1 TIMOTHY 6:8

Don't love money; be satisfied with what you have. HEBREWS 13:5

You will never be content if you focus on your wants, because you will always want more. That is why the Lord promises to supply your needs, not your wants. The more you focus on what the Lord values, the more you will be able to distinguish your wants from your needs. If you constantly feel discontented, you may be focusing more on what you want than on what God knows is best for you.

How can I be sure my needs will be met?

If God is for us, who can ever be against us? Since he did not spare even his own Son but gave him up for us all, won't he also give us everything else? ROMANS 8:31-32

Your greatest need is God himself, and he offers a way for you to be with him forever. God takes great joy in helping you fulfill that need.

Let us come boldly to the throne of our gracious God. There we will receive his mercy, and we will find grace to help us when we need it most. HEBREWS 4:16

Don't hesitate to talk to God about your needs because he welcomes your requests.

God . . . will supply all your needs from his glorious riches, which have been given to us in Christ Jesus. PHILIPPIANS 4:19

God's resources far exceed your greatest needs.

Why does God promise to meet my needs?

God has given us everything we need for living a godly life. We have received all of this by coming to know him, the one who called us to himself by means of his marvelous glory and excellence. 2 PETER 1:3

When the Lord reaches out to supply your needs, you will grow in your trust of him. The problem comes when you look for your wants to be met and completely miss all the needs God is meeting in your life. As you learn to value God's priorities, you will learn not to be seduced by the world's.

One day a man from Baal-shalishah brought the man of God a sack of fresh grain and twenty loaves of barley bread made from the first grain of his harvest. Elisha said, "Give it to the people so they can eat." "What?" his servant exclaimed. "Feed a hundred people with only this?" But Elisha repeated, "Give it to the people so they can eat, for this is what the LORD says: Everyone will eat, and there will even be some left over!" And when they gave it to the people, there was plenty for all and some left over, just as the LORD had promised. 2 KINGS 4:42-44

God gives to you so that you will give to others. He is looking for servants through whom he can express his love and care.

NEGLECT *See also* Abandonment, Apathy, Laziness, Procrastination

Neglect, according to Webster's, is "a lack of due care and concern often resulting in an unintended injury to another." A neglected child, longing for the love of a parent, often suffers extreme emotional trauma. A neglected friend soon drifts away, and a neglected spouse becomes despondent and lonely. Just as tragic is when we neglect our heavenly Father. Patiently, persistently, lovingly, God extends his arms to us each day. But how often do we ignore his overtures? And ironically, in this case the person we hurt the most is ourself.

What can I do when I feel neglected?

Praise God, who did not ignore my prayer or withdraw his unfailing love from me. PSALM 66:20

While others may neglect you, God will never turn away from you. He promises to listen to you when you talk to him and will extend his unfailing love to you at all times.

Rejoice in his presence! PSALM 68:4

Come close to God, and God will come close to you. JAMES 4:8

You may often feel worthless or unlovable when you are neglected, but you must not let these feelings cause you to withdraw from the one who truly loves you the most. Only God can be trusted to keep his promise to never leave you.

What are the consequences of neglect?

Those who shut their ears to the cries of the poor will be ignored in their own time of need. PROVERBS 21:13

Laziness leads to a sagging roof; idleness leads to a leaky house. ECCLESIASTES 10:18

Neglecting your work and other responsibilities can be a sign of laziness. Neglecting those in need is a sign that you are not as passionate about serving God as you should be.

How can I prevent neglect?

"Lord, when did we ever see you hungry and feed you? Or thirsty and give you something to drink?" . . . And the King will say, . . . "When you did it to one of the least of these my brothers and sisters, you were doing it to me!" MATTHEW 25:37, 40

Look after each other so that none of you fails to receive the grace of God. HEBREWS 12:15

Don't forget to show hospitality to strangers. . . . Remember also those being mistreated. HEBREWS 13:2-3

There are so many needs. Begin by helping those people near you who are longing for help. Help those close to you—family and friends—and move out to help those in your church, your community, and even around the world.

How do I neglect God?

Let us not neglect our meeting together, as some people do, but encourage one another. HEBREWS 10:25

You neglect God when you neglect meeting together as a group of believers to worship him and serve one another.

Anyone who hears my teaching and doesn't obey it is foolish, like a person who builds a house on sand. MATTHEW 7:26

We must listen very carefully to the truth we have heard, or we may drift away from it. HEBREWS 2:1

You neglect God when you ignore his Word, the Bible.

What makes us think we can escape if we ignore this great salvation that was first announced by the Lord Jesus himself? HEBREWS 2:3

You neglect God when you ignore his offer of salvation.

Remember, it is sin to know what you ought to do and then not do it. JAMES 4:17

You neglect God when you ignore what you know is right, because you are neglecting God's commands for you.

NEIGHBORS *See also* Community, Fellowship, Love

Most of us think of our neighbors as the people who live next door or across the street. Jesus' teachings expand our neighborhood to include anyone around us who needs his love. This means that the people next to you on the plane, or your coworkers, or the homeless in your town are also your neighbors. It is also important to expand our neighborhood to people around the world who need the love of Christ. When we begin to view people we see or meet or even hear about as our neighbors, we can begin to establish the kind of relationships that allow us to share the love of Christ by offering a helping hand. How will you treat your neighbors today?

Who is my neighbor?

The man . . . asked Jesus, "And who is my neighbor?" Jesus replied with a story: "A Jewish man was traveling on a trip from Jerusalem to Jericho, and he was attacked by bandits. They stripped him of his clothes, beat him up, and left him half dead beside the road. By chance a priest came along . . . and passed him by. A Temple assistant walked over and . . . also passed by on the other side. Then a despised Samaritan came along, and when he saw the man, he felt compassion for him. The Samaritan . . . took care of him. . . . Now which of these three would you say was a neighbor to the man who was attacked by bandits?" Jesus asked. The man replied, "The one who showed him mercy." Then Jesus said, "Yes, now go and do the same." LUKE 10:29-37

Your neighbor is anyone around you who needs help, mercy, forgiveness, compassion, or friendship.

What are my responsibilities to my neighbor? How am I to love my neighbor?

If you see your neighbor's ox or sheep or goat wandering away, don't ignore your responsibility. Take it back to its owner. . . . Do the same if you find your neighbor's donkey, clothing, or anything else your neighbor loses. Don't ignore your responsibility. DEUTERONOMY 22:1-3

If you can help your neighbor now, don't say, "Come back tomorrow, and then I'll help you." PROVERBS 3:28

Help your neighbor in times of need.

Stop telling lies. Let us tell our neighbors the truth, for we are all parts of the same body. EPHESIANS 4:25

Be honest with your neighbor and always tell the truth, even when it is painful. Don't tell lies or gossip about your neighbor.

Do not seek revenge or bear a grudge against a fellow Israelite, but love your neighbor as yourself. LEVITICUS 19:18

The commandments say, "You must not commit adultery. You must not murder. You must not steal. You must not covet." These—and other such commandments—are summed up in this one commandment: "Love your neighbor as yourself." ROMANS 13:9

Never try to get back at your neighbor for some wrong they committed against you. Let the Lord deal with them.

You must not covet your neighbor's wife. You must not covet your neighbor's house or land, male or female servant, ox or donkey, or anything else that belongs to your neighbor. DEUTERONOMY 5:21

Don't covet what your neighbor has.

It is foolish to belittle one's neighbor; a sensible person keeps quiet. PROVERBS 11:12

Don't make fun of your neighbor.

Don't visit your neighbors too often, or you will wear out your welcome. PROVERBS 25:17

A loud and cheerful greeting early in the morning will be taken as a curse! PROVERBS 27:14

Respect your neighbor's time and privacy.

How should I live among my non-Christian neighbors?

Live wisely among those who are not believers, and make the most of every opportunity. Let your conversation be gracious and attractive so that you will have the right response for everyone. COLOSSIANS 4:5-6

Be careful to live properly among your unbelieving neighbors. Then even if they accuse you of doing wrong, they will see your honorable behavior, and they will give honor to God when he judges the world. 1 PETER 2:12

Treat your non-Christian neighbors with love and respect, live honorably and graciously before them, be an example of godliness, and refuse to condemn them. If they don't know God, why should you expect them to live as though they do? Instead of judging them, win them over with friendship.

O

OBEDIENCE *See also* Accountability, Following, Responsibility, Submission

From the six-year-old who leaves her game because her mother has called her in for dinner to the business executive who pays his taxes on time, we all live in a web of relationships dependent upon obedience to authority. Like a loving parent or a responsible government, God sets standards for our good and to protect us from evil and harm. God desires obedience motivated by love and trust, not by fear. Some people defy authority, but ironically obedience actually frees us to enjoy life as God intended because it keeps us from becoming entangled in or enslaved to harmful situations that cause us heartache. Even though God's commandments are sometimes difficult or don't make sense from our human perspective, obedience to him will always bring blessing, joy, and peace.

Is obedience to God really necessary, since I am saved by faith?

If you obey all [God's] decrees and commands . . . then all will go well with you.
DEUTERONOMY 6:2-3

The right thing to do is the smart thing to do. God's commandments are not burdensome obligations but pathways to joyful, meaningful, satisfying lives. God's call for your obedience is based on his own commitment to your well-being. Since God is the Creator of life, he knows how life is supposed to work. Obedience demonstrates your willingness to follow through on what he says is best and your trust that God's way is always best for you.

He is the faithful God who keeps his covenant for a thousand generations and lavishes his unfailing love on those who love him and obey his commands. DEUTERONOMY 7:9

If you love me, obey my commandments. JOHN 14:15

Obedience is the visible expression of your love. Sin is not so much about breaking a law as breaking God's heart.

[The corrupt and unbelieving] claim they know God, but they deny him by the way they live. They are detestable and disobedient, worthless for doing anything good. TITUS 1:16

If you are consistently disobedient to God, your claim to know him is meaningless.

Moses said, "This is what the LORD has commanded you to do so that the glory of the LORD may appear to you." LEVITICUS 9:6

Obedience to God brings you into fellowship with him.

In what ways does God want me to obey him?

Noah did everything exactly as God had commanded him. GENESIS 6:22

You must be careful to obey all the commands of the LORD your God, following his instructions in every detail. DEUTERONOMY 5:32

God wants you to do everything he asks of you. All of his commands are found in the Bible, God's Word to all people. Obedience is not about "generally" following God's commands, or following his instructions that suit you. True obedience is about following every detail of his commands to the best of your ability.

Samuel replied, "What is more pleasing to the LORD: your burnt offerings and sacrifices or your obedience to his voice? Listen! Obedience is better than sacrifice." 1 SAMUEL 15:22

Obedience to God involves listening to what he says and then doing it. Only when you truly listen will you know how to fully obey him.

Peter and the apostles replied, "We must obey God rather than any human authority." ACTS 5:29

Everyone must submit to governing authorities. For all authority comes from God, and those in positions of authority have been placed there by God. ROMANS 13:1

God also commands you to obey your leaders unless what they ask contradicts God's Word.

How will the Lord help me obey him?

Work hard to show the results of your salvation, obeying God with deep reverence and fear. For God is working in you, giving you the desire and the power to do what pleases him. PHILIPPIANS 2:12-13

When God requires something of you, God empowers you. God guides you into the ways that are best for you, then he gives you the power to live according to those ways.

If you love me, obey my commandments. And I will ask the Father, and he will give you another Advocate, who will never leave you. He is the Holy Spirit, who leads into all truth. JOHN 14:15-17

The power God gives you is his own Holy Spirit, who is also called Advocate. As an advocate, he comes alongside you not only to advise and support you, but actually to live and work in you. Even as the air you breathe empowers your physical body, so the Holy Spirit empowers your obedience.

If you look carefully into the perfect law that sets you free, and if you do what it says and don't forget what you heard, then God will bless you for doing it. JAMES 1:25

Following God's Word sets you free from slavery to sin and all its ugly consequences, so that you can be free to obey the Lord and enjoy all his wonderful blessings.

What does God promise to those who obey?

Oh, the joys of those who do not follow the advice of the wicked, or stand around with sinners, or join in with mockers. . . . They are like trees planted along the riverbank, bearing fruit each season. Their leaves never wither, and they prosper in all they do. PSALM 1:1-3

Obedience is the way to a fulfilling and productive life. When you obey, you have a clear conscience and uninterrupted fellowship with God.

The LORD will withhold no good thing from those who do what is right. PSALM 84:11

As a result of your ministry, [the poor] will give glory to God. For your generosity to them and to all believers will prove that you are obedient to the Good News of Christ. 2 CORINTHIANS 9:13

As a river flows freely through an unblocked channel, so God's grace and blessing flow through you when you follow his ways. When you obey God, your life becomes an open channel his love and mercy can flow through to others.

Does obedience to God get me into heaven?

No one will ever be made right with God by obeying the law. GALATIANS 2:16

Obedience to religious laws or rules is not what saves you for eternity. But when you believe in Jesus and decide to follow him, you are increasingly motivated to obey God out of love for him.

How does my disobedience hurt God? Does it really hurt me?

The people of Israel rebelled against me, and they refused to obey my decrees.... They wouldn't obey my regulations even though obedience would have given them life.... I made plans to utterly consume them in the wilderness. But again I held back in order to protect the honor of my name before the nations who had seen my power in bringing Israel out of Egypt. But I took a solemn oath against them in the wilderness. I swore I would not bring them into the land I had given them, a land flowing with milk and honey, the most beautiful place on earth. EZEKIEL 20:13-15

When the Bible talks about disobedience, it means a consistent lifestyle of ignoring God and a regular habit of disregarding what God says is right. Disobedience hurts God because he wants to give you a life full of good things. Ignoring him means that you don't care enough to know God or see what he has planned for you. It hurts you because when you disobey, you forfeit God's best for you and endanger not only your life on earth but your eternal future.

What if I have lived a life of disobedience?

The [criminal on a cross next to] Jesus protested, "... This man hasn't done anything wrong." Then he said, "Jesus, remember me when you come into your Kingdom." And Jesus replied, "I assure you, today you will be with me in paradise." LUKE 23:40-43

It's never too late to stop a life of disobedience to God and start a life of obedience to him. All it takes is to be genuinely sorry for your sins and ask God to forgive you based on Jesus' sacrifice on the cross for your sins.

How can I cultivate the discipline of obeying God?

Commit yourselves wholeheartedly to these words of mine. Tie them to your hands and wear them on your forehead as reminders. Teach them to your children. Talk about them when you are at home and when you are on the road, when you are going to bed and when you are getting up. Write them on the doorposts of your house and on your gates. DEUTERONOMY 11:18-20

Be earnest and disciplined in your prayers. 1 PETER 4:7

For most of us, it is difficult to make obedience a daily habit; we are often tempted to give in to those sins we enjoy the most. Here are four principles in the discipline of obedience: (1) Focus on Scripture by reading and meditating on it daily; (2) teach Scripture to others to motivate you to apply it to your own life; (3) talk about the Bible and spiritual topics every chance you get, telling others what God means to you; and (4) keep a spiritual diary or journal, writing down Scripture passages and what you learn from them. If you follow these four principles every day, you will come to love obedience and it will be part of your everyday life.

OPPORTUNITIES *See also* Challenges, Courage, Risk, Timing of God

In many ways our lives are defined by opportunities seized or missed. According to the Bible, we are to take advantage of opportunities by responding with bold action when we recognize them as God-given chances to participate in his purpose. At all times we must be prepared to recognize and act upon the opportunities that God creates for us to be used by and for him. However, the greatest opportunity is the gift of salvation that God allows us to receive for free if we believe and obey him. We should work hard to make others aware of this gift so they don't miss out on this greatest of opportunities.

How can I prepare for opportunities before they come?

[Jesus] said to his disciples, "The harvest is great, but the workers are few. So pray to the Lord . . . to send more workers into his fields." MATTHEW 9:37-38

Pray that God will prepare you to respond to opportunities as they become available.

Jesus replied, "My light will shine for you just a little longer. Walk in the light while you can, so the darkness will not overtake you." JOHN 12:35

To walk in the light means to stay as close to Jesus as you can through prayer, Bible study, and fellowship with other Christians. Walking in Christ's light will help you more clearly see the opportunities he sends you.

Philip ran over and heard the man reading from the prophet Isaiah. Philip asked, "Do you understand what you are reading?" ACTS 8:30

Make the most of every opportunity in these evil days. EPHESIANS 5:16

God regularly places "divine moments" right in front of us—opportunities to do good, help someone in need, or share what you know about God. Always be on the lookout for these opportunities to be a witness for your faith in word or deed. God will put them in front of you; you need to act on them.

How do I make the most of opportunities?

We must quickly carry out the tasks assigned us by the one who sent us. The night is coming, and then no one can work. JOHN 9:4

Because of my imprisonment, most of the believers here have gained confidence and boldly speak God's message without fear. PHILIPPIANS 1:14

When you see an opportunity to do good, jump on it. The more you think about it the less likely you are to act. Even when you are experiencing personal hardship, helping others can be therapeutic.

Give glory to the LORD your God before it is too late. Acknowledge him before he brings darkness upon you, causing you to stumble and fall on the darkening mountains. JEREMIAH 13:16

Now is the time to respond to God's call and get to know him and his purpose for you. You never know when it will be too late.

Midianite traders . . . sold Joseph to Potiphar. . . . Joseph . . . succeeded in everything he did. . . . This pleased Potiphar, so he . . . gave Joseph complete administrative responsibility over everything he owned. With Joseph there, he didn't worry about a thing. GENESIS 37:36; 39:2-6

Pharaoh sent for Joseph. . . . Pharaoh said to Joseph, "Since God has revealed the meaning of the dreams to you, clearly no one else is as intelligent or wise as you are. You will be in charge of my court, and all my people will take orders from you. Only I, sitting on my throne, will have a rank higher than yours." GENESIS 41:14, 39-40

I will be staying here at Ephesus until the Festival of Pentecost. There is a wide-open door for a great work here. 1 CORINTHIANS 16:8-9

Be willing to be flexible and change your plans in order to take advantage of an opportunity.

The believers who had been scattered during the persecution after Stephen's death traveled as far as Phoenicia, Cyprus, and Antioch of Syria. They preached the word of God. ACTS 11:19

See unexpected change or difficulty as an opportunity to serve God.

How do I know if an opportunity is from God?

Never stop praying. 1 THESSALONIANS 5:17

Stay close to God through prayer and ask for his guidance.

Be careful to obey all the instructions Moses gave you. Do not deviate from them, turning either to the right or to the left. Then you will be successful in everything you do. JOSHUA 1:7

Your word is a lamp to guide my feet and a light for my path. PSALM 119:105

The Bible will not always speak directly in favor of a particular opportunity, but any opportunity that contradicts God's Word or leads you away from its principles is not from the Lord.

Plans go wrong for lack of advice; many advisers bring success. PROVERBS 15:22

Seek the wisdom of trustworthy, mature Christians.

How can I face challenging, sometimes intimidating opportunities?

I can do everything through Christ, who gives me strength. PHILIPPIANS 4:13

Your ability to face challenges is directly proportional to your faith that God can help you. With his help you can make the most of every opportunity.

I know all the things you do, and I have opened a door for you that no one can close. REVELATION 3:8

You can trust that nothing will block you from fulfilling a particular opportunity God has for you. When God opens the door, it will stay open as long as he wants it open. But you must walk through it!

What does God promise to those who make the most of his opportunities?

To those who use well what they are given, even more will be given, and they will have an abundance. But from those who do nothing, even what little they have will be taken away. MATTHEW 25:29

God honors faithfulness in little things which leads to opportunities to be responsible for greater things.

OPPRESSION *See also* Abuse, Control, Power, Spiritual Warfare

Oppression is the abuse or exploitation of someone through the unjust use of power, and it's all too common. Employees taken advantage of by their bosses, racial minorities denied equal access to housing or jobs, political prisoners, children working in sweatshops, women kidnapped into prostitution, those terrorized by demons—all are the victims of oppression. The Bible provides help and hope to those who are oppressed as well as warnings of punishment to those who abuse or take advantage of others.

What is spiritual oppression?

We are not fighting against flesh-and-blood enemies, but against evil rulers and authorities of the unseen world, against mighty powers in this dark world, and against evil spirits in the heavenly places. EPHESIANS 6:12

Satan uses tactics of spiritual oppression to wear down believers until they are led into sin, and then controls them and keeps them from seeking God's help. When Satan has you under his control, you are spiritually oppressed. To defeat you, he focuses on your weak spots, those areas you refuse to give over to God. They are cracks in your spiritual armor at which he takes aim, the areas in which you compromise your convictions. You cannot fight Satan alone. You must use the armor God has given you. You must resist and fight, for you are in the middle of spiritual warfare and the battle is over the welfare of your very soul. So you must use every available weapon God provides for you. But God is a Warrior. He is always ready to fight on your behalf, always ready to come to your defense. But you must join God in the battle or you will be vulnerable and helpless to withstand the enemy. If you join, you are guaranteed victory.

How does God care for people who are oppressed?

He will rescue the poor when they cry to him; he will help the oppressed, who have no one to defend them. PSALM 72:12

God has a special place in his heart for those who are oppressed, and he comforts them in unique ways.

I will deal severely with all who have oppressed you. I will save the weak and helpless ones. ZEPHANIAH 3:19

God promises to judge and punish oppressors and to restore the oppressed.

The Spirit of the LORD *. . . has sent me to proclaim that captives will be released, that the blind will see, that the oppressed will be set free.* LUKE 4:18

Freeing the oppressed was a central component of Jesus' earthly ministry. Jesus came to deliver people who were oppressed by the world or the powers of evil. We see this in the Gospels as he delivered people from spiritual oppression to demons. He delivered them from physical oppression by healing their diseases. He delivered them from intellectual oppression by exposing lies and teaching the truth that sets us free. And he spoke boldly against the injustice of abusive leadership, especially against religious leaders. This is why salvation is also called deliverance. Jesus can deliver you not only from the consequences of your sins, but from those forces that oppress you in this world.

He has brought down princes from their thrones and exalted the humble. LUKE 1:52

When Jesus returns, he will put an end to oppression forever.

What does God call me to do about oppression?

Away with your noisy hymns of praise! I will not listen to the music of your harps. Instead, I want to see a mighty flood of justice, an endless river of righteous living.
AMOS 5:23-24

God urges you to recognize that justice is central to godly living. Wonderful worship and pious prayer are exposed as hypocrisy if they are not accompanied by opposing oppression and aiding the oppressed.

This is what the Sovereign LORD *says: "Enough, you princes of Israel! Stop your violence and oppression and do what is just and right."* EZEKIEL 45:9

Refuse to participate in any form of oppression. Be willing, in whatever way you can, to call those in power to account.

Give your love of justice to the king, O God, and righteousness to the king's son. . . . Help him to defend the poor, to rescue the children of the needy, and to crush their oppressors.
PSALM 72:1, 4

Pray that your leaders will protect the weak and punish any who oppress them. Pray for the leaders of other countries to be fair and just, and to refuse to oppress any of their people.

When you are harvesting your crops and forget to bring in a bundle of grain from your field, don't go back to get it. Leave it for the foreigners, orphans, and widows. Then the LORD *your God will bless you in all you do. When you beat the olives from your olive trees, don't go over the boughs twice. Leave the remaining olives for the foreigners, orphans, and widows. When you gather the grapes in your vineyard, don't glean the vines after they are picked. Leave the remaining grapes for the foreigners, orphans, and widows. Remember that you were slaves in the land of Egypt. That is why I am giving you this command.* DEUTERONOMY 24:19-22

Right now you have plenty and can help those who are in need. Later, they will have plenty and can share with you when you need it. In this way, things will be equal. As the Scriptures say, "Those who gathered a lot had nothing left over, and those who gathered only a little had enough." 2 CORINTHIANS 8:14-15

Throughout the Old Testament, God commands his people to treat the poor with compassion and justice. The powerless and poverty-stricken are often looked upon as incompetent and lazy when, in reality, many are victims of oppression and circumstance. God's people were instructed to leave some of their harvest in the fields so that the poor could have enough to eat. While not many of us harvest fields every year, we do have a God-given responsibility to share from our abundance to minister to the needs of the poor and outcast.

OUTSIDERS *See also* Differences, Prejudice, Rejection

We feel like an outsider when we lack a sense of belonging, when we feel we have no place or value within a specific group. When we feel like we belong to something—a family, club, school, church, city, neighborhood, or nation—we feel more like an insider. There are many reasons why, at certain times, we feel we don't belong, but we can be sure we have a special place and great value in the family of God—the most important place we can belong.

How does God treat outsiders?

The Sovereign LORD, *who brings back the outcasts of Israel, says: "I will bring others, too, besides my people Israel."* ISAIAH 56:8

God includes "outsiders" in his love. "Outsiders" become "insiders." He cares for and protects them. No one is excluded from God's love.

How should I treat outsiders?

Share your food with the hungry, and give shelter to the homeless. Give clothes to those who need them, and do not hide from relatives who need your help. ISAIAH 58:7

You are being faithful to God when you care for the traveling teachers who pass through, even though they are strangers to you. They have told the church here of your loving friendship. Please continue providing for such teachers in a manner that pleases God. 3 JOHN 1:5-6

Outsiders have the same basic physical needs for shelter, clothing, and sustenance as everyone else. Begin by helping to meet these needs. Then, through those relationships, you may be able to discover and minister to their emotional and spiritual needs as well.

I have never turned away a stranger but have opened my doors to everyone. JOB 31:32

Don't forget to show hospitality to strangers, for some who have done this have entertained angels without realizing it! HEBREWS 13:2

Treat outsiders with hospitality.

When you harvest the crops of your land, do not harvest the grain along the edges of your fields, and do not pick up what the harvesters drop. Leave it for the poor and the foreigners living among you. LEVITICUS 23:22

Treat outsiders thoughtfully and generously. Think about how you can use your resources (money, time, skills) to help those on the outside feel accepted and cared for.

I was a father to the poor and assisted strangers who needed help. JOB 29:16

Treat outsiders fairly, justly, and not oppressively. Justice and fair treatment should not be based on social status.

Call them all together—men, women, children, and the foreigners living in your towns—so they may hear this Book of Instruction and learn to fear the LORD your God and carefully obey all the terms of these instructions. DEUTERONOMY 31:12

Include outsiders in worship and share God's good news with them. Assist them in finding God's love and acceptance.

How should I handle being an outsider?

I warn you as "temporary residents and foreigners" to keep away from worldly desires that wage war against your very souls. 1 PETER 2:11

As a Christian you are an "outsider" in this world—your real home is heaven. But on your journey you do have fellow travelers. Through your friendship and accountability, you can encourage each other to obey God.

What blessings await you when people hate you and exclude you and mock you and curse you as evil because you follow the Son of Man. LUKE 6:22

Consider your earthly "outsider" status to be a blessing, not a curse. You can look forward to receiving God's eternal blessing even though you may endure ridicule on earth.

Are there any outsiders in the Kingdom of God?

[The king] said to his servants, "The wedding feast is ready, and the guests I invited aren't worthy of the honor. Now go out to the street corners and invite everyone you see." So the servants brought in everyone they could find, good and bad alike, and the banquet hall was filled with guests. MATTHEW 22:8-10

Everyone who calls on the name of the LORD will be saved. ROMANS 10:13

You Gentiles are no longer strangers and foreigners. You are citizens along with all of God's holy people. You are members of God's family. EPHESIANS 2:19

God does not show preference or favoritism among people. All are invited to be part of his family and live eternally in the Kingdom of Heaven. He welcomes everyone who believes Jesus is the Son of God. But those who don't accept the invitation will remain on the outside forever.

OVERCOMING *See also* Challenges, Courage, Perseverance, Victory

Overwhelmed. Defeated. Powerless. Out of control. Sometimes we feel like there's no way to overcome our circumstances. We are confronted by immense obstacles and invincible opponents. But take heart! Overcoming is the birthright of believers. When Jesus won the ultimate victory by overcoming sin, death, and Satan, he brought hope that we can live triumphantly, too.

How do I overcome obstacles in my life?

I am the LORD, the God of all the peoples of the world. Is anything too hard for me?
JEREMIAH 32:27

Most importantly, know God. He enjoys making the impossible happen.

The ropes of death entangled me; floods of destruction swept over me. The grave wrapped its ropes around me; death laid a trap in my path. But in my distress I cried out to the LORD; yes, I prayed to my God for help. He heard me from his sanctuary; my cry to him reached his ears. PSALM 18:4-6

As soon as I pray, you answer me; you encourage me by giving me strength. PSALM 138:3

Prayer—honestly talking with and intentionally listening to God—helps you face and overcome life's obstacles. Prayer allows God, who has no limits, to work in your situation.

The people of Judah began to complain, "The workers are getting tired, and there is so much rubble to be moved. We will never be able to build the wall by ourselves." Meanwhile, our enemies were saying, "Before they know what's happening, we will swoop down on them and kill them and end their work." NEHEMIAH 4:10-11

The wall was finished—just fifty-two days after we had begun. When our enemies and the surrounding nations heard about it, they were frightened and humiliated. They realized this work had been done with the help of our God. NEHEMIAH 6:15-16

The balance between waiting patiently on God and "building the wall" is courageous obedience to what God calls you to do one day at a time. You may think you can't do the big work God has planned for you, but you can do the little tasks for God today while you wait for him to show you the way. In taking those small steps of obedience each day, you may find you have been building a great work for him one stone at a time.

Let us run with endurance the race God has set before us. We do this by keeping our eyes on Jesus, the champion who initiates and perfects our faith. Because of the joy awaiting him, he endured the cross, disregarding its shame. Now he is seated in the place of honor beside God's throne. Think of all the hostility he endured from sinful people; then you won't become weary and give up. After all, you have not yet given your lives in your struggle against sin. HEBREWS 12:1-4

Having Jesus as your example to follow helps you overcome obstacles. "What would Jesus do?" is more than a cliché; it is a good perspective to take on life's problems.

Be strong and very courageous. Be careful to obey all the instructions Moses gave you. Do not deviate from them, turning either to the right or to the left. Then you will be successful in everything you do. JOSHUA 1:7

David [said] to the Philistine, "You come to me with sword, spear, and javelin, but I come to you in the name of the LORD of Heaven's Armies—the God of the armies of Israel, whom you have defied. Today the LORD will conquer you." 1 SAMUEL 17:45-46

You will have courage to overcome when you are obedient and firm in your faith. Then you can be confident that God is with you and wants to help you.

We are human, but we don't wage war as humans do. We use God's mighty weapons, not worldly weapons, to knock down the strongholds. 2 CORINTHIANS 10:3-4

Be strong in the Lord and in his mighty power. Put on all of God's armor so that you will be able to stand firm against all strategies of the devil. . . . Put on every piece of God's armor so you will be able to resist the enemy in the time of evil. Then after the battle you will still be standing firm. Stand your ground, putting on the belt of truth and the body armor of God's righteousness. EPHESIANS 6:10-14

Every child of God defeats this evil world, and we achieve this victory through our faith. And who can win this battle against the world? Only those who believe that Jesus is the Son of God. 1 JOHN 5:4-5

The devil specializes in putting obstacles in your path. God specializes in helping you overcome them. He equips you to do this with his truth, his righteousness, his peace, his Word, and his gift of salvation.

Lead me in the right path, O LORD, or my enemies will conquer me. Make your way plain for me to follow. PSALM 5:8

You can overcome some obstacles simply by avoiding them when you see them ahead. Living by God's rules will keep you alert to potential obstacles. How often we see an obstacle, and then keep moving right toward it, not believing it could be very dangerous.

What are the traits of an overcomer?

Joseph . . . did as the angel of the Lord commanded and took Mary as his wife. MATTHEW 1:24

An overcomer walks with God in obedience.

When our enemies heard that we knew of their plans and that God had frustrated them, we all returned to our work on the wall. NEHEMIAH 4:15

We can rejoice . . . when we run into problems and trials, for we know that they help us develop endurance. ROMANS 5:3

We are pressed on every side by troubles, but we are not crushed. We are perplexed, but not driven to despair. 2 CORINTHIANS 4:8

An overcomer has the endurance to finish the task before him or her.

I lay down and slept, yet I woke up in safety, for the LORD was watching over me. I am not afraid of ten thousand enemies who surround me on every side. PSALM 3:5-6

God is our refuge and strength, always ready to help in times of trouble. So we will not fear when earthquakes come and the mountains crumble into the sea. PSALM 46:1-2

I am leaving you with a gift—peace of mind and heart. And the peace I give is a gift the world cannot give. So don't be troubled or afraid. JOHN 14:27

An overcomer has peace, even in the middle of hard circumstances.

Are there certain things I'll never overcome? How do I deal with that?

Sin is the sting that results in death, and the law gives sin its power. But thank God! He gives us victory over sin and death through our Lord Jesus Christ. 1 CORINTHIANS 15:56-57

You can never overcome sin by yourself. It is too powerful. Only because Jesus died on the cross for your sins can you overcome sin.

Do not let sin control the way you live; do not give in to sinful desires. Do not let any part of your body become an instrument of evil to serve sin. Instead, give yourselves completely to God, for you were dead, but now you have new life. ROMANS 6:12-13

You cannot overcome your fallen human nature on your own; you need the power of God and his Holy Spirit.

OVERREACTION See also Anger, Emotions, Temper, Self-Control

"I can't believe you did that! What were you thinking?" All too often we jump to conclusions, making assumptions we later learn were wrong. When we overreact, we say and do things we regret, causing hurt and pain to ourselves and others. In extreme cases, like war, overreacting can cost thousands of lives. Sometimes we might wish we had an angel on our shoulder giving us advice and reminding us to use more self-control. God has given us something even better, the Holy Spirit, to be our ever-present Advocate. The Bible promises that when we allow the Holy Spirit to work in us, the result is peace, patience, gentleness, and self-control (see Galatians 5:22-23). And when we do overreact, the Holy Spirit gives us the humility and courage to apologize and prevent hard feelings from escalating into open conflict.

What can cause me to overreact?

Abimelech called for Abraham. "What have you done to us?" he demanded. . . . "No one should ever do what you have done! Whatever possessed you to do such a thing?" Abraham replied, "I thought, 'This is a godless place. They will want my wife and will kill me to get her.'" GENESIS 20:9-11

Not trusting God or basing your actions and reactions on assumptions and fears can cause you to overreact. Basing your actions on truth brings a more accurate and acceptable response.

The men of Dan said, "Watch what you say! There are some short-tempered men around here who might get angry and kill you and your family." JUDGES 18:25

Having an impatient or short-tempered disposition can cause you to overreact.

When Haman saw that Mordecai would not bow down or show him respect, he was filled with rage. He had learned of Mordecai's nationality, so he decided it was not enough to lay hands on Mordecai alone. Instead, he looked for a way to destroy all the Jews throughout the entire empire of Xerxes. ESTHER 3:5-6

Pride can cause you to overreact. When you have an inflated ego, you will do just about anything to protect its image.

The LORD accepted Abel and his gift, but he did not accept Cain and his gift. This made Cain very angry . . . and while they were in the field, Cain attacked his brother, Abel, and killed him. GENESIS 4:4-5, 8

[The Israelite women sang:] "Saul has killed his thousands, and David his ten thousands!" This made Saul very angry. "What's this?" he said. "They credit David with ten thousands and me with only thousands. Next they'll be making him their king!" So from that time on Saul kept a jealous eye on David. 1 SAMUEL 18:7-9

Basing your actions and reactions on unhealthy emotions such as fear, jealousy, hatred, and anger can cause you to overreact. Good emotions like love and joy can also cause you to overreact, too. Be careful that the passions of the moment don't cloud your judgment. Instead, try to rely on what you've learned from God's Word, wise advice, and life experience.

How does it affect other people when I overreact?

"How could you do this to us?" Abimelech exclaimed. "One of my people might easily have taken your wife and slept with her, and you would have made us guilty of great sin." GENESIS 26:10

Jacob's sons . . . plundered the town because their sister had been defiled there. . . . Afterward Jacob said to Simeon and Levi, "You have ruined me! You've made me stink among all the people of this land." GENESIS 34:27, 30

Overreacting can hurt others physically, emotionally, and spiritually. Remember that your actions can begin a chain of rash behavior in others. Think before you talk or act.

How can I avoid overreacting?

The rest of Israel heard that the people of Reuben, Gad, and the half-tribe of Manasseh had built an altar at Geliloth at the edge of the land of Canaan. . . . So the whole community of Israel gathered at Shiloh and prepared to go to war against them. First, however, they sent a delegation led by Phinehas. JOSHUA 22:11-13

Make sure you understand the facts before reacting. If you can resist acting until you've considered the facts, there is a good chance you will react appropriately.

A gentle answer deflects anger, but harsh words make tempers flare. PROVERBS 15:1

A truly wise person uses few words; a person with understanding is even-tempered. PROVERBS 17:27

Be quick to listen, slow to speak, and slow to get angry. JAMES 1:19

Be quick to listen and slow to speak. When a verbal reaction is required, speak with control and wisdom to diffuse an argument rather than stir up passionate emotions in others.

Don't say, "I will get even for this wrong." Wait for the LORD to handle the matter. PROVERBS 20:22

Never pay back evil with more evil. Do things in such a way that everyone can see you are honorable. ROMANS 12:17

He did not retaliate when he was insulted, nor threaten revenge when he suffered. He left his case in the hands of God, who always judges fairly. 1 PETER 2:23

Avoid revenge at all costs; it always makes things worse and demonstrates that you are just as bent on harm as the other party.

The Holy Spirit produces this kind of fruit in our lives: love, joy, peace, patience, kindness, goodness, faithfulness, gentleness, and self-control. GALATIANS 5:22-23

Allow the Holy Spirit to influence your reactions so they will have the greatest positive effect.

"Just kill me now, LORD! I'd rather be dead than alive if what I predicted will not happen." The LORD replied, "Is it right for you to be angry about this? . . . Nineveh has more than 120,000 people living in spiritual darkness, not to mention all the animals. Shouldn't I feel sorry for such a great city?" JONAH 4:3-4, 11

Work to keep a proper perspective. Overreaction puts too much emphasis on yourself and not enough on God, whom you should trust to help you through those situations that don't seem fair or right to you.

OVERWHELMED *See also* Crisis, Pain, Trouble, Overcoming

To be overwhelmed is to feel paralyzed and powerless, like a heavy object sinking in a great ocean of hopelessness. Many things can cause us to feel overwhelmed: when we are worn out, when we're afraid, when there's too much work to do and not enough time, when we feel guilty, when we're grieving. It's overwhelming enough just to deal with the stresses and problems of the day and our immediate circumstances, but if we could look into the future we would be overwhelmed at all the obstacles we have yet to face. The waters of trouble, grief, or stress often trick us into thinking there is no way up or out. God promises to be with us, guiding, comforting, energizing, and restoring hope.

How does God help me when I am overwhelmed?

Nothing can ever separate us from God's love. Neither death nor life, neither angels nor demons, neither our fears for today nor our worries about tomorrow—not even the powers of hell can separate us from God's love. No power in the sky above or in the earth below—indeed, nothing in all creation will ever be able to separate us from the love of God that is revealed in Christ Jesus our Lord. ROMANS 8:38-39

God's love is certain, consistent, ever-present, and victorious. Are you feeling overwhelmed? God's love can overcome whatever overwhelms you.

God is our refuge and strength, always ready to help in times of trouble. So we will not fear when earthquakes come and the mountains crumble into the sea. PSALM 46:1-2

I am leaving you with a gift—peace of mind and heart. And the peace I give is a gift the world cannot give. So don't be troubled or afraid. JOHN 14:27

God's presence gives you peace of mind and heart in overwhelming situations. God's presence can overcome whatever overwhelms you.

If your instructions hadn't sustained me with joy, I would have died in my misery. I will never forget your commandments, for by them you give me life. PSALM 119:92-93

God's Word brings deep joy and contentment in the midst of overwhelming circumstances. God's Word will overcome whatever overwhelms you.

I cry out to the LORD; I plead for the LORD's mercy. I pour out my complaints before him and tell him all my troubles. When I am overwhelmed, you alone know the way I should turn. PSALM 142:1-3

Prayer—honestly talking and listening to God—keeps you in touch with the one whose help you need most. Prayer will overcome whatever overwhelms you.

Wait patiently for the LORD. Be brave and courageous. Yes, wait patiently for the LORD. PSALM 27:14

He gives power to the weak and strength to the powerless. Even youths will become weak and tired, and young men will fall in exhaustion. But those who trust in the LORD will find new strength. They will soar high on wings like eagles. They will run and not grow weary. They will walk and not faint. ISAIAH 40:29-31

When your troubles are overwhelming, continue to look to God and his power to help you. Bravely keep your focus on God, and patiently watch him work. God's power will overcome whatever overwhelms you.

How can I avoid becoming overwhelmed?

Jesus . . . said, "Humanly speaking, it is impossible. But with God everything is possible." MATTHEW 19:26

All glory to God, who is able, through his mighty power at work within us, to accomplish infinitely more than we might ask or think. EPHESIANS 3:20

I can do everything through Christ, who gives me strength. PHILIPPIANS 4:13

Let God put your situation in perspective. There is no problem too big for God. Run to him for comfort and help, and watch him work wonders in your life.

It is not by force nor by strength, but by my Spirit, says the LORD of Heaven's Armies. Nothing, not even a mighty mountain, will stand in Zerubbabel's way; it will become a level plain before him! And when Zerubbabel sets the final stone of the Temple in place, the people will shout: "May God bless it! May God bless it!" ZECHARIAH 4:6-7

Zerubbabel had the overwhelming assignment of rebuilding the Temple in Jerusalem. He completed the task, not by force or by strength, but by God's Spirit. Find strength and power in God living through you; he gloriously overcomes your weaknesses.

Select from all the people some capable, honest men who fear God and hate bribes. Appoint them as leaders over groups of one thousand, one hundred, fifty, and ten. . . . They will help you carry the load, making the task easier for you. If you follow this advice, and if God commands you to do so, then you will be able to endure the pressures." EXODUS 18:21-23

As the time of King David's death approached, he gave this charge to his son Solomon: "I am going where everyone on earth must someday go. Take courage and be a man. Observe the requirements of the LORD your God, and follow all his ways. Keep the decrees, commands, regulations, and laws written in the Law of Moses so that you will be successful in all you do and wherever you go." 1 KINGS 2:1-3

Often the most difficult tasks can be accomplished by consulting God, seeking godly counsel, and then dividing up the task and delegating responsibilities to others. Moses and Solomon both found this to be true in their overwhelming situations.

Why am I discouraged? Why is my heart so sad? I will put my hope in God! I will praise him again—my Savior and my God! Now I am deeply discouraged, but I will remember you. PSALM 42:5-6

When you are overwhelmed, thank God anyway. Praising him for his goodness and power takes your focus off your problems and weaknesses, and reminds you of his ability to handle everything that troubles you.

P

PAIN *See also* Brokenness, Discouragement, Sadness, Suffering

From betrayal, neglect, and abandonment to breaking an arm or failing health—the end result is some kind of emotional or physical pain. When we look back on our lives, we can all remember the physical tension of our aching bodies or the chest-tightening ache that comes from a broken heart. Our greatest hope in times of pain is finding healing from God. Although he does not promise to remove our pain in this life, God does promise to be with us in it and give us hope and purpose in the despair of our aching bodies and souls. And most importantly, God promises to remove our pain forever in eternity.

How does God help me deal with my pain?

Give your burdens to the LORD, and he will take care of you. He will not permit the godly to slip and fall. PSALM 55:22

It is easier to deal with pain when someone is helping you through it, and who better to help than God? This verse is not saying that God will keep you from experiencing pain, but that he will keep you from being defeated by it if you go to him for help and healing. Place your pain on his shoulders so he can help you bear it.

LORD, you know the hopes of the helpless. Surely you will hear their cries and comfort them. PSALM 10:17

God blesses those who mourn, for they will be comforted. MATTHEW 5:4

God listens, loves, blesses, and comforts when we are in pain. While others do this inconsistently, God is unfailing.

The LORD nurses them when they are sick and restores them to health. PSALM 41:3

He heals the brokenhearted and bandages their wounds. PSALM 147:3

God can heal any pain, be it a broken body or a broken heart. As you wait for God's healing, believe that he can and will one day take it all away, whether he does so in this life or in heaven.

In all their suffering he also suffered, and he personally rescued them. In his love and mercy he redeemed them. He lifted them up and carried them through all the years. ISAIAH 63:9

Since he himself has gone through suffering and testing, he is able to help us when we are being tested. HEBREWS 2:18

God feels your pain. He knows what you are going through and is therefore the best one to help you.

Look! He has placed the land in front of you. Go and occupy it as the LORD, the God of your ancestors, has promised you. Don't be afraid! Don't be discouraged! DEUTERONOMY 1:21

Let's not get tired of doing what is good. At just the right time we will reap a harvest of blessing if we don't give up. GALATIANS 6:9

When you feel discouraged, it is easy to turn inward and become paralyzed by your own feelings and pain. It takes great effort, but refocus your attention on God. Every day he opens doors of opportunity that can bring purpose and meaning to you: helping someone in need, giving time to a good cause, writing a note of encouragement. When you lift your eyes from the ground, you will see the door God has opened. Walk through it with courage, and on the other side you will find great encouragement.

What will help to heal my pain?

Since Christ suffered physical pain, you must arm yourselves with the same attitude he had, and be ready to suffer, too. For if you have suffered physically for Christ, you have finished with sin. You won't spend the rest of your lives chasing your own desires, but you will be anxious to do the will of God. 1 PETER 4:1-2

Develop a godly perspective toward pain. This helps you focus less on the pain itself (which can cause bitterness and discouragement) and more on how this pain can help you develop stronger character and greater sensitivity to others who may be hurting.

Come quickly, LORD, and answer me, for my depression deepens. Don't turn away from me, or I will die. Let me hear of your unfailing love each morning, for I am trusting you. Show me where to walk, for I give myself to you. PSALM 143:7-8

Acknowledge your pain honestly to God in prayer. This is how you begin the process of healing.

The king was overcome with emotion. He went up to the room over the gateway and burst into tears. And as he went, he cried, "O my son Absalom! My son, my son Absalom! If only I had died instead of you! O Absalom, my son, my son." 2 SAMUEL 18:33

Express your pain and don't try to keep it in. Expression is healing and brings relief.

I weep with sorrow; encourage me by your word. . . . Your promise revives me; it comforts me in all my troubles. . . . I meditate on your age-old regulations; O LORD, they comfort me. . . . If your instructions hadn't sustained me with joy, I would have died in my misery. PSALM 119:28, 50-52, 92

Immerse yourself in God's Word and find encouragement, revival, comfort, and joy.

The heartfelt counsel of a friend is as sweet as perfume and incense. PROVERBS 27:9

To one person the Spirit gives the ability to give wise advice; to another the same Spirit gives a message of special knowledge. 1 CORINTHIANS 12:8

Seek help from godly counselors. Sometimes it is enough to get advice from trusted friends and family. At other times it is necessary to talk with a trained counselor who can help you pinpoint your pain and provide effective ways, in accordance with God's Word, to deal with it.

If another believer sins, rebuke that person; then if there is repentance, forgive. Even if that person wrongs you seven times a day and each time turns again and asks forgiveness, you must forgive. LUKE 17:3-4

Forgiving those who have sinned against you does wonders in removing the pain of hurt, anger, and bitterness in your heart.

How is pain good for me? What can I learn from it?

[The Lord says] "Don't tear your clothing in your grief, but tear your hearts instead." Return to the LORD your God, for he is merciful and compassionate, slow to get angry and filled with unfailing love. He is eager to relent and not punish. JOEL 2:13

I am not sorry that I sent that severe letter to you, though I was sorry at first, for I know it was painful to you for a little while. Now I am glad I sent it, not because it hurt you, but because the pain caused you to repent and change your ways. . . . For the kind of sorrow God wants us to experience leads us away from sin and results in salvation. There's no regret for that kind of sorrow. 2 CORINTHIANS 7:8-10

Pain can be redemptive. Your broken heart can lead you to God through the recognition, confession, and repentance of sin.

Three different times I begged the Lord to take it away. Each time he said, "My grace is all you need. My power works best in weakness." So now I am glad to boast about my weaknesses, so that the power of Christ can work through me.
2 CORINTHIANS 12:8-9

Pain can reveal God's power. Pain is sometimes a symptom of a weakness in your life, which might be no fault of your own. But God's power works best through our weaknesses. Let God work through your weakness so that your pain can showcase his power.

Jesus said, "Come to me, all of you who are weary and carry heavy burdens, and I will give you rest." MATTHEW 11:28

Pain can bring you closer to God when you turn to him with your hurt.

When troubles come your way, consider it an opportunity for great joy. For you know that when your faith is tested, your endurance has a chance to grow. So let it grow, for when your endurance is fully developed, you will be perfect and complete, needing nothing.
JAMES 1:2-4

Pain can strengthen your character by testing your faith in God and your ability to endure faithfully through troublesome situations.

He comforts us in all our troubles so that we can comfort others. When they are troubled, we will be able to give them the same comfort God has given us. 2 CORINTHIANS 1:4

Pain equips you to comfort others. Remembering how God comforted you in the midst of your pain will help you extend the same care to others.

If I am in debilitating pain, what can give me hope?

Let me reveal to you a wonderful secret. We will not all die, but we will all be transformed! . . . Those who have died will be raised to live forever. And we who are living will also be transformed. For our dying bodies must be transformed into bodies that will never die; our mortal bodies must be transformed into immortal bodies. 1 CORINTHIANS 15:51-53

He will wipe every tear from their eyes, and there will be no more death or sorrow or crying or pain. All these things are gone forever. REVELATION 21:4

You will one day be like Christ. You will not be equal to him in power and authority, but you will be like him in character and perfection, for there will be no sin in those of us God welcomes into heaven. You will never again be in pain or experience sorrow, and evil will be gone forever.

PANIC *See also* Courage, Crisis, Fear, Peace

A mother loses her child in a crowded shopping mall, a teenager feels his car spin out of control on an icy road, a single mom loses her job when a stack of bills is due, a homeowner hears someone break into his house in the middle of the night. Each of these experiences instantly creates a feeling of panic. Panic makes our heart pound in our chest and freezes our mind from thinking. Panic is physically and emotionally paralyzing—it is where worry and fear meet an instant crisis. We've had no time to prepare for it and we're too frozen with fear to deal with it. The closer you are to God, the more you can tap into his courage and peace when panic strikes. Then you will have a clear head and be able to act with purpose.

What causes panic?

Live no longer as the Gentiles do, for they are hopelessly confused. EPHESIANS 4:17

Living life without God will eventually cause panic and confusion because you can't see purpose to your problems or a future beyond this life. When you believe that God is in control of your life, you know he holds it together. Then, if one or two pieces fall out of place, you will not panic that your whole life is falling apart.

A cry was heard in Ramah—weeping and great mourning. Rachel weeps for her children, refusing to be comforted, for they are dead. MATTHEW 2:18

Loss can cause panic. Losing people who were a part of your support system can cause you to panic about your own future.

Troubles surround me—too many to count! My sins pile up so high I can't see my way out. They outnumber the hairs on my head. I have lost all courage. PSALM 40:12

Trouble and fear can cause panic because it feels like your life will never change for the better.

Jesus said to his disciples, "Let's cross to the other side of the lake." So they got into a boat and started out. As they sailed across, Jesus settled down for a nap. But soon a fierce storm came down on the lake. The boat was filling with water, and they were in real danger. The disciples went and woke him up, shouting, "Master, Master, we're going to drown!" When Jesus woke up, he rebuked the wind and the raging waves. Suddenly the storm stopped and all was calm. LUKE 8:22-24

Dangerous, uncontrollable circumstances can cause panic because they make you feel helpless.

What happens to me when I panic?

My life is poured out like water, and all my bones are out of joint. My heart is like wax, melting within me. PSALM 22:14

I said to myself, "I will watch what I do and not sin in what I say. I will hold my tongue when the ungodly are around me." But as I stood there in silence—not even speaking of good things—the turmoil within me grew worse. The more I thought about it, the hotter I got, igniting a fire of words. PSALM 39:1-3

Panic causes emotional, mental, and physical reactions.

The astrologers replied to the king, "No one on earth can tell the king his dream! And no king, however great and powerful, has ever asked such a thing of any magician, enchanter, or astrologer! The king's demand is impossible. No one except the gods can tell you your dream, and they do not live here among people." DANIEL 2:10-11

Panic brings feelings of hopelessness. When your security fades, however misplaced it might be, hope fades too.

When [Peter] saw the strong wind and the waves, he was terrified and began to sink. MATTHEW 14:30

Panic takes your focus off of who God is and what he can do.

What is happening? Why is everyone running to the rooftops? . . . All your leaders have fled. They surrendered without resistance. . . . You never ask for help from [God]. You never considered the One who planned this long ago. ISAIAH 22:1, 3, 11

Panic can cause you to run away from problems instead of bringing them to God and facing them courageously. Running away from problems never solves them.

How should I deal with panic? How do I find peace and perspective in the midst of panic?

Don't worry about anything; instead, pray about everything. Tell God what you need, and thank him for all he has done. Then you will experience God's peace, which exceeds anything we can understand. His peace will guard your hearts and minds as you live in Christ Jesus. PHILIPPIANS 4:6-7

Pray the instant panic hits. Prayer keeps you connected to the God who can overcome the paralysis of panic.

Though the wicked hide along the way to kill me, I will quietly keep my mind on your laws.... How sweet your words taste to me; they are sweeter than honey. Your commandments give me understanding; no wonder I hate every false way of life. Your word is a lamp to guide my feet and a light for my path.... Those who love your instructions have great peace and do not stumble. PSALM 119:95, 103-105, 165

Take comfort in his promises; seek his perspective; relax in his peace.

You will keep in perfect peace all who trust in you, all whose thoughts are fixed on you! ISAIAH 26:3

Let us who live in the light be clearheaded, protected by the armor of faith and love, and wearing as our helmet the confidence of our salvation. 1 THESSALONIANS 5:8

Focus your thoughts clearly and directly on God, contemplating what he would want you to do. Make him part of each solution you are considering.

I lay down and slept, yet I woke up in safety, for the LORD was watching over me. I am not afraid of ten thousand enemies who surround me on every side. PSALM 3:5-6

I trust in the LORD for protection. So why do you say to me, "Fly like a bird to the mountains for safety!" PSALM 11:1

Literally, rest in the Lord. When you realize God is in control you can sleep at night.

PARENTS/PARENTING   *See also* Adoption, Discipline, Family

We all have them, or have had them, and for better or worse they usually influence our lives more than any other single factor—parents. Many of us eventually become parents ourselves and influence the lives of our own children. Every parent learns early on that it's much easier to produce a child than to be a parent. Serving simultaneously as caregiver, nurse, doctor, teacher, coach, disciplinarian, friend, and spiritual role model, wise parents will look to God's Word for encouragement and direction. Fortunately, parents themselves also have a role model—a God who is called Father.

What does the Bible say about the role of parents?

Repeat [these commands] again and again to your children. DEUTERONOMY 6:7

You have been taught the holy Scriptures from childhood, and they have given you the wisdom to receive the salvation that comes by trusting in Christ Jesus. 2 TIMOTHY 3:15

Parents are to take responsibility for teaching their children a love for God and his Word.

Isaac loved Esau ... but Rebekah loved Jacob. GENESIS 25:28

Parents are not to show favoritism between children.

A man of God came to Eli and gave him this message from the LORD: "... Why do you give your sons more honor than you give me?" 1 SAMUEL 2:27-29

Parents are to make sure that God is honored as the head of the household. Too often the home revolves around the children instead of around God. Parents do their children a favor when they make God's desires central, not the children's. Indulgent parents do not help their children develop character.

Filled with love and compassion, he ran to his son, embraced him, and kissed him.
LUKE 15:20

The mark of a loving parent is the willingness to forgive.

How should I discipline my children?

Those who spare the rod of discipline hate their children. Those who love their children care enough to discipline them. PROVERBS 13:24

Discipline your children with love. If you have their safety and well-being in mind, you will need to disciple them in order to protect them.

Discipline your children while there is hope. Otherwise you will ruin their lives.
PROVERBS 19:18

Discipline is almost always most effective when done right away because it makes the cause and effect of the punishment more relevant. Small children may need more discipline when they are younger to teach them what is safe and right. As your children grow up, you will probably need to discipline them less and less as they put into practice the things they've learned from your loving correction.

Fathers, do not provoke your children to anger by the way you treat them. Rather, bring them up with the discipline and instruction that comes from the Lord. EPHESIANS 6:4

Never discipline out of anger because the only thing it teaches a child is to react in anger. If you are angry, calm down before you discipline. When you are calm enough to discipline, be sure to explain to your children what they did wrong, that you love them, and instruct them in how to do better next time. Then they will not only learn from their mistakes but also how to react in love, not anger.

Fathers, do not aggravate your children, or they will become discouraged. COLOSSIANS 3:21

Discipline should be done without causing aggravation and discouragement. Aggravating your children takes the focus off your love and concern for them. This is discouraging for children because they don't see the point of the discipline, only the discipline itself.

How should children relate to parents?

Honor your father and mother. Then you will live a long, full life in the land the LORD your God is giving you. EXODUS 20:12

Children, obey your parents because you belong to the Lord. EPHESIANS 6:1

Even if you disagree with your parents—no matter how old you are—you must still show them honor and respect.

PAST *See also* Heritage, Remembering/Reminders

The past is like a photo album containing snapshots of every moment of our lives. These snapshots are not just of happy moments and celebrations; they also record our failures, tragedies, and acts of deepest shame. Most of us would like to lock some of our past away or tear out the snapshots that expose the parts we'd like to forget. The apostle Paul, whom we consider one of the great leaders in the New Testament, had a past he wished he could forget. His memory album was full of snapshots from his days of persecuting Christians. What immense regret he could have been burdened with. But Paul understood his past had been redeemed through God's healing and forgiveness.

How we view our past will affect how we live our present and future. Some of us have had a good past with a strong spiritual heritage with loving parents and mentors. Don't take that for granted; use it to help and minister to others. Some of us have had a past filled with regrets from activities that were wrong and hurtful. No matter what you've done, God is ready to forgive you, clean you on the inside, and give you a new start—fully forgiven. Some of us have a tragic past where we have been victims of abuse, neglect, violence, and shameful acts. This is the most difficult past to deal with. But God wants to throw away all the bad snapshots and restore you completely—and he can if you'll let him. Regret, guilt, and shame can be removed, and we can be free to live in peace with purpose and joy.

How can I benefit most from the past?

I remember the days of old. I ponder all your great works and think about what you have done. PSALM 143:5

The past helps you remember what God has done for you. Every past work of God is an assurance for the future.

You can tell your children and grandchildren about how I made a mockery of the Egyptians and about the signs I displayed among them—and so you will know that I am the LORD. EXODUS 10:2

The past gives you opportunities to tell others about what God has done.

Don't be like your ancestors who would not listen or pay attention when the earlier prophets said to them, "This is what the LORD of Heaven's Armies says: Turn from your evil ways, and stop all your evil practices." ZECHARIAH 1:4

The past helps you learn from others and prevents you from making the same mistakes they did.

How can I most effectively deal with a hurtful past?

Joseph [said to his brothers], ". . . You intended to harm me, but God intended it all for good." GENESIS 50:19-20

Forgiving is essential to the healing process. As you release those hurts, you are free to be healed and to grow beyond the pain.

I focus on this one thing: Forgetting the past and looking forward to what lies ahead.
PHILIPPIANS 3:13

When you dwell on the past it is hard to forget it and move on. Deal with the pain of the past so you can receive the healing God wants to give you today and so you can move forward toward a future of joy and blessing.

How does my past affect me today?

O God, we have heard it with our own ears—our ancestors have told us of all you did in their day, in days long ago. . . . It was your right hand and strong arm and the blinding light from your face that helped them, for you loved them. PSALM 44:1-3

Seeing how God has worked in the past can give you confidence and hope that he will continue those great works in you in the future.

Think back on those early days when you first learned about Christ. Remember how you remained faithful even though it meant terrible suffering. HEBREWS 10:32

Surviving the past can strengthen you to endure today.

Stop sinning and do what is right. Break from your wicked past and be merciful to the poor. Perhaps then you will continue to prosper. DANIEL 4:27

You have had enough in the past of the evil things that godless people enjoy—their immorality and lust, their feasting and drunkenness and wild parties, and their terrible worship of idols. 1 PETER 4:3

The past can help you avoid temptation today. When you remember past consequences, you will be more motivated to avoid them!

David confessed to Nathan, "I have sinned against the LORD." Nathan replied, "Yes, but the LORD has forgiven you, and you won't die for this sin. Nevertheless, because you have shown utter contempt for the LORD by doing this, your child will die." 2 SAMUEL 12:13-14

Your past decisions have consequences for your future. Each decision you make determines which fork in the road you take. Where you end up depends on the decisions you make along the way.

PATIENCE *See also* Endurance, Perseverance, Self-Control, Testing

If you've ever spent two hours stuck in rush-hour traffic or held a crying baby at 2:00 a.m., you know something about patience. According to the Bible, patience is a form of perseverance and endurance that allows us to respond to frustrating circumstances with grace and self-control. Contrary to popular opinion, patience is not merely a personality trait but is a by-product of the presence and work of the Holy Spirit in the heart and mind of the believer.

Is patience really worth working for?

May God, who gives this patience and encouragement, help you live in complete harmony with each other. ROMANS 15:5

Patience leads to harmony with others, endurance to handle difficult circumstances, and an expectant attitude of hope that things will get better. It demonstrates a thoughtful and careful attitude toward others' feelings. Anyone can be patient, but there is a higher level of patience which comes from God through his Holy Spirit's presence and work in your life.

Love is patient and kind. 1 CORINTHIANS 13:4

Always be humble and gentle. Be patient with each other, making allowance for each other's faults because of your love. EPHESIANS 4:2

Patience is a characteristic of love. The more loving you become, the more you will model the nature of God in your life. God is the perfect example of patience. Every day we fail to measure up to his perfect standard, yet he is slow to get angry and loves us unconditionally.

Patient endurance is what you need now, so that you will continue to do God's will. Then you will receive all that he has promised. HEBREWS 10:36

Patience is evidence of strong character. As you pass each test of your faith, you will build a higher degree of patience for when you are tested again. Patience is the key to achieving many goals. And achieving goals is rarely done with a quantum leap, but rather by small steps.

How do I develop more patience?

If [the end] seems slow in coming, wait patiently, for it will surely take place. It will not be delayed. HABAKKUK 2:3

Consider the farmers who patiently wait for the rains in the fall and in the spring. . . . You, too, must be patient. JAMES 5:7-8

Whether you're waiting for crops to ripen, a traffic jam to unsnarl, a child to mature, or God to perfect you, you can grow in patience by recognizing that these things take time, and there is only so much you can do to speed them up. A key to understanding God's will is to understand God's timing.

Moses went back to the LORD and protested, "Why . . . did you send me?" EXODUS 5:22

Focusing less on your agenda and more on God's agenda for you will give you a "big picture" perspective and help disperse impatience.

I waited patiently for the LORD to help me, and he turned to me and heard my cry. PSALM 40:1

Prayer is a necessary tool in developing your patience and giving you God's perspective on your situation.

The Holy Spirit produces this kind of fruit in our lives: love, joy, peace, patience . . . GALATIANS 5:22

The more you let the Holy Spirit fill and inspire you, the more patient you will become. All fruit takes time to grow and mature, including the fruit of the Holy Spirit.

If we look forward to something we don't yet have, we must wait patiently and confidently. ROMANS 8:25

Patience is produced by the hope a believer has in God's plans. When your long-range future is totally secure, you can be more patient with today's frustrations.

A servant of the Lord must not quarrel but must be kind to everyone, be able to teach, and be patient with difficult people. 2 TIMOTHY 2:24

God develops patience in you through your relationships with others. Abrasive relationships teach you to patiently endure. Even in loving relationships patience is necessary.

What happens when I am patient?

Those who trust in the LORD will find new strength. They will soar high on wings like eagles. They will run and not grow weary. They will walk and not faint. ISAIAH 40:31

Waiting reveals your need for God's strength and gives God the opportunity to exercise his might on your behalf. As an athlete regains strength from sleep and time away from the contest, so you will find strength by abandoning your own efforts and trusting the Lord to work. He will bring what you need when you need it.

Supplement your faith with a generous provision of . . . self-control with patient endurance, and patient endurance with godliness, and godliness with brotherly affection, and brotherly affection with love for everyone. The more you grow like this, the more productive and useful you will be in your knowledge of our Lord Jesus Christ. 2 PETER 1:5-8

Patience is like a chisel, shaping godly character. God patiently sculpts you into a person he can use to show his love to everyone you meet.

PEACE *See also* Confidence, Joy, Salvation, Unity, Will of God

At the heart of peace is harmony. To be at peace with someone—whether a neighbor, a family member, or God—is to be in a harmonious relationship with them. When we ask Christ to cleanse us of our sin and make us new creations, we are asking for peace, a new harmonious relationship with our Creator.

Where can I find peace?

Don't worry about anything; instead, pray about everything. Tell God what you need, and thank him for all he has done. Then you will experience God's peace, which exceeds anything we can understand. His peace will guard your hearts and minds as you live in Christ Jesus. PHILIPPIANS 4:6-7

Peace of mind and heart come from inviting God—the source of peace—to live in you, helping you to understand this world is only temporary. Then you can navigate through any chaos because you know God is ultimately in control. To find this harmony with God, you must ask Jesus Christ to forgive your sins and make you clean in God's sight.

How can I make peace with God?

Turn away from evil and do good. Search for peace, and work to maintain it. PSALM 34:14

There will be glory and honor and peace from God for all who do good. ROMANS 2:10

Peace with God comes from living the way you were created to live. That happens when you develop a relationship with your Creator and live by the standards he has written in his Word, the Bible. When you set aside your sinful lifestyle and work toward a godly lifestyle and loving others, you will experience God's peace as your mind, heart, and actions get into sync with his.

You will keep in perfect peace all who trust in you, all whose thoughts are fixed on you! ISAIAH 26:3

Peace comes from knowing God is in control of your life. Focus your thoughts on God and what he is able to accomplish in your life, rather than focusing on your problems.

The lowly will possess the land and will live in peace and prosperity. PSALM 37:11

Humility before God brings peace because God blesses the humble. Those who are humble understand their place in relationship to God and others. Humility gives you a realistic view of yourself, balanced by the knowledge of how much God loves you.

How can I find peace within?

A child is born to us, a son is given to us. The government will rest on his shoulders. And he will be called: Wonderful Counselor, Mighty God, Everlasting Father, Prince of Peace. His government and its peace will never end. ISAIAH 9:6-7

Lasting peace comes only from Jesus Christ, the Prince of Peace. His rule over all creation as well as in your life ensures it.

I lay down and slept, yet I woke up in safety, for the LORD was watching over me. PSALM 3:5

The LORD gives his people strength. The LORD blesses them with peace. PSALM 29:11

Peace comes from knowing that God is always watching over you day and night. This doesn't mean that your body will never be harmed, but it does mean that God will never let Satan snatch you away from him. You can have absolute confidence that you will be his forever.

Those who love your instructions have great peace and do not stumble. PSALM 119:165

Peace comes from knowing and living according to God's Word. His wisdom and direction guide you into safety and lead you out of conflict, compromise, and deception.

I am leaving you with a gift—peace of mind and heart. And the peace I give is a gift the world cannot give. So don't be troubled or afraid. JOHN 14:27

The Holy Spirit produces this kind of fruit in our lives: . . . peace. GALATIANS 5:22

The Holy Spirit brings peace of mind and heart when given control of your life. Peace of mind comes as the Holy Spirit guides you into God's purpose for your life, giving you an eternal perspective. Peace of heart comes as the Holy Spirit guides you into productive living and comforts you in times of trouble.

How can I make peace with others?

God blesses those who work for peace. MATTHEW 5:9

Peace is not the absence of conflict; it's confident assurance in the midst of conflict. Peace comes from dealing with conflict appropriately. God calls you to pursue peace, which involves hard work.

Grow to maturity. Encourage each other. Live in harmony and peace. Then the God of love and peace will be with you. 2 CORINTHIANS 13:11

Working hard at ridding sin from your own life while diligently building others up helps achieve peace.

Make every effort to keep yourselves united in the Spirit, binding yourselves together with peace. EPHESIANS 4:3

Work toward the unity with others that comes only from the Holy Spirit.

The wisdom from above is . . . peace loving, gentle at all times, and willing to yield to others. It is full of mercy and good deeds. It shows no favoritism and is always sincere. JAMES 3:17

Commit yourself to the gentle deeds that are the mark of a true peacemaker.

Is there any hope for world peace?

The LORD will mediate between peoples and will settle disputes between strong nations far away. They will hammer their swords into plowshares and their spears into pruning hooks. Nation will no longer fight against nation, nor train for war anymore. MICAH 4:3

War is an inevitable consequence of human sin. But when Jesus returns, there will be peace forever.

PEER PRESSURE *See also* Acceptance, Conformity

Because we value others and we long to be valued by others, the people in our lives have an enormous ability to influence us—for better or worse. Peer pressure is the influence of another person, positive or negative, that causes us to think or behave in a certain way so we can gain the approval of another. The best way to ensure positive peer pressure is to surround ourselves with godly friends who will encourage us with wholesome thoughts and actions. However, when we encounter any kind of peer pressure, it is more important to gain God's approval over the approval of others.

What is peer pressure?

No one else so completely sold himself to what was evil in the LORD's sight as Ahab did under the influence of his wife Jezebel. 1 KINGS 21:25

The messenger who went to get Micaiah said to him, "Look, all the prophets are promising victory for the king. Be sure that you agree with them and promise success." 1 KINGS 22:13

The leading priests and the elders persuaded the crowd to ask for Barabbas to be released and for Jesus to be put to death. MATTHEW 27:20

Let us think of ways to motivate one another to acts of love and good works. HEBREWS 10:24

Peer pressure is someone's positive or negative influence on your decisions, actions, thoughts, beliefs, or feelings. When it's negative, it is meant to get you to conform or please, not necessarily do right. When peer pressure is positive, it helps you stay accountable to what is right.

Why is peer pressure so powerful? Why do we tend to want to follow the crowd?

You must not follow the crowd in doing wrong. When you are called to testify in a dispute, do not be swayed by the crowd to twist justice. EXODUS 23:2

Peer pressure often comes from a group—strong in number and in persuasion. You might conform in an effort to belong, to conform so you are like everyone else.

While the Israelites were camped at Acacia Grove, some of the men defiled themselves by having sexual relations with local Moabite women. These women invited them to attend sacrifices to their gods, so the Israelites feasted with them and worshiped the gods of Moab. NUMBERS 25:1-2

Negative peer pressure is an intriguing trap, offering attractive short-term benefits. It tempts you to enjoy small rewards today at the expense of great rewards in the future.

How can I tell the difference between good and bad peer pressure?

Just as you can identify a tree by its fruit, so you can identify people by their actions. MATTHEW 7:20

Don't let this bad example influence you. Follow only what is good. Remember that those who do good prove that they are God's children, and those who do evil prove that they do not know God. 3 JOHN 1:11

Good peer pressure will always encourage you toward living a more godly life while bad peer pressure will always lead you away from godly living. Are your friends encouraging you toward God or away from him?

Stay away from fools, for you won't find knowledge on their lips. PROVERBS 14:7

I am telling you this so no one will deceive you with well-crafted arguments.
COLOSSIANS 2:4

Consider the source of the peer pressure. Are the peers wise, sincere, and authentic? Do they care what God thinks, or not?

How do I best handle peer pressure?

Those who live only to satisfy their own sinful nature will harvest decay and death from that sinful nature. But those who live to please the Spirit will harvest everlasting life from the Spirit. So let's not get tired of doing what is good. GALATIANS 6:8-9

Train yourself to live by God's standards, which will help you develop the conviction to keep strong when tempted. The Bible contains the absolute truths by which all people should live, the truths that lead you on the right path.

Oh, the joys of those who do not follow the advice of the wicked, or stand around with sinners, or join in with mockers. PSALM 1:1

Stay away from fools, for you won't find knowledge on their lips. PROVERBS 14:7

Don't envy evil people or desire their company. PROVERBS 24:1

Perhaps the most obvious and most practical way to resist negative peer pressure is to choose wise peers. If you can't resist friends who constantly persuade you to do wrong, you might need to stay away from them until you have the strength to resist their temptations.

As pressure and stress bear down on me, I find joy in your commands. PSALM 119:143

The people of Berea were more open-minded than those in Thessalonica, and they listened eagerly to Paul's message. They searched the Scriptures day after day to see if Paul and Silas were teaching the truth. ACTS 17:11

Before you do what others want, first think about what God wants. When you take time to consider his advice, as found in the Bible, you will know if your peers are trying to persuade you to do the wrong thing. It is easier to resist bad influences when you are grounded in God's Word and committed to obeying it.

The king regretted what he had said; but because of the vow he had made in front of his guests, he issued the necessary orders. MATTHEW 14:9

Never let pride or the risk of embarrassment keep you from making right choices. Keep your motives pure. Pride and embarrassment are poor motives for your choices.

I will reject perverse ideas and stay away from every evil. PSALM 101:4

The LORD has given me a strong warning not to think like everyone else does.
ISAIAH 8:11

Remember that thinking like everyone else is not always the right way to think. The crowd doesn't always move in the right direction.

PERFECTION *See also* Holiness, Purity, Righteousness

Most of us wish we could be perfect in some way. We want to be the perfect spouse or parent, perform flawlessly, or be supremely skilled or accurate. Christians long to be godly, free from sin and failure. Life on earth will always be a struggle between our longing to be perfect and the reality of our humanness and sinful nature. What we really long for is heaven, where perfection is natural. Thankfully, God understands our struggle and sent his Son, Jesus, to accomplish what we could not. Jesus was perfect, holy, and blameless. Through his death on the cross, he exchanged the burdens of our humanness and sin for his perfect holiness so we can be blameless before God and be prepared for heaven.

How is God perfect?

He is the Rock; his deeds are perfect. Everything he does is just and fair. He is a faithful God who does no wrong; how just and upright he is! DEUTERONOMY 32:4

God is perfect in his character and his nature. As a result, everything he does is perfect, just, fair, compassionate, good, and loving!

God's way is perfect. All the LORD's promises prove true. He is a shield for all who look to him for protection. PSALM 18:30

God's promises are perfect and every one of them comes true.

You know what I am going to say even before I say it, LORD. PSALM 139:4

Who is able to advise the Spirit of the LORD? Who knows enough to give him advice or teach him? Has the LORD ever needed anyone's advice? Does he need instruction about what is good? ISAIAH 40:13-14

Nothing in all creation is hidden from God. Everything is naked and exposed before his eyes, and he is the one to whom we are accountable. HEBREWS 4:13

God is perfect in his knowledge of all things. Therefore you can trust in his perfect wisdom and plan for your life.

The instructions of the LORD are perfect, reviving the soul. The decrees of the LORD are trustworthy, making wise the simple. PSALM 19:7

God's Word is perfect, presented to us exactly the way he wants it. What it says always turns out to be true.

God, for whom and through whom everything was made, chose to bring many children into glory. And it was only right that he should make Jesus, through his suffering, a perfect leader, fit to bring them into their salvation. HEBREWS 2:10

He never sinned, nor ever deceived anyone. 1 PETER 2:22

God is perfect even in human form, as demonstrated when he sent his Son, Jesus, to earth. Jesus was perfect and sinless in everything he did during his earthly life.

Does God really expect me to be perfect?

There once was a man named Job. . . . He was blameless—a man of complete integrity. He feared God and stayed away from evil. JOB 1:1

As you come to know and respect who God is, you are encouraged to aim for the purity of his character in your own daily choices. To be like God, who is perfect, is the goal. But as a human, your best will fall far short of perfection. God knows that and understands. When you live with an attitude of humble obedience, God sees you as blameless.

I don't mean to say that I have . . . reached perfection. But I press on to possess that perfection for which Christ Jesus first possessed me. PHILIPPIANS 3:12

The Christian life is not a flawless imitation of God, but rather a process of maturing into a purer and more godly person. Godliness is becoming more like him, even while falling far short of him. You can look forward to a day when that process of reflecting God's nature will be complete and you will indeed be perfect.

How can I meet God's expectations for me?

He has reconciled you to himself through the death of Christ in his physical body. As a result, he has brought you into his own presence, and you are holy and blameless as you stand before him without a single fault. COLOSSIANS 1:22

By that one offering he forever made perfect those who are being made holy. HEBREWS 10:14

By allowing Jesus to have complete control of your life, you acknowledge that you are imperfect and cannot meet God's expectations without his help.

How foolish can you be? After starting your Christian lives in the Spirit, why are you now trying to become perfect by your own human effort? GALATIANS 3:3

Living every day with the guidance of the Holy Spirit helps you live a blameless life in God's eyes. You can't achieve purity on your own.

All Scripture is inspired by God and is useful to teach us what is true and to make us realize what is wrong in our lives. It corrects us when we are wrong and teaches us to do what is right. God uses it to prepare and equip his people to do every good work. 2 TIMOTHY 3:16-17

Knowing God better as you study his Word teaches you how to strive for perfection in all aspects of life.

What are some of the areas in which I am to strive to be perfect?

Obey this command without wavering. Then no one can find fault with you from now until our Lord Jesus Christ comes again. 1 TIMOTHY 6:14

Make every effort to be found living peaceful lives that are pure and blameless in his sight. 2 PETER 3:14

Obey God's Word, which shows you how to sin less and increase goodness.

If we love each other, God lives in us, and his love is brought to full expression in us.... Such love has no fear, because perfect love expels all fear. If we are afraid, it is for fear of punishment, and this shows that we have not fully experienced his perfect love.
1 JOHN 4:12, 18

Make a conscious effort to be an example of Christ's perfect love to others.

You will keep in perfect peace all who trust in you, all whose thoughts are fixed on you!
ISAIAH 26:3

Don't worry about anything; instead, pray about everything. Tell God what you need, and thank him for all he has done. Then you will experience God's peace, which exceeds anything we can understand. His peace will guard your hearts and minds as you live in Christ Jesus. PHILIPPIANS 4:6-7

Train your mind to think more about God and less about yourself and your problems.

What are some of the dangers of perfectionism?
Not a single person on earth is always good and never sins. ECCLESIASTES 7:20

Everyone has sinned; we all fall short of God's glorious standard. ROMANS 3:23

Perfectionism is a ruthless taskmaster—demanding and unforgiving. It expects perfect performance with no mistakes. This kind of expectation of being perfect puts a great burden on you and others. The goal of perfection is hopeless and sets you up for failure.

I was so zealous that I harshly persecuted the church. And as for righteousness, I obeyed the law without fault. PHILIPPIANS 3:6

Perfectionism can be misdirected. Even a desire to be godly has set some Christians against other Christians. Perfectionism can cause you to strive for religious goals at the expense of godly goals, as with Paul before he became a Christian, or it can cause you to strive for performance goals at the expense of spiritual goals.

Farmers who wait for perfect weather never plant. If they watch every cloud, they never harvest. ECCLESIASTES 11:4

Waiting for perfection can lead to procrastination. You will never be truly perfect, but you can't let that keep you from stepping out and doing what you can.

How should I respond to my own imperfections?
Do not let sin control the way you live; do not give in to sinful desires. Do not let any part of your body become an instrument of evil to serve sin. Instead, give yourselves completely to God, for you were dead, but now you have new life. So use your whole body as an instrument to do what is right for the glory of God. Sin is no longer your master, for you no longer live under the requirements of the law. Instead, you live under the freedom of God's grace. ROMANS 6:12-14

Recognize your own sinfulness, while at the same time aiming to live more and more like Christ. Change comes in small steps. Because you are growing, you will not make consistently perfect choices. Your goal should be to turn more and more from sin and follow the Lord wholeheartedly in each area of your life. When you do sin, confess it and accept God's forgiveness. While sin will inevitably be present in your earthly human existence, you need not be dominated by it.

How should I respond to others' imperfections?

Do not judge others, and you will not be judged. For you will be treated as you treat others. The standard you use in judging is the standard by which you will be judged. And why worry about a speck in your friend's eye when you have a log in your own? How can you think of saying to your friend, "Let me help you get rid of that speck in your eye," when you can't see past the log in your own eye? Hypocrite! First get rid of the log in your own eye; then you will see well enough to deal with the speck in your friend's eye.
MATTHEW 7:1-5

Do not respond with critical judgment, but rather with love, forgiveness, and humility. Then perhaps others will give you love, forgiveness, and humility in the same way.

PERSECUTION *See also* Enemies, Oppression, Prejudice, Suffering

Whether burned alive for the entertainment of a Roman emperor, tortured during the Middle Ages, exiled to a Siberian gulag, or called names by a hateful junior-high peer group, Christians have always faced persecution. While Christians and non-Christians alike suffer unjust treatment, persecution implies an intentional infliction of suffering or hardship because of a person's beliefs.

Why do Christians seem to be the target of so much persecution?

They will do all this to you because of me, for they have rejected the One who sent me.
JOHN 15:21

Sometimes believers are persecuted simply for speaking the truth. Those who don't believe in God, or don't believe God has established absolute truths and communicated them through the Bible, obviously don't recognize truth. To them, truth sounds rigid and intolerant. Others recognize the truth but don't want to live by it. In either case, those who don't live by the truths of the Bible will resist and attack those who do.

Why am I still being persecuted? If I were no longer preaching salvation through the cross of Christ, no one would be offended. GALATIANS 5:11

The bold message that salvation comes only through faith in Jesus threatens those who believe that their own good works are enough to get to heaven.

They are all guilty of treason against Caesar, for they profess allegiance to another king, named Jesus. ACTS 17:7

Because Christians give their ultimate allegiance to God, they have sometimes been accused of treason against their government.

Where can I find hope when I am persecuted?

The apostles left the high council rejoicing that God had counted them worthy to suffer disgrace for the name of Jesus. ACTS 5:41

Everyone who wants to live a godly life in Christ Jesus will suffer persecution.
2 TIMOTHY 3:12

If you are being persecuted for your faith, be encouraged by the fact that many other faithful believers are also standing strong in the face of persecution. The Bible encourages you to see persecution for Jesus' sake as an honor. It is evidence of the depth of your commitment to Jesus and therefore a privilege to suffer for the God you love so much. It also helps you identify with the depth of suffering Jesus went through for you.

God blesses you when people mock you and persecute you and lie about you and say all sorts of evil things against you because you are my followers. MATTHEW 5:11

Jesus promises special blessings to those who are persecuted.

The LORD said to my Lord, "Sit in the place of honor at my right hand until I humble your enemies, making them a footstool under your feet." PSALM 110:1

God will defeat his enemies. You may be persecuted now, but your side will be victorious and your persecution will not be in vain.

How should I respond when I am persecuted for my faith?

Save me, O God. . . . Those who hate me without cause outnumber the hairs on my head.
PSALM 69:1, 4

Prayer is a powerful response in times of persecution. Pray to God, the only One who can give you the strength you need to endure.

Some Jews . . . stoned Paul and dragged him out of town, thinking he was dead. But as the believers gathered around him, he got up and went back into the town. ACTS 14:19-20

Paul's courageous response to persecution enabled him to encourage others. Courage to endure persecution is contagious.

You have been given . . . the privilege of suffering for [Christ]. PHILIPPIANS 1:29

Be very glad—for these trials make you partners with Christ in his suffering, so that you will have the wonderful joy of seeing his glory. 1 PETER 4:13

The Bible encourages you to see the rewards of persecution, which helps you keep going when times get especially tough.

Bless those who curse you. Pray for those who hurt you. LUKE 6:28

Bless those who persecute you. Don't curse them; pray that God will bless them.
ROMANS 12:14

A supernatural love, one that flows from God, allows believers to actually pray for those who persecute them. It may be through your godly response to their persecution that God touches a hard heart and turns it to him.

When the leading priests and the elders made their accusations against him, Jesus remained silent. MATTHEW 27:12

God's holy people must endure persecution patiently, obeying his commands and maintaining their faith in Jesus. REVELATION 14:12

Remain obedient to God and endure the persecution patiently, just as Jesus did when he was persecuted.

[God himself] will wipe every tear from their eyes, and there will be no more death or sorrow or crying or pain. All these things are gone forever. REVELATION 21:4

The knowledge that all suffering will be replaced by the joy of heaven enables believers to endure.

Why is it so important to endure persecution rather than give in to it?

The godly people in the land are my true heroes! I take pleasure in them! PSALM 16:3

We give great honor to those who endure under suffering. For instance, you know about Job, a man of great endurance. You can see how the Lord was kind to him at the end, for the Lord is full of tenderness and mercy. JAMES 5:11

God's heroes are those who hang on to their faith in him no matter what happens. The Bible is full of examples of people who never stopped trusting God even though they were mocked, persecuted, and killed for their faith. God may not ask you to be a martyr for him, but is your faith strong enough to endure even a little derision or scorn? Those who live boldly for God despite opposition will make the greatest impact for eternity.

We can rejoice, too, when we run into problems and trials, for we know that they help us develop endurance. And endurance develops strength of character. ROMANS 5:3-4

I take pleasure in my weaknesses, and in the insults, hardships, persecutions, and troubles that I suffer for Christ. For when I am weak, then I am strong. 2 CORINTHIANS 12:10

Sometimes you suffer because of events outside your control, and your faith is tested. During the hard times, your character is stretched and you are actively learning and growing.

PERSEVERANCE *See also* Commitment, Endurance, Faithfulness

Perseverance has been well defined as "courage stretched out." Although God sometimes delivers his people from difficult or painful circumstances, he often calls us to a courageous and enduring faithfulness in the midst of trials. Perseverance, according to the Bible, is not only enduring situations of suffering but overcoming them with obedience, hope, and joy.

Why is perseverance so important?

Those who remain in me, and I in them, will produce much fruit. JOHN 15:5

Let's not get tired of doing what is good. At just the right time we will reap a harvest of blessing if we don't give up. GALATIANS 6:9

Perseverance leads to a productive life. Giving up always leaves you with the frustration of unfinished work. You can look back with satisfaction on a productive life.

It would be good for you to finish what you started a year ago. Last year you were the first who wanted to give, and you were the first to begin doing it. Now you should finish what you started. 2 CORINTHIANS 8:10-11

Perseverance validates your promises and demonstrates your credibility.

These trials will show that your faith is genuine. It is being tested as fire tests and purifies gold. . . . So when your faith remains strong through many trials, it will bring you much praise and glory and honor on the day when Jesus Christ is revealed to the whole world. 1 PETER 1:7

To stay strong, to persevere, to endure—these characteristics help you to deal with problems. God uses adversity to make you strong. Without adversity, there is nothing to exercise the muscles of your faith. Ask God to give you a glimpse of what he wants you to learn as you persevere through difficult times.

Make every effort to respond to God's promises. Supplement your faith with a generous provision of moral excellence, and moral excellence with knowledge, and knowledge with self-control, and self-control with patient endurance, and patient endurance with godliness, and godliness with brotherly affection, and brotherly affection with love for everyone. The more you grow like this, the more productive and useful you will be in your knowledge of our Lord Jesus Christ. 2 PETER 1:5-8

Perseverance produces, among other things, godliness, love, productivity, usefulness, growth, strength of character, preparedness, strong faith, and eternal rewards.

If we are faithful to the end, trusting God just as firmly as when we first believed, we will share in all that belongs to Christ. HEBREWS 3:14

God blesses those who patiently endure testing and temptation. Afterward they will receive the crown of life that God has promised to those who love him. JAMES 1:12

Those who persevere in their faith will share in the eternal riches of Christ.

How can I develop perseverance?

You and your fighting men should march around the town once a day for six days. Seven priests will walk ahead of the Ark, each carrying a ram's horn. On the seventh day you are to march around the town seven times, with the priests blowing the horns. When you hear the priests give one long blast on the rams' horns, have all the people shout as loud as they can. Then the walls of the town will collapse, and the people can charge straight into the town. JOSHUA 6:3-5

Perseverance is obeying even when God's way doesn't seem to make sense or produce immediate results. Steady obedience develops perseverance.

I am certain that God, who began the good work within you, will continue his work until it is finally finished on the day when Christ Jesus returns. PHILIPPIANS 1:6

Perseverance is based on the promise of God's persistent, faithful work in your life. God never stops working in you, and that should motivate you to always be looking for what he will do next to help you grow and serve others.

We can rejoice, too, when we run into problems and trials, for we know that they help us develop endurance. ROMANS 5:3

When troubles come your way, consider it an opportunity for great joy. For you know that when your faith is tested, your endurance has a chance to grow. So let it grow, for when your endurance is fully developed, you will be perfect and complete, needing nothing. JAMES 1:2-4

Problems, trials, troubles, and the testing of your faith can strengthen your resolve or break you down. It all depends on your attitude. If you see your problems as stepping-stones to something greater, then you can move ahead with anticipation for what you will become—a person of strong character who can handle any obstacle. If you see your problems as giant barriers, you will get discouraged, give up, and turn back, never allowing yourself to become more than you are now.

Let us strip off every weight that slows us down, especially the sin that so easily trips us up. And let us run with endurance the race God has set before us. We do this by keeping our eyes on Jesus, the champion who initiates and perfects our faith. . . . Think of all the hostility he endured from sinful people; then you won't become weary and give up. HEBREWS 12:1-3

Sin will always stunt your spiritual growth. The less you practice sin, the easier it is to persevere through life's problems and challenges. The faithfulness of God's people across the ages and, above all, the example of Jesus give you models of how to reduce the sin in your life and develop the necessary perseverance to help you become all that God wants you to be.

We were crushed and overwhelmed beyond our ability to endure, and we thought we would never live through it. In fact, we expected to die. But as a result, we stopped relying on ourselves and learned to rely only on God, who raises the dead. 2 CORINTHIANS 1:8-9

As we pray to our God and Father about you, we think of your faithful work, your loving deeds, and the enduring hope you have because of our Lord Jesus Christ. 1 THESSALONIANS 1:3

The key to perseverance is having a clear view of heaven as your destination. When you clearly see where you are going, it is easier to endure the hardships along the road. God promises to help you. His persistent and faithful work in your life gives you the supernatural power to keep going when you encounter difficulties.

If I am saved by grace, not works, why do I need to work so hard to persevere?

We give great honor to those who endure under suffering. JAMES 5:11

Perseverance in good works does not produce salvation. Rather, perseverance in doing good is evidence that your faith in God is valid and real.

When your faith is tested, your endurance has a chance to grow. JAMES 1:3

Perseverance turns suffering into maturity. Suffering for the sake of suffering is fruitless. But suffering that leads to maturity is productive.

Will God supply me with more energy when I need to persevere?

It is not by force nor by strength, but by my Spirit, says the LORD of Heaven's Armies. ZECHARIAH 4:6

I pray that from his glorious, unlimited resources he will empower you with inner strength through his Spirit. EPHESIANS 3:16

I can do everything through Christ, who gives me strength. PHILIPPIANS 4:13

The Holy Spirit is the power of God that lives in every believer. When you yield control of your life to the Lord, he releases his power within you—power to resist temptation, to serve and love God and others when you are at the end of your rope, to have wisdom in all circumstances, and to persevere in living for God now with the promise of eternal life later. Through his Spirit, God will give you the energy you need to do all that he asks you to do.

PLANNING *See also* Goals, Preparation, Priorities, Purpose

Homespun wisdom says, "If you fail to plan, you plan to fail." Although you won't find it put just that way in the Bible, you will find many stories of both effective and poor planning. The Bible teaches that God is a God of purpose and planning. His purpose is to draw all humanity to himself in order to forgive and redeem them. His plan—from Creation to the present and on through eternity—is outlined in Scripture. The only question is if we have joined God's plan for our lives on earth and for eternity.

Does God have a plan, or is everything just happening by chance?

[Joseph said to his brothers,] "Don't be angry with yourselves for selling me to this place. It was God who sent me here ahead of you to preserve your lives." GENESIS 45:5

God used even the unjust treatment of Joseph by his own brothers to fulfill a future plan for the nation of Israel.

The wisdom we speak of is the mystery of God—his plan that was previously hidden, even though he made it for our ultimate glory before the world began.
1 CORINTHIANS 2:6-7

God's plan of redemption was established even before Creation itself.

This is God's plan: Both Gentiles and Jews who believe the Good News share equally in the riches inherited by God's children. EPHESIANS 3:6

God's plan to save humankind included a provision for all people, both Jews and non-Jews.

Does God have a specific plan for my life? Can I mess it up?

"I know the plans I have for you," says the LORD. "They are plans for good and not for disaster, to give you a future and a hope." JEREMIAH 29:11

God causes everything to work together for the good of those who love God and are called according to his purpose for them. ROMANS 8:28

When you are tempted by thoughts of hopelessness, remember that God created you and has a specific plan for you. While you may not understand how certain life events fit into God's perfect plan, you can be confident that God is watching over your life and guiding you in a specific direction.

Why is it important to plan ahead?

Those too lazy to plow in the right season will have no food at the harvest.
PROVERBS 20:4

A prudent person foresees danger and takes precautions. PROVERBS 22:3

Don't begin until you count the cost. For who would begin construction of a building without first calculating the cost to see if there is enough money to finish it? LUKE 14:28

Planning prepares you for future needs and challenges. The lazy person will always be caught off guard by difficult circumstances, but the person who plans ahead will be able to face the difficulties of life with confidence. Planning allows you to be productive, even in difficult times.

Doesn't planning ahead conflict with trusting God to lead me?

David also gave Solomon all the plans he had in mind for the courtyards of the LORD's Temple, the outside rooms, the treasuries, and the rooms for the gifts dedicated to the LORD. . . . "Every part of this plan," David told Solomon, "was given to me in writing from the hand of the LORD." 1 CHRONICLES 28:12, 19

Rather than conflicting with trust in God, planning helps you put your faith in God into action. God will lead you, but it is your responsibility to make it happen—to recognize his lead, make a plan, and follow through. God's work doesn't happen simply by chance; he needs capable people who are willing to plan ahead and do the work.

How do I go about planning ahead?

Be sure that you make everything according to the pattern I have shown you here on the mountain. EXODUS 25:40

As he left, however, he said, "I will come back later, God willing." Then he set sail from Ephesus. ACTS 18:21

Follow God's revealed will when you make your plans. If his will is not clear in a specific matter, remember that he has made his will clear in general matters of right and wrong, good and bad, helpful and harmful. So you can move ahead with your plans as long as you are confident they do not go against God's Word. As you do, don't be surprised if God intervenes to alter them.

Trust in the LORD with all your heart; do not depend on your own understanding. Seek his will in all you do, and he will show you which path to take. PROVERBS 3:5-6

As you submit to God, he will guide you in making your plans. Often, in hindsight, you will see how God guided and directed your choices and actions.

I have a plan for the whole earth, a hand of judgment upon all the nations. The LORD of Heaven's Armies has spoken—who can change his plans? When his hand is raised, who can stop him? ISAIAH 14:26-27

God causes everything to work together for the good of those who love God and are called according to his purpose for them. ROMANS 8:28

God will work through your plans, and in spite of them, to accomplish his goals.

Don't worry about tomorrow, for tomorrow will bring its own worries. Today's trouble is enough for today. MATTHEW 6:34

Look here, you who say, "Today or tomorrow we are going to a certain town and will stay there a year. We will do business there and make a profit." How do you know what your life will be like tomorrow? Your life is like the morning fog—it's here a little while, then it's gone. What you ought to say is, "If the Lord wants us to, we will live and do this or that." Otherwise you are boasting about your own plans, and all such boasting is evil. JAMES 4:13-16

Long-range planning is good, but hold those plans loosely. You don't know what the future will bring and where God will take you. So plan ahead, but be flexible as you see God working in your life.

What are some plans I should be making?

[Solomon said,] "I am planning to build a Temple to honor the name of the LORD my God, just as he had instructed my father, David. For the LORD told him, 'Your son, whom I will place on your throne, will build the Temple to honor my name.'" 1 KINGS 5:5

When God calls you to a specific task, you should make plans to obey. Obedience often requires discipline and sacrifice and preparation.

[Paul said] "I planned many times to visit you, but I was prevented until now. I want to work among you and see spiritual fruit, just as I have seen among other Gentiles. For I have a great sense of obligation to people in both the civilized world and the rest of the world, to the educated and uneducated alike. So I am eager to come to you in Rome, too, to preach the Good News." ROMANS 1:13-15

Plan to serve and minister to others. In Paul's case, God didn't always put him where he thought he would serve. But Paul continued to make himself available to serve wherever and whomever God chose. As a result, he developed a passion for helping all kinds of people.

Do not neglect the spiritual gift you received through the prophecy spoken over you when the elders of the church laid their hands on you. Give your complete attention to these matters. Throw yourself into your tasks so that everyone will see your progress. 1 TIMOTHY 4:14-15

Plan to exercise your spiritual gifts. Using your spiritual gifts is both conducive to and a by-product of spiritual growth. If you don't know what your gifts are, meet with godly advisers or people you trust in order to discover the abilities that God has given to you. Then, make plans to throw yourself into your tasks.

Let us not neglect our meeting together, as some people do, but encourage one another, especially now that the day of his return is drawing near. HEBREWS 10:25

Plan for times of worship and fellowship with other Christians. Don't let the busyness of life cause you to neglect these important times of friendship and encouragement.

Do not do your work on the Sabbath, but make it a holy day. JEREMIAH 17:22

Plans for hard work are beneficial but so are plans for times of rest. Work ahead during the week so that you won't feel pressured to work on the Lord's Day. Make it a truly holy day of rest.

Stay alert! Watch out for your great enemy, the devil. He prowls around like a roaring lion, looking for someone to devour. 1 PETER 5:8

Plan ahead of time to stand firm against temptation. Then, when you are tempted, you will be prepared to resist and be ready to do the right thing.

I thought I should send these brothers ahead of me to make sure the gift you promised is ready. But I want it to be a willing gift, not one given grudgingly. 2 CORINTHIANS 9:5

Plan to give your first fruits, or "tithe," to God. This allows you to give cheerfully. Don't neglect this or you'll feel financial pressure later on and be tempted to hold back.

In the future your children will ask you, "What is the meaning of these laws, decrees, and regulations that the LORD our God has commanded us to obey?" Then you must tell them. DEUTERONOMY 6:20-21

Plan to teach your children about God and his commands. Be prepared to talk with them about all he has done in your life.

PLAY *See also* Celebration, Pleasure, Renewal, Rest

It is often said that working hard is the key to success, but more and more we are understanding that play is important to success as well. Numerous psychological studies have confirmed that play relieves stress, increases creativity, and is crucial to mental health. God saw the value of play, too, when he encouraged the Israelites to set aside time for celebration and enjoyment. He also created our world full of things to enjoy. We've all heard the colloquial phrase "work before play" but that doesn't mean that play is not worthy of our time. Playing seems to be important to God. It's hard to define "play," yet we all recognize it. Playing is setting aside time from our routine, feeling unburdened and caught up in the moment, doing something we enjoy, recharging our batteries so that we can better accomplish our work, taking time to relax. It reveals what we choose to do rather than what we have to do. We get to know people in a new way when we see them at play. Studies have also found that we feel safer around people who play because they show us they enjoy being with us. It is encouraging to see that God enjoys and encourages our play as well as our work because he has placed great value on both.

Does God want me to have time to play?

You have six days each week for your ordinary work, but the seventh day is a Sabbath day of complete rest. LEVITICUS 23:3

God set aside one day in seven to rest, to break the routine of work. It is time given to you by God to enjoy him and others more fully.

The master said, "Well done, my good and faithful servant. . . . Let's celebrate together!" MATTHEW 25:23

Task-oriented individuals tend to neglect the opportunity to play and celebrate. The Bible teaches that celebration is both important and necessary. It gives you the opportunity to savor rest from work, to experience the satisfaction of accomplishment, and to enjoy the good things of creation. It creates a spirit of gratitude and renews your energy for the tasks ahead.

What kinds of playing are unnecessary and harmful?

Local Moabite women . . . invited [the Israelites] to attend sacrifices to their gods, so the Israelites feasted with them and worshiped the gods of Moab. NUMBERS 25:1-2

You have had enough in the past of the evil things that godless people enjoy—their . . . feasting and drunkenness and wild parties. 1 PETER 4:3

Play that is self-centered, indulgent, involves sinful acts, or has conditions that can tempt you to sin is wrong.

You [are a] pleasure-loving kingdom, living at ease and feeling secure. ISAIAH 47:8

Making play your ultimate goal is a big mistake. Play and work must be kept in balance for a healthy and productive life.

PLEASURE *See also* Celebration, Joy, Satisfaction, Success

The hedonist believes anything that brings pleasure is good. The ascetic believes all that brings pleasure is evil. Neither position is biblical. Scripture clearly teaches that God intends human life to include physical, emotional, and spiritual pleasure. The Bible warns against the pursuit of certain pleasures such as gluttony, drunkenness, and extramarital sexual relations because they can quickly become our masters and cause us great harm and pain. Scripture teaches that the highest standard for human pleasure is experiencing that which is pleasing to God.

Some seem to think that pleasure and the Christian life don't mix—is that true?

LORD, you alone are my . . . cup of blessing. . . . You will show me the way of life, granting me the joy of your presence and the pleasures of living with you forever. PSALM 16:5, 11

God created you to find pleasure in your relationship with him. The pleasures and blessings that come from knowing God are certainly a wonderful part of the Christian life.

Oh, how beautiful you are! How pleasing, my love, how full of delights!
SONG OF SONGS 7:6

God created husbands and wives to experience the intimate pleasures of marriage. Understanding and experiencing these pleasures as a married couple are part of the Christian life.

Oh, the joys of those who do not follow the advice of the wicked . . . but they delight in the law of the LORD, meditating on it day and night. PSALM 1:1-2

The greatest pleasures come from pleasing God and experiencing the peace and joy that are the rewards of a faithful life.

What gives God pleasure?

The LORD asked Satan, "Have you noticed my servant Job? He is the finest man in all the earth. He is blameless—a man of complete integrity. He fears God and stays away from evil." JOB 1:8

God takes pleasure when you are faithful to him because it demonstrates your commitment to him.

[Jesus said,] "The one who sent me is with me—he has not deserted me. For I always do what pleases him." JOHN 8:29

God is pleased when you obey him because it demonstrates your love for him.

It is impossible to please God without faith. Anyone who wants to come to him must believe that God exists and that he rewards those who sincerely seek him. HEBREWS 11:6

God takes pleasure when you trust him because it demonstrates your faith in him.

God decided in advance to adopt us into his own family by bringing us to himself through Jesus Christ. This is what he wanted to do, and it gave him great pleasure. . . . God has now revealed to us his mysterious plan regarding Christ, a plan to fulfill his own good pleasure. EPHESIANS 1:5, 9

It gives God great pleasure to give eternal life to those who come to him through Jesus Christ.

What kinds of pleasure am I free to enjoy?
There is nothing better than to enjoy food and drink and to find satisfaction in work. . . . These pleasures are from the hand of God. For who can eat or enjoy anything apart from him? ECCLESIASTES 2:24-25

Since everything God created is good, we should not reject any of it but receive it with thanks. For we know it is made acceptable by the word of God and prayer. 1 TIMOTHY 4:4-5

God intends for you to enjoy the life he gave you and the good things he created for all people.

Nehemiah continued, "Go and celebrate with a feast of rich foods and sweet drinks, and share gifts of food with people who have nothing prepared. This is a sacred day before our LORD." NEHEMIAH 8:10

It is good to enjoy occasions of celebrating God's goodness and love.

Children born to a young man are like arrows in a warrior's hands. How joyful is the man whose quiver is full of them! PSALM 127:4-5

God wants you to enjoy the blessing of your family.

Jesus explained: "My nourishment comes from doing the will of God, who sent me, and from finishing his work." JOHN 4:34

The best kind of pleasure is delighting in doing what God wants.

LORD, you alone are my inheritance, my cup of blessing. . . . You will show me the way of life, granting me the joy of your presence and the pleasures of living with you forever. PSALM 16:5, 11

God wants you to take pleasure in him because he knows all of the good blessings he has in store for you.

What kinds of pleasures are wrong?
What sorrow for those who get up early in the morning looking for a drink of alcohol and spend long evenings drinking wine to make themselves flaming drunk. They furnish wine and lovely music at their grand parties . . . but they never think about the LORD or notice what he is doing. ISAIAH 5:11-12

It is wrong to pursue pleasure without also pursuing God's role in it. Pleasure without God is empty, making you need more to feel good. Taking pleasure in what the Lord is doing in your life is a great source of satisfaction.

When you follow the desires of your sinful nature, the results are very clear: sexual immorality, impurity, lustful pleasures. . . . Anyone living that sort of life will not inherit the Kingdom of God. GALATIANS 5:19-21

Pleasure that involves sin leads to eternal destruction.

As I looked at everything . . . it was all so meaningless—like chasing the wind.
ECCLESIASTES 2:11

Not all pleasure is good and often we pursue the wrong pleasures, those that ultimately harm us or that bring no meaning or purpose to life. In pursuing the wrong pleasures, life will eventually seem meaningless when we discover we've been wasting our time chasing after the wrong things.

POOR/POVERTY See also Needs, Oppression, Compassion, Giving

The Bible focuses primarily on two kinds of poverty—people who are in need of basic necessities (like food and clothing) and people who are in need of God (for they lack the Holy Spirit's presence in their life). We are called—commanded—to help both of these kinds of people as much as we possibly can, even if we are in need ourselves.

Does God really care about the poor?

He will rescue the poor when they cry to him; he will help the oppressed, who have no one to defend them. PSALM 72:12

[The Lord our God] lifts the poor from the dust and the needy from the garbage dump. He sets them among princes! PSALM 113:7-8

You are a tower of refuge to the poor, O LORD . . . a refuge from the storm and a shelter from the heat. ISAIAH 25:4

God cares deeply for the poor. He commands all believers to care for them, too. One test of godliness is your care for the poor. Whether you are poor, suffering from a crippling disease, grieving over the loss of a loved one, feeling lonely or abandoned, or living in constant danger, your greatest hope as a believer is that this condition is temporary. God promises that for all eternity you will be free from all trouble as you live with him in heaven. While you may not understand why some people seem to get all the breaks on earth, God assures you that those who love him will get all the breaks for eternity.

He has brought down princes from their thrones and exalted the humble. He has filled the hungry with good things and sent the rich away with empty hands. LUKE 1:52-53

God's righteous purposes will one day be fully accomplished. When Jesus returns, all wrongs will be made right. The hungry will be fed and those whose greed caused their hunger will be judged.

What is my responsibility to the poor?

Feed the hungry, and help those in trouble. Then your light will shine out from the darkness, and the darkness around you will be as bright as noon. ISAIAH 58:10

God has compassion for the poor, so if you would be godly, you must have compassion for the poor. Compassion that does not reach into your checkbook or onto your "to do" list is philosophical passion, not godly passion. Helping the poor is not merely an obligation but a privilege that should bring you great joy.

When you harvest the crops of your land, do not harvest the grain along the edges of your fields, and do not pick up what the harvesters drop. It is the same with your grape crop—do not strip every last bunch of grapes from the vines, and do not pick up the grapes that fall to the ground. Leave them for the poor and the foreigners living among you. LEVITICUS 19:9-10

[A] poor man died and was carried by the angels to be with Abraham. [A] rich man also died and was buried, and his soul went to the place of the dead. There, in torment, he saw Abraham in the far distance with [the poor man] at his side. LUKE 16:22-23

In New Testament times the Pharisees taught that wealth was proof of God's favor and a sign of a person's righteousness. Jesus surprised them with this story of a beggar being blessed in the next life while the rich man was being punished. Through faith in Jesus Christ, those who suffer in this lifetime will experience the full grace of God and vindication in heaven. This is part of our ultimate redemption, but it will not happen apart from faith in Jesus. This fact of heavenly vindication does not excuse any of us from caring for needs whenever and wherever we can. We will not be able to help everyone, but we are to minister to those around us.

POTENTIAL *See also* Abilities, Opportunities, Purpose

How often have you searched drawers and closets for a flashlight only to discover, when you finally find it, that the batteries are dead? Although the flashlight has the potential to provide light, without fresh batteries it is useless. All believers have within them the light of Christ and therefore the potential to shine upon others in such a way as to draw them to God. But if we lose our light, cover our light, or fail to allow the power of the Holy Spirit to illumine our hearts, we will have no more lasting effect than a dead flashlight.

How can I understand my potential?

Don't think you are better than you really are. Be honest in your evaluation of yourselves. ROMANS 12:3

Your full potential is in what God can do through you, not what you can do by yourself. Healthy self-esteem is an honest appraisal of yourself—not too proud because of the gifts and abilities God has given you, yet not so self-effacing that you fail to use your gifts and abilities to their potential for God's glory.

God knew his people in advance, and he chose them to become like his Son, so that his Son would be the firstborn among many brothers and sisters. ROMANS 8:29

You have the potential to be like Jesus if you come to know him and obey his teachings as recorded in the Bible.

We are God's masterpiece. He has created us anew in Christ Jesus, so we can do the good things he planned for us long ago. EPHESIANS 2:10

You have the potential to do the amazing things God has planned for you, if you only let him work through you.

Can I achieve my God-given potential?

Jesus told them, "I tell you the truth, if you have faith and don't doubt, you can do things like this and much more. You can even say to this mountain, 'May you be lifted up and thrown into the sea,' and it will happen." MATTHEW 21:21

Yes, I am the vine; you are the branches. Those who remain in me, and I in them, will produce much fruit. For apart from me you can do nothing. JOHN 15:5

You have the potential for a healthy, fruitful relationship with God. You need to be well connected with your Creator in order to achieve his plans for you.

You are the salt of the earth. But what good is salt if it has lost its flavor? Can you make it salty again? It will be thrown out and trampled underfoot as worthless. You are the light of the world—like a city on a hilltop that cannot be hidden. No one lights a lamp and then puts it under a basket. Instead, a lamp is placed on a stand, where it gives light to everyone in the house. In the same way, let your good deeds shine out for all to see, so that everyone will praise your heavenly Father. MATTHEW 5:13-16

You have the potential to reflect the glory of God when you let others see Jesus in your life.

The LORD [said to Jeremiah], ". . . You must go wherever I send you and say whatever I tell you." JEREMIAH 1:7

You have the potential to fulfill God's plan for your life when you follow God's direction.

If your gift is to encourage others, be encouraging. If it is giving, give generously. If God has given you leadership ability, take the responsibility seriously. And if you have a gift for showing kindness to others, do it gladly. Don't just pretend to love others. Really love them. Hate what is wrong. Hold tightly to what is good. Love each other with genuine affection, and take delight in honoring each other. ROMANS 12:8-10

I am praying that you will put into action the generosity that comes from your faith as you understand and experience all the good things we have in Christ. PHILEMON 1:6

You have the potential to influence others for God. So use whatever God has given you responsibly, generously, and joyfully in loving service to him and others.

How does God encourage me to reach the potential he sees in me?

Gideon . . . was threshing wheat at the bottom of a winepress to hide the grain from the Midianites. The angel of the LORD appeared to him and said, "Mighty hero, the LORD is with you! . . . Go with the strength you have, and rescue Israel from the Midianites. I am sending you!" "But Lord," Gideon replied, "how can I rescue Israel? . . . I am the least in my entire family!" JUDGES 6:11-15

The angel of the Lord greeted Gideon by calling him a "mighty hero." Was God talking to the right person? This was Gideon, hiding in a winepress from his enemies, who saw himself as "the least" in his family. God calls out the best in you, and he sees more in you than you see in yourself. You look at your limitations, but God looks at your potential. If you want to change your perspective, learn to see life from God's eyes. He doesn't put nearly as many limitations on you as you do. He sees you for what he intended you to be as well as for what you are.

It is not that we think we are qualified to do anything on our own. Our qualification comes from God. 2 CORINTHIANS 3:5

I can do everything through Christ, who gives me strength. PHILIPPIANS 4:13

God enables you with strength and unique abilities. Think more about what God can do through you than what you can do through your own abilities.

The LORD asked Moses, "Who makes a person's mouth? Who decides whether people speak or do not speak, hear or do not hear, see or do not see? Is it not I, the LORD? Now go! I will be with you as you speak, and I will instruct you in what to say." EXODUS 4:11-12

God equips you with the abilities and resources you'll need (the Bible, the church, prayer, godly friends) to receive wisdom and knowledge.

All Scripture is inspired by God and is useful to teach us what is true and to make us realize what is wrong in our lives. It corrects us when we are wrong and teaches us to do what is right. 2 TIMOTHY 3:16

Like newborn babies, you must crave pure spiritual milk so that you will grow into a full experience of salvation. Cry out for this nourishment. 1 PETER 2:2

God guides you with his Word.

Caleb tried to quiet the people as they stood before Moses. "Let's go at once to take the land," he said. "We can certainly conquer it!" NUMBERS 13:30

God strengthens you through the encouragement of others.

How will I know when I've reached my potential?

All glory to God, who is able, through his mighty power at work within us, to accomplish infinitely more than we might ask or think. EPHESIANS 3:20

I press on to possess that perfection for which Christ Jesus first possessed me. No, dear brothers and sisters, I have not achieved it, but I focus on this one thing: Forgetting the past and looking forward to what lies ahead, I press on to reach the end of the race and receive the heavenly prize for which God, through Christ Jesus, is calling us. PHILIPPIANS 3:12-14

The bad news is that you will never realize your full potential on this earth because your human nature is sinful and, therefore, you can't be perfect. But God promises that you have far more potential than you think, and that you can achieve this potential if you let him work through you. Reaching your goals will not happen overnight, but with small, steady steps every day in the right direction. Perseverance is the key to reaching your potential.

What can stop me from reaching my potential?

O Israel, when I first found you, it was like finding fresh grapes in the desert. When I saw your ancestors, it was like seeing the first ripe figs of the season. But then they deserted me for Baal-peor, giving themselves to that shameful idol. Soon they became vile, as vile as the god they worshiped. HOSEA 9:10

Few things are so tragic as wasted potential. You are created in the image of a loving and holy God, with the potential to reflect his goodness and grace. You begin to develop your spiritual potential when you recognize the damaging potential of your sinful nature and ask Jesus for forgiveness. The Bible promises that when you give Jesus control of your life, the Holy Spirit comes to live in your heart. The Spirit then begins the work of helping you reach the spiritual potential for which you were created—to become more like Christ and to use your spiritual gifts in helping others. Deciding not to follow Christ is deciding not to live up to the potential for which you were created.

Moses protested to God, "Who am I to appear before Pharaoh? Who am I to lead the people of Israel out of Egypt?" EXODUS 3:11

"O Sovereign LORD," [Jeremiah] said, "I can't speak for you! I'm too young!" The LORD replied, "Don't say, 'I'm too young,' for you must go wherever I send you and say whatever I tell you. And don't be afraid of the people, for I will be with you and will protect you. I, the LORD, have spoken!" JEREMIAH 1:6-8

Thinking your potential is based on and dependent on what you can do (in contrast to what God can do through you) will prevent you from reaching it.

If you can help your neighbor now, don't say, "Come back tomorrow, and then I'll help you." PROVERBS 3:28

A hard worker has plenty of food, but a person who chases fantasies has no sense. PROVERBS 12:11

Procrastination or laziness can hinder your potential. Who you will become is a by-product of what you do today. Don't waste the day.

POWER *See also* Authority, Control, Miracles, Strength, Victory

Imagine the earth's strongest earthquake, tallest tsunami, wildest volcano, and most devastating hurricane—all in one place. This cannot even begin to compare to God's power, because he is the Creator of all these phenomenas, and the created is never more powerful than the Creator. This same God who instantly calmed the storm over the Sea of Galilee has the power to calm the storms in one's heart, dry up a flood of fear, quench the lust for sin, and control the whirlwind of life.

What kind of power does a Christian really have?

I pray that . . . you will understand the incredible greatness of God's power for us who believe him. This is the same mighty power that raised Christ from the dead and seated him in the place of honor at God's right hand in the heavenly realms. EPHESIANS 1:18-20

I can do everything through Christ, who gives me strength. PHILIPPIANS 4:13

The God who created the world and raised Jesus from the dead offers his power to you. If you believe that God sent Jesus Christ to save you from sin, and if you ask him to forgive your sin and remove it, he will replace your sin-filled heart with the power to do good, to accomplish great things, and to resist the forces of evil.

With God's help we will do mighty things, for he will trample down our foes. PSALM 60:12

We use God's mighty weapons, not worldly weapons, to knock down the strongholds of human reasoning and to destroy false arguments. 2 CORINTHIANS 10:4

God gives you his power to resist Satan and to overcome evil with good.

We also pray that you will be strengthened with all his glorious power so you will have all the endurance and patience you need. COLOSSIANS 1:11

God has not given us a spirit of fear and timidity, but of power, love, and self-discipline. 2 TIMOTHY 1:7

God extends his power to you not just to combat evil but also to give you patience and strength in difficult times so you may grow spiritually mature.

How can I have true spiritual power?

It is not that we think we are qualified to do anything on our own. Our qualification comes from God. 2 CORINTHIANS 3:5

Through [Christ] God created everything in the heavenly realms and on earth. He made the things we can see and the things we can't see—such as thrones, kingdoms, rulers, and authorities in the unseen world. Everything was created through him and for him. COLOSSIANS 1:16

Spiritual power comes from God alone.

Three different times . . . [the Lord] said, "My grace is all you need. My power works best in weakness." So now I am glad to boast about my weaknesses, so that the power of Christ can work through me. 2 CORINTHIANS 12:8-9

The more you recognize your weaknesses and limitations, the more you understand God's power at work in you. Strength can make you proud and self-sufficient. You don't feel that you need to rely much on God or others when you are very good at something or have great authority. That is why God often works through your weaknesses—if you let him—because then there is no doubt that it is by his power and not your own that the task is getting done.

The eyes of the LORD search the whole earth in order to strengthen those whose hearts are fully committed to him. 2 CHRONICLES 16:9

I am the vine; you are the branches. Those who remain in me, and I in them, will produce much fruit. For apart from me you can do nothing. JOHN 15:5

God gives strength to those who are fully committed to him. Just as a branch needs to be connected to a tree to grow and thrive, you need to be connected to Jesus to grow and thrive spiritually.

After . . . prayer, the meeting place shook, and they were all filled with the Holy Spirit. Then they preached the word of God with boldness. ACTS 4:31

Pray in the Spirit at all times and on every occasion. Stay alert and be persistent in your prayers for all believers everywhere. EPHESIANS 6:18

Communicating with God fuels your spiritual life. If you want to operate an electric appliance, you must first plug it into the source of power. So it is with spiritual power. You must first connect with God, the source of spiritual power.

Be strong in the Lord and in his mighty power. Put on all of God's armor so that you will be able to stand firm against all strategies of the devil. EPHESIANS 6:10

God gives you all the power you need to stand firm against Satan's attacks. He armors you with truth, righteousness, peace, faith, and salvation (see verses 14-18).

How does God exercise his power?

You formed the mountains by your power. PSALM 65:6

God made the earth by his power, and he preserves it by his wisdom. With his own understanding he stretched out the heavens. JEREMIAH 10:12

The Son . . . sustains everything by the mighty power of his command. HEBREWS 1:3

God exercises his power in creating and sustaining the universe and everything in it.

The devil, who had deceived them, was thrown into the fiery lake of burning sulfur, joining the beast and the false prophet. There they will be tormented day and night forever and ever. REVELATION 20:10

By his power God has conquered our enemy, the devil.

The Son of Man has the authority on earth to forgive sins. MATTHEW 9:6

Jesus uses his power to forgive sins.

I give them eternal life, and they will never perish. No one can snatch them away from me, for my Father has given them to me, and he is more powerful than anyone else. No one can snatch them from the Father's hand. The Father and I are one. JOHN 10:28-30

By his power Jesus gives eternal life to his followers.

What are the dangers of power?

Where now is that great Nineveh . . . ? "Never again will [it] plunder conquered nations," [says the LORD]. NAHUM 2:11-13

Power that does not come from God is fragile. Those who are mighty today will fall tomorrow. You cannot count on any power that is not from God.

One day Korah . . . conspired with Dathan and Abiram. . . . They incited a rebellion against Moses. . . . They united against Moses and Aaron and said, ". . . What right do you have to act as though you are greater than the rest of the LORD's people?" . . . [Moses replied] "The LORD is the one you and your followers are really revolting against!" NUMBERS 16:1-3, 11

The desire for power is seductive and addictive. Self-serving power is always destructive. Don't seek power to get what you want and to control others, but to truly serve them.

"Are you the king of Israel or not?" Jezebel demanded. "Get up and eat something, and don't worry about it. I'll get you Naboth's vineyard!" So she wrote letters in Ahab's name, sealed them with his seal, and sent them. . . . In her letters she commanded: "Call the citizens together for fasting and prayer, and give Naboth a place of honor. And then seat two scoundrels across from him who will accuse him of cursing God and the king. Then take him out and stone him to death." 1 KINGS 21:7-10

Power can be used for evil purposes.

Jehoshaphat enjoyed great riches and high esteem, and he made an alliance with Ahab of Israel by having his son marry Ahab's daughter. A few years later he went to Samaria to visit Ahab, who prepared a great banquet for him and his officials. They butchered great numbers of sheep, goats, and cattle for the feast. Then Ahab enticed Jehoshaphat to join forces with him to recover Ramoth-gilead. "Will you go with me to Ramoth-gilead?" King Ahab of Israel asked King Jehoshaphat of Judah. Jehoshaphat replied, "Why, of course! You and I are as one, and my troops are your troops. We will certainly join you in battle." 2 CHRONICLES 18:1-3

Power can blind you to the truth by blurring the lines between right and wrong alliances, truth and lies.

I will give you one more chance to bow down and worship the statue I have made when you hear the sound of the musical instruments. But if you refuse, you will be thrown immediately into the blazing furnace. And then what god will be able to rescue you from my power? DANIEL 3:15

Power can cause you to act as though you were God. When you have everything you want, and when everyone does whatever you tell them, it's easy to think you are in charge of the universe.

How should I respond to those in power?

All glory to him who alone is God, our Savior through Jesus Christ our Lord. All glory, majesty, power, and authority are his before all time, and in the present, and beyond all time! JUDE 1:25

God alone has ultimate power, so worship only him. He is the only one who perfectly uses his power for the benefit of all.

Everyone must submit to governing authorities. For all authority comes from God, and those in positions of authority have been placed there by God. So anyone who rebels against authority is rebelling against what God has instituted, and they will be punished. ROMANS 13:1-2

Earthly rulers and authorities have power only because God has allowed them to exercise it temporarily. Respect earthly rulers for the power God gave them. But honor God for the ultimate power he has reserved for himself.

PRAISE *See also* Affirmation, Joy, Thankfulness, Worship

It is not unusual for observers to burst into spontaneous applause or cheers when a celebrity enters a room. Such experiences are a natural response to the presence of a person of power, position, or accomplishment. Likewise, when we enter the presence of God through worship, our natural response should be praise and adoration. The Bible teaches that God is the Creator of the universe and provider of salvation and therefore he alone is worthy of our highest praise.

Why is it so important to praise God?

All heaven will praise your great wonders, Lord; myriads of angels will praise you for your faithfulness. PSALM 89:5

It is good to give thanks to the Lord, to sing praises to the Most High. PSALM 92:1

Who can list the glorious miracles of the Lord? Who can ever praise him enough? PSALM 106:2

Consider how great God is—the awesome Creator of the universe. Then consider how sinful and mortal you are. Finally consider how great God's love is for you. How can you help but praise him? He is powerful enough to sustain the universe and loving enough to redeem it.

Let all that I am praise the LORD; may I never forget the good things he does for me. He forgives all my sins and heals all my diseases. He redeems me from death and crowns me with love and tender mercies. He fills my life with good things. PSALM 103:2-5

Praise God for his forgiveness, healing, and salvation which demonstrate his care for you now and forever.

Whatever is good and perfect comes down to us from God our Father, who created all the lights in the heavens. He never changes or casts a shifting shadow. JAMES 1:17

Praise God for his eternal and unchanging qualities which give you the confidence that he will do what he has promised.

How can I express my praise to God?

Each morning and evening they stood before the LORD to sing songs of thanks and praise to him. 1 CHRONICLES 23:30

I will sing to the LORD as long as I live. I will praise my God to my last breath! PSALM 104:33

Express your praise to God through frequent song.

All of you can join together with one voice, giving praise and glory to God, the Father of our Lord Jesus Christ. ROMANS 15:6

Express your praise to God through worship with other believers.

Praise him with a blast of the ram's horn; praise him with the lyre and harp! Praise him with the tambourine and dancing; praise him with strings and flutes! Praise him with a clash of cymbals; praise him with loud clanging cymbals. PSALM 150:3-5

God is the creator of music, and he is pleased when you use it to express your heartfelt praise for him.

I will sacrifice a voluntary offering to you; I will praise your name, O LORD, for it is good. PSALM 54:6

Express your praise with offerings to support God's work.

I hate all your show and pretense. . . . Away with your noisy hymns of praise! . . . Instead, I want to see a mighty flood of justice, an endless river of righteous living. AMOS 5:21-24

Your praise must be sincere and not hypocritical. Be careful not to let your praise become an empty spiritual ritual.

For what should I praise God?

All glory to him who loves us and has freed us from our sins by shedding his blood for us. REVELATION 1:5

For providing salvation through the death and resurrection of Jesus Christ.

The LORD is my strength and my song; he has given me victory. This is my God, and I will praise him—my father's God, and I will exalt him! EXODUS 15:2

For creating you, loving you, and inviting you into a personal relationship with him.

God is awesome in his sanctuary. The God of Israel gives power and strength to his people. Praise be to God! PSALM 68:35

O God, your ways are holy. Is there any god as mighty as you? PSALM 77:13

For his holiness and awesome power.

O my Strength, to you I sing praises, for you, O God, are my refuge, the God who shows me unfailing love. PSALM 59:17

Praise the LORD! Give thanks to the LORD, for he is good! His faithful love endures forever. PSALM 106:1

For his faithful and unfailing love for you.

All praise to God, the Father of our Lord Jesus Christ. God is our merciful Father and the source of all comfort. 2 CORINTHIANS 1:3

For his mercy despite your sinfulness and his comfort in times of sorrow.

Praise the name of God forever and ever, for he has all wisdom and power. DANIEL 2:20

For his wisdom that is far beyond what you can know or understand that he makes available to you in every situation.

Then I bowed low and worshiped the LORD, . . . the God of my master, Abraham, because he had led me straight to my master's niece to be his son's wife. GENESIS 24:48

For his guidance in your life.

O LORD, I will honor and praise your name, for you are my God. You do such wonderful things! You planned them long ago, and now you have accomplished them. ISAIAH 25:1

For all he has done for you and his people.

What is the importance of praising others?

The master was full of praise. "Well done, my good and faithful servant. You have been faithful in handling this small amount, so now I will give you many more responsibilities. Let's celebrate together!" MATTHEW 25:21

There is a difference between praising God, which is worship, and praising others, which is supporting and encouraging them through affirmation. Affirmation gives others a sense of worth, encouraging them to go on.

PRAYER *See also* Communication, Intimacy, Meditation, Worship

The most universally practiced yet least understood of human experiences, prayer is one of the great mysteries of the Christian faith. Its simplest definition is communication with God. Yet so often we approach prayer like a one-way telephone conversation, forgetting that God also wants to speak to us. And how do we pray—on our knees or standing; silently or out loud; alone or with others; by rote or spontaneously? And does prayer really induce God to manipulate events or otherwise act on our behalf? Although the Bible does not always address these questions directly, prayer appears on nearly every page as the very essence of a faith relationship with the living God. Simple enough for a child to understand and yet so profound we could spend a lifetime exploring its depths, prayer assumes that it is possible for us to have an intimate relationship with a God who hears, cares, and answers.

What is prayer?

If my people who are called by my name will humble themselves and pray and seek my face and turn from their wicked ways, I will hear from heaven. 2 CHRONICLES 7:14

Prayer is conversation with God. It is simply talking with God, telling him your thoughts and feelings, praising him, thanking him, confessing sin, asking for his help and advice, and listening for his answers. The essence of prayer is humbly entering the very presence of almighty God.

I confess my sins; I am deeply sorry for what I have done. PSALM 38:18

Prayer often begins with a confession of sin. It is through confession that we demonstrate the humility necessary for open lines of communication with our almighty, holy God.

The priest said, "Let's ask God first." 1 SAMUEL 14:36

David asked the LORD, "Should I go out to fight the Philistines?" 2 SAMUEL 5:19

Prayer is asking God for guidance and waiting for his direction and leading.

Before daybreak . . . Jesus got up and went out to an isolated place to pray. MARK 1:35

Prayer is an expression of an intimate relationship with your heavenly Father, who makes his love and resources available to you. Just as you enjoy being with people you love, you will enjoy spending time with God the more you get to know him and understand just how much he loves you.

I will praise you, LORD, with all my heart. . . . I will sing praises to your name, O Most High. PSALM 9:1-2

Through prayer you praise your mighty God.

Why is prayer important?

Keep on asking, and you will receive what you ask for. Keep on seeking, and you will find. Keep on knocking, and the door will be opened to you. For everyone who asks, receives. Everyone who seeks, finds. And to everyone who knocks, the door will be opened. . . . If you sinful people know how to give good gifts to your children, how much more will your heavenly Father give good gifts to those who ask him. MATTHEW 7:7-8, 11

There's more to prayer than just getting an answer to a question or a solution for a problem. God often does more in your heart through the act of prayer than he does in actually answering your prayer. As you persist in talking and listening you often gain greater understanding of yourself, your situation, your motivation, and God's nature and direction for your life.

How can I know God hears my prayers?

The LORD is close to all who call on him, yes, to all who call on him in truth.
PSALM 145:18

God invites you to make prayer your first response rather than your last resort. He always listens to those who are honest with him.

The eyes of the Lord watch over those who do right, and his ears are open to their prayers.
1 PETER 3:12

Since prayer is conversation with God, approach him with the same love and courtesy you would bring to any relationship you value. Pray with humility, not arrogance, admitting your sin and seeking his forgiveness.

We are confident that he hears us whenever we ask for anything that pleases him.
1 JOHN 5:14

While you may not know God's specific will for every situation, you do know that his will is to empower your obedience, to overcome evil with good, and to equip you to be his witness. You can pray confidently for his power and guidance in these situations and many others, knowing that you are asking for the very things he most longs to give.

Does the Bible teach a "right way" to pray?

David asked the LORD, "Should I go . . . ?" 1 SAMUEL 23:2

For days I mourned, fasted, and prayed to the God of heaven. NEHEMIAH 1:4

Throughout the Bible effective prayer includes elements of adoration, fasting, confession, requests, and persistence.

Pray like this: Our Father in heaven . . . MATTHEW 6:9

Jesus taught his disciples that prayer is an intimate relationship with the Father that includes a dependency for daily needs, commitment to obedience, and forgiveness of sin.

Jesus told his disciples . . . that they should always pray and never give up. LUKE 18:1

Prayer is to be consistent and persistent.

Jesus told this story to some who had great confidence in their own righteousness and scorned everyone else: "Two men went to the Temple to pray. One was a Pharisee, and the other was a despised tax collector. The Pharisee stood by himself and prayed this prayer: 'I thank you, God, that I am not a sinner like . . . that tax collector!' . . . But the tax collector stood at a distance and dared not even lift his eyes to heaven as he prayed. Instead, he beat his chest in sorrow, saying, 'O God, be merciful to me, for I am a sinner.' I tell you, this sinner, not the Pharisee, returned home justified before God. For those who exalt themselves will be humbled, and those who humble themselves will be exalted." LUKE 18:9-14

Prayer is a conversation between you and God, not a public show of spirituality.

Does God always answer prayer?

And God answered Leah's prayers. She became pregnant again and gave birth to a fifth son for Jacob. GENESIS 30:17

When they cry for help, I will not answer. Though they anxiously search for me, they will not find me. For they hated knowledge and chose not to fear the LORD. PROVERBS 1:28-29

The eyes of the Lord watch over those who do right, and his ears are open to their prayers. But the Lord turns his face against those who do evil. 1 PETER 3:12

God listens carefully to every prayer and answers it. His answer may be yes, no, or wait. Any loving parent gives all three of these responses to a child. Answering yes to every request would be dangerous to your well-being. Answering no to every request would be vindictive and stingy and would kill your spirit. Answering wait to every prayer would be frustrating. God always answers based on what he knows is best for you. When you don't get the answer you want, your spiritual maturity will grow as you seek to understand why God's answer is in your best interest.

I love the LORD because he hears my voice and my prayer for mercy. Because he bends down to listen, I will pray as long as I have breath! PSALM 116:1-2

Three different times I begged the Lord to take [the thorn in my flesh] away. Each time he said, "My grace is all you need. My power works best in weakness." 2 CORINTHIANS 12:8-9

God always listens and responds to your prayers. But, as your loving heavenly Father who knows what is best, he does not always give you what you ask for. You must trust his answer of yes, no, or wait. Otherwise, you are playing God and determining what is best for you.

If you remain in me and my words remain in you, you may ask for anything you want, and it will be granted! JOHN 15:7

We are confident that he hears us whenever we ask for anything that pleases him. 1 JOHN 5:14

As you maintain a close relationship with Jesus and consistently study his Word, your prayers will be more aligned with his will. When that happens, God is delighted to grant your requests.

How will God respond to my prayers?

He does not ignore the cries of those who suffer. PSALM 9:12

Give your burdens to the LORD, and he will take care of you. PSALM 55:22

Give all your worries and cares to God, for he cares about you. 1 PETER 5:7

God cares for you and does not ignore a single prayer, no matter how simple it may be. When you bring your burdens to God in prayer, you will often experience real freedom from worry and anxiety in your heart and soul because you are confident he cares and is listening. The assurance of God's love and concern refreshes you and renews your hope.

What role does prayer play in a leader's life?

Moses tried to pacify the LORD his God. "O LORD!" he said. "Why are you so angry with your own people whom you brought from the land of Egypt with such great power and such a strong hand?". . . So the LORD changed his mind about the terrible disaster he had threatened to bring on his people. EXODUS 32:11, 14

Leaders pray for the Lord's mercy on the people. This does not mean that they don't confront the people's sin, however. Moses' intercession saved the disobedient Israelites from the punishment of God's wrath.

Solomon stood before the altar of the LORD in front of the entire community of Israel. He lifted his hands toward heaven, and he prayed, "O LORD, God of Israel, there is no God like you in all of heaven above or on the earth below. You keep your covenant and show unfailing love to all who walk before you in wholehearted devotion." 1 KINGS 8:22-23

Leaders pray publicly at times, reminding their people that they can depend on the promises and power of God.

Jehoshaphat was terrified by this news and begged the LORD for guidance. He also ordered everyone in Judah to begin fasting. . . . He prayed, "O LORD, God of our ancestors, you alone are the God who is in heaven. You are ruler of all the kingdoms of the earth. You are powerful and mighty; no one can stand against you! . . . We are powerless against this mighty army that is about to attack us. We do not know what to do, but we are looking to you for help." 2 CHRONICLES 20:3, 6, 12

Leaders pray when they don't know exactly what to do, or when they don't have the resources they need for a crisis or situation.

Simon, Simon, Satan has asked to sift each of you like wheat. But I have pleaded in prayer for you, Simon, that your faith should not fail. So when you have repented and turned to me again, strengthen your brothers. LUKE 22:31-32

Leaders pray for the spiritual protection of those they lead.

We have not stopped praying for you since we first heard about you. We ask God to give you complete knowledge of his will and to give you spiritual wisdom and understanding. COLOSSIANS 1:9

Leaders pray for the spiritual growth and maturity of those they lead.

PREJUDICE *See also* Assumptions, Diversity, Judging Others, Status

Prejudice is forming a negative opinion about someone without adequate basis. It is judging someone without all the facts, condemning them in the court of personal opinion. Prejudice can be formed against a person or an entire race of people. The Bible speaks out clearly against prejudice. God created all people equally; all humans are unique and special creations formed by the Lord himself. We are not to be judgmental, but loving. We are not to be exclusive, but inviting.

What does God think of prejudice?

"Nazareth!" exclaimed Nathanael. "Can anything good come from Nazareth?"
JOHN 1:46

The woman was surprised, for Jews refuse to have anything to do with Samaritans. She said to Jesus, "You are a Jew, and I am a Samaritan woman. Why are you asking me for a drink?" JOHN 4:9

Jesus broke the judgmental stereotypes of his time. He reached across lines of racial and gender prejudice and division to demonstrate equality and respect for all people.

When [Peter] first arrived, he ate with the Gentile Christians, who were not circumcised. But afterward, when some friends of James came, Peter wouldn't eat with the Gentiles anymore. He was afraid of criticism from these people who insisted on the necessity of circumcision. . . . When I saw that they were not following the truth of the gospel message, I said to Peter in front of all the others, "Since you, a Jew by birth, have discarded the Jewish laws and are living like a Gentile, why are you now trying to make these Gentiles follow the Jewish traditions?" GALATIANS 2:12-14

Any form of prejudice is inconsistent with the Good News of Jesus Christ.

Peter told them, "You know it is against our laws for a Jewish man to enter a Gentile home like this or to associate with you. But God has shown me that I should no longer think of anyone as impure or unclean." ACTS 10:28

God wants you to consider whether you have any racial prejudices. All the goodness of God is available equally to all people.

How can I overcome prejudice?

The LORD said to Samuel, "Don't judge by his appearance or height. . . . The LORD doesn't see things the way you see them. People judge by outward appearance, but the LORD looks at the heart." 1 SAMUEL 16:7

My servant grew up in the LORD's presence like a tender green shoot, like a root in dry ground. There was nothing beautiful or majestic about his appearance, nothing to attract us to him. ISAIAH 53:2

Stereotypes abound—prejudice against all kinds of people exists. But the real person is inside; the body is only the shell, the temporary housing. It is wrong to judge a person by the outward appearance; the real person inside may be a person of incredible beauty. Even Jesus may not have had the tall, handsome body often attributed to him, for Isaiah the prophet said about the coming Savior, "There was nothing beautiful or majestic about his appearance" (Isaiah 53:2).

*The poor are despised even by their neighbors, while the rich have many "friends."...
Blessed are those who help the poor.* PROVERBS 14:20-21

Those who oppress the poor insult their Maker, but helping the poor honors him.
PROVERBS 14:31

If you favor some people over others, you are committing a sin. JAMES 2:9

God condemns prejudice based on financial well-being or socioeconomic class. Money is not a measure of character. Simply treat others as you would like to be treated (see Matthew 7:12).

Don't let anyone think less of you because you are young. 1 TIMOTHY 4:12

Never speak harshly to an older man, but appeal to him respectfully as you would to your own father. Talk to younger men as you would to your own brothers. 1 TIMOTHY 5:1

The Bible forbids prejudice and discrimination based on age. Maturity is not always a function of age. Be attentive to the character and qualifications of the young and old alike.

"Where did he get all this wisdom and the power to perform such miracles?" Then they scoffed, "He's just a carpenter, the son of Mary." Then Jesus told them, "A prophet is honored everywhere except in his own hometown and among his relatives and his own family." MARK 6:2-4

God does not write off families or occupations, and perhaps that is why Jesus chose to come to the family of a carpenter rather than the family of a king. God loves each person, regardless of occupation.

Peter [said], "I see very clearly that God shows no favoritism. In every nation he accepts those who fear him and do what is right." ACTS 10:34-35

When the others heard this, they stopped objecting and began praising God. They said, "We can see that God has also given the Gentiles the privilege of repenting of their sins and receiving eternal life." ACTS 11:18

God condemns racial prejudice. Since God created all ethnic groups and races, they deserve equal respect and treatment.

Can Christians be prejudiced against other Christians?

Why do you look down on another believer? Remember, we will all stand before the judgment seat of God. ROMANS 14:10

There is no longer Jew or Gentile, slave or free, male and female. For you are all one in Christ Jesus. GALATIANS 3:28

Christians are human, and just like everyone else exhibit sinful human nature. But Christians are supposed to be led and controlled by the Holy Spirit and must be careful not to let feelings of prejudice control their thoughts or actions. They, of all people, should understand that God created everyone equal in value and worth.

PREPARATION *See also* Discipline, Planning, Purpose

No one would attempt to run a marathon, or expect to win it, without preparing for the race. Without the proper training and discipline, we can't perform well. Much like training for a marathon, being prepared for anything in life involves thinking ahead, planning, discipline, and developing certain skills. Running the race in our spiritual life is no different. Being prepared spiritually means we've trained ourselves to be ready for the challenges of life, to grow in character, and to be adaptable to whatever God calls us to do.

How do I prepare for life's challenges?

When Abram heard that his nephew Lot had been captured, he mobilized the 318 trained men who had been born into his household. Then he pursued Kedorlaomer's army. . . . Abram recovered all the goods that had been taken, and he brought back his nephew Lot with his possessions and all the women and other captives.
GENESIS 14:14-16

Pharaoh sent for Joseph at once, and he was quickly brought from the prison. After he shaved and changed his clothes, he went in and stood before Pharaoh. GENESIS 41:14

How can you be wise at a moment's notice? The key is to prepare yourself by developing wisdom over time. You can't always anticipate what might happen in a day, but when you are prepared spiritually—when you have developed wisdom—you know the right things to do in God's eyes. This gives you the courage to act swiftly and decisively when necessary because you have a wellspring of wisdom to draw upon.

Moses said to the LORD, "O LORD, you are the God who gives breath to all creatures. Please appoint a new man as leader for the community. Give them someone who will guide them wherever they go and will lead them into battle, so the community of the LORD will not be like sheep without a shepherd." NUMBERS 27:15-17

Anticipating what may be ahead will often show you what needs to be done before the moment arrives.

What should I be prepared for?

Anyone who eats this bread or drinks this cup of the Lord unworthily is guilty of sinning against the body and blood of the Lord. That is why you should examine yourself before eating the bread and drinking the cup. 1 CORINTHIANS 11:27-28

Prepare for worship by getting your heart right with God.

If someone asks about your Christian hope, always be ready to explain it. 1 PETER 3:15

Always be prepared to explain what you believe about your faith in Jesus and why it is important to you.

Don't worry in advance about how to answer the charges against you, for I will give you the right words and such wisdom that none of your opponents will be able to reply or refute you! LUKE 21:14-15

Prepare to defend your faith. When attacks against your faith come, rely on the Holy Spirit to help you speak with authority and courage. If the Holy Spirit spoke to you today, would you hear him and know it was him? Take the time each day to stay in touch with the Spirit so you will be familiar with his voice.

Joshua told the people, "Purify yourselves, for tomorrow the LORD will do great wonders among you." JOSHUA 3:5

If you keep yourself pure, you will be a special utensil for honorable use. Your life will be clean, and you will be ready for the Master to use you for every good work. 2 TIMOTHY 2:21

Purity—keeping your heart as clean as possible from sin—prepares you to be filled with God's wisdom and guidance so that you can serve him and be involved in the work he is doing around you.

Be strong in the Lord and in his mighty power. Put on all of God's armor so that you will be able to stand firm against all strategies of the devil. EPHESIANS 6:10-11

Prepare for spiritual conflict by arming yourself with the defenses that God has given you—truth, righteousness, knowledge of the Scriptures, faith, assurance of salvation, and prayer (see verses 14-18).

What are the benefits of being prepared?

As predicted, for seven years the land produced bumper crops. During those years, Joseph gathered all the crops grown in Egypt and stored the grain from the surrounding fields in the cities. He piled up huge amounts of grain like sand on the seashore. Finally, he stopped keeping records because there was too much to measure. . . . Then the seven years of famine began, just as Joseph had predicted. The famine also struck all the surrounding countries, but throughout Egypt there was plenty of food. GENESIS 41:47-49, 54

Joseph listened to and followed God and, as a result, God showed Joseph how to prepare to save Egypt. God showed Joseph how to prepare for the famine during times of plenty. When you seek God's wisdom, you prepare your heart for future trials by gleaning from your current blessings. Whether that means putting a little extra into the savings account today or spending a little extra time studying God's Word, your preparation will carry you through life's more difficult times.

How does God prepare me to fulfill his call for me?

All Scripture is inspired by God. . . . God uses it to prepare and equip his people to do every good work. 2 TIMOTHY 3:16-17

May the God of peace—who brought up from the dead our Lord Jesus . . . equip you with all you need for doing his will. May he produce in you, through the power of Jesus Christ, every good thing that is pleasing to him. HEBREWS 13:20-21

One of the most frustrating things is to be given an assignment without the resources to accomplish it. But when God calls you to a task, he equips you for it. If you have tuned yourself to hear his call, you can be sure that he will give you the resources to fulfill it. He has given you his Word for counsel and direction, special abilities and gifts to use as you pursue your assignment, and his Holy Spirit to give you strength and guidance along the way. But to be fully prepared, you must tap into all he has given you.

Study this Book of Instruction continually. Meditate on it day and night so you will be sure to obey everything written in it. Only then will you prosper and succeed in all you do. JOSHUA 1:8

What is the Spirit of the Lord preparing you for? The key to recognizing his work in your life is to first obey God's clear instructions for living found in the Bible. If you obey God, your life will go in the right direction and you will walk through the doors of opportunity God opens for you.

How should I prepare for the coming of Christ?

Repent of your sins and turn to God, for the Kingdom of Heaven is near.
MATTHEW 3:2

Think clearly and exercise self-control. Look forward to the gracious salvation that will come to you when Jesus Christ is revealed to the world. So you must live as God's obedient children. Don't slip back into your old ways of living to satisfy your own desires. You didn't know any better then. But now you must be holy in everything you do, just as God who chose you is holy. 1 PETER 1:13-15

Prepare for Christ's coming by committing your life to obeying God's commands and by growing closer in relationship to him. As you do this, you will grow in holiness and be ready when he returns for you.

Learn a lesson from the fig tree. When its branches bud and its leaves begin to sprout, you know that summer is near. In the same way, when you see all these things, you can know his return is very near, right at the door. MATTHEW 24:32-33

Learn the signs of Christ's return and watch for them.

Keep watch! For you don't know what day your Lord is coming. Understand this: If a homeowner knew exactly when a burglar was coming, he would keep watch and not permit his house to be broken into. You also must be ready all the time, for the Son of Man will come when least expected. MATTHEW 24:42-44

Because you can't know when Christ will come again, you must be prepared at all times.

The Good News about the Kingdom will be preached throughout the whole world, so that all nations will hear it; and then the end will come. MATTHEW 24:14

When you take part in proclaiming the Good News of salvation, you help prepare others for the coming of Christ.

PRESENCE OF GOD *See also* Heaven, Holy Spirit, Prayer, Worship

God has promised that he will be with us, and that he will never leave us or forsake us. We can experience God's presence as we become aware of him in our lives, and we can actively pursue his presence by opening our hearts to him. In either case, God is already present.

How can I experience God's presence in my life?

The LORD is close to all who call on him, yes, to all who call on him in truth. PSALM 145:18

The Lord invites you to call on him without hesitation. He will reveal himself to you if your heart is sincere in wanting to know him rather than just wanting to use him as a good-luck charm or magic potion.

If my people . . . will . . . seek my face and turn from their wicked ways, I will hear from heaven and will forgive their sins. 2 CHRONICLES 7:14

The one thing I ask of the LORD—the thing I seek most—is to live in the house of the LORD all the days of my life. PSALM 27:4

Come close to God, and God will come close to you. Wash your hands, you sinners; purify your hearts, for your loyalty is divided between God and the world. JAMES 4:8

You can know God through earnest and sincere worship.

When you pray, I will listen. If you look for me wholeheartedly, you will find me.
JEREMIAH 29:12-13

Looking for and finding God requires purposeful prayer.

With all my faults and failures, how can I enter God's presence?

Because of our faith, Christ has brought us into this place of undeserved privilege where we now stand, and we confidently and joyfully look forward to sharing God's glory. ROMANS 5:2

Because of Christ and our faith in him, we can now come boldly and confidently into God's presence. EPHESIANS 3:12

[God] has reconciled you to himself through the death of Christ in his physical body. As a result, he has brought you into his own presence, and you are holy and blameless as you stand before him without a single fault. COLOSSIANS 1:22

A holy God cannot be in the presence of sin, so how can a sinful person experience God's presence? It is because of Jesus Christ's life, death, and resurrection—and your faith in him. He died and took the punishment for your sins. If you've asked Jesus to forgive your sins, as far as God is concerned, you now stand holy and blameless in his presence. He sees you as if you've never sinned and welcomes you into his presence.

What are some of the benefits of being in God's presence?

God is working in you, giving you the desire and the power to do what pleases him.
PHILIPPIANS 2:13

God's presence helps you to please and obey him.

The Lord is the Spirit, and wherever the Spirit of the Lord is, there is freedom.
2 CORINTHIANS 3:17

God's presence frees you from being a slave to sin.

Be strong and courageous! Do not be afraid or discouraged. For the LORD your God is with you wherever you go. JOSHUA 1:9

Even when I walk through the darkest valley, I will not be afraid, for you are close beside me. Your rod and your staff protect and comfort me. PSALM 23:4

God's presence gives you courage.

I waited patiently for the LORD to help me, and he turned to me and heard my cry. He lifted me out of the pit of despair, out of the mud and the mire. He set my feet on solid ground and steadied me as I walked along. PSALM 40:1-2

God's presence gives you help in your darkest times and security both now and forever.

The LORD is my shepherd; I have all that I need. He lets me rest in green meadows; he leads me beside peaceful streams. He renews my strength. PSALM 23:1-3

God's presence refreshes you with rest, peace, and strength.

I know the LORD is always with me. I will not be shaken, for he is right beside me. No wonder my heart is glad, and I rejoice. My body rests in safety. . . . You will show me the way of life, granting me the joy of your presence and the pleasures of living with you forever. PSALM 16:8-11

God's presence gives you lasting joy.

How do I know God is with me?

Surely your goodness and unfailing love will pursue me all the days of my life.
PSALM 23:6

You go before me and follow me. You place your hand of blessing on my head. . . . I can never escape from your Spirit! I can never get away from your presence! PSALM 139:5-7

I am convinced that nothing can ever separate us from God's love. Neither death nor life, neither angels nor demons, neither our fears for today nor our worries about tomorrow—not even the powers of hell can separate us from God's love. No power in the sky above or in the earth below—indeed, nothing in all creation will ever be able to separate us from the love of God. ROMANS 8:38-39

The Bible, God's Word to you, promises that when you have a relationship with God, his presence is always with you. When you believe this promise, you will start to see events in your life as evidence of his presence with and love for you.

I will ask the Father, and he will give you another Advocate, who will never leave you. He is the Holy Spirit, who leads into all truth. The world cannot receive him, because it isn't looking for him and doesn't recognize him. But you know him, because he lives with you. JOHN 14:16-17

When you place your trust in Jesus, God gives you his Spirit as your constant companion and guide. The Holy Spirit assures you in your heart of God's active presence in your life.

The LORD is a shelter for the oppressed, a refuge in times of trouble. PSALM 9:9

If you are trusting in God, you have his guarantee that his presence is with you regardless of life's circumstances.

The LORD was with Joseph, so he succeeded in everything he did as he served in the home of his Egyptian master. Potiphar noticed this and realized that the LORD was with Joseph, giving him success in everything he did. GENESIS 39:2-3

Was it because God had abandoned Joseph that he became a slave and a prisoner? No, even then God was with him. God remained at work in Joseph's life while he was a slave in Potiphar's household and a prisoner in jail. Regardless of your situation, God is actively present in your life, working to bring good out of every situation. One of the greatest evidences of God's presence is when he redeems good out of bad.

What comfort can I take from God's presence?

The Spirit is God's guarantee that he will give us the inheritance he promised.
EPHESIANS 1:14

The presence of God is a guarantee of his promises.

You have endowed [Israel's king] with eternal blessings and given him the joy of your presence. PSALM 21:6

I love your sanctuary, LORD, the place where your glorious presence dwells. PSALM 26:8

When you live in harmony with God, you will find joy and delight in his presence.

How can others see God's presence in me?

Pharaoh asked his officials, "Can we find anyone else like this man so obviously filled with the spirit of God?" GENESIS 41:38

Joseph used the abilities God gave him and then gave God the credit. Pharaoh immediately recognized Joseph as a man who was filled with the Spirit of God. Although your opportunities may not be as challenging as interpreting dreams for a king, others can see God in you as you use the abilities he has given you in your everyday circumstances. You have positive spiritual influence on others simply by serving them in a way that honors God. When you allow God to work in you, others will then see God's presence in you.

Is it really possible to experience God's presence today?

Let us go right into the presence of God with sincere hearts fully trusting him. . . . Let us think of ways to motivate one another to acts of love and good works.
HEBREWS 10:22-24

During Old Testament times, humans had more limited access to God's presence. For example, the high priest could enter the Holy of Holies only once a year. But when Jesus died for your sins, the veil between you and God was torn away, and you can now enter freely into his presence. Don't take for granted the privilege that is yours to enter directly into the very presence of God.

PRESSURE *See also* Crises, Overwhelmed, Problems, Stress, Work

Pressure puts great stress on our health and relationships. It can stretch us to our limit, and we fear we will snap. But pressure can be positive if we learn to grow from it. Just as a muscle can only grow when stressed, so our wisdom and character can only grow under the pressures of life. As we learn from what God is teaching us in stressful times, we become better equipped to deal with pressure the next time it comes.

What are some dangers of pressure?

The seed that fell among the thorns represents those who hear God's word, but all too quickly the message is crowded out by the worries of this life and the lure of wealth, so no fruit is produced. MATTHEW 13:22

Martha was distracted by the big dinner she was preparing. She came to Jesus and said, "Lord, doesn't it seem unfair to you that my sister just sits here while I do all the work? Tell her to come and help me." But the Lord said to her, "My dear Martha, you are worried and upset over all these details!" LUKE 10:40-41

Pressure can cause you to focus on the trivial and miss the significant. As pressure squeezes your perspective inward, you lose your ability to look outward. Preoccupation with the constant urgency of the moment blinds you to the big picture.

Keep watch and pray, so that you will not give in to temptation. For the spirit is willing, but the body is weak. MARK 14:38

Pressure often makes you vulnerable to temptation because it weakens your resistance.

In Solomon's old age, [his wives and concubines] turned his heart to worship other gods instead of being completely faithful to the LORD his God. 1 KINGS 11:4

Pressure can make you rationalize sin and compromise your beliefs. The pressure of peers and the seduction of riches can so occupy your heart that you leave no room for God. Lust crowds out true love, whether in your relationship with your spouse or with God.

Have mercy on me, LORD, for I am in distress. Tears blur my eyes. My body and soul are withering away. I am dying from grief; my years are shortened by sadness. Sin has drained my strength; I am wasting away from within. PSALM 31:9-10

Pressure can have negative physical effects. The mind, soul, and body are interrelated. As one malfunctions, the others get out of sync. Spiritual distress can induce physical or mental distress, just as physical or mental distress can induce sickness in your soul.

What are some benefits of pressure?

[Hezekiah] built many towns and acquired vast flocks and herds, for God had given him great wealth. . . . However, when ambassadors arrived from Babylon to ask about the remarkable events that had taken place in the land, God withdrew from Hezekiah in order to test him and to see what was really in his heart. 2 CHRONICLES 32:29-31

We can rejoice, too, when we run into problems and trials, for we know that they help us develop endurance. And endurance develops strength of character, and character strengthens our confident hope of salvation. ROMANS 5:3-4

Pressure can develop your strength of character. The question is not whether you will have pressure, but what will you do with pressure when it comes. If you deal with pressure with your own strength, you may be quickly and easily overcome. If you bring God into the picture, his wisdom will show you how to come through the pressure stronger and more joyful.

You must warn each other every day, while it is still "today," so that none of you will be deceived by sin and hardened against God. . . . Remember what it says: "Today when you hear his voice, don't harden your hearts as Israel did when they rebelled." HEBREWS 3:13-15

The urgency of God's pressure can be positive. At the right time, God presses you to a decision about him and about doing his work. To respond to his pressure has eternal benefits. To ignore it will lead to eternal disaster.

Remember that the heavenly Father to whom you pray has no favorites. He will judge or reward you according to what you do. So you must live in reverent fear of him during your time as "foreigners in the land." 1 PETER 1:17

The pressure of the coming Judgment Day can encourage you to right living today. A casual attitude toward God's judgment may allow you to become careless about sin today.

The words of the wise are like cattle prods—painful but helpful. Their collected sayings are like a nail-studded stick with which a shepherd drives the sheep. ECCLESIASTES 12:11

The pressure to learn is sometimes painful, even when learning Scripture, which brings wisdom and life.

The LORD burned with anger against Israel, and he turned them over to the Philistines and the Ammonites, who began to oppress them that year. For eighteen years they oppressed all the Israelites east of the Jordan River in the land of the Amorites (that is, in Gilead). . . . The Israelites were in great distress. Finally, they cried out to the LORD for help, saying, "We have sinned against you because we have abandoned you as our God and have served the images of Baal." JUDGES 10:7-10

Although you probably don't welcome pressure from ungodly sources, it can have great benefit if it turns you to God.

How can I best handle pressure?

[Jesus] took Peter, James, and John with him, and he became deeply troubled and distressed. He told them, "My soul is crushed with grief to the point of death. Stay here and keep watch with me." He went on a little farther and fell to the ground. He prayed that, if it were possible, the awful hour awaiting him might pass him by. "Abba, Father," he cried out, "everything is possible for you. Please take this cup of suffering away from me. Yet I want your will to be done, not mine." MARK 14:33-36

Follow Jesus' example of praying to God, seeking support from other Christians, and focusing on God's will.

As pressure and stress bear down on me, I find joy in your commands. PSALM 119:143

Immerse yourself in and obey God's Word, where you will find the secrets to lasting joy. The more you find joy in the Lord, the less you will feel stress from external pressures.

David was now in great danger because all his men were very bitter about losing their sons and daughters, and they began to talk of stoning him. But David found strength in the LORD his God. 1 SAMUEL 30:6

Focus on God's power and ability to solve your problems. You must believe that he cares and that he will help; otherwise, you won't seek him for help and won't receive it.

Moses' father-in-law exclaimed, . . . "This job is too heavy a burden for you to handle all by yourself." . . . Moses listened to his father-in-law's advice and followed his suggestions. He chose capable men from all over Israel and appointed them as leaders over the people. He put them in charge of groups of one thousand, one hundred, fifty, and ten. These men were always available to solve the people's common disputes. They brought the major cases to Moses, but they took care of the smaller matters themselves. EXODUS 18:17-18, 24-26

Allowing others to help you with the load is often an overlooked solution to the mounting pressure you feel from trying to do everything yourself.

[Joseph said,] "No one here has more authority than I do. [Potiphar] has held back nothing from me except you, because you are his wife. How could I do such a wicked thing? It would be a great sin against God." She kept putting pressure on Joseph day after day, but he refused to sleep with her, and he kept out of her way as much as possible. One day, however, no one else was around when he went in to do his work. She came and grabbed him by his cloak, demanding, "Come on, sleep with me!" Joseph tore himself away . . . [and] he ran from the house. GENESIS 39:9-13

The pressure you feel from the temptation to sin can best be handled by acknowledging sin for what it is and standing firm in your commitment to resist it. Standing firm sometimes means literally running away from temptations that may be too powerful for you to resist in your current condition.

Jesus said, "Come to me, all of you who are weary and carry heavy burdens, and I will give you rest. Take my yoke upon you. Let me teach you, because I am humble and gentle at heart, and you will find rest for your souls. For my yoke is easy to bear, and the burden I give you is light." MATTHEW 11:28-30

Don't worry about anything; instead, pray about everything. Tell God what you need, and thank him for all he has done. Then you will experience God's peace, which exceeds anything we can understand. His peace will guard your hearts and minds as you live in Christ Jesus. PHILIPPIANS 4:6-7

Embrace the peace that comes from knowing that God is in control. Let him carry your burdens to relieve the pressure and help you endure.

Are there ways to prevent or minimize pressure?

LORD, be merciful to us, for we have waited for you. Be our strong arm each day and our salvation in times of trouble. ISAIAH 33:2

The Lord wants to give you strength every day, not just in times of trouble. Calling on his wisdom and power every day will ease the pressures that would otherwise build up if you tried to do things on your own.

Daniel was determined not to defile himself by eating the food and wine given to them by the king. He asked the chief of staff for permission not to eat these unacceptable foods. DANIEL 1:8

Determine to be faithful to God before the time of pressure comes. It is much harder to make that decision after the pressure is already on.

This is what the LORD says—your Redeemer, the Holy One of Israel: "I am the LORD your God, who teaches you what is good for you and leads you along the paths you should follow. Oh, that you had listened to my commands! Then you would have had peace flowing like a gentle river and righteousness rolling over you like waves in the sea." ISAIAH 48:17-18

When you obey God, you avoid the pressures that come from sin and that complicate your life.

Save me, O God, for the floodwaters are up to my neck. PSALM 69:1

Ask God for help with situations before they become catastrophes.

PRETENDING *See also* Appearance, Deceit/Deception, Excuses, Lying

When children play "pretend," they almost always pretend to be someone great—a heroic firefighter, a brave soldier, a brilliant astronaut, or a caring schoolteacher. Their games of pretend are innocent enough and in fact, might inspire them to greatness. This kind of pretending is healthy, but somewhere between childhood and adulthood, the innocence of pretending is lost. The childhood game of pretending turns into a destructive way to hide the parts of us we are ashamed of and pose as someone greater than ourselves. God warns against pretending to be something we're not—especially when we pretend to be spiritually great. True authenticity comes from finding your real value in God's eyes and being honest with yourself and others. It is better to be honest about your failures than to lie about your successes.

Why do I pretend to be something or someone I'm not?

What sorrow awaits you teachers of religious law and you Pharisees. Hypocrites! . . . Outwardly you look like righteous people, but inwardly your hearts are filled with hypocrisy and lawlessness. MATTHEW 23:27-28

Pride—everyone wants to look honorable and important in the eyes of their peers. But looking honorable and having an honorable heart are two different things.

The king regretted what he had said; but because of the vow he had made in front of his guests, he issued the necessary orders. MATTHEW 14:9

Embarrassment—when you are embarrassed to admit what you did, you may be tempted to deceive others into thinking that what you've done is right.

Never once did we try to win you with flattery, as you well know. And God is our witness that we were not pretending to be your friends just to get your money! 1 THESSALONIANS 2:5

Flattery—you may use flattery to pretend you like someone in order to get something from them.

When the people of Gibeon heard what Joshua had done to Jericho and Ai, they resorted to deception to save themselves. . . . They put on worn-out, patched sandals and ragged clothes. . . . "But who are you?" Joshua demanded. "Where do you come from?" They answered, "Your servants have come from a very distant country." JOSHUA 9:3-5, 8-9

Selfishness—you may disguise your true motives in order to get what you want.

In what ways do I pretend before God?

But God says to the wicked: "Why bother reciting my decrees and pretending to obey my covenant? For you refuse my discipline and treat my words like trash." PSALM 50:16-17

She has only pretended to be sorry. JEREMIAH 3:10

[The Lord says,] "I hate all your show and pretense—the hypocrisy of your religious festivals and solemn assemblies." AMOS 5:21

You may pretend with your actions, religious practices, false repentance, and superficial obedience, but God knows your heart.

The Lord says, "These people say they are mine. They honor me with their lips, but their hearts are far from me. And their worship of me is nothing but man-made rules learned by rote." . . . "The LORD can't see us," they say. "He doesn't know what's going on!" ISAIAH 29:13-15

You may pretend with words and even with thoughts. If you keep doing this you can eventually fool even yourself into thinking your motives are sincere, and worse yet, that God does, too.

What are the dangers of pretending to be what I am not?

The LORD detests double standards; he is not pleased by dishonest scales. PROVERBS 20:23

God is so opposed to hypocrisy—pretending to be what you aren't—because it shows a heart of dishonesty. You risk the anger of God when you are a hypocrite.

Get rid of all . . . deceit, hypocrisy, jealousy, and all unkind speech. 1 PETER 2:1

Much of pretending grows out of deceit, which is harmful to your spiritual growth.

The rich among you have become wealthy through extortion and violence. Your citizens are so used to lying that their tongues can no longer tell the truth. MICAH 6:12

Evil people . . . will deceive others and will themselves be deceived. 2 TIMOTHY 3:13

After a while, a habit of deceitful pretending becomes common and even acceptable to you, dulling and even killing your conscience. Eventually deceivers deceive themselves, cutting them off from truth.

How can I take off the mask and stop pretending?

Keep me from lying to myself; give me the privilege of knowing your instructions. PSALM 119:29

Study God's Word. It illuminates deceit and teaches you how to live honestly and transparently.

Don't just pretend to love others. Really love them. Hate what is wrong. Hold tightly to what is good. Love each other with genuine affection, and take delight in honoring each other. ROMANS 12:9-10

The wisdom from above is first of all pure. It is also peace loving, gentle at all times, and willing to yield to others. It is full of mercy and good deeds. It shows no favoritism and is always sincere. JAMES 3:17

God's wisdom can change your thoughts and attitudes, and then produce authentic, godly actions. The closer you are to God the farther away you are from deceit.

I do not spend time with liars or go along with hypocrites. PSALM 26:4

Rescue me, O LORD, from liars and from all deceitful people. PSALM 120:2

Watch the company you keep. Deceitful friends will lead you deeper into deceit.

Don't think you are better than you really are. Be honest in your evaluation of yourselves, measuring yourselves by the faith God has given us. ROMANS 12:3

Be honest with yourself! Ask honest friends to give you a realistic estimate of your life and actions.

PRIDE *See also* Bragging, Hypocrisy, Selfishness, Status

There is a positive, healthy side to pride—finding joy in the accomplishments of your children or spouse, feeling satisfaction about the quality of your work. But the Bible speaks mainly about the destructive side of pride because it has such great power to damage our relationships with others and with God. Pride is destructive when it involves wanting too much recognition, taking too much credit, wanting our own way, thinking our way is best—in summary, thinking too highly of ourselves. It causes us to face the world from a selfish point of view, blinding us to our faults and leading to jealousy, envy, and a judgmental attitude toward others.

Why is pride considered one of the "seven deadly sins" when other things seem so much worse?

Your heart was filled with pride because of all your beauty. EZEKIEL 28:17

The Bible seems to indicate that pride was the sin that resulted in Lucifer (Satan) being cast from heaven. If selfish pride is strong enough to rip an angel away from the very presence of God in heaven, it is certainly strong enough to do much damage in your own life.

When [King Nebuchadnezzar's] heart and mind were puffed up with arrogance, he was brought down from his royal throne. DANIEL 5:20

Pride leads to a hardness of heart, which, in turn, leads to an arrogant disregard of God and sin.

The wicked are too proud to seek God. They seem to think that God is dead. PSALM 10:4

Pride leads to ignoring God (because you think your way is better) and setting a course for a life of disobedience.

[People in the last days] will be boastful and proud. . . . They will be unloving and unforgiving. . . . They will betray their friends. 2 TIMOTHY 3:2-4

Pride can destroy relationships faster than almost anything else because it uses others to strengthen your position at their expense.

The Pharisee stood by himself and prayed this prayer: "I thank you, God, that I am not a sinner like everyone else. . . . I'm certainly not like that tax collector!" LUKE 18:11

Pride blinds you to your own sin.

You have been deceived by your own pride because you live in a rock fortress and make your home high in the mountains. OBADIAH 1:3

Pride finds comfort in false security.

If you pay attention to what I have quoted from the Scriptures, you won't be proud of one of your leaders at the expense of another. 1 CORINTHIANS 4:6

Pride can infect your spiritual life and divide the church.

Why must I beware of pride?

You rescue the humble, but you humiliate the proud. PSALM 18:27

Pride goes before destruction, and haughtiness before a fall. PROVERBS 16:18

Those who exalt themselves will be humbled, and those who humble themselves will be exalted. MATTHEW 23:12

God delivers the humble but humiliates the proud. Don't humiliate yourself by thinking you're above rescuing. If you reject your Savior now, on the Day of Judgment he will reject you because of your arrogance and pride.

When [King Uzziah] had become powerful, he also became proud, which led to his downfall. 2 CHRONICLES 26:16

An inflated estimation of your successes leads to prideful behavior and, ultimately, judgment. King Uzziah, in pride, thought his position and success made him immune from the standards to which all others were subject. God judged him for his presumption.

Instantly, an angel of the Lord struck Herod with a sickness, because he accepted the people's worship instead of giving the glory to God. ACTS 12:23

If left unchecked, pride will delude you into thinking you have almost Godlike qualities that demand the respect and reverence of others. This is especially unacceptable to God.

As Balaam and two servants were riding along, Balaam's donkey saw the angel of the LORD standing in the road. . . . The donkey bolted off the road. . . . It tried to squeeze by and crushed Balaam's foot against the wall. . . . "You have made me look like a fool!" Balaam shouted. "If I had a sword with me, I would kill you!" . . . Then the LORD opened Balaam's eyes, and he saw the angel of the LORD [who said,] "I have come to block your way because you are stubbornly resisting me." NUMBERS 22:22-25, 29-32

The next time your pride is hurt and you feel anger rising up within you, don't assume that you are right and everyone else is at fault. Balaam's anger immediately flared up against his donkey. Balaam assumed that he was right and that the problem was the donkey's fault. Fortunately for Balaam, he finally realized that the donkey had saved his life. Instead of soothing your pride by justifying your actions, see whether you can justify your motives. This will tell you if your anger is warranted or your pride overinflated.

Let's build a great city for ourselves with a tower that reaches into the sky. This will make us famous. GENESIS 11:4

It is not that we think we are qualified to do anything on our own. Our qualification comes from God. 2 CORINTHIANS 3:5

Power is intoxicating—with it comes recognition, control, and often wealth. Each of these feeds pride, and pride leads us away from God and into sin. This is why power so often corrupts. If you are in a position of power or authority, two things will help you use it wisely: accountability and service. When you have to explain your motives to others, you will be more careful in what you do and say. When you determine to serve others with your power rather than be served, you will gain great support and loyalty from those in your care.

When is pride healthy or appropriate?

I have reason to be enthusiastic about all Christ Jesus has done through me in my service to God. ROMANS 15:17

You can feel satisfaction in what God does through you. Paul was not proud of what he had accomplished on his own but of what God had accomplished through him.

Are we commending ourselves to you again? No, . . . it is to bring glory to God. 2 CORINTHIANS 5:12-13

May I never boast about anything except the cross of our Lord Jesus Christ. GALATIANS 6:14

Like Paul, if you take pride in anything, you ought to take pride in the God you serve.

God has united you with Christ Jesus. For our benefit God made him to be wisdom itself. Christ made us right with God; he made us pure and holy, and he freed us from sin. Therefore, as the Scriptures say, "If you want to boast, boast only about the LORD." 1 CORINTHIANS 1:30-31

Pride is appropriate when it causes you to be grateful to God for his gifts. When you look at your spouse, or children, or talents and your heart wells up with gratitude to God, he is pleased. Then your focus is on him and not on yourself.

PRIORITIES *See also* Convictions, Goals, Purpose, Stewardship

You're having a very personal and significant conversation with a friend at the kitchen table. Or you're reading a Bible story with your young child just before tucking her in bed. Then the phone rings. Most of us would answer the phone, because interruptions have become inevitable in our culture. Our lives tend to skip from one urgent interruption to another. And all the while we keep missing what is really important. What are the things that matter most in life, the true priorities of life? How can we distinguish true priorities from false ones, like the ringing phone? The Bible offers some answers.

What should be my highest priority?

Jesus replied, "The most important commandment is this: 'Listen, O Israel! The LORD our God is the one and only LORD. And you must love the LORD your God with all your heart, all your soul, all your mind, and all your strength.' The second is equally important: 'Love your neighbor as yourself.' No other commandment is greater than these." MARK 12:29-31

Jesus clearly stated the two greatest priorities for every person—to love God and to love others, and to do it with all you've got.

Choose today whom you will serve. . . . As for me and my family, we will serve the LORD.
JOSHUA 24:15

God loved the world so much that he gave his one and only Son, so that everyone who believes in him will not perish but have eternal life. JOHN 3:16

Obeying God and accepting Jesus' gift of salvation are also high priorities. Nothing affects your eternal future so significantly, and nothing will alter your immediate future so significantly.

How can I tell if God is really my first priority?

What does the LORD your God require of you? He requires only that you fear the LORD your God, and live in a way that pleases him, and love him and serve him with all your heart and soul. And you must always obey the LORD's commands and decrees . . . for your own good. DEUTERONOMY 10:12-13

Wherever your treasure is, there the desires of your heart will also be. LUKE 12:34

If God is the center of your life, you will make your relationship with him your highest priority. You will long to spend time with him, to talk to him, to listen to him, to think often about him, to please him, and to obey his Word. Your heart will yearn for him. And it's the heart that really matters to God.

Think about the things of heaven, not the things of earth. COLOSSIANS 3:2

If spending eternity with God and others you love is your highest goal, everything you do today should be done to invest in eternity.

How do I know what's really important?

Seek his will in all you do, and he will show you which path to take. PROVERBS 3:6

If all of your priorities focus on what is best for you, you will not achieve God's best for you. Always seek God's input first in any decision. When considering some course of action, ask yourself if it would be a priority to God.

You hoped for rich harvests, but they were poor. And when you brought your harvest home, I blew it away. Why? Because my house lies in ruins, says the LORD of Heaven's Armies, while all of you are busy building your own fine houses. HAGGAI 1:9

Priorities are scales on which your love for God is weighed. Be sure to take care of God's agenda before your own.

How do I set priorities?

Give me an understanding heart so that I can . . . know the difference between right and wrong. 1 KINGS 3:9

Tenaciously seeking after God's wisdom is the way to discern right priorities.

Seek the Kingdom of God above all else, and live righteously, and he will give you everything you need. MATTHEW 6:33

Be intentional about aligning your priorities with the Kingdom of God. Only then will your life have its fullest meaning.

Trust in the LORD with all your heart; do not depend on your own understanding. Seek his will in all you do, and he will show you which path to take. PROVERBS 3:5-6

Putting God first in your life helps put all of your other priorities in order.

What are some of the benefits of living with the right priorities and the dangers of living with the wrong priorities?

How joyful are those who fear the LORD—all who follow his ways! You will enjoy the fruit of your labor. How joyful and prosperous you will be! PSALM 128:1-2

The proper priorities bring lasting joy despite life's circumstances and a deep sense of satisfaction that you are doing the right thing, making a lasting impact, and pleasing God.

Unless the LORD builds a house, the work of the builders is wasted. Unless the LORD protects a city, guarding it with sentries will do no good. It is useless for you to work so hard from early morning until late at night, anxiously working for food to eat; for God gives rest to his loved ones. PSALM 127:1-2

Wrong priorities can lead to useless activity and unproductive anxiety—both a fruitless waste of life.

PROBLEMS See also Challenges, Crisis, Frustration, Stress, Testing

Your life may be filled with problems—troubled relationships, financial difficulties, or physical limitations. The presence of problems doesn't mean that God is absent or that he doesn't love you. Problems come to everyone, but with God, you have the resources to deal with any problem that comes your way.

How does God view my problems?

The LORD helps the fallen and lifts those bent beneath their loads. PSALM 145:14

God is not only aware of your problems, he wants to help you resolve them.

We are hunted down, but never abandoned by God. We get knocked down, but we are not destroyed. 2 CORINTHIANS 4:9

After you have suffered a little while, he will restore, support, and strengthen you, and he will place you on a firm foundation. 1 PETER 5:10

God will never desert those who follow him. He doesn't take the day off and forget about you. He has promised to help you in your difficulties. To abandon you, God would have to cease loving you, and he cannot do that, for he is love.

Moses pleaded with the LORD, "O Lord, I'm not very good with words. I never have been, and I'm not now, even though you have spoken to me. I get tongue-tied, and my words get tangled." Then the LORD asked Moses, "Who makes a person's mouth? Who decides whether people speak or do not speak, hear or do not hear, see or do not see? Is it not I, the Lord? Now go! I will be with you as you speak, and I will instruct you in what to say." EXODUS 4:10-12

God specifically addresses your problems with trustworthy, sure solutions. When you take your problems to God, you can rely on him to deal with them. But expect that he will deal with them his way, which is always in your best interests. Often he uses your problems to help you grow.

The believers who were scattered preached the Good News about Jesus wherever they went. ACTS 8:4

God causes everything to work together for the good of those who love God and are called according to his purpose for them. ROMANS 8:28

Everything that has happened to me here has helped to spread the Good News. For everyone here, including the whole palace guard, knows that I am in chains because of Christ. And because of my imprisonment, most of the believers here have gained confidence and boldly speak God's message without fear. PHILIPPIANS 1:12-14

God may use your problems to lead you in a new direction for a new assignment. He can turn your problems into an avenue for his work.

What are some common mistakes I might make in handling problems?

Sarai, Abram's wife, took Hagar the Egyptian servant and gave her to Abram as a wife. GENESIS 16:3

Impatience can tempt you to take matters into your own hands. Before you make a rash decision, make sure you have talked to God about your problem and that your solution doesn't violate God's Word. Being too quick to try to solve a problem doesn't allow God to work it out in his timing and in his way.

Sarai said to Abram, "This is all your fault! I put my servant into your arms, but now that she's pregnant she treats me with contempt." GENESIS 16:5

You might be tempted to blame others for your problem, even if it was self-inflicted. Blaming others will not resolve the conflict and will only delay getting to the real cause.

After exploring the land for forty days, the men ... reported to the whole community what they had seen and showed them the fruit they had taken from the land. This was their report to Moses: "We entered the land you sent us to explore, and it is indeed a bountiful country. ... But the people living there are powerful, and their towns are large and fortified. We even saw giants there!" NUMBERS 13:25-28

Focusing on all the negative possibilities of your problem prevents you from seeing the positive potential of God at work for you.

The angel said to her, "Hagar, Sarai's servant, where have you come from, and where are you going?" "I'm running away from my mistress, Sarai," she replied. GENESIS 16:8

At times, you may feel like running away from your problems rather than facing them.

How can I best cope with life's problems?

When I am afraid, I will put my trust in you. I praise God for what he has promised. I trust in God, so why should I be afraid? What can mere mortals do to me? PSALM 56:3-4

You will keep in perfect peace all who trust in you, all whose thoughts are fixed on you! ISAIAH 26:3

Don't worry about anything; instead, pray about everything. Tell God what you need, and thank him for all he has done. PHILIPPIANS 4:6

At times your problems might be too big for you. You need someone bigger, wiser, and stronger than you or your problems to help. God should be your first and primary point of contact. Trust him as you honestly communicate with him in prayer about your worries and fears.

Your laws please me; they give me wise advice. PSALM 119:24

When you walk, [these words of] counsel will lead you. When you sleep, they will protect you. When you wake up, they will advise you. PROVERBS 6:22

God's Word is the best source of wise counsel to help you deal with problems.

A mob quickly formed against Paul and Silas, and the city officials ordered them stripped and beaten with wooden rods. They were severely beaten, and then they were thrown into prison. The jailer was ordered to make sure they didn't escape. So the jailer put them into the inner dungeon and clamped their feet in the stocks. Around midnight Paul and Silas were praying and singing hymns to God, and the other prisoners were listening. ACTS 16:22-25

Your problems do not have to weaken your faith, praise, or joy. If this is happening, your trust in God is too small. Seeking God's solutions for your problems should enhance your faith, praise, and joy because you will wait and hope expectantly to see him intervene for you.

How should I learn and grow from my problems?

Those who are wise . . . will see in our history the faithful love of the LORD. PSALM 107:43

The more you see God at work in your problems, the more you learn about his faithful, loving character.

When troubles come your way, consider it an opportunity for great joy. For you know that when your faith is tested, your endurance has a chance to grow. So let it grow, for when your endurance is fully developed, you will be perfect and complete, needing nothing. . . .

God blesses those who patiently endure testing and temptation. Afterward they will receive the crown of life that God has promised to those who love him. JAMES 1:2-4, 12

The more you endure life's problems, the more you will see your own character strengthened. The more you become the kind of person God desires, the more you can do the kind of work God desires.

We live in such a way that no one will stumble because of us, and no one will find fault with our ministry. . . . We patiently endure troubles and hardships and calamities of every kind. . . . We prove ourselves by our purity, our understanding, our patience, our kindness, by the Holy Spirit within us, and by our sincere love. We faithfully preach the truth. God's power is working in us. We use the weapons of righteousness in the right hand for attack and the left hand for defense. We serve God whether people honor us or despise us, whether they slander us or praise us. . . . Our hearts ache, but we always have joy. We are poor, but we give spiritual riches to others. We own nothing, and yet we have everything. 2 CORINTHIANS 6:3-10

The more you endure life's problems, the more you learn what is most important in life. The more you realize what is most important, the more you will put the right things first.

We were crushed and overwhelmed beyond our ability to endure, and we thought we would never live through it. In fact, we expected to die. But as a result, we stopped relying on ourselves and learned to rely only on God, who raises the dead. And he did rescue us from mortal danger, and he will rescue us again. We have placed our confidence in him, and he will continue to rescue us. 2 CORINTHIANS 1:8-10

The more you endure life's problems, the more you see God as the source of your strength and your help. When you realize the source of your strength, the more you rely on God to see you through life's problems.

How can I help others in the midst of their problems?

All praise to God, the Father of our Lord Jesus Christ. God is our merciful Father and the source of all comfort. He comforts us in all our troubles so that we can comfort others. When they are troubled, we will be able to give them the same comfort God has given us. 2 CORINTHIANS 1:3-4

Continue to show deep love for each other, for love covers a multitude of sins. 1 PETER 4:8

You can genuinely love others with your actions, your attitudes, your words, and your presence. Love resolves a thousand problems and prevents a thousand more.

Share each other's burdens, and in this way obey the law of Christ. GALATIANS 6:2

God works through others to show comfort and concern, to restore and refresh, to correct and challenge. While everyone has burdens to bear, one of the great advantages of being part of God's family is that you do not have to bear them alone.

What should I do when problems overwhelm me?

The LORD is my light and my salvation—so why should I be afraid? The LORD is my fortress, protecting me from danger, so why should I tremble? PSALM 27:1

Problems tend to turn your focus away from God and toward the trouble that intimidates you. Use your problems as opportunities to rely on the Lord for his protection, his guidance, and his saving power.

The LORD helps the fallen and lifts those bent beneath their loads. PSALM 145:14

You can't help a person who doesn't want to be helped. God finds the fallen and never passes them by, but they have to want to be helped up. When you feel you can't go another step, allow him to shoulder your load, ease your burden, and heal your pain.

Why am I discouraged? Why is my heart so sad? I will put my hope in God! I will praise him again—my Savior and my God! Now I am deeply discouraged, but I will remember you. PSALM 42:5-6

Spiritual amnesia robs you of the comfort and hope you long for. Remember God's mercy. He has been faithful in the past and will be faithful in the future. Memory of what God has done for you ignites the fire of hope, and praise drives away the darkness of despair.

What are some ways God cares for me in times of trouble?

He will order his angels to protect you wherever you go. PSALM 91:11

Angels are . . . servants—spirits sent to care for people who will inherit salvation. HEBREWS 1:14

In addition to all the other sources of help, God sends his mighty angels to watch over you. Though they are rarely seen, you can trust God's Word that they are watching out for you.

We are pressed on every side by troubles, but we are not crushed. We are perplexed, but not driven to despair. We are hunted down, but never abandoned by God. 2 CORINTHIANS 4:8-9

God shows his care by his constant presence in your life. At the very moment of your greatest trouble or deepest hurt, God is already there taking care of you, tending to your wounds and comforting your fears. Will you let him care for you or will you push him away?

[Jesus said,] "I have told you all this so that you may have peace in me. Here on earth you will have many trials and sorrows. But take heart, because I have overcome the world." JOHN 16:33

We have a priceless inheritance—an inheritance that is kept in heaven for you, pure and undefiled, beyond the reach of change and decay. 1 PETER 1:4

Perhaps the best way God cares for you in times of trouble is to guarantee a future and a place where all problems will end. No matter what the future of this earth holds, you can be sure that heaven will be perfectly free of problems and worries.

PROCRASTINATION See also Fear, Laziness, Goals, Purpose

All of us put off doing certain things: going to the dentist, filing tax returns, writing that letter, fixing the leaky faucet. Why do we avoid that which we know we must do sooner or later? Sometimes we fear discomfort or pain; sometimes we fear failure; often we are just plain lazy. Sometimes our failure to act is itself an act of anger or rebellion. In Scripture, we find encouragement for thoughtful decisions, courageous commitment, and prompt action.

Why do I procrastinate?

A little extra sleep, a little more slumber, a little folding of the hands to rest—then poverty will pounce on you like a bandit. PROVERBS 6:10-11

Procrastination is often a form of laziness which the Bible calls sin.

I was afraid I would lose your money, so I hid it in the earth. MATTHEW 25:25

Fear of failure can make a task hard to get started. However, it's better to try and fail a couple times than to never try at all.

What are the dangers of procrastination?

How long are you going to wait before taking possession of the remaining land? JOSHUA 18:3

Making excuses is an unhealthy habit of the procrastinator. Procrastination, at times, can be a form of disobedience against God.

You . . . must keep watch! For you do not know the day or hour of my return. MATTHEW 25:13

Failure to be prepared for the coming of Christ is the most costly form of procrastination.

Is procrastination a sin?

Work hard and become a leader; be lazy and become a slave. PROVERBS 12:24

Never be lazy, but work hard and serve the Lord enthusiastically. ROMANS 12:11

We often think of sin as doing something we should not do, but sin is also the failure to do what we should. Procrastination is a precursor to laziness, and the Bible says laziness is wrong. The more you procrastinate, the less time you have to help and serve others. The cure for procrastination is purpose. Purpose involves finding a reason and motivation for doing something you know you should do. Purpose requires courage; you must confront yourself or the enemy, and have the discipline to say no to what distracts you from your purpose. Don't let procrastination lead you into sin.

PRODUCTIVITY See also Accomplishments, Goals, Responsibility

Productivity is almost universally measured in numbers. How many widgets were produced; how many sold; how much profit was earned? We measure productivity, even in our personal lives, in quantitative, objective terms. How much has our home gained in equity since we moved in? How many A's do our children receive on their report cards? How many items did we cross off our "to do" list today? This view of productivity is fine and good and helps us evaluate work performance and personal achievement. But the Bible defines productivity not only in terms of numbers but by relationships and character. When all is said and done, these form the only bottom line that really matters.

What does the Bible mean when it says my life is to produce "good fruit"?

Oh, the joys of those who do not follow the advice of the wicked, or stand around with sinners, or join in with mockers. . . . They are like trees planted along the riverbank, bearing fruit each season. Their leaves never wither, and they prosper in all they do.
PSALM 1:1-3

The Bible often uses metaphors of trees and vines to paint a picture of how people should be useful and productive. As God's follower you are to live a life that bears the healthy fruit of righteousness, justice, kindness, love, and truth—all important and productive means of growing God's kingdom on earth. These good deeds served to others will leave a wonderful taste in their mouths for God and his way of living.

A tree is identified by its fruit. . . . A good person produces good things from the treasury of a good heart. LUKE 6:44-45

Just like an apple can look good on the outside but be full of worms, so the fruit God desires in you is not the external appearance of goodness but the internal authenticity of a heart that truly wants to love and serve him. False pretenses or pretending to be spiritual shows a rotten core which cannot be productive. A good heart is the key to producing good deeds.

How can I produce this "good fruit"?

A branch cannot produce fruit if it is severed from the vine, and you cannot be fruitful unless you remain in me. JOHN 15:4

Your life will bear good fruit only when you stay connected to the source of growth. Where else could you be so effectively watered and nurtured than from the nutrients God provides through his Word and himself?

You are united with the one who was raised from the dead. As a result, we can produce a harvest of good deeds for God. ROMANS 7:4

Let the Holy Spirit guide your lives. Then you won't be doing what your sinful nature craves. GALATIANS 5:16

Because of Jesus' power over death and the indwelling of his Holy Spirit, your old nature is put to death, allowing your new nature to produce good fruit. Your old nature prevented you from accomplishing tasks with eternal significance, but with your new nature, there is little to hold you back from great productivity.

Should Christians care how productive they are at work or in business?

A hard worker has plenty of food, but a person who chases fantasies has no sense.
PROVERBS 12:11

The Bible consistently teaches that hard work increases the probability of blessings and success, and guarantees a prosperous character and fulfilling spiritual life.

Stay away from all believers who live idle lives and don't follow the tradition they received from us. . . . We were not idle when we were with you. . . . We worked hard day and night so we would not be a burden to any of you. 2 THESSALONIANS 3:6-8

Christians are expected to be productive so they don't become burdens to others and bad examples to the world.

PROFANITY *See also* Habits, Respect, Self-Control, Words

To profane something, whether the flag of your nation or the name of God, is to make common or to denigrate what is to be respected or holy. It means to pollute that which is pure. When we use the words "God" or "Jesus Christ" as epithets or expletives, we profane his holy name. When we lace our speech with coarse or vulgar language, we profane not only God but ourselves. As Christians with a new nature we are to be pure. Jesus taught that it's not what goes in the mouth that is sin but what comes out.

They're just words. Why is profanity such a big deal?

Fix your thoughts on what is true, and honorable, and right, and pure, and lovely.
PHILIPPIANS 4:8

What you say shows everyone what is in your heart and mind. When foul language comes out of you, it indicates impurity inside of you. Your mind and heart should be filled with good thoughts, not profane.

You must not misuse the name of the LORD your God. EXODUS 20:7

To use the name of God frivolously is to violate God's standard for holiness and shows a lack of respect and reverence for him. This is important enough that God made it one of the Ten Commandments.

Anyone who dishonors father or mother must be put to death. EXODUS 21:17

The Bible says that even to act or speak in a way that dishonors your parents is a very serious offense.

Don't use foul or abusive language. Let everything you say be good and helpful, so that your words will be an encouragement to those who hear them. EPHESIANS 4:29

If you claim to be religious but don't control your tongue, you are fooling yourself, and your religion is worthless. JAMES 1:26

Exercising self-control over your words includes both what you shouldn't say and what you should say. Do you even know what comes out of your mouth most often? Ask a friend to make a mental list of your positive and negative words. If you really want to stop the negative words, ask yourself before you speak, "Is it true? Is it kind? Is it necessary?"

What kinds of words should I speak?

Obscene stories, foolish talk, and coarse jokes—these are not for you. Instead, let there be thankfulness to God. EPHESIANS 5:4

How would it affect other people if you replaced all your negative or unhealthy words with words of kindness, encouragement, and gratitude?

You must commit yourselves wholeheartedly to these commands that I am giving you today. Repeat them again and again to your children. Talk about them when you are at home and when you are on the road, when you are going to bed and when you are getting up. DEUTERONOMY 6:6-7

Talk about God's Word regularly.

[Joseph] reassured them by speaking kindly to them. GENESIS 50:21

Speak kind words to others.

I would encourage you. I would try to take away your grief. JOB 16:5

Let everything you say be good and helpful, so that your words will be an encouragement to those who hear them. EPHESIANS 4:29

Use words that build others up.

A gentle answer deflects anger, but harsh words make tempers flare. PROVERBS 15:1

Gentle words are a tree of life. PROVERBS 15:4

Speak to others with patience and gentleness—particularly in times of conflict.

Don't repay evil for evil. Don't retaliate with insults when people insult you. Instead, pay them back with a blessing. That is what God has called you to do, and he will bless you for it. 1 PETER 3:9

Use your words to bless others, even when others' words injure you.

Tell the truth to each other. Render verdicts in your courts that are just and that lead to peace. ZECHARIAH 8:16

Speak truthfully, in a way that promotes justice and peace.

PROMISES *See also* Commitment, Faithfulness, Integrity, Trust

Among the most common public ceremonies is a wedding. The vows of marriage are breathtaking in beauty and boldness, and they are intended to be binding "as long as we both shall live." Yet divorce statistics prove that today even the most serious of human promises are not taken very seriously. Not so with God. God's promises are anchored in his unchanging character and steadfast love. The Bible is filled with promises upon which the believer can depend. And, in fact, God has never broken a promise he's made. Would you expect less from God? Where even our most heartfelt promises sometimes falter, the Word of God is his promise and never fails.

With so little to depend upon in life, what can I count on from God?

We receive God's promise of freedom only by believing in Jesus Christ. GALATIANS 3:22

Most of God's promises apply to his followers, those who have received his offer of salvation through faith.

I will ask the Father, and he will give you another Advocate, who will never leave you. He is the Holy Spirit. JOHN 14:16-17

Jesus promises to be with you your whole life in the form of his Holy Spirit.

If we confess our sins to him, he is faithful and just to forgive us our sins and to cleanse us from all wickedness. 1 JOHN 1:9

Jesus promises forgiveness when you confess your sin.

When everything is ready, I will come and get you, so that you will always be with me where I am. JOHN 14:3

Jesus promises an eternal home in heaven for those who trust him.

The day of the Lord will come. 2 PETER 3:10

The Bible promises that Jesus will return to judge the world for its deeds and bring his followers to heaven forever.

God causes everything to work together for the good of those who love God and are called according to his purpose for them. ROMANS 8:28

God promises to redeem all the events of your life for your good if you love him.

Why is it so important to keep my promises?

A man who makes a vow to the LORD or makes a pledge under oath must never break it. He must do exactly what he said he would do. NUMBERS 30:2

People rely on your promises. Keeping a promise is the basic foundation for trust in any relationship.

[Jonathan said to David,] "May you treat me with the faithful love of the LORD as long as I live. But if I die, treat my family with this faithful love, even when the LORD destroys all your enemies from the face of the earth." 1 SAMUEL 20:14

"Don't be afraid!" David said [to Jonathan's son]. "I intend to show kindness to you because of my promise to your father, Jonathan. I will give you all the property that once belonged to your grandfather Saul, and you will eat here with me." 2 SAMUEL 9:7

You honor God and others by keeping your promises. David had promised Jonathan to care for his family, and he kept his word when he became king. David took Jonathan's crippled son, Mephibosheth, into his household to care for him, even though he was the grandson of his enemy, King Saul.

What does God expect of me in regard to promises?

Don't trap yourself by making a rash promise to God and only later counting the cost. PROVERBS 20:25

God expects you to keep your promises. If you make a promise or commitment to God or another person, be prepared to follow through regardless of the cost.

Go to the land that I will show you. I will make you into a great nation. . . . So Abram departed as the LORD had instructed. GENESIS 12:1-4

God expects you to respond in faith to his promises.

Don't make rash promises, and don't be hasty in bringing matters before God. . . . Keep all the promises you make to him. It is better to say nothing than to make a promise and not keep it. ECCLESIASTES 5:2-5

Do not make promises quickly or take them lightly.

PROTECTION See also Angels, Boundaries, Safety, Security

Celebrities hire bodyguards, some people take classes in self-defense, and others turn their homes into minifortresses with gates, locks, and alarms. We are all concerned about protection. According to the Bible, God is concerned about our protection too. But how are we to understand God's protection in a world where accidents happen and tragedy strikes? The answer lies in trusting the sovereignty of God. At times God moves in miraculous ways to protect his people from harm (such as with Daniel in the lions' den—see Daniel 6). But usually God seems more concerned about our spiritual protection than our physical safety—guarding our souls from the clutches of the evil one. When we put our earthly life and our eternal future in perspective, the concept of protection takes on a larger and more significant meaning.

If God promises to protect me, why do I sometimes get hurt?

By means of their suffering, he rescues those who suffer. For he gets their attention through adversity. JOB 36:15

He has not ignored or belittled the suffering of the needy. He has not turned his back on them, but has listened to their cries for help. PSALM 22:24

Suffering is not a sign that God doesn't care; it is simply a fact of life in this fallen world. If God took away everyone's suffering, we would not need him or desire heaven. More significantly, we would probably follow God for a magic cure rather than our need for salvation. Some suffering is by chance; some is a consequence of neglect, failure, or sin. Suffering is a universal experience, and God uses it to draw people to him. While the Bible never promises a life free from pain, it does assure you that God is with you in your pain and that for those who believe in him, all pain will one day be gone forever. He protects his people from having to experience pain forever.

Where can I find protection and safety?

My help comes from the LORD, who made heaven and earth! He . . . never slumbers or sleeps. The LORD himself watches over you! PSALM 121:2-5

Your protection is directly related to the character, competence, and capability of your protector. The Maker of heaven and earth is your personal protector. He never sleeps and never turns his attention from you. You can walk securely because he guards your every step.

He will protect his faithful ones. 1 SAMUEL 2:9

The LORD is a shelter for the oppressed, a refuge in times of trouble. PSALM 9:9

Though troubles and threats will find you in this fallen, rebellious world, they are not a surprise to the Lord. He never tires of saving you.

[God's] peace will guard your hearts and minds as you live in Christ Jesus. PHILIPPIANS 4:7

Through consistent and devoted prayer you can know the protection of God's supernatural peace.

If you refuse to obey the LORD your God, . . . the very war and famine you fear will catch up to you. JEREMIAH 42:13-16

Jeremiah taught about the relationship between your obedience and the protection of God. Obedience to God will protect you from the consequences of disobedience. For example, obeying God's command not to cheat will protect you from the embarrassment, loss of friendships, fines, and potential jail time that can come from cheating.

How does the Lord protect me?

You are my hiding place; you protect me from trouble. PSALM 32:7

You can have peace within, despite your circumstances, when you fully trust that God is always watching over your soul. The peace of God will not prevent you from encountering difficulties, but will give you victory over them. God promises to give you eternal life in a perfect heaven, and he promises that Satan cannot steal your soul away from him. When you have total confidence in these two things, then no matter what happens, you can have peace with God.

Don't be afraid. Just stand still and watch the LORD rescue you today. . . . The LORD himself will fight for you. Just stay calm. EXODUS 14:13-14

When enemies come against you, they really come against the Lord. You are continually reminded that victory is assured when you let the Lord fight your battles.

Those who live in the shelter of the Most High will find rest in the shadow of the Almighty. . . . He alone is my refuge, my place of safety; he is my God, and I trust him. . . .

He will cover you with his feathers. He will shelter you with his wings. His faithful promises are your armor and protection. PSALM 91:1-4

God guards you from the dangers that stalk you. God is a refuge, a shadow (like protection from the intense heat of desert sun), a shelter, and a place of safety from all threats. He promises to shield you and inspire your faith and courage.

Be strong in the Lord and in his mighty power. Put on all of God's armor so that you will be able to stand firm against all strategies of the devil. For we are not fighting against flesh-and-blood enemies, but against evil rulers and authorities of the unseen world, against mighty powers in this dark world, and against evil spirits in the heavenly places. Therefore, put on every piece of God's armor so you will be able to resist the enemy in the time of evil. Then after the battle you will still be standing firm. EPHESIANS 6:10-13

Spiritual battles require spiritual protection. God's armor shields you against the schemes of the world, of your own sinful nature, and Satan. You must focus on the Lord's protection instead of evil's threats and stand firm in your faith.

When the Spirit of truth comes, he will guide you into all truth. JOHN 16:13

Stand your ground, putting on the belt of truth and the body armor of God's righteousness. EPHESIANS 6:14

When you believe the truth taught in God's Word and live by it, you will have the upper hand in any battle against evil. When you are loyal to God and ask for his help, he will give you great discernment as protection against Satan and his demons that are fighting even now for your soul. The Word of God and the power of the Holy Spirit are powerful resources that can overpower any enemy. Stand strong and confident in the truth, and you can be certain that God will help you fight your battles so that you will be victorious.

Hold up the shield of faith to stop the fiery arrows of the devil. EPHESIANS 6:16

The Spirit who lives in you is greater than the spirit who lives in the world. 1 JOHN 4:4

Every child of God defeats this evil world, and we achieve this victory through our faith. 1 JOHN 5:4

Your first line of defense is to draw strength from the fact that God is more powerful than your problems or your enemies. Your faith in God is a shield that protects you from the temptations hurled at you every day. Without strong faith, the weapons of Satan and the arrows shot at you by your enemies would pierce and defeat you. So even when life seems overwhelming, hold tightly to your faith like a shield and you will withstand the dangers and discouragements sent at you. And rejoice—you know that God has already won the victory.

How can I guard and protect my heart?

Guard your heart above all else, for it determines the course of your life. PROVERBS 4:23

Keep away from anything that might take God's place in your hearts. 1 JOHN 5:21

Protect your heart from evil influences and temptations by obeying God and by staying away from anything that might tempt you to sin. This is very difficult in today's world. Renew your commitment to love God with all you have. This will help you to step toward him and not away from him when temptations come to call.

PROVISION See also Gifts, Needs, Security, Thankfulness

The heartfelt desire of all parents is to provide adequately for the needs of their family. The question comes when we attempt to discern where to draw the line between needs and wants. Does a child need food, clothing, and emotional support? Most definitely! But does that same child need the latest designer-label jackets and shoes, or a late-model sports car the day they turn sixteen? Probably not. When we speak of the provision of God, we must be careful to differentiate similarly between our needs and our wants. While we are often confused about the difference, God is not. We must trust God both to identify our needs and to meet them by his gracious provision.

What does it mean to trust God's provision? How does he provide for me?

Call on me when you are in trouble, and I will rescue you, and you will give me glory.
PSALM 50:15

God wants you to trust him to supply your needs. Trusting God means you have total faith that he will come through for you in your times of need.

The LORD said to Moses, "Look, I'm going to rain down food from heaven for you."... Moses told[the people], "Do not keep any of it until morning." But some of them didn't listen and kept some of it until morning. But by then it was full of maggots. EXODUS 16:4, 19-20

Too often people trust God for provision, but then think that he hasn't provided because they didn't get everything they wanted when they wanted it and how they wanted it. Trust God for provision, and then be thankful for what he provides.

This same God who takes care of me will supply all your needs from his glorious riches, which have been given to us in Christ Jesus. PHILIPPIANS 4:19

God's supplies are unlimited. He does not dole them out sparingly, but lavishes them on you according to his infinite generosity.

He is so rich in kindness and grace that he purchased our freedom with the blood of his Son and forgave our sins. EPHESIANS 1:7

Through the richness of his grace, God has provided for your greatest need—forgiveness of sin and salvation in Jesus Christ.

Where do I turn when I need provision?

Don't worry about anything; instead, pray about everything. Tell God what you need, and thank him for all he has done. Then you will experience God's peace, which exceeds anything we can understand. PHILIPPIANS 4:6-7

Trust that where God guides, God provides. Release your anxieties to the Lord whose love is certain and whose ability to provide is more than adequate to supply all your needs.

Don't worry about these things, saying, "What will we eat? What will we drink? What will we wear?" These things dominate the thoughts of unbelievers, but your heavenly Father already knows all your needs. Seek the Kingdom of God above all else, and live righteously, and he will give you everything you need. MATTHEW 6:31-33

Keep focused on your priorities and your purpose, trusting that the necessary provisions will be supplied.

God will generously provide all you need. Then you will always have everything you need and plenty left over to share with others. As the Scriptures say, "They share freely and give generously to the poor. Their good deeds will be remembered forever." For God is the one who provides seed for the farmer and then bread to eat. In the same way, he will provide and increase your resources and then produce a great harvest of generosity in you. 2 CORINTHIANS 9:8-10

God's provision to you is also meant to become his provision through you, to continue his work in the world. He provides generously to you so you can share with others.

How is Jesus Christ God's provision for me?

[Jesus said,] "I am the bread of life. Whoever comes to me will never be hungry again. Whoever believes in me will never be thirsty." JOHN 6:35

I am the true grapevine, and my Father is the gardener. . . . Yes, I am the vine; you are the branches. Those who remain in me, and I in them, will produce much fruit. For apart from me you can do nothing. . . . But if you remain in me and my words remain in you, you may ask for anything you want, and it will be granted! When you produce much fruit, you are my true disciples. This brings great glory to my Father. JOHN 15:1, 5-8

Jesus is God's greatest provision for your greatest needs. He will fill your deepest hunger. He is your nourishment, your protection, your redeemer, your direction, your daily companion, and your eternal hope. He is your everything!

Since he did not spare even his own Son but gave him up for us all, won't he also give us everything else? ROMANS 8:32

Since God gave you the ultimate provision of his Son, you can trust him for everything you need to live life for his glory.

PUNISHMENT *See also* Consequences, Discipline

Punishment comes in at least three forms. First, there is the punishment a parent doles out to a child, which is intended for discipline and correction. Then there is the punishment of natural consequences. If a child touches a hot stove, the experience of being burned is generally sufficient punishment. Finally, there is punishment that is vengeful. When a nation responds to a perceived injustice by sending an army to wipe out a village of the offending state, it is punishment with a vengeance. All three are represented in the pages of the Bible, and all are in response to human sin and rebellion. Thankfully, Scripture teaches a fourth approach to punishment. The Lord Jesus Christ, through his sacrificial death on the cross, has absorbed the punishment we deserve.

Why are the punishments in the Old Testament so severe?

Then the LORD God said to the serpent, "Because you have done this, you are cursed more than all animals." GENESIS 3:14

[The LORD said,] "From now on you will be a homeless wanderer on the earth." GENESIS 4:12

[The LORD said] "If any of them offer their children as a sacrifice to Molech, they must be put to death. . . . You must be holy because I, the LORD, am holy." LEVITICUS 20:2, 26

The serpent was punished forever for tempting Eve into sin; Cain's punishment was living alone with the guilt of murdering his brother; people who murdered their children were given the death penalty. The severity of these punishments was designed to impress upon God's people the seriousness of sin.

How does God punish people today?

God's discipline is always good for us, so that we might share in his holiness. HEBREWS 12:10

God disciplines you as a loving Father, by both consequence and rebuke. His desire is always to bring you back to him, not to humiliate or hurt you. Without discipline, and the punishment that may go along with it, people would follow their own sinful desires with abandon.

God abandoned them to do whatever shameful things their hearts desired. ROMANS 1:24

God allows sinners to experience the consequences of their own behavior, especially when their sin is intentional and deliberate.

Will I be punished for my sins?

The LORD is coming from heaven to punish the people of the earth for their sins. ISAIAH 26:21

Judgment and punishment are promised for all sin.

God presented Jesus as the sacrifice for sin. People are made right with God when they believe that Jesus sacrificed his life, shedding his blood. ROMANS 3:25

The good news of the Bible is that Jesus bore the ultimate punishment for your sins—death—when he died in your place. Therefore, when you put your faith in Jesus, while you may still have to live with the consequences of your sins, you will not have to live with the greatest punishment—eternal judgment and separation from God.

God . . . will judge everyone, both the living and the dead. 1 PETER 4:5

O Sovereign Lord, holy and true, how long before you judge the people who belong to this world and avenge our blood for what they have done to us? REVELATION 6:10

For all who reject Jesus, punishment is final and eternal.

PURITY *See also* Holiness, Perfection, Repentance, Righteousness

One dead fly in a pitcher of ice water contaminates the whole thing. It is not enough to remove the fly; you also have to dump out the contaminated water and fill a clean pitcher with clean water. Likewise, Jesus' death on the cross purified our contaminated lives so that we could be pure and clean in the presence of God; something we could not do on our own. Mixing sin into our lives contaminates our relationship with God and with others and causes us to become spiritually sick. But God's forgiveness is like an endless spring of pure water for our lives. When we humbly ask him to forgive us, he removes the contamination and makes us fresh and pure again.

Why is purity so important?

Who may climb the mountain of the LORD? Who may stand in his holy place? Only those whose hands and hearts are pure, who do not worship idols and never tell lies. They will receive the LORD's blessing and have a right relationship with God their savior. Such people may seek you and worship in your presence, O God. PSALM 24:3-6

God blesses those whose hearts are pure, for they will see God. MATTHEW 5:8

If you keep yourself pure, you will be a special utensil for honorable use. Your life will be clean, and you will be ready for the Master to use you for every good work. 2 TIMOTHY 2:21

For a Christian, purity is a desire to be like Jesus in thought, words, and actions. While you can never be fully free of sin in this life, you can strive for that. God will honor you for striving for a pure heart because it demonstrates a sincere commitment to be like Jesus.

How can I possibly be pure when I mess up so often?

Create in me a clean heart, O God. Renew a loyal spirit within me. PSALM 51:10

Teach me your ways, O LORD, that I may live according to your truth! Grant me purity of heart, so that I may honor you. PSALM 86:11

The purpose of my instruction is that all believers would be filled with love that comes from a pure heart, a clear conscience, and genuine faith. 1 TIMOTHY 1:5

God knows you will mess up sometimes. What he desires is for your heart to be pure.

We are made right with God by placing our faith in Jesus Christ. And this is true for everyone who believes, no matter who we are. ROMANS 3:22

Through the death of Christ in his physical body . . . he has brought you into his own presence, and you are holy and blameless as you stand before him without a single fault. COLOSSIANS 1:22

When God forgives you, he sees you as pure.

You can't say that our bodies were made for sexual immorality. They were made for the Lord, and the Lord cares about our bodies. . . . Don't you realize that your bodies are actually parts of Christ? 1 CORINTHIANS 6:13-15

Strive to avoid any sin that violates God's intended plan for your body—sexual immorality, lying, violence, and substance abuse are some of these sins.

What if I have not been living a pure life?

Wash me clean from my guilt. Purify me from my sin. . . . Purify me from my sins, and I will be clean; wash me, and I will be whiter than snow. PSALM 51:2, 7

Let us go right into the presence of God with sincere hearts fully trusting him. For our guilty consciences have been sprinkled with Christ's blood to make us clean, and our bodies have been washed with pure water. HEBREWS 10:22

If we confess our sins to him, he is faithful and just to forgive us our sins and to cleanse us from all wickedness. 1 JOHN 1:9

Christ saves you from any and all sin. Seek his cleansing by being truly sorry for your sin and asking him to forgive you. You will experience the freedom of a clear conscience and a forgiven heart.

PURPOSE *See also* Call of God, Goals, Hope, Vision, Will of God

Do you keep a "to do" list of things you need to accomplish each day, week, or month? Such lists bring purpose to our lives, helping us to stay focused and on target. If we could reduce our entire lives to a short list of only three or four items, what would they be? The top item on that list would come very close to identifying the purpose of our lives. According to the Bible, our purpose is to be inspired by a vision as to how God can best use us to accomplish his purposes.

How do I find true purpose in life?

I take joy in doing your will, my God, for your instructions are written on my heart. PSALM 40:8

Fear God and obey his commands, for this is everyone's duty. ECCLESIASTES 12:13

Meaning in life comes from obeying God and doing his will—both his will for all believers which is found in the Bible, and his will for you personally which is discovered through prayer and your relationship with him. The ultimate goal in life is not to reach the destinations you want for yourself, but to reach the destinations God wants for you.

I brought glory to you here on earth by completing the work you gave me to do. JOHN 17:4

Everything comes from him and exists by his power and is intended for his glory.
ROMANS 11:36

Your purpose in life is to honor, obey, and praise God. All meaningful human effort comes in doing these things and therefore brings glory to God.

Go and make disciples of all the nations, baptizing them in the name of the Father and the Son and the Holy Spirit. Teach these new disciples to obey all the commands I have given you. MATTHEW 28:19-20

Part of your purpose includes taking part in fulfilling the great commission to tell others about Jesus and in building the Kingdom of God.

God knew his people in advance, and he chose them to become like his Son. ROMANS 8:29

Part of your purpose is to become as much like Christ as you can, preparing you for eternal glory.

Does God have a special purpose for me?

I cry out to God Most High, to God who will fulfill his purpose for me. PSALM 57:2

God has a general purpose and a specific purpose for you. If nothing else, you have been chosen by God to let the love of Jesus shine through you to have a positive effect on others. More specifically, God has given you spiritual gifts and wants you to use them to make a unique contribution in your sphere of influence. The more you fulfill your general purpose, the clearer your specific purpose will become.

My life is worth nothing to me unless I use it for finishing the work assigned me by the Lord Jesus—the work of telling others the Good News about the wonderful grace of God.
ACTS 20:24

God has given you work to do, a unique role he created just for you. Part of his purpose for you is to bring his Good News of salvation to all people.

God saved us and called us to live a holy life. He did this, not because we deserved it, but because that was his plan from before the beginning of time—to show us his grace through Christ Jesus. 2 TIMOTHY 1:9

You are called by God to live a holy life and to show the love of Jesus to others by the way you live.

[Jesus said,] "You didn't choose me. I chose you. I appointed you to go and produce lasting fruit, so that the Father will give you whatever you ask for, using my name." JOHN 15:16

As you pursue your purpose as assigned by God, he promises that your life will have lasting significance and eternal results.

How can I discover my personal purpose and fulfill it?

Give your bodies to God because of all he has done for you. Let them be a living and holy sacrifice—the kind he will find acceptable. This is truly the way to worship him. Don't copy the behavior and customs of this world, but let God transform you into a new person by changing the way you think. Then you will learn to know God's will for you, which is good and pleasing and perfect. ROMANS 12:1-2

Discovering God's purpose for you begins with your wholehearted commitment to God. When you give yourself to God, he promises to make his will known to you as you make yourself available to him.

If the LORD is with me, I will drive them out of the land, just as the LORD said. JOSHUA 14:12

God's purpose is best verified by God's presence and God's participation. When Caleb realized he was part of God's purpose to drive out the Canaanites, the strength of his enemies was no longer an obstacle.

Who is this pagan Philistine anyway, that he is allowed to defy the armies of the living God? 1 SAMUEL 17:26

While others saw a fearsome giant, David saw an opportunity for God's mighty work, and his purpose therefore became clear. Don't let obstacles stop you from discovering the purpose God has for you.

Let us rebuild the wall of Jerusalem and end this disgrace! NEHEMIAH 2:17

Nehemiah's passion to rebuild the walls of Jerusalem was rooted in understanding what God wanted for his people. Passionately pursue the process of discovering what God wants for you.

I fully expect and hope that I will . . . continue to be bold for Christ . . . and I trust that my life will bring honor to Christ, whether I live or die. PHILIPPIANS 1:20

I don't mean to say that I have already achieved these things or that I have already reached perfection. But I press on to possess that perfection for which Christ Jesus first possessed me. PHILIPPIANS 3:12

Paul's great purpose, whether by life or death, was to win others to Christ. Your purpose will be something you feel compelled to do regardless of the risks.

As these men were worshiping the Lord and fasting, the Holy Spirit said, "Dedicate Barnabas and Saul for the special work to which I have called them." ACTS 13:2

Worship, prayer, fasting, and relationships with other believers will help you discern God's plan for your life.

Q,R

QUITTING See also Commitment, Perseverance, Victory

Like the boxer, who in the middle of a championship fight said, *"No mas"* (Spanish for "No more") and refused to come out of his corner, most of us have moments when we feel like quitting. Whether the foe has been our job, family, friends, health, or other difficult circumstances, if we've been smacked in the face too many times, we sometimes want to cry, "No more!" The Bible recognizes that life is difficult and at times overwhelming. Faith does not prevent hardship, but it does offer resources, encouragement, and hope to help us persevere when we feel like quitting.

How can I keep going when I feel like quitting?

[Israel's enemy taunted,] "What does this bunch of poor, feeble Jews think they're doing? . . . That stone wall would collapse if even a fox walked along the top of it!"
NEHEMIAH 4:2-3

Faced with an overwhelming task and ridicule from adversaries, Nehemiah kept his eyes on his goal and his call. You can resist quitting when you keep yourself focused on your goals.

I am bound by the Spirit to go to Jerusalem. I don't know what awaits me, except that the Holy Spirit tells me in city after city that jail and suffering lie ahead. But my life is worth nothing to me unless I use it for finishing the work assigned me by the Lord Jesus.
ACTS 20:22-24

Paul faced unimaginable hardship yet never gave up, finishing the work to which God had called him. If you believe the Holy Spirit has called you to do something, let his power and encouragement keep you from quitting when the going gets tough.

Everyone who endures to the end will be saved. MATTHEW 10:22

Let's not get tired of doing what is good. At just the right time we will reap a harvest of blessing if we don't give up. GALATIANS 6:9

You can avoid discouragement and the desire to quit by keeping your eyes on the goal of finishing well and the reward of heaven. Even during times when suffering or difficulties seem never ending, having an eternal perspective can give you hope by reminding you that these times are only temporary and won't last forever.

[Paul and Barnabas] encouraged [the believers] to continue in the faith, reminding them that we must suffer many hardships to enter the Kingdom of God. ACTS 14:22

You have patiently suffered for me without quitting. REVELATION 2:3

Endurance is the antidote to quitting. When you continue to obey God's Word even in difficult times, you demonstrate that your faith is strong. When you refuse to get discouraged and give up, God rewards you. Trusting God means that you confidently expect him to guide you through each day until you see him face-to-face in his heavenly kingdom.

If your boss is angry at you, don't quit! A quiet spirit can overcome even great mistakes.
ECCLESIASTES 10:4

Quitting gives you a reputation of being unreliable and less trustworthy. Be faithful and honest in whatever you do, for when you can be trusted with small things you have a better chance of being trusted with larger responsibilities. Even in the face of criticism, continue to work hard and display a cheerful spirit. Others will notice and your reputation will be enhanced.

We are pressed on every side by troubles, but we are not crushed. We are perplexed, but not driven to despair. . . . We know that God, who raised the Lord Jesus, will also raise us with Jesus and present us to himself together with you. . . . That is why we never give up.
2 CORINTHIANS 4:8, 14-16

When God has called you to a task and you give up, you not only miss the great blessings of reaching your goal, but you might also incur discipline for not trusting God to help you get there. Just because God is in something doesn't make it easy. In fact, the harder the road, the stronger you become. If you know God is leading you and opening doors in a certain direction, don't give up just because the going gets tough. If anything, that should tell you that you are headed in the right direction. Keep moving forward boldly and with faith.

Is there ever a time when I should quit something?

Think carefully about what is right, and stop sinning. 1 CORINTHIANS 15:34

If you are a thief, quit stealing. Instead, use your hands for good hard work, and then give generously to others in need. EPHESIANS 4:28

It is time to quit when you are doing something wrong, when your actions are futile, or when you are hurting yourself or others. Even if an action or behavior is not inherently wrong, if it is absorbing all your time and attention, or is a stumbling block to others, it's time to quit.

R

RAPE *See also* Abuse, Evil, Shame, Violence, Healing

Imagine arriving at church on Sunday morning and entering the sanctuary to find the place ransacked, vandalized, and completely torn apart. In grief you would wonder, *Who could have done such an evil, tragic thing to such a holy place?* Rape is a violent and tragic crime that violates someone's body, which God calls his temple (see 1 Corinthians 6:19). Rape causes not only physical harm but also has devastating emotional consequences. However, just because a church is vandalized doesn't mean that God has left it. And when sin violates what is holy, God can bring restoration and healing to the victim and promises judgment to the violator.

Where is God when rape happens? Doesn't he care enough to prevent it?

LORD, you know the hopes of the helpless. Surely you will hear their cries and comfort them. PSALM 10:17

Let your unfailing love comfort me, just as you promised me. PSALM 119:76

It is hard to know why God allows tragedies to enter your life, especially when you've been faithful to him. But you can know that God hurts deeply with you and loves you more than you'll ever know. God didn't create sin and evil, nor does he condone it. As long as mankind lives on this earth, people's sinful nature will cause them to do sinful and evil acts. God has chosen to allow sin to run its course for now, but that will not be the case forever. God cares so much for all people that he offers anyone who follows him a future place where sin and evil will never, ever, exist again. In the meantime, he comforts you and gives you the strength to work through your pain.

"Rabbi," [Jesus'] disciples asked him, "why was this man born blind? Was it because of his own sins or his parents' sins?" "It was not because of his sins or his parents' sins," Jesus answered. JOHN 9:2-3

Some of the suffering that comes to you is not your fault, as is the case with rape.

What is the Lord's response to rape?

The LORD examines both the righteous and the wicked. He hates those who love violence. PSALM 11:5

The LORD replies, "I have seen violence done to the helpless, and I have heard the groans of the poor. Now I will rise up to rescue them, as they have longed for me to do." PSALM 12:5

God hates all violence, and he hates it when his loved ones suffer at the hands of evil people. God sees all that happens, and he will remember those who have acted violently toward others and judge them accordingly.

In my distress I prayed to the LORD, and the LORD answered me and set me free. PSALM 118:5

God has a special place in his heart for those who are abused, oppressed, or victims of violence and gives an extra measure of comfort and healing.

What is the relationship between evil desires and rape?

Do not let sin control the way you live; do not give in to sinful desires. ROMANS 6:12

When you follow the desires of your sinful nature, the results are very clear: sexual immorality, impurity, lustful pleasures. GALATIANS 5:19

Throw off your old sinful nature and your former way of life, which is corrupted by lust and deception. EPHESIANS 4:22

Lust and evil desires, left unchecked and uncontrolled, will fan into flames of violence, immorality, and rape. It is important, however, for a woman not to fan the flames of lust by wearing provocative clothing or sending provocative signals. That could be the spark that causes a man with evil desires to act. What a woman wears is never an excuse for a man's actions; choosing modest clothing is more for her own protection.

Does the victim of a rape share in the blame of the crime?

If [a] man meets [an] engaged woman out in the country, and he rapes her, then only the man must die. Do nothing to the young woman; she has committed no crime worthy of death. She is as innocent as a murder victim. DEUTERONOMY 22:25-26

Violent people mislead their companions, leading them down a harmful path. PROVERBS 16:29

Rape is a violent act against an innocent victim. There is no excuse for such a terrible crime.

How can the answer possibly be forgiveness? Is forgiveness absolutely necessary?

Love your enemies! Pray for those who persecute you! MATTHEW 5:44

[Peter] asked, "Lord, how often should I forgive someone who sins against me? Seven times?" "No, not seven times," Jesus replied, "but seventy times seven!" MATTHEW 18:21-22

Don't let evil conquer you, but conquer evil by doing good. ROMANS 12:21

Christ forgave those who crucified him. There is nothing harder—or more healing— than forgiving someone who has greatly wronged you. They will still have to face the consequences and punishment for their actions, but forgiveness frees you to move on with your life.

I was raped and now I'm pregnant. How can I possibly love this child?

Love comes from God. Anyone who loves is a child of God and knows God. 1 JOHN 4:7

Even though a child is conceived through a tragedy like rape, the child belongs first and foremost to God. He is the Creator of life, even the life inside you. Only he can fill your heart with love for your child and create joy, even in the worst of circumstances.

REBELLION *See also* Enemies, Power, Sin, Spiritual Warfare

A rebel is a person who opposes or disobeys authority and rejects the expectations, rules, and power of the individual or organization over him or her. Sometimes rebellion is necessary to fight evil and injustice. But many times it is a great tug-of-war between the individual and the authority figure. Rebellion against God is the worst form of rebellion because his expectations and rules were given simply to protect us and keep us from harm. It is rejecting the one who is most able to help.

What does it mean to rebel against God?

The Israelites . . . abandoned the LORD. . . . They went after other gods, worshiping the gods of the people around them. JUDGES 2:11-12

You rebel against God whenever you give your utmost devotion to other things. When this rebellion leads to false worship, your eternal future is in peril. Only God is deserving of your undivided devotion and worship.

Everyone who sins is breaking God's law, for all sin is contrary to the law of God. 1 JOHN 3:4

Sin, deciding not to obey God, is rebellion against him. When you rebel against God, you are cutting yourself off from your Creator because you want to do things your way.

If you rebel against the LORD's commands and refuse to listen to him, then his hand will be as heavy upon you as it was upon your ancestors. 1 SAMUEL 12:15

Rebellion is refusing to listen to and obey God.

Be careful then, dear brothers and sisters. Make sure that your own hearts are not evil and unbelieving, turning you away from the living God. HEBREWS 3:12

The ultimate spiritual rebellion is refusing to accept God's gracious offer of salvation through Jesus Christ.

Can I ever return to God if my past has been very rebellious?

"I will bring them home again," says the LORD. HOSEA 11:11

No matter how far you've strayed, God still loves you with an everlasting love and will gladly welcome you back into his presence when you have a sincere change of heart.

Isn't a certain amount of rebellion to be expected—for example, with teenagers?

[Absolom] sent secret messengers to all the tribes of Israel to stir up a rebellion against the king. 2 SAMUEL 15:10

Jesus told . . . this story: "A man had two sons. The younger son told his father, 'I want my share of your estate now before you die.' So his father agreed to divide his wealth between his sons. A few days later this younger son packed all his belongings and moved to a distant land, and there he wasted all his money in wild living." LUKE 15:11-13

The story of Absalom and David in the Old Testament and the Prodigal Son in the New Testament are classic and heartbreaking stories of the rebellion of son against father. Yes, rebellion is to be expected because all people have a sinful nature, but that doesn't make it right, and it doesn't make it easier to watch.

Is rebellion ever good?

You have had enough in the past of the evil things that godless people enjoy. 1 PETER 4:3

When under pressure to participate in sinful activities, the Christian must rebel against the crowd.

Jesus entered the Temple and began to drive out all the people buying and selling.
MATTHEW 21:12

Jesus himself rebelled against the systematic corruption of the Temple.

How can I change my heart of rebellion to a heart God desires?

Put all your rebellion behind you, and find yourselves a new heart and a new spirit.
EZEKIEL 18:31

I will give you a new heart, and I will put a new spirit in you. I will take out your stony, stubborn heart and give you a tender, responsive heart. EZEKIEL 36:26

God will give you a new heart when you humble yourself before him, turn away from sinful habits, and make a daily effort to connect with him. When you do this, your love for him will grow. He can change even the coldest heart of stone into an obedient and loving heart. Are you willing to change?

God, with undeserved kindness, declares that we are righteous. . . . People are made right with God when they believe that Jesus sacrificed his life, shedding his blood.
ROMANS 3:24-25

Faith is your lifeline to God. When you accept Jesus as your Savior and ask him to forgive your sins, this simple act of faith makes you righteous in God's sight. In other words, God looks at you as though you have never sinned. You can live free from guilt and confident of eternal life.

RECONCILIATION *See also* Acceptance, Fellowship, Forgiveness, Salvation

A relationship has been broken. It may be a husband and wife, parent and child, or two close friends; something has happened to create a chasm that threatens the survival of the relationship. Reconciliation becomes possible only when someone makes the first move; a hand extended, a phone call, a word spoken in forgiveness. In the same way, sin causes a chasm that separates us from God. The relationship is broken, and someone has to make the first move. While it is we who need to be reconciled, it is God who made the move. God extended not just his hand, not just words, but his Son, Jesus Christ, to bridge the chasm between himself and us.

What does it mean to be reconciled to God?

Since our friendship with God was restored by the death of his Son while we were still his enemies, we will certainly be saved through the life of his Son. ROMANS 5:10

God was in Christ, reconciling the world to himself, no longer counting people's sins against them. And he gave us this wonderful message of reconciliation. So we are Christ's ambassadors; God is making his appeal through us . . . [that] God made Christ, who never sinned, to be the offering for our sin, so that we could be made right with God through Christ. 2 CORINTHIANS 5:19-21

One of the most fundamental truths taught in the Bible is that all people are born with a sinful nature and sin separates humankind from God. If you want a personal relationship with him, you must be reconciled to him and that begins with a recognition that without the work of Jesus Christ on the cross, you cannot approach God. God chose to have his Son, Jesus, take your punishment so you could approach God. Accept God's gift of bridging the gap so you can be reconciled to him and have a relationship with him. This is the greatest gift ever offered—and the only way to be reconciled to God.

[God] has reconciled you to himself through the death of Christ in his physical body. As a result, he has brought you into his own presence, and you are holy and blameless as you stand before him without a single fault. COLOSSIANS 1:22

When you have a free pass to a favorite event, you don't hesitate to enter. Jesus' death and resurrection are your free pass into God's presence. When you put your trust in Jesus, you can confidently enter God's presence. You can have an audience with the King of the universe at any time, regardless of your past.

Why is reconciliation with others important?

If you are presenting a sacrifice at the altar in the Temple and you suddenly remember that someone has something against you, leave your sacrifice there at the altar. Go and be reconciled to that person. Then come and offer your sacrifice to God. MATTHEW 5:23-24

Being reconciled with other people is important to God because it demonstrates a humble and forgiving spirit which is essential to healthy relationships.

When you are on the way to court with your adversary, settle your differences quickly. Otherwise, your accuser may hand you over to the judge, who will hand you over to an officer, and you will be thrown into prison. And if that happens, you surely won't be free again until you have paid the last penny. MATTHEW 5:25-26

Working for reconciliation with others is important to your own health and peace of mind.

If another believer sins against you, go privately and point out the offense. If the other person listens and confesses it, you have won that person back. MATTHEW 18:15

God wants you to resolve your differences with others because doing so promotes unity.

Christ himself has brought peace to us. He united Jews and Gentiles into one people . . . he broke down the wall of hostility that separated us. EPHESIANS 2:14

God has, through Christ, made a way for groups at enmity with one another to make peace and be fully reconciled.

How can I mend a broken relationship with a friend?

Make allowance for each other's faults, and forgive anyone who offends you. COLOSSIANS 3:13

I appeal to you to show kindness to my child, Onesimus. I became his father in the faith while here in prison. Onesimus hasn't been of much use to you in the past, but now he is very useful to both of us. I am sending him back to you, and with him comes my own heart. PHILEMON 1:10-12

Reconciliation requires someone to take a first step of kindness. It requires you to make the decision to forgive and show mercy. And sometimes you must decide to forgive before you feel like it.

An offended friend is harder to win back than a fortified city. Arguments separate friends like a gate locked with bars. PROVERBS 18:19

I will go home to my father and say, "Father, I have sinned against both heaven and you." LUKE 15:18

Although making amends for an offense is difficult, your relationships with others are worth your immediate and diligent efforts. "I'm sorry" are two very important words. When you have hurt someone, apologize as quickly as possible and make any needed restitution. Forgiveness is powerful because it frees both parties from bitterness.

REGRETS *See also* Consequences, Grief, Guilt, Mistakes, Shame

If the memories and experiences of our lives were compared to rocks collected and carried in a backpack, surely guilt and regret would be among the heaviest of them all. Guilt is the legitimate spiritual response to sin, while regret is the sorrow over the consequences of our decisions, both the sinful and the simply unfortunate. While God promises to remove the guilt of all who seek his forgiveness, he does not prevent the consequences of our sin. It is the regret over those consequences that we often carry, weighing us down with remorse. God promises to help us deal with our regret so we can move on to the future without carrying a load of regret. He is a God who can bring good out of any situation.

What causes regret?

People who long to be rich fall into temptation and are trapped by many foolish and harmful desires that plunge them into ruin and destruction. . . . Some people, craving money, have wandered from the true faith and pierced themselves with many sorrows. 1 TIMOTHY 6:9-10

Regrets come from a life spent in pursuit of money and possessions. Neither brings lasting happiness, and they are gained at the cost of relationships with God and the people in your life.

Trust in the LORD with all your heart; do not depend on your own understanding. Seek his will in all you do, and he will show you which path to take. PROVERBS 3:5-6

Commit your actions to the LORD, and your plans will succeed. PROVERBS 16:3

Regrets will come from not putting God first in your life because eventually you will realize you have neglected what is most important.

David confessed to Nathan, "I have sinned against the LORD." Nathan replied, "Yes, but the LORD has forgiven you, and you won't die for this sin. Nevertheless, because you have shown utter contempt for the LORD by doing this, your child will die."
2 SAMUEL 12:13-14

What was the result? You are now ashamed of the things you used to do, things that end in eternal doom. ROMANS 6:21

Sin always carries unhappy and unhealthy consequences and regrets you wish you didn't have to live with.

You will say, "How I hated discipline! If only I had not ignored all the warnings! Oh, why didn't I listen to my teachers? Why didn't I pay attention to my instructors? I have come to the brink of utter ruin, and now I must face public disgrace." PROVERBS 5:12-14

Being rebellious, selfish, inattentive, or unteachable brings regrets. These traits can cause wasted months and years which could have been used to develop a better relationship with God and others, as well as greater productivity in living life to its fullest.

[The officials] told the king, "That man Daniel, one of the captives from Judah, is ignoring you and your law. He still prays to his God three times a day." Hearing this, the king was deeply troubled, and he tried to think of a way to save Daniel. He spent the rest of the day looking for a way to get Daniel out of this predicament. . . . At last the king gave orders for Daniel to be arrested and thrown into the den of lions. The king said to him, "May your God, whom you serve so faithfully, rescue you.". . . Then the king returned to his palace and spent the night fasting. He refused his usual entertainment and couldn't sleep at all that night. DANIEL 6:13-18

Making foolish promises brings regrets. In this story the king was persuaded to make a foolish law that put his friend Daniel's life at risk.

How can I deal with the regrets of my life?

Anyone who belongs to Christ has become a new person. The old life is gone; a new life has begun! 2 CORINTHIANS 5:17

When you come to faith in Jesus, he forgives your sins—all of them. Your past is forgotten by him, and he gives you a fresh start. You will still have to live with the consequences of your sins because they cannot be retracted. But because God forgives you, you can move forward without the tremendous guilt that can accompany regret.

Once again you will have compassion on us. You will trample our sins under your feet and throw them into the depths of the ocean! MICAH 7:19

Because God no longer holds your sins against you, you no longer have to hold them against yourself. Now you can be free from self-condemnation.

Have mercy on me, O God, because of your unfailing love. Because of your great compassion, blot out the stain of my sins. Wash me clean from my guilt. Purify me from

my sin. For I recognize my rebellion; it haunts me day and night. . . . The sacrifice you desire is a broken spirit. You will not reject a broken and repentant heart, O God.
PSALM 51:1-3, 17

I know, O LORD, that your regulations are fair; you disciplined me because I needed it.
PSALM 119:75

Ask yourself what God may be communicating through your regrets. God sometimes uses brokenness and remorse to bring spiritual insight and growth. Regrets that drive you to God are redemptive.

I focus on this one thing: Forgetting the past and looking forward to what lies ahead.
PHILIPPIANS 3:13

Focus on God who controls the future, not on regrets of the past. The past is over, so don't live a "what if" life of regret, feeling angry at yourself for what you did and bitter toward God for allowing you to do it. God doesn't cause regrets; he washes them away when you ask him to walk with you into the future.

God had given me the responsibility of preaching the gospel to the Gentiles, just as he had given Peter the responsibility of preaching to the Jews. For the same God who worked through Peter as the apostle to the Jews also worked through me as the apostle to the Gentiles. GALATIANS 2:7-8

Turn your regrets into resolve. Regrets can be so powerful that they disable you from serving God in the future. If Peter had focused on his regret of denying Jesus, he would never have been able to preach the Good News about Jesus so powerfully. Don't let regret paralyze you; instead let it motivate you to positive action in the future.

Restore to me the joy of your salvation, and make me willing to obey you. PSALM 51:12

Give all your worries and cares to God, for he cares about you. 1 PETER 5:7

Let your regrets draw you closer to God. Don't let them pull you away from God. He wants to take your burdens from you and restore your relationship with him and others. Don't cause the biggest regret of your life—withdrawing from God. No matter what you've done, he welcomes you with loving arms.

How can I avoid regrets in the future?

Do to others whatever you would like them to do to you. This is the essence of all that is taught in the law and the prophets. MATTHEW 7:12

When you treat others the way you like to be treated, you will have no regrets.

Cling to your faith in Christ, and keep your conscience clear. For some people have deliberately violated their consciences; as a result, their faith has been shipwrecked.
1 TIMOTHY 1:19

Follow your God-given conscience and always do what is right. This will keep you from getting into situations you will later regret.

When Judas, who had betrayed him, realized that Jesus had been condemned to die, he was filled with remorse. MATTHEW 27:3

Thinking through the full consequences of your decisions in advance will keep you from making decisions you will later regret.

Stay away from every kind of evil. 1 THESSALONIANS 5:22

Stay away from the places and people who tempt you to sin, and you will have less to regret.

Oh, the joys of those who do not follow the advice of the wicked, or stand around with sinners, or join in with mockers. But they delight in the law of the LORD, meditating on it day and night. PSALM 1:1-2

Immerse yourself in Scripture and surround yourself with positive influences who will give you good advice.

People with understanding control their anger; a hot temper shows great foolishness. PROVERBS 14:29

Avoid acting on impulse in the heat of anger. A hasty mistake has lasting effects.

Saul admitted to Samuel, "Yes, I have sinned. I have disobeyed your instructions and the LORD's command, for I was afraid of the people and did what they demanded." 1 SAMUEL 15:24

Let confidence in the Lord, not fear of people or events, determine your course of action.

Fools vent their anger, but the wise quietly hold it back. PROVERBS 29:11

We all make many mistakes. For if we could control our tongues, we would be perfect and could also control ourselves in every other way. . . . In the same way, the tongue is a small thing that makes grand speeches. But a tiny spark can set a great forest on fire. JAMES 3:2, 5

The greatest regrets are often caused by words; once spoken they cannot be taken back. Don't merely avoid hurtful words, but test your words against the standard of truthfulness, goodness, and helpfulness. If you have any thought that you might regret what you are about to say, don't speak.

REJECTION *See also* Abandonment, Blasphemy, Denial, Neglect

To reject is to discard something or someone as unwanted or defective. When a person is rejected, the result is great pain. A fiancé is rejected when the engagement is broken; a student is rejected by his or her peer group; an applicant is rejected for a job; a child is rejected by a parent—in each case the consequences are devastating. Even more devastating is a rejection of God. The painful consequences of rejecting God are not only experienced in this life, but for eternity.

How does God respond to me when I feel rejected?

Even if my father and mother abandon me, the LORD will hold me close. PSALM 27:10

Can a mother forget her nursing child? Can she feel no love for the child she has borne? But even if that were possible, I would not forget you! See, I have written your name on the palms of my hands. ISAIAH 49:15-16

God loves you no matter what you have done or how rejected you feel. If you are feeling lonely and abandoned, know that God is ready to welcome you with open arms.

The angel of the LORD found Hagar beside a spring of water in the wilderness, along the road to Shur. The angel said to her, "Hagar, Sarai's servant, where have you come from, and where are you going?" "I'm running away from my mistress, Sarai," she replied.... Thereafter, Hagar used another name to refer to the LORD, who had spoken to her. She said, "You are the God who sees me." GENESIS 16:7-8, 13

Rejection may cause you to feel lost, like Hagar. But God sees you, and welcomes you with open arms to experience his presence and acceptance, just as Hagar did.

I offered my back to those who beat me and my cheeks to those who pulled out my beard. I did not hide my face from mockery and spitting.... See, the Sovereign LORD is on my side!... All my enemies will be destroyed like old clothes that have been eaten by moths! ISAIAH 50:6, 9

Sometimes rejection comes about through injustice. But God brings justice and mercy to the rejected. Avoid seeking revenge on those who hurt you, knowing God will ultimately judge and bring justice.

How can I recover from rejection in my life?

He was despised and rejected.... We turned our backs on him. ISAIAH 53:3

You have a Savior who understands rejection because he was despised, rejected, and killed by the very people he came to save. Find comfort in your relationship with a God who understands what you are going through.

Give all your worries and cares to God, for he cares about you. 1 PETER 5:7

You don't need to deal with rejection by yourself. Bring your concerns to God and find loving acceptance in him.

Jesus told them, "A prophet is honored everywhere except in his own hometown and among his relatives and his own family." MARK 6:4

Nothing can ever separate us from God's love. ROMANS 8:38

Rejection by others does not change your value or the truth about yourself. Jesus was God's Son regardless of his rejection or acceptance by mankind. Instead of focusing on what other people think about you, focus on God's love for you.

What blessings await you when people hate you and exclude you and mock you and curse you as evil because you follow the Son of Man. When that happens, be happy! Yes, leap for joy! For a great reward awaits you in heaven. And remember, their ancestors treated the ancient prophets that same way. LUKE 6:22-23

If you are rejected for being a Christian, rejoice and persevere because you will receive special blessings from God.

Will God ever reject me?

Jesus [said to the Samaritan woman], "If you only knew the gift God has for you and who you are speaking to, you would ask me, and I would give you living water." JOHN 4:10

Jesus did not reject the sinful Samaritan woman, but rather showed her acceptance by offering her living water. Jesus will never reject anyone who comes to him to be cleansed from sin.

[Jesus asked the woman caught in adultery,] "Where are your accusers? Didn't even one of them condemn you?" "No, Lord," she said. And Jesus said, "Neither do I. Go and sin no more." JOHN 8:10-11

God rejects the sin without rejecting the sinner.

[Jesus said,] "Those the Father has given me will come to me, and I will never reject them." JOHN 6:37

God accepts all who come to him in faith, even those who previously rejected him.

Because of Christ and our faith in him, we can now come boldly and confidently into God's presence. EPHESIANS 3:12

You can approach God knowing that he gladly welcomes you and will always accept you. God will never say, "Sorry, I don't have time for you" or, "I'm busy." He always listens, always hears, always responds, and always loves. Even at your weakest he does not reject you, but rather embraces you so that you can receive strength to be all he intended you to be. In his open arms you will find the ultimate example of how to accept others.

Remove your heavy hand from me, and don't terrify me with your awesome presence. . . . Tell me, what have I done wrong? Show me my rebellion and my sin. Why do you turn away from me? Why do you treat me as your enemy? JOB 13:21-24

Don't misinterpret God's silence as rejection. When God seems silent it could be because you are too busy to hear him. Or it might be that he is being quiet so that you will draw closer to him in order to more fully experience his love and acceptance.

How should I respond to those who reject me?

Then Paul went to the synagogue and preached boldly for the next three months, arguing persuasively about the Kingdom of God. But some became stubborn, rejecting his message and publicly speaking against the Way. So Paul left the synagogue and . . . held daily discussions at the lecture hall of Tyrannus . . . so that people throughout the province of Asia—both Jews and Greeks—heard the word of the Lord. ACTS 19:8-10

When some reject you, they may actually be rejecting the Lord you represent. Continue to follow him and stick to his mission for you. Though others reject you, the Lord will not.

Jesus said, "Father, forgive them, for they don't know what they are doing." LUKE 23:34

Offer forgiveness for those who reject you, just as God offers forgiveness to you.

[One of the debtors] couldn't pay, so his master ordered that he be sold—along with . . . everything he owned—to pay the debt. But the man fell down before his master and begged him, "Please, be patient with me, and I will pay it all." Then his master was filled with pity for him, and he released him and forgave his debt. MATTHEW 18:25-27

Give people, even those who reject you, another chance! Remember, your God is the God of second chances . . . and many more!

[The prodigal son] returned home to his father. And while he was still a long way off, his father saw him coming. Filled with love and compassion, he ran to his son, embraced him, and kissed him. His son said to him, "Father, I have sinned against both heaven and you, and I am no longer worthy of being called your son." But his father said to the servants, "Quick! Bring the finest robe in the house and put it on him. Get a ring for his finger and sandals for his feet. And kill the calf we have been fattening. We must celebrate with a feast, for this son of mine was dead and has now returned to life. He was lost, but now he is found." So the party began. LUKE 15:20-24

Rejection should not negate love. Love is accepting even in the face of rejection.

How can I avoid rejecting others? Is there anyone or anything I should reject?

The LORD said to Samuel, "Don't judge by his appearance or height, for I have rejected him. The LORD doesn't see things the way you see them. People judge by outward appearance, but the LORD looks at the heart." 1 SAMUEL 16:7

Outwardly you look like righteous people, but inwardly your hearts are filled with hypocrisy and lawlessness. MATTHEW 23:28

Appearances can be deceiving. God never accepts or rejects someone based on appearance. Neither should you. God can be the only righteous judge because he alone can see the heart.

I will reject perverse ideas and stay away from every evil. PSALM 101:4

They will act religious, but they will reject the power that could make them godly. Stay away from people like that! 2 TIMOTHY 3:5

You should reject all sinful thoughts and actions. Willfully accepting sin is willfully rejecting God. Willfully rejecting sin opens the door to willfully accepting God and shows God you love him.

RELATIONSHIPS *See also* Family, Fellowship, Marriage, Unity

It has been said that no man is an island, meaning that no one can go through life completely alone. We need relationships and we want relationships because that's how God made us. He "programmed" our DNA with a need to relate to and interact with other people. This is clear from some of the very first words recorded by God in the first book of the Bible: "It is not good for the man to be alone" (Genesis 2:18). Despite the fact that human relationships can sometimes be challenging, hurtful, and highly unpredictable, they fill a deep human need, they can be enormously satisfying, and they are designed to ultimately be an example of our relationship with God. When sin entered the world, relationships were distorted between humans and between humans and God. And so God, because of his desire to be at peace with the people he created, put a plan into action of sending his Son, Jesus, to earth so that all relationships could be restored to the way God originally designed them. This won't be fully realized until we get to heaven, but God has given us the tools and his own Spirit to help us relate effectively here on earth.

What general principles does the Bible give about relationships?

The LORD God said, "It is not good for the man to be alone. I will make a helper who is just right for him." GENESIS 2:18

I will be your Father, and you will be my sons and daughters, says the LORD Almighty.
2 CORINTHIANS 6:18

You are created as a relational being. You live in a world with God and with other people. God intended that you relate to him and others.

Jesus [said], "The most important commandment is this: 'Listen, O Israel! The LORD our God is the one and only LORD. And you must love the LORD your God with all your heart, all your soul, all your mind, and all your strength.' The second is equally important: 'Love your neighbor as yourself.' No other commandment is greater than these."
MARK 12:29-31

Your relationship with God is the most important relationship, although this does not mean you can or should neglect your relationships with others. It is often through others that you learn more about relating to God.

We can rejoice in our wonderful new relationship with God because our Lord Jesus Christ has made us friends of God. ROMANS 5:11

Your relationship with God is made possible through the death of Jesus for your sins and his resurrection and is the beginning of your eternal relationship with him.

How can I build healthy relationships with others?

Never let loyalty and kindness leave you! Tie them around your neck as a reminder. Write them deep within your heart. Then you will find favor with both God and people, and you will earn a good reputation. PROVERBS 3:3-4

Be kind to each other, tenderhearted, forgiving one another, just as God through Christ has forgiven you. EPHESIANS 4:32

Respect everyone, and love your Christian brothers and sisters. 1 PETER 2:17

Most important of all, continue to show deep love for each other, for love covers a multitude of sins. 1 PETER 4:8

The foundation of healthy relationships is love, and the four cornerstones are loyalty, kindness, respect, and forgiveness.

What are some of the benefits of a loving relationship?

Hatred stirs up quarrels, but love makes up for all offenses. PROVERBS 10:12

Love is patient and kind. Love is not jealous or boastful or proud or rude. It does not demand its own way. It is not irritable, and it keeps no record of being wronged. It does not rejoice about injustice but rejoices whenever the truth wins out. Love never gives up, never loses faith, is always hopeful, and endures through every circumstance.
1 CORINTHIANS 13:4-7

The benefits that come from a loving relationship include complete and undivided devotion, forgiveness, patience, kindness, love for truth, love for justice, expecting the best in others, loyalty at any cost, and belief in a person no matter what. Love prohibits jealousy, envy, pride, haughtiness, selfishness, rudeness, demanding one's own way, irritability, and holding grudges.

What types of relationships are best to avoid?

[The people now living in the land] must not live in your land, or they will cause you to sin against me. If you serve their gods, you will be caught in the trap of idolatry. EXODUS 23:33

Don't team up with those who are unbelievers. How can righteousness be a partner with wickedness? How can light live with darkness? What harmony can there be between Christ and the devil? How can a believer be a partner with an unbeliever? 2 CORINTHIANS 6:14-15

God warns against partnerships in which one person loves God and the other doesn't. The potential lack of unity in the relationship and temptation to compromise one's faithfulness to God are dangers which should be avoided if at all possible. (But if you are already in a partnership or marriage relationship where one of you is a believer and one of you is not, you should not try to get out of it.) God also warns against relationships with those who will try to get you to compromise or give up your faith. God does not tell us to avoid friendships with those who don't believe in him; he wants us to be a light to the world. But he does want us to be very careful about binding relationships with those who show animosity toward God.

How can I restore broken relationships with others?

If you are presenting a sacrifice at the altar in the Temple and you suddenly remember that someone has something against you, leave your sacrifice there at the altar. Go and be reconciled to that person. Then come and offer your sacrifice to God. MATTHEW 5:23-24

Reconciliation with others is a priority to God, and thus should also be a priority for you. The first step in restoring broken relationships is honestly evaluating the cause or problem in the relationship. Once you identify the problem, you need to take steps to reconcile it, even if it's not your fault.

I will go home to my father and say, "Father, I have sinned against both heaven and you."
LUKE 15:18

If you have caused hurt or division in a relationship, you need to confess it to God and to whomever you have wronged. Often both sides in a broken relationship are guilty to some degree and both sides need to confess some wrongdoing. But even if the other person refuses to admit fault, never let your pride keep you from confessing yours.

If another believer sins against you, go privately and point out the offense. If the other person listens and confesses it, you have won that person back. MATTHEW 18:15

You may need to confront someone in order to restore a relationship.

Don't sin by letting anger control you. Don't let the sun go down while you are still angry. . . . Get rid of all bitterness, rage, anger, harsh words, and slander, as well as all types of evil behavior. Instead, be kind to each other, tenderhearted, forgiving one another, just as God through Christ has forgiven you. EPHESIANS 4:26-32

You must deal with your own anger before you can truly forgive others.

[Joseph's] brothers came and threw themselves down before Joseph. "Look, we are your slaves!" they said. But Joseph replied, "Don't be afraid of me. Am I God, that I can punish you? You intended to harm me, but God intended it all for good. He brought me to this position so I could save the lives of many people. No, don't be afraid. I will continue to take care of you and your children." So he reassured them by speaking kindly to them. GENESIS 50:18-21

It is through forgiveness that grudges are released and revenge is forgotten.

REMEMBERING/REMINDERS *See also* Heritage, Past, Traditions

Remembering the past is an essential part of living the present and future. Life is a long journey and to live it to the fullest you can't afford to forget some of the important lessons learned along the way. Otherwise you are likely to repeat your mistakes. One way to remember important milestones and lessons of the past is to establish celebrations, events, or special times to pause and reflect on where you've been, who helped you, and what God has done in your life. Try to remember the good and learn from the bad. It is so important to never forget what God has done for you. Share God's faithfulness—both in your life and in the lives of others—with your friends, family, children, and grandchildren, so that you will build a testimony for future generations to remember. God's Word is a book of remembrance about God, reminding us who he is and what he has done so that we will never forget his mercy, presence, and power in our lives. Make his faithfulness memorable to someone else by telling them of your journey. Then you will make an impression on that person not easily forgotten.

How can remembering God help me in my spiritual walk?

I lie awake thinking of you, meditating on you through the night. PSALM 63:6

Remember God day and night. Meditate on him and his great love for you and you will never cease to experience it.

As my life was slipping away, I remembered the LORD. And my earnest prayer went out to you in your holy Temple. JONAH 2:7

Remember God as the source of hope when you're ready to give up. Your limited human mind can only come up with so many solutions before giving up hope. But God's resources and solutions are unlimited.

As [Nehemiah] looked over the situation, [he] called together the nobles and the rest of the people and said to them, "Don't be afraid of the enemy! Remember the Lord, who is great and glorious, and fight for your brothers, your sons, your daughters, your wives, and your homes!" NEHEMIAH 4:14

Remember God as the one who helps you fight and win life's battles. Remembering that he is working through you to accomplish his purposes and defeat sin's grip will help you confidently fight life's battles without fear.

Beware that in your plenty you do not forget the LORD your God and disobey his commands, regulations, and decrees that I am giving you today. . . . Do not become proud at that time and forget the LORD your God, who rescued you from slavery. DEUTERONOMY 8:11,14

Remember God when you have plenty, because he blessed you with it. Remembering God's goodness can help you wait patiently when times are hard.

You must commit yourselves wholeheartedly to these commands that I am giving you today. Repeat them again and again to your children. Talk about them when you are at home and when you are on the road, when you are going to bed and when you are getting up. Tie them to your hands and wear them on your forehead as reminders. Write them on the doorposts of your house and on your gates. DEUTERONOMY 6:6-9

Moses reminded the people to take every opportunity to remember God's Word and to tell family and friends of God's help and blessings. If you do this each day, you will strengthen your love and commitment to God, which will motivate you to be even more faithful in following days. Weave him into the fabric of your life and your spiritual walk will be strong and focused.

If you seek him, you will find him. 1 CHRONICLES 28:9

Remember that God is with you all day, every day, and talk to him about everything that comes up at home, at school, at work, and at play. Share your thoughts, needs, and concerns with him. As you practice remembering his presence, you notice him working in your life more and more.

What is the importance of reminding others about God?

O my people, listen. . . . I will teach you hidden lessons from our past—stories we have heard and known, stories our ancestors handed down to us. PSALM 78:1-3

Recounting God's past faithfulness before others is an act of worship. It can also introduce an unbeliever to your great God. Most importantly, remembering God with others unifies you all because you share something in common.

What are some other ways that I can remember God?

Be careful to keep my Sabbath day, for the Sabbath is a sign of the covenant between me and you from generation to generation. It is given so you may know that I am the LORD, who makes you holy. EXODUS 31:13

As you rest on the Lord's Day, remember his presence. Thank him for providing time for you to rest and play and enjoy his blessings in your life.

When I see the rainbow in the clouds, I will remember the eternal covenant between God and every living creature on earth. GENESIS 9:16

When you see a rainbow, remember God's promises. Reflecting on how God has kept his promises in the past can help you trust him to meet his promises in the future.

[Jesus] took some bread and gave thanks to God for it. Then he broke it in pieces and gave it to the disciples, saying, "This is my body, which is given for you. Do this to remember me." LUKE 22:19

When you participate in Communion, remember Jesus' sacrifice for you. Meditating on what Jesus gave up for you will help you live with a grateful heart.

I will always remind you about these things. . . . It is only right that I should keep on reminding you as long as I live. 2 PETER 1:12-13

When you talk about God with others, you remember his blessings together. Remembering how God has blessed the lives of others helps you depend on God to bless you. In turn, you can remind others to depend on God by sharing how he has blessed your own life.

I have tried to stimulate your wholesome thinking and refresh your memory. I want you to remember what the holy prophets said long ago and what our Lord and Savior commanded through your apostles. 2 PETER 3:1-2

Reading God's Word helps you remember who he is and what he has done for his faithful followers throughout history. This will motivate you to look for ways you can be involved in what he is doing now.

RENEWAL *See also* Change, Confession, Hope

How often we disappoint ourselves. We have such high hopes and good intentions, but inevitably we find ourselves weary and burned out with self-defeat or the burdens of life. The messiness of life can leave us feeling exhausted not only physically, but in our very souls. If only we could start over. So many of us are in desperate need of renewal. Renewal begins with the compassion of God and a heart ready for change. When the two are put together, we find a new beginning, a soul refreshed, and a life revived.

My life is a mess, and I feel like I need to start over again. How can I experience renewal?

I have heard Israel saying, "You disciplined me severely, like a calf that needs training for the yoke. Turn me again to you and restore me, for you alone are the LORD my God."
JEREMIAH 31:18

A heart that truly wants to change is a heart that is ready for the renewal only God's Spirit can bring.

When I refused to confess my sin, my body wasted away, and I groaned all day long. Day and night your hand of discipline was heavy on me. My strength evaporated like water in the summer heat. Finally, I confessed all my sins to you and stopped trying to hide my guilt. I said to myself, "I will confess my rebellion to the LORD." And you forgave me! All my guilt is gone. PSALM 32:3-5

Create in me a clean heart, O God. Renew a loyal spirit within me. PSALM 51:10

Sometimes you are weary because you are clinging to sin and disobedience. If this is the case, confess your sins and let God cleanse your heart and life. He promises to make you a brand-new person! He will give you a fresh, new start.

I will give you a new heart, and I will put a new spirit in you. I will take out your stony, stubborn heart and give you a tender, responsive heart. And I will put my Spirit in you so that you will follow my decrees and be careful to obey my regulations. EZEKIEL 36:26-27

Renewal comes with the gift of a new heart from the Holy Spirit. God will change everything about you if you let him.

In what ways does God renew me?

The instructions of the LORD are perfect, reviving the soul. The decrees of the LORD are trustworthy, making wise the simple. PSALM 19:7

God revives your soul by the safety of the boundaries he gives you.

I lie in the dust; revive me by your word. PSALM 119:25

God revives you by the inspiration, comfort, and encouragement of his Word.

He renews my strength. He guides me along right paths, bringing honor to his name.
PSALM 23:3

God renews your strength by guiding you on new pathways.

When doubts filled my mind, your comfort gave me renewed hope and cheer.
PSALM 94:19

God renews your hope with his comfort.

That is why we never give up. Though our bodies are dying, our spirits are being renewed every day. 2 CORINTHIANS 4:16

God renews your spirit despite your physical troubles.

How can I experience spiritual renewal on a more frequent, even continual, basis?

He renews my strength. He guides me along right paths, bringing honor to his name.
PSALM 23:3

God promises you spiritual refreshment if you dwell in his presence daily. Peace, confidence, and energy flow naturally from fellowship with the Lord.

Throw off your old sinful nature and your former way of life, which is corrupted by lust and deception. Instead, let the Spirit renew your thoughts and attitudes. Put on your new nature, created to be like God—truly righteous and holy. EPHESIANS 4:22-24

Put on your new nature, and be renewed as you learn to know your Creator and become like him. COLOSSIANS 3:10

Through faith in Jesus, you can become a brand-new person, the kind of person you really want to be. As you live with your new nature that longs for what is right, holy, and true, you will experience spiritual refreshment and joy.

REPENTANCE *See also* Change, Confession, Forgiveness

Have you ever had the experience of driving in a strange city and suddenly realizing you were going the wrong way on a one-way street? What you do next is very much like the biblical idea of repentance. You make a U-turn and change your direction as fast as you can. Repentance is motivated by the realization that you have taken the wrong way in life. The Bible calls this wrong way "sin." Repentance is when you admit your sin and make a commitment, with God's help, to change your life's direction. While not a popular concept these days, repentance is essential because it is the only way to arrive at your desired destination—heaven. Because of repentance, change is possible and we can experience God's fullest blessings, both now and for eternity.

What is repentance?

Repent of your sins and turn to God. MATTHEW 3:2

Repentance means being sorry for sin and being committed to a new way of life—that of serving God. It means turning from a life that is ruled by your sinful nature and turning to God for a new nature, which comes when God's Spirit begins to live in you. When God forgives your sins, you will have a new sense of hope for the future.

Zacchaeus stood before the Lord and said, "If I have cheated people on their taxes, I will give them back four times as much!" LUKE 19:8

Repentance is made complete by changed behavior, showing others and God that your life is truly different in a positive way.

When I refused to confess my sin, my body wasted away, and I groaned all day long. Day and night your hand of discipline was heavy on me. My strength evaporated like water in the summer heat. Finally, I confessed all my sins to you and stopped trying to hide my guilt. I said to myself, "I will confess my rebellion to the LORD." And you forgave me! All my guilt is gone. PSALM 32:3-5

One of the first essential steps to repentance is confession, which means being humbly honest with God and sincerely sorry for your sins—the ones you know about and the ones you are unaware of. Confession restores your relationship with God, and this renews your strength and spirit. When you repent, God removes your guilt, restores your joy, and heals your broken soul. A heart that truly longs for change is necessary for repentance to be genuine.

Why does God want me to repent? Why is repentance necessary?

At last my people will confess their sins and the sins of their ancestors for betraying me and being hostile toward me. LEVITICUS 26:40

Everyone has sinned; we all fall short of God's glorious standard. ROMANS 3:23

All people need to repent because everyone has sinned and thus betrayed God.

Samuel said to all the people of Israel, "If you are really serious about wanting to return to the LORD, get rid of your foreign gods. . . . Determine to obey only the LORD; then he will rescue you from the Philistines." 1 SAMUEL 7:3

The LORD your God is gracious and merciful. If you return to him, he will not continue to turn his face from you. 2 CHRONICLES 30:9

Repentance is necessary for an ongoing relationship with God. Turn away from anything that is preventing you from worshiping and obeying God wholeheartedly.

People who conceal their sins will not prosper, but if they confess and turn from them, they will receive mercy. PROVERBS 28:13

This is what the LORD says: "O Israel, my faithless people, come home to me again, for I am merciful. I will not be angry with you forever." JEREMIAH 3:12

God had mercy on me so that Christ Jesus could use me as a prime example of his great patience with even the worst sinners. Then others will realize that they, too, can believe in him and receive eternal life. 1 TIMOTHY 1:16

Repentance is your only hope of receiving God's mercy. Those who refuse to see and admit their own sins can't be forgiven for them and have placed themselves outside God's mercy and blessing.

I will judge each of you, O people of Israel, according to your actions, says the Sovereign LORD. *Repent, and turn from your sins. Don't let them destroy you! Put all your rebellion behind you, and find yourselves a new heart and a new spirit. . . . Turn back and live!* EZEKIEL 18:30-32

This means that anyone who belongs to Christ has become a new person. The old life is gone; a new life has begun! 2 CORINTHIANS 5:17

[God] saved us, not because of the righteous things we had done, but because of his mercy. He washed away our sins, giving us a new birth and new life through the Holy Spirit. TITUS 3:5

Repentance allows you to receive a new life from God, literally, a life where the very spirit of God lives within you.

There is forgiveness of sins for all who repent. LUKE 24:47

Repentance allows you to receive forgiveness of sin. If you are sincere, when you come to God and ask him humbly, he will forgive your sin, no matter how many times you ask.

Jesus began to denounce the towns where he had done so many of his miracles, because they hadn't repented of their sins and turned to God. . . . "You people of Capernaum, will you be honored in heaven? No, you will go down to the place of the dead. For if the miracles I did for you had been done in wicked Sodom, it would still be here today. I tell you, even Sodom will be better off on judgment day than you." MATTHEW 11:20, 23-24

There is no hope for those who refuse to repent of sin. By embracing their sins, they are embracing eternal death by cutting themselves off from the lifeline of Jesus Christ, who offers forgiveness and eternal life.

Is repentance a one-time event, or do I need to repent each time I sin?

The sacrifice you desire is a broken spirit. You will not reject a broken and repentant heart, O God. PSALM 51:17

While salvation is a one-time event, God is pleased by broken and contrite hearts that are willing to continually confess and repent of sin.

If we claim we have no sin, we are only fooling ourselves and not living in the truth. But if we confess our sins to him, he is faithful and just to forgive us our sins and to cleanse us from all wickedness. 1 JOHN 1:8-9

Confession and repentance of sin is a constant mark of the person walking in the light of fellowship with God.

I've done too many horrible things. Could God possibly forgive me?

If wicked people turn away from all their sins and begin to obey my decrees and do what is just and right, they will surely live and not die. All their past sins will be forgotten, and they will live. EZEKIEL 18:21-22

Peter came to [Jesus] and asked, "Lord, how often should I forgive someone who sins against me? Seven times?" "No, not seven times," Jesus replied, "but seventy times seven!"
MATTHEW 18:21-22

No matter how terrible your past, or how many sins you have committed, if you approach God with an attitude of humble sincerity and confess your sins, he will forgive you. To think that some of your sins are "too bad" to be forgiven is to minimize the power of Jesus' death and resurrection on your behalf.

Do not banish me from your presence, and don't take your Holy Spirit from me. Restore to me the joy of your salvation, and make me willing to obey you. Then I will teach your ways to rebels, and they will return to you. . . . You do not desire a sacrifice, or I would bring one. . . . The sacrifice you desire is a broken spirit. You will not reject a broken and repentant heart, O God. PSALM 51:11-13, 16-17

God's grace is greater than your failure. Temptation only wins when it keeps you from turning back to God. No matter how often you fail, God welcomes you back. Recovery begins when you return to God. He will not despise your broken and repentant heart. He promises to forgive you, help you start over, and give you joy.

REPUTATION See also Character, Integrity, Maturity, Respect

We all have a reputation, like it or not. Whether we intentionally try to project a certain image or couldn't care less what others think, people do form an opinion of us through our behavior, personality, and abilities. A good reputation can help us make friends and be respected. A bad reputation can also help us make friends (with others of ill repute) or leave us isolated, shunned, or disrespected. The Bible encourages us to build our reputation on solid character rather than on external image. A reputation built on image without substance is a facade which eventually crumbles.

Why should I care about my reputation?

Choose a good reputation over great riches; being held in high esteem is better than silver or gold. PROVERBS 22:1

A person who plans evil will get a reputation as a troublemaker. PROVERBS 24:8

We are traveling together to guard against any criticism for the way we are handling this generous gift. We are careful to be honorable before the Lord, but we also want everyone else to see that we are honorable. 2 CORINTHIANS 8:20-21

You should care about having a reputation of integrity so that the credibility of your witness for Christ cannot be questioned by anyone. It is sad when the message of Christ is hindered by a believer's damaged reputation.

What is the basis for my reputation?

Christ made us right with God; he made us pure and holy, and he freed us from sin. Therefore, as the Scriptures say, "If you want to boast, boast only about the LORD." 1 CORINTHIANS 1:30-31

Ultimately, you should be known not for what you have done but for what the Lord has done through you and for you. You are "Exhibit A" of God's greatness and goodness.

How can I cultivate and maintain a godly reputation?

My child, never forget the things I have taught you. Store my commands in your heart. If you do this, . . . your life will be satisfying. PROVERBS 3:1-2

Following God's direction in Scripture is the essential ingredient in developing a godly reputation.

Never let loyalty and kindness leave you! Tie them around your neck as a reminder. Write them deep within your heart. Then you will find favor with both God and people, and you will earn a good reputation. PROVERBS 3:3-4

God promises to give a good name to those who show kindness, loyalty, and love to their neighbors.

The Kingdom of God is not a matter of what we eat or drink, but of living a life of goodness and peace and joy in the Holy Spirit. If you serve Christ with this attitude, you will please God, and others will approve of you, too. ROMANS 14:17-18

Focusing less on insignificant external behaviors and more on internal character will please God, and ultimately gain the approval of others, too.

The Holy Spirit produces this kind of fruit in our lives: love, joy, peace, patience, kindness, goodness, faithfulness, gentleness, and self-control. GALATIANS 5:22-23

People often argue that someone's personal life does not matter as long as they perform well on the job or look good in public. God, however, does not make a distinction between your public and private life. Justice, righteousness, integrity, mercy, honesty, fairness, and faithfulness are essential traits of a godly person's character and reputation because they reflect God's character. You will have a good reputation when you display the same godly integrity in private as you do in public.

How can a bad reputation be changed?

[Unbelieving neighbors] will see your honorable behavior, and they will give honor to God when he judges the world. 1 PETER 2:12

The surest way to influence the way others think of you is by consistent, godly behavior.

Some of the traveling teachers recently returned and made me very happy by telling me about your faithfulness and that you are living according to the truth. 3 JOHN 1:3

If you live according to the standards of God's Word, you will have a good reputation.

[The teachers of religious law] asked [Jesus'] disciples, "Why does he eat with such scum?" MARK 2:16

Jesus doesn't accept you on the basis of your past reputation, but because his love can transform you, no matter what you've done. Don't think you have to change your reputation before Jesus will love you.

Don't copy the behavior and customs of this world, but let God transform you into a new person by changing the way you think. Then you will learn to know God's will for you, which is good and pleasing and perfect. ROMANS 12:2

Jesus' love can transform you. When you follow his instructions for your life, eventually your reputation will change, too.

RESENTMENT *See also* Anger, Bitterness, Hatred, Jealousy

Part envy, part spite, part bitterness, resentment is a slow-burning anger that consumes the soul. The experience of pain due to real or perceived injustices is common to all of us, but resentment is clinging to and feeding those hurts until they dominate our lives. The Bible indicates that the cure for resentment is the confession of bitterness and a willingness, with God's help, to forgive the offender.

What causes feelings of resentment?

As the Ark of the LORD entered the City of David, Michal, the daughter of Saul, looked down from her window. When she saw King David leaping and dancing before the LORD, she was filled with contempt for him. 2 SAMUEL 6:16

Disapproving of someone's actions or behavior can cause you to resent them.

When it was time for the harvest, Cain presented some of his crops as a gift to the LORD. Abel also brought a gift—the best of the firstborn lambs from his flock. The LORD accepted Abel and his gift, but he did not accept Cain and his gift. This made Cain very angry, and he looked dejected. . . . One day Cain suggested to his brother, "Let's go out into the fields." And while they were in the field, Cain attacked his brother, Abel, and killed him. GENESIS 4:3-5, 8

Jealousy of another person can cause you to resent them for having what you do not.

"Your brother is back," [servants told the Prodigal Son's older brother], "and your father has killed the fattened calf. We are celebrating because of his safe return." The older brother was angry and wouldn't go in. His father came out and begged him, but he replied, "All these years I've slaved for you and never once refused to do a single thing you told me to. And in all that time you never gave me even one young goat for a feast with my friends. Yet when this son of yours comes back after squandering your money on prostitutes, you celebrate by killing the fattened calf!" LUKE 15:27-30

Feeling left out and unappreciated can cause you to resent those whom you feel have rejected you.

Jacob loved Joseph more than any of his other children because Joseph had been born to him in his old age. So one day Jacob had a special gift made for Joseph—a beautiful robe. But his brothers hated Joseph because their father loved him more than the rest of them. They couldn't say a kind word to him. GENESIS 37:3-4

Favoritism can cause resentment in the least favored person.

What is the danger of resentment?

A stone is heavy and sand is weighty, but the resentment caused by a fool is even heavier. PROVERBS 27:3

If someone says, "I love God," but hates a Christian brother or sister, that person is a liar. 1 JOHN 4:20

Resentment is both self-destructive and destructive for those you resent. Resentment destroys relationships and strips you of joy.

How should I handle my feelings of resentment?

Hatred stirs up quarrels, but love makes up for all offenses. PROVERBS 10:12

Don't sin by letting anger control you. Don't let the sun go down while you are still angry, for anger gives a foothold to the devil. . . . Get rid of all bitterness, rage, anger, harsh words, and slander, as well as all types of evil behavior. Instead, be kind to each other, tenderhearted, forgiving one another, just as God through Christ has forgiven you. EPHESIANS 4:26-32

Only love and forgiveness are strong enough to overcome feelings of resentment. Pray for God's strength to love and forgive until it forces the resentment from your heart. This is an area where you can demonstrate to the world that God's power can make a difference.

RESPECT *See also* Character, Dignity, Trust, Worth/Worthiness

Respect is recognizing the worth of others, honoring them for what they have done and who they are. In a very real sense, it is a gift we bestow on others, a gift of valuing them highly. To honor and respect others requires the ability to recognize their worth as human beings created in God's image.

How do I show respect for God?

[God] requires only that you fear the LORD your God, and live in a way that pleases him, and love him and serve him with all your heart and soul. DEUTERONOMY 10:12

Recognize that the LORD is glorious and strong. Give to the LORD the glory he deserves! Bring your offering and come into his courts. Worship the LORD in all his holy splendor. Let all the earth tremble before him. PSALM 96:7-9

Worshiping and revering God is a demonstration of your respect for him.

As you enter the house of God, keep your ears open and your mouth shut. It is evil to make mindless offerings to God. ECCLESIASTES 5:1

Stand in silence in the presence of the Sovereign LORD. ZEPHANIAH 1:7

Being silent long enough to listen to God shows that you respect him enough to come to him for direction. Seeking God's wisdom is a good way to show your respect for him.

In what ways might I show disrespect to God?

You must not misuse the name of the LORD your God. EXODUS 20:7

I am the LORD. Do not bring shame on my holy name. LEVITICUS 22:31-32

Too often we treat God as ordinary, forgetting that he is completely holy. We must be extremely careful to treat God with the reverence he deserves. Thinking of him as "Santa Claus" or "The Man Upstairs" is disrespectful, as is using his name to swear or spice up your language. Treating God as ordinary shows that you do not understand who God is or how powerful he is. Respect for God means that you show reverence for his name.

What happens when I respect God?

"Don't be afraid," Moses [told the Israelites], "for God has come in this way to test you, and so that your fear of him will keep you from sinning!" EXODUS 20:20

Respect for God often keeps you from sinning because you don't want to hurt the One who loves you so much.

All you who fear the LORD, trust the LORD! He is your helper and your shield. PSALM 115:11

Respect for God helps you trust him when you have doubts or are experiencing troubles.

Here now is my final conclusion: Fear God and obey his commands, for this is everyone's duty. ECCLESIASTES 12:13

Respect for God helps you obey him because you realize his ways are best.

Always think carefully before pronouncing judgment. Remember that you do not judge to please people but to please the LORD. . . . Fear the LORD and judge with integrity, for the LORD our God does not tolerate perverted justice. 2 CHRONICLES 19:6-7

The former governors . . . had laid heavy burdens on the people, demanding a daily ration of food and wine, besides forty pieces of silver. Even their assistants took advantage of the people. But because I feared God, I did not act that way. NEHEMIAH 5:15

Respect for God helps you treat other people with fairness and justice. As you respect God you learn to respect others and treat them with integrity.

He was a devout, God-fearing man, as was everyone in his household. He gave generously to the poor and prayed regularly to God. ACTS 10:2

Respect for God causes you to give generously to help others because God has given generously to you.

How can I show respect to others? How can I gain respect from others?

Jesus [told] a story: "A Jewish man was traveling on a trip from Jerusalem to Jericho, and he was attacked by bandits. They stripped him of his clothes, beat him up, and left him half dead beside the road. . . . A despised Samaritan came along, and when he saw the man, he felt compassion for him. Going over to him, the Samaritan soothed his wounds." LUKE 10:30-33-34

Be humble, thinking of others as better than yourselves. PHILIPPIANS 2:3

How can you claim to have faith in our glorious Lord Jesus Christ if you favor some people over others? JAMES 2:1

Love your Christian brothers and sisters. 1 PETER 2:17

Respect involves showing more concern for people than agendas, thinking highly of others, building them up in love, and treating everyone with fairness and integrity.

[Jonathan said to David,] "If I die, treat my family with this faithful love, even when the LORD destroys all your enemies from the face of the earth." So Jonathan made a solemn pact with David. 1 SAMUEL 20:14-16

Mephibosheth . . . was Jonathan's son and Saul's grandson. . . . He bowed low to the ground in deep respect. David said, "Greetings, Mephibosheth." Mephibosheth replied, "I am your servant." "Don't be afraid!" David said. "I intend to show kindness to you because of my promise to your father, Jonathan." 2 SAMUEL 9:6-7

Your friends will respect you when they know they can trust you. And they will trust you when you prove to be trustworthy. It's as simple as that. When a man became king in ancient days, it was common to kill off the entire family of the preceding king, but David promised he wouldn't do that. Even though Mephibosheth was the grandson of the previous king—and thus a potential threat—David cared for him like a son. When you keep your promises, people will learn they can trust you and will respect you.

Whom should I honor and respect?

Be sure to fear the LORD and faithfully serve him. Think of all the wonderful things he has done for you. 1 SAMUEL 12:24

You are worthy, O Lord our God, to receive glory and honor and power. For you created all things, and they exist because you created what you pleased. REVELATION 4:11

Respect God above anyone else.

Honor your father and mother. Then you will live a long, full life in the land the LORD your God is giving you. EXODUS 20:12

Your parents deserve your deep respect, for they were chosen for you by God to be the ones to raise and teach you.

Honor those who are your leaders in the Lord's work. . . . Show them great respect and wholehearted love because of their work. 1 THESSALONIANS 5:12-13

Spiritual leaders should be treated with respect.

Stand up in the presence of the elderly, and show respect for the aged. LEVITICUS 19:32

Show respect for the elderly.

You must not . . . curse any of your rulers. EXODUS 22:28

Never make light of the king, even in your thoughts. ECCLESIASTES 10:20

Everyone must submit to governing authorities. For all authority comes from God, and those in positions of authority have been placed there by God. ROMANS 13:1

Those in authority over you deserve your respect. Even if they are evil or oppressive, you must at least respect their position.

Slaves, obey your earthly masters with deep respect and fear. Serve them sincerely as you would serve Christ. . . . Masters, treat your slaves in the same way. Don't threaten them; remember, you both have the same Master in heaven, and he has no favorites. EPHESIANS 6:5, 9

Employers and employees should treat each other with respect.

Love each other with genuine affection, and take delight in honoring each other. ROMANS 12:10

Respect everyone, and love your Christian brothers and sisters. 1 PETER 2:17

Treat all people with respect because God created each person with value. Remember that if you are a Christian, your mission is to reflect Jesus to others.

RESPONSIBILITY *See also* Accountability, Integrity, Trust, Wisdom

Denial of personal responsibility is epidemic today. The Bible is very clear: Each and every human being is responsible for his or her own decisions, behavior, and relationships. We are accountable to one another and to the laws of our society, but ultimately we are responsible to the God who will judge the living and the dead.

What does the Bible say about personal responsibility?

Whenever it is time for the Tabernacle to move, the Levites will take it down. And when it is time to stop, they will set it up again. NUMBERS 1:51

Some of your responsibilities may seem boring or dull, but it is important to God that you fulfill them wholeheartedly. It shows that you care about doing a job well and completing a task others have entrusted to you.

Don't be misled—you cannot mock the justice of God. You will always harvest what you plant. GALATIANS 6:7

You are responsible for your own behavior and will bear the consequences for it—now and in eternity.

[Adam said to God,], "It was the woman you gave me who gave me the fruit, and I ate it." Then the LORD God asked the woman, "What have you done?" "The serpent deceived me," she replied. "That's why I ate it." GENESIS 3:12-13

Unfortunately, both Adam and Eve responded by blaming someone else when God confronted them with their sin. You are responsible for your own choices and decisions.

Why is responsibility an important character trait?

The LORD was with Joseph, so he succeeded in everything he did as he served in the home of his Egyptian master. Potiphar noticed this and realized that the LORD was with Joseph, giving him success in everything he did. GENESIS 39:2-3

Pharaoh said to Joseph, "I hereby put you in charge of the entire land of Egypt." GENESIS 41:41

Responsibility will open doors of opportunity. If you are responsible with what you are given, greater opportunities with more responsibility will come your way.

We are each responsible for our own conduct. GALATIANS 6:5

Responsibility is important because you will be held accountable for your own actions. You cannot blame others for what you choose to do.

How do I develop responsibility?

The servant to whom he had entrusted the five bags of silver came forward with five more and said, "Master, you gave me five bags of silver to invest, and I have earned five more." The master was full of praise. "Well done, my good and faithful servant. You have been faithful in handling this small amount, so now I will give you many more responsibilities." MATTHEW 25:20-21

You develop responsibility by conscientiously obeying God's Word, doing what is right, and actively using the gifts God has entrusted to you.

Don't think you are better than you really are. Be honest in your evaluation of yourselves, measuring yourselves by the faith God has given us. ROMANS 12:3

You can become more responsible by assessing how much responsibility you can handle, and not taking on more than you can do well.

Don't reject the LORD's discipline, and don't be upset when he corrects you. For the LORD corrects those he loves, just as a father corrects a child in whom he delights. PROVERBS 3:11-12

God will train you to be more responsible if you submit to his discipline and if you let him work in your heart and life.

What are my responsibilities before God?

To those who use well what they are given, even more will be given. MATTHEW 25:29

You are responsible to invest your life and talents wisely for the Kingdom of God.

Since God loved us that much, we surely ought to love each other. 1 JOHN 4:11

Your two greatest responsibilities are to love God and love others.

O people, the LORD has told you what is good, and this is what he requires of you: to do what is right, to love mercy, and to walk humbly with your God. MICAH 6:8

You are responsible to pursue a personal relationship with the living God, have loving, merciful relationships with others, and to be obedient to God as you make right choices in your daily life.

What are some things for which I am responsible?

The LORD God placed the man in the Garden of Eden to tend and watch over it. GENESIS 2:15

You gave [human beings] charge of everything you made, putting all things under their authority. PSALM 8:6

You are responsible to care for God's creation.

Judah said to his father, "Send the boy with me. . . . I personally guarantee his safety. You may hold me responsible if I don't bring him back to you. Then let me bear the blame forever." GENESIS 43:8-9

You are responsible for keeping your promises.

The words you say will either acquit you or condemn you. MATTHEW 12:37

You are responsible for the words you speak.

His father, King David, had never disciplined him at any time, even by asking, "Why are you doing that?" 1 KINGS 1:6

You are responsible to discipline your children.

All who reject me and my message will be judged on the day of judgment by the truth I have spoken. JOHN 12:48

You are responsible for how you respond to Jesus and his message of salvation.

Should I be held responsible for things that are not my fault?

[Adam] replied, "It was the woman you gave me who gave me the fruit, and I ate it." Then the LORD God asked the woman, "What have you done?" "The serpent deceived me," she replied. "That's why I ate it." GENESIS 3:12-13

Adam and Eve were responsible for their sin, even though they tried to pin the blame on someone else. Similarly, an honest and humble assessment of your behavior may turn up some things that you really are responsible for.

God was very displeased with the census, and he punished Israel for it. Then David said to God, "I have sinned greatly by taking this census. . . . I am the one who called for the census! . . . But these people are as innocent as sheep—what have they done? O LORD my God, let your anger fall against me and my family, but do not destroy your people." 1 CHRONICLES 21:7-8, 17

Sometimes it seems like God punishes innocent people for the sins of the guilty. But in reality, the natural consequences of sin sometimes affect others, even innocent people.

The LORD said . . . "As surely as I live, and as surely as the earth is filled with the LORD's glory, not one of these people will ever enter that land." NUMBERS 14:20-22

Israel violated the instructions about the things set apart for the LORD. A man named Achan had stolen some of these dedicated things, so the LORD was very angry with the Israelites. JOSHUA 7:1

Often the whole community shares responsibility for what an individual or group of individuals has done, particularly if the community supported or did nothing to stop the sin.

All people are mine to judge—both parents and children alike. And this is my rule: The person who sins is the one who will die. EZEKIEL 18:4

In terms of judgment before God, a person is held responsible only for his or her own sins. God will not judge you for someone else's sins.

REST See also Balance, Peace, Renewal, Sabbath, Security

Ours is an age of anxiety and stress because it is an age of perpetual motion. We take pride in explaining to each other how busy we are, and feel vaguely guilty if we relax. God did not intend for his people to live in a state of frenzied activity. From his own example in Genesis to the promises of the New Testament, it is clear that God wants us to discover rest and refreshment for our body and soul.

Why is rest so important for me?

So the creation of the heavens and the earth and everything in them was completed. On the seventh day God had finished his work of creation, so he rested from all his work. And God blessed the seventh day and declared it holy, because it was the day when he rested from all his work of creation. GENESIS 2:1-3

Why would the omnipotent God of the universe rest following his work of creation? Surely, it wasn't because the Almighty was physically tired! The answer is that God, in ceasing from his work, called his rest "holy." God knew that you would need to cease from your work to care for your physical and spiritual needs. Work is good, but it must be balanced by regular rest and attention to the health of your soul. Make sure to carve out regular times for worship and spiritual refreshment.

The LORD is my shepherd; I have all that I need. He lets me rest in green meadows; he leads me beside peaceful streams. He renews my strength. He guides me along right paths, bringing honor to his name. PSALM 23:1-3

It is useless for you to work so hard from early morning until late at night, anxiously working for food to eat; for God gives rest to his loved ones. PSALM 127:2

God provides times of rest. Rest renews you mentally, physically, emotionally, and spiritually, thus giving you more energy for the work ahead. Rest is not only a necessity, but a gift from God you can gladly accept.

What are the dangers of not being rested?

The people of Judah began to complain, "The workers are getting tired, and there is so much rubble to be moved. We will never be able to build the wall by ourselves."
NEHEMIAH 4:10

When you become weary, you can lose your perspective and ability to trust God, becoming vulnerable to discouragement and temptation.

Everything is wearisome beyond description. No matter how much we see, we are never satisfied. No matter how much we hear, we are not content. ECCLESIASTES 1:8

Weariness can blur your vision and purpose. It is hard to look ahead when you feel you can't go on.

I am weary, O God; I am weary and worn out, O God. I am too stupid to be human, and I lack common sense. PROVERBS 30:1-2

Weariness can blur your ability to think. Lack of perception can lead you to make poor decisions. Rest is essential for making smart choices.

What should I do during times of rest?

Tell the people of Israel: "Be careful to keep my Sabbath day, for the Sabbath is a sign of the covenant between me and you from generation to generation. It is given so you may know that I am the LORD, who makes you holy." EXODUS 31:13

Keep the Sabbath day holy. Don't pursue your own interests on that day, but enjoy the Sabbath and speak of it with delight as the LORD's holy day. Honor the Sabbath in everything you do on that day, and don't follow your own desires or talk idly. ISAIAH 58:13

One day a week should be uniquely dedicated to focusing on God. This is a time of rest when you set aside your regular work, if at all possible, and your own agenda to praise, thank, and worship God individually and with other believers. It is a time to stop your normal routine to enjoy the renewal of body, mind, and soul that comes from time spent with God and his people.

I will meditate on your majestic, glorious splendor and your wonderful miracles.
PSALM 145:5

Jesus said, "Let's go off by ourselves to a quiet place and rest awhile." He said this because there were so many people coming and going that Jesus and his apostles didn't even have time to eat. So they left by boat for a quiet place, where they could be alone. MARK 6:31-32

In addition to Sabbath rest, there are times when you will need emotional rest (separation from stress), mental rest (meditation), and physical rest (sleep). These kinds of rest bring renewed energy, mental clarity, healing, and peace of mind and heart.

What gives me spiritual rest?

Those who live in the shelter of the Most High will find rest in the shadow of the Almighty. PSALM 91:1

Jesus said, "Come to me, all of you who are weary and carry heavy burdens, and I will give you rest. Take my yoke upon you. Let me teach you, because I am humble and gentle at heart, and you will find rest for your souls. For my yoke is easy to bear, and the burden I give you is light." MATTHEW 11:28-30

When you visit friends far away and spend the night with them, they've prepared a room for you to make you comfortable and help you rest. God does the same for you. When you come into his presence, he has prepared a place where you can feel safe and rest. At his place, in his presence, the burdens of the world are put into perspective and cares melt away. When you need to be refreshed spiritually, go to the Creator of rest and linger there.

Those who still reject me are like the restless sea, which is never still but continually churns up mud and dirt. ISAIAH 57:20

Sin makes you restless and agitated. Sin clogs your lifeline to God, the source of rest and renewal.

Those who pursue us are at our heels; we are exhausted but are given no rest. LAMENTATIONS 5:5

Satan tries to keep you from rest. The more he can distract you with temptations, the harder it will be to relax and listen to God.

I am overwhelmed with trouble! Haven't I had enough pain already? And now the LORD has added more! I am worn out from sighing and can find no rest. JEREMIAH 45:3

Grief disrupts rest. Suffering and sorrow often distract you from the God who can heal you.

At night my bones are filled with pain, which gnaws at me relentlessly. JOB 30:17

Sickness disrupts rest. When the body suffers, it's hard to think about anything else.

I had no peace of mind because my dear brother Titus hadn't yet arrived with a report from you. So I said good-bye and went on to Macedonia to find him. 2 CORINTHIANS 2:13

When we arrived in Macedonia, there was no rest for us. We faced conflict from every direction, with battles on the outside and fear on the inside. 2 CORINTHIANS 7:5

Anxiety disrupts rest. The combination of conflict and fear can rob you of your sleep.

RESURRECTION See also Body, Death, Eternity, Salvation, Victory

Jesus' resurrection is the key to the Christian faith. Why? Because (1) just as he promised, Jesus rose from the dead. We can be confident, therefore, that he will be able to keep all his promises. (2) Jesus' bodily resurrection proves he is not a false prophet or imposter. (3) We can be certain of our own resurrection because he has power over death. (4) The same power that brought Jesus back to life is available to us for daily living. (5) The Resurrection is the basis for our faith because Jesus proved to be more than just a human leader; he is the Son of God.

How can I have confidence that God will someday resurrect me to live forever in heaven?

Jesus [said], "I am the resurrection and the life. Anyone who believes in me will live, even after dying." JOHN 11:25

Tell me this—since we preach that Christ rose from the dead, why are some of you saying there will be no resurrection of the dead? For if there is no resurrection of the dead, then Christ has not been raised either. And if Christ has not been raised, then all our preaching is useless, and your faith is useless. 1 CORINTHIANS 15:12-14

Eyewitness evidence for any historical event is the most reliable. Hundreds of eyewitnesses claimed to have seen Jesus following the Resurrection. The apostles were willing to risk martyrdom for preaching the truth about it, and millions upon millions of changed lives bear witness to the fact that Jesus rose from the dead and is alive today. Because of the Resurrection, we know that Christ's sacrifice on the cross accomplished God's plan—our sins are forgiven and we will live forever with Jesus in heaven. Christianity, at its heart, is not just another moral or religious code, but resurrection and new life.

What does Jesus' resurrection mean to me?

"Don't be afraid!" [the angel] said. "I know you are looking for Jesus, who was crucified. He isn't here! He is risen from the dead, just as he said would happen. Come, see where his body was lying." MATTHEW 28:5-6

God loved the world so much that he gave his one and only Son, so that everyone who believes in him will not perish but have eternal life. JOHN 3:16

Without the resurrection of Jesus from the dead, there would be no Christianity. The Resurrection is central because it demonstrates God's power over death and assures us that we will also be resurrected. The power of God that brought Jesus back from the dead will also bring you back to life. Jesus' death was not the end. His resurrection is the beginning of eternal life for all who believe in him. Do you believe?

We know that God, who raised the Lord Jesus, will also raise us with Jesus and present us to himself together with you. 2 CORINTHIANS 4:14

Because of Jesus Christ's life, death, and resurrection—and your faith in him—you stand holy and blameless in God's presence. You can come to him confidently. Jesus died for you and rose again with the promise to be with you.

Through Christ you have come to trust in God. And you have placed your faith and hope in God because he raised Christ from the dead and gave him great glory. 1 PETER 1:21

The Lord is our source of hope because his promises are true. We lose hope when we stop believing that. The Resurrection, the greatest event in history, is the foundation of your hope. Jesus promised that he would rise from the dead, and because he did, you can be assured that every other promise God makes to you will also come true.

What will my body be like after it is resurrected?

Our bodies are buried in brokenness, but they will be raised in glory. They are buried in weakness, but they will be raised in strength. They are buried as natural human bodies, but they will be raised as spiritual bodies. For just as there are natural bodies, there are also spiritual bodies. 1 CORINTHIANS 15:43-44

Let me reveal to you a wonderful secret. We will not all die, but we will all be transformed! . . . Our mortal bodies must be transformed into immortal bodies.
1 CORINTHIANS 15:51-53

Your resurrected body will be a physical body like you have now, but it will also have many supernatural characteristics. You may be able to walk through walls, as Jesus did with his resurrected body (see John 20:26). Most importantly, your new body won't decay from the effects of sin. You will never be sick or in pain again, nor will your mind think sinful thoughts. You will be fully and finally perfect in God's sight.

RETIREMENT *See also* Aging/Old Age, Change, Stewardship, Wisdom

From the time we get our first job as teenagers or young adults, we count the days until at last we can retire from the working world and enjoy the fruits of our labors. But just because we retire from a regular job doesn't mean we can retire from doing the Lord's work. In fact, retirement is a wonderful season in life to take your new gift of time and use it for work that has eternal results.

What does the Bible say about retirement?

[The Levites] must retire at the age of fifty. After retirement they may assist their fellow Levites by serving as guards at the Tabernacle. NUMBERS 8:25-26

As you can see, the LORD has kept me alive and well as he promised for all these forty-five years since Moses made this promise—even while Israel wandered in the wilderness. Today I am eighty-five years old. I am as strong now as I was when Moses sent me on that journey, and I can still travel and fight as well as I could then. JOSHUA 14:10-11

The Bible does not give an age for retirement, with the exception of the Levites who served in the Tabernacle. The appropriate retirement age is usually established by each individual company, based on economical concerns or physical limitations. But that doesn't need to dictate your attitude toward other work that still needs to be done.

How can I best transition to retirement?

Grandchildren are the crowning glory of the aged; parents are the pride of their children. PROVERBS 17:6

I will be your God throughout your lifetime—until your hair is white with age. I made you, and I will care for you. I will carry you along and save you. ISAIAH 46:4

The most important aspects of life continue through retirement—relationships. Your relationship with God should continue to grow as you age. And focusing on your personal relationships with others can make your golden years truly golden.

Gray hair is a crown of glory; it is gained by living a godly life. PROVERBS 16:31

Recognizing the benefits of a godly life can help you grow older gracefully.

There is [a] serious tragedy I have seen under the sun, and it weighs heavily on humanity. God gives some people great wealth and honor and everything they could ever want, but then he doesn't give them the chance to enjoy these things. They die, and someone else, even a stranger, ends up enjoying their wealth! This is meaningless— a sickening tragedy. ECCLESIASTES 6:1-2

Realizing that everyone eventually dies, you are wise to plan for the distribution of your inheritance to those you leave behind.

How can I continue to be productive in my retirement years?

Keep on loving others as long as life lasts, in order to make certain that what you hope for will come true. Then you will not become spiritually dull and indifferent. Instead, you will follow the example of those who are going to inherit God's promises because of their faith and endurance. HEBREWS 6:11-12

Continue to love others.

Supplement your faith with a generous provision of moral excellence, and moral excellence with knowledge, and knowledge with self-control, and self-control with patient endurance, and patient endurance with godliness, and godliness with brotherly affection, and brotherly affection with love for everyone. The more you grow like this, the more productive and useful you will be in your knowledge of our Lord Jesus Christ. 2 PETER 1:5-8

Continue to grow and learn spiritually.

Titus, promote the kind of living that reflects wholesome teaching. Teach the older men to exercise self-control, to be worthy of respect, and to live wisely. They must have sound faith and be filled with love and patience. Similarly, teach the older women to live in a way that honors God. They must not slander others or be heavy drinkers. Instead, they should teach others what is good. These older women must train the younger women to love their husbands and their children. TITUS 2:1-4

Live a godly life and teach others to do the same.

After retirement they may assist their fellow Levites by serving as guards at the Tabernacle, but they may not officiate in the service. This is how you must assign duties to the Levites. NUMBERS 8:26

There are different kinds of service, but we serve the same Lord. 1 CORINTHIANS 12:5

Be flexible to changes in your role as you continue to serve the Lord.

Wisdom belongs to the aged, and understanding to the old. But true wisdom and power are found in God; counsel and understanding are his. JOB 12:12-13

The glory of the young is their strength; the gray hair of experience is the splendor of the old. PROVERBS 20:29

Use your experience, wisdom, and understanding as gifts from God to help others.

What must I never stop doing?

Now that I am old and gray, do not abandon me, O God. Let me proclaim your power to this new generation, your mighty miracles to all who come after me. PSALM 71:18

I pray that your love will overflow more and more, and that you will keep on growing in knowledge and understanding. PHILIPPIANS 1:9

I have fought the good fight, I have finished the race, and I have remained faithful. 2 TIMOTHY 4:7

Continue to worship, praise, hope, rejoice, trust, grow, search, obey, do right, serve, and faithfully endure to the end.

REVENGE *See also* Anger, Bitterness, Conflict, Judgment, Forgiveness

Revenge is among the most primitive of human instincts. Whether we have been cut off in traffic, unjustly criticized by a coworker, or made the victim of violent crime, our gut response is to want revenge. While revenge may be a natural reaction, God makes it clear that vengeance is to be left to him alone. Jesus becomes our example of responding to injustice with patience and kindness, leaving judgment and punishment in the hands of God.

What causes the desire to avenge?

One day Dinah, the daughter of Jacob and Leah, went to visit some of the young women who lived in the area. But when the local prince, Shechem son of Hamor the Hivite, saw Dinah, he seized her and raped her.... Jacob's sons ... were shocked and furious that their sister had been raped.... Simeon and Levi, who were Dinah's full brothers, took their swords and entered the town without opposition. Then they slaughtered every male. GENESIS 34:1-2, 7, 25

John had been telling Herod, "It is against God's law for you to marry your brother's wife." So Herodias bore a grudge against John and wanted to kill him. MARK 6:18-19

A spark of anger at a real or perceived injustice.

The people of Philistia have acted against Judah out of bitter revenge and long-standing contempt. Therefore, this is what the Sovereign LORD says: I will raise my fist of judgment against the land of the Philistines. EZEKIEL 25:15-16

Contempt for others.

Surely resentment destroys the fool, and jealousy kills the simple. JOB 5:2

A stone is heavy and sand is weighty, but the resentment caused by a fool is even heavier. PROVERBS 27:3

Bitterness and resentment.

Is revenge ever justified?

Do not seek revenge or bear a grudge against a fellow Israelite, but love your neighbor as yourself. I am the LORD. LEVITICUS 19:18

Taking personal revenge is expressly forbidden by God.

See that no one pays back evil for evil, but always try to do good to each other and to all people. 1 THESSALONIANS 5:15

Not only is personal revenge wrong, but God asks you to repay evil with good.

You have seen the wrong they have done to me, LORD. Be my judge, and prove me right. LAMENTATIONS 3:59

Leave ultimate justice and revenge to God.

You have heard the law that says the punishment must match the injury: "An eye for an eye, and a tooth for a tooth." But I say, do not resist an evil person! If someone slaps you on the right cheek, offer the other cheek also. MATTHEW 5:38-39

The often quoted "eye for an eye" verses are not an excuse for, nor are they a rule for, personal revenge. This principle wasn't established to exact revenge, but rather to make sure the punishment fit the crime. If justice was to prevail, it was necessary that a person neither got off the hook for a crime, nor was punished too severely. An "eye for an eye" was actually a breakthrough for justice and fairness in ancient times because it prevented arbitrary punishment. Revenge is nothing but arbitrary justice. There is no indication that this verse was meant to be taken literally. In fact, in Exodus 21:26-27, if a slave's eye or tooth is knocked out he can go free. The point is that the severity of the punishment should fit the severity of the crime.

Does God ever seek revenge? If revenge is sin, then how can God take vengeance?

The Lord . . . takes revenge on all who oppose him and continues to rage against his enemies! The Lord is slow to get angry, but his power is great, and he never lets the guilty go unpunished. . . . The Lord is good, a strong refuge when trouble comes. He is close to those who trust in him. But he will sweep away his enemies in an overwhelming flood.
NAHUM 1:2-3, 7-8

Can a loving, merciful, and compassionate God also be vengeful? The answer lies in a proper understanding of God's character. Because God is holy, he cannot tolerate sin and evil and therefore must punish all unrighteousness. Because he is merciful, he has not yet destroyed the wicked but allows them the opportunity for repentance and forgiveness. From a human viewpoint, God might appear vengeful. From the viewpoint of true holiness, God is merely administering justice, as is his right to do.

What are the effects of revenge?

[Samson] said, "I'm going into my wife's room to sleep with her," but her father wouldn't let him in. . . . [Samson] went out and caught 300 foxes. He tied their tails together in pairs, and he fastened a torch to each pair of tails. Then he lit the torches and let the foxes run through the grain fields of the Philistines. He burned all their grain to the ground. . . . "Who did this?" the Philistines demanded. "Samson," was the reply. . . . So the Philistines went and got the woman and her father and burned them to death. "Because you did this," Samson vowed, "I won't rest until I take my revenge on you!" So he attacked the Philistines with great fury and killed many of them. . . . The Philistines retaliated by setting up camp in Judah. . . . "We've come to capture Samson. We've come to pay him back for what he did to us." JUDGES 15:1, 4-10

Revenge is the reflex of anger. Someone does you wrong, even if it was an accident, and you think striking back will administer justice and make you feel better. But in the heat of the moment, taking revenge will always cause you to overdo, thus making matters worse. Revenge is a vicious cycle. Revenge demands revenge, and so on in a downward spiral that ends in the destruction of all involved. Beware that when you want to give the next hit, the revenge that comes back may be more than you can take.

If you set a trap for others, you will get caught in it yourself. If you roll a boulder down on others, it will crush you instead. PROVERBS 26:27

Revenge has a boomerang effect that will come back to hurt you.

What are the alternatives to revenge?

[Christ] is your example, and you must follow in his steps. He never sinned, nor ever deceived anyone. He did not retaliate when he was insulted, nor threaten revenge when he suffered. He left his case in the hands of God, who always judges fairly.
1 PETER 2:21-23

Follow Jesus' example not to retaliate. Jesus did not take revenge but fully trusted God to judge fairly. This is the only way for good to come out of a bad situation.

[Love] does not demand its own way. It is not irritable, and it keeps no record of being wronged. 1 CORINTHIANS 13:5

Most important of all, continue to show deep love for each other, for love covers a multitude of sins. 1 PETER 4:8

Show love to those who hurt you. When you love someone, you won't take revenge on them.

Joseph [said], "Don't be afraid of me. Am I God, that I can punish you? You intended to harm me, but God intended it all for good. He brought me to this position so I could save the lives of many people. No, don't be afraid. I will continue to take care of you and your children." So he reassured them by speaking kindly to them. GENESIS 50:19-21

Forgiving erases the reason for revenge.

Do good to those who hate you. Bless those who curse you. Pray for those who hurt you. . . . When things are taken away from you, don't try to get them back. Do to others as you would like them to do to you. LUKE 6:27-31

Pray for your enemies. Prayer helps dissipate the desire for revenge.

Never pay back evil with more evil. Do things in such a way that everyone can see you are honorable. Do all that you can to live in peace with everyone. Dear friends, never take revenge. Leave that to the righteous anger of God. For the Scriptures say, "I will take revenge; I will pay them back," says the LORD. Instead, "If your enemies are hungry, feed them. If they are thirsty, give them something to drink. In doing this, you will heap burning coals of shame on their heads." Don't let evil conquer you, but conquer evil by doing good. ROMANS 12:17-21

You will be held accountable to God for the revenge that you seek and blessed for the good that you do to others. When God balances life's accounts, would you rather weigh in with more good or more vengeance?

REWARDS *See also* Blessings, Consequences, Gifts, Heaven

Rewards are the natural consequences for wise behavior. Productivity on the job brings a bonus or raise, while ineffectiveness, laziness, or unethical practices bring dismissal. Some rewards are intangible, like the inner satisfaction one feels after an act of generosity or compassion. The Bible includes examples and illustrations of each. The greatest reward it talks about, however, is not earned but received as a gift—the gift of salvation.

How does God promise to reward those who believe in him?

How joyful are those who fear the Lord . . . You will enjoy the fruit of your labor. How joyful and prosperous you will be! . . . Your children will be like vigorous young olive trees as they sit around your table. That is the Lord's blessing for those who fear him. PSALM 128:1-4

A life of obedience and wisdom brings natural and supernatural blessings.

God blesses those who patiently endure testing and temptation. Afterward they will receive the crown of life that God has promised to those who love him. JAMES 1:12

It is time to judge the dead and reward your servants the prophets, as well as your holy people, and all who fear your name, from the least to the greatest. REVELATION 11:18

The greatest reward is eternal life with God.

Righteous people will be rewarded for their own righteous behavior. EZEKIEL 18:20

God promises to reward his people on the basis of their deeds.

Salvation is not a reward for the good things we have done, so none of us can boast about it. EPHESIANS 2:9

Salvation is not a reward for good works, but the gift of God is the reward for faith.

Should I work for rewards beyond this world?

I have fought the good fight, I have finished the race, and I have remained faithful. 2 TIMOTHY 4:7

If we are faithful to the end, trusting God just as firmly as when we first believed, we will share in all that belongs to Christ. HEBREWS 3:14

As you work to serve God and others here on earth, you are storing up rewards in heaven. Heavenly rewards await those who are faithful to God now.

Are there rewards in this lifetime for following Jesus?

Anyone who wants to come to him must believe that God exists and that he rewards those who sincerely seek him. HEBREWS 11:6

Knowing Jesus brings personal and spiritual rewards that are beyond anything this world offers.

Give your gifts in private, and your Father, who sees everything, will reward you. MATTHEW 6:4

Acts of devotion—such as giving, prayer, and fasting—bring the reward of pleasing Jesus and the satisfaction of serving him.

Anyone who receives you receives me, and anyone who receives me receives the Father who sent me. If you receive a prophet as one who speaks for God, you will be given the same reward as a prophet. And if you receive righteous people because of their righteousness, you will be given a reward like theirs. And if you give even a cup of cold water to one of the least of my followers, you will surely be rewarded. MATTHEW 10:40-42

Jesus blesses those who bless others. Acts of compassion and caring for others will bring benefits your way.

Before they are appointed as deacons, let them be closely examined. If they pass the test, then let them serve as deacons. 1 TIMOTHY 3:10

If you faithfully serve in the church, you may be given the reward of greater responsibility and leadership.

If you look carefully into the perfect law that sets you free, and if you do what it says and don't forget what you heard, then God will bless you for doing it. JAMES 1:25

If you obey and follow the commands and life principles in the Scriptures, you will be rewarded by experiencing fewer of sin's painful consequences and, thus, a happier and healthier life.

God blesses those who patiently endure testing and temptation. Afterward they will receive the crown of life that God has promised to those who love him. JAMES 1:12

Jesus gives the rewards of security and confidence in guaranteeing eternal life to those who patiently and faithfully endure the difficulties, hardships, tests, and temptations they face in this life.

What are the rewards that await me in heaven?

No eye has seen, no ear has heard, and no mind has imagined what God has prepared for those who love him. 1 CORINTHIANS 2:9

The best rewards you can imagine pale in comparison with what the Lord has in store for you in heaven. Everyone who is a follower of Jesus has much to look forward to. Heaven is more than compensation for faith in Jesus and more than vindication for the ridicule from those who didn't believe. It is fellowship with the Lord and all who have loved and honored him.

God blesses you when people mock you and persecute you and lie about you and say all sorts of evil things against you because you are my followers. Be happy about it! Be very glad! For a great reward awaits you in heaven. And remember, the ancient prophets were persecuted in the same way. MATTHEW 5:11-12

Jesus says there are extra rewards in heaven for those who are persecuted for their faith.

There is a special rest still waiting for the people of God. HEBREWS 4:9

The rest that is promised in heaven is not inactivity. It is the refreshment and satisfaction of savoring a completed, fulfilled work. Like an architect who enjoys living in a building that he or she designed, or a gardener who savors the fruits of hard labor, so you will enjoy the rest and refreshment of the Lord's work in your life.

RIGHTEOUSNESS *See also* Faith, Holiness, Perfection, Purity

Righteousness is not the result of being a good person or doing good things. It is the by-product of deep faith and persistent obedience to God. Nobody can be perfectly righteous on earth, nor can righteousness be achieved by our own efforts. Only a person who lives in close relationship to God, whose heart is tuned to his will and bent on obedience can approach righteousness.

What is righteousness?

Noah was a righteous man, the only blameless person living on earth at the time, and he walked in close fellowship with God. GENESIS 6:9

There once was a man named Job who lived in the land of Uz. He was blameless— a man of complete integrity. He feared God and stayed away from evil. JOB 1:1

Abraham believed God, and God counted him as righteous because of his faith. . . . Abraham never wavered in believing God's promise. In fact, his faith grew stronger, and in this he brought glory to God. He was fully convinced that God is able to do whatever he promises. And because of Abraham's faith, God counted him as righteous. ROMANS 4:3, 20-22

Righteousness is consistently following God's Word and will, being forgiven of sin, walking with God daily, having an unwavering faith in God and his promises, loving him deeply, demonstrating persistent integrity, and avoiding evil. When you sincerely work at this kind of life, God calls you *blameless.* Because he has forgiven your sins, he sees you as though you have no sin.

How can I be considered righteous?

[The] Good News tells us how God makes us right in his sight. This is accomplished from start to finish by faith. As the Scriptures say, "It is through faith that a righteous person has life." ROMANS 1:17

It is by believing in your heart that you are made right with God, and it is by confessing with your mouth that you are saved. ROMANS 10:10

I become righteous through faith in Christ. For God's way of making us right with himself depends on faith. PHILIPPIANS 3:9

You are considered righteous before God when you trust in Jesus Christ to save you from the punishment you deserve for your sins. When you believe in Jesus, confess your sin, and truly turn from sin and turn to living for God, God looks at you as though you had never sinned. You are righteous not because you are perfect, but because God, through his forgiveness, sees you as holy.

How can I pursue and practice righteousness?

Whoever pursues righteousness and unfailing love will find life, righteousness, and honor. PROVERBS 21:21

"Lord, when did we ever see you hungry and feed you? Or thirsty and give you something to drink? Or a stranger and show you hospitality? Or naked and give you clothing? When did we ever see you sick or in prison and visit you?" And the King will say, "I tell you the truth, when you did it to one of the least of these my brothers and sisters, you were doing it to me!" MATTHEW 25:37-40

Pursue righteousness and a godly life, along with faith, love, perseverance, and gentleness. 1 TIMOTHY 6:11

Do your best to follow Jesus' example of living. This means pursuing that which Jesus saw as important.

What are some of the ways the righteous are blessed?

The LORD is far from the wicked, but he hears the prayers of the righteous.
PROVERBS 15:29

The wicked run away when no one is chasing them, but the godly are as bold as lions.
PROVERBS 28:1

The righteous will shine like the sun in their Father's Kingdom. MATTHEW 13:43

Those who are righteous in Jesus' eyes are safe in God's care (their souls cannot be snatched away by Satan), bold in God's work (they have the courage to do the right thing and are not ashamed of their faith), persistent in prayer (they enjoy close fellowship with God), and radiant in their inner beauty (others can see they are different, that something is very attractive about them).

RISK *See also* Challenges, Courage, Opportunities, Planning

Most of us try to minimize risk. We have insurance policies, individual retirement funds, security codes on credit cards, and alarm systems in our homes and cars. This need to protect ourselves is not a bad thing unless it keeps us from doing what we want to do, have to do, or are called to do by God. The Bible tells us that the Christian life is risky; others may not understand us, and spiritual forces are against us. But if we allow ourselves to be vulnerable to God's leading and embrace his teachings wholeheartedly, the rewards of eternal security far outweigh the risks of living with abandon for him.

Why would we take risks?

Faith is the confidence that what we hope for will actually happen; it gives us assurance about things we cannot see. Through their faith, the people in days of old earned a good reputation. . . . It was by faith that Noah built a large boat to save his family from the flood. He obeyed God, who warned him about things that had never happened before. . . . It was by faith that Abraham obeyed when God called him to leave home and go to another land that God would give him as his inheritance. He went without knowing where he was going. And even when he reached the land God promised him, he lived there by faith. HEBREWS 11:1-2, 7-9

Risks in all areas of life are based on odds—are you confident enough that the rewards of achieving your goals outweigh the risks of getting there? In the Christian life, trusting God to lead you is a good risk because he knows what is best for you, and he knows how to get you there. With a loving God who has a perfect plan for you, the odds are definitely in your favor.

Do not be afraid of the terrors of the night, nor the arrow that flies in the day.
PSALM 91:5

Commit everything you do to the LORD. Trust him, and he will help you. PSALM 37:5

When you work in a quarry, stones might fall and crush you. When you chop wood, there is danger with each stroke of your ax. ECCLESIASTES 10:9

Growth and success occur at some risk. Taking foolish chances is not risk—it's stupidity. Taking a risk entails having a good goal, a decent chance of achieving it, and a strong dose of confidence. Risk taking is actually necessary if you want to grow in your relationship with God. When he calls you to do something out of your comfort zone, obey at the risk of failing, while trusting him to help you complete what he has asked you to do.

What kinds of risks should Christians take?

The LORD had said to Abram, "Leave your native country, your relatives, and your father's family, and go to the land that I will show you." GENESIS 12:1

Moses raised his hand over the sea, and the LORD opened up a path through the water with a strong east wind. The wind blew all that night, turning the seabed into dry land. So the people of Israel walked through the middle of the sea on dry ground, with walls of water on each side! EXODUS 14:21-22

Those great in faith are risk takers. Abram left everyone and everything he knew to risk obedience to God. Moses stood before the Red Sea while Pharaoh's armies, thinking the Israelites were trapped, closed in on them. The waters parted and the people risked the journey through the walls of water to freedom. Great things do not happen without some risk. Be prepared to risk your resources, your reputation, and even your closest relationships if that is required to be faithful to God. The only thing more risky than trusting God is not trusting him!

[Elijah] dug a trench around the altar large enough to hold about three gallons. He piled wood on the altar, cut the bull into pieces, and laid the pieces on the wood. Then he said, "Fill four large jars with water, and pour the water over the offering and the wood." After they had done this, he said, "Do the same thing again!" And when they were finished, he said, "Now do it a third time!" . . . The water ran around the altar and even filled the trench. . . . Elijah the prophet walked up to the altar and prayed, "O LORD . . . prove today that you are God." . . . Immediately the fire of the LORD flashed down from heaven and burned up the young bull, the wood, the stones, and the dust. It even licked up all the water in the trench! And when all the people saw it, they fell face down on the ground and cried out, "The LORD—he is God! Yes, the LORD is God!" 1 KINGS 18:32-39

You may be called to take risks to display the glory of God. Such was the case with Elijah on Mount Carmel. Be certain you are following God, as with all risks, or you may make a mockery of your faith and harm others. But when God's call is clear, move forward with confidence.

What blessings await you when people hate you and exclude you and mock you and curse you as evil because you follow the Son of Man. When that happens, be happy! Yes, leap for joy! For a great reward awaits you in heaven. And remember, their ancestors treated the ancient prophets that same way. LUKE 6:22-23

You may risk rejection and the loss of security, but the rewards of loyalty to God are eternal.

[Jesus] bowed with his face to the ground, praying, "My Father! If it is possible, let this cup of suffering be taken away from me. Yet I want your will to be done, not mine." MATTHEW 26:39

Risk doing the right thing, even when it is the hardest thing, because it will earn you a reputation for integrity, which is a priceless quality no one can take from you.

[God said,] "Now go, for I am sending you to Pharaoh. You must lead my people Israel out of Egypt." But Moses protested to God, "Who am I to appear before Pharaoh? Who am I to lead the people of Israel out of Egypt?" EXODUS 3:10-11

You must take the risk of doing things God's way. When God asks you to follow him, he often doesn't give all the information up front about what is happening. When you step out in faith, he gives guidance as you go. Moses risked his life by approaching Pharaoh and leading the Israelites out of captivity. Mary risked her marriage, her reputation, and her future by becoming the mother of Jesus. Following God's will is not without risks, but there is no greater reward.

What are some principles of risk taking I should keep in mind?

Fools think their own way is right, but the wise listen to others. PROVERBS 12:15

Those who trust their own insight are foolish, but anyone who walks in wisdom is safe. PROVERBS 28:26

Fools base their thoughts on foolish assumptions, so their conclusions will be wicked madness. ECCLESIASTES 10:13

There is a difference between being a risk taker and being a fool. The Bible warns us not to take risks that ignore or contradict sound principles. Consulting God and wise, godly friends before taking big steps in life provides a higher likelihood of success. Fools rarely consult others, never consult God, and make plans that are mostly for personal gain or fame. God is looking for wise and obedient risk takers, not foolish people who plunge ahead without first seeking his guidance.

The LORD said to Joshua, "Do not be afraid or discouraged." JOSHUA 8:1

Be strong and courageous, and do the work. Don't be afraid or discouraged, for the LORD God, my God, is with you. . . . He will see to it that all the work related to the Temple of the LORD is finished correctly. 1 CHRONICLES 28:20

Don't be afraid of failing. The only true failure is that which utterly defeats you and makes you unable to try again. Failure wins when you accept defeat and give up. Joshua was defeated at the battle of Ai. He dealt with the causes of defeat head-on, then led his army out once again into the danger of battle, and then won a great victory. You must have the courage to face failure and take risks again. The lessons you learn from your failures will make you better able to assess risk in the future. If you don't give up, yesterday's failure will turn into tomorrow's victory.

ROLES *See also* Church, Diversity, Marriage, Work

Roles signal responsibilities. In a work environment, defining the roles of each employee gives meaning and purpose to their work and helps them identify and accomplish those tasks for which they are responsible. The more clearly roles are defined, the better idea we have of what needs to be done and how we're gifted to meet those. God has also given each of his people a role in the church. It is particularly fulfilling to find our role and be satisfied and motivated with the role he wants us to play in moving his kingdom work forward.

What is my role in the body of Christ?

Just as our bodies have many parts and each part has a special function, so it is with Christ's body. We are many parts of one body, and . . . God has given us different gifts for doing certain things well. ROMANS 12:4-6

[Jesus] makes the whole body fit together perfectly. As each part does its own special work, it helps the other parts grow, so that the whole body is healthy and growing and full of love. EPHESIANS 4:16

God assigns a variety of servant roles based on abilities and the needs of his church. Just a few of the wide variety of roles God assigns to people are: preachers, teachers, administrators, prophets, elders, deacons, and musicians.

How should I respond to my role?

Commit your actions to the LORD, and your plans will succeed. PROVERBS 16:3

I planted the seed in your hearts, and Apollos watered it, but it was God who made it grow. 1 CORINTHIANS 3:6

Remember it is God's work in which you are allowed to be involved.

All of you together are Christ's body, and each of you is a part of it. 1 CORINTHIANS 12:27

Appreciate the importance of your role and of the roles of others as you are interdependent with one another. Don't try to do too much by taking over a role that is not meant for you.

My life is worth nothing to me unless I use it for finishing the work assigned me by the Lord Jesus—the work of telling others the Good News about the wonderful grace of God. ACTS 20:24

God has given us different gifts for doing certain things well. So if God has given you the ability to prophesy, speak out with as much faith as God has given you. If your gift is serving others, serve them well. If you are a teacher, teach well. If your gift is to encourage others, be encouraging. If it is giving, give generously. If God has given you leadership ability, take the responsibility seriously. And if you have a gift for showing kindness to others, do it gladly. ROMANS 12:6-8

When you discover your role in the church, make it a priority to fulfill it well so that you can maximize your efforts for God.

Martha was distracted by the big dinner she was preparing. She came to Jesus and said, "Lord, doesn't it seem unfair to you that my sister just sits here while I do all the work? Tell her to come and help me." But the Lord said to her, "My dear Martha, you are worried and upset over all these details! There is only one thing worth being concerned about. Mary has discovered it, and it will not be taken away from her." LUKE 10:40-42

Don't let your "role" in serving God interfere with your relationship with him.

Never be lazy, but work hard and serve the Lord enthusiastically. ROMANS 12:11

Do everything without complaining and arguing. PHILIPPIANS 2:14

Work willingly at whatever you do, as though you were working for the Lord rather than for people. COLOSSIANS 3:23

No matter what your role is, be a dedicated, hard worker who serves the Lord enthusiastically and willingly without complaining or arguing.

ROMANCE *See also* Desires, Intimacy, Love, Marriage, Relationships

Romance is what draws two people together in love. What a wonderful feeling when someone expresses affection for you, enjoys your company, and is captivated by you. You feel happy, confident, and interesting to another. As you read through the Bible, you learn that God himself is the original romantic. He created the concept of intimate love between a husband and wife, and loves a "happily ever after" story. He also created an even deeper kind of love, the love between the Creator and the created. God "romances" you, not in a sexual way of course, but in a way that says he longs to have a deeper relationship with you, to be your God, to captivate you with interest, to give you joy and peace. He wants your relationship with him to be a "happily ever after" story that truly lasts for all eternity. Romantic love between a husband and wife is a picture of this even deeper love that God desires all his people to experience.

What is the connection between love and romance?

Place me like a seal over your heart, like a seal on your arm. For love is as strong as death, its jealousy as enduring as the grave. Love flashes like fire, the brightest kind of flame. Many waters cannot quench love, nor can rivers drown it. If a man tried to buy love with all his wealth, his offer would be utterly scorned. SONG OF SONGS 8:6-7

Three things will last forever—faith, hope, and love—and the greatest of these is love. 1 CORINTHIANS 13:13

Love is the source of all true romance.

Love is patient and kind. Love is not jealous or boastful or proud or rude. It does not demand its own way. It is not irritable, and it keeps no record of being wronged. It does not rejoice about injustice but rejoices whenever the truth wins out. Love never gives up, never loses faith, is always hopeful, and endures through every circumstance.
1 CORINTHIANS 13:4-7

True love is extremely attractive and inspires good romance.

Why is romance important?

Like a lily among thistles is my darling among young women. . . . Like the finest apple tree in the orchard is my lover among other young men. I sit in his delightful shade and taste his delicious fruit. SONG OF SONGS 2:2-3

Romance expresses the value of both individuals in a loving relationship.

Drink water from your own well—share your love only with your wife. Why spill the water of your springs in the streets, having sex with just anyone? You should reserve it for yourselves. Never share it with strangers. PROVERBS 5:15-17

You are my private garden, my treasure, my bride, a secluded spring, a hidden fountain.
SONG OF SONGS 4:12

Romance is a guard for intimacy and promotes faithfulness.

What does it mean to be romantic in a married relationship?

Oh, how beautiful you are! How pleasing, my love, how full of delights! . . . May your kisses be as exciting as the best wine, flowing gently over lips and teeth. I am my lover's, and he claims me as his own. SONG OF SONGS 7:6, 9-10

Romance means being purposeful about enjoying your mate and expressing that enjoyment.

Let your wife be a fountain of blessing for you. Rejoice in the wife of your youth. She is a loving deer, a graceful doe. Let her breasts satisfy you always. May you always be captivated by her love. PROVERBS 5:18-19

True romance in a marriage relationship is in finding and enjoying the things about your spouse that captivate you.

Kiss me and kiss me again, for your love is sweeter than wine. SONG OF SONGS 1:2

Strengthen me with raisin cakes, refresh me with apples, for I am weak with love. His left arm is under my head, and his right arm embraces me. SONG OF SONGS 2:5-6

Romance involves expressing desire for your mate's affection.

You are as exciting, my darling, as a mare among Pharaoh's stallions. How lovely are your cheeks; your earrings set them afire! How lovely is your neck, enhanced by a string of jewels. We will make for you earrings of gold and beads of silver. . . . How beautiful you are, my darling, how beautiful! Your eyes are like doves.... You are so handsome, my love, pleasing beyond words! SONG OF SONGS 1:9-11, 15-16

Romance involves expressing how attractive your mate is to you.

Don't be concerned about the outward beauty of fancy hairstyles, expensive jewelry, or beautiful clothes. You should clothe yourselves instead with the beauty that comes from within, the unfading beauty of a gentle and quiet spirit, which is so precious to God. This is how the holy women of old made themselves beautiful. They trusted God and accepted the authority of their husbands. 1 PETER 3:3-5

Romance involves getting to know the inner beauty of your spouse.

Don't be selfish; don't try to impress others. Be humble, thinking of others as better than yourselves. PHILIPPIANS 2:3

You husbands must give honor to your wives. Treat your wife with understanding as you live together. She may be weaker than you are, but she is your equal partner in God's gift of new life. Treat her as you should so your prayers will not be hindered.... Sympathize with each other. Love each other as brothers and sisters. Be tenderhearted, and keep a humble attitude. 1 PETER 3:7-8

Treating your spouse with respect, selflessness, and understanding is romantic.

Her husband praises her: "There are many virtuous and capable women in the world, but you surpass them all!" Charm is deceptive, and beauty does not last; but a woman who fears the LORD will be greatly praised. Reward her for all she has done. Let her deeds publicly declare her praise. PROVERBS 31:28-31

He escorts me to the banquet hall; it's obvious how much he loves me. SONG OF SONGS 2:4

It is romantic to publicly declare your affection for your spouse.

Is God "romantic" toward me?

For your Creator will be your husband. ISAIAH 54:5

The LORD said to Israel: "I have loved you, my people, with an everlasting love. With unfailing love I have drawn you to myself." JEREMIAH 31:3

I will win her back once again. I will lead her into the desert and speak tenderly to her there.... I will make you my wife forever, showing you righteousness and justice, unfailing love and compassion. I will be faithful to you and make you mine, and you will finally know me as the LORD. HOSEA 2:14, 19-20

Then the LORD said to [Hosea], "Go and love your wife again, even though she commits adultery with another lover. This will illustrate that the LORD still loves Israel, even though the people have turned to other gods and love to worship them." HOSEA 3:1

God's romantic love for you is evidenced throughout Scripture in his desire for a loving, intimate relationship with you.

What are the dangers of romance?

A seductive woman is a trap more bitter than death. Her passion is a snare, and her soft hands are chains. Those who are pleasing to God will escape her, but sinners will be caught in her snare. ECCLESIASTES 7:26

Be cautious of whom and what you allow to entertain your affections. Being romanced is intoxicating and sexually tempting, so outside of marriage it can easily lead to sexual immorality.

ROUTINE *See also* Consistency, Discipline, Habits, Priorities

Routine is defined as "a regular course of action." A routine can be a habit, a job, a workout schedule, or any number of things done consistently. There is nothing basically good or bad about routine; but what routines you follow and why determine their value. For example, a bad habit or an addiction is a routine that will bring much harm. But regular exercise or consistent time spent in God's Word will yield wonderful benefits. The key to any routine is having the discipline to persistently pursue important goals while maintaining the flexibility to be open to important interruptions, the most important being God asking you to change direction.

What should always be a part of my routine?

Sing to the LORD; praise his name. Each day proclaim the good news that he saves. PSALM 96:2

Praising God daily for who he is and what he has done will help you appreciate him and put your hope in him for tomorrow.

If you are wise and understand God's ways, prove it by living an honorable life, doing good works with the humility that comes from wisdom. JAMES 3:13

Your life should be a routine of good deeds.

Listen to my voice in the morning, LORD. Each morning I bring my requests to you and wait expectantly. PSALM 5:3

Never stop praying. 1 THESSALONIANS 5:17

Make prayer and communication with God a daily habit.

Give me understanding and I will obey your instructions; I will put them into practice with all my heart. . . . I will keep on obeying your instructions forever and ever. . . . This is how I spend my life: obeying your commandments. . . . Oh, how I love your instructions! I think about them all day long. PSALM 119:34, 44, 56, 97

Jesus [said], "Blessed are all who hear the word of God and put it into practice." LUKE 11:28

Read, meditate on, and obey God's Word every day.

You must set aside a tithe of your crops—one-tenth of all the crops you harvest each year. DEUTERONOMY 14:22

Routinely give to the Lord. Following the principle of the "tithe" (giving the first tenth of your paycheck) is a routine that demonstrates the priority of God in your life.

Let us not neglect our meeting together, as some people do, but encourage one another, especially now that the day of his return is drawing near. HEBREWS 10:25

Routinely participate with other believers in worshiping God.

What should never be part of my routine?

Those who have been born into God's family do not make a practice of sinning, because God's life is in them. So they can't keep on sinning, because they are children of God. 1 JOHN 3:9

We know that God's children do not make a practice of sinning, for God's Son holds them securely, and the evil one cannot touch them. 1 JOHN 5:18

A routine of sinful living is not compatible with a godly lifestyle and is unacceptable to our holy God.

When is routine good?

The men in charge of the renovation worked hard and made steady progress. They restored the Temple of God according to its original design and strengthened it. 2 CHRONICLES 24:13

Be strong and immovable. Always work enthusiastically for the Lord, for you know that nothing you do for the Lord is ever useless. 1 CORINTHIANS 15:58

Routine is good when it accomplishes the Lord's work. Often productivity is the result of steady and conscientious work.

Endurance develops strength of character, and character strengthens our confident hope of salvation. ROMANS 5:4

Routine is good when it builds godly character. Routine can help you learn perseverance and endurance, which are elements of strong character.

God anointed Jesus of Nazareth with the Holy Spirit and with power. Then Jesus went around doing good and healing all who were oppressed by the devil, for God was with him. ACTS 10:38

When God's people are in need, be ready to help them. Always be eager to practice hospitality. ROMANS 12:13

Get into the habit of identifying and meeting the needs of others. Then your daily routine will be a blessing to you and those around you.

What is the danger of routine?

Can an Ethiopian change the color of his skin? Can a leopard take away its spots? Neither can you start doing good, for you have always done evil. JEREMIAH 13:23

[False teachers] promise freedom, but they themselves are slaves of sin and corruption. For you are a slave to whatever controls you. 2 PETER 2:19

Bad habits and sinful lifestyle choices are routines that are difficult to break and can be controlling.

My people come pretending to be sincere and sit before you. They listen to your words, but they have no intention of doing what you say. Their mouths are full of lustful words, and their hearts seek only after money. EZEKIEL 33:31

Routines are hypocritical and insincere when you are merely going through the motions for all the wrong reasons.

What are God's "routines" concerning you and all of his people?

Each day the LORD pours his unfailing love upon me, and through each night I sing his songs, praying to God who gives me life. PSALM 42:8

Loving you.

If we confess our sins to him, he is faithful and just to forgive us our sins and to cleanse us from all wickedness. 1 JOHN 1:9

Forgiving you.

Praise the LORD; praise God our savior! For each day he carries us in his arms. PSALM 68:19

Caring for, supporting, and sustaining you.

Great is his faithfulness; his mercies begin afresh each morning. LAMENTATIONS 3:23

Showing mercy.

I, the LORD, will watch over [the vineyard], watering it carefully. Day and night I will watch so no one can harm it. ISAIAH 27:3

Protecting you.

That is why we never give up. Though our bodies are dying, our spirits are being renewed every day. 2 CORINTHIANS 4:16

Renewing your spirit.

S

SABBATH *See also* Balance, Renewal, Rest, Work, Worship

The idea of Sabbath, or taking one day of the week to rest and worship, was first introduced by God on the seventh day of his world, after he had finished the work of Creation. He further emphasized his desire for people to observe a Sabbath by making it the fourth commandment. Why would an almighty God need to take a day off? Because he knew humans would need to restore their bodies and souls, and so he personally set in motion a rhythm of life which includes a healthy balance between work, rest, and worship.

Why did God institute the Sabbath?

On the seventh day God had finished his work of creation, so he rested from all his work. And God blessed the seventh day and declared it holy, because it was the day when he rested from all his work of creation. GENESIS 2:2-3

For in six days the LORD made the heavens, the earth, the sea, and everything in them; but on the seventh day he rested. That is why the LORD blessed the Sabbath day and set it apart as holy. EXODUS 20:11

God instituted a weekly Sabbath (day of rest) because it honors his creative work and the blessing that he gave when he finished Creation.

You have six days each week for your ordinary work, but on the seventh day you must stop working. This gives your ox and your donkey a chance to rest. It also allows your slaves and the foreigners living among you to be refreshed. EXODUS 23:12

The weekly Sabbath allowed an opportunity for both people and animals to rest from their work and be refreshed.

Be careful to keep my Sabbath day, for the Sabbath is a sign of the covenant between me and you from generation to generation. It is given so you may know that I am the LORD, who makes you holy. EXODUS 31:13

The weekly Sabbath gave the Israelites a regular opportunity to remember their covenant with God and to worship him.

Keep the Sabbath day holy. Don't pursue your own interests on that day, but enjoy the Sabbath and speak of it with delight as the LORD's holy day. Honor the Sabbath in everything you do on that day, and don't follow your own desires or talk idly. Then the LORD will be your delight. I will give you great honor and satisfy you with the inheritance I promised to your ancestor Jacob. I, the LORD, have spoken! ISAIAH 58:13-14

God gave Sabbath rest to his people for his honor as well as for their welfare and delight. Allow yourself the joy and luxury of spending one day a week restoring your body and soul.

Remember to observe the Sabbath day by keeping it holy. You have six days each week for your ordinary work, but the seventh day is a Sabbath day of rest dedicated to the LORD your God. On that day no one in your household may do any work. This includes you. EXODUS 20:8-10

The primary principle of the Sabbath is to take time away from the pressures of everyday routines so that you can more intently focus on the Lord in worship as you rest and renew your spirit.

The law permits a person to do good on the Sabbath. MATTHEW 12:12

Jesus said . . . , "The Sabbath was made to meet the needs of people, and not people to meet the requirements of the Sabbath." MARK 2:27

The Sabbath was not meant to keep people from doing good.

Am I required to keep the Sabbath today?

You are trying to earn favor with God by observing certain days or months or seasons or years. I fear for you. GALATIANS 4:10-11

Don't let anyone condemn you for what you eat or drink, or for not celebrating certain holy days or new moon ceremonies or Sabbaths. COLOSSIANS 2:16

You cannot become righteous or gain God's approval by observing the Sabbath or celebrating certain holy days. Jesus provides true spiritual rest for your soul through faith in him. Jesus gave new meaning to the Sabbath by emphasizing what you can do on the Sabbath rather than what you can't do.

On the first day of the week, we gathered with the local believers to share in the Lord's Supper. ACTS 20:7

It was the Lord's Day, and I was worshiping in the Spirit. REVELATION 1:10

Since the time of the early Christians, the first day of the week has been the Lord's Day and has replaced the Jewish Sabbath (Saturday) as a special day of worship.

Some think one day is more holy than another day, while others think every day is alike. You should each be fully convinced that whichever day you choose is acceptable. ROMANS 14:5

There is no hard-and-fast rule for Christians with regard to the Sabbath.

Don't misunderstand why I have come. I did not come to abolish the law of Moses or the writings of the prophets. No, I came to accomplish their purpose. I tell you the truth, until heaven and earth disappear, not even the smallest detail of God's law will disappear until its purpose is achieved. MATTHEW 5:17-18

The principle that you need weekly rest and an opportunity to set aside a regular time to worship God is still true.

What are the benefits of taking Sabbath time?

The apostles returned to Jesus from their ministry tour and told him all they had done and taught. Then Jesus said, "Let's go off by ourselves to a quiet place and rest awhile." MARK 6:30-31

There is great value to rest, especially after hard work. Rest is not only for the recovery of energy, but also for the savoring of the work you have completed. Even Jesus took the time to rest. Though forces and demands will conspire against your rest, you must continually make it your goal to pursue time for a break from your regular routine.

SACRIFICE *See also* Abstinence, Fasting, Giving, Sharing, Surrender

A sacrifice is a kind of substitution. We give up one thing in order to obtain something of greater value. Parents may sacrifice a new car to save money for a child's education. A baseball player executes a "sacrifice bunt" to give a teammate an opportunity to score a run. In the Old Testament, a sacrifice was an act of worship by which the blood of an animal was shed as a substitute for the punishment a person deserved for his or her sin. All the sacrifices of the Old Testament anticipated God's ultimate sacrifice of Jesus on the cross for the sins of the world. Anytime we make a sacrifice, we are reminded, in a small way, of God's greatest sacrifice of all.

Why did God require animal sacrifices in the Old Testament—and why were they so bloody?

Moses took the blood from the basins and splattered it over the people, declaring, "Look, this blood confirms the covenant the LORD has made with you in giving you these instructions." EXODUS 24:8

Lay your hand on the animal's head, and the LORD will accept its death in your place to purify you, making you right with him. LEVITICUS 1:4

It is the blood, given in exchange for a life, that makes purification possible. LEVITICUS 17:11

The sacrificial system reminded the Israelites of the seriousness of sin before their holy God. Sin separates us from God and earns eternal death (see Colossians 1:21). Forgiveness and salvation restore us to God and bring eternal life. The offering of a sacrifice symbolized a person's desire to be forgiven for sin and restored to fellowship with God. In Old Testament times, a life had to be given up (the animal's) so that a life could be spared (the person's). The blood of the sacrificed animal represented one life being poured out in substitution for another. This idea of a "substitute" foreshadowed Jesus' death on the cross for our sins. Just as an animal died so a person wouldn't have to, so Jesus died so we wouldn't have to (see Romans 5:6-11). The sacrifice of the animal was bloody and grotesque, but it reminded the sinner how serious sin is and how grotesquely it can damage one's soul.

What is the significance of Jesus' sacrifice?

God presented Jesus as the sacrifice for sin. People are made right with God when they believe that Jesus sacrificed his life, shedding his blood. ROMANS 3:25

He personally carried our sins in his body on the cross so that we can be dead to sin and live for what is right. By his wounds you are healed. 1 PETER 2:24

Jesus Christ took the punishment you deserve for your sins and made atonement for you (made you "at one" with God), not by covering up your sins, but by taking them away.

As they were eating, Jesus took some bread and blessed it. Then he broke it in pieces and gave it to the disciples, saying, "Take this and eat it, for this is my body." And he took a cup of wine and gave thanks to God for it. He gave it to them and said, "Each of you drink from it, for this is my blood, which confirms the covenant between God and his people. It is poured out as a sacrifice to forgive the sins of many." MATTHEW 26:26-28

Jesus' death and resurrection began a new covenant between God and those who come to him by faith. Now you can have an intimate relationship with God because Jesus removed your sin by his sacrificial death.

The law of Moses was unable to save us because of the weakness of our sinful nature. So God did what the law could not do. He sent his own Son in a body like the bodies we sinners have. And in that body God declared an end to sin's control over us by giving his Son as a sacrifice for our sins. ROMANS 8:3

Animal sacrifices could not take away sin; only Jesus' sacrifice for you could take away your sin and make it possible for you to have eternal life.

Jesus [said], "I am the way, the truth, and the life. No one can come to the Father except through me." JOHN 14:6

There is salvation in no one else! God has given no other name under heaven by which we must be saved. ACTS 4:12

There is only one God and one Mediator who can reconcile God and humanity—the man Christ Jesus. 1 TIMOTHY 2:5

Because Jesus is the only means by which forgiveness can been obtained, faith in him is the only means of salvation.

What kinds of sacrifices am I called to make?

Wherever you go, I will go; wherever you live, I will live. Your people will be my people, and your God will be my God. RUTH 1:16

You may be called to give up your favorite place, your friends, or your favorite things in order to be with the one you love. Such a sacrifice shows your commitment of love and your understanding of what is truly important.

[Jesus said,] "The world would love you as one of its own if you belonged to it, but you are no longer part of the world. I chose you to come out of the world, so it hates you. Do you remember what I told you? 'A slave is not greater than the master.' Since they persecuted me, naturally they will persecute you." JOHN 15:19-20

You might have to give up popularity and what the world calls security in order to stay loyal to Jesus.

Give your bodies to God because of all he has done for you. Let them be a living and holy sacrifice—the kind he will find acceptable. This is truly the way to worship him.
ROMANS 12:1

You have to sacrifice what is comfortable or pleasurable for doing what is right.

Live a life filled with love, following the example of Christ. He loved us and offered himself as a sacrifice for us, a pleasing aroma to God. EPHESIANS 5:2

Just as Jesus gave himself for you, he wants you to give yourself to serve other people—even to the point of giving your life for them if necessary.

What kinds of sacrifices are dangerous for me to make?

The LORD said to Samuel, "I am about to do a shocking thing in Israel. I am going to carry out all my threats against Eli and his family, from beginning to end. I have warned him that judgment is coming upon his family forever, because his sons are blaspheming God and he hasn't disciplined them. So I have vowed that the sins of Eli and his sons will never be forgiven by sacrifices or offerings." 1 SAMUEL 3:11-14

[David's] letter instructed Joab, "Station Uriah on the front lines where the battle is fiercest. Then pull back so that he will be killed." 2 SAMUEL 11:15

Eli sacrificed his family life for his career. David sacrificed the life of another man to hide his adultery. Some things are not worth the sacrifice, and some things are simply wrong to sacrifice in the name of convenience or sinful pleasure. Those sacrifices always produce devastating consequences.

SADNESS *See also* Discouragement, Hurts/Hurting, Loneliness

One of the most common denominators of human experience is sadness. Guaranteed. From the loss of a pet in childhood, to the loss of innocence through abuse or neglect, or the loss of a parent, child, friend, or spouse, sorrow is inevitable. Whether predictable and necessary or random and tragic, the losses of life affect us profoundly for the rest of our days. The Bible acknowledges that sorrow and grief are part of human life, even for those who love God. But Scripture does not give sorrow the last word. God redeems our losses with his promises of comfort and hope.

Is God concerned about my sadness?

He was despised and rejected—a man of sorrows, acquainted with deepest grief.
ISAIAH 53:3

Through the pain and sorrow of Jesus' experiences on earth, God experienced the depth of human grief.

Lazarus had died. . . . Jesus wept. The people who were standing nearby said, "See how much he loved him!" JOHN 11:13, 35-36

The tears of Jesus demonstrate that he relates to your sadness. Great grief comes from great love.

Give all your worries and cares to God, for he cares about you. 1 PETER 5:7

God cares not only about your eternal future, but also about your present troubles.

Should faith in God eliminate my sorrow?

My son, my son Absalom! If only I had died instead of you! 2 SAMUEL 18:33

King David's reaction to the loss of his son was an acute response of grief. God himself called David a man after his own heart, yet David still experienced great sorrow. Sorrow is a regular part of our earthly existence. Although faith in God does not erase our sorrow on earth, it does give us hope and a longing for heaven when there will be no sorrow.

[Jesus said], "My soul is crushed with grief to the point of death. Stay here and keep watch with me." MARK 14:34

Even Jesus suffered great sorrow and pain on earth.

The disciples were filled with grief. MATTHEW 17:23

Even though Jesus promised he would rise from the dead, the disciples still grieved his death.

How can I find hope in my times of sadness?

Weeping may last through the night, but joy comes with the morning. PSALM 30:5

You will grieve, but your grief will suddenly turn to wonderful joy. JOHN 16:20

[God himself] will wipe every tear from their eyes, and there will be no more death or sorrow or crying or pain. All these things are gone forever. REVELATION 21:4

God promises to relieve your sorrow and one day replace it with joy that lasts forever.

We want you to know what will happen to the believers who have died so you will not grieve like people who have no hope. 1 THESSALONIANS 4:13

The promise of heaven brings hope in the midst of your grief.

The Holy Spirit prays for us with groanings that cannot be expressed in words. ROMANS 8:26

When your suffering is so great that you don't know what to pray, the Holy Spirit prays for you.

What should I do when I'm sad?

[Elijah] went on alone into the wilderness, traveling all day. He sat down under a solitary broom tree and prayed that he might die. "I have had enough, LORD," he said. "Take my life, for I am no better than my ancestors who have already died." Then he lay down and slept under the broom tree. But as he was sleeping, an angel touched him and

told him, "Get up and eat!" He looked around and there beside his head was some bread baked on hot stones and a jar of water! So he ate and drank and lay down again.
1 KINGS 19:4-6

Recovery from deep sadness involves a number of factors, including a new perspective. Elijah was tired, hungry, and feeling completely alone. A period of rest, good food, and reengagement with God helped him to regain a proper perspective and to reconnect with God's purpose for his life. Sorrow can lead to depression when you've lost the hope God offers you and the big picture of God's purpose for you. Sadness for a time over a loss is natural and appropriate. But if it goes on too long it becomes unhealthy. Begin with rest, good nutrition, and reengagement with God. If you still need help, a godly counselor can help you regain a right perspective.

Look! He has placed the land in front of you. Go and occupy it as the LORD, the God of your ancestors, has promised you. Don't be afraid! Don't be discouraged!
DEUTERONOMY 1:21

Let's not get tired of doing what is good. At just the right time we will reap a harvest of blessing if we don't give up. GALATIANS 6:9

When you feel discouraged, it is easy to turn inward and become paralyzed by your sadness and pain. It takes some effort, but you need to refocus your attention on God. Every day he opens doors of opportunity that can bring purpose and meaning to you: helping someone in need, volunteering time to a good cause, writing a note of encouragement. When you lift your eyes from the ground, you will see the door God has opened. Walk through it with courage, and on the other side you will find relief from your sorrow.

SAFETY *See also* Caution/Cautiousness, Protection, Security

From terrorist attacks to the abduction of children in broad daylight, random acts of violence seem to fill the news reports night after night. Is anyone really safe anymore? Does faith in God offer any guarantees that our children will be safe at the bus stop or as we drive the highways? Scripture reveals God to be concerned about and committed to our safety. But to understand the concept of safety more fully, we must recognize who we are—eternal beings wrapped in mortal bodies. While God is concerned about what happens to our body, he is much more concerned about the safety of our soul. Once we have confessed faith in Jesus and the Holy Spirit comes to live in us, God is at work protecting our soul from being snatched away by Satan. This is the essence of God's promise for protection. Yes, God is also concerned about the safety of our physical body, and we probably experience his hand of protection more often than we realize. But ultimately, physical protection will be certain only when we are given our new body in heaven.

Does God protect those who love him from physical harm?

[The Lord] will order his angels to protect you wherever you go. PSALM 91:11

My God sent his angel to shut the lions' mouths so that they would not hurt me.
DANIEL 6:22

Sometimes God protects you and delivers you in miraculous ways in order to preserve you so you can continue to serve him.

I was given a thorn in my flesh, a messenger from Satan to torment me and keep me from becoming proud. 2 CORINTHIANS 12:7

Sometimes, like Paul, you may experience devastating physical hardship and suffering. These are the times when your faith is put to the test, and you have to keep your eternal perspective.

If you love and obey the LORD, you will live long in the land the LORD swore to give your ancestors Abraham, Isaac, and Jacob. DEUTERONOMY 30:20

Through his Word, God offers wisdom that helps you avoid needless peril.

If God doesn't guarantee physical safety, what's the point of faith?

Even when I walk through the darkest valley, I will not be afraid, for you are close beside me. Your rod and your staff protect and comfort me. PSALM 23:4

The path of the virtuous leads away from evil; whoever follows that path is safe.
PROVERBS 16:17

Faith has more to do with the eternal safety of your soul than the physical safety of your body.

Once you were like sheep who wandered away. But now you have turned to your Shepherd, the Guardian of your souls. 1 PETER 2:25

Jesus, the Shepherd of your soul, guards you from the enemy's attacks.

Christ . . . died for sinners to bring you safely home to God. 1 PETER 3:18

Faith in Jesus gives you safe passage to your eternal home.

Is it wrong to pray for safety for myself and my loved ones?

While Peter was in prison, the church prayed very earnestly for him. ACTS 12:5

God always welcomes the expression of your desires when offered in submission to his will.

One of the things I always pray for is the opportunity, God willing, to come at last to see you. ROMANS 1:10

Paul's desire for safety in travel was rooted in his desire to minister to others.

You are helping us by praying for us. Then many people will give thanks because God has graciously answered so many prayers for our safety. 2 CORINTHIANS 1:11

The early apostles depended on the prayers for safety offered by the churches. There may be people in your life who are depending on your prayers.

SALVATION *See also* Eternity, Faith, Forgiveness, Grace, Repentance

The scene is played out before us many times every year: A man is dramatically rescued from a swollen river; a child is pulled by firefighters from a burning apartment building; a woman is delivered from a would-be assailant by a brave bystander. Each scenario includes a situation of impending peril or destruction, a rescuer or deliverer who intervenes, and a second chance at life for the one saved. Although the word is rarely used in the media, each is a picture of salvation. The Bible teaches that sin threatens us with broken relationships, judgment, and spiritual death. When sin controls us, we are in grave danger. But God, through the death and resurrection of Jesus Christ, has provided a way to rescue us from sin's consequences. He offers us salvation so that we can have a second chance at life, an opportunity to experience a spiritual rebirth into a new and abundant life, and ultimately, eternal life with him forever.

What does it mean to be saved?

He has removed our sins as far from us as the east is from the west. PSALM 103:12

God, with undeserved kindness, declares that we are righteous. ROMANS 3:24

What joy for those whose record the LORD has cleared of sin. ROMANS 4:8

Spiritually speaking, being saved means your sins no longer count against you. By the kindness of God, you are forgiven and have eternal life. Being saved does not spare you from earthly troubles, but it does spare you from eternal judgment.

Remove the stain of my guilt. Create in me a clean heart, O God. PSALM 51:9-10

Being saved means the stain of guilt has been washed away. Guilt not only appears to be gone, it *is* gone! You are given a clean slate!

Those who listen to my message and believe in God who sent me have eternal life. JOHN 5:24

I give them eternal life, and they will never perish. No one can snatch them away from me, for my Father has given them to me, and he is more powerful than anyone else. No one can snatch them from the Father's hand. JOHN 10:28-29

Being saved means you are assured of eternal life in heaven. What greater hope could you have?

Why is salvation necessary?

The LORD observed the extent of human wickedness on the earth, and he saw that everything they thought or imagined was consistently and totally evil. . . . So God said to Noah, "I have decided to destroy all living creatures." GENESIS 6:5, 13

For the wages of sin is death. ROMANS 6:23

Salvation is necessary because sin against a holy God separates you from him, bringing judgment and spiritual death. An unholy being cannot live forever in the presence of a holy God.

There is salvation in no one else! God has given no other name under heaven by which we must be saved. ACTS 4:12

Although it may sound exclusive, the Bible's claim of "one way" to salvation is actually an expression of the grace and kindness of God in letting all people know how to escape eternal judgment. God invites anyone and everyone to come to him.

How can I be saved?

Everyone who calls on the name of the Lord will be saved. ROMANS 10:13

God's Word promises salvation to anyone who calls on Jesus' name for forgiveness. Call out to him in prayer and tell him that you want him to save you. He promises he will.

God loved the world so much that he gave his one and only Son, so that everyone who believes in him will not perish but have eternal life. JOHN 3:16

Believe in the Lord Jesus and you will be saved. ACTS 16:31

God has shown us a way to be made right with him without keeping the requirements of the law, as was promised in the writings of Moses and the prophets long ago. We are made right with God by placing our faith in Jesus Christ. And this is true for everyone who believes, no matter who we are. ROMANS 3:21-22

Jesus promised that those who believe in him will be saved. All you have to do is accept what Jesus did for you. God sent Jesus Christ to take your place and receive the punishment that you deserved for your sins. When you believe that he died to save you from your sins and rose again to give you eternal life, then you will be saved.

If you confess with your mouth that Jesus is Lord and believe in your heart that God raised him from the dead, you will be saved. For it is by believing in your heart that you are made right with God, and it is by confessing with your mouth that you are saved. ROMANS 10:9-10

God saved you by his grace when you believed. And you can't take credit for this; it is a gift from God. EPHESIANS 2:8

It seems too easy. The greatest gift God could ever offer—salvation—is absolutely free. You just have to accept it by (1) agreeing with God that you have sinned, (2) acknowledging that your sin cuts you off from God, (3) asking Jesus to forgive your sins, and (4) believing that Jesus is Lord over everything and that he is the Son of God. The gift is yours.

"Save me, Lord!" [Peter] shouted. Jesus immediately reached out and grabbed him. MATTHEW 14:30-31

You cannot save yourself from sin, guilt, judgment, and spiritual death. Only Jesus Christ can save you.

Since it is through God's kindness, then it is not by their good works. For in that case, God's grace would not be what it really is—free and undeserved. ROMANS 11:6

You cannot earn your way to heaven by being good and doing kind deeds. Salvation comes only through faith in Jesus.

How can I be sure of my salvation?

If you confess with your mouth that Jesus is Lord and believe in your heart that God raised him from the dead, you will be saved. ROMANS 10:9

You can be sure of your salvation because God has promised that you are saved if you believe in Jesus Christ as your Savior.

All who are led by the Spirit of God are children of God. ROMANS 8:14

When you believed in Christ, he identified you as his own by giving you the Holy Spirit, whom he promised long ago. The Spirit is God's guarantee that he will give us the inheritance he promised and that he has purchased us to be his own people. EPHESIANS 1:13-14

When you are God's child, the Holy Spirit takes up residence in your heart and is God's guarantee that you belong to him.

To all who believed him and accepted him, he gave the right to become children of God. JOHN 1:12

Just as a child cannot be "unborn," God's children—those who have believed in Jesus Christ—cannot be "unborn-again."

How does salvation affect my daily life?

Anyone who belongs to Christ has become a new person. The old life is gone; a new life has begun! 2 CORINTHIANS 5:17

Salvation not only gives you hope for eternity, but also hope for today. You have been given a new life and new power for living.

Our old sinful selves were crucified with Christ so that sin might lose its power in our lives. We are no longer slaves to sin. For when we died with Christ we were set free from the power of sin. And since we died with Christ, we know we will also live with him. ROMANS 6:6-8

Being saved means being freed from the power of sin and being free to live a new life.

He has created us anew in Christ Jesus, so we can do the good things he planned for us long ago. EPHESIANS 2:10

God created you for a purpose. Salvation enables you to fulfill that purpose by the power of God at work within you.

What is the connection between salvation and hope?

Humans can reproduce only human life, but the Holy Spirit gives birth to spiritual life. JOHN 3:6

Salvation brings the hope of real and lasting change in your life.

Since we have been made right in God's sight by faith, we have peace with God.
ROMANS 5:1

Salvation brings the hope of an intimate relationship with God. Salvation is more than being rescued from sin; it is a new relationship with God.

Christ died for us so that, whether we are dead or alive when he returns, we can live with him forever. 1 THESSALONIANS 5:10

For those who are saved, even death holds the promise of hope. Although death is considered your worst enemy, it is death that helps you graduate into your eternal reward.

SATISFACTION *See also* Confidence, Contentment, Joy, Peace, Trust

Human beings are creatures of both simple and complex needs. A newborn child cries out every few hours with hunger that needs to be satisfied. That same child will suffer emotional starvation if his or her needs for love, affection, and affirmation go unmet. Teenagers and adults crave social acceptance, material success, and personal significance. How do we know which needs must be satisfied and which are selfish "wants" that should be denied? The Bible tells us that God is the source of all true and lasting satisfaction. If we learn to trust him, he will guide us in discerning our healthy needs from our harmful desires.

Why do so many people seem so unhappy?
O God, you are my God. . . . My soul thirsts for you. . . . You satisfy me more than the richest feast. PSALM 63:1, 5

No matter how much we see, we are never satisfied. No matter how much we hear, we are not content. ECCLESIASTES 1:8

Those who drink the water I give will never be thirsty again. It becomes a fresh, bubbling spring within them, giving them eternal life. JOHN 4:14

Too many people try to meet their deepest needs in ways that just don't satisfy. Sometimes when you're hungry, the worst thing you can do is eat the wrong thing. For example, if you haven't eaten in a while and you quickly gobble down three donuts, you'll be satisfied for only a few minutes until you start to shake from the sugar rush. The same principle applies to satisfying the hungry soul. Fill it with only fun and pleasure and sin and you'll always be craving more and never getting enough. Your soul will get the "shakes." Without taking nourishment from God's spiritual food, you will never feel satisfied and always wonder what is wrong with your life.

Does God promise to satisfy all my needs?
Give me just enough to satisfy my needs. PROVERBS 30:8

Often God first redefines your needs. There is a vast difference between your needs and wants. Don't confuse the two.

When I awake, I will see you face to face and be satisfied. PSALM 17:15

Spiritual need finds satisfaction in intimacy with God. Since he created you for this purpose, the only way you'll be satisfied is to pursue a relationship with him.

God blesses those who are poor and realize their need for him, for the Kingdom of Heaven is theirs. MATTHEW 5:3

Jesus promised that the heart hungry for righteousness will be satisfied.

Is there any danger to being satisfied?

I fed my people until they were full. But they thanked me by committing adultery. JEREMIAH 5:7

The sinful heart may take advantage of God's goodness.

In the spring of the year, when kings normally go out to war, David sent Joab and the Israelite army to fight the Ammonites. . . . However, David stayed behind in Jerusalem. Late one afternoon, after his midday rest, David got out of bed and was walking on the roof of the palace. As he looked out over the city, he noticed a woman of unusual beauty taking a bath. He sent someone to find out who she was, and he was told, "She is Bathsheba, the . . . wife of Uriah the Hittite." Then David sent messengers to get her; and when she came to the palace, he slept with her. . . . Then she returned home. 2 SAMUEL 11:1-4

Satisfaction tends to lead to complacency, which leads to sin.

Their silver and gold won't save them on that day of the LORD's anger. It will neither satisfy nor feed them, for their greed can only trip them up. EZEKIEL 7:19

When you had eaten and were satisfied, you became proud and forgot me. HOSEA 13:6

Although affluence can be a blessing, it can also be dangerous, leading you into the sins of pride and greed.

SECURITY *See also* Eternity, Peace, Protection, Safety, Salvation

From retirement investment portfolios to home protection systems, we spend vast amounts of time and money on security. Financial security, personal security, job security, relational security, and even national security are sooner or later threatened by the unpredictable nature of the world in which we live. The Bible teaches that we can trust God as our source of lasting security, for he is changeless and his love endures forever.

With so much change and instability in the world, how does my faith give me security?

Those who trust in the LORD are as secure as Mount Zion; they will not be defeated but will endure forever. PSALM 125:1

All who listen to me will live in peace, untroubled by fear of harm. PROVERBS 1:33

Anyone who listens to my teaching and follows it is wise, like a person who builds a house on solid rock. MATTHEW 7:24

When you build your faith day by day with the truths of God's Word, you have built a solid foundation that will not easily crack under the world's pressure. As life's battles come your way, some may be strong enough to knock down a few walls, but your foundation remains strong, steady, and not easily moved because God's truths are eternal. A secure foundation gives you greater courage to face whatever troubles come your way.

God is our refuge and strength, always ready to help in times of trouble. So we will not fear when earthquakes come and the mountains crumble into the sea. Let the oceans roar and foam. Let the mountains tremble as the waters surge! PSALM 46:1-3

The name of the LORD is a strong fortress; the godly run to him and are safe. PROVERBS 18:10

No matter how much the storms of life batter you, you are eternally secure when you put your faith in God. Nothing can ever separate you from his eternal presence and security.

How can I feel secure about the future?

Don't worry about anything; instead, pray about everything. . . . Then you will experience God's peace, which exceeds anything we can understand. PHILIPPIANS 4:6-7

Your greatest security comes from knowing the peace of God. When you find it, your perspective on life will change. And you find it when you pray and hand your problems over to God for him to resolve.

Nothing in all creation will ever be able to separate us from the love of God that is revealed in Christ Jesus our Lord. ROMANS 8:39

The most powerful security in the world is knowing that nothing can separate you from God's love.

We have a priceless inheritance—an inheritance that is kept in heaven for you, pure and undefiled, beyond the reach of change and decay. And through your faith, God is protecting you by his power until you receive this salvation. 1 PETER 1:4-5

We know that God's children do not make a practice of sinning, for God's Son holds them securely, and the evil one cannot touch them. 1 JOHN 5:18

All who are victorious will be clothed in white. I will never erase their names from the Book of Life, but I will announce before my Father and his angels that they are mine. REVELATION 3:5

God has promised to save you from judgment and eternal death when you accept his Son, Jesus Christ, as your Savior. When Jesus holds you securely, Satan cannot get his hands on you.

How do I deal with my feelings of insecurity?

We are God's masterpiece. He has created us anew in Christ Jesus, so we can do the good things he planned for us long ago. EPHESIANS 2:10

I pray that from his glorious, unlimited resources he will empower you with inner strength through his Spirit. Then Christ will make his home in your hearts as you trust in him. Your roots will grow down into God's love and keep you strong. And may you have the power to understand, as all God's people should, how wide, how long, how high, and how deep his love is. . . . All glory to God, who is able, through his mighty power at work within us, to accomplish infinitely more than we might ask or think. EPHESIANS 3:16-20

God, who began the good work within you, will continue his work until it is finally finished on the day when Christ Jesus returns. PHILIPPIANS 1:6

Insecurity can be a sign that you are measuring your value by the wrong things. The only thing that matters—and the only way to be secure—is to find your value as a creation of God, one of his masterpieces. When you understand how much God loves you, you can feel secure in yourself as a person.

SEDUCTION *See also* Deceit/Deception, Temptation, Vulnerability

Most often we think of seduction occurring in a sexual encounter, but seduction is actually a common tactic used by Satan to disguise sin in beauty, power, riches, pleasure, and even righteousness. God intends for his people to experience pleasure, but in the right context. For example, sexual pleasure is a gift to be enjoyed, but only in a marriage relationship. Seduction takes pleasure out of context and makes it the highest goal. When we begin to pursue pleasure just because we want to or because it makes us feel good, we have been lured into the trap of seduction. Pleasure must have the higher goal of pleasing God and blessing others. Seduction is all about deception, self-gratification, and disguising wrong motives for good ones.

How can I avoid being seduced into doing wrong?

[Potiphar's wife] kept putting pressure on Joseph day after day, but he refused to sleep with her, and he kept out of her way as much as possible. GENESIS 39:10

If someone is trying to seduce you, stay away from that person as much as possible!

One day, however, no one else was around when he went in to do his work. [Potiphar's wife] came and grabbed him by his cloak, demanding, "Come on, sleep with me!" Joseph tore himself away, but he left his cloak in her hand as he ran from the house. GENESIS 39:11-12

Never stray from what I am about to say: Stay away from [an immoral woman]! Don't go near the door of her house! PROVERBS 5:7-8

Stay away from temptation! Sometimes you need to do more than ignore the situation; you must remove yourself from it.

Guard your heart above all else, for it determines the course of your life. PROVERBS 4:23

Don't let yourself become emotionally intimate with anyone of the opposite sex other than your spouse.

I am writing these things to warn you about those who want to lead you astray. 1 JOHN 2:26

Study God's Word in order to keep from being seduced by those who teach falsehood.

King Solomon loved many foreign women. . . . The LORD had clearly instructed the people of Israel, "You must not marry them, because they will turn your hearts to their gods." Yet Solomon insisted on loving them anyway. . . . And in fact, they did turn his heart away from the LORD. 1 KINGS 11:1-3

Behind every seduction is a temptation to sin, and behind every temptation is a direct violation of a truth found in the Bible. Satan wants to seduce you into seeing sin as lovely and attractive and fun. Sin is so seductive because, at the time, it is almost always pleasurable. The Old Testament was clear that God's people should not marry foreigners who worshiped others gods because they would be seduced to abandon their God. It was also clear that marriage was reserved for one man and one woman. But Solomon couldn't overcome the seduction of these beautiful women and the political alliances they would secure. He was seduced by lust, pleasure, and power, and soon this choked out his character, integrity, and reputation. Beg God for the power not to give temptation a second look for that is when the power of seduction becomes so strong.

Delilah pouted, "How can you tell me, 'I love you,' when you don't share your secrets with me?" . . . She tormented him with her nagging day after day until he was sick to death of it. Finally, Samson shared his secret with her. JUDGES 16:15-17

Do not let sin control the way you live; do not give in to sinful desires. ROMANS 6:12

God is faithful. He will not allow the temptation to be more than you can stand. When you are tempted, he will show you a way out so that you can endure. 1 CORINTHIANS 10:13

The crafty Philistines knew they couldn't match Samson's brute strength, so they aimed at his weakness—his inability to stay away from seductive women. Temptation always strikes at your weak spots, not your strengths. Your weak spots are those areas you refuse to give over to God. They are cracks in your spiritual armor at which the enemy takes aim, the areas in which you compromise your convictions and are seduced for a few moments of pleasure. In those areas of weakness, you must ask God to cover your weaknesses with his strength. You must understand your weaknesses so you can arm yourself against Satan's attacks.

SELF-CONTROL *See also* Accountability, Discipline, Habits

Self-control is one of the hardest character traits to achieve because it means denying what comes naturally to our sinful nature and replacing it with a controlled, godly response. Self-control is a lifelong endeavor, because just when you think you have one area of your life mastered, another area gets out of control. Some of the hardest things to control are our thoughts, our words, and our physical appetites. It is only with the help of the Holy Spirit that we achieve self-control. But when we do, we are pleasing to God and pleasing to others. Self-control involves disciplining ourselves, making an intentional effort to be the kind of person who walks with God and others the way we should.

Why can't I seem to control certain desires?

I have discovered this principle of life—that when I want to do what is right, I inevitably do what is wrong. I love God's law with all my heart. But there is another power within me that is at war with my mind. This power makes me a slave to the sin that is still within me. Oh, what a miserable person I am! Who will free me from this life that is dominated by sin and death? Thank God! The answer is in Jesus Christ our Lord. ROMANS 7:21-25

Because you were born with a sinful nature, you will always struggle to do what is right and to not do what is wrong. Thankfully, God understands your weaknesses and gives you the desire to please him. As you obey God, you will develop more self-control, and the battle with your sinful nature will lessen.

I plead with you to give your bodies to God because of all he has done for you. Let them be a living and holy sacrifice—the kind he will find acceptable. ROMANS 12:1

You must truly want to give up the wrong desires you have. If you try to hang on to just a little sinful habit, it will eventually rule you.

Is it possible to exercise self-control?

Just as sin ruled over all people and brought them to death, now God's wonderful grace rules. ROMANS 5:21

According to the Bible, sin will reign in your life, controlling every aspect of you, until Jesus Christ breaks its power. If Jesus has power over sin itself, he has the power to help you fight against it.

Wherever the Spirit of the Lord is, there is freedom. 2 CORINTHIANS 3:17

The Holy Spirit produces this kind of fruit in our lives: love, joy, peace, patience, kindness, goodness, faithfulness, gentleness, and self-control. GALATIANS 5:22-23

Self-control is promised through the power of the Holy Spirit. He works in you to bring freedom from the drives and desires that distract you from living for God.

What are some steps to exercising self-control?

How can a young person stay pure? By obeying your word. PSALM 119:9

Athletes cannot win the prize unless they follow the rules. 2 TIMOTHY 2:5

To develop self-control, you first need to know God's guidelines for right living as found in the Bible. You need to know what you must control before you can keep it under control. Reading God's Word consistently—preferably every day—keeps his guidelines for right living fresh in your mind. God's Word guides and empowers your obedience.

Train yourself to be godly. Physical training is good, but training for godliness is much better, promising benefits in this life and in the life to come. 1 TIMOTHY 4:7-8

Self-control begins with God's work in you, but it requires your effort as well. Just as a talented musician or athlete must develop his or her gifts through intentional effort, spiritual fitness must be intentional as well. God promises to reward such effort.

Take control of what I say, O LORD, and guard my lips. PSALM 141:3

Those who control their tongue will have a long life; opening your mouth can ruin everything. PROVERBS 13:3

You exercise self-control by watching what you say. How often do you wish you could take back words as soon as they have left your mouth?

When I need help beyond my own self-control, what should I do?

Those who belong to Christ Jesus have nailed the passions and desires of their sinful nature to his cross and crucified them there. GALATIANS 5:24

When you feel like your sinful nature is getting the best of you, you must constantly ask the Holy Spirit to fill your life with his goodness. Those who have put their faith in Jesus Christ have tapped into a whole new power source to help them control unhealthy desires.

When I am afraid, I will put my trust in you. I praise God for what he has promised. I trust in God, so why should I be afraid? What can mere mortals do to me? PSALM 56:3-4

With God's help we will do mighty things, for he will trample down our foes. PSALM 60:12

The Bible tells you that God's power is greatest in your times of weakness. Your problems become God's opportunities if you allow him to work through you. When you face a problem or temptation too big for you to handle on your own, run to God for help.

The temptations in your life are no different from what others experience. . . . When you are tempted, he will show you a way out so that you can endure. 1 CORINTHIANS 10:13

It helps to know others are facing the same temptations you are. Sometimes it is necessary to confess your struggles to a godly friend or a counselor so they can partner with you in your specific struggle. It helps to have people around you who can hold you accountable.

What are the rewards of self-control?

God blesses those who patiently endure testing and temptation. Afterward they will receive the crown of life that God has promised to those who love him. JAMES 1:12

Self-control saves you from the consequences of giving in to sin and bad habits. Self-control in faithfully following God brings you the ultimate reward of eternal life in heaven.

SELFISHNESS *See also* Coveting, Desires, Greed, Pride

It is the divisive force threatening every relationship, the weakness allowing healthy pursuits to become destructive obsessions, and the selfishness behind all sin. It is not anger, pride, hatred, or malice—although it can be found in all four. It is simple, everyday selfishness. From Adam and Eve, who ate from the forbidden tree because they desired knowledge reserved only for God, to Judas, who betrayed his Lord for thirty pieces of silver, the Bible warns of the seductive power of selfishness. Fortunately Scripture also leads us to Jesus Christ, the one whose redemptive work can transform selfishness to selflessness.

Why is selfishness so destructive?

Isaac said, "Your brother was here, and he tricked me. He has taken away your blessing." Esau exclaimed, "No wonder his name is Jacob, for now he has cheated me twice. First he took my rights as the firstborn, and now he has stolen my blessing. Oh, haven't you saved even one blessing for me?" Isaac said to Esau, "I have made Jacob your master and have declared that all his brothers will be his servants.". . . From that time on, Esau hated Jacob. . . . And Esau began to scheme. GENESIS 27:35-41

Selfishness can destroy relationships and tear families apart.

When Simon saw that the Spirit was given when the apostles laid their hands on people, he offered them money to buy this power. ACTS 8:18

Selfish ambition can cause you to do almost anything for personal gain.

How can I address the selfishness in my own life?

Calling the crowd to join his disciples, [Jesus] said, "If any of you wants to be my follower, you must turn from your selfish ways, take up your cross, and follow me." MARK 8:34

My old self has been crucified with Christ. It is no longer I who live, but Christ lives in me. So I live in this earthly body by trusting in the Son of God, who loved me and gave himself for me. GALATIANS 2:20

When you surrender to God, you give up what you think is best for your life and do what he knows is best. You put aside your self-fulfilling ambitions so that you can do the job Jesus has for you. You ask Jesus, through the power of the Holy Spirit, to live in you and through you.

If others have reason for confidence in their own efforts, I have even more! . . . I once thought these things were valuable, but now I consider them worthless because of what Christ has done. Yes, everything else is worthless when compared with the infinite value of knowing Christ Jesus my Lord. PHILIPPIANS 3:4, 7-8

Selfishness is all about you and what you can get now. The Christian life is all about obeying God, serving others, and delaying rewards until the future. Put your energy into something that will last forever.

Don't look out only for your own interests, but take an interest in others, too.
PHILIPPIANS 2:4

Unselfishness is learning to put others first.

SENSITIVITY *See also* Compassion, Empathy, Sympathy

Who enjoys the company of an insensitive person who couldn't care less about others? Who enjoys being around an overly sensitive person who always seems to get hurt by whatever is said? Sensitivity in proper balance, however, is a beautiful quality. We are attracted to sensitive people because they care deeply about others without smothering or manipulating them. Sensitivity is awareness, being awake to others, being a person who feels and responds. The Bible encourages us to be sensitive to the physical, emotional, and spiritual needs of others, especially their need for God.

In what areas do I probably need to develop more sensitivity?

If there are any poor Israelites in your towns when you arrive in the land the LORD your God is giving you, do not be hard-hearted or tightfisted toward them. DEUTERONOMY 15:7

Always try to be sensitive and openhearted to the needs of the poor and oppressed.

A loud and cheerful greeting early in the morning will be taken as a curse! PROVERBS 27:14

Take special care to be sensitive toward your neighbors.

Blessed are those who fear to do wrong, but the stubborn are headed for serious trouble.
PROVERBS 28:14

Be sensitive to sin in your life to keep your conscience clear.

The Holy Spirit had prevented them from preaching the word in the province of Asia at that time. Then . . . they headed north for the province of Bithynia, but again the Spirit of Jesus did not allow them to go there. . . . That night Paul had a vision: A man from Macedonia in northern Greece was standing there, pleading with him, "Come over to Macedonia and help us!" So we decided to leave for Macedonia at once, having concluded that God was calling us to preach the Good News there. ACTS 16:6-10

Sensitivity to the Holy Spirit will guide you throughout your life.

How can I develop sensitivity to God and to his Word?

The ear tests the words it hears just as the mouth distinguishes between foods. JOB 12:11

Open my eyes to see the wonderful truths in your instructions. PSALM 119:18

They stumble because they do not obey God's word, and so they meet the fate that was planned for them. 1 PETER 2:8

Spiritual sensitivity comes from eyes that are open to God's Word and ears willing to hear it. Develop the art of listening to God through his Word. Then use your hands to put it to action!

What will dull my spiritual sensitivity?

[Unbelievers] have no sense of shame. They live for lustful pleasure and eagerly practice every kind of impurity. EPHESIANS 4:19

Giving up on fighting evil and giving in to sinful desires will dull your spiritual sensitivity.

Anyone who wanders away from [Christ's] teaching has no relationship with God. 2 JOHN 1:9

Time away from God dulls your spiritual sensitivities. The more time you spend ignoring God, the less sensitive you will be toward his presence and his leading.

You tolerate some among you whose teaching is like that of Balaam, who showed Balak how to trip up the people of Israel. He taught them to sin by . . . committing sexual sin. REVELATION 2:14

Compromising with sin will eventually dull your sensitivity to it.

Is God sensitive toward me?

When he saw the crowds, he had compassion on them because they were confused and helpless, like sheep without a shepherd. MATTHEW 9:36

Jesus Christ knows your needs and is ready to meet them when you ask.

The temptations in your life are no different from what others experience. And God is faithful. He will not allow the temptation to be more than you can stand. When you are tempted, he will show you a way out so that you can endure. 1 CORINTHIANS 10:13

God is sensitive to the temptations you face and has offered you ways to avoid it.

SERVICE See also Help, Hospitality, Support, Thoughtfulness

A popular notion of success in life is being able to afford the luxury of having servants. Jesus turns this thinking on its head by teaching that the highest goal in life is to *be* a servant. He places such a high value on serving because it is others-centered rather than self-centered, which is the essence of effective Christian living.

What does it mean to be a servant?

Though [Christ Jesus] was God, he did not think of equality with God as something to cling to. . . . In human form, he humbled himself in obedience to God. PHILIPPIANS 2:6-8

A servant is humble and obedient to God.

Whoever wants to be a leader among you must be your servant, and whoever wants to be first among you must become your slave. MATTHEW 20:26-27

A servant ministers to others regardless of their status in life.

Then [Jesus] began to wash the disciples' feet. JOHN 13:5

A servant gladly performs tasks that others consider beneath them.

Give yourselves completely to God. . . . Use your whole body as an instrument to do what is right for the glory of God. ROMANS 6:13

Servants use all of their energy and talents for the benefit of God and others.

How did Jesus serve?

Whoever wants to be a leader among you must be your servant. . . . For even the Son of Man came not to be served but to serve others and to give his life as a ransom for many. MATTHEW 20:26-28

He served to the point of sacrificing his very life for you and all people.

[Christ] gave up his divine privileges; he took the humble position of a slave and was born as a human being. PHILIPPIANS 2:7

This High Priest of ours [Jesus] understands our weaknesses, for he faced all of the same testings we do, yet he did not sin. HEBREWS 4:15

Because Jesus humbled himself, becoming human, he is able to understand human life with all of its struggles and temptations. Are you willing to humble yourself to the level of those you wish to serve?

When Jesus heard [the blind men shouting to him for help], he stopped and called, "What do you want me to do for you?" MATTHEW 20:32

He made himself available to serve people who needed him.

What is meant by having a servant heart? How can I have a servant heart?

You must have the same attitude that Christ Jesus had. Though he was God, he did not think of equality with God as something to cling to. Instead, he gave up his divine privileges; he took the humble position of a slave and was born as a human being. When he appeared in human form, he humbled himself in obedience to God and died a criminal's death on a cross. PHILIPPIANS 2:5-8

A servant's heart comes through humbling yourself as Jesus did, and obediently doing what God wants. The more you obey, the more you condition your heart to become like Jesus'.

Use your whole body as an instrument to do what is right for the glory of God. ROMANS 6:13

By submitting yourself to obey Jesus' commands and live by his words, you put your heart in a position ready for heartfelt action.

"My lord," [Rebekah said,] "have a drink." And she quickly lowered her jug from her shoulder and gave him a drink. When she had given him a drink, she said, "I'll draw water for your camels, too, until they have had enough to drink." So she quickly emptied her jug into the watering trough and ran back to the well to draw water for all his camels. GENESIS 24:18-20

Look for opportunities to help those who need you. If you wait until you feel like helping, you will rarely help anyone. The best way to change your attitude is to start helping. Then your heart will follow.

SEX/SEXUALITY See also Adultery, Intimacy, Marriage, Seduction

God created us as sexual beings. It was his design for reproduction and continuation of the human race and also his gift to married couples to allow them to enjoy each other in the most intimate of ways. The intimacy of sex strengthens our faithfulness to each other, and thus enables us to better trust each other. As we learn about faithfulness and commitment with our spouse, we learn much about faithfulness and commitment to God. Sexuality, therefore, is not evil, but good and sacred. It is the misuse and abuse of sexuality—taking something designed by God for our enjoyment and using it only to gratify our sinful desires—that is evil. The holiness of sexuality is seen in the direct comparison God makes between the marriage relationship and our relationship with him. It is seen also in his direct commands for a man and woman to join together in love for each other and produce a new generation that lives for the Lord.

What does God think about sex?

God created human beings in his own image. In the image of God he created them; male and female he created them. Then God blessed them and said, "Be fruitful and multiply. Fill the earth and govern it." GENESIS 1:27-28

A man leaves his father and mother and is joined to his wife, and the two are united into one. GENESIS 2:24

God created sex. He made men and women as sexual beings, giving them the ability to reproduce and to express love to and delight in one another. The sexual relationship is a key part of a husband and wife becoming one. God intended sex to be a good thing within the context of a marriage relationship.

Rejoice in the wife of your youth. She is a loving deer, a graceful doe. Let her breasts satisfy you always. May you always be captivated by her love. PROVERBS 5:18-19

God clearly allows you to enjoy and delight in sex within marriage. Sex is not for reproduction only, but for a bonding of love and enjoyment between husbands and wives.

What rights do husbands and wives have to each other's body?

The husband should fulfill his wife's sexual needs, and the wife should fulfill her husband's needs. The wife gives authority over her body to her husband, and the husband gives authority over his body to his wife. 1 CORINTHIANS 7:3-4

Husbands and wives do not completely own their own bodies. When they marry, each mate has a loving claim to the other's body.

The prevailing attitude about sex before marriage seems to be that as long as both people agree, it's okay. What does the Bible have to say about premarital sex?

Give honor to marriage, and remain faithful to one another in marriage. God will surely judge people who are immoral and those who commit adultery. HEBREWS 13:4

As Scripture describes the role of sexuality in marriage, it is clear that the full expression of your physical desires—sexual intercourse—is to be reserved for the commitment of marriage.

God's will is for you to be holy, so stay away from all sexual sin. Then each of you will control his own body and live in holiness and honor. 1 THESSALONIANS 4:3-4

The world's attitude says, "If it feels good, do it." God calls you to exercise control over your passions and your body. The fact that something feels good doesn't mean that you should do it. Only if it honors God should you do it. Practically, this avoids health risks, but from a spiritual point of view, God designed marriage to be a picture of your relationship to him. Just as spiritual adultery is worshiping anything other than God, physical adultery is having sex with anyone who is not your spouse.

Potiphar's wife soon began to look at [Joseph] lustfully. "Come and sleep with me," she demanded. But Joseph refused. . . . "How could I do such a wicked thing? It would be a great sin against God." GENESIS 39:7-9

Joseph drew his boundaries early, knowing that sex outside of marriage is "a great sin against God." When temptation came, he was prepared and he knew how to handle it. Even though everyone around you seems to assume that premarital sex is okay, they ignore the whole picture: unplanned pregnancy, disease, guilt, shame, and secrets from their future spouse. The Bible sets boundaries—not to curb your fun, but to protect you and show you how to have the greatest joy and fulfillment in a relationship. It's interesting that virtually all sex surveys (even those conducted among unbelievers) show greater sexual satisfaction among married couples than unmarried couples. God knew what he was doing when he asked us to reserve sex for marriage.

Is it so bad if I just think about sex with someone other than my spouse? I didn't really do anything.

You have heard the commandment that says, "You must not commit adultery." But . . . anyone who even looks at a woman with lust has already committed adultery with her in his heart. MATTHEW 5:27-28

Lust is adultery in the heart. While it is technically true that when you only imagine having sex with someone you have not actually sinned with that person physically, it is still true that in your heart you have committed adultery.

It is what comes from inside that defiles you. For from within, out of a person's heart, come evil thoughts, sexual immorality, . . . lustful desires. MARK 7:20-22

What you think about doesn't just come from your mind; it comes from your heart. Your thoughts tell you the condition of your heart and your every action begins as a thought. Left unchecked, wrong thoughts will eventually result in wrong actions. If you continue to think about having sex with someone, your heart will begin to convince your mind that what you want to do is okay. The Bible says that the heart is "desperately wicked" (Jeremiah 17:9). In other words, don't trust your emotions to tell you what is right and good. Trust God's Word, for it comes from God's heart, which is good and perfect.

Will God forgive my past sexual sins? Can I truly start over?

Through this man Jesus there is forgiveness for your sins. Everyone who believes in him is declared right with God. ACTS 13:38-39

God will forgive any sexual sin if there is sincere repentance, turning away from that sin and seeking forgiveness.

But isn't my body my own, to do with as I choose?

You can't say that our bodies were made for sexual immorality. They were made for the Lord, and the Lord cares about our bodies. 1 CORINTHIANS 6:13

Don't you realize that your body is the temple of the Holy Spirit, who lives in you and was given to you by God? You do not belong to yourself, for God bought you with a high price. So you must honor God with your body. 1 CORINTHIANS 6:19-20

When you become a Christian, you dedicate yourself to the Lord, and that includes your body. It is no longer truly yours; it is his temple. Also, in marriage, your body also belongs to your mate (see 1 Corinthians 7:4).

Why is virginity so important?

If you keep yourself pure, you will be a special utensil for honorable use. Your life will be clean, and you will be ready for the Master to use you for every good work.
2 TIMOTHY 2:21

Give honor to marriage, and remain faithful to one another in marriage. God will surely judge people who are immoral and those who commit adultery. HEBREWS 13:4

God gave you the gift of your virginity, and he allows you to choose whom you will give it to. You can give it to only one person in the whole world. Don't give this precious gift away to just anyone, but save it for the person who commits to you by marrying you. This is why God commands you not to have sex before marriage—he is trying to protect you from people who will hurt you by stealing your purity without committing to you.

SHAME *See also* Guilt, Regrets

Shame and embarrassment are similar but not the same. We feel embarrassed over silly or mindless actions; we feel shame when we commit sinful actions as well as when some sinful actions (like rape) are committed against us. Embarrassment can be laughed off later when the moment has passed, but shame digs deep into our hearts and can last a long time. We can carry shame around like a load of rocks for a lifetime unless we deal purposefully with it. Ridding ourselves of shame involves repentance, confession, long-term revision of our actions, and many times restitution for those we have hurt. When we have been hurt by others, ridding ourselves of shame requires releasing unnecessary guilt to God in order to once again experience the joy and freedom of a pure relationship with him.

What can I do with my recurring feelings of shame?

Finally, I confessed all my sins to you and stopped trying to hide my guilt. I said to myself, "I will confess my rebellion to the LORD." And you forgave me! All my guilt is gone.
PSALM 32:5

Anyone who belongs to Christ has become a new person. The old life is gone; a new life has begun! 2 CORINTHIANS 5:17

Feelings of shame are usually the result of sin. Shame increases with unreleased guilt. God wants to release you from shame and restore you to a pure and holy relationship with himself. When you confess your sin to God and ask for his forgiveness, he takes your shame away.

What can help me live without shame and avoid shameful feelings in the future?

I cling to your laws. LORD, don't let me be put to shame! PSALM 119:31

Remain in fellowship with Christ so that when he returns, you will be full of courage and not shrink back from him in shame. 1 JOHN 2:28

The best way to avoid feeling shame is to avoid sin! When you obey God and live a clean life, you will rarely feel shame. The pain of past shame should be a great motivation to strive for honesty and integrity in all areas of life from now on.

Cling to your faith in Christ, and keep your conscience clear. For some people have deliberately violated their consciences; as a result, their faith has been shipwrecked.
1 TIMOTHY 1:19

Your conscience is a gift from God, an instinct he placed inside you to make you aware of your sins and give you an appropriate sense of guilt and shame. To keep your conscience working properly, you need to receive forgiveness from God and others, and then repair your wrongs. Ignoring your conscience dulls it and allows sin's consequences to grow unchecked without you feeling bad about it. This is like ignoring warning lights at a railroad crossing when a freight train is barreling down on you.

Of what should I not be ashamed?

I am not ashamed of this Good News about Christ. It is the power of God at work, saving everyone who believes. ROMANS 1:16

Never be ashamed to tell others about our Lord. 2 TIMOTHY 1:8

It is no shame to suffer for being a Christian. Praise God for the privilege of being called by his name! 1 PETER 4:16

Never be ashamed of Jesus, your faith in him, the good news he brings, telling others about him, or the privilege of bearing his name. He is the only one who can heal you and take away your shame.

You will no longer live in shame. . . . There is no more disgrace for you. ISAIAH 54:4

If you have been victimized by someone through no fault of your own, you do not need to feel shame. Often people who have been abused, molested, or raped carry undeserved shame. God can remove your burden of shame and set you free to live victoriously again.

SHARING *See also* Generosity, Giving, Stewardship, Support, Tithing

Ever since we were little children we've been taught to share. Yet for most of us it remains as hard as ever to share our resources and ourselves. Why? Because at the very core of sinful human nature is the desire to get, not give; to accumulate, not relinquish; to look out for ourselves, not others. The Bible calls us to share many things—our resources, our faith, our love, our time, our talents, our money. Those who generously share discover that the benefits of giving are far greater than the temporary satisfaction of receiving.

Why should I share?

Do to others whatever you would like them to do to you. MATTHEW 7:12

I always thank my God for you and for the gracious gifts he has given you, now that you belong to Christ Jesus. 1 CORINTHIANS 1:4

As each part does its own special work, it helps the other parts grow, so that the whole body is healthy and growing and full of love. EPHESIANS 4:16

You are to share because God shares so generously with you. Sharing is an expression of love. Share because God has given you special gifts, and by sharing them with others, you pass them on and bless others.

In what ways should I share with others?

Share your food with the hungry, and give shelter to the homeless. Give clothes to those who need them, and do not hide from relatives who need your help. ISAIAH 58:7

All the believers were united in heart and mind. And they . . . shared everything they had. ACTS 4:32

I long to visit you so I can bring you some spiritual gift that will help you grow strong in the Lord. ROMANS 1:11

Be happy with those who are happy, and weep with those who weep. ROMANS 12:15

God asks that you share your money, your home, your resources, your love, your faith, your sympathy, your joys and sorrows. When you share, you connect with others in relationship and demonstrate your Christian love.

What special things does God share with me?

Since we are his children, we are his heirs. In fact, together with Christ we are heirs of God's glory. But if we are to share his glory, we must also share his suffering.
ROMANS 8:17

When Christ, who is your life, is revealed to the whole world, you will share in all his glory. COLOSSIANS 3:4

God shares his love, peace, and comfort. God shares forgiveness of sins and salvation. And one day God will share heaven, his eternal home, with those who believe in him.

How much of my resources am I expected to share with others?

On the first day of each week, you should each put aside a portion of the money you have earned. Don't wait until I get there and then try to collect it all at once.
1 CORINTHIANS 16:2

You must each decide in your heart how much to give. And don't give reluctantly or in response to pressure. For God loves a person who gives cheerfully. 2 CORINTHIANS 9:7

To try to set tight or fixed boundaries on how much you should share, or give, represents the wrong attitude. God's desire is that you will want to give to others generously. The exact amount that you give is not as important to God as the fact that you trust him with all of your resources and are willing to share generously with people in need.

SICKNESS *See also* Pain, Suffering, Healing

From a little cold to the dreaded news of cancer, sickness often strikes unexpectedly. It attacks our bodies and makes us unable to function at full capacity. It makes us feel lousy. And, in the worst cases, it takes our life. When we are sick, we know we are infected with germs that are attacking our body, trying to hurt us. Quickly our immune system kicks in, sending white blood cells and other agents to fight the bad germs, kill them, and wash them out of our system. While the battle rages, we are often left exhausted physically, mentally, and emotionally. This should remind us that another infectious disease is raging within our body all the time. It is called sin. Sin is a disease that not only takes a physical, mental, and emotional toll, but also a spiritual one. Sin is a sickness every human has and must learn to keep in check and seek to overcome. When we come to Jesus with this sin problem, he prescribes forgiveness. When you ask, he forgives your sin, and it can no longer control the way you live. It will still lurk in your heart, trying to attack your body and bring you down.

Ultimately, it is sin that causes everyone to die. But then a miraculous healing takes place for those who have received the antidote of Jesus' forgiveness. At the moment of death, sin is washed from your body forever. For the rest of eternity you live in a body that will never again be sick from any physical or spiritual disease. Our job as Christians is to do the best we can to keep sin from infecting us and to serve as "nurses for the soul," bringing others to God, the Great Physician, who has the eternal antidote for any sickness and can ultimately heal it all.

Does God care when I am sick?

The LORD nurses them when they are sick and restores them to health. PSALM 41:3

God has full authority over all sickness, and he cares deeply when you are sick.

What is a positive way I can respond in times of personal sickness?

Let all that I am praise the LORD; may I never forget the good things he does for me. He forgives all my sins and heals all my diseases. PSALM 103:2-3

Praise the Lord for his ability to forgive your sins and heal your diseases—even if he chooses not to. Praise the Lord when he uses your sickness to move you closer to him.

Three different times I begged the Lord to take [the thorn in my flesh] away. Each time he said, "My grace is all you need. My power works best in weakness." So now I am glad to boast about my weaknesses, so that the power of Christ can work through me. That's why I take pleasure in my weaknesses, and in the insults, hardships, persecutions, and troubles that I suffer for Christ. For when I am weak, then I am strong. 2 CORINTHIANS 12:8-10

Are any of you sick? You should call for the elders of the church to come and pray over you, anointing you with oil in the name of the Lord. JAMES 5:14

Pray for healing and be content with God's decision. If he chooses not to heal you then look for ways you can minister to others through your sickness. You might wind up having a greater effect on them than if you were healthy.

My health may fail, and my spirit may grow weak, but God remains the strength of my heart; he is mine forever. PSALM 73:26

Our bodies are buried in brokenness, but they will be raised in glory. They are buried in weakness, but they will be raised in strength. 1 CORINTHIANS 15:43

Regardless of the condition of your health, whether you are well or sick, you can rejoice that God faithfully remains your strength. Your frail earthly body will one day be gloriously transformed for eternity.

How can I minister to the sick?

When they were ill, I grieved for them. I denied myself by fasting for them, but my prayers returned unanswered. I was sad, as though they were my friends or family, as if I were grieving for my own mother. PSALM 35:13-14

You can pray for those who are sick. Some will be healed, and some will be strengthened spiritually even though they are not healed.

Four men arrived carrying a paralyzed man on a mat. They couldn't bring him to Jesus because of the crowd, so they dug a hole through the roof above his head. Then they lowered the man on his mat, right down in front of Jesus. Seeing their faith, Jesus said to the paralyzed man, "My child, your sins are forgiven." MARK 2:3-5

Often, there are practical ways you can help those who are sick get the help and healing they need.

I was naked, and you gave me clothing. I was sick, and you cared for me. I was in prison, and you visited me. MATTHEW 25:36

You can meet the physical, emotional, social, and spiritual needs of the sick.

Why does God heal some and not others?

My suffering was good for me, for it taught me to pay attention to your decrees. PSALM 119:71

Jesus met a man with an advanced case of leprosy. When the man saw Jesus, he bowed with his face to the ground, begging to be healed. "Lord," he said, "if you are willing, you can heal me and make me clean." Jesus reached out and touched him. "I am willing," he said. "Be healed!" And instantly the leprosy disappeared. LUKE 5:12-13

Jesus . . . said, "Lazarus's sickness will not end in death. No, it happened for the glory of God so that the Son of God will receive glory from this." JOHN 11:4

God possesses the ability to heal all diseases. He heals, or does not heal, for reasons you cannot always comprehend right now. But you can be assured that God's love for you is the greatest love you can experience, and trust that God's plan for your life really is the best for you. It is because of this great love that he is preparing a place in heaven where sickness will be gone forever.

Are there ways to avoid sickness?

[God] said, "If you will listen carefully to the voice of the LORD your God and do what is right in his sight, obeying his commands and keeping all his decrees, then I will not make you suffer any of the diseases I sent on the Egyptians; for I am the LORD who heals you." EXODUS 15:26

Run from sexual sin! No other sin so clearly affects the body as this one does. For sexual immorality is a sin against your own body. 1 CORINTHIANS 6:18

Obedience to God's Word can help you avoid some sickness because the Bible provides guidelines to good health. For example, God's warning to avoid sexual immorality will prevent you from the possibility of contracting sexually transmitted diseases.

You have six days each week for your ordinary work, but on the seventh day you must stop working, even during the seasons of plowing and harvest. EXODUS 34:21

Maintaining a balance between work and rest will often help you avoid sickness.

No one hates his own body but feeds and cares for it, just as Christ cares for the church. EPHESIANS 5:29

Physically caring for your body will often help you avoid sickness.

SIMPLICITY *See also* Contentment, Self-Control, Stewardship

Simplicity is not just a lifestyle but a tangible expression of an inner attitude of the heart. There are three main components that contribute to an attitude of simplicity:

(1) thankfulness—viewing every possession and good thing as a gift from God; (2) trust—that your life and everything about it is ultimately under the care of God, not you; and (3) generosity—being willing to share all that you have with others. When we are thankful, we expect nothing but are delighted with everything and live dependently on God. When we trust God to care for our needs, we free ourselves from worry and anxiety. Finally, when we share as an expression of God's own generosity toward us, we don't hold things tightly. When these three attitudes work together, we are freed from the slavery of materialism and delivered into a life of true contentment.

What kind of simplicity should I develop in my life?

LORD, my heart is not proud; my eyes are not haughty. . . . Like a weaned child is my soul within me. O Israel, put your hope in the LORD—now and always. PSALM 131:1-3

At that time Jesus prayed this prayer: "O Father, Lord of heaven and earth, thank you for hiding these things from those who think themselves wise and clever, and for revealing them to the childlike." MATTHEW 11:25

Strive for a faith that, like a small child, eagerly and completely trusts whatever your loving Father says and that he always wants the best for you.

[Jesus] called his twelve disciples together and began sending them out two by two, giving them authority to cast out evil spirits. He told them to take nothing for their journey except a walking stick—no food, no traveler's bag, no money. He allowed them to wear sandals but not to take a change of clothes. MARK 6:7-9

Jesus said, "I tell you not to worry about everyday life—whether you have enough food to eat or enough clothes to wear. For life is more than food, and your body more than clothing." LUKE 12:22-23

Cultivate an attitude that focuses less on material possessions and more on the riches of a life filled with God's Spirit.

When I first came to you, dear brothers and sisters, I didn't use lofty words and impressive wisdom to tell you God's secret plan. 1 CORINTHIANS 2:1

Talk to others in a clear and uncomplicated way about your faith in Jesus.

What kind of simplicity should I avoid?

These proverbs will give insight to the simple, knowledge and discernment to the young. PROVERBS 1:4

Only simpletons believe everything they're told! The prudent carefully consider their steps. PROVERBS 14:15

Don't be childish in your understanding of these things. Be innocent as babies when it comes to evil, but be mature in understanding matters of this kind. 1 CORINTHIANS 14:20

Avoid being a simpleton by cultivating wisdom. Without wisdom you are in danger of being seduced by clever people who want to take advantage of you.

SIN *See also* Backsliding, Deceit/Deception, Evil, Judgment

Sin will always be an offensive word. We can talk openly and impersonally about crimes like rape and murder; we can cite statistics about adultery, unwed pregnancies, and divorces; we can trivialize greed, selfishness, and lust—or raise them as cultural values—but to call anything sin makes us uncomfortable. The word *sin* implies the violation of an objective and absolute standard of behavior established by God. We almost instinctively feel that such rules are an infringement on our rights. Yet this kind of attitude displays a terrible misunderstanding of sin and an underestimation of God. When a doctor correctly diagnoses a disease in our body, we do not accuse him of impinging on our freedom; rather, we are grateful because he will know how to treat the disease before it destroys our life. The Bible teaches that sin is a disease of the soul that will destroy our life now and forever if we do not treat it. God's standard of behavior is preventative medicine prescribed not to limit our freedom but to counteract the disease of sin.

What is sin?

We all fall short of God's glorious standard. ROMANS 3:23

Sin is falling short of the standards set forth by our holy God.

[Unbelievers] demonstrate that God's law is written in their hearts, for their own conscience and thoughts either accuse them or tell them they are doing right. ROMANS 2:15

Sin is violating God's moral law.

Do not let sin control the way you live. ROMANS 6:12

Sin is a power that seeks to influence, enslave, and destroy you.

You used to live in sin, just like the rest of the world, obeying the devil. EPHESIANS 2:2

Sin is obedience to Satan rather than to God.

You will always harvest what you plant. GALATIANS 6:7

Sin is always a liability, not an asset. It is always wrong, so it always produces bad consequences.

It's your sins that have cut you off from God. Because of your sins, he has turned away and will not listen anymore. ISAIAH 59:2

Sin is a wall that separates you from God.

Do not let sin control the way you live; do not give in to sinful desires. ROMANS 6:12

When you follow the desires of your sinful nature, the results are very clear: sexual immorality, impurity, lustful pleasures, idolatry, sorcery, hostility, quarreling, jealousy, outbursts of anger, selfish ambition, dissension, division, envy, drunkenness, wild parties, and other sins like these. Let me tell you . . . that anyone living that sort of life will not inherit the Kingdom of God. GALATIANS 5:19-21

Sin is often alluring and attractive, offering short-term pleasure in exchange for long-term consequences.

When I want to do what is right, I inevitably do what is wrong. I love God's law with all my heart. But there is another power within me that is at war with my mind. This power makes me a slave to the sin that is still within me. ROMANS 7:21-23

Sin is warfare of the soul, a constant battle inside you.

Remember, it is sin to know what you ought to do and then not do it. JAMES 4:17

Sin is not only doing wrong things, but failing to do the right things.

Calling the crowd to join his disciples, [Jesus] said, "If any of you wants to be my follower, you must turn from your selfish ways, take up your cross, and follow me." MARK 8:34

Sin is selfishness.

What are the consequences of sin?

It's your sins that have cut you off from God. Because of your sins, he has turned away and will not listen anymore. ISAIAH 59:2

Sin alienates and separates you from God so that you are not able to enjoy a relationship with him.

The words you speak come from the heart—that's what defiles you. For from the heart come evil thoughts, murder, adultery, all sexual immorality, theft, lying, and slander. MATTHEW 15:18-19

Your sins make you impure and your heart bent on doing wrong.

I lavish unfailing love to a thousand generations. I forgive iniquity, rebellion, and sin. But I do not excuse the guilty. EXODUS 34:7

God will judge us for everything we do, including every secret thing, whether good or bad. ECCLESIASTES 12:14

Sin brings God's punishment because it is a violation of his laws and holiness.

For the wages of sin is death. ROMANS 6:23

Those who refuse to obey the Good News of our Lord Jesus . . . will be punished with eternal destruction, forever separated from the Lord and from his glorious power. 2 THESSALONIANS 1:8-9

Death is the penalty for sins—physical death as well as eternal separation from God.

Is everyone sinful?

Not a single person on earth is always good and never sins. ECCLESIASTES 7:20

When Adam sinned, sin entered the world. Adam's sin brought death, so death spread to everyone, for everyone sinned. ROMANS 5:12

All people have sinned against God.

I was born a sinner— yes, from the moment my mother conceived me. PSALM 51:5

Everyone is born with a sinful nature. It is a condition at birth, and not something that can be avoided with the right training.

The human heart is the most deceitful of all things, and desperately wicked. Who really knows how bad it is? JEREMIAH 17:9

The human heart is far more sinful than you want to believe.

How can I be free from sin's guilt and power?

How can I know all the sins lurking in my heart? Cleanse me from these hidden faults. PSALM 19:12

Wash me clean from my guilt. Purify me from my sin. For I recognize my rebellion; it haunts me day and night. PSALM 51:2-3

Search me, O God, and know my heart; test me and know my anxious thoughts. Point out anything in me that offends you, and lead me along the path of everlasting life. PSALM 139:23-24

Ask God to cleanse your heart from sin.

"Come now, let's settle this," says the LORD. "Though your sins are like scarlet, I will make them as white as snow. Though they are red like crimson, I will make them as white as wool." ISAIAH 1:18

God made Christ, who never sinned, to be the offering for our sin, so that we could be made right with God through Christ. 2 CORINTHIANS 5:21

God has made it possible for the stain of your sin to be removed through the death and resurrection of Jesus Christ.

If we confess our sins to him, he is faithful and just to forgive us our sins and to cleanse us from all wickedness. 1 JOHN 1:9

Confessing your sins to God and turning away from them to obey God is the only way to be free from sin's power and your guilt. When you confess your sins to God he forgives you and forgets them.

Our old sinful selves were crucified with Christ so that sin might lose its power in our lives. We are no longer slaves to sin. . . . Now you are free from your slavery to sin, and you have become slaves to righteous living. ROMANS 6:6, 18

Because of Jesus' death and resurrection, those who have faith in him are free from the power of sin. This doesn't mean you will no longer sin, but that sin's power to enslave you has been defeated.

Am I really a Christian if I still sin?

Here on earth you will have many trials and sorrows. But take heart, because I have overcome the world. JOHN 16:33

If I do what I don't want to do, I am not really the one doing wrong; it is sin living in me that does it. ROMANS 7:20

Throughout your earthly life you will continue to struggle with sin, but if you place your faith in Jesus, he guarantees victory over it.

SINGLENESS *See also* Dating, Divorce, Loneliness, Will of God

Singles include those who have never married, those who are divorced, and those who are widowed. The Bible does not set forth either singleness or marriage as the absolute standard for everyone. Rather, Scripture teaches that each individual should seek the will of God for his or her life. For some, this will lead to marriage. For others, it will lead to a single life. Single or married, our purpose is the same: to honor and serve God and to help others. But without the help and support of a mate, singles face some unique challenges and questions. As always, God offers answers in Scripture.

Is God's plan for everyone to marry? If I'm single, am I missing out on God's plan for me?

Some choose not to marry for the sake of the Kingdom of Heaven. MATTHEW 19:12

I wish everyone were single, just as I am. But God gives to some the gift of marriage, and to others the gift of singleness. 1 CORINTHIANS 7:7

Either marriage or singleness can be a gift from God. Is it all right to remain single? Yes. Is it all right to marry? Yes. There are advantages to both.

An unmarried man can spend his time doing the Lord's work and thinking how to please him. 1 CORINTHIANS 7:32

In your singleness, serve the Lord wholeheartedly. Do not succumb to the feeling that your life is incomplete without a spouse.

What if I want to marry? Is that wrong?

The LORD God said, "It is not good for the man to be alone. I will make a helper who is just right for him." GENESIS 2:18

The person who marries his fiancée does well. 1 CORINTHIANS 7:38

God made man and woman for each other. It is good when the right mates find each other, but tragic when a marriage falls short of God's glorious plan. People should not feel pressured to marry or to remain single. Ask God to lead you concerning marriage and the right marriage partner.

How can God help me accept my singleness?

I wish everyone were single, just as I am. But God gives to some the gift of marriage, and to others the gift of singleness. So I say to those who aren't married and to widows—it's better to stay unmarried, just as I am. 1 CORINTHIANS 7:7-8

Each of you should continue to live in whatever situation the Lord has placed you.
1 CORINTHIANS 7:17

Sometimes, when you desperately want something, it is easy to forget the gifts of your current situation. Paul found that his singleness was an advantage in pursuing his call of establishing churches. Step back and look for how God might want to use your singleness in a way that he could not if you were married.

How can I deal with the loneliness of being single?
Be sure of this: I am with you always, even to the end of the age. MATTHEW 28:20

You are never alone. You can take comfort in knowing that God is with you and will never leave you.

Let us not neglect our meeting together, as some people do, but encourage one another, especially now that the day of his return is drawing near. HEBREWS 10:25

The best way to avoid loneliness is to get together with other believers. Get involved in a local church. Get busy with God's people doing God's work. You don't have to be married to do that.

SPIRITUAL DISCIPLINES *See also* Fasting, Meditation, Prayer, Stewardship

We get close—and stay close—to God through regular practice of the spiritual disciplines. The spiritual disciplines are not ends in themselves; rather, they are means by which we strengthen our connection with God and become more like him. The spiritual disciplines include prayer, fasting, solitude, stewardship, simplicity, and meditating on Scripture, to name a few. As we make these practices a regular part of our lives, our relationship with God will be more vital and life-changing.

Are the spiritual disciplines really important?
For forty days and forty nights he fasted. MATTHEW 4:2

Before daybreak . . . , Jesus got up and went out to an isolated place to pray. MARK 1:35

Jesus often withdrew to the wilderness for prayer. LUKE 5:16

The spiritual disciplines were central to Jesus' earthly life. If the Son of God relied on them to stay connected to God, they must be important.

How can I maintain spiritual discipline?
Guard your heart above all else, for it determines the course of your life. PROVERBS 4:23

Every aspect of life is affected by the spiritual condition of your heart. Because of the impact you can make on others, you must care for your inner life. Otherwise, your weaknesses, wounds, and weariness will likely affect those around you in negative ways. Likewise, your spiritual vitality will inspire and sustain those around you. The spiritual disciplines are the ways you can care for your heart and soul. They are not practiced to impress God, but rather to allow God to impress himself on you. They are not achievements you perform for God, but ways you make yourself available to him.

Don't you realize that in a race everyone runs, but only one person gets the prize? So run to win! All athletes are disciplined in their training. They do it to win a prize that will fade away, but we do it for an eternal prize. So I run with purpose in every step. I am not just shadowboxing. I discipline my body like an athlete, training it to do what it should.
1 CORINTHIANS 9:24-27

An athlete trains over and over again so that fundamental actions become almost automatic. In the same way, spiritual discipline needs to be developed until it becomes a reflex.

Can the spiritual disciplines be misused?

When you pray, don't babble on and on as people of other religions do. They think their prayers are answered merely by repeating their words again and again. MATTHEW 6:7

You misuse spiritual disciplines when you think you can use them to get leverage with God or to manipulate God into blessing you.

When you fast, don't make it obvious, as the hypocrites do, for they try to look miserable and disheveled so people will admire them for their fasting. I tell you the truth, that is the only reward they will ever get. MATTHEW 6:16

You misuse spiritual disciplines if you do them only to seek praise for your spirituality.

"We have fasted before you!" they say. "Why aren't you impressed? We have been very hard on ourselves, and you don't even notice it!" "I will tell you why!" [God responds.] "It's because you are fasting to please yourselves. Even while you fast, you keep oppressing your workers." ISAIAH 58:3

You misuse spiritual disciplines when you act as if they are the goal in themselves rather than a means to godly living.

SPIRITUAL DRYNESS *See also* Apathy, Complacency, Sin, Stress

Scorching temperatures, blazing sun, and days without rain will bring a drought. Plants wilt, streams dry up—everything is dry and thirsty. We can all relate to that parched feeling where we long for a cup of cold water. Our souls can become dry, too, thirsting for something that will be truly fulfilling. Seasons of drought come to our spiritual lives when we experience the blazing pressures of the world or the heat of temptation. Our desire to know God and serve him dries up. Just as a gardener must take extra care of plants in a drought, so we must take care of our souls in times of spiritual dryness—watering them with God's Word and reviving them with a sense of renewed purpose. Just as God sends the rains to refresh the earth, he also sends us living water, showers of blessings, to refresh our souls and restore our passion for him.

What causes spiritual dryness?

As soon as they were at peace, your people again committed evil in your sight, and once more you let their enemies conquer them. NEHEMIAH 9:28

Success and complacency can lead to spiritual dryness.

We are merely moving shadows, and all our busy rushing ends in nothing. We heap up wealth, not knowing who will spend it. PSALM 39:6

The busyness of life and survival can crowd out time for spiritual refreshment and cause dryness of the soul.

What are the symptoms of spiritual dryness?

I know all the things you do, that you are neither hot nor cold. I wish that you were one or the other! But since you are like lukewarm water, neither hot nor cold, I will spit you out of my mouth! . . . I correct and discipline everyone I love. So be diligent and turn from your indifference. REVELATION 3:15-19

A lack of enthusiasm toward God.

To whom can I give warning? Who will listen when I speak? Their ears are closed, and they cannot hear. They scorn the word of the LORD. They don't want to listen at all. JEREMIAH 6:10

Refusing to hear God's Word.

LORD, you are searching for honesty. You struck your people, but they paid no attention. You crushed them, but they refused to be corrected. They are determined, with faces set like stone; they have refused to repent. JEREMIAH 5:3

Unresponsiveness to God's discipline.

Our ancestors in Egypt were not impressed by the LORD's miraculous deeds. They soon forgot his many acts of kindness to them. Instead, they rebelled against him at the Red Sea. . . . Yet how quickly they forgot what he had done! They wouldn't wait for his counsel! PSALM 106:7, 13

Forgetting God's past acts of kindness and mercy.

Watch out! Don't let your hearts be dulled by carousing and drunkenness, and by the worries of this life. LUKE 21:34

Careless living and worrying about life.

I hate all your show and pretense—the hypocrisy of your religious festivals and solemn assemblies. I will not accept your burnt offerings and grain offerings. I won't even notice all your choice peace offerings. Away with your noisy hymns of praise! I will not listen to the music of your harps. Instead, I want to see a mighty flood of justice, an endless river of righteous living. AMOS 5:21-24

Show and pretense in worship.

"When you give blind animals as sacrifices, isn't that wrong? And isn't it wrong to offer animals that are crippled and diseased? Try giving gifts like that to your governor, and see how pleased he is!" says the LORD of Heaven's Armies. MALACHI 1:8

Not giving your best to God.

Why can't I always be on fire for God?

Everyone has sinned; we all fall short of God's glorious standard. ROMANS 3:23

When sin takes a foothold in your life, it will always lead you away from God, and the more apathetic you will become toward him. Satan will use all his power to keep you from getting excited about following God.

The woman was convinced. She saw that the tree was beautiful and its fruit looked delicious, and she wanted the wisdom it would give her. So she took some of the fruit and ate it. Then she gave some to her husband, who was with her, and he ate it, too. GENESIS 3:6

The combination of your sinful nature and temptation will quench your enthusiasm for God.

I will destroy those who used to worship me but now no longer do. They no longer ask for the LORD's guidance or seek my blessings. ZEPHANIAH 1:6

A tendency toward self-sufficiency can stifle your relationship with God.

"You say, 'It's too hard to serve the LORD,' and you turn up your noses at my commands," says the LORD of Heaven's Armies. MALACHI 1:13

We must listen very carefully to the truth we have heard, or we may drift away from it. HEBREWS 2:1

As is true in all relationships, your relationship with God takes effort. God is fully committed to you. In order for your relationship with him to grow, you must be diligent in your dedication to knowing him.

How can I prevent spiritual dryness?

O God, you are my God; I earnestly search for you. My soul thirsts for you; my whole body longs for you in this parched and weary land where there is no water. PSALM 63:1

A tree by a riverbank grows full and tall because it is always near the water. In the same way, if you stay close to God you will grow to spiritual maturity. You will not hunger or thirst for meaning in life because God will nourish you with his Word and his presence. Stay close to God by being with him consistently and persistently through Bible reading, prayer, time with other believers, and serving him in a church and other ministries.

Dear children, keep away from anything that might take God's place in your hearts. 1 JOHN 5:21

Keep sin from taking a foothold in your life. Sin always leads away from God. To avoid drifting from God, guard your affection and devotion to him.

When I refused to confess my sin, my body wasted away, and I groaned all day long. Day and night your hand of discipline was heavy on me. My strength evaporated like water in the summer heat. PSALM 32:3-4

Confess any sin right away, and ask God to forgive you and turn your heart back toward him.

Don't look out only for your own interests, but take an interest in others, too. PHILIPPIANS 2:4

Practice genuine, active love for others. Love waters a dry soul.

How do I recover from spiritual dryness?

As the deer longs for streams of water, so I long for you, O God. PSALM 42:1

Thirst for God, and your soul will be watered.

I confessed all my sins to you and stopped trying to hide my guilt. I said to myself, "I will confess my rebellion to the LORD." And you forgave me! All my guilt is gone. PSALM 32:5

Confess and repent of any known sin. Sin will parch a thirsty soul.

The rain and snow come down from the heavens and stay on the ground to water the earth. They cause the grain to grow, producing seed for the farmer and bread for the hungry. It is the same with my word. I send it out, and it always produces fruit. It will accomplish all I want it to, and it will prosper everywhere I send it. ISAIAH 55:10-11

Commit to faithful obedience to God and his Word. From the springs of God's Word come refreshment for your soul.

Work willingly at whatever you do, as though you were working for the Lord rather than for people. COLOSSIANS 3:23

Work diligently and enthusiastically for the Lord. Serving God refreshes your soul.

Our great desire is that you will keep on loving others as long as life lasts, in order to make certain that what you hope for will come true. Then you will not become spiritually dull and indifferent. Instead, you will follow the example of those who are going to inherit God's promises because of their faith and endurance. HEBREWS 6:11-12

Practice loving others, and follow the example of other spiritually mature believers. Loving others refreshes your soul.

SPIRITUAL WARFARE *See also* Angels, Evil, Oppression, Victory

In order to be effective on the battlefield, a soldier must be both well trained and properly equipped. The warrior must also have access to both a defensive stronghold and offensive weaponry. He or she must know the enemy and be alert for surprise attacks. So it is in our spiritual battle with Satan. Determined to destroy our faith by leading us into sin and discouragement, Satan attacks with blatant temptation and deceptive lies. The Bible trains you in using the best weapons and tactics for this very real and very dangerous spiritual warfare.

Is spiritual warfare a reality?

The serpent was the shrewdest of all the wild animals the LORD God had made. One day he asked the woman, "Did God really say you must not eat the fruit from any of the trees in the garden?" GENESIS 3:1

Jesus was led by the Spirit into the wilderness to be tempted there by the devil. MATTHEW 4:1

From the beginning of time and from the beginning of Jesus' own ministry, the Bible clearly teaches that human beings are involved in a spiritual battle. Far from excluding you from spiritual battles, faith puts you right in the midst of them. Those who fail to realize and plan for this put themselves in jeopardy.

What does the Bible say about spiritual warfare?

Put on every piece of God's armor so you will be able to resist the enemy in the time of evil. EPHESIANS 6:13

Spiritual warfare requires preparation—through prayer, unwavering faith, and knowledge of biblical truth—to defeat your spiritual enemy.

Stay alert! Watch out for your great enemy, the devil. 1 PETER 5:8

You must be alert at all times for the sneak attacks of the devil.

Resist the devil, and he will flee from you. JAMES 4:7

When you resist the devil in the name and power of Jesus, he will flee from you. At the name of Jesus, Satan has no power.

Jesus was led by the Spirit into the wilderness to be tempted there by the devil. For forty days and forty nights he fasted and became very hungry. During that time the devil came and said to him, "If you are the Son of God, tell these stones to become loaves of bread." But Jesus told him, "No! The Scriptures say, . . ." MATTHEW 4:1-4

When under attack by Satan, Jesus relied on the Word of God to resist the lies of his adversary.

How does spiritual warfare affect me?

The serpent was the shrewdest of all the wild animals the LORD God had made. One day he asked the woman, "Did God really say you must not eat the fruit from any of the trees in the garden?" GENESIS 3:1

[The devil] was a murderer from the beginning. He has always hated the truth, because there is no truth in him. When he lies, it is consistent with his character; for he is a liar and the father of lies. JOHN 8:44

Satan's first tactic is to distort God's Word. If he can raise suspicion about the integrity of Scripture, he can get you to question God's will and intentions for you. Study the Bible so you know it well enough that you can recognize the lies that most often come in the guise of cultural mores and worldviews.

Satan rose up against Israel and caused David to take a census of the people of Israel.
1 CHRONICLES 21:1

A big part of spiritual warfare is getting you to rely only on yourself and not on God, who has the greater power. Satan will tempt you to rely on your own resources—on the tangible, measurable assets you can count. While it is wise to understand your resources, it is unwise to think that your ultimate security is in them. David's census was an egotistical inventory of his military might and was in direct contradiction to David's experience of God's provision and protection throughout his lifetime.

The devil came and said to [Jesus], "If you are the Son of God, tell these stones to become loaves of bread." . . . Then the devil took him to the holy city, Jerusalem, to the highest point of the Temple, and said, "If you are the Son of God, jump off!" . . . Next the devil took him to the peak of a very high mountain and showed him all the kingdoms of the world and their glory. "I will give it all to you," he said, "if you will kneel down and worship me." MATTHEW 4:3-5, 8-9

In spiritual battle, you may be tempted by offers of personal gain, pride, and power.

In spiritual warfare, how do I fight back?

I have hidden your word in my heart, that I might not sin against you. PSALM 119:11

"Get out of here, Satan," Jesus told [the devil]. "For the Scriptures say . . ." Then the devil went away. MATTHEW 4:10-11

Take the sword of the Spirit, which is the word of God. EPHESIANS 6:17

Your best offensive weapon is the Word of God. It's odd to think of the Bible as a weapon, but in it, God reveals his plan of attack and defense against anyone or anything that tries to bring you down. It's your battle plan; if you don't read it, you won't know how to fight the battle that literally determines your destiny both here on earth and for eternity. Only by knowing whom you are fighting, where the battle is, and how to defend yourself will you be able to win. It is vital to read God's Word as regularly as possible. This weapon will send Satan running for cover and leave him defenseless.

Be strong in the Lord and in his mighty power. Put on all of God's armor so that you will be able to stand firm against all strategies of the devil. For we are not fighting against flesh-and-blood enemies, but against evil rulers and authorities of the unseen world, against mighty powers in this dark world, and against evil spirits in the heavenly places. Therefore, put on every piece of God's armor so you will be able to resist the enemy in the time of evil. Then after the battle you will still be standing firm. Stand your ground, putting on the belt of truth and the body armor of God's righteousness. For shoes, put on the peace that comes from the Good News so that you will be fully prepared. In addition to all of these, hold up the shield of faith to stop the fiery arrows of the devil. Put on salvation as your helmet, and take the sword of the Spirit, which is the word of God. Pray in the Spirit at all times and on every occasion. Stay alert and be persistent in your prayers for all believers everywhere. EPHESIANS 6:10-18

When a dog threatens you, he will chase you if you run. But if you stand your ground, the dog will usually back down. The same principle applies in spiritual warfare. Stand your ground because you have the power of the Lord Jesus Christ with you. See beyond the human antagonists to the spiritual enemy, often working through the unaware parties involved. Prepare yourself with the resources God provides, and count on God's protection, not your own intellect or cleverness.

STATUS *See also* Appearance, Peer Pressure, Reputation

Status, by itself, is neither good nor bad. What we do with our status is what counts. The greatest lesson we can learn about status is from Jesus. The Bible tells us that as the Son of the all-powerful, all-knowing, almighty God, Jesus was very rich and powerful. Yet, he gave all that up to live on earth as a human being, taking on the frailties of a human body and then giving himself over to die a criminal's death so the sins of the world could be forgiven.

How important is my status in life?

[Abraham said,] "Here I am, a stranger and a foreigner among you. Please sell me a piece of land so I can give my wife a proper burial." The Hittites replied to Abraham, "Listen, my lord, you are an honored prince among us. Choose the finest of our tombs and bury her there. No one here will refuse to help you in this way." GENESIS 23:4-6

Choose a good reputation over great riches; being held in high esteem is better than silver or gold. PROVERBS 22:1

Status certainly has its advantages, at least on this earth.

When Isaac planted his crops that year, he harvested a hundred times more grain than he planted, for the LORD blessed him. He became a very rich man, and his wealth continued to grow. . . . The Philistines became jealous of him. So the Philistines filled up all of Isaac's wells with dirt. . . . Finally, Abimelech ordered Isaac to leave the country. "Go somewhere else," he said, "for you have become too powerful for us." GENESIS 26:12-16

Status also has its share of headaches and difficulties.

Many who are the greatest now will be least important then, and those who seem least important now will be the greatest then. MATTHEW 19:30

Status in this world matters very little in God's eternal kingdom.

How can I use my status to glorify God?

[Joseph said to his brothers,] "[God] brought me to this position so I could save the lives of many people." GENESIS 50:20

You can use your status to bring blessing to other people.

The queen of Sheba heard of Solomon's fame, which brought honor to the name of the LORD. 1 KINGS 10:1

Use your status to build a good reputation that brings honor to God's name.

The king went up to the Temple of the LORD *with all the people of Judah and Jerusalem. . . . There the king read to them the entire Book of the Covenant that had been found in the* LORD's *Temple.* 2 KINGS 23:2

Status and position provide prime opportunities to point people to God.

STEALING *See also* Cheating, Deceit/Deception

No culture anywhere on earth treats stealing as acceptable behavior. Taking something that does not belong to you is universally considered wrong. Yet there is no society in which stealing does not occur. Stealing, from armed robbery to inflated expense accounts, from teenage shoplifting to price fixing on Wall Street, is epidemic. The Bible offers insight into why stealing is so common—and so harmful.

In what ways do I steal from others?

When you make an agreement with your neighbor to buy or sell property, you must not take advantage of each other. . . . Show your fear of God by not taking advantage of each other. I am the LORD *your God.* LEVITICUS 25:14, 17

You must use accurate scales when you weigh out merchandise, and you must use full and honest measures . . . so that you may enjoy a long life in the land the LORD *your God is giving you.* DEUTERONOMY 25:13-15

The cartoon version of a thief is usually a sinister figure in a black mask that robs banks, snatches purses, and breaks into homes after dark. Although theft and violent crime are a real part of our world, most of us will be tempted by more subtle and "civilized" forms of stealing, such as padding an expense account, adding false deductions to an income-tax statement, or taking advantage of someone's gullibility or goodness. Whether we rob a widow at knifepoint or skim so smoothly that our victims never know it, stealing is detestable in the eyes of a holy God. Make a commitment to be completely honest in all you do and say.

Do not spread slanderous gossip among your people. LEVITICUS 19:16

When you gossip about someone you are stealing something from them—their honorable reputation. You are also using information that belongs to them without their permission.

Never be lazy, but work hard and serve the Lord enthusiastically. ROMANS 12:11

Wasting time on the job is stealing from your employers.

Give honor to marriage, and remain faithful to one another in marriage. God will surely judge people who are immoral and those who commit adultery. HEBREWS 13:4

Having sex before or outside of marriage is stealing the purity of another.

What if I have been guilty of stealing in some way?
Suppose . . . you steal or commit fraud. . . . You must give back whatever you stole. . . . You must make restitution. LEVITICUS 6:2-7

Quit stealing. Instead, use your hands for good hard work, and then give generously to others in need. EPHESIANS 4:28

Make restitution for what you have stolen, seek God's forgiveness, and be generous toward others.

The commandments say, "You must not commit adultery. You must not murder. You must not steal. You must not covet." These . . . are summed up in this one commandment: "Love your neighbor as yourself." ROMANS 13:9

Avoid stealing and dishonesty by learning to love others as God loves you. This builds trust and respect. It's harder to steal from those you trust and respect.

STEWARDSHIP See also Giving, Money, Responsibility, Tithing
Most of us think about money every day. Will we have enough to pay the bills? Are we saving enough? Can we pay less for this item somewhere else? How much will our monthly payments be? When we think carefully about our money and try to spend and save it wisely, we are showing good stewardship of our financial resources. But often we forget that God calls us to be good stewards of all the resources and gifts he has provided for us to use and enjoy. For example, God has given us the earth and all its resources to manage responsibly. Since he has invested so much in us, as evidenced by his amazing plan of salvation and eternal life, we should invest our time and talents in his work until he returns. The goal of stewardship is to make the best possible use of what we have in order to have the greatest possible effect on others so that God's purpose and plan can move forward as efficiently and effectively as possible.

What does it mean to be a good steward?
The heavens are yours, and the earth is yours; everything in the world is yours—you created it all. PSALM 89:11

Stewardship begins by acknowledging that the Lord owns everything. Since everything belongs to God, you should consult him before you use what he has given to you.

God said, *"Let us make human beings in our image, to be like us. They will reign over the fish in the sea, the birds in the sky, the livestock, all the wild animals on the earth, and the small animals that scurry along the ground."* GENESIS 1:26

Part of the reason you were created was to manage God's world for him.

How does God want me to use the resources available to me?
The master was full of praise. "Well done, my good and faithful servant. You have been faithful in handling this small amount, so now I will give you many more responsibilities. Let's celebrate together!" MATTHEW 25:21

God wants you to use what you are given to serve him faithfully.

Plant your seed in the morning and keep busy all afternoon, for you don't know if profit will come from one activity or another—or maybe both. ECCLESIASTES 11:6

Prepare for the future by wisely managing what is entrusted to you.

All must give as they are able, according to the blessings given to them by the LORD your God. DEUTERONOMY 16:17

As you are able, give to God's work.

Don't you realize that your body is the temple of the Holy Spirit, who lives in you and was given to you by God? You do not belong to yourself, for God bought you with a high price. So you must honor God with your body. 1 CORINTHIANS 6:19-20

Take care of your body so you will be strong and healthy to serve God and others.

STRENGTH *See also* Power, Victory
A weightlifter's strength is defined by the number of pounds he can lift. The strength of a building is measured by its resistance to external forces exerted by wind or earthquake. The strength of a corporation is often defined by its net assets. But what is spiritual strength? The Bible teaches that spiritual strength has the faith to move mountains, the power to lift burdens, a foundation deep enough to resist the pressures of temptation, and the security of salvation for eternity.

What is the evidence of God's strength? How strong is he?
Who else has held the oceans in his hand? Who has measured off the heavens with his fingers? Who else knows the weight of the earth or has weighed the mountains and hills on a scale? . . . "To whom will you compare me? Who is my equal?" asks the Holy One. Look up into the heavens. Who created all the stars? He brings them out like an army, one after another, calling each by its name. Because of his great power and incomparable strength, not a single one is missing. ISAIAH 40:12, 25-26

God's mighty power is evident in creation. God created and sustains the universe. There is no greater strength.

The LORD does whatever pleases him throughout all heaven and earth, and on the seas and in their depths. PSALM 135:6

God's strength is revealed in his sovereign providence over all things. Nothing happens without God directing it or allowing it. God not only provides all good things, but he continually manages them as well.

All who heard [Paul] were amazed. "Isn't this the same man who caused such devastation among Jesus' followers . . . ?" they asked. ACTS 9:21

A life transformed is evidence of God's power.

Jesus [said], "I am the resurrection and the life. Anyone who believes in me will live, even after dying. Everyone who lives in me and believes in me will never ever die." JOHN 11:25-26

When our dying bodies have been transformed into bodies that will never die, this Scripture will be fulfilled: "Death is swallowed up in victory. O death, where is your victory? O death, where is your sting?" 1 CORINTHIANS 15:54-55

The present heavens and earth have been stored up for fire. They are being kept for the day of judgment, when ungodly people will be destroyed. 2 PETER 3:7

Only God has the power over death, the authority to judge sin, and the right to determine people's eternal fate.

How can I experience the strength of God in my life?

I pray that your hearts will be flooded with light so that you can understand the confident hope he has given to those he called. . . . I also pray that you will understand the incredible greatness of God's power for us who believe him. This is the same mighty power that raised Christ from the dead. EPHESIANS 1:18-20

God's power to raise Jesus from the dead is the same power that will one day raise you from the dead if you believe in him. And that same power is available to you now to live more effectively and courageously for him.

I pray that from his glorious, unlimited resources he will empower you with inner strength through his Spirit. . . . Now all glory to God, who is able, through his mighty power at work within us, to accomplish infinitely more than we might ask or think. EPHESIANS 3:16, 20

God promises to give you inner strength powered by his own Holy Spirit when you depend on him and trust him to do what is best for you.

The joy of the LORD is your strength! NEHEMIAH 8:10

Strength starts in your heart long before it is exerted in other aspects of life. The joy that comes from your hope in all God promises gives you strength to obey, to endure, and to triumph in all circumstances.

As soon as I pray, you answer me; you encourage me by giving me strength. PSALM 138:3

God's strength comes through prayer, your lifeline to God.

What can I do in God's strength?

I can do everything through Christ, who gives me strength. PHILIPPIANS 4:13

There are no limits to what God can do in and through you.

All glory to God, who is able, through his mighty power at work within us, to accomplish infinitely more than we might ask or think. EPHESIANS 3:20

With God's strength you have the power to accomplish things you could never do on your own.

God is our refuge and strength, always ready to help in times of trouble. So we will not fear when earthquakes come and the mountains crumble into the sea. PSALM 46:1-2

By God's strength you can live without fear, even in times of trouble. God's strength drives out fear.

What are the signs of spiritual strength?

My health may fail, and my spirit may grow weak, but God remains the strength of my heart; he is mine forever. PSALM 73:26

The signs of spiritual strength may not be evident in your physical body. Spiritual strength goes past the bone and into the soul.

It is not that we think we are qualified to do anything on our own. Our qualification comes from God. 2 CORINTHIANS 3:5

A sign of spiritual strength is depending on God more than on yourself or others.

Anyone who becomes as humble as this little child is the greatest in the Kingdom of Heaven. MATTHEW 18:4

A sign of spiritual strength is humility and gentleness.

I am not ashamed of this Good News about Christ. It is the power of God at work, saving everyone who believes. ROMANS 1:16

A sign of spiritual strength is courage to stand up for God and not be ashamed of your faith.

Be strong and immovable. Always work enthusiastically for the Lord, for you know that nothing you do for the Lord is ever useless. 1 CORINTHIANS 15:58

A sign of spiritual strength is a passion to serve God.

[A church leader] must have a strong belief in the trustworthy message he was taught; then he will be able to encourage others with wholesome teaching and show those who oppose it where they are wrong. TITUS 1:9

A sign of spiritual strength is encouraging others with wholesome teaching.

STRESS *See also* Burnout, Busyness, Crisis, Fear, Trouble, Work

Life sometimes causes us to feel like a rubber band stretched tight. Pressures build up and pull us in different directions and strain our sense of well-being. Trying to do too much in too little time with too few resources stretches us beyond our capacity to cope. The financial demands of life, difficult relationships, health problems, and just trying to survive all bring on stress. What is the solution? Giving God your burdens and allowing him to administer peace and rest.

What are some of the dangers of stress?

Moses was also very aggravated. And Moses said to the LORD, "Why are you treating me, your servant, so harshly? Have mercy on me! What did I do to deserve the burden of all these people? . . . Where am I supposed to get meat for all these people? They keep whining to me, saying, 'Give us meat to eat!' I can't carry all these people by myself! The load is far too heavy! If this is how you intend to treat me, just go ahead and kill me. Do me a favor and spare me this misery!" NUMBERS 11:10-15

The intense demands of life have the potential to overwhelm you. The expectations, the criticism, the scope of the need and responsibility can threaten to crush even the strongest person.

The seed that fell among the thorns represents those who hear God's word, but all too quickly the message is crowded out by the worries of this life and the lure of wealth, so no fruit is produced. MATTHEW 13:22

Martha was distracted by the big dinner she was preparing. She came to Jesus and said, "Lord, doesn't it seem unfair to you that my sister just sits here while I do all the work? Tell her to come and help me." But the Lord said to her, "My dear Martha, you are worried and upset over all these details!" LUKE 10:40-41

Stress can cause you to focus on the trivial and miss the important. As pressure squeezes your perspective inward, you lose the big picture. Preoccupation with the issues of the moment blinds you to what's really important.

Should I be surprised by the stress of life?

I have told you all this so that you may have peace in me. Here on earth you will have many trials and sorrows. But take heart, because I have overcome the world. JOHN 16:33

Jesus warned us to expect stress. This world is filled with trials and sorrows that will generate stress in your life. The key to dealing with stress is to not be surprised when it comes, but learn how to deal with it. While there are many healthy and positive ways to handle stress, never neglect the spiritual help the Holy Spirit is waiting to provide if you ask.

How can I deal with stress?

We are hunted down, but never abandoned by God. We get knocked down, but we are not destroyed. 2 CORINTHIANS 4:9

Keep going! Knowing that God is by your side during times of trouble and stress can help you to keep from giving up.

Give your burdens to the LORD, and he will take care of you. He will not permit the godly to slip and fall. PSALM 55:22

Jesus said, "Come to me, all of you who are weary and carry heavy burdens, and I will give you rest. Take my yoke upon you. Let me teach you, because I am humble and gentle at heart, and you will find rest for your souls." MATTHEW 11:28-29

I have told you all this so that you may have peace in me. Here on earth you will have many trials and sorrows. But take heart, because I have overcome the world. JOHN 16:33

When you allow Jesus to carry your burdens and teach you from his humble and gentle spirit, you will find your stress melting away and experience peacefulness in your soul instead. Jesus' humility and gentleness counteract the pride and irritability that fuel so much of the conflict and stress in life.

In my distress I cried out to the LORD; yes, I cried to my God for help. He heard me from his sanctuary; my cry reached his ears. 2 SAMUEL 22:7

I will call to you whenever I'm in trouble, and you will answer me. PSALM 86:7

Be persistent in prayer.

Jesus said, "Let's go off by ourselves to a quiet place and rest awhile." He said this because there were so many people coming and going that Jesus and his apostles didn't even have time to eat. MARK 6:31

Take time to slow down and take a break from pressure-packed situations.

Don't you realize that your body is the temple of the Holy Spirit, who lives in you and was given to you by God? You do not belong to yourself, for God bought you with a high price. So you must honor God with your body. 1 CORINTHIANS 6:19-20

Take care of your body. Adequate rest, regular exercise, and proper nutrition are essential to dealing effectively with stress.

Is stress ever positive?

We can rejoice, too, when we run into problems and trials, for we know that they help us develop endurance. And endurance develops strength of character, and character strengthens our confident hope of salvation. ROMANS 5:3-4

When troubles come your way, consider it an opportunity for great joy. For you know that when your faith is tested, your endurance has a chance to grow. So let it grow, for when your endurance is fully developed, you will be perfect and complete, needing nothing. JAMES 1:2-4

Stress and pressure can make you stronger, teach you endurance, and develop strength of character.

What can I learn from stress?

We were crushed and overwhelmed beyond our ability to endure, and we thought we would never live through it. In fact, we expected to die. But as a result, we stopped relying on ourselves and learned to rely only on God, who raises the dead. 2 CORINTHIANS 1:8-9

Stress exposes your limitations and forces you to rely on God's limitless power and unconditional love.

I will call to you whenever I'm in trouble, and you will answer me. PSALM 86:7

Stress puts great pressure on your health and relationships. It is a warning sign that you are being stretched to your limit, and that beyond that limit you will snap. But stress can be positive if you learn and grow from it. Just as a muscle can only grow under stress, so your wisdom and character can only grow under the pressures of life. As you look for what God is teaching you in your stressful times, you will become better equipped to deal with stressful situations in the future.

STUBBORNNESS *See also* Denial, Pride, Selfishness, Humility, Submission

Stubbornness comes out of pride—we think our way is best, and we refuse to budge. Stubbornness is not a respecter of others' thoughts or ideas. When we know what God wants and refuse to do it, we show our stubborn rebellion against him. Stubbornness is unyielding, refusing to move, refusing to change. It is hardened resistance to others and to God himself. Not only that, stubbornness often keeps us from doing what is best for us, and thus in the end we hurt ourselves.

What makes people stubborn?

You again rebelled against the LORD's command and arrogantly went into the hill country to fight. DEUTERONOMY 1:43

Stubbornness is almost always rooted in pride, thinking you always know best.

When the judge died, the people returned to their corrupt ways, behaving worse than those who had lived before them. They went after other gods, serving and worshiping them. And they refused to give up their evil practices and stubborn ways. JUDGES 2:19

Stubbornness can come from resisting authority. Those who enjoy a lifestyle of sin and don't want to give up sinful habits are stubbornly resisting God's authority.

The people refused to listen to Samuel's warning. "Even so, we still want a king," they said. 1 SAMUEL 8:19

Stubbornness can come from a fiercely independent spirit that causes you to be overly self-reliant.

Where does stubbornness lead?

My people wouldn't listen. Israel did not want me around. So I let them follow their own stubborn desires, living according to their own ideas. PSALM 81:11-12

If you persist in stubbornness, God may let you have your way and allow you to suffer the consequences that follow.

Your ancestors did not listen or even pay attention. Instead, they stubbornly followed their own evil desires. And because they refused to obey, I brought upon them all the curses described in this covenant. JEREMIAH 11:8

Those who are stubborn against God will be punished.

The king insisted that they take the census, so Joab and the commanders of the army went out to count the people of Israel. . . . So the LORD sent a plague upon Israel that morning, and it lasted for three days. 2 SAMUEL 24:4, 15

When the leaders of a nation are stubborn, it can lead to national disaster.

It is impossible to bring back to repentance those who were once enlightened . . . and who then turn away from God. HEBREWS 6:4-6

Persistent stubbornness may bring eternal separation from God.

How can I keep from being stubborn?

Do not be stubborn . . . but submit yourselves to the LORD. 2 CHRONICLES 30:8

Submit to God's leading in your life by obeying him and not insisting on doing things your way.

Search for the LORD and for his strength; continually seek him. 1 CHRONICLES 16:11

Seek God's wisdom and guidance first, before you form opinions and make decisions.

You must warn each other every day, while it is still "today," so that none of you will be deceived by sin and hardened against God. HEBREWS 3:13

Fellowship with other believers, including exhorting and warning one another, can keep you accountable for your actions and preserve you from developing a hard heart.

How are people stubborn in their relationship to God?

"This is the finger of God!" the magicians exclaimed to Pharaoh. But Pharaoh's heart remained hard. He wouldn't listen to them, just as the LORD had predicted. EXODUS 8:19

They are stubborn toward God when they see God's work around them and refuse to believe it is God doing the work.

The LORD hardened Pharaoh's heart. EXODUS 9:12

A habit of stubbornly refusing to acknowledge God may cause him to leave you alone. What hope do you have then?

How do I deal with stubbornness in someone else?

The LORD ordered the fish to spit Jonah out onto the beach. Then the LORD spoke to Jonah a second time. JONAH 2:10–3:1

God dealt with Jonah's stubbornness with both patience and confrontation.

If any place refuses to welcome you or listen to you, shake its dust from your feet as you leave to show that you have abandoned those people to their fate. MARK 6:11

Jesus recognized there are times, regrettably, when you must leave people to the consequences of their own stubbornness.

SUBMISSION *See also* Accountability, Humility, Obedience, Surrender

Unfortunately, the word *submission* is taboo in today's culture. Many people believe that submission—to God, family, friends, spouse—is a sign of either weakness or imbalance of power. However, we learn from the Bible that the keys to submission are signs of great strength of character—profound respect, genuine love and appreciation, and the willingness to help others. Submission out of obligation doesn't benefit anyone. When done out of love and appreciation for others, submission reveals inner strength and is wonderfully freeing.

What is submission to God? Why is it important?

The LORD had said to Abram, "Leave your native country, your relatives, and your father's family, and go to the land that I will show you."... So Abram departed as the LORD had instructed. GENESIS 12:1, 4

Submission to God is obedience to him—learning to find joy in doing what he commands. It involves seeking God's will and following it wholeheartedly out of a genuine love and deep respect for him.

Obey me, and I will be your God, and you will be my people. Do everything as I say, and all will be well! JEREMIAH 7:23

Obedience is defined as "being submissive to an authority." Ironically, obedience to God's ways actually frees you to enjoy life as he originally created it, keeping you from becoming entangled or enslaved to the sinful things that distract or hurt you. It protects you from the evil that God knows is there, leads you on right paths where you will find blessing, and directs you into service that will please him.

Should I submit to anyone other than the Lord?

Submit to one another out of reverence for Christ. EPHESIANS 5:21

Christians are to submit to one another, to put others' needs and rights above one's own needs and rights.

For wives, this means submit to your husbands as to the Lord.... For husbands, this means love your wives, just as Christ loved the church. He gave up his life for her. EPHESIANS 5:22, 25

Husbands and wives should submit to each other.

Children, obey your parents because you belong to the Lord, for this is the right thing to do. EPHESIANS 6:1

Children should submit to their parents.

Slaves, obey your earthly masters with deep respect and fear. Serve them sincerely as you would serve Christ. EPHESIANS 6:5

Employees should submit to their employers.

Everyone must submit to governing authorities. For all authority comes from God, and those in positions of authority have been placed there by God. ROMANS 13:1

You younger men must accept the authority of the elders. And all of you, serve each other in humility, for "God opposes the proud but favors the humble." 1 PETER 5:5

Submit to those in authority over you as long as they do not ask you to disobey the commands of God.

How should I submit?

Do not let any part of your body become an instrument of evil to serve sin. Instead, give yourselves completely to God, for you were dead, but now you have new life. So use your whole body as an instrument to do what is right for the glory of God. ROMANS 6:13

Submit your body to God so he can help you become all he created you to be.

He went on a little farther and bowed with his face to the ground, praying, "My Father! If it is possible, let this cup of suffering be taken away from me. Yet I want your will to be done, not mine." MATTHEW 26:39

Submit yourself to God's will so that you can be connected to God's great plan for you.

Since we respected our earthly fathers who disciplined us, shouldn't we submit even more to the discipline of the Father of our spirits, and live forever? HEBREWS 12:9

Submit to authority and discipline so you will be spared from the consequences of foolish behavior.

Obey your spiritual leaders, and do what they say. Their work is to watch over your souls, and they are accountable to God. Give them reason to do this with joy and not with sorrow. That would certainly not be for your benefit. HEBREWS 13:17

Submit to spiritual leaders and pray for them.

What are some ways to show submission?

Love each other with genuine affection, and take delight in honoring each other. ROMANS 12:10

Love and respect are two key components in showing submission in a relationship.

Be humble, thinking of others as better than yourselves. Don't look out only for your own interests, but take an interest in others, too. PHILIPPIANS 2:3-4

Submission results from a humble heart, respect for others, and the willingness to serve them and treat them as you would like to be treated.

The wisdom from above is first of all pure. It is also peace loving, gentle at all times, and willing to yield to others. It is full of mercy and good deeds. It shows no favoritism and is always sincere. JAMES 3:17

Be peace loving and gentle, merciful and full of good deeds.

SUCCESS *See also* Accomplishments, Productivity, Purpose, Victory

In most cultures, success is defined by how much we own and how much we achieve. Success by God's standards is not measured by material assets, but by godliness and all that is associated with it. Many people are successful both materially and by God's standards. But we get into trouble when we gain material or worldly success at the expense of godly success. On the day of our death, when we lay aside all material assets, what we own and how we achieved it has no value. But how we have succeeded in godly matters counts in every way.

What is true success in God's eyes?

You must love the LORD your God with all your heart, all your soul, and all your mind. MATTHEW 22:37

This is the way to have eternal life—to know you, the only true God, and Jesus Christ, the one you sent to earth. JOHN 17:3

Success is knowing God and loving him with everything you have—your heart, soul, and mind. The more you know him, the more you will love him because he is love.

Whether we are here in this body or away from this body, our goal is to please him. For we must all stand before Christ to be judged. We will each receive whatever we deserve for the good or evil we have done in this earthly body. 2 CORINTHIANS 5:9-10

Success is pleasing God. Form your agenda from God. Your goals should be ultimately rooted in what you can achieve with integrity and with ways consistent with loving God and others.

Believe in the Lord Jesus and you will be saved. ACTS 16:31

Faith in Jesus is success because only through faith will you find salvation and eternal life.

Study this Book of Instruction continually. Meditate on it day and night so you will be sure to obey everything written in it. Only then will you prosper and succeed in all you do. JOSHUA 1:8

Encourage me by your word. PSALM 119:28

Your decrees have been the theme of my songs wherever I have lived. PSALM 119:54

Knowing and following God's Word brings success, for it reveals God's will for your life and his path is the most successful one you can take. God's Word teaches you truth, and whatever is true can be counted on, and whatever can be counted on will give you a strong foundation on which to live your life and will equip you with the skills and understanding to live life to the fullest.

Whoever wants to be a leader among you must be your servant. MATTHEW 20:26

Serving and helping others brings success, for in serving others you find true joy.

When you produce much fruit, you are my true disciples. This brings great glory to my Father. . . . You didn't choose me. I chose you. I appointed you to go and produce lasting fruit, so that the Father will give you whatever you ask for, using my name. JOHN 15:8, 16

Success is being productive in the things that matter to God. The Bible calls this "bearing fruit." This kind of fruit comes as a result of your relationship with Jesus and commitment to living by his principles of success.

What are the dangers of living for worldly success?

Lot took a long look at the fertile plains of the Jordan Valley in the direction of Zoar. The whole area was well watered everywhere, like the garden of the LORD or the beautiful land of Egypt. . . . Lot chose for himself the whole Jordan Valley to the east of them. . . . So Abram settled in the land of Canaan, and Lot moved his tents to a place near Sodom and settled among the cities of the plain. But the people of this area were extremely wicked and constantly sinned against the LORD. GENESIS 13:10-13

It is easy to be seduced by appearances and overlook the evil beneath. Lot chose the fertile valley of Sodom, not caring that its cash crop was wickedness. It would later cost him his family.

What do you benefit if you gain the whole world but are yourself lost or destroyed? LUKE 9:25

The greatest danger in being a success by the world's standards is failing to live by God's standards. To gain the world and lose your soul is the ultimate failure.

All too quickly the message is crowded out by the worries of this life, the lure of wealth, and the desire for other things, so no fruit is produced. MARK 4:19

Being consumed by worldly things can smother the success that comes from God. When you focus all your attention on gaining money, position, power, or fame, you will spend all your energies getting them and miss out on the blessings from God.

Is it okay to try to be successful in this life?

The LORD God is our sun and our shield. He gives us grace and glory. The LORD will withhold no good thing from those who do what is right. PSALM 84:11

Work hard and become a leader; be lazy and become a slave. PROVERBS 12:24

Do you see any truly competent workers? They will serve kings rather than working for ordinary people. PROVERBS 22:29

There are many godly character traits that, if applied to life, often bring material success (hard work, integrity, commitment, serving others, planning).

The LORD was with Joseph, so he succeeded in everything he did as he served in the home of his Egyptian master. GENESIS 39:2-3

The LORD blessed Job in the second half of his life even more than in the beginning. . . . Job lived 140 years after that, living to see four generations of his children and grandchildren. Then he died, an old man who had lived a long, full life. JOB 42:12, 16-17

Throughout the Scriptures, there are frequent references to God's material blessings for his people. God allows his people to have material blessing but urges them never to forget the one who gave them. It is always a bad investment to sacrifice spiritual success for worldly wealth.

How do I keep my focus on godly success?

Commit your actions to the LORD, and your plans will succeed. PROVERBS 16:3

The first step toward success is being willing to let go of your own agenda and commit to God's.

Don't store up treasures here on earth. . . . Store your treasures in heaven, where moths and rust cannot destroy, and thieves do not break in and steal. Wherever your treasure is, there the desires of your heart will also be. MATTHEW 6:19-21

Set your priorities and measure your accomplishments by God's standards, not worldly criteria. You cannot always ignore worldly standards, but you must keep them in perspective.

Train yourself to be godly. "Physical training is good, but training for godliness is much better, promising benefits in this life and in the life to come." This is a trustworthy saying, and everyone should accept it. This is why we work hard and continue to struggle, for our hope is in the living God, who is the Savior of all people and particularly of all believers. 1 TIMOTHY 4:7-10

Spiritual fitness keeps you vigorous for spiritual success.

I press on to possess that perfection for which Christ Jesus first possessed me. No, dear brothers and sisters, I have not achieved it, but I focus on this one thing: Forgetting the past and looking forward to what lies ahead, I press on to reach the end of the race and receive the heavenly prize for which God, through Christ Jesus, is calling us. PHILIPPIANS 3:12-14

Constant awareness of your heavenly rewards helps you remain faithful.

SUFFERING *See also* Grief, Hurts/Hurting, Pain, Sickness, Tragedy

Suffering is a universal experience. Some suffering comes by chance, like a car accident that maims or an illness that ravages a loved one or even takes his or her life. Some suffering happens by neglect, such as our failure to prepare for times of pressure. Sometimes it is by design, like when we willingly take on enormous responsibilities in order to achieve a goal. Other times it is by sin, when we willingly go against God's commands and then must suffer the consequences. Whatever the source, we all feel the dark shadow of suffering. While the Bible never promises a life free from suffering, it does assure us that God is with us in our pain.

Why am I suffering?

When the Ishmaelites, who were Midianite traders, came by, Joseph's brothers pulled him out of the cistern and sold him to them for twenty pieces of silver. GENESIS 37:28

A man named Achan had stolen some of these dedicated things, so the LORD was very angry with the Israelites. JOSHUA 7:1

Sometimes you may suffer because of the sins of others.

"The house collapsed, and all your children are dead."... Job stood up and tore his robe in grief.... In all of this, Job did not sin by blaming God. JOB 1:19-22

"Rabbi," his disciples asked [Jesus], "why was this man born blind? Was it because of his own sins or his parents' sins?" "It was not because of his sins or his parents' sins," Jesus answered. JOHN 9:2-3

Sometimes the suffering that comes to you is not your fault. It happens for reasons unknown to you. How you react to the suffering is what matters.

My child, don't reject the LORD's discipline, and don't be upset when he corrects you. For the LORD corrects those he loves, just as a father corrects a child in whom he delights. PROVERBS 3:11-12

Sometimes God sends suffering as punishment for sin. He disciplines you because he loves you and wants to correct and restore you. Thank God for this kind of suffering, because his actions to get your attention could save you from even greater consequences later.

Does suffering mean that God doesn't care about me?

You keep track of all my sorrows. You have collected all my tears in your bottle. You have recorded each one in your book. PSALM 56:8

Your suffering matters to God because you matter to God. He created you personally, and he created you for a purpose. God's care is such that not even a single tear goes unnoticed. He knows your every pain and will one day bring an end to all suffering.

[God] has not ignored or belittled the suffering of the needy. He has not turned his back on them, but has listened to their cries for help. PSALM 22:24

Suffering is not a sign of God's absence; it is a fact of life in this fallen world. God is with you in the midst of life's struggles. He may not remove them from you, but he does promise to help you get through them.

Can any good come from my suffering?

Consider the joy of those corrected by God! Do not despise the discipline of the Almighty when you sin. For though he wounds, he also bandages. He strikes, but his hands also heal. JOB 5:17-18

Each time [the Lord] said, "My grace is all you need. My power works best in weakness." So now I am glad to boast about my weaknesses, so that the power of Christ can work through me. 2 CORINTHIANS 12:9-10

During times of suffering you have the opportunity to learn and grow, so take advantage of each opportunity. It will help you to deal better with suffering in the future, and it will teach you to recognize and avoid certain troubles down the road.

When the storms of life come, the wicked are whirled away, but the godly have a lasting foundation. PROVERBS 10:25

LORD, be merciful to us, for we have waited for you. Be our strong arm each day and our salvation in times of trouble. ISAIAH 33:2

God doesn't want to see you suffer. The great message of the Bible is that God promises to bring renewal, healing, and spiritual maturity through your suffering so that you can be stronger and better equipped to help others and to live with purpose and meaning.

God is our merciful Father and the source of all comfort. He comforts us in all our troubles so that we can comfort others. When they are troubled, we will be able to give them the same comfort God has given us. For the more we suffer for Christ, the more God will shower us with his comfort through Christ. 2 CORINTHIANS 1:3-5

Suffering can make you more sensitive to God's presence in your life and also to the suffering of others.

How do I stay close to God in times of suffering?

Wasn't it clearly predicted that the Messiah would have to suffer all these things before entering his glory? LUKE 24:26

God loved the world so much that he gave his one and only Son, so that everyone who believes in him will not perish but have eternal life. JOHN 3:16

Recognize that Jesus himself suffered for you. He suffered the agonies of the cross, which was not only incredible physical suffering, but he also bore the unthinkable weight of the sins of the world.

What are God's promises in the midst of suffering?

Do not be afraid, for I have ransomed you. I have called you by name; you are mine. When you go through deep waters, I will be with you. When you go through rivers of difficulty, you will not drown. When you walk through the fire of oppression, you will not be burned up; the flames will not consume you. ISAIAH 43:1-2

You belong to the Lord. He knows you by name and will not allow anything to cause you eternal harm. You may go through deep waters of trouble and intense fires of trial and testing, but you will not go through them alone.

Weeping may last through the night, but joy comes with the morning. PSALM 30:5

Those who plant in tears will harvest with shouts of joy. They weep as they go to plant their seed, but they sing as they return with the harvest. PSALM 126:5-6

He heals the brokenhearted and bandages their wounds. PSALM 147:3

No suffering will last forever. Sometimes the only thing that keeps you going is the reminder that this time of suffering will pass. Trust that one day you will look back and it will be a memory. If you stay close to God, even your suffering can be a testimony to God's faithfulness and a reason to rejoice in what he has done through the hard times and what he is going to do for you in the future.

He will wipe every tear from their eyes, and there will be no more death or sorrow or crying or pain. All these things are gone forever. REVELATION 21:4

God promises that all suffering will one day end. There will be no more.

How can I respond to the suffering of others?

If one part suffers, all the parts suffer with it, and if one part is honored, all the parts are glad. 1 CORINTHIANS 12:26

When one Christian suffers, it should hurt us all, for we are all members of Christ's body—unified. If one part of your body hurts, it sends up sympathetic pain throughout your entire body. So it should be in the body of Christ. If you know someone who is hurting, come alongside that person to bring comfort and hope.

Going over to him, the Samaritan soothed his wounds with olive oil and wine and bandaged them. Then he put the man on his own donkey and took him to an inn, where he took care of him. LUKE 10:34

Seek to provide whatever practical support you can for a person who is suffering.

SUICIDE *See also* Coping, Death, Suffering, Worth/Worthiness

Although the Bible gives us reasons not to fear death, we should never try to end our life. Life is especially difficult for some. They may feel abandoned, or have lost everything, or be burdened with a load of guilt. But even in times when death seems like the only way out, it is important to remember that we have already been promised delivery from our troubles through Jesus Christ. Ending life, which is a precious gift from God, does not put us at peace because it deeply offends God by destroying his very own creation. Seek peace with God, and although the troubles may not immediately end, you will find the strength to live.

What does God say about suicide?

God bought you with a high price. So you must honor God with your body.
1 CORINTHIANS 6:20

Jesus paid the ultimate sacrifice for you so that you could have life. Taking your own life would go against everything Jesus taught and sacrificed.

God created human beings in his own image. In the image of God he created them; male and female he created them. GENESIS 1:27

You made all the delicate, inner parts of my body and knit me together in my mother's womb. Thank you for making me so wonderfully complex! Your workmanship is marvelous—how well I know it. You watched me as I was being formed in utter seclusion, as I was woven together in the dark of the womb. You saw me before I was born. PSALM 139:13-16

I knew you before I formed you in your mother's womb. Before you were born I set you apart. JEREMIAH 1:5

These words are not just nice poetry—they are inspired words that describe God's creation of each individual. Every person ever born was known by God before his or her birth. Human beings are God's workmanship, created by God for a purpose. Human life is God's to create and God's to end. Suicide is making a decision to end life, a decision that is God's alone.

How can I deal with thoughts I have about suicide?

Be sure of this: I am with you always, even to the end of the age. MATTHEW 28:20

Even when death seems to be the only answer, it is important to remember that you are not alone on this earth. When it seems everyone has abandoned you, God is by your side, ready to comfort and help you.

"I know the plans I have for you," says the LORD. "They are plans for good and not for disaster, to give you a future and a hope." JEREMIAH 29:11

When you are tempted by thoughts of hopelessness, remember that God created you for a reason and has a plan for you. He has plans for your future and will help you get there through the dark times.

You will search again for the LORD your God. And if you search for him with all your heart and soul, you will find him. DEUTERONOMY 4:29

If you look for God, you will find him. He loves you.

Do not be afraid or discouraged. For the LORD your God is with you wherever you go. JOSHUA 1:9

Remember that if you are a believer, you have God's Spirit within you and you can draw from God's almighty power. You don't have to win every battle on your own—God doesn't even want you to. When you ask for his help in your struggles, God will fight for you.

SUPPORT *See also* Affirmation, Giving, Help, Sharing

When building a house, the workers must build a strong foundation and a sturdy frame. Whoever will live in that house doesn't want to worry that the slightest wind will cause it to collapse on them. In fact, the future homeowners want to be sure the house will stand even in the middle of a violent storm. Our lives need a similar kind of support system—a strong foundation on which to build and a sturdy frame to keep us from falling apart when the storms of adversity pass through. Having no support system feels a lot like standing alone on a hill in a lightning storm; without shelter we will eventually be struck and will fall. God has given each of the members of his spiritual family a unique gift to share with the other members as a means of supporting one another. When each of us is offering support in the way we're designed to, the church (all those who believe in Jesus) is more solid than the strongest of buildings and ready to weather any storm.

What are some of the ways God supports me?

Answer my prayers, O LORD, for your unfailing love is wonderful. Take care of me, for your mercy is so plentiful. PSALM 69:16

You are supported by the very character of God. When you know God loves you unconditionally, that he wants what is good for you, that he forgives your sins, and that he is merciful to you even when you mess up, you feel truly supported.

Give your burdens to the LORD, and he will take care of you. He will not permit the godly to slip and fall. PSALM 55:22

When doubts filled my mind, your comfort gave me renewed hope and cheer. PSALM 94:19

God's care and comfort support you.

The LORD [said], "I will personally go with you, Moses, and I will give you rest— everything will be fine for you." EXODUS 33:14

You take care of the earth and water it, making it rich and fertile. The river of God has plenty of water; it provides a bountiful harvest of grain, for you have ordered it so. PSALM 65:9

You are supported by God's provision. He knows what you need before you ask and already has plans to meet those needs at the perfect time.

Don't be afraid, for I am with you. Don't be discouraged, for I am your God. I will strengthen you and help you. I will hold you up with my victorious right hand. ISAIAH 41:10

God's help and protection support you. In all that you do and in all that you face, you can be confident that God will strengthen you for the task and help you through it.

I will ask the Father, and he will give you another Advocate, who will never leave you. JOHN 14:16

You are supported by the Holy Spirit. In the most difficult of times, the presence of his friendship and wisdom can uplift and encourage you.

Whom should I support?

Speak up for those who cannot speak for themselves; ensure justice for those being crushed. Yes, speak up for the poor and helpless, and see that they get justice.
PROVERBS 31:8-9

The poor, helpless, and weak need to experience God's love through the giving of your time and resources.

Pure and genuine religion in the sight of God the Father means caring for orphans and widows in their distress and refusing to let the world corrupt you. JAMES 1:27

All are called to lend support to orphans and widows.

Those who won't care for their relatives, especially those in their own household, have denied the true faith. Such people are worse than unbelievers. 1 TIMOTHY 5:8

You have a special job to care for and support your family.

When God's people are in need, be ready to help them. Always be eager to practice hospitality. ROMANS 12:13

Believers need to support one another in the task of serving God.

I was hungry, and you fed me. I was thirsty, and you gave me a drink. I was a stranger, and you invited me into your home. I was naked, and you gave me clothing. I was sick, and you cared for me. I was in prison, and you visited me. . . . When you did it to one of the least of these my brothers and sisters, you were doing it to me!
MATTHEW 25:35-36, 40

As a child of God you are to be especially sensitive toward helping anyone in need.

How can I support others?

All of you should be of one mind. Sympathize with each other. Love each other as brothers and sisters. Be tenderhearted, and keep a humble attitude. 1 PETER 3:8

You can support others by being sympathetic, loving, and humble.

Confess your sins to each other and pray for each other so that you may be healed. The earnest prayer of a righteous person has great power and produces wonderful results.
JAMES 5:16

You can support others in prayer.

Jonathan went to find David and encouraged him to stay strong in his faith in God.
1 SAMUEL 23:16

All his brothers, sisters, and former friends came and feasted with him in his home. And they consoled him and comforted him because of all the trials the LORD had brought against him. And each of them brought him a gift of money and a gold ring. JOB 42:11

You can support others by encouraging them.

Moses' arms soon became so tired he could no longer hold them up. So Aaron and Hur found a stone for him to sit on. Then they stood on each side of Moses, holding up his hands. So his hands held steady until sunset. EXODUS 17:12

You can support others through your physical assistance.

Right now you have plenty and can help those who are in need. Later, they will have plenty and can share with you when you need it. In this way, things will be equal. 2 CORINTHIANS 8:14

You can support others by practically and unselfishly sharing what you have.

SURRENDER *See also* Repentance, Submission, Vulnerability

Many great battles in history concluded with surrender. One side realized it was powerless against the other, and to save themselves the soldiers admitted defeat and raised the white flag. In the spiritual realm, we fight two great battles, and surrender plays a part in both. On the one hand, we fight against sin and its control in our lives. If we are not allied with God, we will be forced to surrender to sin and its deadly consequences. On the other hand, we often foolishly fight against God and his will for us because we want to have ultimate control over our lives. This is a time when surrender is necessary and positive. Surrender to God comes when we at last realize we are powerless to defeat sin by ourselves and we give control of our life to God. It is when we are in alliance with God and when the Holy Spirit lives in us that we are able to be victorious in our battle to defeat sin and experience the greatest freedom possible.

What did Jesus Christ surrender for me?

You must have the same attitude that Christ Jesus had. Though he was God, he did not think of equality with God as something to cling to. Instead, he gave up his divine privileges; he took the humble position of a slave and was born as a human being. When he appeared in human form, he humbled himself in obedience to God and died a criminal's death on a cross. Therefore, God elevated him to the place of highest honor and gave him the name above all other names, that at the name of Jesus every knee should bow, in heaven and on earth and under the earth, and every tongue confess that Jesus Christ is Lord, to the glory of God the Father. PHILIPPIANS 2:5-11

[Christ] never sinned, but he died for sinners to bring you safely home to God. 1 PETER 3:18

Jesus Christ willingly and obediently surrendered his will to God, his Father, and his life on the cross so that you can live forever in heaven.

What does it mean to surrender my life to God?

Calling the crowd to join his disciples, [Jesus] said, "If any of you wants to be my follower, you must turn from your selfish ways, take up your cross, and follow me." MARK 8:34

When you surrender to God, you give up what you think is best for you to receive what God knows is best for you.

Since we believe that Christ died for all, we also believe that we have all died to our old life. He died for everyone so that those who receive his new life will no longer live for themselves. Instead, they will live for Christ, who died and was raised for them.
2 CORINTHIANS 5:14-15

When you surrender to God, you ask Jesus Christ to live in you and through you. What greater honor could you have than to have the Son of God accomplish his divine purposes through you?

Why surrender? Why must I give anything up?

The Kingdom of Heaven is like a treasure that a man discovered hidden in a field. In his excitement, he hid it again and sold everything he owned to get enough money to buy the field. MATTHEW 13:44-45

You gain by giving up. When you give up your agenda for God's, when you give up control of your soul to God, you gain eternal life and eternal rewards. You also gain a sense of peace and security you will never otherwise have.

If you try to hang on to your life, you will lose it. But if you give up your life for my sake, you will save it. MATTHEW 16:25

You receive life by giving up your life. When you give your temporary life here on earth to God, he gives you eternal life in exchange.

What must I surrender to God?

[The religious leader said,] "I've obeyed all these commandments since I was young." When Jesus heard his answer, he said, "There is still one thing you haven't done. Sell all your possessions and give the money to the poor, and you will have treasure in heaven. Then come, follow me." But when the man heard this he became very sad, for he was very rich. LUKE 18:21-23

Surrender anything and everything that threatens to take God's place in your heart. Anything that takes God's place of top priority in your life is an idol, a false god you have chosen to follow instead of him.

Those who belong to Christ Jesus have nailed the passions and desires of their sinful nature to his cross and crucified them there. Since we are living by the Spirit, let us follow the Spirit's leading in every part of our lives. GALATIANS 5:24-25

Surrender your sinful desires and passions to God's forgiveness, for you cannot live in the presence of a holy God with the filth of sin infecting your heart.

How do I surrender to God?

Jesus . . . prayed, "My Father! If this cup cannot be taken away unless I drink it, your will be done." MATTHEW 26:42

This world is fading away, along with everything that people crave. But anyone who does what pleases God will live forever. 1 JOHN 2:17

Ask God to help you put his will above yours. When your will takes precedence over God's will, you are proudly announcing that you know what is best for you and therefore know more than God.

God loved the world so much that he gave his one and only Son, so that everyone who believes in him will not perish but have eternal life. JOHN 3:16

If we confess our sins to him, he is faithful and just to forgive us our sins and to cleanse us from all wickedness. 1 JOHN 1:9

Believe that Jesus Christ is who he says he is—the Son of God who came to earth to show you how to get to heaven. Then accept his message as true that all people are infected with sin and need forgiveness of sin to be acceptable in God's sight. This takes humility and surrender.

If you love me, obey my commandments. . . . Those who accept my commandments and obey them are the ones who love me. And because they love me, my Father will love them. And I will love them and reveal myself to each of them. JOHN 14:15, 21

God is working in you, giving you the desire and the power to do what pleases him. PHILIPPIANS 2:13

Obedience to God requires that you surrender what you want to do and do what God wants you to do, for that is the way to a happy and fulfilled life.

We are confident that he hears us whenever we ask for anything that pleases him. 1 JOHN 5:14

Pray. Prayer requires that you surrender your desires to God's desires, that you move from asking for things for yourself to asking what you can do for others. Prayer is bringing your life into harmony with your Creator by surrendering to his will.

You must love the LORD your God with all your heart, all your soul, and all your mind. This is the first and greatest commandment. MATTHEW 22:37-38

Love God with your whole being. Surrender all of yourself—your heart, your soul, your mind—to him.

Since you have been raised to new life with Christ, set your sights on the realities of heaven, where Christ sits in the place of honor at God's right hand. Think about the things of heaven, not the things of earth. For you died to this life, and your real life is hidden with Christ in God. COLOSSIANS 3:1-3

Live life thinking about heaven. This will help you have the proper perspective on all you do.

SYMPATHY *See also* Compassion, Empathy, Sensitivity, Thoughtfulness

A sympathetic person reaches out in compassion to one in need and stands beside that person to be of comfort and help. We appreciate sympathy from others, and others appreciate sympathy from us. Love flows from a heart of sympathy like a refreshing spring, spilling over into the thirsty heart of the needy.

What is sympathy?

Did I not weep for those in trouble? Was I not deeply grieved for the needy? JOB 30:25

Be happy with those who are happy, and weep with those who weep. ROMANS 12:15

Share each other's burdens, and in this way obey the law of Christ. GALATIANS 6:2

Sympathy is putting yourself in the shoes of another. Whatever affects them affects you. Whatever they feel, you feel. When you do this, you will understand their pain and have compassion for them when they are hurting, and rejoice with them when they are happy.

Does God really sympathize with me in my time of need?

He will rescue the poor when they cry to him; he will help the oppressed, who have no one to defend them. He feels pity for the weak and the needy, and he will rescue them . . . for their lives are precious to him. PSALM 72:12-14

The LORD is like a father to his children, tender and compassionate to those who fear him. PSALM 103:13

There is no trouble that comes to you without the watchful eye of your heavenly Father seeing it and sympathizing with you. Just knowing he cares is the beginning of healing.

When he saw the crowds, he had compassion on them because they were confused and helpless, like sheep without a shepherd. MATTHEW 9:36

Jesus felt sorry for [the two blind men] and touched their eyes. Instantly they could see! Then they followed him. MATTHEW 20:34

When the Lord saw [the woman mourning], his heart overflowed with compassion. "Don't cry!" he said. LUKE 7:13

The life of Jesus is a story of tender compassion toward those in need. There is no temptation, hurt, or pain that comes into your life that does not touch his sympathetic heart.

Since he himself has gone through suffering and testing, he is able to help us when we are being tested. HEBREWS 2:18

Jesus became human and is therefore able to sympathize with your every need, including your need for strength when you are being tested.

Why is being sympathetic important?

You must show sincere love to each other as brothers and sisters. Love each other deeply with all your heart. 1 PETER 1:22

All of you should be of one mind. Sympathize with each other. Love each other as brothers and sisters. Be tenderhearted, and keep a humble attitude. 1 PETER 3:8

To be sympathetic or tenderhearted toward others is a mark of being like Jesus, which is the goal and calling of every Christian.

Four men arrived carrying a paralyzed man on a mat. They couldn't bring him to Jesus because of the crowd, so they dug a hole through the roof above his head. Then they lowered the man on his mat, right down in front of Jesus. Seeing their faith, Jesus said to the paralyzed man, "My child, your sins are forgiven." MARK 2:3-5

When I am with those who are weak, I share their weakness, for I want to bring the weak to Christ. Yes, I try to find common ground with everyone, doing everything I can to save some. 1 CORINTHIANS 9:22

Being sympathetic is a way to bring others to Jesus so that they can know him, too.

How can I show sympathy to others?

Remember those in prison, as if you were there yourself. Remember also those being mistreated, as if you felt their pain in your own bodies. HEBREWS 13:3

By feeling deeply what another person is going through. A sympathetic heart and mind more naturally reaches out to those in need.

When three of Job's friends heard of the tragedy he had suffered, they got together and traveled from their homes to comfort and console him. . . . They sat on the ground with him for seven days and nights. No one said a word to Job, for they saw that his suffering was too great for words. JOB 2:11-13

By being there. Explanations and clichés are rarely comforting. Love, sympathy, and the power of your presence are urgently needed. Sometimes the best comfort you can give is to just be there.

Many of the people had come to console Martha and Mary in their loss. JOHN 11:19

He comforts us in all our troubles so that we can comfort others. When they are troubled, we will be able to give them the same comfort God has given us. 2 CORINTHIANS 1:4

By sharing words of sympathy and encouragement.

Share your food with the hungry, and give shelter to the homeless. Give clothes to those who need them, and do not hide from relatives who need your help. ISAIAH 58:7

"Now which of these three would you say was a neighbor to the man who was attacked by bandits?" Jesus asked. The man replied, "The one who showed him mercy." Then Jesus said, "Yes, now go and do the same." LUKE 10:36-37

Let's not merely say that we love each other; let us show the truth by our actions. 1 JOHN 3:18

By helping a person in need. Sympathy is more than thoughts and feelings; it is also actions.

TEAMWORK *See also* Relationships, Sharing, Unity

Have you ever watched an enormous plane soar into the air and wonder how it does that? This large body of metal composed of thousands of complex, moving parts seems to fly effortlessly in the sky while carrying hundreds of people, monitoring hundreds of different systems, and knowing exactly where it's going. Christians should be like that plane. We are part of a larger body of believers, and each person is a complex and important piece of the body. The better each piece works, and the less it has to fight against the other pieces, the more efficiently and effortlessly the larger body functions. When we are all in our correct place and working with others as we should be, we advance the cause of the church to new heights and carry many others with us. All this is accomplished through teamwork.

What are some of the keys to successful teamwork?

Can two people walk together without agreeing on the direction? AMOS 3:3

A clear vision and mutual goals are keys to successful teamwork.

Live in harmony with each other. Let there be no divisions in the church. Rather, be of one mind, united in thought and purpose. 1 CORINTHIANS 1:10

Harmony and unity are vital in order to cooperate and work efficiently together.

At last the wall was completed to half its height around the entire city, for the people had worked with enthusiasm. NEHEMIAH 4:6

The determination and enthusiasm of a team can accomplish incredible things, especially when they have a common goal and encourage one another through the process.

Just as our bodies have many parts and each part has a special function, so it is with Christ's body. We are many parts of one body, and we all belong to each other. ROMANS 12:4-5

Genuine appreciation for the gifts and abilities of each team member, and humility to realize you're just once piece of the puzzle, promotes good teamwork. Using your gifts to fulfill your role and encouraging others to use their gifts to fulfill their role are also essential to teamwork.

Joshua did what Moses had commanded and fought the army of Amalek. Meanwhile, Moses, Aaron, and Hur climbed to the top of a nearby hill. As long as Moses held up the staff in his hand, the Israelites had the advantage. But whenever he dropped his hand, the Amalekites gained the advantage. Moses' arms soon became so tired he could no longer hold them up. So Aaron and Hur found a stone for him to sit on. Then they stood on each side of Moses, holding up his hands. So his hands held steady until sunset. As a result, Joshua overwhelmed the army of Amalek in battle. EXODUS 17:10-13

Teamwork means helping one another finish the job. Creative solutions are often the result of several people working together to solve a problem.

You are being faithful to God when you care for the traveling teachers who pass through, even though they are strangers to you. They have told the church here of your loving friendship. Please continue providing for such teachers in a manner that pleases God.
3 JOHN 1:5-6

Teamwork means supporting and encouraging each other to continue to serve and not give up.

How is teamwork an important part of the Christian life?

[Apollos and Paul] are both God's workers. And you are God's field. You are God's building. 1 CORINTHIANS 3:9

[A Christian leader's] responsibility is to equip God's people to do his work and build up the church, the body of Christ. EPHESIANS 4:12

All who serve God serve the same God. It is important that you work together to support and encourage each other. This will motivate you to greater service and help to avoid burnout. Make sure that you are well supported and that you support others in order to continue serving God. You will do your individual work better as you work together with others.

How can I team up with God in his work?

I am the vine; you are the branches. Those who remain in me, and I in them, will produce much fruit. For apart from me you can do nothing. JOHN 15:5

Recognize your dependency on God.

[Jesus prayed,] "My Father! If it is possible, let this cup of suffering be taken away from me. Yet I want your will to be done, not mine.". . . Then Jesus left them a second time and prayed, "My Father! If this cup cannot be taken away unless I drink it, your will be done." . . . So he went to pray a third time, saying the same things again. MATTHEW 26:39, 42-44

Align yourself with God's will. When your vision aligns with his, you can work for God with purpose knowing that his plans are being carried out through you.

Jesus [said], "All who love me will do what I say. My Father will love them, and we will come and make our home with each of them." JOHN 14:23

Be obedient to what God tells you to do. When you respect God in this way, he promises to support you with his presence and care.

Work willingly at whatever you do, as though you were working for the Lord rather than for people. Remember that the Lord will give you an inheritance as your reward, and that the Master you are serving is Christ. COLOSSIANS 3:23-24

Willingly accomplish whatever task God assigns to you using the talents he has given you. Be grateful that God has given you an assignment and equipped you to succeed in your tasks.

TEMPER *See also* Anger, Emotions, Overreaction, Violence

A person with a short temper is like a room filled with invisible, flammable gas; it only takes a tiny spark to cause a devastating explosion. It is important that we practice self-control, especially when it comes to our tempers. When we have our tempers under control, and someone causes a spark, our initial anger won't burst into an uncontrollable fire that threatens to consume those around us.

What causes a hot temper?

When you follow the desires of your sinful nature, the results are very clear: . . . hostility, quarreling, jealousy, outbursts of anger, selfish ambition, dissension, division . . . and other sins like these. GALATIANS 5:19-21

Your sinful nature can cause a hot temper when things don't go your way or when you don't get what you want.

Finishing is better than starting. Patience is better than pride. Control your temper, for anger labels you a fool. ECCLESIASTES 7:8-9

Impatience brings your temper to the surface.

What are some of the consequences of a hot temper?

People with understanding control their anger; a hot temper shows great foolishness. PROVERBS 14:29

A hot temper can cause you to make mistakes you will later regret. Self-control allows you to think about a situation before acting.

[Naaman said,] "Aren't the rivers of Damascus, the Abana and the Pharpar, better than any of the rivers of Israel? Why shouldn't I wash in them and be healed?" So Naaman turned and went away in a rage. But his officers tried to reason with him and said, "Sir, if the prophet had told you to do something very difficult, wouldn't you have done it? So you should certainly obey him when he says simply, 'Go and wash and be cured!'" So Naaman went down to the Jordan River and dipped himself seven times, as the man of God had instructed him. And his skin became as healthy as the skin of a young child's, and he was healed! 2 KINGS 5:12-14

A hot temper can cause you to act foolishly. Naaman's temper almost cost him his opportunity to be healed.

A person without self-control is like a city with broken-down walls. PROVERBS 25:28

An angry person starts fights; a hot-tempered person commits all kinds of sin. PROVERBS 29:22

A hot temper can lead to fights. Ironically, a short-tempered person is not prepared for confrontation.

How does a temper affect relationships?

The tongue is a small thing that makes grand speeches. But a tiny spark can set a great forest on fire. JAMES 3:5

A temper causes a great deal of damage to yourself and others. Words spoken in anger are often the most hurtful and the most memorable. Self-control is a sure defense against angry words that can alienate those you love.

Don't befriend angry people or associate with hot-tempered people, or you will learn to be like them and endanger your soul. PROVERBS 22:24-25

A mighty roar rose from the crowd, and with one voice they shouted, "Kill him, and release Barabbas to us!"... Pilate argued with them, because he wanted to release Jesus. But they kept shouting, "Crucify him! Crucify him!" For the third time he demanded, "Why? What crime has he committed? I have found no reason to sentence him to death. So I will have him flogged, and then I will release him." But the mob shouted louder and louder, demanding that Jesus be crucified, and their voices prevailed. LUKE 23:18-23

Short tempers can be contagious with like-minded people. They will join voices and soon a whole group of people have been whipped into a frenzy. Much violence has been caused by the contagious temper of one person.

How can I better control my temper?

You, O LORD, are a God of compassion and mercy, slow to get angry and filled with unfailing love and faithfulness. PSALM 86:15

Now is the time to get rid of anger, rage, malicious behavior, slander, and dirty language. Don't lie to each other, for you have stripped off your old sinful nature and all its wicked deeds. Put on your new nature, and be renewed as you learn to know your Creator and become like him. COLOSSIANS 3:8-10

God is even tempered. As you come to know God more and live under the control of his Spirit, you will be able to keep your temper in check. You will model Jesus' example through your new nature.

Always be humble and gentle. Be patient with each other, making allowance for each other's faults because of your love.... And "don't sin by letting anger control you." Don't let the sun go down while you are still angry, for anger gives a foothold to the devil. EPHESIANS 4:2, 26-27

As you rid yourself of your old sinful nature, you will treat others differently. Your new nature, rather than angry and impatient, will be humble, patient, forgiving, and peaceful.

A fool is quick-tempered, but a wise person stays calm when insulted. PROVERBS 12:16

Fools vent their anger, but the wise quietly hold it back. PROVERBS 29:11

Remain calm and do not be controlled by anger. Small personal injustices are usually not worth getting upset over.

You must all be quick to listen, slow to speak, and slow to get angry. Human anger does not produce the righteousness God desires. JAMES 1:19-20

Your anger can never make things right in God's sight.

A truly wise person uses few words; a person with understanding is even-tempered. PROVERBS 17:27

Think before speaking, and use few and gentle words until you get your anger in check.

TEMPTATION *See also* Sin, Spiritual Warfare, Testing, Vulnerability

We most often associate temptation with giving in to sin and evil. The Bible teaches that temptation to sin is Satan's main activity in our lives—although our own selfishness and appetites certainly make the tempter's work easier. Just as blood attracts a shark, so our weaknesses attract Satan's attacks. The key is to identify where you are most vulnerable—where you have the greatest tendency to sin. Then, as you work with God's help to strengthen yourself in those areas, you will be stronger to defend yourself against future attacks from Satan.

Is temptation sin?

Jesus was led by the Spirit into the wilderness to be tempted there by the devil. MATTHEW 4:1

This High Priest of ours . . . faced all of the same testings we do, yet he did not sin. HEBREWS 4:15

Jesus was severely tempted, yet he never gave in to it. Since Jesus was tempted and remained sinless, being tempted is not the same as sinning. You don't have to feel guilty about the temptations you wrestle with. Rather, you can devote yourself to resisting them.

Where does temptation come from?

The serpent was the shrewdest of all the wild animals the LORD God had made. One day he asked the woman, "Did God really say you must not eat the fruit from any of the trees in the garden?" GENESIS 3:1

Satan rose up against Israel and caused David to take a census of the people of Israel. 1 CHRONICLES 21:1

Jesus was led by the Spirit into the wilderness to be tempted there by the devil. MATTHEW 4:1

All temptation ultimately comes from Satan.

I know that nothing good lives in me, that is, in my sinful nature. I want to do what is right, but I can't. I want to do what is good, but I don't. I don't want to do what is wrong, but I do it anyway. But if I do what I don't want to do, I am not really the one doing wrong; it is sin living in me that does it. ROMANS 7:18-20

Temptation can be nurtured in your sinful human nature, and at times your decisions may invite temptation into your life.

What sorrow awaits the world, because it tempts people to sin. Temptations are inevitable, but what sorrow awaits the person who does the tempting. MATTHEW 18:7

Other people become agents of Satan when they allow him to use them as conduits of temptation. Be careful that you never cause someone to sin by tempting them.

Do not love this world nor the things it offers you, for when you love the world, you do not have the love of the Father in you. For the world offers only a craving for physical pleasure, a craving for everything we see, and pride in our achievements and possessions. These are not from the Father, but are from this world. 1 JOHN 2:15-16

The pleasures and distractions of this world are a rich source of temptation because you can easily be lured by them and find yourself paying a high price to get them.

What makes temptation so enticing?

[The woman] saw that the tree was beautiful and its fruit looked delicious . . . so she took some of the fruit and ate it. GENESIS 3:6

Satan's favorite strategy is to make that which is sinful appear to be desirable and good. In contrast, he also tries to make good look evil. If he can make evil look good and good look evil, then giving in to temptation appears right instead of wrong. You must constantly beware of this confusion he desires to create in you.

King Solomon loved many foreign women. . . . The LORD had clearly instructed the people of Israel, "You must not marry them, because they will turn your hearts to their gods." . . . And in fact, they did turn his heart away from the LORD. 1 KINGS 11:1-3

Often temptation begins in seemingly harmless pleasure, soon gets out of control, and progresses to full-blown idolatry. But the reality is that the kind of pleasure that leads to sin is never harmless. Before you give in to something that seems innocent, take a look at God's Word to see what it says. If Solomon had done this, he would have been reminded that his "pleasure" was really sin. Maybe he would have been convicted enough to stop.

Jesus was led by the Spirit into the wilderness to be tempted there by the devil. For forty days and forty nights he fasted and became very hungry. During that time the devil came and said to him, "If you are the Son of God, tell these stones to become loaves of bread." MATTHEW 4:1-3

Temptation often offers short-term attractive benefits, but with destructive, even deadly, long-term consequences. Temptation is often convincingly seasoned with partial truths twisted into lies.

How can I resist temptation?

The devil took [Jesus] to the holy city, Jerusalem, to the highest point of the Temple, and said, "If you are the Son of God, jump off! For the Scriptures say, 'He will order his angels to protect you. And they will hold you up with their hands so you won't even hurt your foot on a stone.'" Jesus responded, "The Scriptures also say, 'You must not test the Lord your God.'" MATTHEW 4:5-7

Resist the devil, and he will flee from you. JAMES 4:7

The devil has less power than you think. The devil can tempt you, but he cannot coerce you. He can dangle the bait in front of you, but he cannot force you to take it. You can resist the devil as Jesus did: by responding to the lies of temptation with the truth of God's Word.

The Spirit who lives in you is greater than the spirit who lives in the world. 1 JOHN 4:4

Every child of God defeats this evil world, and we achieve this victory through our faith. And who can win this battle against the world? Only those who believe that Jesus is the Son of God. 1 JOHN 5:4-5

Instead of thinking about your weakness, fill your mind with the promise of God's strength. Instead of thinking about what you're missing out on, think about what you'll be gaining by moving in a different direction. You have far more power available to you than you think. The Holy Spirit within you is great enough to overcome any threat against you.

Do not waste time arguing. . . . Instead, train yourself to be godly. "Physical training is good, but training for godliness is much better, promising benefits in this life and in the life to come." 1 TIMOTHY 4:7-8

The time to prepare for temptation is before it presses in on you. Train yourself in the quieter times so that you will have the spiritual wisdom, strength, and commitment to honor God in the face of intense desires and temptation.

[Joseph] ran from the house. GENESIS 39:12

If possible, remove yourself from the tempting situation. Sometimes you must literally flee.

Daniel was determined not to defile himself by eating the food. DANIEL 1:8

A solid commitment made before temptation strikes is the best prevention to sin. A certain temptation has less power over you if you have already determined that you will not yield to it.

Don't let us yield to temptation. MATTHEW 6:13

Make resisting temptation a constant focus of prayer.

A person standing alone can be attacked and defeated, but two can stand back-to-back and conquer. Three are even better, for a triple-braided cord is not easily broken. ECCLESIASTES 4:12

Enlisting a Christian friend as an accountability partner will give you far more spiritual strength than you have on your own.

The temptations in your life are no different from what others experience. . . .
When you are tempted, [God] will show you a way out so that you can endure.
1 CORINTHIANS 10:13

The Lord can lead you away from temptations. He can help you see the lies of deception that blind you. He can help you anticipate the terrible consequences that will result from giving in to what you know is wrong. He can also bring to mind the name of a friend or spiritual leader you can call to support you. Instead of thinking you have no hope for resisting, call on the Lord to lead you out of temptation.

How do I recover when I have given in to temptation?

If we confess our sins to him, he is faithful and just to forgive us our sins and to cleanse us from all wickedness. 1 JOHN 1:9

God's grace is greater than your failure. His forgiveness overcomes your sin. Temptation only wins when it keeps you from turning back to God. No matter how often you fail, God welcomes you back through the love of Jesus Christ.

Have mercy on me, O God, because of your unfailing love. Because of your great compassion, blot out the stain of my sins. Wash me clean from my guilt. . . . Purify me from my sins, and I will be clean; wash me, and I will be whiter than snow. . . . Create in me a clean heart, O God. Renew a loyal spirit within me. . . . Restore to me the joy of your salvation, and make me willing to obey you. PSALM 51:1-2, 7, 10-12

Confess your sin to God, ask for his forgiveness, accept it, and recommit yourself to obedience. Then make every effort to stay away from what got you into trouble.

TERRORISM *See also* Enemies, Evil, Fear, Persecution, Violence

While people in many parts of the world have been living for years with terrorism, the events of September 11, 2001, have impressed on Americans that terrorist attacks are a possibility for anyone in this world. The goal of terrorism is to plant fear in the hearts of people and drive a wedge of distrust between the people and their leaders. Terrorists' goals are to disrupt the economy and cause a breakdown of the society. Even though terrorism is a violent outward act of aggression, its real purpose is to destroy a people and culture from within by the fear, insecurity, and despair it produces. Satan and his demons have used these same terrorist tactics on people's souls since the beginning of time, trying to cause chaos in our lives so that we will live afraid, insecure, and more and more distrusting of God's presence and help in our daily lives. God's Word presents a whole range of counterterrorism tactics to help us avoid fear and learn to live with peace of mind and heart, whether our attackers are physical or spiritual forces.

How can I avoid living in constant fear?

The LORD is my light and my salvation—so why should I be afraid? The LORD is my fortress, protecting me from danger, so why should I tremble? PSALM 27:1

Trusting that God is in control of the world, that he is all-powerful, and that he will one day judge all people and punish the wicked can free you from crippling fear. Without this confident trust, you have no choice but to live with a great deal of insecurity. When the Bible says God protects us from danger, it means that sometimes God protects us from physical danger, but always God protects his people from the spiritual danger of losing their soul to Satan. When you commit your life to follow Jesus Christ, your eternal future is secure.

Don't be afraid of those who want to kill your body; they cannot touch your soul.
MATTHEW 10:28

The thought of dying at the hands of a terrorist attack can ironically bring peace instead of fear when you remember that your eternity is secure. When you place your allegiance with Jesus Christ, your soul is untouchable by terrorists. This can allow you to go about your life with a greater degree of normalcy.

Don't worry about tomorrow, for tomorrow will bring its own worries. Today's trouble is enough for today. MATTHEW 6:34

Refuse to panic about what might happen. You can do this by making a conscious effort to not think about what you can't control and to think only about what you can control. Fretting about the unknowable future is paralyzing and debilitating. The "what if" worries are not only a waste of your God-given imagination, but they will demoralize both your body and spirit.

Does living by faith mean I should not take precautions?

[Paul] debated with some Greek-speaking Jews, but they tried to murder him. When the believers heard about this, they took him down to Caesarea and sent him away to Tarsus, his hometown. ACTS 9:29-30

Faith is different from foolishness. Taking precautions against outside threats is wise. God calls us to combat the enemy for our own good and the long-term good of those we care about.

How should I pray with regard to terrorism?

Arise, O LORD, in anger! Stand up against the fury of my enemies! Wake up, my God, and bring justice! PSALM 7:6

It is appropriate to be outraged by acts of terrorism and to pray that God will protect you and bring terrorists to justice.

You have heard the law that says, "Love your neighbor" and hate your enemy. But I say, love your enemies! Pray for those who persecute you! MATTHEW 5:43-44

You can pray that terrorists will find God's love and that their lives will be transformed. This is complementary, not contradictory, to the prayer that God will judge terrorists.

May your Kingdom come soon. May your will be done on earth, as it is in heaven.
MATTHEW 6:10

It is important to pray not just against terrorism, but for God's purposes, and to look forward to the fulfillment of God's kingdom at the return of Jesus.

TESTING *See also* Challenges, Character, Limitations, Maturity

Students are tested regularly for retention and understanding of the material they are learning. Auto consumers routinely take "test drives" to determine the quality of the vehicle they want to purchase. Companies invest vast sums in testing their new products to guarantee they will perform as advertised. So also our character and spiritual commitments are tested by the fires of hardship, persecution, or suffering. The Bible distinguishes between temptation, which is used by Satan to lead us into sin, and testing, which is used by God to purify us and move us toward maturity and growth.

What good comes out of being tested?

God tested Abraham's faith. GENESIS 22:1

Out of Abraham's testing came a more committed faith. Just as commercial products are tested to strengthen their performance, so also God tests your faith to strengthen its resolve so that you can accomplish all God wants you to.

Jeremiah, I have made you a tester of metals, that you may determine the quality of my people. JEREMIAH 6:27

Spiritual testing reveals the impurities and sin in your heart. Once you are able to recognize your shortcomings, you can let God forgive and remove them. Testing, therefore, can result in your cleansing.

The LORD your God is testing you to see if you truly love him with all your heart and soul. DEUTERONOMY 13:3

God's testing reveals your love for him.

Remember how the LORD your God led you through the wilderness for these forty years, humbling you and testing you to prove your character, and to find out whether or not you would obey his commands. DEUTERONOMY 8:2

Testing proves character. Character is not strengthened through ease, but through adversity.

When troubles come your way, consider it an opportunity for great joy. For you know that when your faith is tested, your endurance has a chance to grow. So let it grow, for when your endurance is fully developed, you will be perfect and complete, needing nothing. JAMES 1:2-4

Testing gives you the opportunity to develop endurance. It trains you to persist to the end rather than give up before you get there.

What are some of the ways that God tests me?

When ambassadors arrived from Babylon to ask about the remarkable events that had taken place in the land, God withdrew from Hezekiah in order to test him and to see what was really in his heart. 2 CHRONICLES 32:31

God may test you through silence. Sometimes what God *doesn't* say may be more effective in getting your attention. God's eloquence is the effectiveness of his communication, not the quantity of his words.

God tested Abraham's faith. "Abraham!" God called. "Yes," he replied. "Here I am." "Take your son, your only son—yes, Isaac, whom you love so much—and go to the land of Moriah. Go and sacrifice him as a burnt offering on one of the mountains, which I will show you."... When they arrived at the place where God had told him to go, Abraham built an altar and arranged the wood on it. Then he tied his son, Isaac, and laid him on the altar on top of the wood. And Abraham picked up the knife to kill his son as a sacrifice. At that moment the angel of the LORD called to him from heaven, "Abraham! Abraham!... Don't lay a hand on the boy!" the angel said. "Do not hurt him in any way, for now I know that you truly fear God. You have not withheld from me even your son, your only son." GENESIS 22:1-2, 9-12

God may test you through sacrifice. What you're willing to give up for God reveals more than what you keep for yourself.

Trials will show that your faith is genuine. It is being tested as fire tests and purifies gold. ... So when your faith remains strong through many trials, it will bring you much praise and glory and honor on the day when Jesus Christ is revealed to the whole world. 1 PETER 1:7

God may test you through problems and trials. While no one wants troubles in life, most of us desire the healthy benefits and rewards they bring.

I have refined you, but not as silver is refined. Rather, I have refined you in the furnace of suffering. ISAIAH 48:10

God may test you through suffering. The depth of your faith will be revealed during times of suffering.

To keep me from becoming proud, I was given a thorn in my flesh, a messenger from Satan to torment me and keep me from becoming proud. Three different times I begged the Lord to take it away. Each time he said, "My grace is all you need. My power works best in weakness." So now I am glad to boast about my weaknesses, so that the power of Christ can work through me. 2 CORINTHIANS 12:7-9

God may test you through your weaknesses. Only when you acknowledge your weaknesses can you invite God's strength to work through you.

Put me on trial, LORD, and cross-examine me. Test my motives and my heart. For I am always aware of your unfailing love, and I have lived according to your truth. PSALM 26:2-3

God may test you through life choices. The road you choose will always determine the destination you reach. The choices you make will always determine the consequences.

How can I know when I have passed God's tests?

Merely listening to the law doesn't make us right with God. It is obeying the law that makes us right in his sight. ROMANS 2:13

We can be sure that we know him if we obey his commandments. If someone claims, "I know God," but doesn't obey God's commandments, that person is a liar and is not living in the truth. 1 JOHN 2:3-4

You know you have passed one of God's tests when you have obeyed his Word rather than given in to sin. God has given you the gift of your conscience to confirm whether you have passed his test or failed it.

THANKFULNESS *See also* Blessings, Praise, Satisfaction, Worship

A loving mate works hard all day at the office or at home. Do we bother to say thanks? Think about how often in a day someone does something for us, however small. Do we remember to thank them? Now think about how often God helps us in life. Think about how much God has given us. When we pause to thank God, we recognize that he has a track record of blessing us, providing for us, and protecting us. How often do we say thanks to him? Giving thanks is a way to celebrate both the giver and the gift. Celebrate often!

Why should I give thanks to God?

Give thanks to the LORD, for he is good! His faithful love endures forever. 1 CHRONICLES 16:34

Give thanks to God because he is good, kind, and loving. Thanking God for his character helps you more fully appreciate and respect those qualities in him and in others.

[The man cured of leprosy] fell to the ground at Jesus' feet, thanking him for what he had done. LUKE 17:16

A thankful heart shows that you recognize God's work in your life.

Thank God for this gift too wonderful for words! 2 CORINTHIANS 9:15

Thank God because of the gift of his Son, Jesus, who paid the price for your sin and calls you his friend.

Give thanks to the LORD and proclaim his greatness. Let the whole world know what he has done. 1 CHRONICLES 16:8

By giving thanks to God, you can show others what he has done in your life and invite them into relationship with him.

Let your roots grow down into him, and let your lives be built on him. Then . . . you will overflow with thankfulness. COLOSSIANS 2:7

A life characterized by thankfulness is pleasing to God and others.

Even though the fig trees have no blossoms, and there are no grapes on the vines; even though the olive crop fails, and the fields lie empty and barren; even though the flocks die in the fields, and the cattle barns are empty, yet I will rejoice in the LORD! I will be joyful in the God of my salvation! HABAKKUK 3:17-18

A spirit of gratitude and praise changes the way you look at life. Complaining connects you to your unhappiness; gratitude and praise connect you to the source of real joy. When you make thanksgiving a regular part of your life, you stay focused on all God has done and continues to do for you. Expressing gratitude for God's help is a form of worship.

What can I be thankful for?

Jesus took the five loaves and two fish, looked up toward heaven, and blessed them. MARK 6:41

You can thank God for providing life's basic needs, such as food, clothing, shelter, oxygen, and life itself.

I trust in your unfailing love. I will rejoice because you have rescued me. I will sing to the LORD because he is good to me. PSALM 13:5-6

You can thank God for helping you through your troubles. It is often through the difficult times that you grow the most.

You are the one who gives us victory. PSALM 44:7

You can thank God when you have experienced success.

Whatever is good and perfect comes down to us from God our Father, who created all the lights in the heavens. He never changes or casts a shifting shadow. JAMES 1:17

You can thank God for everything good in your world and in your life.

God loved the world so much that he gave his one and only Son, so that everyone who believes in him will not perish but have eternal life. JOHN 3:16

Anyone who belongs to Christ has become a new person. The old life is gone; a new life has begun! 2 CORINTHIANS 5:17

You can thank God for his gift of salvation which brings a new start to life and peace with God.

Why is it important to have a thankful attitude?

O my people, listen as I speak. . . . I am God, your God! . . . Giving thanks is a sacrifice that truly honors me. If you keep to my path, I will reveal to you the salvation of God. PSALM 50:7, 23

It is good to give thanks to the LORD, to sing praises to the Most High. PSALM 92:1

When you give thanks to God, you honor and praise him for what he has done—in your life, in the lives of others, in the church, and in the world. Similarly, you honor others when you give thanks to them, respecting them for who they are and what they have done. This attitude of gratitude prevents you from expecting others to serve you and allows you to enjoy whatever blessings come your way.

How do I develop an attitude of thanksgiving in myself and my family?

I will praise you, Lord, with all my heart; I will tell of all the marvelous things you have done. PSALM 9:1

Since everything God created is good, we should not reject any of it but receive it with thanks. 1 TIMOTHY 4:4

Cultivate thankfulness by giving thanks regularly—to God and also to others. Set aside time every day to think about things you are thankful for. Make a mental list of God's blessings in your life—especially the most recent ones—and thank him for them. Don't wait to feel thankful before giving thanks. Giving thanks will lead you to feel thankful.

How can I express my thankfulness?

David gave to Asaph and his fellow Levites [a] song of thanksgiving to the Lord. 1 CHRONICLES 16:7

Sing psalms and hymns and spiritual songs to God with thankful hearts. COLOSSIANS 3:16

With music and singing.

Enter his gates with thanksgiving; go into his courts with praise. Give thanks to him and praise his name. PSALM 100:4

Praise the Lord! I will thank the Lord with all my heart as I meet with his godly people. How amazing are the deeds of the Lord! All who delight in him should ponder them. PSALM 111:1-2

Through worship and praise with other believers.

As I learn your righteous regulations, I will thank you by living as I should! PSALM 119:7

Through obedience and service.

When should I give thanks to the Lord?

It is good to proclaim your unfailing love in the morning, your faithfulness in the evening, PSALM 92:2

Every morning and evening.

Jesus took the five loaves and two fish, looked up toward heaven, and blessed them. LUKE 9:16

When you are about to eat.

Always be thankful. COLOSSIANS 3:15

Constantly and consistently.

How can I thank God when life is difficult?
Be thankful in all circumstances, for this is God's will for you who belong to Christ Jesus.
1 THESSALONIANS 5:18

Life can be difficult for many reasons. You may experience the consequences of your own sin; you may suffer because of someone else's sin; you may be caught in circumstances that are no one's fault but are nonetheless unfortunate. God may be testing your faith, or you may be a target of Satan, who wants to disrupt your godly influence and discourage you. In any of these tough circumstances, there is a reason to thank God. He redeems your mistakes, teaches you wisdom through adversity, promises to help you through tough times, and guarantees eternal life free from suffering for all who are his followers. A God who redeems all trouble is a God worthy of praise and thanksgiving.

What are the consequences of an unthankful heart?
People will love only themselves and their money. They will be boastful and proud, scoffing at God, disobedient to their parents, and ungrateful. They will consider nothing sacred. They will be unloving and unforgiving; they will slander others and have no self-control. . . . They will act religious, but they will reject the power that could make them godly. Stay away from people like that! 2 TIMOTHY 3:2-5

A consistently ungrateful attitude will eventually turn you into a bitter and mean-spirited person.

Hezekiah did not respond appropriately to the kindness shown him, and he became proud. So the LORD's anger came against him. 2 CHRONICLES 32:25

An unthankful heart leads to pride and cynicism, which builds a wall to keep you from God.

THOUGHTFULNESS   *See also* Caring, Kindness, Sensitivity, Service
Thoughtfulness is shown through selfless acts of kindness that flow from an attitude of genuine love and affection for others. Selfish people cannot be thoughtful because they think only of themselves. They do things for others as a means of getting what they want, and their acts are self-serving at best and will soon be forgotten. But thoughtful people are attentive to others, focusing on their needs and finding ways to meet them. A thoughtful act helps someone else feel valued, important, and cared for, and those acts of kindness will be remembered. Are you kind to others for your own gain or for theirs? That is the true test of thoughtfulness.

How is God thoughtful toward me?
How precious are your thoughts about me, O God. They cannot be numbered!
PSALM 139:17

O LORD, what are human beings that you should notice them, mere mortals that you should think about them? PSALM 144:3

God loved the world so much that he gave his one and only Son, so that everyone who believes in him will not perish but have eternal life. JOHN 3:16

God does more than notice you; he thinks continually about you and constantly acts on your behalf. God cares for you with the deepest kind of love. His compassion moves him to meet your needs as best evidenced by the sending of his Son, Jesus, to die for your sins.

What does it mean to be thoughtful?

Don't be selfish; don't try to impress others. Be humble, thinking of others as better than yourselves. Don't look out only for your own interests, but take an interest in others, too. PHILIPPIANS 2:3-4

Since God chose you to be the holy people he loves, you must clothe yourselves with tenderhearted mercy, kindness, humility, gentleness, and patience. COLOSSIANS 3:12

Thoughtful people meet the needs of others with mercy, kindness, humility, gentleness, and patience.

How can I be thoughtful of others?

Sympathize with each other. Love each other as brothers and sisters. Be tenderhearted, and keep a humble attitude. 1 PETER 3:8

You can be more thoughtful of others by trying to understand their point of view so that you can sympathize with them.

We who are strong must be considerate of those who are sensitive about things like this. We must not just please ourselves. We should help others do what is right and build them up in the Lord. ROMANS 15:1-2

You can be more thoughtful of others by considering what bothers their conscience. If you are confident that something you are doing is okay with God, but your friend is not, then don't do it when you are together.

As apostles of Christ we certainly had a right to make some demands of you, but instead we were like children among you. Or we were like a mother feeding and caring for her own children. 1 THESSALONIANS 2:7

You can be thoughtful of others by giving up some of your "rights" of power or authority in order to come alongside them and help them.

Be quick to listen, slow to speak, and slow to get angry. JAMES 1:19

You can be thoughtful of others by carefully listening and thinking before speaking.

Worry weighs a person down; an encouraging word cheers a person up. PROVERBS 12:25

You can be thoughtful by encouraging others with cheerful and positive words.

Do not withhold good from those who deserve it when it's in your power to help them.
PROVERBS 3:27

If your gift is to encourage others, be encouraging. If it is giving, give generously. If God has given you leadership ability, take the responsibility seriously. And if you have a gift for showing kindness to others, do it gladly. ROMANS 12:8

You can be thoughtful by remembering that God has equipped you to meet the needs of others. This gives you a different perspective on being more sensitive to others and reaching out to them with the gifts God has already given you.

What are the results of thoughtfulness?

God has put the body together such that extra honor and care are given to those parts that have less dignity. This makes for harmony among the members, so that all the members care for each other. If one part suffers, all the parts suffer with it, and if one part is honored, all the parts are glad. 1 CORINTHIANS 12:24-26

Thoughtfulness brings harmony and equal concern for all.

I was naked, and you gave me clothing. I was sick, and you cared for me. I was in prison, and you visited me. MATTHEW 25:36

Someone's needs will be met through your thoughtfulness.

Ruth fell at his feet and thanked him warmly. "What have I done to deserve such kindness?" she asked. "I am only a foreigner." "Yes, I know," Boaz replied. "But I also know about everything you have done for your mother-in-law since the death of your husband. I have heard how you left your father and mother and your own land to live here among complete strangers." RUTH 2:10-11

Others notice thoughtfulness. Your thoughtfulness inspires others to respond with thoughtfulness.

Your kindness will reward you, but your cruelty will destroy you. PROVERBS 11:17

You reward yourself when you are kind to others.

THOUGHTS *See also* Attitude, Character, Heart, Motives, Wisdom

Our mind is something we consider to be private—a place where we can retreat into. But there is one person who knows our every thought—God. We can appear to be as pure as gold on the outside, but deep down in our core, our thought life is who we really are. Even without verbalizing them, our thoughts have a way of revealing themselves through our actions. Our thoughts come from our heart, so if we're unhappy with our thoughts, we've got to go to the source of our thought life—the heart—to begin changing there.

How can I please God with my thoughts?

I lie awake thinking of you, meditating on you through the night. Because you are my helper, I sing for joy in the shadow of your wings. PSALM 63:6-7

May all my thoughts be pleasing to him, for I rejoice in the LORD. PSALM 104:34

God is pleased when you think about him. What you think about reveals what you're really like on the inside. In other words, the quality of your thoughts is an important measure of the quality of your heart. For example, if you are consistently grateful for what you have, those thoughts of gratitude come from a grateful heart. If you are constantly complaining about your circumstances, the negative thoughts are coming to your mind from an ungrateful heart. When you change your heart to focus on thankfulness, praise, love, and joy then your thoughts will soon follow.

Oh, the joys of those who do not follow the advice of the wicked, or stand around with sinners, or join in with mockers. But they delight in the law of the LORD, meditating on it day and night. PSALM 1:1-2

God is pleased when you think about his Word, because his Word reveals who he is.

Remember the wonders he has performed, his miracles, and the rulings he has given. 1 CHRONICLES 16:12

I recall all you have done, O LORD; I remember your wonderful deeds of long ago. They are constantly in my thoughts. I cannot stop thinking about your mighty works. PSALM 77:11-12

God is pleased when you think about all he has done for you—the beauty of his creation, his miracles, and his care for you.

Since you have been raised to new life with Christ, set your sights on the realities of heaven, where Christ sits in the place of honor at God's right hand. Think about the things of heaven, not the things of earth. For you died to this life, and your real life is hidden with Christ in God. COLOSSIANS 3:1-3

God is pleased when you think about his ways—the principles by which he set the world in motion, how good will prevail over evil, the wonder of salvation, and the promise of eternal life.

Don't be concerned for your own good but for the good of others. 1 CORINTHIANS 10:24

Let us think of ways to motivate one another to acts of love and good works. HEBREWS 10:24

God is pleased when you think of ways to help and motivate others.

How can I improve my thoughts so they are pleasing to God?

I have hidden your word in my heart, that I might not sin against you. PSALM 119:11

Focus on reading the Scriptures to the church, encouraging the believers, and teaching them. . . . Give your complete attention to these matters. 1 TIMOTHY 4:13-15

Study and think about God's Word continually, and let his thoughts fill your mind. As your mind becomes more and more in harmony with his, your heart will, too.

It is what comes from inside that defiles you. For from within, out of a person's heart, come evil thoughts, sexual immorality, theft, murder, adultery, greed, wickedness, deceit, lustful desires, envy, slander, pride, and foolishness. All these vile things come from within; they are what defile you. MARK 7:20-23

Don't let your mind dwell on sinful thoughts. Bad thoughts will inevitably pop into your mind at times; it's when you encourage them to stay that you get in trouble. When bad thoughts come to mind, don't entertain them but immediately turn to God in prayer.

Search me, O God, and know my heart; test me and know my anxious thoughts. PSALM 139:23

Develop a real desire to invite God into your thought life to hold you more accountable.

Fix your thoughts on what is true, and honorable, and right, and pure, and lovely, and admirable. Think about things that are excellent and worthy of praise. PHILIPPIANS 4:8

Make a conscious effort to practice thinking good thoughts, just like you might practice some other skill. These thoughts might be about the good in your life that you can be thankful for, the good in others that you appreciate, the good that you might do for others, and the goodness of God in providing your earthly blessings and in promising you eternal life.

Think about the things of heaven, not the things of earth. For you died to this life, and your real life is hidden with Christ in God. COLOSSIANS 3:2-3

Think more about heaven, because someday it will be your eternal home.

Let God transform you into a new person by changing the way you think. Then you will learn to know God's will for you, which is good and pleasing and perfect. ROMANS 12:2

Be prepared to let God radically change what you think about and the way you think.

Is it sinful to think about committing sin?

There are six things the LORD hates—no, seven things he detests: . . . a heart that plots evil . . . PROVERBS 6:16-18

You have heard the commandment that says, "You must not commit adultery." But I say, anyone who even looks at a woman with lust has already committed adultery with her in his heart. MATTHEW 5:27-28

It is possible to sin without committing a physical act. Both the Old and New Testaments clearly point out that your thoughts are as important as your actions.

How can I discipline my mind to think more like God?

Who can know the LORD's thoughts? Who knows enough to teach him? But we understand these things, for we have the mind of Christ. 1 CORINTHIANS 2:16

Make a deliberate commitment to seek the help of the Holy Spirit to regularly cleanse your mind of bad thoughts and renew your mind with good thoughts.

Those who are dominated by the sinful nature think about sinful things, but those who are controlled by the Holy Spirit think about things that please the Spirit. ROMANS 8:5

"Don't handle! Don't taste! Don't touch!" Such rules are mere human teachings about things that deteriorate as we use them. These rules may seem wise because they require strong devotion, pious self-denial, and severe bodily discipline. But they provide no help in conquering a person's evil desires. COLOSSIANS 2:21-23

A disciplined mind will not come by just obeying rules, or on your own strength. It will be the result of seeking God's supernatural help in taking control over your mind.

What are the benefits of a more godly thought life?

You will keep in perfect peace all who trust in you, all whose thoughts are fixed on you! ISAIAH 26:3

Peace of mind.

We have not stopped praying for you since we first heard about you. We ask God to give you complete knowledge of his will and to give you spiritual wisdom and understanding. COLOSSIANS 1:9

Understanding, wisdom, and discernment.

Since you have been raised to new life with Christ, set your sights on the realities of heaven, where Christ sits in the place of honor at God's right hand. Think about the things of heaven, not the things of earth. COLOSSIANS 3:1-2

A more godly perspective on life.

The way you live will always honor and please the Lord, and your lives will produce every kind of good fruit. All the while, you will grow as you learn to know God better and better. COLOSSIANS 1:10

Actions that are more pure because of a deepened relationship with God.

TIME *See also* Busyness, Eternity, Priorities, Timing of God

Time is a lot like battery energy—we rarely know how much is left until it's gone. With time, unlike batteries, we cannot buy more or borrow more from someone else. That is why time is so valuable to us, and yet we often live as though it means so little. All of us would admit we waste far too much time in doing things that aren't important or significant. We know we should be more purposeful about how we spend our time, but we're often unsure just what that is. The Bible is clear that how we use our precious little time on earth will have an effect that lasts for eternity. We seem to live by the phrase, "So much to do, so little time." But God does not ask us to do everything, just everything he has called us to do, and he assures us that there is time for whatever this is. The more we can invest in discovering the purpose for which God created us and how to live out that purpose with obedience and responsibility, the more meaningful and significant our time on earth will become.

How does God view time?

For everything there is a season, a time for every activity under heaven.... [God] has planted eternity in the human heart, but even so, people cannot see the whole scope of God's work from beginning to end. ECCLESIASTES 3:1, 11

You must not forget this one thing, dear friends: A day is like a thousand years to the Lord, and a thousand years is like a day. 2 PETER 3:8

While God is eternal and not bound by time, he honors time and your careful use of it.

How can I best use my time?

Teach us to realize the brevity of life, so that we may grow in wisdom. PSALM 90:12

Valuing time begins with seeing it from God's perspective. When you do, you learn that although life is short, there is always time for accomplishing God's plans.

Be careful how you live. Don't live like fools, but like those who are wise. Make the most of every opportunity in these evil days. Don't act thoughtlessly, but understand what the Lord wants you to do. Don't be drunk with wine, because that will ruin your life. Instead, be filled with the Holy Spirit, singing psalms and hymns and spiritual songs among yourselves, and making music to the Lord in your hearts. EPHESIANS 5:15-19

When you use your time to do good, no opportunity is wasted.

God blesses the one who reads the words of this prophecy to the church, and he blesses all who listen to its message and obey what it says, for the time is near. REVELATION 1:3

Live each day as though it may be your last. The promise of Jesus' return should inspire your commitment to faithfulness and help you keep a proper perspective on the fleeting nature of earthly life.

You can make many plans, but the LORD's purpose will prevail. PROVERBS 19:21

A prudent person foresees danger and takes precautions. The simpleton goes blindly on and suffers the consequences. PROVERBS 22:3

Don't begin until you count the cost. For who would begin construction of a building without first calculating the cost to see if there is enough money to finish it? LUKE 14:28

Planning demonstrates your desire to use your time wisely and makes you a good steward of the time and resources God has given you. So make your plans, but hold them loosely so that you can adjust them if God gives you new marching orders.

How can I find the time I need?

Remember to observe the Sabbath day by keeping it holy. You have six days each week for your ordinary work, but the seventh day is a Sabbath day of rest dedicated to the LORD your God.... For in six days the LORD made the heavens, the earth, the sea, and everything in them; but on the seventh day he rested. That is why the LORD blessed the Sabbath day and set it apart as holy. EXODUS 20:8-11

Believe it or not, the best way to have the time you need is to devote time to God for worship and to yourself for rest. Devoting time to God gives you spiritual refreshment and the opportunity to hear his priorities for you. Devoting time to rest gives you physical refreshment and the energy to do what you are called to do.

TIMING OF GOD *See also* Guidance, Opportunities, Will of God

How we hate to wait! Even trivial delays like red lights or slow cashier lines can make us edgy, even angry. And it can be especially frustrating when God does not act, even though we have prayed and it seems obvious that what we are praying for is right and good. How hard it is to accept that God's timing is usually different from ours. And it's even harder to accept that his timing is best for us because we can't see what's up ahead. We want what's best for us now. As the old saying puts it: God is rarely early, but he's never late.

How was Jesus' life an example of God's perfect timing?

The leaders tried to arrest [Jesus]; but no one laid a hand on him, because his time had not yet come. JOHN 7:30

Christ came at just the right time and died for us sinners. ROMANS 5:6

When the right time came, God sent his Son. GALATIANS 4:4

The Hebrew people had been longing for the Messiah for centuries, yet God sent Jesus to earth at just the right time. You may not fully understand why this was perfect timing until you get to heaven and see God's complete plan, but you can be assured that God sent Jesus at the time when the most people would be reached with the Good News of salvation.

At the right time he will bring everything together under the authority of Christ— everything in heaven and on earth. EPHESIANS 1:10

If Jesus' first coming was timed exactly right, we can be confident that his second coming will also be right on schedule.

Can I trust God's timing in my life?

You saw me before I was born. Every day of my life was recorded in your book. Every moment was laid out before a single day had passed. PSALM 139:16

O LORD, I will honor and praise your name, for you are my God. You do such wonderful things! You planned them long ago, and now you have accomplished them. ISAIAH 25:1

Many times God will intervene in your life at a special time and in a special way. Watch for those times, and then praise God that you can play a part, even if it is a small one, in the movement of God in this world.

What are the benefits of waiting for God's timing?

I waited patiently for the LORD to help me, and he turned to me and heard my cry. PSALM 40:1

I wait quietly before God, for my victory comes from him. . . . Let all that I am wait quietly before God, for my hope is in him. PSALM 62:1, 5

The ability to wait quietly for something is evidence of a strong character. Waiting on the Lord is the patient confidence that what he promises for your life now and in the future will come true. When you are able to wait quietly for God to act without becoming restless and agitated, you show that you fully trust his timing. What a confident and peaceful way to live!

My life seems to be on hold right now. Has God forgotten me?

Pharaoh's chief cup-bearer, however, forgot all about Joseph, never giving him another thought. GENESIS 40:23

David was thirty years old when he began to reign, and he reigned forty years in all. 2 SAMUEL 5:4

I cry out to God Most High, to God who will fulfill his purpose for me. PSALM 57:2

Jesus was about thirty years old when he began his public ministry. LUKE 3:23

I know the one in whom I trust, and I am sure that he is able to guard what I have entrusted to him until the day of his return. 2 TIMOTHY 1:12

Because of a cupbearer's forgetfulness, Joseph spent two additional years in prison. David was anointed as the next king of Israel when he was just a boy, but he did not reign until he was thirty years old. Much of that time was spent in running from King Saul. Jesus began his ministry when he was thirty. Paul spent much time in prison for his faith. While you might think God shouldn't have "wasted" their time, God knew better. David's waiting prepared him for the great work God called him to do. Paul's waiting gave him time to write several books of the New Testament. Your time "on hold" is not wasted if you are serving God right where you are. Trust that God's timing is better than your own. He is actively working in your life to help you become all he made you to be.

I keep praying to you, LORD, hoping this time you will show me favor. In your unfailing love, O God, answer my prayer with your sure salvation. PSALM 69:13

Rejoice in our confident hope. Be patient in trouble, and keep on praying. ROMANS 12:12

Keep praying, be patient, and stay alert as you wait for God to show you your next assignment.

TIREDNESS *See also* Balance, Limitations, Rest, Spiritual Dryness

God made us flesh-and-blood human beings. He set aside one full day of rest in seven at Creation because he knew we would need it. Jesus lived in a human body, so he understands what it means to be tired. He understood the limitations of his disciples and took them away for regular breaks. Life is full and busy, and must be balanced by regular attention to the health of our body and soul. Being overly tired is dangerous because it can keep us from thinking clearly and cause us to do or say something we'll regret. But when it's impossible to get enough rest, our weariness is an opportunity to experience God's faithfulness.

Why am I so tired?

Is not all human life a struggle? Our lives are like that of a hired hand, like a worker who longs for the shade, like a servant waiting to be paid. I, too, have been assigned months of futility, long and weary nights of misery. JOB 7:1-3

The struggles of life can be tiring when they are relentless and seem futile.

I have worked hard and long, enduring many sleepless nights. I have been hungry and thirsty and have often gone without food. I have shivered in the cold, without enough clothing to keep me warm. 2 CORINTHIANS 11:27

You may be tired because you are constantly lacking necessities.

Don't wear yourself out trying to get rich. Be wise enough to know when to quit. In the blink of an eye wealth disappears, for it will sprout wings and fly away like an eagle. PROVERBS 23:4-5

You may be tired because you are striving too hard for something that isn't worth it.

We grow weary in our present bodies, and we long to put on our heavenly bodies like new clothing. 2 CORINTHIANS 5:2

We, too, are weak. 2 CORINTHIANS 13:4

You may be tired because your body is aging and slowing down. As you grow older and face the limitations of your body, you long for the new body you will receive in heaven.

I am dying from grief; my years are shortened by sadness. Sin has drained my strength; I am wasting away from within. PSALM 31:10

You may be tired because grief has drained your strength.

It is useless for you to work so hard from early morning until late at night, anxiously working for food to eat; for God gives rest to his loved ones. PSALM 127:2

Always being tired may mean you are trying to do too much. It may be God's way of telling you to slow down.

Who can help me when I grow tired?

The Sovereign LORD is my strength! He makes me as surefooted as a deer, able to tread upon the heights. HABAKKUK 3:19

Be strong in the Lord and in his mighty power. EPHESIANS 6:10

When you are weary, tap into the Lord's power and strength. It is not some fable or fairy tale, but real supernatural power from the one who created you and sustains you.

Think of all the hostility [Jesus] endured from sinful people; then you won't become weary and give up. . . . Take a new grip with your tired hands and strengthen your weak knees. HEBREWS 12:3, 12

When you are most tempted to give up, it helps to remind yourself of the endurance of Jesus Christ. Though fully divine, Jesus was also fully human. At times he felt hungry, sad, and tired. He looked to his Father for strength and found the power for his every need. That same power is available to you if you seek it.

They brought sleeping mats, cooking pots, serving bowls, wheat and barley, flour and roasted grain, beans, lentils, honey, butter, sheep, goats, and cheese for David and those who were with him. For they said, "You must all be very hungry and tired and thirsty after your long march through the wilderness." 2 SAMUEL 17:28-29

As [Elijah] was sleeping, an angel touched him and told him, "Get up and eat!". . . So he ate and drank and lay down again. Then the angel of the LORD came again and touched him and said, "Get up and eat some more, or the journey ahead will be too much for you." So he got up and ate and drank. 1 KINGS 19:5-8

Take good care of your body: Exercise, rest, and eat nutritious meals. These activities will help you overcome weariness. Poor nutrition or health habits invite burnout.

What do I have to watch out for when I'm tired?

Let's not get tired of doing what is good. At just the right time we will reap a harvest of blessing if we don't give up. GALATIANS 6:9

Being tired makes you more susceptible to discouragement, temptation, and sin and causes you to lose hope that things will change in the future.

I am weary, O God; I am weary and worn out, O God. I am too stupid to be human, and I lack common sense. PROVERBS 30:1-2

Being tired causes you to lose perspective. When you're weary is not a good time to try to make important decisions.

Everything is wearisome beyond description. No matter how much we see, we are never satisfied. ECCLESIASTES 1:8

Being tired can cause you to lose your vision and purpose.

Ahithophel urged Absalom, "Let me choose 12,000 men to start out after David tonight. I will catch up with him while he is weary and discouraged. He and his troops will panic, and everyone will run away. Then I will kill only the king." 2 SAMUEL 17:1-2

Weariness makes you vulnerable to your enemies. When your guard is down, it's easier for them to attack you.

TITHING *See also* Giving, Money, Priorities, Stewardship

Tithing is not just a religious law. Tithing is both practical and symbolic. Practically, tithing is a means of supporting the church and the work of God around the world. When we give, we do so because we believe in the church and the work it is doing. Symbolically, giving the first part of our earnings to the Lord demonstrates that he is our number one priority and that we are grateful for the blessings he has given us. When we tithe, we are not only supporting one another, we are showing our commitment to God and honoring him for his provision and faithfulness. A habit of regular tithing helps keep God at the top of your priority list and gives you a proper perspective on the rest of your paycheck. Instead of asking, "How much of my money do I need to give to God?" ask yourself, "How much of God's money do I need to keep for myself?"

Why did God require tithes from Israel in the Old Testament?

The LORD said, . . . "I am your share and your allotment. . . . The Levites will receive no allotment of land among the Israelites, because I have given them the Israelites' tithes, which have been presented as sacred offerings to the LORD. This will be the Levites' share. That is why I said they would receive no allotment of land among the Israelites."
NUMBERS 18:20, 23-24

The tithes were necessary to support the priesthood—the ordained spiritual leaders who were responsible for Israel's worship and spiritual life.

You must set aside a tithe of your crops—one-tenth of all the crops you harvest each year. . . . Doing this will teach you always to fear the LORD your God.
DEUTERONOMY 14:22-23

Giving one-tenth of their income to God taught the Israelites to make him a priority, to acknowledge their dependence on him, to keep him a regular part of their lives, and to learn to sacrifice for the well-being of others.

Am I required to tithe to God today?

Elders who do their work well should be respected and paid well, especially those who work hard at both preaching and teaching. For the Scripture says, "You must not muzzle an ox to keep it from eating as it treads out the grain." 1 TIMOTHY 5:17-18

The need to support the spiritual leaders of the church financially has not changed from the Old to the New Testament.

At the moment I have all I need—and more! I am generously supplied with the gifts you sent me with Epaphroditus. They are a sweet-smelling sacrifice that is acceptable and pleasing to God. PHILIPPIANS 4:18

While you may wonder what value the little bit that you can offer God could have, remember that the purpose of tithing is to give you the privilege of participating in God's work. Giving to God can help you learn, like Israel in the Old Testament, to give to meet the needs of others just as God gives to meet your needs.

Honor the LORD with your wealth and with the best part of everything you produce.
PROVERBS 3:9

Giving the firstfruits of your income to God honors him by demonstrating that he has first priority in your life.

[Jesus said to the religious leaders,] "You should tithe." MATTHEW 23:23

The amount you give will determine the amount you get back. LUKE 6:38

You must each decide in your heart how much to give. And don't give reluctantly or in response to pressure. "For God loves a person who gives cheerfully." 2 CORINTHIANS 9:7

Old Testament law made it clear that God wanted his people to tithe—to give him the first tenth of their income to demonstrate obedience and trust that he would provide for them. When Jesus came, he made it clear that God loves a cheerful giver. This means that he loves a generous heart. Whatever the amount, you should honor the Lord with your resources so that his work on earth can continue. God promises to bless you lavishly if you give lavishly.

How does tithing affect my own finances?

"Bring all the tithes into the storehouse so there will be enough food in my Temple. If you do," says the LORD of Heaven's Armies, "I will open the windows of heaven for you. I will pour out a blessing so great you won't have enough room to take it in! Try it! Put me to the test!" MALACHI 3:10

God promises to meet your needs far above your gifts to him. Tithing is God's means of supplying for a variety of needs for his people. As you fulfill his command to meet others' needs, he graciously meets—and exceeds—your own.

Give, and you will receive. Your gift will return to you in full—pressed down, shaken together to make room for more, running over, and poured into your lap. The amount you give will determine the amount you get back. LUKE 6:38

You cannot out-give God. While you do not give in order to get, God blesses you in response to your giving.

Can I tithe my time?

Be careful how you live. . . . Make the most of every opportunity in these evil days. Don't act thoughtlessly, but understand what the Lord wants you to do. EPHESIANS 5:15-17

It's so easy to waste time. How many times have you said, "I don't know where my day went"? Here's a suggestion for using your time more wisely. You've heard people tell you to tithe your money (by giving one-tenth of your money to God). Try tithing your time by giving one-tenth of your time to God each day. If you're awake sixteen hours in a day, that's about an hour and a half. Use that time (you can break it up) reading your Bible, praying, volunteering at church, working at a soup kitchen, or serving some other way. Give ten percent of your time to God, and you will discover that the rest of your time is more wisely spent as well.

TOLERANCE *See also* Acceptance, Love, Judging Others, Prejudice

Many think that the Bible's claim of Jesus being the only way to heaven is intolerant and exclusive. But tolerance is about treating others with kindness and civility. Even as a teacher grading a test is "intolerant" of wrong answers, or the concept of gravity is "intolerant" to those who jump off buildings, so those who reject God will experience the "intolerance" of their mistaken choice. In actuality, the Bible is thoroughly tolerant because it teaches that God gladly welcomes all who accept the truth that Jesus Christ is God's Son and the only way to heaven. God asks us to be completely intolerant of sin and remove it from our lives. But he also asks that we be tolerant of people who hold differing views by showing love to all. We should not condone beliefs or practices that lead people away from God's standards of living, but we should not condemn or punish those who do—that job is left to God.

What things should I never tolerate?

When the LORD your God hands these nations over to you and you conquer them, you must completely destroy them. Make no treaties with them and show them no mercy. You must not intermarry with them. . . . They will lead your children away from me to worship other gods. Then the anger of the LORD will burn against you.
DEUTERONOMY 7:2-4

You must never tolerate idolatry and sin in your life. Society has many idols—not statues but other gods that take the place of priority that the one true God should have in your life. Never allow devotion to these idols to enter your heart.

The Jewish leaders . . . said, "Many of the people of Israel, and even some of the priests and Levites, have not kept themselves separate from the other peoples living in the land. They have taken up the detestable practices of the Canaanites, Hittites, Perizzites, Jebusites, Ammonites, Moabites, Egyptians, and Amorites." EZRA 9:1

You should not be tolerant of adopting pagan lifestyle choices just because "everyone is doing it."

Do not fall into the trap of following their customs and worshiping their gods.
DEUTERONOMY 12:30

There is only one true God. You should not tolerate in yourself the worship of anything or anyone but God.

I will not tolerate people who slander their neighbors. I will not endure conceit and pride.
PSALM 101:5

You should not tolerate pride in yourself. Pride clouds your judgment and your ability to distinguish right from wrong and truth from lies.

Why is tolerance dangerous?

He had 700 wives of royal birth and 300 concubines. And in fact, they did turn his heart away from the LORD. 1 KINGS 11:3

Tolerance in spiritual matters will lead you away from God. Even though King Solomon had been blessed with great wisdom from God, he put himself in the dangerous position of having to make daily choices to please his pagan wives and therefore allowed their sinful practices. When compromise negatively affects your commitment to obeying God, you have become too tolerant.

TRAGEDY *See also* Crisis, Hurts/Hurting, Suffering, Trouble

Natural disasters, terrorism, death, illness, loss—these are all tragedies that invade human life and leave us with the plaguing question, why? Tragedy leaves in its wake the realization that this world is not just. Because of this, many people mistakenly blame God. Although God can cause or allow tragedy to occur, he is the only source of true justice. In our own efforts, we can never rebuild what tragedy has destroyed in our lives. Only God can redeem the ruins of life into something more glorious than the original.

What causes tragedy?

The LORD . . . said, "I have discovered a conspiracy against me among the people of Judah and Jerusalem. They have returned to the sins of their forefathers. They have refused to listen to me and are worshiping other gods. Israel and Judah have both broken the covenant I made with their ancestors. Therefore, this is what the LORD says: I am going to bring calamity upon them, and they will not escape. Though they beg for mercy, I will not listen to their cries." JEREMIAH 11:9-11

Tragedy sometimes occurs because of sin—your own sin or others' sins.

Listen! Today I am giving you a choice between life and death, between prosperity and disaster. For I command you this day to love the LORD your God and to keep his commands, decrees, and regulations by walking in his ways. If you do this, you will live and multiply, and the LORD your God will bless you and the land you are about to enter and occupy. But if your heart turns away and you refuse to listen, and if you are drawn away to serve and worship other gods, then I warn you now that you will certainly be destroyed. DEUTERONOMY 30:15-18

Tragedy is sometimes caused by ignoring God's wisdom. The rules and laws he gives are not meant to squelch pleasure or fun, but to keep you out of trouble and bring you life and health.

Jehoahaz . . . began to rule over Israel in the twenty-third year of King Joash's reign in Judah. . . . He did what was evil in the LORD's sight. He followed the example of Jeroboam son of Nebat, continuing the sins that Jeroboam had led Israel to commit. So the LORD was very angry with Israel, and he allowed King Hazael of Aram and his son Ben-hadad to defeat them repeatedly. 2 KINGS 13:1-3

Tragedy is sometimes caused by ungodly leadership.

"All right, you may test [Job]," the LORD said to Satan. "Do whatever you want with everything he possesses, but don't harm him physically." So Satan left the LORD's presence. . . . Job stood up and tore his robe in grief. Then he shaved his head and fell to the ground to worship. He said, "I came naked from my mother's womb, and I will be naked when I

leave. The Lord gave me what I had, and the Lord has taken it away. Praise the name of the Lord!" In all of this, Job did not sin by blaming God. JOB 1:12, 20-22

Tragedy is sometimes allowed to test your faith and your response to adversity. While you may not always understand the reason for life's tragic circumstances, don't give up trusting God or his ability to bring good out of the situation. If you do give up, you will become bitter and hopeless because you will see no value to life whatsoever.

How does God help in times of tragedy?

In my distress I prayed to the Lord, and the Lord answered me and set me free. PSALM 118:5

God responds to your calls for help.

The Lord . . . will still be with you to teach you. You will see your teacher with your own eyes. ISAIAH 30:20

God walks with you, teaching you and giving you strength.

I am counting on the Lord; yes, I am counting on him. I have put my hope in his word. PSALM 130:5

God restores hope for the future.

Can anything ever separate us from Christ's love? Does it mean he no longer loves us if we have trouble or calamity, or are persecuted, or hungry, or destitute, or in danger, or threatened with death? . . . I am convinced that nothing can ever separate us from God's love. Neither death nor life, neither angels nor demons, neither our fears for today nor our worries about tomorrow—not even the powers of hell can separate us from God's love. No power in the sky above or in the earth below—indeed, nothing in all creation will ever be able to separate us from the love of God that is revealed in Christ Jesus our Lord. ROMANS 8:35, 38-39

God continues to love you with an intensity that no tragedy can ever quench.

How should I handle tragedy?

Whenever we are faced with any calamity such as war, plague, or famine, we can come to stand in your presence before this Temple where your name is honored. We can cry out to you to save us, and you will hear us and rescue us. 2 CHRONICLES 20:9

Go directly and immediately to God—to listen to him, trust him, and find strength in him.

When [the son] finally came to his senses, he said, . . . "I will go home to my father and say, 'Father, I have sinned against both heaven and you, and I am no longer worthy of being called your son. Please take me on as a hired servant.'" So he returned home to his father. And while he was still a long way off, his father saw him coming. Filled with love and compassion, he ran to his son, embraced him, and kissed him. . . . His father said to

the servants, "Quick! . . . We must celebrate with a feast, for this son of mine was dead and has now returned to life. He was lost, but now he is found." So the party began.
LUKE 15:17-24

If your tragedy is brought on by your own sin, confess, repent, return to God, and receive his forgiveness.

Be strong and courageous, all you who put your hope in the LORD! PSALM 31:24

LORD, where do I put my hope? My only hope is in you. PSALM 39:7

Allow tragedy to bring you closer to God, not farther away from him. Tragedy can destroy your faith or help you walk more closely with God—the choice is yours.

They are being tested by many troubles, and they are very poor. But they are also filled with abundant joy, which has overflowed in rich generosity. 2 CORINTHIANS 8:2

In times of tragedy, it is easy to focus inward, looking only at yourself and the bitter pill you have to swallow. Instead of feeling depressed or sorry for yourself, look outward to others' needs. As you respond to the needs of others, you will find your own troubles put into perspective and weighing less.

Call on me when you are in trouble, and I will rescue you, and you will give me glory. PSALM 50:15

Trust God, and then be ready to give him credit for all he does to care for you. Tragedy is not new, but that doesn't make it any less surprising or painful. Ask God to give you strength to endure so that your life glorifies him.

How can I help others cope with tragedy?

Elijah cried out to the LORD, "O LORD my God, why have you brought tragedy to this widow who has opened her home to me, causing her son to die?" 1 KINGS 17:20

You can intercede in prayer for people in distress.

[Nehemiah] said to them, "You know very well what trouble we are in. Jerusalem lies in ruins, and its gates have been destroyed by fire. Let us rebuild the wall of Jerusalem and end this disgrace!" NEHEMIAH 2:17

You can encourage others to keep going.

When three of Job's friends heard of the tragedy he had suffered, they got together and traveled from their homes to comfort and console him. JOB 2:11

You can comfort and console the hurting. Sometimes your presence is better than words.

The believers in Macedonia and Achaia have eagerly taken up an offering for the poor among the believers in Jerusalem. ROMANS 15:26

You can meet others' physical needs in practical, compassionate ways. Small gifts often turn into great blessing.

TROUBLE *See also* Challenges, Conflict, Perseverance, Testing

The various biblical words translated "trouble" convey a range of meanings. Perhaps the closest word in our language would be *stress*. Trouble in our lives creates stress, and stress, in turn, often creates more trouble. The Bible indicates that trouble enters our lives from a variety of sources—including our own decisions and behavior. Whatever the source, God makes his resources for comfort, peace, and rest available to us through his Spirit.

What causes trouble in my life?

[God said to Adam,] "The ground is cursed because of you. All your life you will struggle to scratch a living from it. It will grow thorns and thistles for you, though you will eat of its grains. By the sweat of your brow will you have food to eat until you return to the ground from which you were made." GENESIS 3:17-19

Trouble is the inevitable by-product of sin entering the world, so you should not be surprised by it.

My guilt overwhelms me—it is a burden too heavy to bear. My wounds fester and stink because of my foolish sins. I am bent over and racked with pain. All day long I walk around filled with grief. PSALM 38:4-6

Trouble can be self-inflicted as the consequence of your own poor decisions and sin.

Jonah got up and went in the opposite direction to get away from the LORD. He . . . found a ship leaving for Tarshish. . . . But the LORD hurled a powerful wind over the sea. JONAH 1:3-4

Expect to find yourself in deep trouble if you insist on running away from God.

So many enemies against one man—all of them trying to kill me. . . . They delight in telling lies about me. PSALM 62:3-4

Trouble is sometimes undeserved and caused by others.

If you suffer . . . it must not be for murder, stealing, making trouble, or prying into other people's affairs. But it is no shame to suffer for being a Christian. Praise God for the privilege of being called by his name! 1 PETER 4:15-16

The trouble you experience may be related to your commitment to God. Satan will try to stop you from accomplishing anything for God.

What can help me avoid trouble?

Here on earth you will have many trials and sorrows. But take heart, because I have overcome the world. JOHN 16:33

In this life there will always be trouble, but God offers hope and peace in the midst of it. This helps put trouble in perspective.

If you do not listen to me or obey all these commands . . . I will punish you. LEVITICUS 26:14-16

God wants to keep you away from sin and trouble, and that is best accomplished when you listen to his voice and obey his commands.

People who despise advice are asking for trouble; those who respect a command will succeed. PROVERBS 13:13

Seeking wise advice can help you avoid trouble.

Blessed are those who fear to do wrong, but the stubborn are headed for serious trouble. PROVERBS 28:14

Listen to your conscience, for through that still, small voice God speaks wisdom to you.

How should I respond when trouble comes?

The ropes of death entangled me; floods of destruction swept over me. The grave wrapped its ropes around me; death laid a trap in my path. But in my distress I cried out to the LORD; yes, I prayed to my God for help. He heard me from his sanctuary; my cry to him reached his ears. PSALM 18:4-6

Go immediately to God with honesty and faith. He promises to listen to you and act on your behalf—not always to take your trouble away, but to help you grow from it and give you peace during it.

As pressure and stress bear down on me, I find joy in your commands. PSALM 119:143

Dive into God's Word. He has given you his Word as a source of comfort, joy, guidance, and strength. If you want to hear him speak to you, open his book and read his words.

Don't worry about tomorrow, for tomorrow will bring its own worries. Today's trouble is enough for today. MATTHEW 6:34

Don't allow yourself to be overcome by worry. Borrowing trouble from tomorrow through worry can deplete you physically, spiritually, and emotionally.

There is a time and a way for everything, even when a person is in trouble. ECCLESIASTES 8:6

Be open to options and look for God's creative solutions.

The LORD of Heaven's Armies . . . says: "If you are determined to go to Egypt and live there, the very war and famine you fear will catch up to you, and you will die there. . . . None of you will escape the disaster I will bring upon you there." JEREMIAH 42:15-17

Be obedient to what you know is God's will—even if you don't know exactly what to do in a particular situation. Sometimes you might think running away from trouble will make it go away—but some kinds of trouble will follow you wherever you go. The best course of action is usually to stay and work through it with God's help and guidance.

Shadrach, Meshach, and Abednego replied, "O Nebuchadnezzar, we do not need to defend ourselves before you. If we are thrown into the blazing furnace, the God whom we serve is able to save us. He will rescue us from your power, Your Majesty. But even if he doesn't, we want to make it clear to you, Your Majesty, that we will never serve your gods or worship the gold statue you have set up." DANIEL 3:16-18

Be fully committed to God and trust him with the outcome. If you are unstable in your relationship to God, you will be unsure of God's help in times of trouble.

How does God help in times of trouble?

When you go through deep waters, I will be with you. When you go through rivers of difficulty, you will not drown. When you walk through the fire of oppression, you will not be burned up; the flames will not consume you. ISAIAH 43:2

God promises to go through the trouble with you.

I hold you by your right hand—I, the LORD your God. And I say to you, "Don't be afraid. I am here to help you." ISAIAH 41:13

God offers to replace your fear with his peace.

The righteous person faces many troubles, but the LORD comes to the rescue each time. PSALM 34:19

The LORD rescues the godly; he is their fortress in times of trouble. PSALM 37:39

God promises to rescue and save you for all eternity.

When we arrived in Macedonia, there was no rest for us. We faced conflict from every direction, with battles on the outside and fear on the inside. But God, who encourages those who are discouraged, encouraged us by the arrival of Titus. 2 CORINTHIANS 7:5-6

God encourages you through his Word and through other Christians.

What can I learn from my troubles? What good can come from times of trouble?

Those who are wise will take all this to heart; they will see in our history the faithful love of the LORD. PSALM 107:43

God causes everything to work together for the good of those who love God and are called according to his purpose for them. ROMANS 8:28

God is always working in your life. Although you may not see his plan or even his activity in the midst of your trouble, you can trust him to work on your behalf. When you look back through your own history, you will remember how God has faithfully shown his love to you, especially through times of trouble.

Saul was going everywhere to destroy the church. He went from house to house, dragging out both men and women to throw them into prison. But the believers who were scattered preached the Good News about Jesus wherever they went. ACTS 8:3-4

God can use your difficult circumstances for his kingdom's growth and for the good of others.

When troubles come your way, consider it an opportunity for great joy. For you know that when your faith is tested, your endurance has a chance to grow. So let it grow, for when your endurance is fully developed, you will be perfect and complete, needing nothing. . . . God blesses those who patiently endure testing and temptation. Afterward they will receive the crown of life that God has promised to those who love him. JAMES 1:2-4, 12

Trouble may bring growth. Times of trouble, which lead to the testing of your faith and the increasing of your endurance, help to strengthen your character and better prepare you to adapt to whatever the future holds. Use times of trouble to grow rather than give in to defeat.

What are some common mistakes to avoid when dealing with troubles?

Sarai, Abram's wife, took Hagar the Egyptian servant and gave her to Abram as a wife. GENESIS 16:3

You might be tempted to be impatient and take matters into your own hands instead of allowing God to work in his way, in his time.

Sarai said to Abram, "This is all your fault! I put my servant into your arms, but now that she's pregnant she treats me with contempt." GENESIS 16:5

You might try to blame others for your self-inflicted troubles and even your self-inflicted failed solution.

After exploring the land for forty days, the men returned. . . . This was their report to Moses: "We entered the land you sent us to explore, and it is indeed a bountiful country—a land flowing with milk and honey. . . . But the people living there are powerful, and their towns are large and fortified. We even saw giants there!" NUMBERS 13:25-28

In the middle of trouble it's easy to focus too much on the negative possibilities of what might happen rather than the positive potential of what God can do.

The angel said to her, "Hagar, Sarai's servant, where have you come from, and where are you going?" "I'm running away from my mistress, Sarai," she replied. GENESIS 16:8

You can sometimes yield to the temptation to run away from your troubles.

TRUST *See also* Confidence, Faith, Integrity, Promises

A three-year-old boy stands hesitantly on the edge of the pool. His father, waist deep in the water, stretches out his hands and says, "Jump! I'll catch you!" The child might believe his father can catch him, but without trust he will never jump. Trust is the critical element of faith. The Bible teaches that we trust God by believing his Word is true, by obeying his will, and by depending on Jesus Christ alone for salvation. We can trust God completely because he is completely trustworthy.

What does it mean to trust God?

In him our hearts rejoice, for we trust in his holy name. PSALM 33:21

You are worthy, O Lord our God, to receive glory and honor and power. For you created all things, and they exist because you created what you pleased. REVELATION 4:11

Trusting God means recognizing that God is worthy of your trust and then giving him control of your life.

Build a large boat. . . . I am about to cover the earth with a flood that will destroy every living thing that breathes. . . . So Noah did everything exactly as God had commanded him. GENESIS 6:14, 17, 22

Trusting God means obeying his commands even when you don't fully understand why.

We are made right with God by placing our faith in Jesus Christ. And this is true for everyone who believes, no matter who we are. ROMANS 3:22

Trusting God means placing your faith in Jesus Christ and believing he alone makes you right with God.

Mary responded [to the angel], "I am the Lord's servant. May everything you have said about me come true." LUKE 1:38

Trusting God is acknowledging that he knows what is best and surrendering to his plan.

Don't worry about anything; instead, pray about everything. Tell God what you need, and thank him for all he has done. PHILIPPIANS 4:6

Trusting God means you believe he has everything under control.

What makes God trustworthy?

This truth gives them confidence that they have eternal life, which God—who does not lie—promised them before the world began. TITUS 1:2

You can trust God because he always tells the truth.

The faithful love of the LORD never ends! LAMENTATIONS 3:22

God showed his great love for us by sending Christ to die for us while we were still sinners. ROMANS 5:8

You can trust God because he loves you and therefore always has your best interests at heart. The supreme evidence of God's love is the sacrifice of his Son for you so that you can be forgiven and live forever with him in heaven.

The instructions of the LORD are perfect, reviving the soul. The decrees of the LORD are trustworthy, making wise the simple. PSALM 19:7

All he does is just and good, and all his commandments are trustworthy. PSALM 111:7

You can trust God because everything he says and does is just and good.

Oh, the joys of those who trust the LORD, who have no confidence in the proud or in those who worship idols. PSALM 40:4

It is better to take refuge in the LORD than to trust in people. PSALM 118:8

You can trust God because he is perfect. While it is good and necessary to trust others, God is the only one in whom you can completely trust. You can have absolute assurance that what he says is true and what he does is reliable. People, who are not perfect, will sometimes fail you, but God, who is perfect, will never fail you.

When the people of Israel saw the mighty power that the LORD had unleashed against the Egyptians, they were filled with awe before him. They put their faith in the LORD and in his servant Moses. EXODUS 14:31

God's power and strength have been demonstrated in your own life and in the lives of those around you. The undeniable facts of changed lives should give you confidence that you can trust who God is and what he can accomplish.

How do I know if I am trusting God? What are the signs of trusting God?

Look what happens to mighty warriors who do not trust in God. They trust their wealth instead and grow more and more bold in their wickedness. But I am like an olive tree, thriving in the house of God. I will always trust in God's unfailing love. PSALM 52:7-8

A thriving love relationship with God.

Taste and see that the LORD is good. Oh, the joys of those who take refuge in him! PSALM 34:8

Joy.

You will keep in perfect peace all who trust in you, all whose thoughts are fixed on you! Trust in the LORD always, for the LORD GOD is the eternal Rock. ISAIAH 26:3-4

Peace.

Wait patiently for the LORD. Be brave and courageous. Yes, wait patiently for the LORD. PSALM 27:14

Patience.

Build a large boat. . . . I am about to cover the earth with a flood. . . . So Noah did everything exactly as God had commanded him. GENESIS 6:14, 17, 22

Obedience.

Trust in the LORD with all your heart; do not depend on your own understanding. Seek his will in all you do, and he will show you which path to take. PROVERBS 3:5-6

A desire for God's guidance.

Even when I walk through the darkest valley, I will not be afraid, for you are close beside me. Your rod and your staff protect and comfort me. PSALM 23:4

We can say with confidence, "The LORD is my helper, so I will have no fear. What can mere people do to me?" HEBREWS 13:6

Courage and confidence.

The LORD is my strength and shield. I trust him with all my heart. He helps me, and my heart is filled with joy. I burst out in songs of thanksgiving. PSALM 28:7

An attitude of praise and worship.

How can I become more trustworthy?

"Well done!" the king exclaimed. "You are a good servant. You have been faithful with the little I entrusted to you, so you will be governor of ten cities as your reward." LUKE 19:17

Take responsibilities seriously, regardless of their size or importance. Faithfulness to small tasks will lead to being trusted with greater responsibilities.

A man who makes a vow to the LORD or makes a pledge under oath must never break it. He must do exactly what he said he would do. NUMBERS 30:2

Do exactly what you say you will do.

A gossip goes around telling secrets, but those who are trustworthy can keep a confidence. PROVERBS 11:13

Keep a confidence.

Slaves must always obey their masters and do their best to please them. They must not talk back or steal, but must show themselves to be entirely trustworthy and good. Then they will make the teaching about God our Savior attractive in every way. TITUS 2:9-10

Be respectful to those in authority.

An honest answer is like a kiss of friendship. PROVERBS 24:26

Trustworthy messengers refresh like snow in summer. They revive the spirit of their employer. PROVERBS 25:13

Prove yourself over time to be trustworthy and honest.

The other administrators and high officers began searching for some fault in the way Daniel was handling government affairs, but they couldn't find anything to criticize or condemn. He was faithful, always responsible, and completely trustworthy. DANIEL 6:4

Consistently demonstrate that you are responsible with what God has entrusted to you.

What are the benefits of being trustworthy?

I thank Christ Jesus our Lord, who has given me strength to do his work. He considered me trustworthy and appointed me to serve him. 1 TIMOTHY 1:12

You can be used by God for his service.

To those who use well what they are given, even more will be given, and they will have an abundance. But from those who do nothing, even what little they have will be taken away. MATTHEW 25:29

You will be rewarded by God for your faithfulness to him.

[Joseph said to Pharaoh,] "Please allow me to go and bury my father. After his burial, I will return without delay." Pharaoh agreed to Joseph's request. "Go and bury your father, as he made you promise," he said. . . . So Joseph and his brothers and their families continued to live in Egypt. Joseph lived to the age of 110. GENESIS 50:5-6, 22

Your good reputation will afford you privileges and freedoms.

TRUTH *See also* Absolutes, Bible, Honesty, Integrity, Promises

Few things affect our daily lives as much as the concept of truth. First, there's "telling the truth." We gravitate toward those who tell the truth because we know they can be trusted. Without trust, relationships fall apart. We have to be truthful if we want relationships to work, companies to work, and government to work. Second, there's absolute truth—fundamental principles of nature, science, and human behavior that were built into the universe from the beginning of time. For example, the truth (or law) of gravity is that when you drop an object it will fall. A truth of mathematics is that two plus two equals four. A truth of biology is that the right combination of hydrogen and oxygen makes water. A truth about life in general is that every person enters this world as a baby and someday exits this world through death. Only a fool would argue that these truths aren't absolute. There is nothing any person can do to change these fundamental truths about how the world works.

The Bible claims there is a third kind of truth: spiritual truth—moral and supernatural principles about human relationships with God and others that are absolute and constant despite our feelings and beliefs to the contrary. Human beings have always wanted to reserve the right to determine this kind of truth for themselves or to believe it doesn't exist at all. Ironically, it's this kind of truth that, while more difficult to discover, will most affect the way we live both here on earth and our eternal destiny. Just as you can't reject the truth about gravity and expect to function well in this world, so you can't ignore or reject truth about God and how he has determined human life should work. It's wise to discover and study this kind of truth because it so completely affects the life of every human being on the planet. We are free to ignore truth if we so choose, but we do so at our own risk, both now and for eternity.

What do we know to be true about God?

Truly, God will not do wrong. The Almighty will not twist justice. JOB 34:12

God's way is perfect. All the LORD's promises prove true. He is a shield for all who look to him for protection. PSALM 18:30

The instructions of the LORD are perfect, reviving the soul. The decrees of the LORD are trustworthy, making wise the simple. PSALM 19:7

For the word of the LORD holds true, and we can trust everything he does. PSALM 33:4

Truthful words stand the test of time, but lies are soon exposed. PROVERBS 12:19

The grass withers and the flowers fade, but the word of our God stands forever. ISAIAH 40:8

In their book *Right from Wrong*, Josh McDowell and Bob Hostetler define absolute truth as "that which is true for all people, for all times, for all places. Absolute truth is truth that is objective, universal, and constant."* Therefore, absolute truth must originate from God, who is the only being who spans all people, places, and time and the only being who is objective, universal, and constant. In other words, God didn't just create truth; he is truth itself.

Anyone who accepts his testimony can affirm that God is true. JOHN 3:33

Even if everyone else is a liar, God is true. As the Scriptures say about him, "You will be proved right in what you say, and you will win your case in court." ROMANS 3:4

Put on your new nature, created to be like God—truly righteous and holy. EPHESIANS 4:24

Absolute truth originates from God as the creator of the laws and principles that govern the world, life, and relationships. Without absolute principles on which you can rely, the world would not be able to exist or function.

You came down at Mount Sinai and spoke to them from heaven. You gave them regulations and instructions that were just, and decrees and commands that were good. NEHEMIAH 9:13

Each of your commandments is right. That is why I hate every false way.... Your justice is eternal, and your instructions are perfectly true.... But you are near, O LORD, and all your commands are true. PSALM 119:128, 142, 151

All Scripture is inspired by God and is useful to teach us what is true and to make us realize what is wrong in our lives. It corrects us when we are wrong and teaches us to do what is right. 2 TIMOTHY 3:16

There must be some standards upon which human life is based, standards that, if followed, create peace, harmony, and unity in relationships. God has set these standards, and if you follow them, you will experience joy and purpose. You can argue they don't exist or aren't relevant to you, but that doesn't change the fact that they are true and right.

---

*Josh McDowell and Bob Hostetler, *Right from Wrong: What You Need to Know to Help Youth Make Right Choices* (Dallas: Word, 1994), 17.

Many say there is no such thing as absolute truth. How can I know the Bible is true?

The Father . . . will give you another Advocate, who will never leave you. He is the Holy Spirit, who leads into all truth. JOHN 14:16-17

When the Holy Spirit enlightens your mind, your heart recognizes the truth.

[Jesus said,] "I was born and came into the world to testify to the truth. All who love the truth recognize that what I say is true." JOHN 18:37

The human quest for truth finds fulfillment in Jesus Christ.

We saw him with our own eyes and touched him with our own hands. 1 JOHN 1:1

You can trust the New Testament's claim of Christ's resurrection because the story is told by eyewitnesses.

How does seeking truth affect my relationship with God?

Those who know your name trust in you, for you, O LORD, do not abandon those who search for you. PSALM 9:10

Your unfailing love will last forever. Your faithfulness is as enduring as the heavens. PSALM 89:2

You can trust God because he always tells the truth. Nothing he has said in his Word, the Bible, has ever been proven wrong or false. He specifically created you in order to have a relationship with you for all eternity. If God—who always tells the truth—says he loves you, you can be sure he desires a relationship with you.

Jesus [said], "I am the way, the truth, and the life. No one can come to the Father except through me." JOHN 14:6

God shows his anger from heaven against all sinful, wicked people who suppress the truth by their wickedness. ROMANS 1:18

This truth gives them confidence that they have eternal life, which God—who does not lie—promised them before the world began. TITUS 1:2

God wants you to accept the ultimate truth that only by following Jesus can you spend eternity with him. He wants to spare you from the terrible consequences of pushing this most important truth away.

Why is telling the truth so important?

The LORD detests lying lips, but he delights in those who tell the truth. PROVERBS 12:22

If you are faithful in little things, you will be faithful in large ones. But if you are dishonest in little things, you won't be honest with greater responsibilities. LUKE 16:10

Telling the truth is the litmus test to see if you are trying to model your life after the God of truth. If you are truthful in even little things, you will have the reputation of being an honest person.

Stop telling lies. Let us tell our neighbors the truth, for we are all parts of the same body.
EPHESIANS 4:25

Telling the truth promotes good relationships.

God is not a man, so he does not lie. He is not human, so he does not change his mind. Has he ever spoken and failed to act? Has he ever promised and not carried it through?
NUMBERS 23:19

He who is the Glory of Israel will not lie, nor will he change his mind, for he is not human that he should change his mind! 1 SAMUEL 15:29

Honesty is God's nature. He can't tell a lie. If you are to follow God, you must strive to be as much like him as possible.

Who may climb the mountain of the LORD? Who may stand in his holy place? Only those whose hands and hearts are pure, who do not worship idols and never tell lies. They will receive the LORD's blessing and have a right relationship with God their savior.
PSALM 24:3-5

Telling the truth is necessary for a relationship with God.

Cling to your faith in Christ, and keep your conscience clear. For some people have deliberately violated their consciences; as a result, their faith has been shipwrecked.
1 TIMOTHY 1:19

Always telling the truth keeps a clear conscience.

U, V

UNITY *See also* Church, Fellowship, Marriage, Purpose

An orchestra can be transformed from cacophony to symphony by following the composer's score and the conductor's baton. In the same manner, when believers follow God's plan for their life and allow the Holy Spirit to lead them, great diversity within the church can be dynamically unified in service to God. The Bible extols unity as one of the highest goals of Christian relationships—whether in marriage, families, communities, work, or church. God desires his people to live and work together in harmony because then his people are at peace and great things can be accomplished.

What is true unity?

Just as our bodies have many parts and each part has a special function, so it is with Christ's body. We are many parts of one body, and we all belong to each other.
ROMANS 12:4-5

Unity is not the same as uniformity. Everyone has unique gifts and personalities. It is the celebration and appreciation of these differences to reach the common goal of serving God that is true unity.

Why is unity important?

All the believers devoted themselves to the apostles' teaching, and to fellowship, and to sharing in meals (including the Lord's Supper), and to prayer. A deep sense of awe came over them all, and the apostles performed many miraculous signs and wonders.
ACTS 2:42-43

Unity allows you to share a sense of fellowship and devotion and to work together with a common purpose.

May God . . . help you live in complete harmony with each other. . . . Then all of you can join together with one voice, giving praise and glory to God. ROMANS 15:5-6

Unity creates a more beautiful worship experience.

Abram said to Lot, "Let's not allow this conflict to come between us or our herdsmen. After all, we are close relatives!" GENESIS 13:8

How wonderful and pleasant it is when brothers live together in harmony!
PSALM 133:1

As the Scriptures say, "A man leaves his father and mother and is joined to his wife, and the two are united into one." EPHESIANS 5:31

Unity is not just for the church. God desires for you to live in unity in your marriage, in your family, and in your friendships.

How can I help achieve unity?

May God, who gives this patience and encouragement, help you live in complete harmony with each other, as is fitting for followers of Christ Jesus. ROMANS 15:5

By working hard to develop the same kind of attitude Jesus has, one of patience and encouragement, one of uniting not dividing.

[The church leaders'] responsibility is to equip God's people to do his work and build up the church, the body of Christ. This will continue until we all come to such unity in our faith and knowledge of God's Son that we will be mature in the Lord, measuring up to the full and complete standard of Christ. EPHESIANS 4:12-13

By exercising your God-given gifts to build others up.

All of you should be of one mind. Sympathize with each other. Love each other as brothers and sisters. Be tenderhearted, and keep a humble attitude. 1 PETER 3:8

By sympathizing with others.

Always be humble and gentle. Be patient with each other, making allowance for each other's faults because of your love. Make every effort to keep yourselves united in the Spirit, binding yourselves together with peace. EPHESIANS 4:2-3

By being humble and gentle.

Make allowance for each other's faults, and forgive anyone who offends you. . . . Above all, clothe yourselves with love, which binds us all together in perfect harmony. COLOSSIANS 3:13-14

By loving and forgiving others.

Does unity mean everyone has to agree?

The body has many different parts, not just one part. . . . Yes, there are many parts, but only one body. 1 CORINTHIANS 12:14, 20

Unity does not mean everyone's opinion has to be the same, or even that their goals must be exactly the same. God has created everyone different, which means there will be differences of opinion. But your common purpose should be the same—to serve and honor God. Unity is ruined when selfish interests take priority over godly interests.

Search for peace, and work to maintain it. PSALM 34:14

Never pay back evil with more evil. . . . Do all that you can to live in peace with everyone. ROMANS 12:17-18

Make every effort to keep yourselves united in the Spirit, binding yourselves together with peace. EPHESIANS 4:3

To live peaceably with others does not mean avoiding conflict, but handling conflict appropriately. Conflict handled poorly leads to fractured relationships. Avoiding conflict altogether leads to the same end because there is unresolved hurt or anger. Rather, when conflict arises, don't retaliate in anger, but respond with love, relying on the Holy Spirit to give you the kind of patient endurance that leads to the resolution of the problem.

If the church is to be unified, why are there so many different denominations?

Live in harmony with each other. Let there be no divisions in the church. Rather, be of one mind, united in thought and purpose. 1 CORINTHIANS 1:10

Although Scripture discourages divisions in the church, diversity can be positive if all are striving for a united purpose of serving and glorifying God.

VALUES *See also* Character, Convictions, Priorities, Truth

How do you spend most of your free time? Who is your favorite entertainer? Who are your best friends? What do you think about most? How do you spend your money? Your answers to these questions will show what you value most. Whatever we consider important, useful, and worth a lot is what we value. We've heard it said, "He doesn't have any values." But that's never true. Everyone has values, good or bad. The problem comes when we don't value what should be most important to us, but instead let the world's values shape us. Our values are crystal clear to those around us, because what we do, where we spend our time and money, and what we talk about shows exactly what we value the most. This is true even for God. What he does and says shows what he values most. For example, God made you in his own image, so he must value you highly! Your soul is so valuable to God that he sacrificed the life of his own Son so that you can live forever with him. Jesus said that our actions reveal our values. What we do shows what we really believe. Do your actions clearly show you are living by the values God feels are most important?

How can I cultivate godly values?

Joseph . . . told her, "My master trusts me with everything in his entire household. . . . How could I do such a wicked thing? It would be a great sin against God."
GENESIS 39:8-9

Refuse to value the kind of life choices the Bible says are worthless or dangerous to your long-term well-being. To obey God's Word is to align your values with God's.

The LORD has told you what is good, and this is what he requires of you: to do what is right, to love mercy, and to walk humbly with your God. MICAH 6:8

The Holy Spirit produces this kind of fruit in our lives: love, joy, peace, patience, kindness, goodness, faithfulness, gentleness, and self-control. GALATIANS 5:22-23

Godly living simply means valuing what God values and living accordingly. If you want godly values, you need God living in you. He promises his Holy Spirit will literally live in you if you ask, helping you value what is truly important and then living it.

How do I know if my current values align with God's?

Help me never to tell a lie. PROVERBS 30:8

Their lives became full of every kind of wickedness, sin, greed, hate, envy, murder, quarreling, deception, malicious behavior, and gossip. ROMANS 1:29

Obscene stories, foolish talk, and coarse jokes—these are not for you. Instead, let there be thankfulness to God. EPHESIANS 5:4

How do you view acts the Bible calls sin, such as gossip, flattery, profanity, lying, or cheating? If you don't see these as sin, you must face up to the fact that your values are different than God's.

From the heart come evil thoughts, murder, adultery, all sexual immorality, theft, lying, and slander. MATTHEW 15:19

The heart is the source of moral or immoral behavior. If your actions don't regularly match up with what God says is most important, then you need a change of heart before you can change your behavior.

VICTORY *See also* Courage, Eternity, Overcoming, Resurrection

The ticker-tape parades that follow a nation's triumph in war, the wild celebration that accompanies a sports team upon winning the championship game, the deep satisfaction of a student finally conquering a difficult subject to receive an A+ on the final exam—each is a picture of glorious victory. Most of us will never have the experience of winning a professional sports championship, but the Bible promises us a victory far greater—and more lasting. We can experience spiritual victory over sin and death, the reward of which is eternal life in heaven. What makes the victory even more amazing is that it doesn't come by lots of hard work on your part, but rather it's a free gift resulting from God's hard work on your behalf.

What does it mean to live a victorious Christian life?

Every child of God defeats this evil world, and we achieve this victory through our faith. 1 JOHN 5:4

Responding to God's invitation to follow him by believing that his way is the right way leads to victorious living.

Put on every piece of God's armor. EPHESIANS 6:13

God equips you with all the spiritual weapons you need to defeat Satan and temptation.

I run with purpose in every step. 1 CORINTHIANS 9:26

To experience daily victories in the difficult struggles of life, you must be willing to commit yourself to vigorous spiritual training and preparation.

Overwhelming victory is ours through Christ. ROMANS 8:37

Thank God! He gives us victory over sin and death through our Lord Jesus Christ.
1 CORINTHIANS 15:57

Your greatest victory is ultimately conquering death to live for eternity. Only through Jesus can you achieve this victory.

What are some of the victories I can achieve day by day?

Study this Book of Instruction continually. Meditate on it day and night so you will be sure to obey everything written in it. Only then will you prosper and succeed in all you do. JOSHUA 1:8

When you consistently obey God's Word, you will experience victory over your fears, over Satan's tactics to derail your relationship with God, and ultimately, over sin and death.

Trials will show that your faith is genuine. It is being tested as fire tests and purifies gold—though your faith is far more precious than mere gold. So when your faith remains strong through many trials, it will bring you much praise and glory and honor on the day when Jesus Christ is revealed to the whole world. 1 PETER 1:7

If you can trust God with your pain, confusion, and loneliness, you will win a spiritual victory because you will have defended yourself against the temptation of the enemy to let anger, bitterness, or discouragement defeat you. The next time you face trouble or hardship, see it as an opportunity to rely on God for strength and endurance.

In peace I will lie down and sleep, for you alone, O LORD, will keep me safe. PSALM 4:8

The LORD gives his people strength. The LORD blesses them with peace. PSALM 29:11

God's peace does not prevent us from encountering difficulties, but it gives us victory over them.

I try to faithfully follow Jesus. Why won't he give me more victories over the everyday problems I face?

The LORD your God will drive those nations out ahead of you little by little. You will not clear them away all at once, otherwise the wild animals would multiply too quickly for you. DEUTERONOMY 7:22

Be still in the presence of the LORD, and wait patiently for him to act. Don't worry about evil people who prosper or fret about their wicked schemes. PSALM 37:7

God often asks you to wait while leading you along the path of progressive, not immediate, victory. Why? Sometimes this keeps you from the pride that often comes after success. Sometimes it saves you from defeat. And sometimes God makes you wait to prepare you for a special task he has for you. Waiting is never time wasted by God, so don't waste it by being anxious. Serve God as you wait for him to accomplish the next good thing in your life.

Sometimes it feels like I'm under attack. How can I achieve victory?

Hold up the shield of faith to stop the fiery arrows of the devil. EPHESIANS 6:16

The Spirit who lives in you is greater than the spirit who lives in the world. 1 JOHN 4:4

Every child of God defeats this evil world, and we achieve this victory through our faith.
1 JOHN 5:4

Your first line of defense is to draw strength from the fact that God is more powerful than your problems or your enemies. Your faith in God is a shield that protects you from the temptations and criticisms hurled at you every day. Without strong faith, the weapons of Satan and the arrows shot at you by your enemies would pierce and defeat you. So even when life seems overwhelming, hold tightly to your faith like a shield and you will withstand the dangers and discouragements sent at you. And rejoice—you know that God has already won the victory.

The LORD is a warrior; Yahweh is his name! EXODUS 15:3

This is what the LORD says: Do not be afraid! Don't be discouraged by this mighty army, for the battle is not yours, but God's. 2 CHRONICLES 20:15

The LORD will march forth like a mighty hero; he will come out like a warrior, full of fury. He will shout his battle cry and crush all his enemies. ISAIAH 42:13

Put on all of God's armor. EPHESIANS 6:11

The purpose of evil is to defy God and to wear down believers until they are led into sin. This pleases Satan and gives him greater power over the earth. But God is a warrior. A battle rages in the spiritual realm and, as a believer, you are right in the thick of it. God is always ready to fight on your behalf, always ready to come to your defense. In addition, he provides you with armor so that you can fight alongside him (see Ephesians 6:11-18). But you must join God in the battle or you will be vulnerable and helpless to withstand the enemy. If you join, you are guaranteed victory.

How can I expect victory when the odds are stacked high against me?

The chief of staff stood and shouted in Hebrew to the people on the wall, "Listen to this message from the great king of Assyria! This is what the king says: Don't let Hezekiah deceive you. He will never be able to rescue you from my power. Don't let him fool you into trusting in the LORD.". . . When King Hezekiah heard their report, he tore his clothes and put on burlap and went into the Temple of the LORD. . . . "O LORD our God, rescue us from his power." 2 KINGS 18:28-30; 19:1, 19

The LORD sent an angel who destroyed the Assyrian army. 2 CHRONICLES 32:21

The odds were definitely stacked against the little nation of Judah. The mighty Assyrian army had already destroyed every nation in its path . . . and Judah was next. So King Hezekiah did the only thing he could do—he went to the Temple and prayed. Assyria's mighty army was no match for God. You, too, will succeed at whatever God has called you to if you humbly and faithfully follow him, no matter how the odds seem stacked against you.

VIOLENCE *See also* Abuse, Persecution, Rape, Rebellion, War

War, destruction, murder, and assault—every day we hear new stories of violence in our world. But violence is nothing new. The first act of murder occurred in the second generation of mankind when Cain killed his brother Abel. In the Old Testament it seemed God not only condoned but even encouraged some violence (see Joshua 10–11, for example). How are we to reconcile these gruesome Old Testament images with the teachings of Christ in the New Testament to refrain from returning evil for evil and to turn the other cheek? Although it is difficult to fully explain the bloodshed and brutality found in parts of the Old Testament, when taken as a whole the Bible clearly teaches that violence is evil and that God is a God of peace and reconciliation.

The Old Testament seems filled with violence; does God really condone such behavior?

God saw that the earth had become corrupt and was filled with violence. GENESIS 6:11

God's disapproval of violence is seen when he sent the Great Flood to judge and expunge the violence of humanity.

The LORD . . . hates those who love violence. PSALM 11:5

God condemns all violence.

Anyone who assaults and kills another person must be put to death. EXODUS 21:12

Violence in relationships is abuse and must be stopped immediately. Attacking someone, whether out of anger or revenge, creates fear, animosity, injury, and hatred in the victim. That is why it is so detestable to God—nothing good can come out of violence in a relationship.

What does the New Testament teach about violence?

Those who use the sword will die by the sword. MATTHEW 26:52

A life of violence brings its own destruction.

If someone slaps you on the right cheek, offer the other cheek also. MATTHEW 5:39

According to Jesus, violence is to be replaced by a willingness to love even your enemies.

If your enemies are hungry, feed them. ROMANS 12:20

Instead of plotting revenge, you are to be proactive in creating peace.

What causes violence?

Jacob loved Joseph more than any of his other children because Joseph had been born to him in his old age. So one day Jacob had a special gift made for Joseph—a beautiful robe. But his brothers hated Joseph because their father loved him more than the rest of them. They couldn't say a kind word to him. . . . When Joseph's brothers saw him coming, they recognized him in the distance. As he approached, they made plans to kill him. . . .

"Come on, let's kill him and throw him into one of these cisterns. We can tell our father, 'A wild animal has eaten him.'" GENESIS 37:3-4, 18-20

Envy, anger, and resentment, if left unresolved, spread like wildfire and can lead to violence and even murder.

Is violence always wrong?

[Abimelech] went to his father's home at Ophrah, and there, on one stone, they killed all seventy of his half brothers, the sons of Gideon. But the youngest brother, Jotham, escaped and hid. . . . God sent a spirit that stirred up trouble between Abimelech and the leading citizens of Shechem, and they revolted. . . . In this way, God punished Abimelech for the evil he had done against his father by murdering his seventy brothers. God also punished the men of Shechem for all their evil. JUDGES 9:5, 23, 56-57

"Put away your sword," Jesus told him. "Those who use the sword will die by the sword." MATTHEW 26:52

Violence is the use of force to possess or destroy something or someone, whether it is one nation taking land from another, a thief robbing someone's home, a murderer ending someone's life, or an abusive spouse trying to destroy his or her mate's self-esteem. The Bible is clear that violence for personal gain ends in self-destruction and will be judged by God. But sometimes, as in the Old Testament, violence is necessary to combat or defeat evil and defend good.

VISION *See also* Call of God, Discernment, Goals, Purpose

Vision is a picture of the future that produces a passion in the present. Lack of vision is like trying to see underwater without a mask—everything is blurry, nothing makes sense, and we feel impossibly lost. If we want to have purpose, if we want to see our way clearly in life, if we want to be motivated to do something that counts, we need a vision—a picture of where we and those with us (family, church, employees, neighbors) should be at some point in the future. Spiritual vision is God's picture of the future he created for us. How do we capture God's vision of what he created us to accomplish and where he wants us to be in the future? It's only when we empty ourselves of our own opinions and dreams of the future that God can fill us up with his picture of the future.

Why is vision important?

This is what the LORD of Heaven's Armies says: Once again old men and women will walk Jerusalem's streets with their canes and will sit together in the city squares. And the streets of the city will be filled with boys and girls at play. . . . All this may seem impossible to you now, a small remnant of God's people. But is it impossible for me? says the LORD of Heaven's Armies. ZECHARIAH 8:4-6

Vision motivates us to get things done. The Temple in Jerusalem still needed to be rebuilt after long years of exile, but the people weren't motivated to finish it. God gave

Zechariah a vision of the city of Jerusalem once again filled with joyful people, and that vision, in turn, motivated the people to complete their task. If a tough task hangs over you, ask God to give you a vision for the finished project and the sense of joy you will have when the job is done.

[Peter] saw the sky open, and something like a large sheet was let down by its four corners. In the sheet were all sorts of animals, reptiles, and birds. Then a voice said to him, "Get up, Peter; kill and eat them." "No, Lord," Peter declared. "I have never eaten anything that our Jewish laws have declared impure and unclean." But the voice spoke again: "Do not call something unclean if God has made it clean." ACTS 10:11-15

Vision helps you see things you would never have seen before, giving you a different perspective. In this vision given to Peter, God was revealing something startling to Peter's point of view. God was nullifying the Jewish dietary laws to prepare Peter to meet a Gentile (a non-Jew) who was very unlike him and yet a strong fellow believer.

Elisha prayed, "O LORD, open his eyes and let him see!" The LORD opened the young man's eyes, and when he looked up, he saw that the hillside around Elisha was filled with horses and chariots of fire. 2 KINGS 6:17

Spiritual vision can encourage you by helping you see God's presence and readiness to help all around you.

I, Nebuchadnezzar, looked up to heaven. My sanity returned, and I praised and worshiped the Most High and honored the one who lives forever. His rule is everlasting, and his kingdom is eternal. DANIEL 4:34

Vision helps you see things in their true and proper perspective.

If you obey, you will enjoy a long life in the land the LORD swore to give to your ancestors and to you, their descendants—a land flowing with milk and honey! DEUTERONOMY 11:9

Vision inspires hope.

Why is it important for me to seek God's vision for the future?

"My thoughts are nothing like your thoughts," says the LORD. "And my ways are far beyond anything you could imagine. For just as the heavens are higher than the earth, so my ways are higher than your ways and my thoughts higher than your thoughts."
ISAIAH 55:8-9

Anyone who believes in me will do the same works I have done, and even greater works, because I am going to be with the Father. JOHN 14:12

All glory to God, who is able, through his mighty power at work within us, to accomplish infinitely more than we might ask or think. EPHESIANS 3:20

You already have some vision of the future. Seeking God's vision breaks your bondage to small ideas that are not worthy of God or representative of God's work in the world. God's vision expands your mind to greater possibilities. By aligning your vision with God's vision for your life, you will be inspired to navigate your future with purpose and clarity.

Don't copy the behavior and customs of this world, but let God transform you into a new person by changing the way you think. Then you will learn to know God's will for you, which is good and pleasing and perfect. ROMANS 12:2

When your vision aligns with God's, you can work for him with enthusiasm knowing that his plans are being carried out through you.

How can I align my vision with God's plan for me?

Open my eyes to see the wonderful truths in your instructions. PSALM 119:18

God blesses those whose hearts are pure, for they will see God. MATTHEW 5:8

You can find God's vision for your life through his Word, through the conscience he has built into you, through the counsel of other godly people, and through prayer. God wants to reveal his vision for your life. Believe in his power, seek his guidance each day, and be alert to the ways that he answers you.

How is vision essential to leadership?

The LORD had said to Abram, "Leave your native country, your relatives, and your father's family, and go to the land that I will show you. I will make you into a great nation. I will bless you and make you famous, and you will be a blessing to others. I will bless those who bless you and curse those who treat you with contempt. All the families on earth will be blessed through you." GENESIS 12:1-3

God's strategy has always been to give his people a vision of a new reality. This kind of vision inspires teamwork and awakens courage when the leader is in tune with God's vision.

One night Joseph had a dream. GENESIS 37:5

Vision sustains during the delays in reaching your goals. Joseph never lost hope because he kept God's vision before him.

How do I obtain good spiritual vision?

The people's minds were hardened, and to this day whenever the old covenant is being read, the same veil covers their minds so they cannot understand the truth. And this veil can be removed only by believing in Christ. 2 CORINTHIANS 3:14

It seems ironic that, for many of us, the only way to see better is to cover our eyes with glass lenses. With spiritual vision, you need the lens of faith—the ability to believe that there is much more happening than you can see. When you face difficulties that seem insurmountable, remember that spiritual armies are fighting for your soul. Open your spiritual eyes to view God's power.

As these men were worshiping the Lord and fasting, the Holy Spirit said, "Dedicate Barnabas and Saul for the special work to which I have called them." So after more fasting and prayer, the men laid their hands on them and sent them on their way. ACTS 13:2-3

Vision comes from the inspiration of the Holy Spirit. As you learn to be more sensitive to the nudges of the Holy Spirit, and respond in faith, your vision becomes more clear.

This is what the LORD says: . . . Ask me and I will tell you remarkable secrets you do not know about things to come. JEREMIAH 33:2-3

If you need wisdom, ask our generous God, and he will give it to you. He will not rebuke you for asking. JAMES 1:5

He hears us whenever we ask for anything that pleases him. 1 JOHN 5:14

Prayer is an essential means for developing spiritual vision because it connects you to God who sees everything.

Open my eyes to see the wonderful truths in your instructions. PSALM 119:18

I send [my word] out, and it always produces fruit. It will accomplish all I want it to, and it will prosper everywhere I send it. ISAIAH 55:11

God's Word is one of the greatest sources for vision and inspiration.

Because I am righteous, I will see you. When I awake, I will see you face to face and be satisfied. PSALM 17:15

God blesses those whose hearts are pure, for they will see God. MATTHEW 5:8

Purity of heart and mind will enable you to have a stronger spiritual vision because there is less to cloud your spiritual eyesight.

How can I know if a particular vision is from God?

All Scripture is inspired by God and is useful to teach us what is true and to make us realize what is wrong in our lives. It corrects us when we are wrong and teaches us to do what is right. 2 TIMOTHY 3:16

The Word of God is authoritative. No dream or vision from God would ever contradict the clear teaching and intent of the Scriptures. No vision can override the authority of the Word of God or be a new word from God. Thus, a vision can only confirm what you know to be true or untrue from God's Word.

Plans go wrong for lack of advice; many advisers bring success. PROVERBS 15:22

Consult other wise and mature believers to help interpret a vision. Even then only time will tell if it is truly from the Lord.

VULNERABILITY *See also* Humility, Intimacy, Submission, Trust

What if others could know who we really are? Is there anyone to whom we can or should reveal our deepest fears, hurts, or doubts? The Bible teaches that every human being has a need for intimate relationships but that we are to choose carefully to whom we reveal our heart. True vulnerability occurs in only the most intimate relationships because it requires us to reveal the dark things we had hoped would never come out in the open. We often resist being vulnerable to God about our sins, especially the ones we don't want to give up, but vulnerability requires full disclosure, not hiding or covering up. But it is only through being vulnerable that we find true healing, restoration, renewal, and forgiveness. When we admit and confess our sin, seek forgiveness, and commit ourselves to taking the high road, our relationship with God and others is restored and a great weight is lifted from us. While we cannot become intimately vulnerable with everyone, we can trust God and should be able to trust a few others to handle our deepest feelings with care.

It's very difficult for me to share my feelings with others. How can I learn to become vulnerable in the right way?

Have mercy on me, LORD, for I am in distress. . . . Sin has drained my strength; I am wasting away from within. PSALM 31:9-10

You can start by being vulnerable with God when you pray.

If we confess our sins to him, he is faithful and just to forgive us our sins and to cleanse us from all wickedness. 1 JOHN 1:9

Be vulnerable to God about your sins and failures, for he is absolutely trustworthy and he will offer unconditional forgiveness.

To you who are willing to listen, I say, love your enemies! LUKE 6:27

As you understand God's great love for you, despite your mistakes, you will want to pass on this same love to others. Loving others always makes you vulnerable, but it is the best way to live.

As you share in our sufferings, you will also share in the comfort God gives us. 2 CORINTHIANS 1:7

A great privilege of believers is to share the vulnerability of offering comfort and understanding to one another. If you see vulnerability as a negative thing, you will always have trouble sharing with others. If you see it as the way to deeper and healthier relationships, you will learn to develop it.

Are there ways in which I should be vulnerable?

The man and his wife were both naked, but they felt no shame. GENESIS 2:25

Besides your relationship with God, your next most vulnerable relationship should be with your spouse, if you are married. There should be nothing hidden between the two of you.

The word of God is alive and powerful. It is sharper than the sharpest two-edged sword, cutting between soul and spirit, between joint and marrow. It exposes our innermost

thoughts and desires. Nothing in all creation is hidden from God. Everything is naked and exposed before his eyes, and he is the one to whom we are accountable.
HEBREWS 4:12-13

It is essential to open your heart and life fully to God and let him do his work in you to help you become all he created you to be. If you hold back from God and don't allow him to help, you will never reach your God-given potential.

God blesses you when people mock you and persecute you and lie about you and say all sorts of evil things against you because you are my followers. Be happy about it! Be very glad! For a great reward awaits you in heaven. And remember, the ancient prophets were persecuted in the same way. MATTHEW 5:11-12

Sometimes you were exposed to public ridicule and were beaten, and sometimes you helped others who were suffering the same things. HEBREWS 10:33

Allow yourself to be vulnerable enough to experience humiliation and ridicule for believing in Jesus.

How can I help those who are vulnerable?

Ham, the father of Canaan, saw that his father was naked and went outside and told his brothers. Then Shem and Japheth took a robe, held it over their shoulders, and backed into the tent to cover their father. As they did this, they looked the other way so they would not see him naked. GENESIS 9:22-23

Don't cheat your neighbor by moving the ancient boundary markers; don't take the land of defenseless orphans. PROVERBS 23:10

When someone is vulnerable they are easily taken advantage of. Do what you can to "cover" those who are vulnerable, to protect them from being exploited.

Share your food with the hungry, and give shelter to the homeless. Give clothes to those who need them, and do not hide from relatives who need your help.
ISAIAH 58:7

Help those who are vulnerable in order to restore them to a stronger position. You do this by treating them with mercy, compassion, and kindness, and providing whatever resources you can.

Rescue the poor and helpless; deliver them from the grasp of evil people. PSALM 82:4

Speak up for the poor and helpless, and see that they get justice. PROVERBS 31:9

God wants you to rescue the vulnerable so others will not take advantage of them.

How do I keep myself from being vulnerable to harm?

Jerusalem has sinned greatly, so she has been tossed away like a filthy rag. All who once honored her now despise her, for they have seen her stripped naked and humiliated. All she can do is groan and hide her face. LAMENTATIONS 1:8

Keep yourself from being vulnerable to harm by obeying God and staying within his plan and revealed will. Shame and humiliation are the direct consequences of disobedience to God.

We had told the king, "Our God's hand of protection is on all who worship him, but his fierce anger rages against those who abandon him." So we fasted and earnestly prayed that our God would take care of us, and he heard our prayer. EZRA 8:22-23

Prayer strengthens a wall of spiritual protection around you.

I placed armed guards behind the lowest parts of the wall in the exposed areas. I stationed the people to stand guard by families, armed with swords, spears, and bows. NEHEMIAH 4:13

Keep from being vulnerable by joining together with others and standing together against danger.

I will come as unexpectedly as a thief! Blessed are all who are watching for me, who keep their clothing ready so they will not have to walk around naked and ashamed. REVELATION 16:15

If you are fully prepared for Christ's coming, you will not be vulnerable to judgment when he comes.

WILL OF GOD *See also* Discernment, Guidance, Wisdom

"What is God's will for my life?" Is there a Christian who has not asked this question? Sometimes "God's will" seems so vague, so hard to know. Perhaps the problem is that we're expecting God to reveal something special to us, while ignoring the revelation he's already given in his written Word. The Bible has dozens of clear commands for us to follow: Worship God only, love your neighbors and your enemies, use your spiritual gifts, do not lie, do not covet, do not steal, be sexually pure, remain faithful, teach your children spiritual truths, don't gossip, be generous, don't take God's name in vain, read his Word regularly, don't let money control you, let the Holy Spirit control your life—and the list goes on and on. Isn't that God's will for our lives? While God created each of us for a purpose and might call us to do certain specific tasks, his will is really that we do the things he calls every person to do. When we are ushered into eternity will it really matter what house, what car, or maybe even what job we had? The real issues will be whether we have been faithful, loved others, and come to know God in a life-changing way. God is vitally interested in the details of our lives, but his will for all people is simply obedience.

Does God really have a plan for my life?

The LORD will work out his plans for my life. PSALM 138:8

I am certain that God, who began the good work within you, will continue his work until it is finally finished on the day when Christ Jesus returns. PHILIPPIANS 1:6

God has a plan for your life. It is not an unthinking, automated script that you must follow. It is a journey with various important destinations and appointments, but also a great deal of freedom as to the pace and scope of the travel. God's plan for you will always have a sense of mystery, but you can be certain that he will guide you as long as you rely on his leading.

Who knows if perhaps you were made queen for just such a time as this? ESTHER 4:14

"I know the plans I have for you," says the LORD. "They are plans for good and not for disaster, to give you a future and a hope." JEREMIAH 29:11

God's plans for you are always good. Unknown plans can be frightening, but when they are designed by God, you can expect something marvelous.

The LORD says, "I will guide you along the best pathway for your life. I will advise you and watch over you." PSALM 32:8

God wants to help you follow the path that will be most pleasing to him, and in the long run, it will be the most fulfilling to you, too.

How can I discover God's will for my life?

Give your bodies to God because of all he has done for you. Let them be a living and holy sacrifice—the kind he will find acceptable. This is truly the way to worship him. Don't copy the behavior and customs of this world, but let God transform you into a new person by changing the way you think. Then you will learn to know God's will for you, which is good and pleasing and perfect. ROMANS 12:1-2

Knowing God's will begins with knowing God. He holds nothing good back from those who hold nothing back from him. As he transforms you into a new person, you come to understand his ways and enjoy the habit of living out his purpose for your life.

Seek his will in all you do, and he will show you which path to take. PROVERBS 3:6

If you need wisdom, ask our generous God, and he will give it to you. He will not rebuke you for asking. JAMES 1:5

You can't sit around waiting for God to reveal his will for you; you must proactively look for it. Actively seek God's will through prayer, reading the Bible, conversation with mature believers and reliable advisors, and by discerning the circumstances around you.

When it was clear that we couldn't persuade him, we gave up and said, "The Lord's will be done." ACTS 21:14

Sometimes God's will for you becomes evident through circumstances beyond your control. You do the seeking, but allow God to work out his will in the way he deems best. You will discover that you like where he takes you.

Well done, my good and faithful servant. You have been faithful in handling this small amount, so now I will give you many more responsibilities. MATTHEW 25:21

To those who use well what they are given, even more will be given, and they will have an abundance. MATTHEW 25:29

The natural abilities you have are gifts from God, and they are often a clue to what God wants you to do. Why would God give you certain talents and spiritual gifts, and then not ask you to use them? You may have natural gifts in the areas of cooking, entertaining, managing a business, teaching, handling money, playing an instrument, or many other things. Use whatever gifts you have been given to bring honor and glory to God, and you will be right where you need to be to discover God's will for you.

What are some of the things I can know are God's will for me?

Commit your actions to the LORD, and your plans will succeed. PROVERBS 16:3

God's will is that you do everything as if you were doing it for him. God has not revealed everything to his followers, but he has revealed all you need to know to live for him now.

I want to see a mighty flood of justice, an endless river of righteous living. AMOS 5:24

God's will is that you seek justice at all times and do what is right.

Let love be your highest goal! 1 CORINTHIANS 14:1

God's will is that you always love others.

Even the Son of Man came not to be served but to serve others and to give his life as a ransom for many. MARK 10:45

God's will is that you serve others, putting them above yourself.

God gave the people all these instructions . . . (See Exodus 20:1-17 for a list of the Ten Commandments.)

God's will is that you obey his laws for living.

The Holy Spirit produces this kind of fruit in our lives: love, joy, peace, patience, kindness, goodness, faithfulness, gentleness, and self-control. GALATIANS 5:22-23

God's will is that you live under the power and guidance of the Holy Spirit.

Why is discerning God's will important?

Paul and Silas traveled through the area of Phrygia and Galatia, because the Holy Spirit had prevented them from preaching the word in the province of Asia at that time. . . . Instead, they went on through Mysia to the seaport of Troas. That night Paul had a vision: A man from Macedonia in northern Greece was standing there, pleading with him, "Come over to Macedonia and help us!" So we decided to leave for Macedonia at once, having concluded that God was calling us to preach the Good News there. ACTS 16:6-10

In life, you will have innumerable opportunities. Discerning God's will helps you recognize the opportunities with the most potential from the mediocre ones.

WISDOM *See also* Bible, Discernment, Holy Spirit, Maturity

Solving a complex problem in trigonometry or writing a computer program that will guide a nuclear missile both require great intelligence. But such intelligence does not guarantee a fulfilling, balanced, or productive life. Success in relationships, raising godly children, and spiritual maturity are less dependent on intellect than wisdom. The Bible has an enormous amount to say about wisdom (and even devotes the entire book of Proverbs to it) because successfully navigating through life requires so much of it.

How will having wisdom help me?

Fear of the LORD is the foundation of wisdom. Knowledge of the Holy One results in good judgment. PROVERBS 9:10

Wisdom is not simply knowing facts and figures; it is understanding the filter through which those facts and figures should be used. Wisdom recognizes that an all-powerful, all-knowing God has designed a moral universe with consequences for good or sinful choices. Wisdom begins with understanding your accountability to and your full dependence on your Creator. It's not what you know, but who you know.

Don't copy the behavior and customs of this world, but let God transform you into a new person by changing the way you think. Then you will learn to know God's will for you, which is good and pleasing and perfect. ROMANS 12:2

Wisdom transforms head knowledge into commonsense action. Wisdom from God helps you develop a biblical outlook that penetrates the deceptive and distorted thoughts of the world.

Don't lose sight of common sense and discernment. Hang on to them, for they will refresh your soul. They are like jewels on a necklace. They keep you safe on your way, and your feet will not stumble. You can go to bed without fear; you will lie down and sleep soundly . . . for the LORD is your security. He will keep your foot from being caught in a trap.
PROVERBS 3:21-26

Wisdom will help preserve you from trouble and disaster. Wise people know the difference between right and wrong and choose to do what's right, which often helps them avoid trouble. More than that, wisdom is choosing to apply God's truth and principles to your daily relationships and situations.

Using a dull ax requires great strength, so sharpen the blade. That's the value of wisdom; it helps you succeed. ECCLESIASTES 10:10

Wisdom gives you an edge that will help you succeed.

Be careful how you live. Don't live like fools, but like those who are wise.
EPHESIANS 5:15

Wisdom helps you know how to live.

Wisdom will multiply your days and add years to your life. If you become wise, you will be the one to benefit. If you scorn wisdom, you will be the one to suffer.
PROVERBS 9:11-12

Wisdom will allow you to lead a longer, healthier, happier life.

How do I obtain wisdom?

I, Wisdom, live together with good judgment. I know where to discover knowledge and discernment. . . . I love all who love me. Those who search will surely find me.
PROVERBS 8:12, 17

You find wisdom when you seek it wholeheartedly. Like many other good things in life, to find wisdom you must pursue it.

If you need wisdom, ask our generous God, and he will give it to you. He will not rebuke you for asking. JAMES 1:5

God promises to give wisdom to anyone who asks. You need not be embarrassed to ask God for the wisdom and direction you need.

The fear of the LORD is true wisdom; to forsake evil is real understanding. JOB 28:28

Giving God first place in your life is a prerequisite for God's guidance. Asking God for wisdom is a hollow request if you are not willing to let God rule in your heart. Wisdom comes from honoring God.

Let the message about Christ, in all its richness, fill your lives. Teach and counsel each other with all the wisdom he gives. COLOSSIANS 3:16

Obedience to God's Word will make you wise. It is your most reliable source of wisdom and insight because it is the very counsel of God himself and therefore speaks to all situations.

You have received the Holy Spirit, and he lives within you, so you don't need anyone to teach you what is true. For the Spirit teaches you everything you need to know, and what he teaches is true—it is not a lie. So just as he has taught you, remain in fellowship with Christ. 1 JOHN 2:27

Wisdom comes from the Holy Spirit who lives in you when you believe in Jesus Christ.

What are some of the characteristics of a wise person?

Only fools say in their hearts, "There is no God." PSALM 14:1

Fear of the LORD is the foundation of true knowledge, but fools despise wisdom and discipline. PROVERBS 1:7

A wise woman builds her home, but a foolish woman tears it down with her own hands. PROVERBS 14:1

Fools have no interest in understanding; they only want to air their own opinions. PROVERBS 18:2

The Bible describes fools as having the following characteristics: (1) refusing to acknowledge the existence of a loving God; (2) making no attempt to develop wisdom and self-discipline; (3) being entertained by making fun of what is good and moral; (4) speaking carelessly and thoughtlessly about others; and (5) thinking you are always right. Therefore, a wise person must have the opposite characteristics: (1) acknowledging a loving God who deeply cares about you; (2) actively disciplining yourself to pursue wisdom; (3) respecting what is good and right and standing up to wrong; (4) finding the good in others and encouraging them; and (5) being humble enough to know you don't have all the answers.

WITNESSING *See also* Communication, Courage, Faith, Love

A friend mentions in casual conversation that she enjoyed a terrific meal at a new restaurant and thinks you would like it, too. A stranger overhears you and your spouse wondering if a certain movie would be good to rent for a family night and offers that his kids thought it was great. Both the friend and the stranger are witnesses. Although the word tends to conjure images of courtrooms or awkward religious proselytizing, to "witness" means simply to tell about something you have experienced. According to the Bible, every believer shares the privilege and responsibility of witnessing. We should always be ready to tell the story of how we met and grew to love Jesus. That story is the greatest story you could tell.

Is witnessing really necessary?

Has the LORD redeemed you? Then speak out! Tell others he has redeemed you from your enemies. PSALM 107:2

Go into all the world and preach the Good News to everyone. MARK 16:15

God wants us to tell others about what he has done.

[Jesus] ordered us to preach everywhere and to testify that [he] is the one appointed by God to be the judge of all—the living and the dead. ACTS 10:42

Telling others the story of Jesus is an essential part of being a follower of Jesus. Simply tell others why you love him.

This is a day of good news, and we aren't sharing it with anyone! . . . Come on, let's go back and tell the people. 2 KINGS 7:9

How can [anyone] call on him to save them unless they believe in him? And how can they believe in him if they have never heard about him? And how can they hear about him unless someone tells them? ROMANS 10:14

It is not right to keep the Good News to yourself. Your witness may be the only way some people will ever hear the Good News. Being a Christian isn't about getting "in" to some exclusive group. It's about experiencing something so wonderful that you can't wait to invite others to experience it, too. Is this how you feel about being a Christian?

How will God help me be a witness to my faith?

Jesus called out to them, "Come, follow me, and I will show you how to fish for people!" MARK 1:17

Sharing your faith is a natural expression of your relationship with Jesus. When you pray for sensitivity to know what to say, God will make you aware of people around you who are ready to hear his Good News.

You will receive power when the Holy Spirit comes upon you. And you will be my witnesses, telling people about me everywhere—in Jerusalem, throughout Judea, in Samaria, and to the ends of the earth. ACTS 1:8

The Holy Spirit will empower you and help you to speak.

When we brought you the Good News . . . the Holy Spirit gave you full assurance that what we said was true. 1 THESSALONIANS 1:5

Go ahead and speak, and the Holy Spirit will do the work in people's hearts and minds.

One night the Lord spoke to Paul in a vision and told him, "Don't be afraid! Speak out! Don't be silent! For I am with you." ACTS 18:9-10

You are not alone when you witness. God is there to give you the words and the strength to proclaim the message.

What if I find it difficult to share my faith?

Those who are wise will shine as bright as the sky, and those who lead many to righteousness will shine like the stars forever. DANIEL 12:3

Everyone who acknowledges me publicly here on earth, the Son of Man will also acknowledge in the presence of God's angels. LUKE 12:8

God will honor those who honor him by proclaiming the Good News of what he has done. There is no greater purpose in life than sharing the message that could make the eternal difference in someone's life.

God has not given us a spirit of fear and timidity, but of power, love, and self-discipline. So never be ashamed to tell others about our Lord. And don't be ashamed of me, either, even though I'm in prison for him. With the strength God gives you, be ready to suffer with me for the sake of the Good News. 2 TIMOTHY 1:7-8

When the enemy tries to intimidate you with lies about your inadequacies, you can summon that same power God used to transform your life to boldly share your faith.

What should my witnessing include?

"I don't know whether he is a sinner," the man replied. "But I know this: I was blind, and now I can see!" JOHN 9:25

Your witness should include telling others how God has rescued you and freed you from the burden of sin.

Praise the LORD! For he has heard my cry for mercy. PSALM 28:6

Tell others about the prayers God has answered.

You brought me up from the grave, O LORD. You kept me from falling into the pit of death. PSALM 30:3

Explain how God has saved you from spiritual death.

We testify and proclaim to you that he is the one who is eternal life. 1 JOHN 1:2

Tell others the terrific news that anyone can have the gift of eternal life in a perfect world. It's not too good to be true.

The apostles testified powerfully to the resurrection of the Lord Jesus, and God's great blessing was upon them all. ACTS 4:33

Be sure to tell others about the resurrection of Jesus, for this is the basis for our hope in eternal life.

[Jesus] ordered us to preach everywhere and to testify that [he] is the one appointed by God to be the judge of all—the living and the dead. ACTS 10:42

Warn people about God's ultimate judgment ahead. Eventually there will only be two sides. It's important to be on God's side.

If someone asks about your Christian hope, always be ready to explain it. 1 PETER 3:15

Be ready to explain why you have hope.

I decided that . . . I would forget everything except Jesus Christ, the one who was crucified. 1 CORINTHIANS 2:2

Tell how Jesus Christ died on the cross to take away the punishment that we deserve for our sins.

It was also written that this message would be proclaimed in the authority of his name to all the nations, beginning in Jerusalem: "There is forgiveness of sins for all who repent." LUKE 24:47

Explain the message of repentance, forgiveness, and reconciliation with God.

If you confess with your mouth that Jesus is Lord and believe in your heart that God raised him from the dead, you will be saved. ROMANS 10:9

Make clear the need to confess Jesus Christ as Lord and believe in his resurrection.

Let your good deeds shine out for all to see, so that everyone will praise your heavenly Father. MATTHEW 5:16

How you live is an important element of your witness for Jesus. Make sure your actions match your words.

What do I do when people aren't interested in hearing about Jesus?

Your unbelieving neighbors . . . will see your honorable behavior, and they will give honor to God. 1 PETER 2:12

Your actions are, in themselves, a testimony to the world.

The Pharisees . . . asked [Jesus'] disciples, "Why does your teacher eat with such scum?" MATTHEW 9:10-11

Believers must build relationships with the lost—as Jesus did—in order to have opportunity to minister.

A farmer went out to plant his seed. LUKE 8:5

Sometimes your role is simply to plant the seed of faith and trust God to bring the harvest.

When they heard Paul speak about the resurrection of the dead, some laughed in contempt, but others said, "We want to hear more about this later." That ended Paul's discussion with them, but some joined him and became believers. ACTS 17:32-34

The majority may seem disinterested or hostile, but you never know when someone will believe—so you should never give up.

Whether they listen or refuse to listen—for remember, they are rebels—at least they will know they have had a prophet among them. . . . You must give them my messages whether they listen or not. EZEKIEL 2:5-7

Preach the word of God. Be prepared, whether the time is favorable or not.
2 TIMOTHY 4:2

Even if attitudes or circumstances are not favorable, courageously speak out anyway. In this way you honor God.

WORDS *See also* Communication, Gossip, Lying, Promises, Truth

Our words are gifts that we give to God and others. The things we say and the meaning behind them have an enormous effect on those who hear. We wouldn't give an obscene gift to the president, or even a friend, and it would certainly be a bad idea to give an insulting gift to an enemy. Our words are no different. In fact, the greatest gift you will ever give someone is not in a box covered with paper and bows, but in the words you use to encourage, inspire, comfort, and challenge them. Don't let your words be annoying, insulting, demeaning, or simply useless. Make your words truly matter.

Do my words really matter?

Once you have voluntarily made a vow, be careful to fulfill your promise to the LORD your God. DEUTERONOMY 23:23

When you say you will do something, people should be able to trust that you will do it. Otherwise, you can't be counted on and you make a poor example of a Christian.

Who may worship in your sanctuary, LORD? Who may enter your presence on your holy hill? Those who lead blameless lives and do what is right, speaking the truth from sincere hearts. Those who refuse to gossip or harm their neighbors or speak evil of their friends.
PSALM 15:1-3

Your words matter to God; only those whose motives are pure and who lovingly speak truth can enter his presence.

If you claim to be religious but don't control your tongue, you are fooling yourself, and your religion is worthless. JAMES 1:26

Your words show what kind of a person you really are. You cannot live a double standard of speaking one way in church and another way on the job or in the community.

Upright citizens are good for a city and make it prosper, but the talk of the wicked tears it apart. PROVERBS 11:11

A gentle answer deflects anger, but harsh words make tempers flare. PROVERBS 15:1

Gentle words and words of anger are powerful. You can greatly help or hinder those around you by what you say.

You must give an account on judgment day for every idle word you speak. The words you say will either acquit you or condemn you. MATTHEW 12:36-37

The words you speak during your life can condemn or acquit you on Judgment Day.

What kinds of words should I speak?

You must commit yourselves wholeheartedly to these commands that I am giving you today. Repeat them again and again to your children. Talk about them when you are at home and when you are on the road, when you are going to bed and when you are getting up. DEUTERONOMY 6:6-7

Continually share God's words from the Bible.

[Joseph] reassured them by speaking kindly to them. GENESIS 50:21

Speak kind words to others.

Giving thanks is a sacrifice that truly honors [God]. PSALM 50:23

All of you can join together with one voice, giving praise and glory to God, the Father of our Lord Jesus Christ. ROMANS 15:6

Speak words of thanks and praise to God.

I would encourage you. I would try to take away your grief. JOB 16:5

Don't use foul or abusive language. Let everything you say be good and helpful, so that your words will be an encouragement to those who hear them. EPHESIANS 4:29

Use words that encourage and build others up.

Gentle words are a tree of life. PROVERBS 15:4

Speak to others with gentleness and patience.

Timely advice is lovely, like golden apples in a silver basket. PROVERBS 25:11

When the time is right, giving good advice can be very beneficial.

Don't retaliate with insults when people insult you. Instead, pay them back with a blessing. That is what God has called you to do, and he will bless you for it. 1 PETER 3:9

Use your words to bless even those who injure you.

Tell the truth to each other. Render verdicts in your courts that are just and that lead to peace. ZECHARIAH 8:16

Speak truthfully.

We can't help but thank God for you, because your faith is flourishing and your love for one another is growing. 2 THESSALONIANS 1:3

Compliment others with words of gratitude.

What kinds of words should I avoid speaking?

You must not misuse the name of the LORD your God. The LORD will not let you go unpunished if you misuse his name. DEUTERONOMY 5:11

Don't swear using God's name.

Never make light of the king, even in your thoughts. And don't make fun of the powerful, even in your own bedroom. For a little bird might deliver your message and tell them what you said. ECCLESIASTES 10:20

Don't make fun of those in leadership.

Does anyone want to live a life that is long and prosperous? Then keep your tongue from speaking evil and your lips from telling lies! PSALM 34:12-13

Avoid saying anything that is deceptive or false.

Rumors are dainty morsels that sink deep into one's heart. PROVERBS 18:8

Avoid spreading gossip or slander about other people.

Fools vent their anger, but the wise quietly hold it back. PROVERBS 29:11

Avoid speaking in the heat of anger; you will usually regret it later.

Don't speak evil against each other, dear brothers and sisters. If you criticize and judge each other, then you are criticizing and judging God's law. JAMES 4:11

Avoid criticizing other people.

WORK *See also* Call of God, Productivity, Responsibility, Success

Work is God's plan for our lives and our work matters to God. Those who work diligently experience many benefits in their own lives and are able to pass them on to others. At its best, work honors God and brings meaning and joy to life. We should emulate the character traits we see in God's work, such as excellence, concern for the well-being of others, purpose, beauty, and service. When we have the perspective that we are actually working for God, the focus moves off the task and onto our motives—to help people know God. The excitement and interest that come from having this perspective are not primarily from the work but from the one for whom we work. God promises two basic rewards for faithful work: (1) a more credible witness to nonbelievers and (2) having our needs met without having to depend financially on others. There is immense dignity in all honest human labor, for our work is an opportunity to serve God and others.

How should I view work?

God created human beings in his own image. In the image of God he created them; male and female he created them. Then God blessed them and said, "Be fruitful and multiply. Fill the earth and govern it. Reign over the fish in the sea, the birds in the sky, and all the animals that scurry along the ground." GENESIS 1:27-28

There is value and honor in work. God created people and gave them dominion over his creation. In other words, God created you for work. Even before the Curse, humanity was given the opportunity to transform the raw materials of earth into things that would enhance life. Work has always been meant to honor the Lord, to give people the dignity of having something important to do, and to bring blessings to others.

Make it your goal to live a quiet life, minding your own business and working with your hands, just as we instructed you before. Then people who are not Christians will respect the way you live, and you will not need to depend on others. 1 THESSALONIANS 4:11-12

Your attitude toward work should include the goal of honoring God by the way you work, as well as supporting yourself and others.

What are the benefits of faithful work?

Jeroboam was a very capable young man, and when Solomon saw how industrious he was, he put him in charge of the labor force from the tribes of Ephraim and Manasseh, the descendants of Joseph. 1 KINGS 11:28

Faithful work often brings opportunities to do more satisfying work.

Lazy people are soon poor; hard workers get rich. PROVERBS 10:4

A hard worker has plenty of food, but a person who chases fantasies has no sense. PROVERBS 12:11

Hard work usually yields enough success to meet your needs; often it yields much more.

What kind of work should I do?

By the sweat of your brow will you have food to eat until you return to the ground from which you were made. GENESIS 3:19

You know that these hands of mine have worked to supply my own needs and even the needs of those who were with me. And I have been a constant example of how you can help those in need by working hard. ACTS 20:34-35

Choose work that will enable you to provide for your own and your family's needs and to give generously to God and others.

[Jesus said,] "I was hungry, and you fed me. I was thirsty, and you gave me a drink. I was a stranger, and you invited me into your home. I was naked, and you gave me clothing. I was sick, and you cared for me.". . . Then these righteous ones will reply, "Lord, when did we ever see you hungry and feed you? Or thirsty and give you something to drink? Or a stranger and show you hospitality? Or naked and give you clothing?" . . . And the King will say, "I tell you the truth, when you did it to one of the least of these my brothers and sisters, you were doing it to me!" MATTHEW 25:35-40

Whatever work you do, do it to honor God and advance the values of God's kingdom.

Wealth from get-rich-quick schemes quickly disappears; wealth from hard work grows over time. PROVERBS 13:11

Honest, hard work is much better than schemes to get rich quickly.

If your gift is to encourage others, be encouraging. If it is giving, give generously. If God has given you leadership ability, take the responsibility seriously. And if you have a gift for showing kindness to others, do it gladly. ROMANS 12:8

Do work in which you can use your gifts and abilities.

I take joy in doing your will, my God, for your instructions are written on my heart. PSALM 40:8

My life is worth nothing to me unless I use it for finishing the work assigned me by the Lord Jesus—the work of telling others the Good News about the wonderful grace of God. ACTS 20:24

You don't need to accomplish earthshaking tasks in order to have your work be meaningful. Your life has meaning when you do the work that God has given you to do. Whether you are changing diapers, running a company, cleaning houses, or pastoring a church, your work has meaning when you are doing it for God.

What if my work has nothing to do with anything "Christian"— how can God be glorified in my work?

On the seventh day God had finished his work of creation, so he rested from all his work. . . . The LORD God placed the man in the Garden of Eden to tend and watch over it. GENESIS 2:2, 15

A Jew named Aquila . . . had recently arrived from Italy with his wife, Priscilla. . . . Paul lived and worked with them, for they were tentmakers just as he was. ACTS 18:2-3

Work is anchored in God's very character. Part of being made in God's image is sharing in the industrious and creative aspects of his nature. Christians are needed in all kinds of vocations. Gardening was the very first job given to humans, and Paul's "day job" was tent making. Whatever your job, believe that God has placed you there for a reason, and then do your work well as a service to him and as a way to serve others.

How should I work?

Do you see any truly competent workers? They will serve kings rather than working for ordinary people. PROVERBS 22:29

Whatever you do, do well. ECCLESIASTES 9:10

Be industrious and do the best work you can.

Using a dull ax requires great strength, so sharpen the blade. That's the value of wisdom; it helps you succeed. ECCLESIASTES 10:10

Be smart in how you work.

Try to please them all the time, not just when they are watching you. As slaves of Christ, do the will of God with all your heart. Work with enthusiasm, as though you were working for the Lord rather than for people. EPHESIANS 6:6-7

Work with enthusiasm at whatever you do, even when no one is watching, because you are ultimately serving God.

If you are wise and understand God's ways, prove it by living an honorable life, doing good works with the humility that comes from wisdom. JAMES 3:13

Work honorably with an attitude of humility, rather than continually pointing at your own accomplishments.

Slaves must always obey their masters and do their best to please them. They must not talk back or steal, but must show themselves to be entirely trustworthy and good. Then they will make the teaching about God our Savior attractive in every way. TITUS 2:9-10

Be trustworthy and faithful in your work.

What does the Lord promise to those who work hard?
Good planning and hard work lead to prosperity, but hasty shortcuts lead to poverty. PROVERBS 21:5

Work willingly at whatever you do, as though you were working for the Lord rather than for people. . . . The Lord will give you an inheritance as your reward. COLOSSIANS 3:23-24

God promises a reward to those who work hard. That reward can sometimes, but not always, include financial reward. It may also include the even more significant rewards of respect, personal satisfaction, and the joy of contributing to the welfare of others.

Can I work too hard?
All our busy rushing ends in nothing. PSALM 39:6

Too much activity gives you restless dreams. ECCLESIASTES 5:3

While you are called to work hard, make sure that your work doesn't so preoccupy you that you endanger your health, your relationships, or your time with God.

This is what the LORD commanded: Tomorrow will be a day of complete rest. EXODUS 16:23

Jesus said [to his disciples], "Let's go off by ourselves to a quiet place and rest awhile." MARK 6:31

There is a time to stop your work in order to rest, to celebrate, and to worship God.

WORRY *See also* Fear, Stress, Trouble, Faith
To worry is human. We worry about job security. We worry about unexpected expenses. We worry about our children. We worry about the future. Worry is a natural part of life. It is a normal response to threatening situations, but often we imagine far worse scenarios than ever happen. Too much worry can distract and paralyze—and can even lead to a sinful denial of God's presence and grace in our lives. The Bible teaches that we find rest from

inappropriate worry when we admit we can't control the future and, instead, entrust ourselves—and our loved ones—to the God who does.

When does worry become sin?

The seed that fell among the thorns represents those who hear God's word, but all too quickly the message is crowded out by the worries of this life. MATTHEW 13:22

Think about the things of heaven, not the things of earth. COLOSSIANS 3:2

Worry is like thorny weeds—left uncontrolled, it crowds out what is good. Worry over the concerns of life becomes sin when it prevents the Word of God from taking root in your life. Worry is the misuse of your God-given imagination.

How can I worry less?

He alone is my rock and my salvation, my fortress where I will not be shaken.
PSALM 62:2

Remembering that God's love and care for you are as solid as a rock can help keep your worries in perspective. He has everything under control.

Can all your worries add a single moment to your life? MATTHEW 6:27

Realize that instead of adding more time or better quality of life, worry robs your health, kills your joy, and accomplishes nothing positive.

Don't worry about anything; instead, pray about everything. PHILIPPIANS 4:6

Give all your worries and cares to God, for he cares about you. 1 PETER 5:7

Talk to God openly about your worries. Hand them off to him as if to a consultant you totally trust, or a supervisor you have the utmost confidence in.

Fix your thoughts on what is true, and honorable, and right, and pure, and lovely, and admirable. Think about things that are excellent and worthy of praise. Keep putting into practice all you learned and received from me—everything you heard from me and saw me doing. Then the God of peace will be with you. PHILIPPIANS 4:8-9

Fix your thoughts on the power of God, not the problems of life. Worry will always change you for the worse; God has the power to change you and your circumstances for the better. Turn your attention away from negative, unbelieving thoughts to the positive, constructive thoughts of faith and hope.

Moses told the people, "Don't be afraid. Just stand still and watch the LORD rescue you."
EXODUS 14:13

Combat worry and anxiety by remembering and trusting what God, in his Word, has already promised to do for you.

"Don't worry about this Philistine," David told Saul. "I'll go fight him!" "Don't be ridiculous!" Saul replied. "There's no way you can fight this Philistine." . . . But David

persisted. "I have been taking care of my father's sheep and goats," he said. "When a lion or a bear comes to steal a lamb from the flock, I go after it with a club . . . and I'll do it to this pagan Philistine, too, for he has defied the armies of the living God! The LORD who rescued me from the claws of the lion and the bear will rescue me from this Philistine!"
1 SAMUEL 17:32-37

When your own problems and obstacles consume you, you give in to fear—that you will fail, that you will let others down, and that God will not help you when you most need him. Fear will tempt you to focus on the size of the problem rather than on the size of your God. When you focus on God instead, you will see him fighting by your side.

[Jesus said,] "Don't let your hearts be troubled. Trust in God, and trust also in me. There is more than enough room in my Father's home. If this were not so, would I have told you that I am going to prepare a place for you? When everything is ready, I will come and get you, so that you will always be with me where I am. And you know the way to where I am going." JOHN 14:1-4

If you had ten million dollars in the bank, you wouldn't worry about providing for your family if you lost your job. In the same way, you know that God has provided for your future by preparing a perfect place for you in heaven. Let that assurance keep you from panicking in today's storms. The outcome is certain.

Where can I turn when worry overwhelms me?

I tell you not to worry about everyday life—whether you have enough food and drink, or enough clothes to wear. Isn't life more than food, and your body more than clothing? Look at the birds. They don't plant or harvest or store food in barns, for your heavenly Father feeds them. And aren't you far more valuable to him than they are? Can all your worries add a single moment to your life? . . . These things dominate the thoughts of unbelievers, but your heavenly Father already knows all your needs. Seek the Kingdom of God above all else, and live righteously, and he will give you everything you need. So don't worry about tomorrow, for tomorrow will bring its own worries. Today's trouble is enough for today. MATTHEW 6:25-27, 32-34

Jesus' words suggest three questions you can ask yourself when you start to worry about something: (1) Is it important? Many of our anxieties revolve around issues that are even less important than food and clothing. (2) Is it helpful? Worrying is useless; in fact, it's usually counterproductive. (3) Who is in charge? God is in control, and your heavenly Father delights to meet your needs.

WORSHIP *See also* Praise, Presence of God, Thankfulness

We do not think of ourselves as a worshiping culture, let alone an idolatrous culture, but our behavior suggests otherwise. Consider our weekly gatherings of up to one hundred thousand frenzied fans observing a ceremony of men dressed in strange garb acting out a violent drama of conquest. Others stay at home and join in by way of a small glowing shrine set up in the family room. Fans of professional football are probably not even aware that their behavior could be described as worship. Or consider the way thousands of young people scream and throw themselves at the stage where their rock-star idols are performing. Human beings were created to worship. To worship is to ascribe ultimate value to an object, person, or God—and then to revere, adore, pay homage to, and obey by ordering the priorities of our lives around that which we worship. The Bible teaches that God alone is worthy of our real worship. Worship, more than anything else, will connect us with God, our only source of lasting hope.

What is the ultimate purpose of my worship?

David praised the LORD in the presence of the whole assembly: "O LORD, the God of our ancestor Israel, may you be praised forever and ever! Yours, O LORD, is the greatness, the power, the glory, the victory, and the majesty. Everything in the heavens and on earth is yours, O LORD, and this is your kingdom. We adore you as the one who is over all things. Wealth and honor come from you alone, for you rule over everything. Power and might are in your hand, and at your discretion people are made great and given strength. O our God, we thank you and praise your glorious name!" 1 CHRONICLES 29:10-13

Worship is the recognition of who God is, and of who you are in relation to him. Ultimately, everything we do should be based on what we think of and how we worship the almighty God. If our actions don't pay homage to him, then we are paying homage to someone or something else.

Honor the LORD with your wealth and with the best part of everything you produce. PROVERBS 3:9

Giving the firstfruits of your income to God honors him as your number one priority. Your offerings demonstrate that your work is for God and that his work is most important.

Whenever the living beings give glory and honor and thanks to the one sitting on the throne (the one who lives forever and ever), the twenty-four elders fall down and worship the one sitting on the throne (the one who lives forever and ever). And they lay their crowns before the throne and say, "You are worthy, O Lord our God, to receive glory and honor and power. For you created all things, and they exist because you created what you pleased." REVELATION 4:9-11

Your worship of God is a foretaste of heaven.

Why is worship important? How is it integral to my relationship with God?

Moses immediately threw himself to the ground and worshiped. EXODUS 34:8

Worship only the LORD, who brought you out of Egypt with great strength and a powerful arm. Bow down to him alone, and offer sacrifices only to him. 2 KINGS 17:36

Great is the LORD! He is most worthy of praise! No one can measure his greatness.
PSALM 145:3

Worship is recognizing God's gracious character and his many acts of love toward you, and then returning love to him.

When Solomon finished praying, fire flashed down from heaven and burned up the burnt offerings and sacrifices, and the glorious presence of the LORD filled the Temple.
2 CHRONICLES 7:1

God meets his people in a unique and powerful way when they worship him together.

You must read this Book of Instruction to all the people of Israel when they assemble before the LORD your God at the place he chooses. DEUTERONOMY 31:11

Come, let us go up to the mountain of the LORD, to the house of Jacob's God. There he will teach us his ways, and we will walk in his paths. MICAH 4:2

Something very powerful and unique happens when God's people get together to sing, praise, hear his Word, and worship him. There is a sense of community and fellowship that can only happen when believers worship together.

Shout with joy to the LORD, all the earth! Worship the LORD with gladness. Come before him, singing with joy. Acknowledge that the LORD is God! He made us, and we are his. We are his people, the sheep of his pasture. Enter his gates with thanksgiving; go into his courts with praise. Give thanks to him and praise his name. PSALM 100:1-4

Worship is a fitting response to God's holiness, power, love, and grace.

What does worshiping God involve? How should I worship God?

Great is the LORD! He is most worthy of praise! He is to be feared above all gods.
PSALM 96:4

Worship only God because he alone is worthy of your utmost devotion.

"Do not come any closer," the LORD warned. "Take off your sandals, for you are standing on holy ground." EXODUS 3:5

When you approach God in worship, recognize that wherever you are, you are standing on holy ground. In other words, you come to God with an attitude of respect and humility for almighty God, wherever you are.

Sing praises to the LORD who reigns in Jerusalem. Tell the world about his unforgettable deeds. PSALM 9:11

Your worship should include praise and thanks to God for what he has done.

Praise him with a blast of the ram's horn; praise him with the lyre and harp! Praise him with the tambourine and dancing; praise him with strings and flutes! Praise him with a clash of cymbals; praise him with loud clanging cymbals. PSALM 150:3-5

Worship can take the form of a joyous celebration with musical instruments.

David also ordered the Levite leaders to appoint a choir of Levites who were singers and musicians to sing joyful songs to the accompaniment of harps, lyres, and cymbals.
1 CHRONICLES 15:16

Sing to the LORD, all you godly ones! Praise his holy name. PSALM 30:4

Singing is an important part of your worship to God.

Come, let us worship and bow down. Let us kneel before the LORD our maker.
PSALM 95:6

Kneeling and bowing are appropriate postures for worship.

Since we are receiving a Kingdom that is unshakable, let us be thankful and please God by worshiping him with holy fear and awe. HEBREWS 12:28

Holy respect and awe should accompany thanksgiving as appropriate attitudes in worship.

I hate all your show and pretense—the hypocrisy of your religious festivals and solemn assemblies. AMOS 5:21

Public worship is useless if it is done without sincerity and the desire to live whole-heartedly for God. Worship out of a genuine love for God, not out of a sense of guilt. God wants a heartfelt response.

In every place of worship, I want men to pray with holy hands lifted up to God, free from anger and controversy. 1 TIMOTHY 2:8

Public prayer is an important part of corporate worship.

Call them all together—men, women, children, and the foreigners living in your towns—so they may hear this Book of Instruction and learn to fear the LORD your God and carefully obey all the terms of these instructions. Do this so that your children who have not known these instructions will hear them and will learn to fear the LORD your God. DEUTERONOMY 31:12-13

It is good to worship as a family.

They entered the house and saw the child with his mother, Mary, and they bowed down and worshiped him. Then they opened their treasure chests and gave him gifts of gold, frankincense, and myrrh. MATTHEW 2:11

Worship should be accompanied by generous giving.

How can I make worship a part of my daily life?

God is Spirit, so those who worship him must worship in spirit and in truth. JOHN 4:24

Worship is not confined to formal places and times. The only thing that is required is that you worship God in spirit (through authentic faith inspired by the Holy Spirit) and in truth (according to God's true person and nature). You can do that anytime and anywhere.

Be filled with the Holy Spirit, singing psalms and hymns and spiritual songs among yourselves, and making music to the Lord in your hearts. EPHESIANS 5:18-19

Worship, in addition to being an act of the people of God, is also a part of ordinary life. One way to bring worship into your daily life is through music—whether you sing to yourself or listen to it.

Oh, how great are God's riches and wisdom and knowledge! How impossible it is for us to understand his decisions and his ways! For who can know the LORD's thoughts? Who knows enough to give him advice? And who has given him so much that he needs to pay it back? For everything comes from him and exists by his power and is intended for his glory. All glory to him forever! Amen. ROMANS 11:33-36

Take a moment to praise God whenever you see his wisdom, power, direction, care, and love in your life. Worship then becomes a way of life.

WORTH/WORTHINESS *See also* Character, Dignity, Respect, Worship

Most of us find our sense of self-worth from a combination of our looks, accomplishments, careers, possessions, and social status. But this is precarious because if we age or become ill, if our next performance doesn't exceed our last, if we lose our job or retire, if we meet with misfortune and our assets disappear, or if our friends are shallow and fickle, we also lose our sense of worthiness. The more secure and lasting place to find worth is in our relationship with God. Since he created us and knew us intimately before we were born and loved us enough to rescue us from eternal punishment for our sins through Jesus' death and resurrection, we know we have tremendous value and worth in God's eyes. Because of the magnitude of God's forgiveness, and his grace and love for us, he is worthy of our praise, gratitude, and love in return.

In what ways is God worthy?

Honor the LORD, you heavenly beings; honor the LORD for his glory and strength. Honor the LORD for the glory of his name. Worship the LORD in the splendor of his holiness. PSALM 29:1-2

The word of the LORD holds true, and we can trust everything he does. PSALM 33:4

You are worthy, O Lord our God, to receive glory and honor and power. For you created all things, and they exist because you created what you pleased. REVELATION 4:11

In every way, God is worthy of your praise, worship, respect, and trust. In the limited human perspective on life and the world, it is common to assign worth to created things rather than the Creator of all things. When you do this, you lose perspective on who God is, on what he has done for you, and on what life is all about.

What am I worth? What is my value to God?

God created human beings in his own image. In the image of God he created them; male and female he created them. GENESIS 1:27

You made them only a little lower than God and crowned them with glory and honor.
PSALM 8:5

We are God's masterpiece. He has created us anew in Christ Jesus, so we can do the good things he planned for us long ago. EPHESIANS 2:10

God made you in his own image, so he must value you highly! You are his treasure and masterpiece. You are invaluable to him, which is why he sent his own Son to die for your sins so that you could live forever in heaven.

God paid a high price for you, so don't be enslaved by the world. 1 CORINTHIANS 7:23

You are worthy because God paid a high price for you. He loved you enough to die for you. That's how important you are to him!

Even before he made the world, God loved us and chose us in Christ to be holy and without fault in his eyes. God decided in advance to adopt us into his own family by bringing us to himself through Jesus Christ. This is what he wanted to do, and it gave him great pleasure. So we praise God for the glorious grace he has poured out on us who belong to his dear Son. He is so rich in kindness and grace that he purchased our freedom with the blood of his Son and forgave our sins. EPHESIANS 1:4-7

Before God made the world he chose you to be born as his unique creation, holy and forgiven.

How can I develop a healthier sense of self-worth?

How precious are your thoughts about me, O God. They cannot be numbered!
PSALM 139:17

Be honest in your evaluation of yourselves, measuring yourselves by the faith God has given us. ROMANS 12:3

God has given each of you a gift from his great variety of spiritual gifts. Use them well to serve one another. 1 PETER 4:10

Healthy self-esteem comes from an honest appraisal of yourself—not too proud, because your gifts and abilities were given to you by God, yet not so self-effacing that you fail to use your gifts and abilities to their potential. Using your gifts to bless and serve others actually increases your self-worth because it takes the focus off of you and allows God to work more effectively through you.

What does God consider to be of worth?

Three things will last forever—faith, hope, and love—and the greatest of these is love.
1 CORINTHIANS 13:13

The enduring characteristics of faith, hope, and love.

Getting wisdom is the wisest thing you can do! And whatever else you do, develop good judgment. PROVERBS 4:7

Wisdom and good judgment.

Physical training is good, but training for godliness is much better, promising benefits in this life and in the life to come. 1 TIMOTHY 4:8

A persistent and disciplined desire to know and follow him.

A good reputation is more valuable than costly perfume. ECCLESIASTES 7:1

A good reputation.

Wise words are more valuable than much gold and many rubies. PROVERBS 20:15

Wise and helpful words.

Who can find a virtuous and capable wife? She is more precious than rubies. PROVERBS 31:10

Virtue and exemplary conduct.

If you love me, obey my commandments. JOHN 14:15

Your obedience.

God loved the world so much that he gave his one and only Son, so that everyone who believes in him will not perish but have eternal life. JOHN 3:16

Your love for him and gratitude for your salvation.

ABOUT THE AUTHORS

RONALD A. BEERS has been with Tyndale House Publishers since 1987, serving as a Bible editor, editorial director, vice president, and currently as senior vice president and group publisher. In his present position, he has been responsible for developing and publishing many of Tyndale's Bibles and books. Since 1988, Ron has been a member of the central Bible translation committee for the *New Living Translation,* working as executive director and one of the stylists. Ron was also the creator and general editor of *The Life Application Bible* (the bestselling study Bible in the world for the past ten years). He also developed the TouchPoint series, which has sold more than 2.5 million copies since 1996. He was also fortunate to marry a woman whom he calls "the best editor I've ever worked with." His wife, Becki, carefully reads and edits everything he works on, and Ron wishes to acknowledge all her fine work on this project. His daughter, Amy, is also in the publishing business as a freelance editor. She pared down this manuscript from its original two thousand pages.

V. GILBERT BEERS has been writing and developing Bible reference materials for more than fifty years. Gil began his publishing career as editorial director at David C. Cook Publishing Company in the early 1960s, developing the children's curriculum that the company used for decades and that became the standard for the industry. From there he struck out on his own to become a full-time author, writing more than 150 books, with total sales of more than 13 million copies. Gil also served as editor of *Christianity Today* magazine, from 1982–1985. He holds three master's degrees and two earned doctorates. Among his many projects, Gil developed the twenty-three-volume Family Bible Library—a Bible study and devotional program for families—and the *Victor Handbook of Bible Knowledge,* and he worked side by side with his son Ron on the *TouchPoint Bible* and the TouchPoint series. His latest book is titled *What Everyone Should Know about the Bible* (Tyndale, 2007).

Books in The Complete Book Popular Reference Series

 The Complete Book of Bible Trivia contains more than 4,500 questions and answers about the Bible.

 The Complete Book of Christian Heroes is an in-depth popular reference about those who have suffered for the cause of Christ throughout the world.

 The Complete Book of When and Where in the Bible and throughout History focuses on more than 1,000 dates that illustrate how God has worked throughout history to do extraordinary things through ordinary people.

 The Complete Book of Zingers is an alphabetized collection of one-sentence sermons.

 The Complete Book of Who's Who in the Bible is your ultimate resource for learning about the people of the Bible.

 The Complete Book of Bible Basics identifies and defines the names, phrases, events, stories, and terms from the Bible and church history that are familiar to most Christians.

 In **The Complete Book of Bible Secrets and Mysteries** Stephen Lang, an expert on the Bible, serves up secrets and mysteries of the Bible in a fun, entertaining way.

 The Complete Book of Bible Trivia: Bad Guys Edition, an extension of Stephen Lang's best-selling book *The Complete Book of Bible Trivia,* focuses on facts about the "bad guys" in the Bible.

 The Complete Book of Hymns is the largest collection of behind-the-scenes stories about the most popular hymns and praise songs.

 The Complete Book of Wacky Wit is filled with more than 1,500 humorous sayings to live by.